PRIVACY AND FREEDOM OF EXPRESSION
SECOND EDITIO

BPP

PRIVACY AND FREEDOM OF EXPRESSION

SECOND EDITION

Editors

RICHARD CLAYTON QC
Barrister, 4–5 Gray's Inn Square, Associate Fellow,
Centre for Public Law, University of Cambridge

HUGH TOMLINSON QC
Barrister, Matrix Chambers

Contributing Editor

Mathew Purchase, *Barrister, Matrix Chambers*

International Contributing Editors

Andrew Butler, *Partner, Russell McVeagh, New Zealand*
Simon Heeney, *Associate, Blakes, Canada*
Dr Petra Butler, *Senior Lecturer, Faculty of Law,*
Victoria University of Wellington, New Zealand
Gilbert Marcus SC, *Advocate, South Africa*
Aidan O'Neill QC (Scot.), *Associate, Matrix Chambers*
Robin Reinertson, *Associate, Blakes, Canada*

OXFORD
UNIVERSITY PRESS

OXFORD

UNIVERSITY PRESS

Great Clarendon Street, Oxford OX2 6DP

Oxford University Press is a department of the University of Oxford.
It furthers the University's objective of excellence in research, scholarship,
and education by publishing worldwide in

Oxford New York

Auckland Cape Town Dar es Salaam Hong Kong Karachi
Kuala Lumpur Madrid Melbourne Mexico City Nairobi
New Delhi Shanghai Taipei Toronto

With offices in

Argentina Austria Brazil Chile Czech Republic France Greece
Guatemala Hungary Italy Japan Poland Portugal Singapore
South Korea Switzerland Thailand Turkey Ukraine Vietnam

Oxford is a registered trade mark of Oxford University Press
in the UK and in certain other countries

Published in the United States
by Oxford University Press Inc., New York

British Library Cataloguing in Publication Data
Data available

Library of Congress Cataloging in Publication Data
Data available

Typeset by Glyph International, Bangalore, India
Printed in Great Britain
on acid-free paper by the
MPG Books Group, Bodmin and King's Lynn

ISBN 978–0–19–957973–0

1 3 5 7 9 10 8 6 4 2

PREFACE AND UPDATE

The rights

The Convention rights to privacy and to freedom of expression were two of the most important rights introduced into English law by the Human Rights Act 1998 ('the HRA'). The Article 8 right to respect for private life has provided a focus for the development of 'privacy' rights in English law. The Article 10 right to freedom of expression reinforces the well-established domestic right. The question of the balancing of these two rights has been central to the development of the new law of privacy and is, increasingly, influencing the development of the English law of defamation.

The present book is a reprint of the chapters on Privacy and Freedom of Expression from the second edition of our book, *The Law of Human Rights*. It sets out to provide a comprehensive and systematic treatment of human rights law and practice in the UK in relation to these areas.

The book contains two parts: the chapters from the *Law of Human Rights* relating to privacy and freedom of expression respectively. Each chapter is, itself, divided into three sections. After an introduction, there is a discussion of the right in English law which includes an analysis of the various Articles 8 and 10 cases decided under the Human Rights Act 1998. This is followed by an analysis of the case law under the European Convention on Human Rights. Each chapter ends with Appendices examining the United Kingdom cases under Articles 8 and 10, the Scottish cases, the Canadian Charter of Rights, the New Zealand Bill of Rights Act, the South African Constitution Act, and human rights cases in other jurisdictions.

The second edition covered the law up to 31 December 2008. In the remainder of this introduction we shall briefly consider the case law concerning Articles 8 and 10 up to 30 November 2009, both in relation to the European Court of Human Rights and the English courts. In particular, we will deal with the rapidly developing case law concerning the 'balancing' of the two rights when both 'privacy' and 'expression' interests are involved.

Recent Article 8 case law

The Court of Human Rights

Article 8 of the Convention contains a right to respect for 'private and family life, home and correspondence'. These are 'qualified rights': restrictions on the rights are permitted provided that they are 'prescribed by law' and 'necessary in a democratic society'.[1] The right to family life is not considered in the present book.[2]

---

[1] For a full discussion of these concepts, see *The Law of Human Rights*, para 6.215ff.
[2] It forms the subject matter of Chapter 13 of *The Law of Human Rights*.

The Court has considered a number of cases concerning photographs. In *Reklos v Greece*[3] the applicants complained that a photograph had been taken of their baby in hospital. The Court held that there was a violation of Article 8 because the right to protection of image was an essential component of personal development and presupposed the right to control the use of that image. That included the right to object to the reproduction of the image. The baby was not a public figure; therefore, there was no issue of public interest.

In *Nikolaishvili v Georgia*[4] contrary to domestic law, the authorities posted the applicant's photograph on a board of 'wanted persons'. This was held to be a breach of Article 8, because it was not 'in accordance with law' and, in addition, there was a breach of the positive obligation to carry out effective inquiries to rectify the matter as far as possible.

In *Egeland v Norway*[5] the applicants were editors of two national newspapers who had published photographs of a person, B, who had just been convicted of a major crime, outside the court house without B's permission. They were convicted of an offence of taking photographs of a defendant outside court under domestic law. They contended that the conviction was a breach of Article 10. The Court held that although the photographs had been taken in a public place and in relation to a public event, their publication had represented a particularly intrusive portrayal of B. The need to protect B's privacy was equally important as that of safeguarding due process. The interests in restricting publication of the photographs outweighed those of the press in informing the public on a matter of public concern. As a result, there had been no breach of Article 10.

Article 8 also gives rise to a right of access to personal data. In *K H v Slovakia*[6] the Court held that the positive obligation under Article 8 included a duty, in the absence of compelling reasons to the contrary, to allow a person to make photocopies of his or her personal data.

Article 8 also provides protection for tenants who are subject to possession proceedings. In *Paulic v Croatia*[7] it was held that an order for eviction was a violation of Article 8. The domestic court had simply considered whether he had a right to occupy and, having decided that he did not, 'made no further analysis of the proportionality of his eviction'. It was held that 'any person at risk of an interference with his rights under Article 8 should be able to have the proportionality and reasonableness of the measure determined by an independent tribunal applying the relevant principles under Article 8'.[8] This approach appears to be inconsistent with the approach of the English courts to this issue.[9]

---

[3] [2009] EMLR 16.

[4] Judgment, 13 January 2009.

[5] Judgment, 16 April 2009.

[6] (2009) 49 EHRR 34 (request for referral to Grand Chamber pending).

[7] Judgment, 22 October 2009; see also *Ćosić v Croatia* Judgment, 15 January 2009.

[8] Ibid, para 43.

[9] See *Doherty v Birmingham City Council* [2009] 1 AC 367, and see para 12.192 below. Note that on 5 November 2009, the Supreme Court refused permission to appeal in the case of *Central Bedfordshire v Taylor* [2009] EWCA Civ 613, which again raised this issue.

Finally, there has been one finding of violation in a recent United Kingdom Article 8 case in the past 12 months. In *Szuluk v United Kingdom*[10] it was held that the monitoring of a Category A prisoner's confidential medical correspondence was an unjustified interference with his right to respect for correspondence.

The HRA case law

The domestic courts continue to deal with a wide range of Article 8 issues. In *Wood v Commissioner of Police*[11] the claimant complained about the taking and retention of photographs of him by the police in circumstances in which he had never been arrested or charged with any offence. The Court of Appeal held that in the circumstances the retention of the photographs was an interference with Article 8. The majority went on to hold that this interference was not justified under Article 8(2).

In *R (Wright) v Secretary of State for Health*[12] the House of Lords held that placing of a person on a provisional list of people unsuitable to work with vulnerable adults could be an interference with the person's Article 8 rights. The lack of fair procedures for dealing with listing meant that the relevant statutory provisions were incompatible with Article 8. A similar issue arose in the case of *R (L) v Commissioner of Police*.[13] The Supreme Court considered the question as to whether the regime for 'enhanced criminal record certificates' under section 115(7) of the Police Act 1997 was compatible with Article 8. It was held that Article 8 was engaged and that, provided that proper consideration was given to the applicant's rights, the regime could be applied proportionately so that the interferences would be justified under Article 8(2).

In the well known case of *R (Purdy) v DPP*[14] the House of Lords held that the offence of assisting suicide was an interference with the Article 8 rights of a person who had declared her wish to travel to a country where assisted suicide was lawful when her life became unbearable. In the absence of an 'offence specific' policy relating to prosecution for this offence, the interference was not 'in accordance with law'. As a result, the DPP was required to promulgate such a policy and later did so.

However, the courts have sometimes been reluctant to extend the scope of Article 8 into new areas. In *Treharne v Secretary of State for Work and Pensions*[15] it was held that Article 8 could not be extended to found any claim for damages for the failure of the Child Support Agency properly to pursue maintenance assessments. In *R (N) v Secretary of State for Health*[16] a majority of the Court of Appeal held that the smoking ban in a secure hospital did not engage the Article 8 rights of detainees.

---

[10] Judgment, 2 June 2009.
[11] [2010] EMLR 1.
[12] [2009] 1 AC 739.
[13] [2009] UKSC 3.
[14] [2009] 3 WLR 403.
[15] [2009] 1 FLR 853.
[16] [2009] EWCA Civ 795.

Recent Article 10 case law

Court of Human Rights Article 10 case law

In *Manole v Moldova*[17] a violation of the state's positive obligations under Article 10 was found because domestic law did not provide any guarantee of political balance in the composition of the senior management and supervisory body of the State radio and television station. The Court held that Article 10 placed a duty on the State to ensure, first, that the public has access through television and radio to impartial and accurate information and a range of opinion and comment, reflecting, inter alia, the diversity of political outlook within the country and, secondly, that journalists and other professionals working in the audiovisual media are not prevented from imparting this information and comment.[18]

In *Europapress Holding DOO v Croatia*[19] the applicant newspaper had been ordered to pay damages in defamation to a politician who it had accused of making an inappropriate joke by pointing a handgun at a journalist and saying 'I will kill you now.' The Court dismissed the application, agreeing with the assessment of the domestic court that the newspaper had taken insufficient steps to verify the published statements.

The Court of Human Rights has found a number of violations of Article 10 in cases in which the domestic courts have failed to properly investigate the truth of the allegations made or have imposed excessive penalties. For example, in *Marchenko v Ukraine*[20] the Court accepted that a conviction for defamation was necessary where he had organized picketing accusing a public official of misappropriating funds and property. However, imposition of a suspended prison sentence of one year was disproportionate and a violation of Article 10.[21] In *Porubova v Russia*[22] the applicant had published an article concerning a homosexual relationship between the head of the regional government and a young man employed in the region's office in Moscow. There were also allegations of embezzlement. The articles concerned professional politicians and contributed to a debate on an issue of public concern and in the circumstances the conviction of the applicant for criminal insult and a sentence of one and half year's correctional work was a violation of Article 10.

The protection of journalistic sources is an important element of freedom of expression. However, in *Sanoma Uitgevers BV v Netherlands*[23] the Court held that an order that a magazine should deliver to the police a CD-ROM which could reveal the identity of journalistic sources was not a violation. The Court pointed out that the domestic authorities are entitled to balance the conflicting interests served by prosecuting crimes concerned and the protection of journalistic privilege: relevant considerations will include the nature and seriousness of the crimes, the nature and content of the information demanded, the existence of alternative possibilities of obtaining the information, and any restraints on the authorities'

---

[17] Judgment, 17 September 2009.
[18] Ibid, para 100.
[19] Judgment, 22 October 2009.
[20] Judgment, 19 February 2009.
[21] See also *Bodrožić v Serbia* Judgment, 23 June 2009; *Bodrožić and Vujin v Serbia* Judgment, 23 June 2009 and *Romanenko v Russia*, Judgment, 8 October 2009.
[22] Judgment, 8 October 2009.
[23] Judgment, 31 March 2009.

procurement and use of the materials concerned. The information had been relevant and capable of identifying the perpetrators of crimes and, as a result, the Court found, by a majority of four to three, that there had been no violation. The case has been heard by the Grand Chamber.

Article 10 applies to the workplace and civil servants but this must be qualified by the duty of 'loyalty, reserve and discretion' owed by employees. In *Kudeshkin v Russia*[24] the applicant was a judge who was dismissed after expressing strong criticisms of the judicial system in media interviews, raising fears about the impartiality of the Moscow City Court. The Court said that these were comments on matters of great public importance and that the manner in which the sanction was imposed did not secure important procedural gurantees. As a result, there was a violation of Article 10.

Although Article 10 includes a right to 'receive information', the Court has held on a number of occasions that this does not include a right of freedom of information.[25] However, recent case law suggests that a different approach may be developing. In the Hungarian Civil Liberties Union case[26] the Court commented that it had:

> recently advanced towards a broader interpretation of the notion of 'freedom to receive information' . . . and thereby towards the recognition of a right of access to information.

In that case, the Court found a violation of Article 10 when the domestic courts had refused access to a complaint which sought constitutional scrutiny of certain amendments to the Criminal Code. It concluded that obstacles to hinder access to information of public interest might discourage the media and other public interest organisations from pursuing their vital role as 'public watchdogs'.[27]

There have been no new findings of violation of Article 10 in United Kingdom cases. In *Times Newspapers v United Kingdom*[28] the applicant complained that the rule that each time material was downloaded from the internet there was a new publication was a violation of Article 10. The application was dismissed. The Court held that responsible journalists had a duty to ensure accuracy of historical information and a requirement to publish an appropriate qualification to an article contained in an internet archive was not a disproportionate interference. In *Wall Street Journal v United Kingdom*[29] the applicant complained, inter alia, that the common law presumption of falsity in libel actions was incompatible with Article 10. The Court noted that it had previously accepted that this presumption was consistent with Article 10 and that its use aimed to protect the right to reputation guaranteed by Article 8. Furthermore, bearing in mind the fact that the applicant's 'responsible journalism' defence had succeeded they could not claim to be victims. As a result, the complaint was inadmissible.

---

[24] Judgment, 26 February 2009.
[25] See *Leander v Sweden* (1987) 9 EHRR 433, para 74.
[26] *Társaság a Szabadságjogokért v Hungary*, Judgment, 14 April 2009, para 35; see also *Kenedi v Hungary* Judgment, 26 May 2009.
[27] Ibid, para 38.
[28] [2009] EMLR 14.
[29] (2009) 48 EHRR SE 19.

Article 10 cases under the HRA

In *Ajinomoto Sweeteners Europe SAS v Asda Stores Ltd*[30] it was held that, having regard to Article 10, the 'single meaning rule' could be adapted to the tort of malicious falsehood so that where there were two possible meanings, one true and one false, the court should adopt the former.

In *Tabernacle v Secretary of State for Defence*[31] the Court of Appeal held that a bye-law which prevented a member of the Aldermaston Women's Peace Camp from camping in an area owned by the Secretary of State was an unjustified interference with her Article 10 rights (and her right to freedom of assembly under Article 11). However, in *A-G v Seckerson*[32] the Court rejected an argument based on Article 10 to the effect that the statutory prohibition on the disclosure of jury deliberations should be restricted to disclosures which interfered with the administration of justice.

Balancing Articles 8 and 10

The rights to privacy and to freedom of expression are both of fundamental importance but in many cases they are in potential conflict. The freedom of expression of the media often involves an infringement of the right to privacy of the person whose affairs are being discussed. Any extension of the protection of privacy poses problems for the protection of freedom of expression.

Both the Court of Human Rights and the domestic courts have grappled with the issue of the 'balancing' of the rights in recent cases. In *Karakó v Hungary*[33] the Court considered a complaint by a Hungarian MP that his Article 8 right to reputation had not been properly protected because his private prosecution for libel had been dismissed. His claim failed but the Court appeared to cast doubt on the contention that the right to reputation was protected under Article 8. Much of the recent case law[34] was not cited and the concurring judgment of Judge Jociene which refuses to agree with the majority on this point is to be preferred. The case is aberrant and should be treated with caution.

The well-established recent approach of the Court to the balancing of Articles 8 and 10 is illustrated by two recent cases. In *A v Norway*[35] the applicant complained of newspaper articles and photographs concerning his arrest on suspicion of murder. His domestic defamation proceedings failed on the basis that there was a public interest in the crime in question. The Court of Human Rights found a violation of Article 8 on the basis that the domestic court had not struck a fair balance between the newspaper's freedom of expression under Article 10 and the applicant's right to respect for his private life under Article 8. In *Standard Verlags GmbH v Austria (No 2)*[36] the Court was concerned with an article in the Austrian press which related to the marriage of the then Federal president. He had brought successful

---

[30] [2009] EWHC 1717 (QB).
[31] [2009] EWCA Civ 23.
[32] [2009] EMLR 20.
[33] Judgment, 28 April 2009.
[34] See, in particular, the decision of the Grand Chamber in *Lindon v France* (2008) 46 EHRR 35.
[35] Judgment, 9 April 2009.
[36] Judgment, 4 June 2009.

domestic proceedings for 'insult' and the applicant newspaper contended that this was a breach of Article 10. The Court considered that what was in issue was a balance between Article 8 and Article 10. It found that the reasons given by the domestic courts were 'relevant' and 'sufficient' to justify the interference. They have properly considered the claimants' status as public figures but found that the article at issue failed to contribute to any debate of general interest. The information published was 'idle gossip' which did not contribute to any public debate in respect of which the press has to fulfil its role of 'public watchdog', but merely serves to satisfy the curiosity of a certain readership.

The domestic courts have also considered the balance between Articles 8 and 10 in several recent cases. In *Re Stedman*[37] the judge was concerned with an injunction relating to the publication of images of a 13-year-old boy who was said to be the father of a child born to a 15-year-old girl and of DNA test results which showed he was not the father. Although there was substantial interference with Article 8 rights, in balancing these against Article 10 rights, a prohibition on publication of the DNA results, or of pictures and images already in the public domain, would be disproportionate. The court had to consider the interferences which had already happened on a consensual basis. An order prohibiting publication would be both disproportionate and, in the light of the previous publicity, futile.

In the case of *Re British Broadcasting Corporation*[38] the House of Lords considered whether or not to continue an anonymity order made on an Attorney-General's reference. They approach the matter on the basis that it was necessary to balance the Article 8 rights of the defendant against the Article 10 rights of the media. It was accepted that the former included the right to 'reputation'.[39] The same issue was considered by a seven-judge panel of the Supreme Court in *A v HM Treasury*.[40] Judgment is awaited.

The issue of 'balancing' has also been considered in the defamation context. In *Clift v Slough BC*[41] the claimant sued a local authority in defamation after it placed her name on its 'Violent Persons Register'. The defendant relied on the defence of qualified privilege but the judge held that her Article 8 rights were engaged and, as a result, privilege was only available in respect of publications which were necessary and proportionate. The local authority's obligations under Article 8 had the effect of removing the requirement that qualified privilege could only be rebutted by proof of malice and replacing it with a 'proportionality' test.

In *Gary Flood v Times Newspapers*[42] the judge was considering a *Reynolds* qualified privilege defence in a libel action. He held that the balance between the protection of reputation and freedom of expression requires the same approach in whatever legal context it arises.[43] As a result, in libel cases it was necessary to carry out a 'parallel analysis' and 'ultimate balancing'

---

[37] [2009] 2 FLR 852.
[38] [2009] 3 WLR 142.
[39] Ibid, Lord Hope at s22 and Lord Brown at s69.
[40] Heard on 22 October 2009.
[41] [2010] EMLR 4.
[42] [2009] EWHC 2375 (QB).
[43] Ibid, para 138.

in accordance with the analysis in *Re S (A Child)*[44] and *Re British Broadcasting Corporation.*[45] Neither freedom of expression nor the right to reputation could be accorded 'presumptive priority'.[46]

Conclusion

The importance of the two fundamental rights covered by this book is illustrated by the large volume of case law over recent years. English law is continuing to fashion a law of privacy, drawing on Article 8. The balancing of privacy and freedom of expression is now central to most 'media publication' cases. The development of the case law continues and requires close attention.

Richard Clayton QC
4–5 Gray's Square
Gray's Inn
London WC1R 5AH

Hugh Tomlinson
Matrix Chambers
Gray's Inn
London WC1R 5LN
30 November 2009

---

[44] [2005] 1 AC 593.
[45] n 38 above.
[46] *Flood* (n 42 above), para 148.

CONTENTS

12. The Right to Respect for Privacy and the Home

A. The Nature of the Rights   12.01

B. The Rights in English Law   12.08
   (1) Introduction   12.08
   (2) Personal information   12.21
   (3) Privacy rights and employment   12.78
   (4) Privacy and the media   12.91
   (5) Intrusion into the home: entry, search, and seizure   12.117
   (6) Photography, surveillance, telephone tapping, and intercepting letters   12.138
   (7) Housing law and respect for the home   12.180
   (8) Other privacy rights in English law   12.203

C. The Law under the European Convention   12.234
   (1) Introduction   12.234
   (2) Negative and positive obligations   12.240
   (3) Scope of 'Private life'   12.264
   (4) 'Home'   12.303
   (5) 'Correspondence'   12.313
   (6) Justification under Article 8(2)   12.324

Appendix 1: United Kingdom Cases Under Article 8   12.370

Appendix 2: Scottish Cases on Privacy and the Home   12.399

Appendix 3: The Canadian Charter of Rights   12.435

Appendix 4: The New Zealand Bill of Rights Act   12.472

Appendix 5: South African Constitutional Cases   12.494

Appendix 6: Human Rights Cases in Other Jurisdictions   12.506

15. Freedom of Expression

A. The Nature of the Right   15.01

B. The Right in English Law   15.06
   (1) Introduction   15.06
   (2) Prior restraint   15.25
   (3) Protection of reputation and private life   15.49
   (4) Comment on court proceedings: contempt of court   15.80
   (5) Orders that restrict court reporting   15.103
   (6) Protection of journalistic sources   15.145
   (7) Obscenity and indecency   15.153
   (8) Media regulation and censorship   15.170

(9) Freedom of expression and the criminal law   15.188

(10) Expression and government secrecy   15.212

(11) Freedom of expression in other areas   15.219

(12) Freedom of expression in Community law   15.234

C. The Law under the European
Convention   15.236

(1) Introduction   15.236

(2) Scope of the right   15.241

(3) The licensing power   15.262

(4) 'Interference' with the right to freedom of expression   15.267

(5) Justifying interferences with freedom of expression:
general considerations   15.273

(6) Justifying interferences with media expression   15.310

(7) Justifying interferences with expression for
specific legitimate aims   15.359

Appendix 1: United Kingdom Article 10 Cases in Strasbourg   15.386

Appendix 2: Human Rights Case in Scotland   15.412

Appendix 3: The Canadian Charter of Rights   15.426

Appendix 4: The New Zealand Bill of Rights Act   15.467

Appendix 5: Human Rights Cases in South Africa   15.499

Appendix 6: Human Rights Cases from Other Jurisdictions   15.514

Index   371

Contents of The Law of Human Rights   391

12

THE RIGHT TO RESPECT FOR PRIVACY AND THE HOME

A. **The Nature of the Rights**	12.01	(3) Scope of 'private life'	12.264
B. **The Rights in English Law**	12.08	(4) 'Home'	12.303
(1) Introduction	12.08	(5) 'Correspondence'	12.313
(2) Personal information	12.21	(6) Justification under Article 8(2)	12.324
(3) Privacy rights and employment	12.78	**Appendix 1: United Kingdom**	
(4) Privacy and the media	12.91	**Cases under Article 8**	12.370
(5) Intrusion into the home: entry, search, and seizure	12.117	**Appendix 2: Scottish Cases on Privacy and the Home**	12.399
(6) Photography, surveillance, telephone tapping, and intercepting letters	12.138	**Appendix 3: The Canadian Charter of Rights**	12.435
(7) Housing law and respect for the home	12.180	**Appendix 4: The New Zealand Bill of Rights Act**	12.472
(8) Other privacy rights in English law	12.203	**Appendix 5: South African Constitutional Cases**	12.494
C. **The Law under the European Convention**	12.234	**Appendix 6: Human Rights Cases in Other Jurisdictions**	12.506
(1) Introduction	12.234		
(2) Negative and positive obligations	12.240		

A. The Nature of the Rights

The rights to privacy and respect for the home are less well established in human rights **12.01**
jurisprudence than traditional civil rights such as life, liberty or freedom from slavery.
Although the right of persons to be secure in their homes from unreasonable searches
has long been acknowledged,[1] a more general right to privacy and respect for the home
was only clearly recognized in the twentieth century.[2] Most modern international human
rights instruments now protect the right of the individual to 'privacy' or 'private life', but
the limits of the right are still not clearly defined.

---

[1] See eg, Fourth Amendment, US Constitution which reflected the English common law, cf A Amar, *The Bill of Rights* (Yale University Press, 1998) 65ff and see para 12.508 below; for a recent discussion of the position under the Fourth Amendment, see *Minnesota v Carter* (1998) 5 BHRC 457.

[2] It has been suggested that the need to recognize privacy did not arise earlier because, in small rural communities, there was less distinction between 'private' and 'public' life, see F Schoeman, *Privacy and Social Freedom* (Cambridge University Press, 1992), Chap 7.

12.02   Article 12 of the Universal Declaration provides that:

> No one shall be subjected to arbitrary interference with his privacy, family, home, or correspondence, nor to attacks upon his honour and reputation. Everyone has the right to protection of the law against such interference or attacks.

Article 17 of the International Covenant on Civil and Political Rights describes it in similar terms.[3] Article 8 of the Convention refers to 'respect for private and family life, home and correspondence'.

12.03   At the heart of the right to privacy lies the notion of personal liberty and autonomy.[4] There is an enormous literature on 'privacy rights'[5] in which a variety of different definitions of the scope of the rights have been suggested. In addition to the 'right to be let alone',[6] privacy rights have been said to cover matters as diverse as an individual's dignity or moral integrity,[7] the unauthorized circulation of portraits,[8] the control of personal information,[9] the establishment and development of emotional relationships with others[10] and the freedom from media intrusion.[11] The wide range of areas in which the right has been invoked have led to scepticism as to whether it is helpful to speak of a general 'right to privacy' at all.[12] However, in analysing privacy rights it is important to distinguish between the 'human right' to privacy as against the state and the right to privacy as against private individuals or organizations.[13] Although the two are closely connected, the range of the former has been greater than that of the latter because of the greater power of the state over all aspects of private life as compared to private organizations.

12.04   The right to respect for private life in human rights instruments has its origin in traditional human rights concerns about state interference with the individual. Thus, in the United States, the constitutional right to privacy arises as an 'emanation'[14] derived from liberty

---

[3] See App J in Vol 2, Art 17 refers to 'arbitrary *or unlawful* interference . . .'. For the effect of the latter term, see Human Rights Committee, General Comment 16, Doc A 43/40, 181–3.

[4] See generally, D Feldman, *Civil Liberties and Human Rights in England and Wales* (2nd edn, Oxford University Press, 2002), Chap 9; see also E Barendt, 'Privacy as a Constitutional Right and Value' in B Markesinis (ed), *Protecting Privacy* (Oxford University Press, 1999) and James Q Whitman 'The Two Western Cultures of Privacy: Dignity Versus Liberty' (2004) 113 Yale LJ 1151.

[5] See eg, A Westin, *Privacy and Freedom* (Bodley Head, 1967); JUSTICE Report, *Privacy and the Law* (Stevens, 1970); R Wacks, *The Protection of Privacy* (Sweet & Maxwell, 1980); R Wacks *Privacy and Press Freedom* (Blackstone, 1995); Daniel Solove 'Conceptualizing Privacy' (2002) 90 Cal L Rev 1087; N A Moreham 'Privacy in the Common Law: A Doctrinal and Theoretical Analysis' (2005) 121 LQR 628, Daniel Solove 'A Taxonomy of Privacy' (2006) 154 U Pa L Rev 477. For a full discussion of privacy in the human rights context, see D Feldman, (n 4 above) Pt III.

[6] S Warren and L Brandeis, 'The Right to Privacy' (1890) 4 Harv LR 193.

[7] See eg, JC Inness; *Privacy, Intimacy and Isolation* (Oxford University Press, 1992); S Stoljar, 'A Re-examination of Privacy' (1984) 4 LS 67; D Feldman, 'Secrecy, Dignity or Autonomy? Views of Privacy as a Social Value' (1994) 47 CLP 41; *Pretty v United Kingdom* (2002) 35 EHRR 1.

[8] See Warren and Brandeis (n 6 above) 195.

[9] See eg, Westin, (n 5 above); R Wacks, *The Protection of Privacy* (Sweet & Maxwell, 1980).

[10] *X v Iceland* (1976) 5 DR 86, EComm HR; *Von Vondel v Netherlands* (Judgment of 4 October 2007), para 48.

[11] See eg, *Kaye v Robertson* [1991] FSR 62; *Von Hannover v Germany* (2005) 40 EHRR 1.

[12] See eg, R Wacks, 'The Poverty of "Privacy"' (1980) 96 LQR 73.

[13] For a discussion about the debate between proponents of the vertical as against the horizontal approach towards human rights, see para 5.92ff above.

[14] Or a 'penumbra' or 'shadow'; see *Whalen v Roe* (1977) 429 US 589.

rights enshrined in the Bill of Rights.[15] The protection of the home from unreasonable searches has expanded to protection from surveillance and interception of telephones.[16] The constitutional right to privacy has been invoked in cases concerning state interference with private decisions relating to birth control[17] and abortion,[18] clothing and appearance[19] and sexual conduct.[20]

In the private law sphere, the right to privacy has been more limited. It was first suggested **12.05** at the end of the nineteenth century in the United States,[21] where it has been extensively analysed and developed in the case law.[22] It has, however, usually been restricted to the four areas summarized in the *Restatement of the Law of Torts*[23] which states that:

> The right to privacy is invaded by
> (a) the unreasonable intrusion upon the seclusion of another;
> (b) the appropriation of the other's name or likeness;
> (c) unreasonable publicity given to the other's private life;
> (d) publicity that unreasonably places the other in a false light before the public.

Private law privacy issues most commonly arise in the context of media intrusion into a person's private life. This can take a wide variety of forms including intrusive photography, the publication of personal information and 'harassment' by journalists and photographers. Such activities may give rise to causes of action in private law. However, they also indirectly bring the 'human right' to privacy into play as a result of the state's positive obligations to ensure that the private lives of its citizens are protected. The extent to which these obligations require the courts, as emanations of state to provide the individual with private law remedies for 'breach of privacy' is of fundamental importance in English law because of its failure to provide full protection for private law privacy rights.[24]

The issues arising in relation to the right to privacy in the context of human rights law can **12.06** be conveniently considered under four heads:

> **Misuse of personal information**: A right to restrict the use of 'personal' or 'private' information about an individual is central to the right to privacy. A large volume of such information is held by public bodies and is, potentially, open to misuse. The extent to which the use of this information is controlled or restricted is one of the most important 'privacy' issues.

> **Intrusion into the home**: The right of the individual to respect for his home is fundamental to any notion of privacy. The issues which arise under this head include, in particular, protection

---

[15] The right has evolved, for example, from due process clauses of the Fifth and Fourteenth Amendments (see *Roe v Wade* (1973) 410 US 113, 153), the Ninth Amendment (see *Griswold v Connecticut* (1965) 381 US 479, 486–499) (Goldberg J concurring); see generally, L Tribe, *American Constitutional Law* (2nd edn, Foundation Press, 1988), 15–03.

[16] See eg, the Convention cases, para 12.321ff below.

[17] *Griswold v Connecticut* (1965) 381 US 479.

[18] *Roe v Wade* (1973) 410 US 113, see para 12.507 below.

[19] See eg, *Kelley v Johnson* (1976) 425 US 238 (police department regulations on officers' hair styles).

[20] See eg, *Dudgeon v United Kingdom* (1981) 4 EHRR 149.

[21] See S Warren and L Brandeis, 'The Right to Privacy', (1890) 4 Harv L Rev 193.

[22] See *Restatement of the Law of Torts*, 2nd edn, para 625Aff.

[23] Ibid, 2nd edn, para 625A; save for the right in para 2(b), an action for invasion of privacy can be maintained only by a living individual whose privacy is invaded (ibid, para 652I).

[24] See para 12.08ff below.

of the citizen against unreasonable entries, searches and seizures by public officials and against surveillance by the state or the media.

Photography, surveillance and telephone tapping: The 'private sphere' is not only invaded by physical intrusion into the home. The right of privacy is generally understood to extend to private 'correspondence'. Modern technology provides a wide range of means of surveillance including telephone tapping, 'bugging' and photography of various forms. When surveillance is carried out by public officials there is potentially a 'direct' infringement of privacy rights. However, surveillance may also be carried out by private organizations, in particular, the media. This gives rise to difficult issues as to the applicability of human rights instruments in the private sphere.[25]

The extent of other privacy rights: Finally, there are a range of other 'privacy rights' to be considered. These cover all forms of interference in the 'private sphere' including appropriation of a person's image, interference with private sexual behaviour and questions of the sexual identity of transsexuals.

12.07 Difficulties arise in each of these areas as to the extent to which interference with the privacy rights of the individual can be justified by the interests of society as a whole in, for example, the investigation of suspected criminal offences or the exposing of wrongdoing.

B. The Rights in English Law

(1) Introduction

(a) The common law position

12.08 The English common law does not recognize a right to privacy as such.[26] In *Kaye v Robertson*,[27] a prominent actor had undergone extensive surgery and was in hospital when he was photographed and allegedly interviewed by a tabloid newspaper. He sought an injunction to restrain publication of the interview. The case was argued on a number of bases, the most straightforward of which was infringement of privacy. In rejecting this head of claim, Glidewell LJ remarked that the case was:

> a graphic example of the desirability of Parliament considering whether and in what circumstances statutory provision should be made to protect the privacy of individuals.[28]

12.09 The courts have, on a number of occasions considered whether the development of a common law right to privacy would be appropriate. In *Malone v Commissioner of Police*[29] Sir Robert Megarry V-C rejected a claim that telephone tapping breached the 'right to privacy', holding that such a new right could only be created by parliament. In *Wainwright v Secretary of State for the Home Department*[30] the House of Lords rejected the contention that,

---

[25] See generally, para 5.50ff above.
[26] See the remarks of Lord Denning MR in *Re X (A Minor)* [1975] Fam 47, 58; *Malone v Metropolitan Police Commissioner* [1979] Ch 344, 372.
[27] [1991] FSR 62.
[28] Ibid, 66 (an injunction was granted on the basis of a potential claim in malicious falsehood).
[29] [1979] Ch 344, 372; see also *Kaye v Robertson* (n 27 above) and *R v Khan* [1997] AC 558.
[30] [2004] 2 AC 406 (rejecting suggestions in some earlier cases that the courts might be willing to develop such a tort (see eg, *Douglas v Hello!* [2001] QB 967, *H (A Healthcare Worker) v Associated Newspapers* [2002] EMLR 23 para 40, *Campbell v MGN* [2004] 2 AC 457, para 70).

as a result of the United Kingdom's accession to the Convention,[31] domestic law should recognize a general right to privacy. Lord Hoffmann noted that:

> there are a number of common law and statutory remedies of which it may be said that one at least of the underlying values they protect is a right of privacy. . . .Common law torts include trespass, nuisance, defamation and malicious falsehood; there is the equitable action for breach of confidence and statutory remedies under the Protection from Harassment Act 1997 and the Data Protection Act 1998. There are also extra-legal remedies under Codes of Practice applicable to broadcasters and newspapers. But there are gaps; cases in which the courts have considered that an invasion of privacy deserves a remedy which the existing law does not offer. Sometimes the perceived gap can be filled by judicious development of an existing principle.[32]

As a result, a claim for invasion of privacy by requiring two visitors to a prisoner to strip naked, in front of a window, was dismissed. The Court of Human Rights subsequently held that the United Kingdom was in breach of Article 8[33] and, as a result, the position under domestic law remains uncertain.

The consequences of the refusal of the courts to recognize a right of privacy was vividly illustrated in the *Kaye* case and in the case of *R v Brentwood Borough Council, ex p Peck*,[34] in which the release to the media of CCTV footage of the claimant just before he attempted suicide was held to be lawful.[35] The question of reform of the English law in this area has received considerable attention over the last forty years.[36] The impetus for reform has come largely from the perceived need to curb the excesses of the tabloid press. In response to a 1969 private members bill on the subject, the Younger Committee on Privacy was established. In 1972, the Committee decided, by a majority, against creating a 'general right to privacy', primarily because it would confer upon the courts an exceedingly wide discretion to enforce the law.[37] An attempt to introduce a Protection of Privacy Bill in the 1988–89 session of Parliament failed to achieve a Third Reading. In 1990, the Calcutt Committee on Privacy concluded that no tort of infringement of privacy should be introduced,[38] but recommended the establishment of a Press Complaints Commission. This Commission was established but attracted considerable criticism, and in his 1993 Review of Press Self-Regulation Sir David Calcutt QC recommended that further consideration be given to the introduction of a tort of infringement of privacy.[39] However, nothing concrete emerged from these various proposals.

12.10

---

[31] The case concerned matters which had taken place before the HRA had come into force.
[32] Ibid, para 18.
[33] *Wainwright v United Kingdom* (2006) 42 EHRR 41; see N Moreham (2007) 66 CLJ 35.
[34] *The Times*, 18 December 1997.
[35] This was held by the Court of Human Rights to be a breach of Article 8: *Peck v United Kingdom* (2003) 36 EHRR 41, see para 12.396 below.
[36] For general discussions, see D Eady, 'A Statutory Right to Privacy' [1996] EHRLR 243; Lord Bingham, 'Should there be a Law to Protect Rights of Personal Privacy?' [1996] EHRLR 450.
[37] *Report of the Committee on Privacy*, Cmnd 5012 (1972) paras 33–44 and 661–666.
[38] See *Report of the Committee on Privacy and Related Matters*, Cmnd 1102 (1990).
[39] (1993) Cm 2315, para 17; see also the House of Commons, National Heritage Committee, Fourth Report on Privacy and Media Intrusion, Mar 1993, (1992–93) HC Papers 294; and Lord Chancellor's Consultation Paper, *Infringement of Privacy* (Jul 1993).

(b) Private life and the Human Rights Act

12.11   With the enactment of the HRA the capacity of English law to protect privacy rights has radically improved. The HRA requires public authorities[40] to respect Article 8 privacy rights and it has been accepted that section 6(3) of the Act requires a court in private litigation to act in a way which is compatible with the Article 8 privacy rights.[41]

12.12   The possibility that the courts would use Article 8 to develop privacy remedies (in particular, granting injunctions to prevent publication of private information), was of such concern to the media that the Government was persuaded to introduce a new clause into the Human Rights Bill headed 'freedom of expression'. This ultimately became section 12 of the HRA, which was designed to provide stricter tests for the granting of interlocutory injunctions to restrain interference with privacy.[42] Section 12(4) provides that the court must have 'particular regard' to the importance of the Convention right to freedom of expression.[43] The issues which arise from this provision are considered in Chapter 15.[44]

12.13   The protection of privacy has been one of the most controversial and dynamic areas of development under the HRA. Ironically, in *Wainwright*[45] Lord Hoffman considered that the availability of statutory remedies under the HRA mitigated against the need for the common law to develop a new tort of invasion of privacy. The result so far has been a legal recognition that personal privacy should be appropriately protected[46] without going so far as to create a new tort of invasion of privacy. The recognition of a need to protect privacy has accordingly generally expressed itself in the development and application of existing causes of action, as anticipated by Lord Irvine LC in the course of the debates on the Human Rights Bill:

> I believe that the true view is that the courts will be able to adapt and develop the common law by relying on existing domestic principles in the laws of trespass, nuisance, copyright, confidence and the like to fashion a common law right to privacy.[47]

(c) Article 8 in the English courts

12.14   **Introduction.**   The provisions of Article 8 have been considered by the English courts on a very large number of occasions since the HRA came into force. In a number of cases the courts have made general observations about the nature and scope of Article 8. It has been emphasized that there are no bright line rules to be applied to the generality of cases because Article 8 requires a difficult fact sensitive evaluative exercise.[47a]

12.15   **'Respect'.**   The concept of 'respect' is not analysed in the Convention case law. In general, any state action which disrupts an individual's enjoyment of private life, home or

---

[40]   See para 5.03ff above.

[41]   See generally, para 5.107ff above.

[42]   See *Hansard*, HC col 535 (2 Jul 1998) (Home Secretary introducing s 12). And see paras 12.110ff below.

[43]   It does not, however, give priority to Article 10 over Article 8, see para 12.108 below.

[44]   See para 15.22ff below; section 12 does not give Article 10 precedence over Article 8: *In Re S (A Child)(Identification: Restrictions on Publication)* [2005] 1 AC 593, para 17.

[45]   n 30 above.

[46]   *Douglas v Hello! Ltd* [2001] QB 967, para 110 per Sedley LJ.

[47]   *Hansard*, HC col 785; see also Lord Bingham, 'Should there be a Law to Protect Rights of Personal Privacy?' [1996] EHRLR 450.

[47a]   *EB (Kosovo) v Secretary of State for the Home Department* [2008] 3 WLR 178, para 12; see also para 21, pointing out that consideration of an appeal under Article 8 calls for a broad and informed judgment which is not to be constrained by a series of prescriptive rules.

correspondence is treated as an 'interference' with Article 8 rights which requires justification.[48] However, in *M v Secretary of State for Work and Pensions*[49] Lord Walker suggested that an interference with Article 8 rights requires a 'failure to accord respect' and that less serious matters would not constitute interferences at all. This is not consistent with Convention case law which does not require interferences with Article 8 rights to be 'serious' before justification is required.

'Private life'. The English courts have recognized the breadth of the rights protected by **12.16**
Article 8. No attempt has been made to provide a comprehensive definition of 'private life'. It clearly extends to physical and psychological integrity and to those features which are integral to a person's identity or ability to function socially as a person.[50] It also covers the right to share what would otherwise be private with others; so that the right to tell one's story is protected by Article 8.[50a] Private life issues therefore arise in a wide variety of contexts including areas as diverse as medical treatment,[51] the exercise of police stop and search powers,[52] and the health impact of deportation decisions.[53] It has been accepted that Article 8 covers 'personal autonomy.'[53a]

However, the Courts have recognized a number of limits to the concept of private life. In **12.17**
R (Pretty) v DPP[54] the House of Lords held that Article 8 was not engaged in relation to a decision as to how an individual wished to die. This restrictive view was not accepted by the Court of Human Rights.[55] Thus, it has been held that the conditions imposed on a homeless person provided with local authority accommodation are not within the private sphere.[56] Furthermore, the Courts have shown considerable reluctance in extending the concept of private life; to activities conducted in public with social aspects involving the wider community such as hunting with dogs.[57] The reasoning in support of this conclusion

---

[48] But note that it has been said that 'not every act or measure which adversely affects moral or physical integrity will interfere with the right to respect for private life' (*Bensaid v United Kingdom* (2001) 33 EHRR 205 para 46); where a 'positive obligation' is relied on where it has been said that Article 'cannot be considered applicable each time an individual's everyday life is disrupted', *Šečić v Croatia*, Decision of 15 June 2006, see para 12.328 below.

[49] [2006] 2 AC 91, para 83; and see also *R v G* [2008] 1 WLR 1379, para 54 where Baroness Hale said that Article 8 does not mean 'that every sexual relationship, however brief or unsymmetrical is worthy of respect, nor is every sexual act which a person wishes to perform' (although this approach does not seem to have been supported by the other members of the House).

[50] *R (Razgar) v Secretary of State for the Home Department* [2004] 2 AC 368, para 9; in *R (Countryside Alliance) v Attorney-General* ([2008] 1 AC 719) Baroness Hale described this as 'the personal and psychological space within which each individual develops his own sense of self and relationships with other people' (para 116).

[50a] *Torbay BC v News Group Newspapers* [2004] EMLR 8.

[51] See *R (Burke) v General Medical Council* [2006] QB 424, discussed at para 12.216 below.

[52] See *R (Gillan) v Commissioner of Police for the Metropolis* [2006] 2 AC 307, discussed at para 12.219 below.

[53] See para 12.225 below.

[53a] See *R (Purdy) v DPP* [2008] EWHC 2565 (Admin) para 54; in which it was said that the *Countryside Alliance* case (n 50 above) 'gave general support for broadening the scope of Art 8(1) to cover personal autonomy'.

[54] [2002] 1 AC 800, noted by Keown (2002) 61 CLJ 8.

[55] *Pretty v United Kingdom* (2002) 35 EHRR 1, para 65, see generally A Pedain (2002) 61 CLJ 511 and A Pedain 'The human rights dimension of the Diane Pretty case' (2003) 61 CLJ 181; in *R (Purdy) v DPP* (n 53a above) (Administrative Court held that it was bound by the decision of the House of Lords and that, as a result, Article 8 was not engaged in relation to a decision by the DPP as to whether to issue guidance concerning prosecutions for assisting suicides) and see para 12.299 below.

[56] *Orejudos v RB Kensington and Chelsea* [2003] EWCA Civ 1967 (the reasoning in this case is difficult to follow and the alternative basis for the decision, justification under Art 8(2), is to be preferred).

[57] *R (Countryside Alliance) v Attorney-General* (n 50 above).

is not entirely convincing[58] and, arguably, fails to give sufficient weight to the recent Convention jurisprudence concerning Article 8 and the right to self-fulfilment. It is, at first sight, difficult to see why the fact that certain individual's self-fulfilment takes the form of participation in public spectacles prevents it from falling within the scope of Article 8 which is, increasingly recognized as extending to 'social' activities.[59]

12.18 **Article 8 and misuse of private information.** The HRA has led to a profound change in the approach of the courts to cases involving the publication of private information. The values enshrined in Article 8 have been absorbed into the cause of action for breach of confidence to provide protection against the misuse of private information, with the claim being renamed 'misuse of private information'.[60] The inherent jurisdiction of the High Court to protect the interests of children has also been affected. In *Re S (A Child) (Identification: Restrictions on Publication)*,[61] the House of Lords made it clear that the HRA entitles the court to restrain publicity in cases where an Article 8 interest outweighs the freedom of expression of the media enshrined in Article 10. Nevertheless, the case law was held to reveal that the approach adopted in the past under the inherent jurisdiction of the court to grant injunctions was remarkably similar to that to be adopted under the Convention.

12.19 **Article 8 and reputation.** Alongside the development of a new cause of action for misuse of private information, the English courts have also acknowledged that the right to reputation is protected by Article 8.[62] This means that a similar 'balancing exercise' between Article 8 and 10 should be carried out in both privacy and defamation cases.[63] This, in turn, suggests that that the tort of defamation – which has developed to take account of Article 10 rights of defendants[64] may now have to be further adapted to take into account the Article 8 rights of claimants. The English courts have not yet directly engaged with these issues.[65]

(d) The contents of this section

12.20 In this section we will consider the English law in law in the following areas where 'privacy and the home' are protected by a variety of common law and statutory remedies:

• Personal information—including the private law remedies in confidence and misuse of private information, the law concerning the use and disclosure of private information by public bodies and the available rights of access to private information held by others.

---

[58] Each of the members of the Judicial Committee approached the point in a slightly different way, see para 12.207 below.

[59] See, para 12.299ff below. Note that these arguments, of course, only go to the first stage—whether there is an interference—although at the 'justification' stage the fact that an activity is public (thus impacting on the rights of others) may well be a relevant consideration.

[60] *Campbell v MGN* [2004] 2 AC 457, para 17, per Lord Nicholls; *A v B plc* [2003] QB 195, para 11, per Lord Woolf CJ, see para 12.24ff below.

[61] [2005] 1 AC 593, para 23.

[62] See eg, *W v Westminster* [2005] 1 FLR 816, para 38; *Greene v Associated Newspapers* [2005] QB 972, para 68.

[63] Cf the comments of Eady J in *Prince Radu of Hohenzollern v Houston* [2007] EWHC 2735 (QB) para 44; at present these two wrongs are approached in very different ways by the Courts with very little discussion of 'balancing' in the defamation cases.

[64] Particularly in relation to media publication, see para 15.65 below.

[65] The Art 8 cases were cited in the House of Lords in *Jameel (Mohammed) v Wall Street Journal Europe Sprl* [2007] 1 AC 359 but not considered in the speeches, see para 15.66 below.

- Privacy rights in employment—the rights of employees to maintain privacy and of employers to deal with private information relating to their employees.
- Privacy and the media—the regulation of the media to prevent unwarranted intrusions into private life and the availability of private law remedies.
- Intrusion into the home—the law relating to entry search and seizure.
- Photography, surveillance, telephone tapping, and intercepting letters.
- Other privacy rights in English law.

(2) Personal information[66]

(a) Introduction

The common law did not provide comprehensive protection against the misuse of personal information. The equitable claim for 'breach of confidence' provided protection against the misuse of some categories of personal information. Public law has gradually developed analogous principles of protection in relation to information held by public authorities. A patchwork of statutory prohibitions on the misuse of personal information has provided additional protection. In 1984 the Data Protection Act provided a general regime for regulating the use of personal information held on automated systems. This has been strengthened by the Data Protection Act 1998.
    12.21

(b) Breach of confidence and misuse of personal information

INTRODUCTION

History.   The nineteenth century case law on 'breach of confidence' was the inspiration for the development of the right of privacy in the United States. The doctrine derives from a case in which Prince Albert obtained an injunction on the basis of breach of confidence to prevent an exhibition of etchings by him and Queen Victoria: the injunction was granted against a defendant who had acquired copies without their consent.[67] As the case law developed it was established that, in order to establish a breach of confidence a 'three part test' had to be satisfied:
    12.22

> First, the information itself . . . must have the necessary quality of confidence about it. Secondly, that information must have been imparted in circumstances importing an obligation of confidence. Thirdly, there must be an unauthorized use of that information to the detriment of the party communicating it.[68]

The doctrine proved to be extremely flexible and came to protect not merely trade secrets, but also confidential information about an individual's private life such as marital secrets,[69] sexual relationships,[70] or a medical condition (such as having AIDS),[71] as well as artistic confidences.[72] The approach of the courts was pragmatic and breach of
    12.23

---

[66] See generally, H Fenwick, *Civil Liberties and Human Rights* (4th edn, Routledge-Cavendish, 2007), Chap 17.

[67] *Prince Albert v Strange* (1848) 2 De G & Sm 652; the decision was heavily relied on by S Warren and L Brandeis, 'The Right to Privacy' (1890) 4 Harv LR 193.

[68] *Coco v A N Clark (Engineers) Ltd* [1969] RPC 41, 47–48.

[69] *Argyll (Duchess) v Argyll (Duke)* [1967] 1 Ch 302.

[70] *Stephens v Avery* [1988] Ch 449; *Barrymore v News Group* [1997] FSR 600.

[71] *X v Y* [1990] 1 QB 220.

[72] See eg, *Gilbert v Star Newspapers* (1894) 11 TLR 4.

confidence developed into an adaptable remedy for the protection of privacy in an important class of cases.[73]

12.24 **Impact of Article 8.** This development has continued under the influence of the section 6 of the HRA,[74] as a means for Article 8 to be brought to bear on privacy disputes between individuals.[75] In *A v B plc*,[76] Lord Woolf CJ commented that Article 8 and Article 10, are:

> the new parameters within which the court will decide, in an action for breach of confidence, whether a person is entitled to have his privacy protected by the court or whether the restriction of freedom of expression which such protection involves cannot be justified'. . . This involves giving a new strength and breadth to the action [for breach of confidence][77]

In *Campbell v MGN*[78] the House of Lords confirmed that

> This cause of action has now firmly shaken off the limiting constraint of the need for an initial confidential relationship. In doing so it has changed its nature. In this country this development was recognized clearly in the judgment of Lord Goff of Chieveley in *Attorney General v Guardian Newspapers Ltd (No 2)* [1990] 1 AC 109, 281. Now the law imposes a 'duty of confidence' whenever a person receives information he knows or ought to know is fairly and reasonably to be regarded as confidential. Even this formulation is awkward. The continuing use of the phrase 'duty of confidence' and the description of the information as 'confidential' is not altogether comfortable. Information about an individual's private life would not, in ordinary usage, be called 'confidential'. The more natural description today is that such information is private. The essence of the tort is better encapsulated now as misuse of private information . . . The time has come to recognize that the values enshrined in articles 8 and 10 are now part of the cause of action . . .'

12.25 As a result the cause of action for breach of confidence no longer depends on the establishment of a 'duty of confidence'. It focuses on the one hand upon the protection of human autonomy and dignity, the right to control the dissemination of information about one's private life and the right to the esteem and respect of other people; and, on the other hand, on the right to freedom of expression and the public interest in receiving information.[79] As Buxton LJ said in *McKennitt v Ash*,[80] 'articles 8 and 10. . .are now not merely of persuasive or parallel effect but. . .are the very content of the domestic tort that the English court now has to enforce'. Neither Article 8 nor Article 10 has 'presumptive priority'.[81]

12.26 When a claim for misuse of private information is made the matter is approached in two stages. At the first stage the court considers whether the claimant has a reasonable expectation of privacy in respect of the disclosed facts in all the circumstances. If so there is a *prima facie* right to protection of the information. Once this has been established, the second stage

---

[73] See generally, F Gurry, *Breach of Confidence* (Oxford University Press, 1984), and R Toulson and C Phipps, *Confidentiality* (2nd edn, Sweet & Maxwell, 2006).

[74] See para 5.50ff above.

[75] See eg, *Campbell v Mirror Group Newspapers Ltd* [2004] 2 AC 457, *Venables v News Group Newspapers* [2001] Fam 430.

[76] [2003] QB 195.

[77] Ibid, para 4.

[78] [2004] 2 AC 457, paras 11–22 per Lord Nicholls.

[79] Ibid, para 51; see also *Douglas v Hello! Ltd (No 1)* [2001] QB 967, 1001 per Sedley LJ.

[80] [2008] QB 73, para 11.

[81] Campbell (n 75 above) 10 para 113 (Lord Hope), paras 138–141 (Baroness Hale).

must be considered. The Court must look at the Article 8(2) justifications for interference with the claimant's privacy rights. If another Convention right (for example Article 10) is in play the court must carry out what has been referred to as 'ultimate balancing' or 'parallel analysis': looking at the position under Article 8 and Article 10 in turn, considering the justification under each article in parallel on the basis of presumptive parity.[82] These two stages will be considered in turn.

FIRST STAGE: REASONABLE EXPECTATION OF PRIVACY

Introduction. At the first stage, the question is whether the information in question is   **12.27** private or confidential. It has been said that:

> Essentially the touchstone of private life is whether in respect of the disclosed facts the person in question had a reasonable expectation of privacy.[83]

The Court of Appeal has held that private information includes:

> information that is personal to the person who possesses it and that he does not intend shall be imparted to the general public. The nature of the information, or the form in which it is kept, may suffice to make it plain the information satisfies those criteria.[84]

This represents a significant expansion upon the type of information protected by the old tort of breach of confidence. The tort now protects certain rights to both privacy and secrecy; information which would previously have been protected as 'confidential'[85] remains protected, even though that information might not fall within the scope of Article 8.[86] In what follows we will focus on the protection of *private* information.

The question whether the relevant information is sufficiently private or confidential to   **12.28** warrant protection must be kept separate from the question as to whether the disclosure of such information is justified,[87] although the factors relevant to the two issues will clearly overlap. There is no determinative factor in deciding whether or not information is private: it will depend on all the circumstances.[88] Relevant factors include the nature of the information, the circumstances in which it is obtained, the identity of the claimant and the extent to which the information is in the public domain.

The nature of the information. The nature and content of the information itself is plainly   **12.29** of great importance. As the Court of Appeal held in *Douglas v Hello! (No 3)* this in itself may be sufficient to show that the information is private.[89] An obvious example is medical

---

[82] Mc Kennitt (n 80 above), para 48; and see *A Local Authority v W* [2006] 1 FLR 1, para 53.

[83] *Campbell v MGN Limited* [2004] 2 AC 457, para 21. See also para 85 (per Lord Hope), para 134 (per Baroness Hale), and para 165 (per Lord Carswell).

[84] *Douglas v Hello! Ltd (No 3)* [2006] QB 125, para 83. See also para 55. The case was appealed to the House of Lords on other grounds: see [2008] 1 AC 1.

[85] That is, information having the necessary quality of confidence about it and being imparted in circumstances importing a obligation of confidence: see *Coco v AN Clark (Engineers) Ltd* [1969] RPC 41, 47.

[86] *OBG v Allan* [2008] 1 AC 1, paras 118 (per Lord Hoffman) and para 255 (per Lord Nicholls). See also *Prince of Wales v Associated Newspapers* [2008] Ch 57, CA, paras 28–29 and 67.

[87] *Campbell v MGN Limited* (n 83 above), para 21; and see *Attorney General v Guardian Newspapers Ltd (No 2)* [1990] 1 AC 109.

[88] See also *Lord Browne of Madingley v Associated Newspapers* [2008] QB 103, para 31.

[89] See para 12.27 above.

information because 'a person's health is in any event a private matter'.[90] The recording of personal opinions in diary form might also be clearly private: the musings of the Prince of Wales in his journals, recording his impressions of overseas visits, were held to be obviously private regardless of the existence of any pre-existing relationship between the Prince and the individual who disclosed the information.[91] But information need not be intimate or embarrassing to qualify for protection.[92] Information may be protected even though it concerns business affairs[93] or was intended to be used for commercial gain.[94] Further, personal experiences, including relationships, do not necessarily lose their private character simply because they were shared with others and one of the parties wishes to disclose those experiences.[95]

12.30 Special considerations apply to photographs, video tapes or tape recordings. Photographs:

> are not merely a method of conveying information that is an alternative to verbal description . . . As a means of invading privacy, a photograph is particularly intrusive.[96]

As a result, a court may restrain the publication of a photograph even if the taker is free to describe the information in the photograph.[97]

12.31 It has been said that the action of breach of confidence did not protect 'trivial or useless information'[98] or to 'tittle tattle or gossip'.[99] However, the position is less clear cut when the information is private. In *McKennitt v Ash*[100] Eady J:

> the mere fact that information concerning an individual is 'anodyne' or 'trivial' will not necessarily mean that Article 8 is not engaged. For the purpose of determining that initial question, it seems that the subject–matter must be carefully assessed. If it is such as to give rise to a 'reasonable expectation of privacy', then questions such as triviality or banality may well need to be considered at the later stage of bringing to bear an 'intense focus' upon the comparative importance of the specific rights being claimed in the individual case.

---

[90] *McKennitt v Ash* [2008] QB 73, para 23.

[91] *Prince of Wales v Associated Newspapers* [2008] Ch 57, para 36.

[92] *Murray v Express Newspapers* [2007] EWHC 1908 (Ch), para 37, interpreting *Von Hannover v Germany* (2005) 40 EHRR 1.

[93] *Lord Browne of Madingley v Associated Newspapers* [2008] QB 103, paras 34 and 50; see also *Long Beach Limited v Global Witness Limited* [2007] EWHC 1980 (QB), para 20, in which it was held that Article 8 was 'undoubtedly engaged' by the disclosure of information (including credit card statements) about the allegedly corrupt business activities of the son of the President of the Republic of Congo.

[94] *OBG v Allan* [2008] 1 AC 1, para 118.

[95] See *McKennitt v Ash* (n 90 above) paras 28–30 and 50–51; *CC v AB* [2006] EWHC 3083 (QB), para 21. This point is usually likely to be more relevant to the balancing exercise required by the second question, rather than the question of whether the information is private at all.

[96] *Douglas v Hello! (No 3)* [2006] QB 125, para 84.

[97] See *D v L* [2004] EMLR 1, para 23; see eg, *Theakston v MGN* [2002] EMLR 22 (court permitted story to be published, but not photographs of claimant in a brothel) and *Mosley v News Group Newspapers* [2008] EMLR 20, paras 16–23.

[98] See *McNicol v Sportsman's Books* (1930) McG CC 116; *Attorney General v Guardian Newspapers Ltd (No 2)* [1990] 1 AC 109.

[99] Cf *Stephens v Avery* [1988] Ch 449.

[100] [2006] EMLR 178, para 58 see also paras 131 to 158; the judge's approach was approved by the Court of Appeal, see *McKennitt v Ash* (n 90 above) paras 12 and 18 to 26.

In *Lord Browne v Associated Newspapers*[101] the Court of Appeal held that 'the fact that a **12.32** piece of information can be regarded as trivial does not seem to us to be decisive'. In fact, recent dicta suggest that the fact that private information is used to promote 'vapid tittle-tattle' (as opposed to, say, political comment) will make the courts *more* likely to restrain publication.[102] Although there has been some suggestion that there is no reasonable expectation of privacy in relation to casual sexual encounters[103] the modern approach is that:

> anyone indulging in sexual activity is entitled to a degree of privacy—especially if it is on private property and between consenting adults (paid or unpaid).[104]

The decision of Court of Human Rights Case in the *Von Hannover* case[105] has had an **12.33** important impact on the approach of the English courts. In *Von Hannover*, Princess Caroline of Monaco complained of the publication of photographs of her engaging in ordinary activities in public places, such as eating out at a restaurant and undertaking sporting activities. The Court held that there had been a breach of Article 8. The English courts have accepted that this case cannot be confined as merely an example of media harassment: 'an individual. . . may have a legitimate expectation of privacy in relation to private family and personal activities which are not in themselves either embarrassing or intimate in a sexual or medical sense'.[106] In *Murray v Big Pictures (UK) Limited*[107] the Court of Appeal held that even routine activities such as taking a bus ride might, depending on the circumstances, form part of 'private life'.

Information may be 'private' for these purposes even though it is untrue. In *McKennitt v* **12.34** *Ash*,[108] a successful musician brought proceedings for misuse of private information when a former friend wrote a book containing personal and private information about her. Some of that information was said to be false. The Court held that this did not prevent the claimant from bringing her claim in breach of confidence, rather than defamation. Longmore LJ considered the argument 'untenable' and held that:

> The question in a case of misuse of private information is whether the information is private not whether it is true or false. The truth or falsity of the information is an irrelevant inquiry in deciding whether information is entitled to be protected . . .

However, Buxton LJ, with whom Latham and Longmore LJJ agreed, pointed out that:

> If it could be shown that a claim in breach of confidence was brought when the nub of the case was a complaint of the falsity of the allegations, and that that was done in order to avoid the rules of the tort of defamation, then objections could be raised in terms of abuse of process.

---

[101] [2008] QB 103, para 33.

[102] *Campbell v MGN* [2004] 2 AC 457, paras 148–149; *Jameel v Wall Street (Europe)* [2007] 1 AC 359, para 147; *CC v AB* (n 95 above) para 36.

[103] See *Theakston v MGN Ltd* [2002] EMLR 398; *McKennitt v Ash*, (n 90 above) paras 29–30; *X v Y* [2003] ICR 1138.

[104] *Mosley v News Group Newspapers* [2008] EWHC 1777 (QB), para 99; see also *CC v AB* (n 95 above) para 30 (reasonable expectation of privacy in relation to adulterous relationship).

[105] *Von Hannover v Germany* (2005) 40 EHRR 1; see para 12.260 below and see also the discussion of the case in H Fenwick and G Phillipson, *Media Freedom under the Human Rights Act* (Oxford University Press, 2006), 677–683.

[106] *McKennitt v Ash*, (n 90 above) para 41.

[107] [2008] EMLR 12, para 56.

[108] (n 90 above).

The fact that the claimant is not named will not prevent an action being brought provided that he is identifiable from the published material.[109] Thus, summary judgment and a final injunction were granted to restrain the publication of a proposed account of fictional sexual activity between 'transparently disguised' individuals.[110]

12.35 **The circumstances in which the information was obtained.** It remains highly relevant to consider whether the information was disclosed in circumstances connoting confidentiality,[111] although this is no longer a necessary component of the tort. Nor is it determinative,[112] but the existence of a relationship of trust and confidence between the parties will reinforce a claim for misuse of private information. It has been suggested, for example, that contractual documents innocently discovered might not be self-evidently private, but that the position would be different if they were discovered in the course of a relationship of confidence.[113] A relationship of confidence can arise in many circumstances and has been held to exist, for example, between doctor and patient,[114] journalist and source,[115] husband and wife[116] and between the parties to any sexual relationship.[117] However, the court will consider not just the general nature of the relationship, but also specific details of the relationship in question and the circumstances in which the particular information was communicated.

12.36 In *Murray v Big Pictures (UK) Limited*,[118] the Court of Appeal took into account the fact that the photographs of JK Rowling's child in a public street were taken with a view to profit and would encourage further intrusion in the future. It was also relevant that the photographers acted covertly in the knowledge that the taking of the photographs would be objected to.[119] Accordingly, while this kind of consideration would be reserved for the second stage of the analysis, it might also be of relevance to whether there is a reasonable expectation of privacy.

12.37 **The identity of the claimant.** The identity of the claimant may be relevant to the extent to which there is a reasonable expectation of privacy in relation to a particular item of information. In the *Murray*[120] case the claim was brought by the well known author JK Rowling and her husband on behalf of their infant son, in respect of photographs taken of him. The Court of Appeal held that it was of particular importance that the claimant was a child.[121]

---

[109] It appears that, in contrast to the position in libel where publication to at least one third party is required, because the action concerns damage to the claimant's own Article 8 rights it will be sufficient if he can identify himself from the published information.

[110] *P, Q and R v Quigley* [2008] EWHC 1051 (QB).

[111] See, for instance, *Prince of Wales v Associated Newspapers* [2008] Ch 57, para 48; *McKennitt v Ash* [2008] QB 73, para 15; and *Lord Browne of Madingley v Associated Newspapers* [2008] QB 103, paras 26 and 31.

[112] *Lord Browne of Madingley v Associated Newspapers* (n 111 above) para 29.

[113] *McKennitt v Ash*, (n 111 above) para 24.

[114] *W v Edgell* [1990] 1 Ch 359.

[115] *A-G v Mulholland* [1963] 2 QB 477, and see *In re an Inquiry under the Company Securities(Insider Dealing) Act 1985* [1988] AC 660.

[116] *Argyll (Duchess) v Argyll (Duke)* [1967] 1 Ch 302.

[117] *Barrymore v News Group Newspapers* [1997] FSR 600.

[118] [2008] EMLR 12, para 50.

[119] Ibid, para 57.

[120] Ibid.

[121] Ibid, para 46.

It said that the issue was whether the child had a reasonable expectation of privacy, not whether his parents did.[122] A similar approach would apply in cases involving adults who lack the mental capacity for 'expectations'. The fact that a claimant is a 'public figure' does not reduce expectations of privacy but may enhance them because, in 'respect of such persons the public takes an interest in information about them that is relatively trivial'.[123]

The claimant's conduct. The conduct of the claimant is, in general, not relevant at the first stage. The suggestion in the cases that a person who seeks favourable publicity cannot complain of an invasion of privacy by subsequent unfavourable publicity[124] is no longer good law. Neither is there a doctrine that there can be a 'zonal forfeiture of privacy rights'[125] This notion was trenchantly dismissed by the Court of Appeal in *McKennitt v Ash*[126] which agreed with Eady J's statement that there is 'a significant difference between choosing to reveal aspects of private life with which one feels 'comfortable' and yielding up to public scrutiny every detail of personal life, feelings, thoughts and foibles of character.'[127] The Court rejected the contention that a person should not be able to limit publication of private information that which he wishes to be published, holding that: **12.38**

> If information is my private property, it is for me to decide how much of it should be published. The 'zone' argument completely undermines that reasonable expectation of privacy.

Public domain. In an action for breach of confidence, a claim cannot be maintained in relation to information which is already in the public domain. In a well known passage in the *Spycatcher* case in the House of Lords Lord Goff said: **12.39**

> . . . the principle of confidentiality only applies to information to the extent that it is confidential. In particular, once it has entered what is usually called the public domain (which means no more than that the information in question is so generally accessible that, in all the circumstances, it cannot be regarded as confidential) then, as a general rule, the principle of confidentiality can have no application to it.[128]

This principle continues to apply in breach of confidence cases[129] but the question as to whether the publication of information has been so extensive as destroy its confidential character is 'a question of degree depending on the facts of the particular case'.[130] The Court of Appeal has suggested that there is an important distinction between making information available to a circle of friends and colleagues, and publishing information

---

[122] Ibid, para 56.
[123] *Prince of Wales v Associated Newspapers* [2008] Ch 57, para 70 (however, the fact that such a person has 'public functions' may well be highly relevant at the second 'justification' stage).
[124] See *Woodward v Hutchins* [1977] 1 WLR 760, 765; for criticism of this decision see *Douglas v Hello! Ltd (No 1)* [2001] QB 967, para 96 (Brooke LJ); *Campbell v Frisbee* [2003] EMLR 3, para 34 and see M Tugendhat and I Christie, *The Law of Privacy and the Media*, (2002), paras 9.30–9.31, p 343.
[125] Sometimes said to derive from the decision of Eady J in *A v B* [2005] EMLR 36.
[126] [2008] QB 73, para 53; see also *X v Persons Unknown* ([2006] EWHC 2783 (QB), para 28.
[127] [2006] EMLR 178 at paras 79–80.
[128] *Attorney-General v Guardian Newspapers (No 2)* [1990] 1 AC 109 at 282.
[129] *McKennitt v Ash* (n 111 above) para 53; *OBG v Allan* [2008] 1 AC 1, para 122.
[130] *Franchi v Franchi* [1967] RPC 149, 153; *Lord Browne of Madingley v Associated Newspapers* [2008] QB 103, para 61. For a discussion as to the effect of foreign publication see *A-G v Guardian Newspapers Ltd (No 2)* [1990] 1 AC 109; and see R Toulson and C Phipps, *Confidentiality* (2nd edn, Sweet & Maxwell, 2006), Chap IV.

widely in a newspaper.[131] An exclusive agreement with a single publication to publish wedding photographs did not remove all confidentiality, and the photographs were protected from subsequent unauthorized publication.[132] Information which is disclosed in open court may lose its private nature, probably even if the court is in another country;[133] however, documents disclosed during the course of civil[134] or criminal[135] proceedings are subject to an implied undertaking that they cannot be used for a collateral purpose. It has been held that previous convictions and sentences cannot be confidential information,[136] but this may be an overstatement of the position.[137]

12.40   In relation to private information even if material is already generally available it does not necessarily lose its protection. An important factor is whether republication of material which is already generally accessible would have significant additional effects.[138] Since photographs, video footage and tape recordings can be particularly intrusive, it is in general no answer to a claim to restrain publication of such material that the information is already in the public domain.[139] Particular care may be needed in respect of intimate photographs which have already been published, for further publication may still be highly embarrassing.[140] Further, the fact that a matter has once been in the public domain does not necessarily mean it can never become private again; the determination is matter of fact and degree.[141] On the other hand, confidentiality may also be *lost* by the passage of time or a change of circumstances.[142]

Second stage: justifications for interference and parallel analysis

12.41   **Introduction.**   Once it is determined that the information in question is private or confidential, the next step is to balance the rights of the subject of the information against the rights of the person who has used, or is seeking to use, it. Since the complaint is usually against publication or disclosure of some form, Article 10 of the Convention often comes into play. Ordinarily in misuse of private information cases, therefore, the balance is

---

[131] *Lord Browne of Madingley v Associated Newspapers* [2008] QB 103, para 61.

[132] *Douglas v Hello! Ltd (No 3)* [2006] QB 125, paras 103–107.

[133] *Long Beach Limited v Global Witness Limited* [2007] EWHC 1980 (QB).

[134] *Home Office v Harman* [1983] AC 280; and see *Crest Homes plc v Marks* [1987] AC 829; and *Sybron Corporation v Barclays Bank plc* [1985] Ch 299.

[135] *Taylor v Director of the Serious Fraud Office* [1998] 1 WLR 1040.

[136] *Elliott v Chief Constable of Wiltshire, The Times*, 5 December 1996.

[137] Cf *Melvin v Reid* (1931) 112 Cal App 285 (a film identifying the plaintiff as a prostitute who, seven years earlier, had been acquitted of murder was a breach of privacy after she had 'abandoned her life of shame, had rehabilitated herself'); and see W Prosser, 'Privacy', (1960) 48 Calif Rev 383, 396.

[138] *Green Corns Ltd v Claverley Group* [2005] EMLR 31, paras 78–81. This reflects Lord Hoffman's view in *OBG v Allan* [2008] 1 AC 1, para 122, that the principle rests on 'whether there is still a point in enforcing the obligation of confidence'.

[139] *D v L* [2004] EMLR 1 at para 23.

[140] *Mosley v News Group Newspapers Limited* [2008] EWHC 687 (QB), para 33; (the publication of a video of sexual activities was already so widespread that there would have been no purpose in an injunction – however, the judge appears to have been strongly influenced by the fact that an injunction against the defendant would not prevent the continuing publication by third parties, see para 34).

[141] *R v Broadcasting Complaints Commission, ex p Granada TV* [1995] EMLR 163, 168; see also *R v Chief Constable of North Wales Police, ex p Thorpe* [1999] QB 396, 429A.

[142] See eg, *A-G v Jonathan Cape Ltd* [1976] 1 QB 752 (the confidentiality of Cabinet discussions lost after 10 years; publication of 'Crossman Diaries' not restrained).

between Article 8 rights and Article 10 rights. This is the language used by the House of Lords in *Campbell v MGN* and adopted in most of the following cases.

The applicable principles.　It is now well established[143] that the following principles **12.42** apply:

- neither article has as such precedence over the other;
- where conflict arises between the values under articles 8 and 10, an 'intense focus' is necessary upon the comparative importance of the specific rights been claimed in the individual case;
- the court must take into account the justification for interfering with or restricting each right; and
- so, too, the proportionality test must be applied to each.

In some cases, however, the information in question may not attract the protection of **12.43** Article 8 but might still be confidential for the purposes of the tort. Similarly, the use to which the information is put might not involve freedom of expression under Article 10, but might involve, say, the actual application of trade secrets in manufacture. In such cases, a similar balancing act of the interests in question still needs to be carried out,[144] albeit that where Convention rights are engaged on only one side of the balance, the starting point should be that any interference with that right must be justified as proportionate.

Factors to be taken into account.　The factors which come into the balance will be many **12.44** and varied. The nature of the intrusion into privacy will be relevant. The deeper the intrusion and the wider its dissemination or proposed dissemination, the more likely that privacy will prevail. Thus, for example, if private information is disclosed in breach of an undertaking of confidence, the court will be less likely to allow its subsequent publication than if it is picked up innocently.[145] The court will also look beyond the specific interference with private life to the possible *consequences* of disclosure and the likelihood of those coming about. For example, disclosure might be likely to cause mental distress or illness or, in some cases, physical reprisals which might seriously jeopardize the well-being of the claimant.[146] The court may also consider the effects on third parties, including the claimant's family.[147]

On the other hand there are a series of factors tending towards permitting publication. **12.45** Such factors are often loosely described as 'the public interest' in disclosure, although it should be borne in mind that disclosure to a limited section of the public may be justified

---

[143] See *McKennitt v Ash* [2008] QB 73, para 46.

[144] This appears to be the view taken by the Court of Appeal: see *Prince of Wales v Associated Newspapers* [2008] Ch 57, paras 64–69; however, the speeches of the House of Lords in *OBG v Allan* [2008] 1 AC 1 might arguably be read as taking a more traditional approach where commercial confidence as opposed to privacy is at issue.

[145] *Prince of Wales* (n 144 above) para 69.

[146] This danger was a major factor leading to the grant of an injunction preventing the disclosure of the new identity and whereabouts of Thompson and Venables, the killers of Jamie Bulger: *Venables v News Group Newspapers* [2001] Fam 340; see also *Maxine Carr v News Group Newspapers* [2005] EWHC 971 (QB), para 4.

[147] *CC v AB* [2006] EWHC 3083 (QB), para 43.

in circumstances where wider publication, for example, in the media would not be justified.[148] The English courts have always recognized that there may be occasions on which the public interest in the preserving of confidence is outweighed by other public interests. This was sometimes known as a 'defence',[149] although its broad ambit was criticized and it was not recognized in Australia.[150] However, if 'defence' were ever an accurate description of this feature of English law, the term is no longer apposite in the context of private information. The various elements of the public interest are now simply factors to be taken into account in the balancing exercise.

12.46 An important factor will obviously be whether the information in question reveals 'wrongdoing', although this term has a very broad meaning. Traditionally, the courts have refused as a matter of principle to intervene in such cases: it was said that this:

> extends to any misconduct of such a nature that it ought to be in the public interest to disclose it to others. . .The exception should extend to crimes, frauds, misdeeds, both those actually committed as well as those in contemplation provided always—and this is essential—that the disclosure is justified in the public interest. The reason is because 'no private obligation can dispense with that universal one which lies on every member of society to discover every design which be formed contrary to the laws of society, to destroy the public welfare.[151]

However, under the modern law the test is now a broader one of 'justification' under Article 8(2) (as compared to justification under Article 10(2)). Nevertheless, the breach of confidence cases still provide useful guidance. The interest in exposing and preventing wrongdoing has been held to justify disclosure of suspected criminal conduct,[152] disclosure by the police of a photograph of a suspect where they make reasonable use of it for the purpose of the prevention and detection of crime and the apprehension of suspects or persons unlawfully at large,[153] disclosure of fraudulent business practices,[154] alleged miscarriages of justice and corrupt and disgraceful police practices,[155] alleged corruption by a local authority,[156] dangerous medical practices which endanger the public,[157] dangerous medical hazards[158] and information about 'cults'.[159] It has been said that 'once there is good reason to doubt the propriety of the financial affairs of a public official, there is a public interest in those

---

[148] See eg, *Mosley v News Group Newspapers* [2008] EMLR 20, para 122 (in which it was suggested that if the 'S&M' activities in that case had had a Nazi theme 'there could be a public interest in that being revealed at least to those in [the international organization of which the claimant was the president] to whom he is accountable').

[149] See *Beloff v Pressdram Ltd* [1973] 1 All ER 241, 260; but see *Price Waterhouse v BCCI* [1992] BCLC 583.

[150] See *Castrol Australia v Emtech Associates* (1980) 33 ALR 31, 54; and *Corrs Pavey Whiting and Byrne v Collector of Customs* (1987) 74 ALR 428, 445–50.

[151] *Initial Services v Putterill* [1968] 1 QB 398, 405.

[152] *Malone v Metropolitan Police Commissioner* [1979] Ch 344.

[153] *Hellewell v Chief Constable of Derbyshire* [1995] 1 WLR 804.

[154] *Gartside v Outram* (1857) 26 LJ Ch 113.

[155] *Cork v McVicar, The Times*, 31 October 1984.

[156] *Preston Borough Council v McGrath, The Times*, 19 May 2000.

[157] *Schering Chemicals Ltd v Falkman Ltd* [1982] 1 QB 1.

[158] *W v Egdell* [1990] 1 Ch 359.

[159] *Hubbard v Vosper* [1972] 2 QB 84 (in relation to a book about Scientology).

affairs being open to public scrutiny'.[160] The principle has also been held to justify the voluntary disclosure of confidential information to an inquiry set up under the Banking Act 1987[161] and to regulators[162] (including disclosure of information acquired from police interview).[163] The exposure of hypocrisy on the part of public figures might also justify disclosure of private information;[164] however, it has been suggested that a high level of misconduct is necessary to make out this justification.[165]

In matters of sexual conduct the court will not refuse to enforce a duty of confidence simply **12.47** because some people might regard the conduct as immoral.[166] It has been held that 'sexual relationships of those who are in the public eye . . . are generally likely to be interesting to the public, but they will not necessarily be of genuine public interest'; whether they are so will depend upon the facts and the context.[167] As Eady J put it in *Mosley v News Group*:[168]

> it is not for the state or for the media to expose sexual conduct which does not involve any significant breach of the criminal law. That is so whether the motive for such intrusion is merely prurience or a moral code

The courts have emphasized in several cases that it does not follow from the fact that the public is interested in information that the disclosure of that information is in the public interest.[169]

It is important to note that reliance on public interest as justifying disclosure does not depend **12.48** upon proof of iniquity on the part of the person claiming breach of confidence; it involves balancing the public interest in favour of publication against the public interest in maintaining the right to privacy or confidentiality.[170] However, bad faith on the part of the *informer* might be put into the balance by the court: it has been held that 'selling the story to the tabloids (whether for revenge, money or any other reason) should be accorded lower priority'.[171]

(c) Disclosure of information by public bodies

Introduction. At common law a public body was under a strict obligation of confidence **12.49** and where it acquires information relating to a member of the public which is not generally available and is potentially damaging:

> the body ought not to disclose such information save for the purpose of and to the extent necessary for performance of its public duty or enabling some other public body to perform its public duty.[172]

---

[160] *Long Beach Limited v Global Witness Limited* [2007] EWHC 1980 (QB), para 52.
[161] See *Price Waterhouse v BCCI* [1992] BCLC 583.
[162] See *Re A Company's Application* [1989] Ch 477.
[163] *Woolgar v Chief Constable of Sussex* [2000] 1 WLR 25.
[164] *Campbell v MGN* [2004] 2 AC 467.
[165] *McKennitt v Ash* [2008] QB 73, para 69.
[166] *Stephens v Avery* [1988] Ch 449 (a married woman's lesbian relationship).
[167] *CC v AB* [2006] EWHC 3083 (QB), para 37. The court offered the Profumo affair as an example of a case which would be in the public interest.
[168] [2008] EMLR 20, para 127.
[169] See, for example, *Prince of Wales v Associated Newspapers* [2008] Ch 57, para 51.
[170] *Lion Laboratories Ltd v Evans* [1985] QB 526: injunction refused in relation to information suggesting doubts about the accuracy of a breathalyser device; see also *X v Y* [1988] 2 All ER 648: injunction granted to restrain publication of information from medical records that two doctors were suffering from AIDS.
[171] *CC v AB*, (n 167 above) paras 6 and 36.
[172] *R v Chief Constable of North Wales Police, ex p Thorpe* [1999] QB 396, 409H.

This principle did not rest on a duty of confidence but on a 'fundamental rule of good administration'.[173] This approach was approved by the Court of Appeal who said that:

> The issue here is not the same as it would be in private law. The fact that the convictions of the applicants had been in the public domain did not mean that the police as a public authority were free to publish information about their previous offending absent any public interest in this being done.[174]

12.50 The general principle is that a public body should not disclose information which is confidential or of a confidential character[175] unless there is a 'pressing need'[176] for disclosure in the interests of public health or safety,[177] the exposure or prevention of corruption[178] or similar purposes.[179] A balance must be struck between the competing public interests in maintaining confidentiality and in disclosure: the duty imposed on public authorities under Article 8 to respect the private lives of individuals is reflected in this exercise.[180]

12.51 **Statutory presumptions in favour of disclosure.** The common law presumption against disclosure of sensitive personal information by public bodies can be reversed by statute. In *R (X) v Chief Constable of the West Midlands Police*[181] the Court of Appeal held that this was the effect of the Enhanced Criminal Record Certificate regime under the Police Act 1997. Such certificates concern those who seek employment in the course of which they would care for or be responsible for children or vulnerable adults. The Court of Appeal held that the statutory scheme required a Chief Constable to disclose any information which he considered relevant to the particular application, even if it only might be true, and that this was compatible with Article 8.[182] However, the Court accepted that in some cases disclosure might be disproportionate: the information might be as to some trifling matter, for example, or the evidence might be such that it was so unlikely that the information was correct as to make it disproportionate to reveal.[183]

12.52 **Criminal conduct.** The disclosure of information concerning criminal conduct is likely to be found to be justified. In the leading case of *R v Chief Constable of North Wales Police*,

---

[173] Ibid, 410.

[174] [1999] QB 396, 429A–B, per Lord Woolf MR.

[175] For example, information which has been in the public domain at some earlier date and which may not, therefore, attract the protection of the private law: see Toulson and Phipps (n 73 above) para 3–08ff.

[176] *Re L (Sexual Abuse: Disclosure)* [1999] 1 WLR 307, 306A (in that case, the Court of Appeal quashed the decision to disclose findings made in care proceedings because there were no pending investigations); *R v A Police Authority, ex p LM* [2000] 1 FLR 612 (decision to disclose past unproven allegations of sex abuse quashed).

[177] See *Woolgar v Chief Constable of Sussex Police* [2000] 1 WLR 25.

[178] *Preston Borough Council v McGrath, The Times*, 19 May 2000.

[179] See also *R v Secretary of the State for the Home Department, ex p Amnesty International*, (15 Feb 2000, unrep) where the Divisional Court held that fairness required that medical reports concerning General Pinochet be disclosed to the states who had requested his extradition.

[180] Ibid, paras 29 and 36.

[181] [2005] 1 WLR 65.

[182] Ibid, para 37. See also *R (B) v Secretary of State for the Home Department* [2006] EWHC 579 (Admin). The information in question in the *X* case concerned a criminal charge and a prosecution, which had been discontinued; Mummery LJ made it clear that the court had made no decision that such information engaged Article 8 rights at all: para 57. In any event, the information need not relate to criminal or suspected criminal activity: *R (L) v Commissioner of Police for the Metropolis* [2007] 4 All ER 128.

[183] *R (X)* (n 181 above) para 41.

ex p Thorpe[184] the Divisional Court and the Court of Appeal dismissed an application by convicted sex offenders for judicial review of a decision to inform the owner of a caravan site where they were living of their convictions. The Court went on to say that both under Article 8 and public law, the police were entitled to use information when they reasonably conclude that this is what is required in order to protect the public. In *R (J & P) v West Sussex County Council*[185] it was held that a decision by a local authority to reveal to the daughter of the claimant's partner that he had been convicted of sexually abusing children was justified. Similarly, the disclosure of finding in care proceedings that the claimant presented a considerable risk to children to his housing association landlord was justified.[186] In *R (Stanley) v Commissioner of Police of the Metropolis*[187] the police had distributed leaflets and publicizing of information containing the claimants' photographs, names and ages, and details of anti-social behaviour orders issued against them. The Court held that, although anti-social behaviour orders were civil and not criminal orders, they needed such publicity in order to operate effectively.

Disclosure of information concerning suspected criminal conduct has also often been held **12.53** to be justified. In *R (Kent Pharmaceuticals) v Serious Fraud Office*,[188] the Court of Appeal held that the Serious Fraud Office was entitled to disclose documents pertaining to the business of selling pharmaceuticals[189] to the Department of Health when requested as evidence in relation to allegations of anti-competitive practices. However, in *W v Westminster City Council*[190] the publication a child protection case conference of a report at suggesting that there were serious grounds for suspecting that the claimant was grooming the child for prostitution was held to be unlawful. The court held that, although the disclosure was protected by qualified privilege, there was no need for the publication and that it had breached the claimant's rights under Article 8. Similarly, there was no justification for a disclosure by the police of information about a pending prosecution to a third party.[191]

It is relatively easy to justify the disclosure of information concerning suspected criminal **12.54** conduct to employers. In *R v C & D, ex p A*[192] Turner J held that a police authority was entitled to pass to a local education authority information concerning allegations of sex abuse against an individual who had applied to be a school teacher.[193] Checks provided by a consultancy service which advised local authorities and voluntary organizations on the suitability of those they proposed to employ in childcare posts have also been found to

---

[184] [1999] QB 396.

[185] [2002] 2 FLR 1192.

[186] *Re C (Sexual Abuse: Disclosure)* [2002] 2 FLR 375.

[187] [2005] EMLR 3.

[188] [2005] 1 WLR 1302.

[189] These commercial documents were held to fall within the scope of Article 8(1): ibid, para 5; a subsequent application to Strasbourg was inadmissible, *Kent Pharmaceuticals v United Kingdom* Decision of 11 October 2005.

[190] [2005] EWHC 102 (QB).

[191] *Wood v Chief Constable of West Midlands* [2005] EMLR 20 (as a result there was no defence of qualified privilege available in a libel case), see also the decision at first instance by Tugendhat J [2003] EWHC 2971 (QB).

[192] [2001] 1 WLR 461.

[193] Declining to follow *R v Local Police Authority in the Midlands, ex p L M* [2000] 1 FLR 612.

be lawful.[194] In *Brent Council v SK*[195] Silber J held that the local authority was entitled to disclose to the care home where the defendant worked the fact that she had assaulted her eight-year-old daughter with sufficient force to cause bruising and marks. In *R (D) v Secretary of State for Health*,[196] the Court of Appeal held that it was justifiable for a health authority to circulate an 'alert letter' warning NHS Trusts of allegations of sexual assault made against a doctor even though they had not been proven. However, in *Mersey Care NHS Trust v Ackroyd*,[197] the Court of Appeal upheld Tugendhat J's refusal to order the disclosure of the source of leaked confidential information about Ian Brady, even though the source was suspected to be an employee of the mental health facility at which he was detained.

12.55 **Personal information.** The impact of Article 8 on the way in which public bodies disclose information was considered in *R (Robertson) v City of Wakefield Metropolitan Council*,[198] which concerned the sale of the electoral register to commercial concerns who utilized it for direct marketing purposes. Maurice Kay J held that the information on the register was private within the meaning of Article 8, taking into account the anticipated use to which the information would be put,[199] and that Article 8 was breached because individuals who wished to be on the register could not object to the sale of their details. After the first *Robertson* judgment, the government introduced an edited register for those voters who objected to their details being generally available, but the edited register remained available for purchase by credit reference agencies for the purposes of taking risk assessments and complying financial services rules on money laundering. In *R (Robertson) v Lord Chancellor's Department*[200] Maurice Kay J held that this limited disclosure was a proportionate interference with Article 8 rights.

12.56 **Medical information.** The disclosure of medical information can raise acute issues under Article 8. In *A Health Authority v X*[201] the Court of Appeal approved comments made by Munby J to the effect that a GP has a duty to preserve patient confidentiality other than in compliance with a judicial order. In *R (TB) v Crown Court*,[202] it was held that it is a fundamental principle that medical records are confidential. Accordingly, the Crown Court had breached Article 8 by ordering disclosure of the medical records of a witness without inviting that witness to make representations. However, in *Sayers v Smithkline Beecham*,[203] the court held that, provided medical reports used in litigation were sufficiently anonymized, no interference with Article 8 would arise from their disclosure to the government for use in other litigation.

---

[194] *R v Secretary of State for Health, ex p C* [2000] HRLR 400 and *R v Worcester County Council, ex p SW* [2000] HRLR 702.
[195] [2007] EWHC 120 (Fam).
[196] [2006] Lloyd's Rep Med 457.
[197] [2007] EWCA Civ 101.
[198] [2002] QB 1052.
[199] Ibid, para 34.
[200] [2003] EWHC 1760 (Admin).
[201] [2002] 2 All ER 780.
[202] [2007] 1 WLR 1524.
[203] [2007] EWHC 1346 (QB).

In *R (E) v Bristol City Council*,[204] the claimant challenged the local authority's decision to **12.57**
defy her wishes and inform her sister of her treatment. Under section 11(3) of the Mental
Health Act, a local authority is required, where 'practicable', to inform a patient's nearest
relative of her treatment. Bennett J held that 'practicable' had to be construed in accordance
with Article 8 so as to take into account the claimant's wishes.

In *A London Borough Council v N*[205] the Council sought guidance as to whether it could **12.58**
disclose to the natural father of a child in care the fact that the child's foster father was HIV
positive. The court held that there was in general an obligation to share information relating to a child in care with its parents, but that the disclosure would in this case be a disproportionate interference with the foster father's Article 8 rights. Although the consequences
of infection were serious, the risks were negligible. Further, they would not affect the placement of the child with the foster parents in question.

The case of *R (Stone) v South East Coast Strategic Health Authority*[206] shows that the publica- **12.59**
tion of medical records may be justified if the public interest considerations are sufficiently
compelling. The case concerned the publication of an independent inquiry report into the
care, treatment and supervision of a convicted murderer. The report was a very serious
interference with the claimant's Article 8 rights, but this was outweighed by the strong
public interest in knowing how he had been treated and cared for. In addition, the judge
took into account that the inquiry and the publicity had arisen out of the claimant's own
criminal acts – although he did not forfeit Article 8 rights the information related solely to
an investigation foreseeably arising out of his murders.

(d) Personal information and the Data Protection Act 1998

Introduction.   Public bodies hold on file very large quantities of personal information **12.60**
about individuals. This is often, but not always, stored on computer. Error or misuse can
have serious consequences. Under section 64 of the Police and Criminal Evidence Act
1984, for instance, the police may maintain on file DNA and fingerprint samples of individuals, even if those individuals have not been convicted of any crime. In *R (Marper) v
Chief Constable of South Yorkshire*[207] the House of Lords held that the scheme was compatible with Article 8, concluding that there was no interference with Article 8 rights and that,
even if there was, the interference was not substantial and was justified. However, when
the case went to Strasbourg this approach was decisively rejected by a unanimous
Grand Chamber[207a] and it is now clear that a blanket power to collect DNA samples of
nonconvicted persons is not compatible with Article 8.

Without statutory intervention it would have been very difficult for individuals to check **12.61**
the accuracy of personal data held by public bodies and the only potential remedy for misuse of this information would be a finding of breach of confidence: the claimant had to
show that the information concerned was originally acquired 'in confidence' and that the

---

[204] [2005] EWHC 74.
[205] [2006] 1 FLR 310.
[206] [2007] UKHRR 137.
[207] [2004] 1 WLR 2196.
[207a] *S and Marper v United Kingdom*, Judgment of 4 December 2008 (GC), see paras 12.281 and 12.362 below.

recipient had notice of its confidential nature. The scope of an action for breach of confidence—or misuse of private information, as it is now known—has now developed so as to remove these strict requirements, but the tort remains an inadequate means of regulating the retention of personal data.

12.62 The Younger Committee on Privacy[208] recommended legislation to keep under review the techniques of collecting and processing personal information on computer. In 1975, a white paper was published proposing a permanent statutory agency to protect data subjects and the Lindop Committee on Data Protection was appointed the following year. In 1978, this Committee recommended the establishment of a Data Protection Authority.[209] The proposal was not accepted. In 1984, however, the Data Protection Act 1984 was passed in order to comply with the provisions of the European Convention for the Protection of the Individual with Regard to the Automatic Processing of Personal Data.[210] The Act has now been replaced by the Data Protection Act 1998 ('the DPA'), which gave effect to the European directive of 1995 [211] on the processing and free movement of personal data. The Court of Appeal has held[212] that:

> the primary objective of the 1995 Directive is to protect individuals' fundamental rights, notably the right to privacy and accuracy of their personal data held by others . . . in computerized form or similarly organized manual filing systems . . ., whilst at the same time facilitating the free movement of such data between Member States of the European Union.

12.63 **Personal data.**   The DPA protects 'personal data', which is data relating to a living individual who can be identified from the data, whether taken alone or read with other information which is in the possession (or is likely to come into the possession) of the data controller.[213] Expressions of personal opinion may be 'personal data'.[214] In light of this, it might be thought that 'personal' has a broader meaning than 'private', but the Court of Appeal has more or less equated the two terms. In *Durant v Financial Services Authority*,[215] the Court held that the Act is concerned with:

> information that affects [an individual's] privacy, whether in his personal or family life, business or professional capacity.

So, the mere mention of a data subject in a document will not necessarily create 'personal data': whether it does so 'will depend on where it falls in a continuum of relevance or proximity to the data subject as distinct, say, from transactions or matters in which he may have been involved to a greater or lesser degree'.[216] Relevant factors include whether the information is biographical and the extent to which it focuses on the individual in question.

---

[208] *Report of the Committee on Privacy*, Cmnd 5012 (1972), para 621.
[209] *Report of the Committee on Data Protection* (1978) Cmnd 7341.
[210] See R Austin, 'The Data Protection Act 1984: The Public Law Implications' [1984] PL 618.
[211] EC Directive (EC) 95/46.
[212] *Durant v Financial Services Authority* [2004] FSR 28, para 4.
[213] As defined by s 1(1) of the 1998 Act.
[214] Ibid, s 1(3).
[215] Ibid, para 28.
[216] *Durant*, (n 212 above) para 28.

In *Murray v Express Newspapers*[217] it was held that photographs can amount to personal data.

Types of data.   The definition of date under the DPA includes information which is **12.64** recorded as part of a relevant filing system (or with the intention of forming a relevant filing system) or part of an accessible record.[218] The Court of Appeal has interpreted the scope of a relevant filing system very narrowly, placing much weight on the perceived need to render the DPA workable by allowing data subjects to obtain and check only that information which is relatively easy and swift to access.[219] Accordingly, the DPA applies only to systems:[220]

(1) in which the files forming part of it are structured or referenced in such a way as clearly to indicate at the outset of the search whether specific information capable of amounting to personal data of an individual requesting it. . .is held within the system and, if so, in which file or files it is held; and

(2) which has, as part of its own structure or referencing mechanism, a sufficiently sophisticated and detailed means of readily indicating whether and where in an individual file or files specific criteria or information about the applicant can readily be obtained.

Many manual filing systems would appear to fall outside this highly restrictive reading, which arguably undermines the aims of the Directive and the DPA. It also appears to reward those organizations which badly manage their records: these are arguably the kinds of records which are most likely to be out of date or inaccurate and whose subjects are therefore most in need of protection.

Data protection principles.   The DPA provides that data must be processed in accord- **12.65** ance with the data protection principles. Part I of Schedule I of the Act lists these principles; guidance concerning their interpretation is contained in Part II of the Schedule. The data protection principles are as follows:

- personal data shall be processed fairly[221] and lawfully and, in particular, shall not be processed unless at least one of the conditions in Schedule 2 is met and, in the case of sensitive personal data,[222] at least one of the conditions in Schedule 3 is met;[223]
- personal data shall be obtained only for one or more specified and lawful purposes, and shall not be processed in any manner incompatible with that purpose or those purposes;
- personal data held shall be adequate, relevant and not excessive in relation to the purpose or purposes for which they are processed;

---

[217] [2007] EWHC 1908 (Ch); there was no appeal on this point, for the appeal see [2008] EMLR 12.

[218] See s 1(1) of the DPA.

[219] *Durant* (n 212), para 45.

[220] Ibid, para 50.

[221] In *Johnson v Medical Defence Union* (2007) 96 BMLR 99 para 62 per Buxton LJ 'fairness requires consideration not only of data subjects but data users'.

[222] As defined by s 2 of the DPA.

[223] The data subject must give his consent (para 1); the processing must be necessary for the purposes of exercising rights or obligations conferred by law on the date controller in connection with his employment (para 2); the processing must be necessary to protect the vital interests of the data subject (para 3); the processing is carried out by a non profit making body (para 4); the information is public as a result of steps deliberately taken by the data subject (para 5); the processing is necessary in connection with legal proceedings or advice (para 6), the administration of justice, statutory functions or governmental functions (para 7) or medical purposes (para 8); the processing consists of information relating to racial or ethnic origin (para 9) or is processed in circumstances specified by the Secretary of State (para 10).

- personal data shall be accurate and, where necessary, kept up to date;
- personal data processed for any purpose or purposes shall not be kept longer than is necessary for that purpose or those purposes;
- personal data shall be processed in accordance with the rights of data subjects under the DPA;
- appropriate technical and organizational measures shall be taken against unauthorized or unlawful processing of personal data and against accidental loss or destruction of, or damage to, personal data; and
- personal data shall not be transferred to a country or territory outside the European Economic Area unless that country or territory ensures an adequate level of protection for the rights and freedoms of data subjects in relation to the processing of personal data.

12.66 **Individual rights.**   An individual who is the subject of personal data is entitled[224] if he makes a request in writing to a data controller[225] to be promptly informed of whether there is any personal data which is being processed. The concept of processing is very broadly defined in section 1(1) of the DPA to include, 'obtaining, recording and holding the information or data or carrying out any operation or set of operations on the information or data'. However, this concept has been given a narrow interpretation by the Court of Appeal. In *Johnson v Medical Defence Union*,[226] the claimant had been ejected from his trade union on the basis of a number of allegations made against him. The report upon which the decision to expel the claimant was based had been compiled by a person who extracted information from a set of files on the claimant. The claimant alleged that the process of selection was 'unfair processing' because the report failed to include either his own responses to the allegations or details of the outcomes of the investigations into those allegations. The Court held by a majority that the DPA did not cover the human selection of material from a file for compilation in a report, even if that report is then input into a computer.[227] The claimant's complaint accordingly fell outside the scope of the DPA. Arguably this outcome turned on the manner in which the claim was pleaded:[228] there seems to be little doubt that actually holding the information on the computer—or subsequently retrieving the report from the computer—would amount to 'processing' within the meaning of the DPA,[229] and there seems no obvious reason why the fairness argument could not apply to the processing of the fruits of an unfair selection as much as to the process of selection itself.[230]

12.67   The data controller may charge a fee for providing information about any personal data he is processing. Where the processing of personal data is causing (or is likely to cause) unwarranted and substantial damage to the data subject[231] or another, the data subject is entitled

---

[224] Under s 7 of the DPA.
[225] As defined by s 1(1) of the DPA.
[226] (2007) 96 BMLR 99.
[227] Ibid, paras 43 and 155.
[228] Buxton LJ placed some weight on this: see, for instance, ibid, para 21.
[229] Further, in *Lindqvist* [2004] QB 1014, the ECJ held that uploading information onto the internet amounted to processing within the meaning of the Directive.
[230] It should, however, be noted that this would not on the face of it meet Buxton LJ's concerns about the impropriety of subjecting human judgment to the DPA: see, ibid, paras 44–47; and see his comments at para 23.
[231] As defined by s 1(1) of the DPA.

to require the data controller, after the expiry of a reasonable period, to cease processing[232] (or not to begin processing) unless one of several specified exceptions apply.[233] He may also apply to the court[234] to rectify, block, erase or destroy personal data if the court is satisfied[235] that the data processed by the data controller is incorrect or misleading as to any matter of fact.[236] Any individual who suffers damage as a result of a data controller contravening the Act is entitled to compensation.[237]

Exemptions. The DPA contains exemptions in the following areas: **12.68**

- national security;[238]
- crime and taxation;[239]
- health education and social work;[240]
- regulatory activity;[241]
- journalism, literature and art;[242]
- research, history and statistics;[243]
- information available to the public by or under any enactment;[244]
- disclosures required by law or made in connection with legal proceedings;[245]
- domestic purposes;[246] and

there are also a number of other miscellaneous exemptions[247] and the Secretary of State has power to make further orders for exemptions.[248]

The Commissioner and the Tribunal. The Information Commissioner[249] has power to **12.69** ensure that data controllers comply with the Act by using the enforcement procedures in Part V of the Act. The Act also creates a number of criminal offences,[250] though prosecutions can only be instituted by the Commissioner or the Director of Public Prosecutions.

In *Baker v Secretary of State for the Home Department*[251] the Information Tribunal held **12.70** that the Home Secretary did not have reasonable grounds for issuing a national security

---

[232] Ibid, As defined by s 1(1) of the DPA.
[233] Ibid, s 10 of the 1998 Act.
[234] Ibid, s 15.
[235] Under ibid, s 14.
[236] Ibid, s 70(2) of the 1998 Act.
[237] Ibid, s 13.
[238] Ibid, s 28.
[239] Ibid, s 29.
[240] Ibid, s 30.
[241] Ibid, s 31.
[242] Ibid, s 32.
[243] Ibid, s 33.
[244] Ibid, s 34.
[245] Ibid, s 35.
[246] Ibid, s 36.
[247] Ibid, s 37 and Sch 7.
[248] Ibid, s 38.
[249] Formerly the Data Protection Commissioner. Changed by para 1 of Schedule 2 to the Freedom of Information Act 2000.
[250] Such as unlawfully obtaining or disclosing personal data and selling or offering to sell personal data: see s 55.
[251] [2001] UKHRR 1275.

certificate giving the Security Service blanket exemption from revealing in response to a request under section 7(1)(a) of the Data Protection Act 1998 whether it was holding or processing personal data about an individual. The exemption was found to be wider than was necessary to protect national security and as a result failed the proportionality test. In *R (Secretary of State for the Home Department) v Information Commissioner*,[252] the Divisional Court confirmed that, if a data controller relied on the national security exemption to refuse to disclose information to a data subject, the Information Commissioner was entitled to inquire into whether that exemption was properly claimed and request relevant supporting material from the Secretary of State.[253] It was then open to the Secretary of State to refuse to disclose that supporting material to the Information Commissioner if he believed that *that* disclosure would also imperil national security, but the Commissioner had a right of appeal against such a decision.[254]

12.71 **The DPA and Article 8.** The word 'necessary' as used in the Schedules to the DPA involves similar considerations to those which arise under Article 8(2): a pressing social need is involved and that the measure employed is proportionate to the legitimate aim being pursued.[255] This is because Article 8 is an important source of inspiration for the Data Protection Directive. When applying the Directive the Court of Justice has interpreted it in the light of Article 8. Interference with private life can only be justified where it is in accordance with the law, is necessary in a democratic society for the pursuit of legitimate aims, and is not disproportionate to the objective pursued.[256]

12.72 The Information Tribunal referred to Article 8 when deciding that old conviction data could legitimately be retained on the Police National Computer, but only if access was limited to police officers[257] and in deciding whether information relating to MPs expenses should be disclosed.[258]; and the High Court considered Article 8 in deciding that the taking, holding and sale of photographs of JK Rowling and her family in public by a photographic agency was 'necessary for the purpose of legitimate interests'.[259]

(e) Other rights of access to personal information

12.73 **Introduction.** The Data Protection Act 1998 is the primary means by which individuals may seek access to personal information about them held by others. The Access to Personal

---

[252] [2007] 2 All ER 703.

[253] Ibid, para 38.

[254] Ibid, para 41.

[255] See *Stone v South East Coast Strategic Health Authority* [2007] UKHRR 137, at para 60; and see also *Corporate Officer of the House of Commons v Information Commissioner*, Information Tribunal Decision of 26 February 2008, para 56.

[256] Joined Cases C-465/00, C-138/01, and C-139/01 *Österreichisher Rundfunk and Others* [2003] ECR I-4989 at paras 64–72.

[257] *Chief Constables of West Yorkshire, South Yorkshire and North Wales Police v Information Commissioner* (Judgment of 12 October 2005).

[258] See *Corporate Officer of the House of Commons* (n 255 above), the House of Commons' appeal was dismissed by the Divisional Court, [2008] EWHC 1084 (Admin).

[259] *Murray v Associated Newspapers and Big Pictures Limited* [2008] 1 FLR 704, para 76. The court found against the second defendant on the ground that they were has not registered as data controllers under section 17 of the 1998 Act and failed to provide to the claimant the information required by Schedule 1 of the Act; however, the court refused to award any damages on causation grounds. See also *igroup Ltd v Ocwen* [2004] 1 WLR 451,

Files Act 1987 has, for instance, now been repealed. However, there remain specific statutory provisions which give individuals a right of access to health records: the Access to Health Records Act 1990 and the Access to Medical Reports Act 1988.[260]

Freedom of information. The Freedom of Information Act 2000 also allows individuals   **12.74** to obtain information held by public authorities. However, there are a number of exceptions set out in Part II of the Act and section 40 exempts personal data of which the applicant is the data subject. Accordingly, the Freedom of Information Act cannot be used to obtain information already available under the Data Protection Act 1998; nor on the face of it could it be used to obtain information which *would* fall within the Data Protection Act 1998 but for the fact that it is not computerized or in a relevant filing system. However, it is possible in some cases that the Act could be used to seek data pertaining to individuals which falls outside the fairly narrowly-interpreted scope of 'personal data' in the Data Protection Act.[261]

Section 40 of the Freedom of Information Act 2000 also prevents the disclosure of personal   **12.75** information about *others* if that disclosure would breach the data protection principles. And, by virtue of section 41, information cannot be disclosed under the Act if it was obtained from another person and its disclosure would be a breach of confidence.[262]

Access to information under Article 8. Article 8 may also create a right of access to   **12.76** personal information held by public authorities.[263] Although the Court of Human Rights in *Gaskin v United Kingdom*[264] declined to express a view on that point, it held that information concerning highly personal aspects of the applicant's childhood, development and history created a right of access to that information. In *McGinley and Egan v United Kingdom*,[265] however, the Court held that where the government engages in hazardous activities with hidden consequences for health, respect for private and family life requires an effective and accessible procedure to ensure that all relevant and appropriate information is made available. There is no positive obligation to provide access to documents which do not concern a person's identity or personal history.[266]

Thus, Article 8 was held to be engaged in circumstances in which a child born through arti-   **12.77** ficial insemination wishes to discover the identity of his biological parents.[267] However, in *R (Addinell) v Sheffield City Council*[268] Sullivan J took the view that it was an unwarranted

---

[260] See also, Access to Health Records (Control of Access) Regulations 1993, SI 1993/746.

[261] See para 12.63 above.

[262] See para 12.22 above.

[263] Thus reversing the effect of *R v Mid-Glamorgan Family Health Services Authority, ex p Martin* [1995] 1 WLR 110. This right of access to personal information should be distinguished from the right to freedom of information which may arise under Article 10 because of the obligation on a public authority to impart information. The latter right arises because Article 10 prohibits a government from restricting a person from receiving information that others wish or may be willing to impart to him. See *Leander v Sweden* (1987) 9 EHRR 433, para 74; *Guerra v Italy* (1998) 26 EHRR 357, para 53; and see generally, para 15.248ff below.

[264] (1989) 12 EHRR 36. See para 12.254 below.

[265] (1998) 27 EHRR 1; and see *Roche v United Kingdom* (2006) 42 EHRR 30.

[266] *Smith v United Kingdom*, Decision of 4 January 2007.

[267] *R (Rose) v Secretary of State for Health* [2002] 2 FLR 962.

[268] [2000] ACD 331.

extension of *Gaskin* for a parent to obtain access to the social services files of his son who had died in council care. In *R (Gunn-Russo) v Nugent Care Society*[269] Scott Baker J held that *Gaskin* was very much dependant on its facts, and that the disclosure of adoption records by a voluntary adoption agency required a balancing exercise to be conducted between disclosure and confidentiality.[270]

(f) Legal privilege and correspondence

12.77A **Privilege.** Legal privilege is a 'fundamental human right long established at common law'.[270a] It is also protected as an aspect of the right to respect for private life and correspondence under Article 8. The principles behind Convention law and the common law have been described as 'virtually identical'.[270b]

12.77B Where documents are sought under a request for mutual assistance including private and professional correspondence subject to legal privilege Article 8 was engaged. The documents had to be reviewed by the court with the participation of those whose Article 8 rights were affected to determine whether the interferences were justified under Article 8(2).[270c]

12.77C **Correspondence.** The personal correspondence of a bankrupt is of nature peculiarly personal to him and his life as a human being and did not constitute property which vested in his trustee in bankruptcy.[270d] Confidential business correspondence falls within the scope of Article 8. As a result, where a trustee in bankruptcy seeks personal correspondence then Article 8 is engaged and disclosure of particular documents must be justified under Article 8(2).[270e]

(3) Privacy rights and employment

(a) Introduction

12.78 The HRA means that employees of core public authorities, in effect, have a 'right of privacy' against their employer. They will also have a right to respect for family life under Article 8.[271] It is also clear that the courts will be required, under the interpretative obligation in section 3, to have regard to Article 8 in claims against private employers, at least in cases where the State has a positive obligation to protect Article 8 rights.[272] There are several important areas in which violations of Article 8 might take place: the monitoring of the activities of employees at work, the regulation of 'private aspects' of employees' conduct, the collection of personal data on employees and sexual orientation discrimination.[273] Article 8 also has a role to play in determining whether employers are entitled to be told

---

[269] [2002] 1 FLR 1.

[270] See para 13.70 below.

[270a] *R (Morgan Granfell) v Special Commissioners* [2003] 1 AC 563, para 7 [Lord Hoffmann].

[270b] *Bowman v Fels* [2005] 1 WLR 3083, para 82; see generally, C Passmore, *Privilege* (2nd edn, XPL. 2006), para 1.162ff; for a discussion of the position in relation to prisoners, see para 12.230ff below.

[270c] *R (Halner) v Wastminster Magistrates Court* [2008] EWHC 524 (Admin) (the court commented that where disclosure was necessary for the prevention of crime the interference was likely to be justified).

[270d] *Haig v Aitken* [2000] BPIR 462 (in construing the Insolvency Act 1986, the Judge relied on Art 8).

[270e] See *In the Estate of Rivkin, Warner v Verfides* [2008] EWHC 2609 (Ch).

[271] See para 13.151ff below.

[272] *X v Y (Employment:Sex Offender)* [2004] IRLR 625.

[273] Sexual orientation discrimination is discussed also below at para 12.206.

about personal information about employees or prospective employees which might be relevant to the job.[274]

(b) Monitoring in the workplace

Monitoring employees. The monitoring of employees at the workplace will engage **12.79** Article 8. The important question is whether an employee has a 'reasonable expectation of privacy'[275] in relation to a particular work activity. In *Copland v United Kingdom*[276] the Court of Human Rights confirmed that employees ordinarily have a reasonable expectation of privacy in using telephones, emails and the internet in the workplace. Violations of Article 8 may also occur if a public authority employer monitors its premises by closed circuit television, or searches personal desk space.[277]

However, if employers expressly warn employees that they monitor telephone calls or inter- **12.80** net usage, then surveillance is unlikely to breach Article 8 because the reasonable expectation of privacy will be removed.[278] If the warning is given in a policy document, it should be clear and expressly drawn to the attention of employees. However, it is suggested there must still be limits on what employers can legitimately monitor, even they do give notice. There is, for example, a strong argument that an expectation of privacy will arise in relation to telephones in employee rest rooms or staff canteens, regardless of whether the employers give a warning.

Further, Convention rights may in principle be waived in the contract of employment.[279] **12.81** However, it is well established under Convention case law that any waiver of a Convention right must be established in an unequivocal manner.[280] Simply signing a contract may not be sufficient to amount to a waiver;[281] we suggest that in order to rely on a waiver of Convention rights, an employer will be obliged to draw the provision specifically to the attention of the employees. In the Convention cases a distinction has been made between employees who have the choice of whether or not to accept a job[282] and employees in post who are put at risk of losing their jobs if they refuse to sign a waiver.[283]

Covert recordings of employers. The Courts have been called on to consider the propri- **12.82** ety of covertly recording employers on a number of occasions. In *XXX v YYY*[284] the Employment Appeal Tribunal considered a challenge to the public airing in court of a video which showed sexual advances made by the defendant employer to his former nanny, in the

---

[274] For which, see para 12.52ff above.
[275] See para 12.27ff above; and for a discussion of the Canadian case law considering this phrase, see para 12.442ff below.
[276] (2007) 45 EHRR 37; see also *Halford v United Kingdom* (1997) 24 EHRR 523.
[277] In *Peev v Bulgaria* (Judgment of 26 July 2007), para 39, the Court confirmed that the test is whether the employee has a reasonable expectation of privacy. It held that the applicant did have a reasonable expectation that his own filing cabinet and desk were private, although this might not extend to the rest of the office.
[278] See, for example, *Fosh v Cardiff University* (EAT, 23 January 2008).
[279] See eg, *Vereinigung Rechtswinkels Utrecht v Netherlands* (1986) 46 DR 200, EComm HR; *Deweer v Belgium* (1980) 2 EHRR 439, para 49; see generally, para 6.263ff above.
[280] See para 6.265ff above.
[281] See eg, *Rommelfanger v Germany* (1989) 62 DR 151, EComm HR.
[282] See eg, *Glasenapp v Germany* (1986) 9 EHRR 25; *Kosiek v Germany* (1986) 9 EHRR 328.
[283] See eg, *Knudsen v Norway* (1985) 42 DR 247, EComm HR.
[284] [2004] IRLR 137.

presence of his son. The video had been secretly recorded. The Employment Appeal Tribunal held that the video should be viewed in private to avoid severely embarrassing the employer's son and breaching his rights under Article 8. In *Amwell View School v Dogherty*[285] the Employment Appeal Tribunal held that the private discussions of the schools governors when deciding whether or not to dismiss an employee were not protected by Article 8; however, there was a public interest in not admitting covertly recorded evidence of that process.[286]

12.83 **Regulation of Investigatory Powers Act.** The Investigatory Powers Tribunal has held that Part II of the Regulation of Investigatory Powers Act 2000 does not apply to surveillance of employees for employment purposes, even by public authorities.[287] The Tribunal took the view that this kind of behaviour could be dealt with under other regimes, although it expressed no opinion as to whether such monitoring would, absent the applicability of the legal regime set out in RIPA, be in accordance with the law for the purposes of Article 8.[288] The Telecommunications (Lawful Business Practice) (Interception of Communications) Regulations 2000[289] are likely to provide a sufficient legal basis for the interception of communications but there is now a clear gap in the regulation of employee surveillance.

12.84 It is arguable that compliance with the *Employment Practices Data Protection Code*, issued by the Information Commissioner under the Data Protection Act 1998, will be sufficient to render employee monitoring in accordance with the law in relation to the collection of data which falls within the scope of the Act.[290] Part 3 of the code takes a very restrictive view as to the extent to which monitoring and surveillance can be conducted in the workplace. The core principles of the code are:

- It will usually be intrusive to monitor your workers.
- Workers have legitimate expectations that they can keep their personal lives private and that they are also entitled to a degree of privacy in the work environment.
- If employers wish to monitor their workers, they should be clear about the purpose and satisfied that the particular monitoring arrangement is justified by real benefits that will be delivered.
- Workers should be aware of the nature, extent and reasons for any monitoring, unless (exceptionally) covert monitoring is justified.
- In any event, workers' awareness will influence their expectations.

(c) Regulation of 'private aspects' of employees' conduct

12.85 **Introduction.** The HRA may also affect the ability of public authority employers to restrict personal conduct by means of provisions such as dress codes. The EAT has held that

---

[285] [2007] IRLR 178.

[286] The Court of Appeal has also confirmed that absolute immunity attached to proceedings of the police disciplinary board and that this is compatible with Article 8: *Heath v Commissioner of Police for the Metropolis* [2005] ICR 329.

[287] *C v The Police* [2006] 1 Pol LR 151, paras 85–89 (interceptions of employees' communications would still be covered under Part I of the 2000 Act).

[288] Ibid, para 91.

[289] SI 2000/2699.

[290] See *Silver v United Kingdom* (1983) 5 EHRR 347 and *R (Munjaz) v Mersey NHS Trust* [2006] 2 AC 148, paras 34 and 92, holding that clear non-legislative codes can in some cases provide a sufficient legal basis for Convention purposes.

a dress code preventing male employees from wearing their hair in pony tails did not constitute sex discrimination.[291] However, it could be argued that such dress codes are capable of constituting interference with the 'private life' of the employees.[292] The right to privacy will also have an impact on the scope of the implied term of mutual trust and confidence[293] and may be relevant to issues such as random drug tests. Furthermore it is likely to be a breach of Article 8 for health checks to be carried out on an employee without 'informed consent' having been given.[294]

As public authorities Employment Tribunals must take Article 8 rights[295] into account **12.86** deciding cases involving, for example, dress regulations,[296] no smoking rules, private conduct outside the workplace which is alleged to affect working relationships (such as homosexuality[297] and mental illness)[298] or medical (including HIV and psychological) testing. However, the positive duty on public authorities to take 'reasonable and appropriate measures' to secure Article 8 rights[299] does not oblige the courts to create a general right to privacy.[300] The tribunal is not obliged to apply Article 8 directly to the acts of private employers.

Although the termination of employment in itself will not ordinarily engage Article 8, it **12.87** has been held that it may have a sufficient impact on personal relationships and private life to do so in certain circumstances. In *R (Wright) v Secretary of State for Health*[301] Stanley Burnton J held that the provisional placement of the claimant on a list of individuals unsuitable to work with vulnerable adults engaged Article 8 because it effectively prevented her from carrying out her work as a nurse and had a sufficiently serious effect on her

---

[291] *Smith v Safeway plc* [1996] ICR 686; see also *Schmidt v Austicks Bookshops Ltd* [1978] ICR 85 and *Department of Work and Pensions v Thompson* [2004] IRLR. It has been argued that *Safeway* is inconsistent with the 'but for' approach taken in *Jones v Eastleigh Borough Council* [1990] 2 AC 751 (see R Wintemute, 'Recognising New Kinds of Direct Sex Discrimination: Transsexualism, Sexual Orientation and Dress Codes' (1997) 60 MLR 334, 353ff); and see G Clayton and G Pitt, 'Dress Codes and Freedom of Expression' [1997] EHRLR 54. However, it is now established that the 'but for' approach is not the appropriate test in direct discrimination cases: see, for example, *Nagarajan v London Regional Transport* [1999] IRLR 572 and *B v A* [2007] IRLR 576.

[292] Cf *McFeeley v United Kingdom* (1980) 20 DR 44, 91, EComm HR (a case concerning prison dress); *Kara v United Kingdom* (1998) 27 EHRR CD 272 (a bisexual male transvestite who wore female clothes to express his identity established that restrictions placed on his dress breached the right to private life; however, the Commission took the view that the interference was legitimate and proportionate); there has been considerable litigation in the United States on the question as to whether the control of dress or grooming is unconstitutional: see L Tribe, *American Constitutional Law*, (2nd edn, Foundation Press, 1988), para 15–15 (he points to over 200 cases in the two decades up to 1988).

[293] *Mahmud v Bank of Credit and Commerce International SA* [1998] AC 20.

[294] See *X v Commission* [1995] IRLR 320 and generally, B Watt, 'The Legal Protection of HIV and Health Care Workers and the Human Rights Jurisprudence of the European Court of Justice' [1998] EHRLR 301.

[295] For an instructive article on the approach of the American courts to privacy in the employment relationship, see eg, M Finkin, 'Employee Privacy, American Values and the Law' (1996–97) 72 Chicago-Kent LR 222.

[296] See eg, *Boychuk v Symons Holdings* [1977] IRLR 395; see Clayton and Pitt (n 648 above) which relies on *Stevens v United Kingdom* (1986) DR 245, EComm HR to argue that the right of dress and appearance is a manifestation of the right of freedom of expression (see generally, para 15.241 below).

[297] See eg, *Saunders v Scottish National Camps Association* [1980] IRLR 174.

[298] See eg, *O'Brien v Prudential Assurance* [1979] IRLR 140.

[299] See para 12.240ff above.

[300] See para 12.09ff above.

[301] [2007] 1 All ER 825, para 65; the point was left open on appeal: [2008] QB 422, paras 73 and 115.

personal relationships. In *R (A) v B Council*[302] the local authority refused to allow a contractor engaged to provide transport services for children with special educational needs to use a particular employee with a distant history of serious criminal activity. Although the council's position was justified on the facts, the court held that Article 8 was engaged because of the stigma attached to the decision, the impact on the claimant's personal relationships and the fact that she had been reduced to taking work as a toilet attendant. However, in *Security Industry Authority v Stewart*,[303] the Divisional Court held that the licensing of doormen did not involve Article 8 at all. And in *R v Worcester County Council, ex p SW*,[304] Newman J held that material gathered by an employer about the suitability of the applicant as a teacher was merely recording the public performance of the teacher, and did not involve an element of private life.

12.88 A claim for unfair dismissal against a private employer under the Employment Rights Act 1996 might also require consideration of Article 8 if, say, the reason for the dismissal, or the means of obtaining evidence, breach privacy rights. However, it seems likely that it will be sufficient in most cases for the tribunal to continue to decide unfair dismissal cases against private employers by applying the well established 'reasonable responses test'[305] for determining whether a dismissal is unfair.[306]

12.89 **Collection and use of personal data on employees.** Employers hold and collect substantial amounts of personal data on employees which may be subject to misuse. The International Labour Organization has expressed concern about the need to protect such data from misuse.[307] Security checks on employees which involve the collection of information about their private affairs would be a breach of Article 8 unless justified.[308] References to an applicant's personal life in a letter of instruction sent to a medical expert in an unfair dismissal case were, however, held not to breach Article 8.[309]

12.90 **Sexual orientation discrimination.** Discrimination by public employers in connection with sexual orientation breaches Article 8.[310] In *Lustig-Prean v United Kingdom*[311] and *Smith and Grady v United Kingdom*[312] the Court held that the investigation and dismissal of homosexuals from the armed forces was a breach of Article 8. Public authorities will violate the right to private life if they conduct intrusive investigations into the sexuality of employees; and, in practice, they will be acting unlawfully by dismissing employees on the grounds of their sexual orientation. Although the Sex Discrimination Act 1975 could not

---

[302] [2007] EWHC 1529 (Admin).
[303] [2008] 2 All ER 1003.
[304] [2000] HRLR 702, 716–20.
[305] As set out in *Post Office v Foley* [2000] IRLR 827.
[306] See the guidance set out in *X v Y* [2004] IRLR 625, para 63.
[307] For the concerns expressed by the ILO see: *Protection of Workers' Personal Data: An ILO Code of Practice* (ILO, 1997).
[308] See *Hilton v United Kingdom* (1998) 57 DR, EComm HR.
[309] *De Keyser v Wilson* [2000] IRLR 234.
[310] See generally, R Wintemute, *Sexual Orientation and Human Rights* (Clarendon Press, 1995) Chap 4; and see R Wintemute, 'Lesbian and Gay Britons, the Two Europes and the Bill of Rights Debate' [1997] EHRLR 466. R Wintemute, 'Lesbian and Gay Inequality 2000: The Potential Impact of the HRA 1998 and the Need for an Equality Act 2002' [2000] EHRLR 603.
[311] (1999) 29 EHRR 449.
[312] (2000) 29 EHRR 493.

be interpreted so as to render sexual orientation discrimination unlawful,[313] the Employment Equality (Sexual Orientation) Regulations 2003[314] now plug the gap.

(4) Privacy and the media[315]

(a) Introduction

A large proportion of all complaints of invasion of privacy relate to the activities of the **12.91** media. Many advocates of a tort of invasion of privacy have been motivated by the perceived need to curb the excesses of the tabloid press.[316] Reporting of private information is now generally regulated by the tort of misuse of private information.[317] In addition, some protection against invasion of privacy by the press is contained in the Code of Practice adopted by the Press Complaints Commissions. Invasion of privacy by radio or television broadcasters is regulated by Ofcom under the provisions of the Communications Act 2003. In *Campbell v Mirror Group Newspapers Ltd*[318] Lord Hoffmann observed in relation to the application of Article 8 to complaints against the media that there was no logical ground for saying that a person should have less protection against a private individual than he would have against the state for the publication of personal information for which there is no justification.[319]

It is strongly arguable that both the regulatory bodies dealing with the media are hybrid **12.92** public authorities[320] and, as a result, must act in conformity with Article 8. As a result, if they fail to establish and effectively police a regulatory regime which provides proper protection for Article 8 rights, their actions may be unlawful under section 6 of the HRA. A 'victim' could be entitled to damages or injunctive relief. The effect of 'privacy rights' in the media law context, however, gives rise to complex issues of balancing of rights under the Convention. In every case where privacy rights are relied on to challenge publication, media defendants respond by relying on the right to freedom of expression. In considering a conflict between these two rights the result of section 12(4) of the HRA is that the court must have particular regard to any relevant privacy codes.[321] Neither Article 8 nor Article 10 has, as such, precedence over the other.[322] The issues which arise are considered above.[323]

---

[313] *Macdonald v Ministry of Defence* [2003] 1 ICR 937.

[314] SI 2003/1661; see generally, para 17.92ff below.

[315] For a detailed treatment of the issues dealt with in this section see G Robertson and A Nicol, *Media Law* (5th edn, Sweet & Maxwell, 2007); Chap 14 'Media Self-Regulation' and Chap 16 'Broadcasting Law' and H Fenwick and G Phillipson, *Media Freedom under the Human Rights Act* (Oxford University Press, 2006), Chap 17 'Regulation of the Broadcast Media and the Protection of Privacy'.

[316] See para 12.10 above.

[317] See paras 12.24ff above.

[318] [2004] 2 AC 457.

[319] Ibid, para 50. On privacy and freedom of expression in relation to private parties, such as the media, see A Young, 'Remedial and Substantive Horizontality: The Common Law and *Douglas v Hello! Ltd*' [2002] PL 232 and I Hare, 'Verticality Challenged: Private Parties, Privacy and the HRA' [2001] EHRLR 526. Generally, on the law relating to privacy and freedom of expression, see H Tomlinson (ed), *Privacy and the Media: The Developing Law* (Matrix, 2002); M Tugendhat and I Christie (eds), *The Law of Privacy and the Media* (Oxford University Press, 2002); and H Fenwick and G Phillipson (n 315 above) Chaps 13 to 17.

[320] See para 5.17ff above and *R v Press Complaints Authority, ex p Stewart-Brady* (1997) 9 Admin LR 274.

[321] See *Douglas v Hello! Ltd* [2001] QB 967; *A v B plc* [2003] QB 195, para 11(iv).

[322] See *In Re S (A Child)(Identification: Restrictions on Publication)* [2005] 1 AC 593, para 17.

[323] See para 12.24ff above.

(b) Press regulation

12.93 **Introduction.**   The Press Complaints Commission ('PCC') was established in 1991 on the recommendation of the Calcutt Committee.[324] It is a non-statutory body established by the press. The Commission has 16 members, the majority of whom are from outside the industry. One of the most important functions of the Commission is the enforcing of a Code of Practice for newspapers and periodicals. This was adopted in April 1994; the current edition is dated 1 August 2007.

12.94 **The Code of Conduct.**   The Code of Conduct contains a number of provisions dealing with privacy issues.[325] Paragraph 3 is headed 'Privacy' and provides:

> (i) Everyone is entitled to respect for his or her private and family life, home, health and correspondence, including digital communications. Editors will be expected to justify intrusions into any individual's private life without consent.

> (ii) It is unacceptable to photograph individuals in private places without their consent.
> Note—Private places are public or private property where there is a reasonable expectation of privacy.

Paragraph 4 is headed 'Harassment' and provides:

> (i) Journalists must not engage in intimidation, harassment or persistent pursuit.
> (ii) They must not persist in questioning, telephoning, pursuing or photographing individuals once asked to desist; nor remain on their property when asked to leave and must not follow them.
> (iii) Editors must ensure these principles are observed by those working for them and take care not to use non-compliant material from other sources.

Paragraph 5 states that enquiries in cases involving grief or shock should be made with sympathy and discretion. Paragraph 10 deals with listening devices and surveillance and states:

> The press must not seek to obtain or publish material acquired by using hidden cameras or clandestine listening devices; or by intercepting private or mobile telephone calls, messages or emails; or by the unauthorized removal of documents or photographs; or by accessing digitally-held private information without consent.

The Code provides that exceptions may be made to all of these clauses 'where they can be demonstrated to be in the public interest'. The public interest is not exhaustively defined but is said to *include*:

> (i) Detecting or exposing crime or a serious impropriety;
> (ii) Protecting public health and safety;
> (iii) Preventing the public from being misled by an action or statement of an individual or organization.

12.95 If a complaint of breach of the Code is brought to the PCC, it will make an adjudication. Any publication which is criticized by the PCC is required to print the adjudication in full and with due prominence. The PCC has no power to award compensation. There is no

---

[324] *Report of the Committee on Privacy and Related Matters* (1990) Cm 1102.
[325] For a valuable commentary on these provisions of the Code and robust criticism of the PCC, see Robertson and Nicol (n 315 above), para 14-014, 773–782.

procedure for appeal from a decision of the PCC. However, the PCC is arguably a 'public authority' and as such susceptible to judicial review.[326] The PCC has attracted considerable public criticism: it is all too willing to defer to the views of newspaper editors and often seems to be strongly influenced by the status of the complainant rather than the nature of the intrusion.[327] In his second report on self-regulation, Sir David Calcutt concluded that the press freedom had been emphasized by the PCC to the detriment of fairness to the individual.[328]

Judicial oversight of the PCC.   It seems clear that the PCC is exercising a public adjudicative function but there have been few attempts to review its decisions in the courts. As one leading textbook says, few have regarded its decisions as important enough to quash.[329] In *R (Ford) v Press Complaints Commission*[330] the court refused permission to proceed with a judicial review of the PCC's dismissal of a privacy complaint on the basis that even after the HRA came into force the court should defer to the views of regulators in privacy matters. This approach is difficult to justify, bearing in mind the fact that the obvious lack of expertize of the PCC in privacy matters and the important legal rights involved. The positive obligation of the Court under Article 8 should lead to a stricter scrutiny of such decisions by the Courts which are best equipped to decide whether privacy rights have been infringed.[331]   **12.96**

(c) Regulation of broadcasting

Introduction.   Radio and television broadcasting has long been subject to statutory control in relation to standards and complaints. The Communications Act 2003 merged, the Broadcasting Standards Commission ('the BSC') (which regulated all television and radio services provided by the BBC and other television and radio companies in the United Kingdom) and the Independent Television Commission (which regulated all non-BBC television) into a single regulator—Ofcom. The 2003 transferred to Ofcom the BSC's function of drawing up a code of practice in relation to privacy[332] and its power to compel broadcasters to carry apologies and statements of findings in relation to complaints. Independent broadcasters are directly bound by the fairness and privacy codes[333] and the BBC's Agreement with the Government now contains an obligation to comply with the codes.[334]   **12.97**

The Ofcom Board has delegated the discharge of functions in relation to fairness and privacy complaints to a committee known as the Fairness Committee, chaired by the deputy   **12.98**

---

[326] The point was accepted as being 'at least arguable' in *R v Press Complaints Authority, ex p Stewart-Brady* (1997) 9 Admin LR 274; see the debate in House of Lords on the Human Rights Bill, *Hansard*, HL cols 771–787 (24 Nov 1997) in which Lord Irvine LC expressed the view that the PCC might well be a 'public authority' under the HRA.
[327] See the striking examples given by Robertson and Nicol (n 315 above) 775–776.
[328] See *Review of Press Self-Regulation* (1993) Cm 2315.
[329] G Robertson and A Nicol, *Media Law* (5th edn, Sweet & Maxwell, 2007), para 14-007; but see *R (Pro-Life Alliance) v BBC* [2004] 1 AC 185 in which the House of Lords endorsed the notion of deference to the regulator in a matter of 'taste', see the discussion in H Fenwick, *Civil Liberties and Human Rights* (4th edn, Routledge-Cavendish, 2007), 850–851.
[330] [2002] EMLR 5 (the court proceeded on the basis that it was strongly arguable that the PCC was a public authority); for criticism of this decision see H Fenwick and G Phillipson, *Media Freedom under the Human Rights Act* (Oxford University Press, 2006), 866–868.
[331] See the comments of Robertson and Nicol in relation to Ofcom (n 329 above) 924.
[332] Communications Act 2003, Sch 1, para 14—the function of drawing up a privacy code arose under s107 of the Broadcasting Act 1996.
[333] Communications Act 2003, s 326.
[334] BBC Agreement, cl 5A.

chair of Ofcom's Content Board. The guidelines for the handling of complaints, dated June 2004, were drafted in light of the Article 6 but do not mention Article 8. Ofcom does not have a power to award damages to complainants and, as a result, cannot provide an 'effective remedy' for violations of Article 8 rights.[335]

12.99　**Ofcom Code.**　Section 8 of the Ofcom Broadcasting Code deals with 'Privacy'. It provides that any infringement of privacy in programmes, or in connection with obtaining material included in programmes, must be 'warranted' (clause 8.1). In other words, the Code not only covers what is broadcast but the means used to obtain material.[336]

12.100　The Ofcom Code used term 'warranted' in place of the reference in the BSC Code to justification in by 'an overriding public interest'.[337] This term is explained as follows:

> It means that where broadcasters wish to justify an infringement of privacy as warranted, they should be able to demonstrate why in the particular circumstances of the case, it is warranted. If the reason is that it is in the public interest, then the broadcaster should be able to demonstrate that the public interest outweighs the right to privacy. Examples of public interest would include revealing or detecting crime, protecting public health or safety, exposing misleading claims made by individuals or organisations or disclosing incompetence that affects the public.

The Code explains 'legitimate expectations of privacy' in the following terms:

> Legitimate expectations of privacy will vary according to the place and nature of the information, activity or condition in question, the extent to which it is in the public domain (if at all) and whether the individual concerned is already in the public eye. There may be circumstances where people can reasonably expect privacy even in a public place. Some activities and conditions may be of such a private nature that filming or recording, even in a public place, could involve an infringement of privacy. People under investigation or in the public eye, and their immediate family and friends, retain the right to a private life, although private behaviour can raise issues of legitimate public interest.

It then contains, inter alia, the following provisions:

> **8.2** Information which discloses the location of a person's home or family should not be revealed without permission, unless it is warranted.

> **8.3** When people are caught up in events which are covered by the news they still have a right to privacy in both the making and the broadcast of a programme, unless it is warranted to infringe it. This applies both to the time when these events are taking place and to any later programmes that revisit those events.

> **8.4** Broadcasters should ensure that words, images or actions filmed or recorded in, or broadcast from, a public place, are not so private that prior consent is required before broadcast from the individual or organization concerned, unless broadcasting without their consent is warranted.

> Consent

> **8.5** Any infringement of privacy in the making of a programme should be with the person's and/or organization's consent or be otherwise warranted.

---

[335] See *Peck v United Kingdom* (2003) 36 EHRR 41, para 109 (which found that the lack of power of ITC and BSC to award damages meant that complaints to them did not provide an effective remedy) the problem was not remedied when Ofcom was established, see the discussion in Fenwick and Phillipson (n 330 above) 863–864.

[336] It should, however, be noted that Ofcom only considers complaints in relation to the making of a programme if it is broadcast, see Ofcom Broadcasting Code Guidance Notes.

[337] This wider term was chosen because the legislation does not specify that public interest is the only way of justifying an infringement of privacy; see the discussion in Fenwick and Phillipson (n 330 above) 874.

8.6 If the broadcast of a programme would infringe the privacy of a person or organization, consent should be obtained before the relevant material is broadcast, unless the infringement of privacy is warranted. (Callers to phone-in shows are deemed to have given consent to the broadcast of their contribution.)

8.7 If an individual or organization's privacy is being infringed, and they ask that the filming, recording or live broadcast be stopped, the broadcaster should do so, unless it is warranted to continue.

In relation to the gathering of material for broadcast, the Code provides that means used 'must be proportionate in all the circumstances and in particular to the subject matter of the programme'.[338] The Code also provides that permission should be obtained when recording in institutions (unless filming without permission is warranted)[339] and makes detailed provision in relation to 'doorstepping'[340] and surreptitious filming.[341]   **12.101**

Judicial oversight. In *R v BSC ex p BBC*[342] the Court of Appeal held that the BSC was entitled to find that a company could make privacy complaint under the BSC code. The fact that a programme was made in accordance with the provisions of the Ofcom code will be an important factor when considering whether injunctive relief should be granted to prevent a broadcast.[343]   **12.102**

(d) Photography by the media[344]

Introduction. The taking of photographs on behalf of the media without the consent of the subject does not engage any common law right.[345] However, a person who is photographed by the media now has two potential remedies: an action for harassment and an action for misuse of private information. These will be considered in turn.   **12.103**

Harassment. Under the Protection from Harassment Act 1997, a tort and a crime may be committed by a person who pursues a course of conduct which amounts to harassment of another: a course of conduct must involve conduct on at least two occasions and harassment includes alarming a person or causing them distress.[346] There is a defence of 'reasonableness'.[347] Harassment can be caused by taking photographs of a person[348] and pursuit by   **12.104**

---

[338] Clause 8.9.

[339] Clause 8.8.

[340] Clause 8.11. 'Doorstepping' is defined as 'the filming or recording of an interview or attempted interview with someone, or announcing that a call is being filmed or recorded for broadcast purposes, without any prior warning'.

[341] Clause 8.13, which 'includes the use of long lenses or recording devices, as well as leaving an unattended camera or recording device on private property without the full and informed consent of the occupiers or their agent. It may also include recording telephone conversations without the knowledge of the other party, or deliberately continuing a recording when the other party thinks that it has come to an end.

[342] [2001] QB 885; see also *R v BCC, ex p Barclay Brothers*, *The Times*, 11 October 1996 and *R v BCC, ex p Granada* [1995] EMLR 163.

[343] See eg, *Leeds City Council v Channel 4 Television* [2007] 1 FLR 678, para 25.

[344] See generally, C Michalos, *The Law of Photography and Digital Images* (Sweet & Maxwell, 2004).

[345] See para 12.142 below.

[346] Protection from Harassment Act 1977, s 1 and s 7.

[347] Ibid, s 3(c)—it is also a defence to show that the course of conduct was pursued for the purposes of preventing or detecting crime, s 3(a).

[348] See eg, *DPP v Ramsdale*, *The Independent*, 19 March 2001 (harassment included taking photographs and a video).

press photographers could plainly constitute both the crime and the tort. A person who is being pursued by press photographers could, in appropriate circumstances, obtain an injunction to restrain the taking of photographs.

12.105 **Misuse of private information.** Although, there will usually not be a relationship of confidence between a photographer and the person photographed express or implied obligation not to take photographs may give rise to action for breach of confidence. The case of *Hellewell v The Chief Constable of Derbyshire*,[349] dealt with the use which police officers could make of photographs taken of persons in custody. Laws J held that there was undoubtedly an obligation of confidence between the plaintiff and police, as the photograph was not a 'public fact' and could be described as a 'piece of confidential information'. Nevertheless, the public interest in the prevention of crime outweighed the public interest in maintaining confidentiality. Laws J said, *obiter*, that:

> If someone with a telephoto lens were to take from a distance, and with no authority, a picture of another engaged in some private act, his subsequent disclosure of the photograph would in my judgment as surely amount to a breach of confidence as if he had found or stolen a letter or diary in which the act was recounted, and proceeded to publish it. In such a case the law would protect what might reasonably be called a right of privacy, though the name accorded to the cause of action would be breach of confidence.[350]

In *Campbell v MGN Limited*[351] it was held that the publication of photographs of a fashion model attending a drug rehabilitation group was in breach of confidence, or a 'misuse of private information'. This cause of action now reflects the values enshrined in Article 8

12.106 The position as to photographs taken in public places remains unclear. In *Campbell v Mirror Group Newspapers Ltd*,[352] it was held that the activity photographed must itself be private. Accordingly, photographs of a fashion model leaving a meeting of Narcotics Anonymous was a breach of confidence. But Baroness Hale suggested there could have been no complaint had the model simply been going about her business in a public street. This is, however, questionable in light of the ruling of the Court of Human Rights in *Von Hannover v Germany*.[353] In *Murray v Big Picture (UK) Limited*[354] the Court of Appeal confirmed that, depending on the circumstances, even routine activities such as taking the bus could be protected.

12.107 It is now well established that special considerations apply to photographs as they are 'particularly intrusive' as a 'means of invading privacy'.[355] This means that a court may restrain the publication of a photograph even if the taker is free to describe the information in the photograph.[356]

---

[349] [1995] 1 WLR 804.
[350] Ibid, 807.
[351] [2004] 2 AC 457.
[352] Ibid.
[353] (2005) 40 EHRR 1, see para 12.260 below.
[354] [2008] EMLR 12, para 56.
[355] *Douglas v Hello! (No 3)* [2006] QB 125, para 84.
[356] See *D v L* [2004] EMLR 1, para 23; see eg, *Theakston v MGN* [2002] EMLR 22 (court permitted story to be published, but not photographs of claimant in brothel) and *Mosley v News Group Newspapers* [2008] EMLR 20, paras 16–23, and see generally, para 12.30 above.

(e) Privacy and reporting judicial proceedings

12.108 Those acting on behalf of children sometimes seek to restrict the media's ability freely to report on criminal and other proceedings where that reporting is perceived to have potential ill effects on the child's well-being or to expose his or her private life to undue publicity. The House of Lords took the opportunity in the case of *In re S (Identification: Restrictions on Publication)*[357] to emphasize that reporting restrictions will rarely be appropriate in criminal cases where the child is not directly involved. Lord Steyn held[358] that, although when balancing Article 8 and Article 10 rights neither has precedence as such, the particular context mattered:

> the ordinary rule is that the press, as the watchdog of the public, may report everything that takes place in a criminal court. I would add that in European and in domestic practice this is a strong rule. It can only be displaced by unusual or exceptional circumstances.

The House of Lords upheld the refusal of an injunction to protect the identity of a child whose mother was to undergo trial on charges of murdering his brother by salt poisoning. This principle has since been robustly applied in a number of cases.[359]

(f) Restraining publication of private information

12.109 **Introduction.** An important aspect of the law concerning private information and the media concerns the availability of injunctive relief to restrain the publication of information. This is a draconian measure – involving a total restriction on the Article 10 rights and will be closely scrutinized. In each case, the court must now consider the provisions of section 12 of the HRA and balance the competing Convention rights which are in play.

12.110 **Section 12 of the HRA.**[360] Section 12 of the HRA applies when a court is considering whether to grant any relief which, if granted, might affect the exercise of Article 10 rights and provides that the court must have 'particular regard' to the importance of this right. Section 12(3) applies to the grant of interim relief and provides that no such relief is to be granted 'unless the court is satisfied that the applicant is likely to establish that publication should not be allowed'. In *Cream Holdings Ltd v Banerjee*[361] the House of Lords held that, on its proper construction, the effect of section 12(3) of the HRA was that the court was not to make an interim restraint order unless satisfied that an applicant's prospects of success at trial were sufficiently favourable to justify such an order being made in the particular circumstances of the case. As to what degree of likelihood made the prospects of success 'sufficiently favourable', the general approach should be that courts would be exceedingly slow to make interim restraint orders where an applicant had not satisfied the court that he would probably, as in 'more likely than not', succeed at trial.[362]

---

[357] [2005] 1 AC 593.
[358] Ibid, paras 17–18; see also para 30.
[359] *In re Trinity Mirror* [2008] QB 770 *Crawford v CPS* [2008] EWHC 854 (Admin).
[360] See generally, para 15.15ff below.
[361] [2005] 1 AC 253.
[362] In *Greene v Associated Newspapers* [2005] 1 QB 971, the Court of Appeal confirmed that section 12 did not affect the existing test to be applied when considering whether to grant an interim injunction in defamation cases.

12.111 **Interim injunctions.** Injunctions are commonly sought on an interim basis, since preventing publication is often the principal aim of litigation: indeed, the outcome of an interim application for an injunction is likely to be vital for both parties. In *Cream Holdings*[363] Lord Nicholls commented that confidentiality, once breached, 'is lost for ever, so that the granting or withholding of a pre-trial injunction is of critical importance to a claimant'.

12.112 The courts have refused interim injunctions in a number of private information cases. The first 'guideline case' was *A v B plc*,[364] in which the Court of Appeal discharged an interim injunction to restrain publication of a story about the sexual activities of a premiership footballer. The Court took into account the fact that the relationship had been a transient one, that the other parties to the relationship wished to disclose it and the contention that the claimant was a 'role model'. This case is of doubtful authority. In *Campbell v MGN*[365] the Court of Appeal said:

> We do not see why it should necessarily be in the public interest that an individual who has been adopted as a role model, without seeking this distinction, should be demonstrated to have feet of clay.

In the subsequent case of *McKennitt v Ash*[366] the Court of Appeal commented that the approach in *A v B plc*[367] could not be reconciled with that of the Court of Human Rights in *Von Hannover* and that it could not be regarded as 'any sort of binding authority on the content of articles 8 and 10'.

12.113 In *Tillery Valley Foods v Channel Four Television*[368] the claimant sought to prevent the airing of footage taken covertly by a journalist who was employed in a factory that produced frozen meals for distribution to the healthcare and public sector markets. The court held that the claimant had no real likelihood of being able to maintain a claim for an injunction at trial based on misuse of confidential information. In *Mills v Mirror Group Newspapers*[369] an injunction restraining the publication of the claimant's home address was refused in the absence of evidence of apprehended harm. In *Long Beach v Global Witness*[370] the court refused an interim injunction to restrain publication on the website of a non-governmental organization of documents alleged to reveal corrupt business practices on the part of the son of the President of the Republic of Congo, who was also a government minister.

12.114 **Information concerning children.** The earlier case law about the existence and scope of the inherent jurisdiction of the Court to restrain the publication of information relating to children has been superseded by the HRA. The foundation of the jurisdiction to restrain publicity in relation to children is now derived from Article 8.[371] A number of applications have been brought with a view to restraining the publication of material in criminal trials which indirectly impacts on children. In *Re S (A Child) (Identification: Restrictions on*

---

[363] See n 361 above, para 18.
[364] [2003] QB 195.
[365] *Campbell v MGN* [2003] QB 633, para 41.
[366] [2008] QB 73, para 64.
[367] See n 364 above.
[368] [2004] EWHC 1075 (Ch).
[369] [2001] EMLR 957.
[370] [2007] EWHC 1980 (QB).
[371] *Re S (A Child) (Identification: Restrictions on Publication)* [2005] 1 AC 593.

Publication),[372] the House of Lords held that the privacy interests of a child whose mother was being tried for the murder of his brother were not sufficient to justify an injunction against publishing the names of his mother or deceased brother.[373] However, an injunction was granted in *A Local Authority v W*[374] to prevent the publication of the identity of a defendant and her victim in a criminal trial, and that they were suffering from the HIV virus, in order to protect the privacy of their children.

12.115 In a number of cases attempts have been made to restrain publication in the media of information relating to children. In *Leeds City Council v Channel 4*,[375] the Council and representatives of a number of children sought to restrain Channel 4 from showing a documentary in which surreptitious filming portrayed 'a situation, seemingly on an endemic basis, of children approximately 13 to 16 years old out of control'. The broadcast obscured the faces of the children, but the judge accepted that they would still be recognisable to friends, relatives and locals and that the filming and broadcast of the programme would interfere with their privacy rights. However, due to the 'very powerful public interest' the judge refused the injunction, taking the view that 'the case comes down fairly heavily in favour of Channel 4'.[376] This case can be contrasted with *T v BBC*[377] the BBC wished to broadcast a programme about a form of foster parenting known as 'concurrent planning', where a child is placed with foster parents with a view to adoption should return to her natural parents prove to be unrealistic. The programme showed the tearful final meeting between a child and her natural mother and suggested that the mother had been rough with her daughter and had problems with anger management. In a claim brought by the mother, the court held that the programme could only be broadcast if she was not identified. The public interest in the issue could be satisfied without revealing the mother's identity.

12.116 ***Contra mundum* injunctions.** Where an 'unqualified convention right' is in play then it will be much easier to justify the grant of an injunction in wide terms. If the publication of private information will put the life or safety of the claimant at risk there is jurisdiction to grant an injunction not just against named parties but against the whole world, *contra mundum*.[378] The first such order was made in *Venables v News Group Newspapers*[379] in favour of two claimants who had been convicted of a notorious child murder and were about to be released. The Court held that there was jurisdiction to grant an injunction for breach of confidence against the whole world. There was a 'strong possibility' that if the claimants were identified their lives would be at risk.[380] An injunction was granted to pre-

---

[372] Ibid.

[373] See also *In re Trinity Mirror* [2008] QB 770 (no jurisdiction for a Crown Court judge to grant an injunction restraining publicity but, in any event, no order should be made to protect children from 'misery, shame and disadvantage' in ordinary criminal cases) and see *Crawford v CPS* [2008] EWHC 854 (Admin).

[374] [2006] 1 FLR 1 (this appears to be the only case in which an order has been made under Art 8 to prevent the reporting of the name of a defendant in a criminal trial); see also *Re LM (Reporting Restrictions: Coroner's Inquest)* [2008] 1 FLR 1360 (order granted to prevent the identification of a child the death of whose sister was the subject of the inquest).

[375] [2007] 1 FLR 678.

[376] Ibid, para 34.

[377] [2008] 1 FLR 281.

[378] *Venables v News Group Newspapers* [2001] Fam 340, paras 98–100.

[379] Ibid.

[380] Ibid, para 94.

vent the publication of information which might lead to their identification. Similar relief was granted in the *Mary Bell* case,[381] to prevent the publication of the present name and address of the applicant who had assumed a new identity.

(5) Intrusion into the home: entry, search, and seizure

(a) Introduction

12.117 The common law has always treated the right to freedom from interference with personal property[382] as fundamental.[383] It has given rise to perhaps the most well-known of all maxims of the English law:

> 'An Englishman's home is his castle' is one of the few principles of law known to every citizen . . . The rule is, of course, subject to exceptions, but they are few . . .[384]

In fact, the principle has always been subject to numerous limitations: by 1604 it provided protection only against the forcible entry of outer doors of dwelling houses, and gave way to legal process in the name of the King.[385] Nevertheless, it remains the case that the police or other public officials can enter premises only in the limited situations defined by statute or common law and that the burden is on them to justify the entry.

12.118 In the famous constitutional case of *Entick v Carrington*,[386] it was argued that an entry and seizure by the King's messengers was justified by a warrant issued by one of the four principal secretaries of state. Lord Camden CJ dismissed this defence in stirring words:

> The great end, for which men entered into society was to secure their property. That right is preserved sacred and incommunicable in all instances, where it has not been taken away or abridged by some public law for the good of the whole. . . . By the laws of England every invasion of private property, be it ever so minute, is a trespass.

This approach, which applies both to searches of property and seizures of goods has been applied, somewhat unevenly, ever since. Search, seizure and retention by public officials will be unlawful unless justified by some common law or statutory power.[387]

12.119 The idea of 'respect for the home' under Article 8(1)[388] of the Convention has rather broader implications in the public law field. Article 8(1) has been successfully utilized in judicial review cases, such as *R v North and East Devon District Health Authority, ex p Coughlan*,[389] where the Court of Appeal held that moving a disabled person out of a long stay residence after giving her an express assurance that she could remain there for life con-

---

[381] *X, A Woman Formerly Known as Mary Bell v O'Brien* [2003] EMLR 37; see also *Maxine Carr v News Group Newspapers* [2005] EWHC 971 (QB).

[382] For a fuller treatment, see eg, D Feldman, *The Law Relating to Entry, Seizure and Search* (Butterworths, 1986); R Clayton and H Tomlinson, *Civil Actions Against the Police* (3rd edn, Sweet & Maxwell, 2001), Chap 7.

[383] R Kerr (ed), *Blackstone's Commentaries on the Laws of England* (4th edn, John Murray, 1876), 100ff.

[384] *McLorie v Oxford* [1982] 1 QB 1290 per Donaldson LJ.

[385] See D Feldman, *Civil Liberties and Human Rights in England and Wales* (2nd edn, Oxford University Press, 2002), 573–574.

[386] (1765) 2 Wils 275; 19 State Trials 1029.

[387] For an illuminating general discussion see Feldman (n 382 above).

[388] See para 12.303ff below.

[389] [2001] QB 213.

stituted an interference with the right to her home, which required the public body to comply with its duty to act fairly.

(b) Interference with land and goods

Any unjustified direct physical intrusion onto land in possession of another is a trespass at common law. The slightest entry, such as putting a foot in the door or a microphone on a window, is sufficient. The person who enters must justify the entry. Honest belief in a right to enter is not a defence.[390] A public official who enters under an authority given by law becomes a trespasser *ab initio* if he abuses that authority.[391] This means that the occupier of the land can recover damages for the whole period that the wrongdoer is on the land and not just for the period after the abuse.[392]   **12.120**

Any interference with a person's goods is also, *prima facie*, tortious. An unjustified direct physical interference with goods in the possession of a person will be sufficient to constitute a trespass to goods.[393] A person's right of possession to goods is entitled to legal protection regardless of whether possession was obtained unlawfully, even by theft.[394] If the person interfering with the goods acts in a manner inconsistent with the rights of the person in possession, he will be guilty of conversion. Conversion covers actions such as keeping and refusing to return, using, destroying, and returning the goods to a third party. Proceedings can be brought for trespass to goods when goods are removed, damaged or even touched. Conversion will be more appropriate if the plaintiff is prevented from gaining access to his goods, if lawfully seized goods are lost or damaged, or if there is a refusal to return goods which are no longer needed for the purpose for which they were seized.   **12.121**

(c) Powers of entry under warrant

Introduction.   A warrant is a legal authority to carry out acts which would, otherwise, be unlawful.[395] A large number of statutes empower justices of the peace to issue search warrants to police officers and other public officials.[396] The Serious Organized Crime and Police Act 2005 significantly extended the powers of magistrates to grant search orders, expanding the scope of section 8 of PACE.[397] Constables who act 'in obedience' to such a warrant are protected from claims in trespass if the warrant is issued without jurisdiction.[398] However, where police officers have acted maliciously in procuring the search war-   **12.122**

---

[390] *Hewlitt v Bickerton* (1947) 150 EG 421; and see *Entick v Carrington* (n 386 above) 1066G: 'No man can set his foot upon my ground without my licence, but he is liable to an action, though the damage be nothing'.

[391] *Six Carpenters Case* (1610) 8 Co Rep 146a; and see *Cinnamond v British Airports Authority* [1980] 1 WLR 582, 588; and generally, Clayton and Tomlinson (n 382 above) Chap 6.

[392] See *Shorland v Govett* (1826) 5 B & C 485.

[393] *Fouldes v Willoughby* (1841) 8 M & W 540, 549.

[394] *Costello v Chief Constable of Derbyshire* [2001] 1 WLR 1437.

[395] For comprehensive discussions, see D Feldman, *The Law Relating to Entry Search and Seizure* (Butterworths, 1986) and R Stone, *The Law of Entry, Search and Seizure* (4th edn, Oxford University Press, 2005).

[396] A Centre for Policy Studies study has listed 266 powers, see H Snook, *Crossing the Threshold* (Centre for Policy Studies, 2007).

[397] The Joint Committee on Human Rights expressed doubt as to the compatibility of the new powers with Article 8 (Scrutiny Fourth Progress Report, 23 February 2005, HL Paper 60, HC 338).

[398] Constables Protection Act 1750, s 6; see generally, Clayton and Tomlinson, (n 382 above) Chap 7.

rant, they will be liable in damages.[399] It is, further, clear that the police will breach Article 8 if the intrusion is unjustified, regardless of whether they act with malice.[400]

12.123 **Applications for search warrants.**   Applications for search warrants by police officers must be made in accordance with the procedure laid down in section 15 of the Police and Criminal Evidence Act 1984 ('PACE'). An application must be supported by an 'information' in writing.[401] The warrant must specify the name of the person who applies for it, the date on which it is issued, the enactment under which it is issued, the premises to be searched[402] and the articles or persons to be sought.[403] The execution of warrants by police officers is governed by section 16 of PACE. The constable must, if the occupier is present, identify himself, produce the warrant and supply a copy.[404] If the occupier is not present, a copy of the warrant must be left at the premises.[405] A warrant does not permit a 'general search' of the premises:[406] a search under a warrant may only be a search 'to the extent required for the purpose for which the warrant was issued'.[407] The warrant must be endorsed, stating whether the articles which were sought were found and what other articles were seized.[408] The safeguards imposed by sections 15 and 16 of PACE are 'stringent in effect'.[409] Any search which is not carried out in accordance with these provisions will be unlawful.[410] Thus, searches have been held to be unlawful where copies of the schedules to the warrants were not supplied to the applicant at the time of the search[411] and where the enactment under which the warrant was issued was not specified.[412]

12.124 Special provisions apply to 'items subject to legal privilege',[413] 'excluded material'[414] and 'special procedure material'.[415] A provision of any enactment, passed prior to PACE, which permits searches for any of these three types of material, is of no effect.[416] A constable can, however, obtain access to excluded material or special procedure material by obtaining an appropriate order from a circuit judge if a number of special access conditions are fulfilled.[417] It has been emphasized that this procedure is 'a serious inroad upon the liberty of

---

[399] See, most recently, *Gibbs v Rea* [1998] AC 786 and see generally, Clayton and Tomlinson (n 382 above) Chap 8.

[400] *Keegan v United Kingdom* (2007) 44 EHRR 33.

[401] See s 15(3).

[402] *R v Southwestern Magistrates' Court, ex p Cofie* [1997] 1 WLR 885.

[403] See s 15(6).

[404] See s 16(5).

[405] See s 16(7).

[406] See eg, *R v Chief Constable of Warwick Constabulary, ex p Fitzpatrick* [1999] 1 WLR 564.

[407] See s 16(8).

[408] See s 16(9).

[409] *R v Central Criminal Court, ex p AJD Holdings* [1992] Crim LR 669.

[410] See s 15(1) which covers the composite process of entering and searching; *R v Chief Constable of Lancashire, ex p Parker* [1993] QB 577.

[411] Ibid.

[412] *R v Reading Justices, ex p South West Meats* (1992) 4 Admin LR 401.

[413] As defined in s 10(1); a person's name, address and contact details are not covered by legal privilege, see: *R v Minshull Street Crown Court, ex p Miller Gardner* [2002] EWHC 3077 (QB).

[414] That is personal records, human tissue or journalistic material held in confidence: see s 11(1).

[415] That is, non-confidential journalistic material and confidential business material, s 14(1); for the impact of freedom of expression under Art 10 on these applications, see para 15.208 below.

[416] s 9(2) of PACE.

[417] Ibid, s 9 and Sch 1.

the subject' and that 'it is of cardinal importance that circuit judges should be scrupulous in discharging that responsibility'.[418] There is no power to search for or seize items subject to legal privilege. PACE provides, however, that this privilege is lost if the material is held 'with the intention of furthering a criminal purpose'.[419] The relevant provision[420] was given a very broad interpretation by the House of Lords in *R v Central Criminal Court, ex p Francis and Francis*[421] in which it was found that, although the material was held innocently, the privilege was lost as a result of the 'criminal purpose' of a third party.[422]

Balancing and Article 8. In cases involving the use of warrants, the courts have empha- **12.125**
sized the need to carry out a balancing exercise between, the public interest in the effective investigation and prosecution of crime and the public interest in protecting the personal and property rights of citizens against infringement and invasion:[423]

> [PACE] . . . seeks to effect a carefully judged balance between these interests and that it why it is a detailed and complex Act. If the scheme intended by Parliament is to be implemented it is important that the provisions laid down in the Act should be fully and fairly enforced.[424]

This approach has led to warrants being quashed in a number of cases.[425] However, there is no domestic law obligation on magistrates to give reasons for the grant of a warrant[426] and no record of the proceedings. As a result, it remains extremely difficult, in practice, to mount a successful challenge to a search warrant.[427]

The provisions of PACE in relation to warrants are, in general, in conformity with **12.126**
the Convention. An issue may arise, however, as to whether the procedure for the issue of search warrants by magistrates conforms to Article 8, because the procedure is arguably little more than a 'rubber stamping exercise', with refusals being exceedingly rare.[428] A warrant does not show the grounds on which it was issued and the 'information in writing' is usually formal in nature. Justices have no clear obligation in domestic law to give reasons for the grant of a warrant and or to keep a record of proceedings.[429] This

---

[418] *R v Maidstone Crown Court, ex p Waitt* [1988] CLR 384; as a result, there is an implied obligation to give reasons for the decision: see *R v Southampton Crown Court, ex p J and P* [1993] Crim LR 962.
[419] See s 10(2).
[420] Ibid.
[421] [1989] AC 346.
[422] The dispute arose when solicitors were ordered to produce material, comprising advice to a client, to assist in the tracing of proceeds of crime; the police argued that the material was held by the solicitors as a result of the plan of suspected drug traffickers for laundering their criminal gains. This decision has been subject to considerable criticism: see A Newbold, 'The Crime/Fraud Exception to Legal Professional Privilege' (1990) 53 MLR 472; and see generally, D Feldman, *Civil Liberties and Human Rights in England and Wales* (2nd edn, Oxford University Press, 2002), 637–638.
[423] *R v Crown Court at Lewes, ex p Hill* (1990) 93 Cr App R 60, 65.
[424] Ibid per Bingham LJ.
[425] See eg, *R v Lewes Crown Court, ex p Nigel Weller & Co*, unreported, 12 May 1999.
[426] Although it is desirable, see *R v Marylebone Magistrates' Court, ex p Amdrell Ltd (trading as 'Get Stuffed')* (1998) 162 JP 719.
[427] See eg, ibid; in that case, the fact that the police did not disclose an intention to invite the media to attend the execution of a warrant did not invalidate its issue or execution.
[428] D Dixon, C Coleman, and K Bottomley 'PACE in Practice' (1991) 141 NLJ 1586. Note, though, that in *Wareham v Purbeck District Council* [2006] LGR 151, para 10, the Divisional Court refused to hold that magistrates were granting anti-social behaviour orders 'without a proper consideration of their merits' even though official statistics showed that between 1999 and 2004, 3069 had been granted and only 42 refused.
[429] *Ex p Amdrell Ltd* (n 426 above).

makes legal challenges extremely difficult. If a warrant is issued without proper grounds, then the person whose property is searched has no remedy in domestic law absent malice. No action for malicious procurement of a search warrant has been successful in England in modern times.[430] These factors lead Feldman to conclude:

> one is left with an impression that justices of the peace do not provide the independent judicial scrutiny of proposed entries and searches under warrants which is needed to ensure that interferences with the right to respect for a person's private life and home are justified. . .The formal trappings of scrutiny are there, but the substance is sadly lacking in most cases.[431]

As a result, it is arguable that the procedure for the grant of search warrants is in breach of Article 8. However, a challenge to the issue of a warrant under Article 8 was unsuccessful in the Scottish case of *Birse v HM Advocate*.[432] In any event, the English courts have repeatedly stated that it is preferable for magistrates to make a note of evidence and give reasons for their decisions,[433] and it now appears clear that Article 8 does indeed oblige them to do so at least where the evidence or reasons go beyond those which are obvious on the face of the information.[434]

12.127 The execution of search warrants in the presence of the media also raises significant Article 8 concerns. A search warrant involves a serious interference with a person's home and private life. Media involvement and the publication of material relating to the search, including films of police entry, means that there is a much greater degree of interference. Although the Divisional Court has stated that any general practice of inviting the media to attend on the execution of warrants is deplorable,[435] it refused to quash a warrant on the ground that television cameras had been invited to attend. In the United States, in contrast, the practice of inviting the media to attend the execution of a warrant, known as 'ride-along', has been held to be unconstitutional.[436] The Supreme Court held that media 'ride-alongs' could not be justified by matters such as the need to publicize law enforcement activities, minimize police abuses and protect suspects and officers: the right to the privacy of the home prevailed. It is strongly arguable that a similar approach should be taken under Article 8.

12.128 Police powers to seize material which is subject to legal professional privilege give rise to potential issues under Article 8. Although there is no statutory power to search for or seize such material, in *R v Chesterfield Justices, ex p Bramley*,[437] it was held that it is not unlawful to seize privileged documents if the police officer who did so did not have reasonable grounds for believing they were privileged. Further, privilege is lost if the material is held 'with the intention of furthering a criminal purpose',[438] and case law establishes that the

---

[430] But see *Gibbs v Rea* [1998] AC 786, PC (successful claim in Cayman Islands). See generally, R Clayton and H Tomlinson, *Civil Actions Against the Police* (3rd edn, Sweet & Maxwell, 2004), Chap 7.

[431] D Feldman, *Civil Liberties and Human Rights in England and Wales* (2nd edn, Oxford University Press, 2002), 583.

[432] 2000 JC 503.

[433] *R v Marylebone Magistrates Court, ex p Amdrell Ltd (trading as 'Get Stuffed')* (1998) 162 JP 719; *R (Cronin) v Sheffield Justices* [2003] 1 WLR 752; *R (Energy Financing Team) v Director of SFO* [2006] 1 WLR 1316.

[434] *Cronin v UK* (Decision of 6 January 2004).

[435] *R v Marylebone Magistrates Court, ex p Amdrell Ltd (trading as 'Get Stuffed')* (1998) 162 JP 719.

[436] *Wilson v Layne* (1999) 7 BHRC 274 held there was violation of Fourth Amendment rights.

[437] [2000] 1 All ER 411.

[438] PACE, s 10(2).

privilege may be lost even when the material was held innocently for a third party's 'criminal purpose'.[439] However, there is a good argument that an interference with legal professional privilege will be disproportionate unless it can be shown that the solicitor, or perhaps his client, was intending to further a criminal purpose.[440] The Court of Human Rights requires strict justification for the seizure of legally privileged documents. In *Niemetz v Germany*[441] a search of a lawyer's office was held to be a breach of Article 8, as disproportionate to the aim of prevention of crime and protection of rights of others.[442]

Not all legal material is protected. In *R (Pamplin) v Law Society*,[443] for example, Newman J   **12.129**
held that the disclosure by the police to the Law Society of the prosecution file relating to the applicant solicitor was not a breach of his Article 8 rights. The mere fact that the information was confidential did not engage Article 8 because the file centred on the applicant's public life as a provider of legal services. In *R (Miller Gardner) v Crown Court*,[444] it was held that client contact details held by a solicitor were not privileged; further, while accepting the concession that the seizure of those details interfered with Article 8 rights, the court held the interference to be proportionate.

(d) Powers of entry without warrant

Introduction.   A police officer has a common law power of entry into premises 'to deal   **12.130**
with or prevent a breach of the peace'.[445] The power allows police officers to enter whether the breach is actually in progress or merely apprehended.[446] They may also enter in the fresh pursuit of someone suspected of a breach of the peace committed elsewhere. When the pursuit ends, however, and there is no likelihood of the breach recurring, the common law power to enter is terminated.[447]

PACE provides police officers with a number of statutory powers of entry. Officers may   **12.131**
enter to:

- execute an arrest warrant;[448]
- arrest for an indictable offence;[449]
- arrest for certain specified offences;[450]
- arresting a child or young person remanded or committed to local authority accommodation;[451]

---

[439] See *R v Central Criminal Court, ex p Francis and Francis* [1989] AC 346.
[440] See Feldman (n 431, above) 636–638.
[441] (1992) 16 EHRR 97; cf D Harris, M O'Boyle, and C Warbrick, *Law of the European Convention on Human Rights* (Butterworths, 1995), 345.
[442] Such a search may, however, be justifiable provided there are safeguards against the taking of legally privileged documents: see para 12.347 below.
[443] [2001] EWHC Admin 300.
[444] [2002] EWHC 3077 (Admin).
[445] PACE, s 17(6); for a discussion of the meaning of breach of the peace, see para 16.13 below.
[446] See *Thomas v Sawkins* [1935] 2 KB 249; and see *McLeod v Commissioner of Police of the Metropolis* [1994] 4 All ER 553. Only exceptional circumstances can justify entry onto premises to prevent anticipated breaches of the peace: *Friswell v Chief Constable of Essex Police* [2004] EWHC 3009 (QB).
[447] *R v Marsden* (1868) LR 1 CCR 131.
[448] PACE, s 17(1)(a).
[449] Ibid, s 17(1)(b).
[450] Ibid, s 17(1)(c) and (caa).
[451] Ibid, s 17(1)(ca).

- recapture a person unlawfully at large;[452]
- save life, limb or property;[453]
- search the premises of a person under arrest for evidence;[454] and
- search premises attended by a person immediately prior to or at the time of his arrest.[455]

The first five of these powers are only exercisable if the constable has reasonable grounds to believe that the person sought is on the premises.[456] The last requires reasonable grounds for believing that evidence which would justify the search is located on the premises. In *R (Paul Da Costa & Co) v Thames Magistrates' Court*,[457] a search of a private residence, which was committed without a warrant and was admitted to have been illegal, was held to breach Article 8.[458]

(e) Powers of seizure and retention of goods

12.132 Police officers have a common law power to seize the 'fruits', 'evidence' or 'instruments' of serious crime from anyone 'implicated' in the crime or who unreasonably refuses to hand them over.[459] These powers have been superseded, but not replaced, by powers of seizure under PACE which are 'in addition to any power otherwise conferred'.[460]

12.133 Police officers have powers to enter premises and seize goods under a wide range of statutes. PACE provides for seven powers of seizure without warrant. The police may seize:

- items obtained through crime which may be disposed of;[461]
- evidence of crime which may be disposed of;[462]
- information on a computer which may be disposed of;[463]
- evidence found on the premises of a person under arrest for an indictable offence;[464]
- evidence obtained through a stop and search procedure;[465]
- evidence found after arrest;[466]
- property located on a person brought to a police station.[467]

12.134 When the police seize large quantities of goods they must consider each item separately and decide whether or not there are reasonable grounds for believing that it is seizable. If proper

---

[452] Ibid, s 17(1)(d) and (cb).
[453] Ibid, s 17(1)(e).
[454] Ibid, s 18(1).
[455] Ibid, s 32(2)(b).
[456] Ibid, s 17(2)(a).
[457] [2002] Crim LR 504.
[458] Para 23.
[459] *Ghani v Jones* [1970] 1 QB 693, 708–709; the last category was added by Lord Denning MR when revising the Judgment and is of dubious authority: see Jackson [1970] CLJ 1; and see generally, D Feldman, *The Law Relating to Entry Search and Seizure* (Butterworths, 1986), 409–416.
[460] PACE, s 19(5); see also *R v Commissioner of Police for the Metropolis, ex p Rottman* [2002] 2 AC 692.
[461] Ibid, s 19(2).
[462] Ibid, s 19(3).
[463] Ibid, s 19(4).
[464] Ibid, s 18(1).
[465] Ibid, s 1(6).
[466] Ibid, s 32(2)(a).
[467] Ibid, s 54(1) and (3).

consideration is not given to each item, a trespass to goods will result.[468] Where the search or seizure is unlawful, the goods must be returned.[469] As the Divisional Court stressed in *R v Chesterfield Justices, ex p Bramley*,[470] it is not unlawful to seize documents which are legally privileged if the police officer who did so did not have reasonable grounds for believing they were. However, under Part 2 of the Criminal Justice Act 2001, enacted to reverse the effect of the *Chesterfield Justices'*, decision, the police are entitled to remove documents to carry out a preliminary sift to investigate whether they are entitled to seize them.

Even if goods have been lawfully seized, the police will be guilty of wrongful interference **12.135** with goods if they cannot justify the continued retention of them.[471] When the police seize an item under their common law powers they must not keep it for longer than is reasonably necessary for their investigations.[472] The property must be returned when charges are dropped or the proceedings have been disposed of.

The common law position is confirmed by section 22 of PACE, under which any material **12.136** seized may be retained for 'so long as is necessary in all the circumstances'. Goods may be retained if there are reasonable grounds for believing they are the fruits of crime.[473] If goods are seized from a person in custody, on grounds that they might be used to cause injury, damage to property, interfere with evidence or assist in escape, they must be returned when the person is released from custody.[474] No goods can be retained for use as evidence at a trial or for investigation if a photograph or a copy would be sufficient.[475] Section 21 of PACE provides that the owner of documents has rights of access and copying. There is also a right of access to anything retained for the purpose of investigation of an offence, unless the police have reasonable grounds for believing that to give access would prejudice the investigation.[476] Owners of documents nevertheless often experience considerable practical difficulty in obtaining access or copies.

The powers to seize and retain documents are conferred for the performance of public **12.137** functions and cannot be used to make information available to private individuals for private purposes. This is because:

> Search and seizure under statutory powers constitute fundamental infringements of the individual's immunity from interference by the state with his property and privacy—fundamental human rights.[477]

---

[468] *Reynolds v Commissioner of Police of the Metropolis* [1985] QB 881.
[469] See *R v Chief Constable of Lancashire, ex p Parker* [1993] QB 577.
[470] [2000] 1 All ER 411.
[471] *Gough v Chief Constable of West Midlands Police* [2004] 1 Pol LR 164.
[472] *Ghani v Jones* [1970] 1 QB 693.
[473] PACE, s 22(2)(b).
[474] Ibid, s 22(3).
[475] Ibid, s 22(4).
[476] Ibid, s 21(8).
[477] See *Marcel v Commissioner of Police of the Metropolis* [1992] Ch 225, 235D–E per Browne-Wilkinson J; approved by the Court of Appeal, 256D; and see also *Taylor v Director of the Serious Fraud Office* [1999] 2 AC 177.

The police must nevertheless respond to a subpoena to produce documents to the court for the purposes of a civil action.[478]

(6) Photography, surveillance, telephone tapping, and intercepting letters

(a) Introduction

12.138 There has been a substantial increase in the surveillance of citizens by both public and private bodies over recent decades. This has been supported by technological advances in the gathering and processing of information.[479] Surveillance can take many forms and can be carried out by both private and public bodies.

12.139 One important way in which privacy may be invaded is by the taking of closed circuit television ('CCTV') recording or the making of unauthorized photographs or film of a person or his home.[480] A person may be photographed or filmed in a 'private setting', such as while sunbathing at home, or in a public place. The CCTV, photographs or films may be taken by public officials such as police officers or by private parties such as journalists or private investigators.

12.140 Closely related is the invasion of privacy by means of 'listening devices'. Devices can be placed in the home or fixed to a telephone line; they can also take the form of 'long range' listening devices which record conversation in a building without any form of physical intrusion. Such surveillance may, again, be carried out by public officials or third parties. During the year ended 31 December, 2007, public authorities made 519,260 requests for communications data.[481]

12.141 In both these situations, the right to respect for private life under Article 8 may be engaged. If a public authority is responsible for the surveillance, or sufficiently involved in monitoring carried out by a private party, there will be an interference with Article 8 rights. The public authority may not be able to succeed in justifying the interference under Article 8(2) on the basis that it is necessary for the protection of the rights of others, because the Investigatory Powers Tribunal has held that the Regulation of Investigatory Powers Act 2000 does not apply to such monitoring:[482] it is accordingly doubtful that surveillance of this nature could be said to be in accordance with the law (at least outside of the employment context). However, evidence obtained in breach of Article 8 may still be admissible in court.[483]

---

[478] See *Marcel v Commissioner of Police* (n 477 above) 257D, 265D–G (the Court of Appeal overruling Browne-Wilkinson J on this point).

[479] See generally, Home Affairs Select Committee, *A Surveillance Society?* (5th Report of Session 2007–2008, HC 58-I).

[480] This was one of the areas of mischief mentioned by S Warren and L Brandeis in 'The Right to Privacy' (1890) 4 Harv Law Rev 193.

[481] *Report of Interception of Communications Commissioner for 2007* (HC 947, July 2008), para 3.7.

[482] *C v The Police* [2006] 1 Pol LR 151, paras 85–89.

[483] See para 12.153 below. However, in *St Merryn Meat v Hawkins* [2001] C.P. Rep. 116 the court discharged search and freezing orders on the ground that it had not been informed of surreptitious telephone taps placed by the claimant on the defendant's telephone.

(b) Photography and film

General. The traditional view is that the English law gives a person no 'right to his own **12.142** image'[484] or to an image of his home[485] as 'the eye cannot by the laws of England be guilty of a trespass'.[486] It remains that case that the taking[487] of a photograph of a person without their consent—whether done overtly or covertly—is not actionable at common law.

It is, however, clear that the publication of photographs taken by public authorities is **12.143** potentially actionable as a misuse of private information. Thus in *Djerdjar v Commissioner of Police*[488] the police released photographs of the claimant as a 'suspect' with inaccurate information to the media. There had been an inadequate police investigation and despite disclaimers those who saw the photographs could not have doubted that the claimant was guilty of criminal conduct. The Court awarded damages of £7,500 for breach of the claimant's Article 8 rights.

It is, however, arguable that the taking of photographs and the retention of the images will **12.144** also engage Article 8. In *R v Loveridge*[489] it was held that secret filming in a place to which the public had access could infringe Article 8 of the Convention, even where the events filmed contained no private elements. However, the opposite conclusion was reached in relation to photographs in *Wood v Commissioner of Police*.[490] The claimant had been photographed by police officers in the street whilst attending a meeting. He complained that the taking and retention of his photograph was an interference with his Article 8 rights which was not 'in accordance with law'. It was held that the taking and retention of photographs (in contrast to their publication) was not an interference with the claimant's Article 8 rights.[491] The Court went on to hold that, in any event, there was a lawful basis for the taking of the photographs at common law[492] and that their collection and retention was regulated by the Data Protection Act 1998. Finally, the Court held that any interference was 'necessary in a democratic society'. This decision is difficult to follow. The collection and storage of information by state agencies clearly engages Article 8[493] and the identified legal basis for the actions of the police was extremely slim. It is difficult to see how, on the facts of the case, the taking and retention of photographs of an innocent person, suspected of no crime, could be justified under Article 8(2).

Closed circuit television. It has been estimated that there are 4.2 million CCTV cam- **12.145** eras in the United Kingdom.[494] Many of these are operated by public authorities. This use is not specifically regulated by statute. Local authorities have a specific power to install

---

[484] See *Sports Press Agency v Our Dogs* [1916] 2 KB 880.
[485] *Baron Bernstein of Leigh v Skyways View and General Ltd* [1978] 1 QB 479.
[486] *Entick v Carrington* (1765); 19 St Tr 1029, 1066.
[487] As opposed to the publication of such a photograph, see para 12.105 above.
[488] Central London County Court, 22 February 2005 (HHJ Collins).
[489] [2002] Cr App R 591.
[490] [2008] HRLR 34.
[491] Ibid, para 43.
[492] Ibid, paras 66–70 (relying on certain comments in *Murray v UK* (1994) 19 EHRR 193).
[493] See para 12.282 below.
[494] Surveillance Studies Network, *A Report on the Surveillance Society: Public Discussion Document* (September 2006), pp 7–8; it is not clear how reliable this estimate is.

closed circuit cameras for surveillance purposes.[495] The use of these powers is not, however, regulated by statute.[496] The use of CCTV is regulated by the Information Commissioner under the Data Protection Act 1998 who has published a Code of Practice.[497] This suggests that public authorities will have to justify the use of CCTV in accordance with Article 8(2)[498] that the images should only be used for the purpose for which they were taken and should only be stored for as long as is strictly necessary. The Code requires that people be notified that CCTV is being used but there is no requirement for advance authorization of the installation of cameras and no mechanism for monitoring their use.

(c) Surveillance, intercepting letters, and telephone tapping

12.146 **Position at common law.**   The common law has provided very limited protection to the victims of visual or aural surveillance. If an individual is kept under constant observation he might have a claim for harassment.[499] If his conversation is recorded by surveillance devices, he may have an action for breach of confidence or misuse of private information.[500] The most obvious remedies are found in nuisance and trespass to land but these suffer from important limitations.

12.147 If any person enters onto another's land to observe him or to plant a listening device, he will be guilty of trespass. Damages have accordingly been awarded for trespass where a defendant secretly installed a microphone in the flat of the plaintiff[501] and under a marital bed.[502] The significance of an action in trespass has, however, been undermined by the highly sophisticated nature of surveillance devices. Such technology has made it a simple matter to eavesdrop on a home without entering the premises to install the device.

12.148 A nuisance will be committed if an act or omission of one person unreasonably interferes with the enjoyment of land of another. In *Victoria Park Racing v Taylor*,[503] the High Court of Australia held that spying is not an actionable nuisance. It refused to prevent racing broadcasts from a high platform built to gain an unimpeded view over the race track of the plaintiff, since the activities of the defendant neither interfered with nor were intended to interfere with the land of the plaintiff, but merely rendered his business less profitable. Another action in nuisance failed in a case in which a dentist in Balham sought an injunction against neighbours who installed large mirrors to observe his study and surgery.[504]

12.149 In *Bernstein v Skyways*[505] it was held that aerial photography over the plaintiff's land did not constitute a trespass because the rights of the landowner in the airspace above his property

---

[495] Criminal Justice and Public Order Act 1984, s 163; see *R v Brentwood BC, ex p Peck* [1998] EMLR 697.

[496] It is not directed or intrusive surveillance for the purposes of the Regulation of Investigatory Powers Act 2000 (see para 12.166ff below) because it is not undertaken for specific purpose.

[497] *CCTV Code of Practice* (Revised Edition, 2008).

[498] Ibid, Section 4, p 7.

[499] See now Protection from Harassment Act 1997, para 12.178 below.

[500] See para 12.22ff above.

[501] *Greig v Greig* [1966] VR 376.

[502] *Sheen v Clegg*, *Daily Telegraph*, 22 June 1961.

[503] (1937) 58 CLR 479.

[504] C Kenny, *Cases on Tort* (4th edn, 1926), 367.

[505] [1978] 1 QB 479.

are limited to such a height as is necessary for the ordinary use and enjoyment of the land. However, Griffiths J went on to say that:

> if the circumstances were such that the plaintiff was subjected to the harassment of constant surveillance of his house, accompanied by the photographing of his every activity, I am far from saying that the court would not regard such a monstrous invasion of his privacy as an actionable nuisance for which they would give relief.

In *Khorasandjian v Bush*,[506] it was held that persistent and protracted harassment by telephone constituted a nuisance. This attempt to extend the tort of nuisance to cover interference with privacy rights was, however, criticized by the House of Lords in *Hunter v Canary Wharf*[507] on the basis that the essence of the tort is injury to land. Harassment is now a statutory tort,[508] but a tort of harassment might have developed independently on the basis of an extension of the tort in *Wilkinson v Downton*[509] to cover cases in which the claimant only suffers distress or discomfort.[510]

The interception of a letter does not constitute a trespass unless the letter is actually touched   **12.150** in an unauthorized manner. However, the publication or disclosure of private information contained in the letter would plainly constitute breach of confidence and misuse of private information. Similarly, the publication or disclosure of private information obtained that by the use of unauthorized listening devices[511] would be actionable under both heads.

SURVEILLANCE BY THE POLICE, SECURITY SERVICES, AND OTHER STATE AGENCIES

Introduction. Until 1985 the surveillance of citizens by the security services or the police   **12.151** was entirely unregulated by statute. Police surveillance was regulated by Home Office Guidelines[512] which did not provide a lawful authority for the placing of listening devices on private premises. The interception of letters by warrant of the Home Secretary is also a practice of long standing, in spite of the absence of clear authority for it.[513] The lawfulness of telephone tapping was unsuccessfully challenged in *Malone v Commissioner of Police for the Metropolis*.[514] Sir Robert Megarry V-C rejected a number of arguments based on a 'right to privacy'[515] and the 'direct effect of the Convention'.[516]

However, the lawfulness of the power of the Home Secretary to authorize telephone tap-   **12.152** ping was the subject of review in slightly different circumstances in *R v Secretary of State for Home Affairs, ex p Ruddock*.[517] An official of the Campaign for Nuclear Disarmament

---

[506] [1993] QB 727.
[507] [1997] AC 655, 691G–692B, per Lord Goff; 706B–7–7E, per Lord Hoffmann.
[508] See Protection from Harassment Act 1997, discussed at para 12.178 below.
[509] [1897] 2 QB 57.
[510] At present, the tort requires the claimant to have suffered nervous shock, see *Hunter v Canary Wharf* (n 239 above) 707E–G, per Lord Hoffmann; and see the discussion of the tort in R Wacks, *Privacy and Press Freedom* (Blackstone, 1995), 80–89.
[511] See *Francome v Mirror Group Newspapers Ltd* [1984] 1 WLR 892.
[512] *The Guidelines on the Use of Equipment in Police Surveillance Operations*, 19 Dec 1984, Dep NS 1579.
[513] See *Report of Committee of Privy Councillors* (1957) Cmnd 283, 'the Birkett Committee'.
[514] [1979] Ch 344. The European Court of Human Rights subsequently found a violation of Article 8 in this case: *Malone v United Kingdom* (1984) 7 EHRR 14.
[515] See para 12.09 above.
[516] See para 2.41ff above.
[517] [1987] 1 WLR 1482.

unsuccessfully alleged that the Home Secretary had acted unlawfully by authorizing MI5 to tap her telephone for party political purposes. Taylor J accepted that the court had jurisdiction to hear the case. He held that, as the Home Secretary was under a duty to act fairly, the official must act in accordance with the published criteria governing the issuance of warrants. He was not prepared, however, to infer from the evidence that the Home Secretary had issued a warrant in breach of his criteria.

12.153 Further, the courts refused to exclude surveillance evidence from proceedings purely on the ground that it had been obtained outside of a statutory regime. In *R v Khan*[518] the defendant sought to exclude evidence obtained by the use of a listening device on the basis that the device had been illegally installed. Even though it was accepted that the surveillance had been illegal, the evidence was admitted as the result of an exercise of judicial discretion in accordance with section 78 of PACE. Similarly, the Court of Appeal in *R v Mason*[519] held that evidence obtained through the covert taping of the applicants, was not obtained 'in accordance with the law' for the purposes of Article 8.[520] Nevertheless, the Court of Appeal that this did not mean that the tape-recordings could not be relied upon as evidence. A number of other cases reached similar views on evidence obtained through unregulated surveillance.[521] Finally, in *R v P*[522] the House of Lords decided that recordings of telephone conversations between a national of another country and the appellants which had been lawfully intercepted in that country by its prosecuting authorities were admissible in evidence at the appellants' trial in England.

12.154 The absence of a statutory basis for official surveillance has been described by the courts as unsatisfactory on a number of occasions. Several Strasbourg judgments went against the United Kingdom on the basis that the interference by the police with the Article 8 rights of those on whom they carried out surveillance operations was not 'in accordance with the law'.[523] As a result, in a more or less piecemeal fashion, legislation has been passed to deal with those judgments.

12.155 In response to the decision in the *Malone* case the Government published a White Paper.[524] The result was the Interception of Communications Act 1985, to regulate the interception of communications by post and public telecommunications systems.[525] The introduction of the Social Security Service Acts of 1989 and 1996 and the Intelligence Services Act 1994 went some way to regulating the activities of the security and intelligence services. Part III of the Police Act 1997 was introduced to regulate forms of police surveillance involving interference with property.

---

[518] [1997] AC 558; see para 11.289 above.
[519] [2002] 2 Cr App R 38.
[520] Ibid, para 73, citing *PG v United Kingdom* (2008) 46 EHRR 51, see para 12.322 below.
[521] See, for example, *R v Loveridge* [2002] Cr App R 591 and *R v McLeod* [2002] EWCA Crim 989.
[522] [2002] 1 AC 146.
[523] See para 12.374ff below.
[524] *The Interception of Communications in the United Kingdom* (1985) Cmnd 9438.
[525] See s 1.

Provoked by the decision in *Halford v United Kingdom*[526] and technological advances, **12.156**
the Government proposed significant changes to the Interception of Communications Act
in the 1990 Consultation Paper 'Interception of Communications in the United
Kingdom'.[527] As a result the 1985 Act was repealed and replaced by the Regulation of
Investigatory Powers Act 2000 ('RIPA'). RIPA covers the whole field of interception and
other forms of surveillance. It has been described as 'longer and even more perplexing' than
the 1985 Act.[528]

Police Act 1997. Those forms of police surveillance involving 'interference with prop- **12.157**
erty' are regulated by Part III of the Police Act 1997, entitled 'Authorization of Action in
Respect of Property'. Section 92 provides that:

> No entry on or interference with property or with wireless telegraphy shall be unlawful if it
> is authorized by an authorisation having effect under this Act.

The authorization may be given by a chief officer of police or equivalent senior officer[529] or,
if that is not reasonably practicable, by a designated deputy.[530] The authorization should,
save in an urgent case, be provided in writing.[531] Authorization may be given in cases where
the authorizing officer believes that the action is necessary because it is likely to be of
substantial value in the protection or detection of serious crime[532] and that what the action
seeks to achieve cannot reasonably be achieved by other means.[533]

In some cases an authorization is not permitted to take effect until it has been approved by **12.158**
a Commissioner[534] appointed under the provisions of the Act.[535] Such approval is required
where the property to which the authorization relates is a dwelling house, hotel bedroom
or office or in which:

> it is likely to result in any person acquiring knowledge of
> (i) matters subject to legal privilege;[536]
> (ii) confidential personal information;[537] or
> (iii) confidential journalistic material.[538]

These provisions do not, however, apply to an authorization 'where the person who gives it
believes that the case is one of urgency'.[539] The Act provides for the Secretary of State to
issue a Code of Practice in relation to the issuing of authorizations. It also provides for a

---

[526] (1997) 24 EHRR 523.
[527] CM 4368.
[528] *AG's Reference No 5 of 2002* [2005] 1 AC 167, para 9.
[529] Police Act 1997, s 93(5).
[530] Police Act 1997, s 94.
[531] Ibid, s 95.
[532] Ibid As defined in ibid, s 93(4).
[533] Ibid, s 93(2).
[534] Ibid, s 97(1).
[535] See ibid, s 91; the Commissioners are appointed from the Senior Judiciary.
[536] Defined in ibid, s 98.
[537] Defined in ibid, s 99.
[538] Defined in ibid, s 100; s 97(2).
[539] Ibid, s 97(3); there is no requirement that this belief is based on reasonable grounds.

'complaints procedure'. Such complaints are to be investigated by a Commissioner.[540] A Commissioner who is satisfied that there are no reasonable grounds for believing the specified matters may quash the authorization or renewal.[541] There is no provision for the independent review of authorizations in the Courts. It has been held that this procedure is compatible with Article 8.[542]

12.159 **RIPA—Introduction.** All interception of telecommunications and postal communications, directed surveillance, intrusive surveillance and the use of covert intelligence sources are now governed by RIPA.[543] For the first thing there is a comprehensive statutory code for the use of covert surveillance. RIPA covers a very wide range of public authorities. Part I of RIPA deals with the interception of communications and Part II covers surveillance.

12.160 **RIPA—Part I.** Part I of RIPA deals with communications. Under section 1 it is an offence for anyone, without lawful authority, to intercept any communication in the course of its transmission by a public post office or by a public or private telecommunications system. A communication can be lawfully intercepted both with and without a warrant. Section 5 of the Act states that the Secretary of State shall not issue an interception warrant unless he believes that the warrant is necessary on the following grounds:[544]

(a) in the interests of national security;

(b) for the purpose of preventing or detecting serious crime;

(c) for the purpose of safeguarding the economic well-being of the United Kingdom; or

(d) for the purpose, in circumstances appearing to the Secretary of State to be equivalent to those in which he would issue a warrant by virtue of paragraph (b), of giving effect to the provisions of any international mutual assistance agreement.

The conduct authorized by the warrant must be proportionate to what is sought to be achieved by that conduct.[545]

12.161 A communication can be lawfully intercepted without a warrant in the limited circumstances defined by sections 3 or 4 and under the rather broader conditions under the Telecommunications (Lawful Business Practice) (Interception of Communications) Regulations 2000,[546] which, for example, may entitle interception to establish the existence of facts to detect unauthorized use of the telecommunications system.

12.162 A warrant permits the interception of communications sent to or from one or more specific addresses. The addresses specified are those to or from which communications are likely to be made by the persons identified in the warrant. The interception of other communications is, however, permissible as necessary to intercept the communications described in

---

[540] See s 107 and Sch 7.
[541] See s 103.
[542] *R v Lawrence* [2002] Crim 584.
[543] See generally, Y Akendiz, N Taylor, and C Walker, 'Big Brother.gov.uk: State surveillance in the age of information and rights' [2001] Crim LR 73–90.
[544] RIPA, ss 5(2) and 5(3).
[545] Ibid, s 5(2)(b).
[546] SI 2000/2699.

the warrant.[547] A warrant issued by the Home Secretary is normally valid for a period of two months.[548] Warrants issued on the grounds of national security or economic well-being may be renewed for up to six months if they are endorsed to this effect; other warrants only benefit from a one-month renewal period.[549] The warrant may be modified by the Home Secretary at any time.[550]

A complaint in relation to an intercepted communication or in relation to the acquisition **12.163** and disclosure of communications data under Chapter II of the Act must be made to the Tribunal established by section 65 of the Act. The Tribunal applies the same principles for making a determination as would be applied by a court on an application for judicial review.[551] Section 67(8) of the Act further states that, except to such extent as the Secretary of State may by order otherwise provide, determinations, awards, orders and other decisions of the Tribunal (including decisions as to whether they have jurisdiction) shall not be subject to appeal or liable to be questioned in any court.

Even if the warrant is found to have been properly authorized, the tribunal is not at **12.164** liberty to concern itself with the way in which the material intercepted is subsequently handled. There is therefore no remedy under the Act for improper disclosure of material following its interception (though such improper disclosure might be challengeable in public law[552] or in private law by the tort of misuse of private information[553]). Furthermore, by section 7(8):

> The decision of the Tribunal (including any decision as to its jurisdiction) shall not be subject to appeal or liable to be reviewed in any court.

If the tribunal finds that there has been a contravention of the Act, it may quash the relevant **12.165** warrant (or certificate), direct that copies of the intercepted material be destroyed and direct that the Secretary of State pay compensation in a specified sum.[554]

RIPA—Part II. The key aim of Part II of RIPA is to meet the 'legality' requirement of **12.166** Article 8. It deals with covert surveillance and the use of covert intelligence.[555] Unlike Part I, Part II does not in itself render it unlawful to carrying out covert surveillance without authorization: rather, it sets up an authorization procedure which, if properly followed, renders such surveillance lawful for all purposes.

By section 26(3) of RIPA, 'intrusive' surveillance takes place when a surveillance device is **12.167** used or the person undertaking surveillance is present on residential premises or in a private vehicle. 'Residential' premises are defined as premises used as living accommodation (but does not cover office premises or the common parts of shared premises). Intrusive surveillance

---

[547] RIPA, s 3(1).
[548] Ibid, s 4.
[549] Ibid, s 4(6)(c).
[550] Ibid, s 5.
[551] Ibid, s 67(2).
[552] See para 12.49ff above.
[553] See para 12.24ff above.
[554] RIPA, s 7(5).
[555] See *R v GS* [2005] EWCA Civ 887, paras 4–12 for a summary of the legislative scheme governing surveillance.

can only be authorized in the interests of national security, for the purposes of preventing or detecting serious crime or preventing disorder or in the interests of the economic well-being of the United Kingdom.[556] The authorizing person must be satisfied that the action to be taken is proportionate to what is sought to be achieved by carrying it out.[557] Authorizations are granted by the Home Secretary or by senior authorizing officers.[558] The authorization mechanism is similar to that under Part I in respect of communications and it appears that it is accordance with the requirements of Article 8.[559] There were 2,493 property interference and 355 intrusive surveillance authorizations in 2007.[560]

12.168 If covert surveillance is not 'intrusive' and is undertaken 'otherwise than by way of immediate response to events and circumstances' such that authorization is impracticable, it is 'directed surveillance'.[561] Surveillance carried out by means of a device in relation to anything taking place on any residential premises or in any private vehicle without the device being present on the premises or in the vehicle is not intrusive 'unless the device is such that it consistently provides information of the same quality and detail as might be expected to be obtained from a device actually present on the premises or in the vehicle'.[562] Directed surveillance may be authorized in the interests of national security, for the purposes of preventing or detecting crime, preventing orders, in the interests of the economic well-being of the United Kingdom, in the interests of public safety, for the purposes of protecting public health and for the purposes of assessing or collecting taxes.[563] The conduct and use of covert human intelligence sources (that is, informants) can be authorized on the same grounds.[564] There is a 'proportionality' requirement.[565] Authorizations of directed surveillance must be by a 'designated person'.[566] In the period 1 April 2007 to 31 March 2008 there were 18,767 'directed surveillance authorizations' and 4,498 covert human intelligence sources were recruited by law enforcement agencies.[567]

12.169 The Court of Appeal has held that the material obtained may be used as evidence in a criminal trial even though the request for authorization did not specifically state that it would be so used.[568] The mere fact that police officers are aware of video surveillance being carried out by members of the public does not mean that the police have to obtain authorization

---

[556] RIPA, s 32(3); serious crime is defined in s 81(3) (in the substantially the same terms as s 93(4) of the Police Act 1997).

[557] RIPA, s 32(2).

[558] Ibid, ss 41 and 32(6).

[559] See the discussion in H Fenwick, *Civil Liberties and Human Rights* (4th edn, Routledge-Cavendish, 2007), 1027–1028 and 1061.

[560] See *Annual Report of Chief Surveillance Commissioner 2007–2008* (HC 659, July 2008), paras 6.3 and 6.7.

[561] RIPA s 26(2).

[562] Ibid, s 26(5).

[563] Ibid, s 28(3); the last of these does not derive from Art 8(2) but is likely to be held to be within its terms.

[564] Ibid, s 29(3).

[565] Ibid, s 28(2) and s 29(2).

[566] Ibid, s 30—such persons include the Home Secretary, and the relevant persons set out in the Regulation of Investigatory Powers Act 2000 (Prescription of Offices, Ranks and Positions) Order 2000, SI 2000/2417.

[567] See *Annual Report of Chief Surveillance Commissioner 2007–2008* (HC 659, July 2008), paras 7.2 and 7.4.

[568] *R v Kelly* [2007] EWCA Crim 1715.

under RIPA, and the evidence obtained may be used by the police and prosecuting authorities.[569] Covert surveillance in a police cell, which was the subject of several challenges under Article 8,[570] is now governed by RIPA.

Use of material obtained under RIPA.   RIPA places restrictions on the use of intercept   **12.170** material obtained under Part I in legal proceedings,[571] although it includes broad exceptions aimed mostly at immigration and terrorism related hearings.[572] There is no similar restriction on the use of material obtained using the surveillance methods controlled by Part II. It has been held that the use of a listening device which overhears a telephone conversation is not an interception within the meaning of Part I of the Act.[573] Nor does the use of a mobile phone as a surveillance device amount to the interception of a telecommunications system within the meaning of the Act.[574] Accordingly, such evidence was admissible in criminal proceedings.

Scrutiny of RIPA powers.[575]   RIPA provides the necessary legal framework for interfer-   **12.171** ence with Article 8 rights by the state and was held to be compliant with Article 8 by the Court of Appeal in *R v E*.[576] A failure to comply with the provisions of the Act will obviously render any surveillance in breach of Article 8 because to would not have been obtained in accordance with the law. In such cases, the courts have continued to hold evidence may still be admissible. The Court of Appeal in *R v Bailey*[577] took the view that tape recordings made by the police in breach of various statutory requirements which did by that time exist might nevertheless be admissible under section 78.[578] In *R v Button*[579] the Court of Appeal held that evidence admitted in breach of Article 8 does not necessarily render a trial unfair under Article 6 and that a court is not itself complicit in any breach of Article 8 by admitting that evidence.

It is extremely difficult for a subject of surveillance to establish and obtain a remedy for an   **12.172** interference with Article 8 rights in relation to surveillance which has been authorized under RIPA. The statutory scheme is designed to prevent recourse to the ordinary courts by the subjects of surveillance.[580] Part IV of RIPA establishes a mechanism for scrutinizing the powers under the Act. It creates three commissioners, who must have held high judicial office.[581]

---

[569] *R v Rosenberg* [2006] EWCA Crim 6. However, the Court suggested that any active police involvement, or even encouragement, would require authorization.

[570] See para 12.279 below.

[571] RIPA, s 17.

[572] Ibid s 18.

[573] *R v E* [2004] 1 WLR 3279; it appears that this includes a recording device in the ear of the officer making a telephone call, *R v McDonald* Woolwich Crown Court, 23 April 2002 (Astill J).

[574] *R v Allsopp* [2005] EWCA Crim 703.

[575] See generally, H Fenwick, *Civil Liberties and Human Rights* (4th edn, Routledge-Cavendish, 2007), 1080–1090.

[576] [2004] 2 Cr App R 29, paras 37–46.

[577] [2001] EWCA Crim 733.

[578] See also *R v GS* [2005] EWCA Crim 887, para 12.

[579] *R v Button* [2005] Crim LR 571.

[580] See generally, Y Akendiz, N Taylor, and C Walker, 'Big Brother.gov.uk: State surveillance in the age of information and rights' [2001] Crim LR 89–90.

[581] RIPA, s 57.

In addition, it establishes a Regulation of Investigatory Powers Tribunal[582] which can hear complaints about the conduct of intelligence services or in relation to surveillance and covert human intelligence sources. This Tribunal is designated as the 'only appropriate tribunal' before which claims under the HRA relating to such surveillance may be brought.[583] The Court of Appeal has held that it is not for the criminal courts to look into the lawfulness of an authorization made under Part II: this is the role of the Tribunal.[584]

12.173 Complaints to the Tribunal are rarely made because, in general, individuals subject to interception or surveillance have no way of knowing that it has taken place. It is noteworthy that the United Kingdom is the only member state to have entered a derogation to Principle 2(2) of the Council of Europe Recommendation Regulating the use of Data in the Police Sector[585] which provides that:

> Where data concerning an individual have been collected and stored without his knowledge, and unless the data are deleted, he should be informed, where practicable, that information is held about him as soon as the object of the police activities is no longer likely to be prejudiced.

The subjects of surveillance are, therefore, not informed that it has taken place. The Interception of Communications Tribunal never found a breach under the Interception of Communications Act 1985. Between 2 October 2000 and 31 December 2006 the Investigatory Powers Tribunal dealt with 554 complaints, only one of which was upheld.[586]

12.174 The Investigatory Powers Tribunal has held that RIPA only regulates surveillance under Part II if it is carried out as part of the 'core functions' of public authorities, as opposed to 'the ordinary functions of public authorities shared by all authorities, such as the employment of staff and the making of contracts'.[587] The Tribunal accordingly held that it had no jurisdiction to consider a complaint about police surveillance of a former officer whose claim to an 'enhanced injury on duty award' as a result of tripping over while at work was mistrusted. This interpretation leaves the UK vulnerable to further breaches of Article 8 on the ground that surveillance has been carried out by arms of the state without a sufficient regulatory basis to be in accordance with the law. The Tribunal pointed to the availability of other means of challenging interferences with Article 8 rights—presumably having in mind section 7 of the HRA—but, as the Tribunal implicitly recognized, the incorporation of Article 8 into domestic law does not of itself provide the necessary legal framework so as to render interferences with private life in accordance with the law.[588] It is possible that the Information Commissioner's *Employment Practice Data Protection Code* will go some way

---

[582] RIPA s 65; this replaces the Interception of Communications Tribunal and the Intelligence and Security Services Tribunal. It has also taken over the complaints role of the Commissioners under the Police Act 1997.

[583] s 65(2)(a), referring to s 7(1)(a) of the HRA.

[584] *R v GS* [2005] EWCA Civ 887, paras 32 and 35.

[585] R (87) 15, adopted by the Committee of Ministers on 17 September 1987.

[586] See Written Answer, Hansard HC 21 July 2008, Col 970W; the complaint concerned the interception of calls of black and Asian officers by the Metropolitan Police, see 'Met chief oversaw illegal bugging of black officers' *Sunday Times*, 10 December 2006.

[587] *C v The Police* [2006] 1 Pol LR 151, para 85.

[588] Ibid, paras 89 and 91.

to meeting that requirement in employment cases. The Data Protection Act 1998, under which the Code was made, does cover the 'obtaining' of personal data. However, the Act protects only information which is, or is intended to be, placed on a computer or equivalent manual filing system and the courts have generally taken a restrictive approach to its scope.[589] Accordingly, it appears that the Investigatory Powers Tribunal decision does leave the UK without a full legal framework covering all surveillance carried out by public authorities.

Security services. Surveillance by the security and intelligence services is also governed **12.175** by statute. In *Hewitt and Harman v United Kingdom*[590] the Commission on Human Rights declared admissible a complaint by two former officials of Liberty who had allegedly been under surveillance by MI5. This resulted in the enactment of the Security Service Act 1989 which establishes MI5 as a statutory body and defines its functions.[591] By section 5, the Home Secretary is authorized to issue warrants for entry onto or interference with property or for interference with wireless telegraphy. Similar provisions relating to MI6 and GCHQ are to be found in the Intelligence Services Act 1994.

The Security Service Act 1996 extended the function of the Security Service to allow it to **12.176** act in support of the activities of police forces and other law enforcement agencies in the prevention and detection of serious crime.[592] The Act also extends the power of the Home Secretary to issue warrants authorizing entry onto or interference with property or interference with wireless telegraphy for the purposes of this function. These warrants may relate to property in the British Islands if either:

(a) the conduct concerned involves the use of violence, results in substantial financial gain or is conduct by a large number of persons in pursuit of a common purpose, or
(b) the offence or one of the offences is an offence for which a person who has attained the age of 21 and has no previous convictions could reasonably be expected to be sentenced to imprisonment of three years or more.[593]

These provisions involve an executive power to issue warrants which is not controlled by the courts.[594] It has, therefore, been forcefully argued that the power to issue warrants may be in breach of Article 8 because the Secretary of State is given a broad discretion which does not satisfy the requirements of 'foreseeability' and 'precision'.[595] The various bodies established under the Security Service and Intelligence Service Acts are also immune from judicial review. It has been forcefully argued that, in cases in which the purpose of the surveillance is not the protection of national security, these bodies do not provide an adequate substitute for judicial supervision.[596]

---

[589] *Durant v Financial Services Authority* [2004] FSR 28; *Johnson v Medical Defence Union* (2007) 96 BMLR 99.
[590] (1989) 67 DR 88, EComm HR.
[591] Security Service Act 1989, s 1(1).
[592] Security Service Act 1996, s 1(1), amending s 1 of the Security Service Act 1989.
[593] Ibid, s 2, adding s 5(3B) to the Intelligence Services Act 1994.
[594] See P Duffy and M Hunt, 'Goodbye *Entick v Carrington*: the Security Service Act 1996', [1997] EHRLR 11.
[595] Ibid, 15–16.
[596] Ibid, 18–19.

12.177 **Anti-Terrorism Crime and Security Act 2001.**   This statute was passed by Parliament in the immediate aftermath of the of the attacks on the World Trade Centre on 9 September 2001 and contains a number of draconian provisions.[597] Section 17 relates to the disclosure of information under 66 different statutory provisions.[598] It provides that:

> (2) Each of the provisions to which this section applies shall have effect, in relation to the disclosure of information by or on behalf of a public authority, as if the purposes for which the disclosure of information is authorized by that provision included each of the following—
>> (a) the purposes of any criminal investigation whatever which is being or may be carried out, whether in the United Kingdom or elsewhere;
>> (b) the purposes of any criminal proceedings whatever which have been or may be initiated, whether in the United Kingdom or elsewhere;
>> (c) the purposes of the initiation or bringing to an end of any such investigation or proceedings;
>> (d) the purpose of facilitating a determination of whether any such investigation or proceedings should be initiated or brought to an end.

It should be noted that this provision is not confined to issues relating to national security or terrorism. It is, however, subject to a proportionality requirement.[599] Fenwick comments that:

> in a startling fashion s 17(2) destroys the balance created by a large number of existing carefully considered and often highly detailed schemes permitting disclosure and preserving confidentiality . . . it provides a regime allowing the police, security services and other public authorities to obtain a vast range of personal and other information.[600]

There is no mechanism for ensuring that the individuals whose information has been disclosed are made aware that this has taken place and so very limited opportunity to obtain redress if there is wrongful disclosure.[601]

OTHER REMEDIES IN RELATION TO SURVEILLANCE

12.178 **Harassment.**   There are a number of other potential remedies in relation to surveillance by private and public bodies. An individual who is subject to a 'course of conduct' which causes alarm or distress may have a claim under the Protection from Harassment Act 1997. A tort and a crime may be committed by a person who pursues a course of conduct which amounts to harassment of another: a course of conduct must involve conduct on at least two occasions and harassment includes alarming a person or causing them distress.[602] It is a defence to show that the course of conduct was pursued for the purposes of preventing or detecting crime,[603] or that the conduct was 'reasonable'.[604] It is likely that prolonged and intrusive surveillance by journalists or other private individuals would constitute harassment unless some strong justification can be provided.[605] It seems likely that properly authorized surveillance by state agencies would attract the 'reasonableness' defence.

---

[597] For the relationship between this statute, RIPA and the DPA see C Walker and Y Akdeniz, 'Anti-Terrorism Laws and Data Retention: the War is Over?' (2003) 54 NILQ 159.
[598] Listed in Anti-Terrorism Crime and Security Act 2001, Sch 4.
[599] Ibid, s 17(5).
[600] H Fenwick, *Civil Liberties and Human Rights* (4th edn, Routledge-Cavendish, 2007), 1093.
[601] Ibid, 1094.
[602] Protection from Harassment Act 1977, s 1 and s 7.
[603] Ibid, s 3(b).
[604] Ibid, s 3(c).
[605] But note, no claim would lie if the subject of the surveillance was unaware that it was taking place.

Article 8. Where a public authority is responsible for surveillance then its conduct **12.179** could be challenged under section 6 of the HRA on the basis that it was incompatible with the subject's Article 8 rights. If Article 8 is engaged then the public authority would have to justify the interference with the right constituted by the surveillance under Article 8(2).[606]

(7) Housing law and respect for the home

(a) Introduction

Concept of 'home'. The protection of the home has been recognized as a matter of **12.180** fundamental importance as 'few things are more central to the enjoyment of human life than having somewhere to live'.[607] Article 8 does not create a right to a home as such:[608] the right is to *respect* for an existing home. Such respect, demanded of public authorities, is an aspect of the right to private life; the proprietary aspects of the home are protected under Article 1 of the First Protocol.[609]

The notion of 'home' in Article 8 is an autonomous concept,[610] which has been held to **12.181** involve pragmatic considerations of whether the place in question is that where a person 'lives and to which he returns and which forms the centre of his existence'.[611] However, 'the expression can cover premises other than the places where a person lays his or her head at night'.[612] 'Home' is thus not a legal term of art, and is not determined by property interests or contractual rights. In *Qazi v London Borough of Harrow*,[613] the House of Lords held unanimously that, for the purposes of Article 8, the concept of a home depends on whether an individual has a sufficient and continuous link with premises, and not on questions of legal title.[614] Premises can thus be a 'home' notwithstanding that the claimant has no legal or equitable interest in them. A resident of local authority or NHS accommodation for the mentally ill or elderly can rely on his or her right to respect for her home to resist being moved to s different facility.[615]

No right to acquire a home. In general, the right to respect for home relates only to an **12.182** existing home. As the Court of Appeal said *Anufrijeva v Southwark County Council*,[616] 'the

---

[606] For an example of an unsuccessful claim made on this basis see *Wood v Commissioner of Police* [2008] EWHC 1105 (Admin) discussed at para 12.144 above.

[607] Per Lord Bingham in *Qazi v London Borough of Harrow* [2004] 1 AC 983, para 8.

[608] See para 12.82 below.

[609] See Chapter 18 below.

[610] See, for example, *Sheffield City Council v Smart; Central Sunderland Housing Company Ltd v Wilson* [2002] HLR 639, para 26.

[611] Per Lord Millett in *Uratemp Ventures Ltd v Collins* [2002] 1 AC 301, para 31. Cited with approval in relation to Article 8 per Lord Bingham in *Qazi v London Borough of Harrow* [2004] 1 AC 983, para 8.

[612] *R (Countryside Alliance) v Attorney General* [2008] 1 AC 719, para 15(3).

[613] [2004] 1 AC 983.

[614] Ibid, paras 8 to 10.

[615] *R (Coughlan) v North East Devon Health Authority* [2001] QB 213, in which the application was successful; *R (C) v Brent NHS Trust* [2002] Lloyd's Rep Med 321, in which the application was unsuccessful. However, an attendee of a day centre cannot claim that the day centre is her home: *R (Bishop) v Bromley Council* [2006] EWHC 2148 (Admin).

[616] [2004] QB 1124.

Court of Human Rights has always drawn back from imposing on States the obligation to provide a home'.[617] However, Lord Woolf went on to point out that:[618]

> Strasbourg has recognized the possibility that Article 8 may oblige a State to provide welfare support, such as housing, in special circumstances.

The Court concluded that such support would not ordinarily have to be provided to an individual unless his predicament was sufficiently serious to engage Article 3.[619]

12.183 Nevertheless, the English courts have rejected a number of arguments, based on Article 8, to the effect that there is a right to acquire a home:

- Article 8 does not provide any remedy solely because an individual is homeless.[620] Article 8 does not confer a right to be provided with a home nor to succeed to a tenancy.
- Article 8, read in conjunction with Article 14, cannot be used to interpret the Housing Act 1985 so as to permit a claimant outside the class of relatives so entitled under the 1985 Act to succeed to the tenancy of a dead relative.[621]
- Given the competing claims to the resources of a local authority, Article 8 cannot be used to interpret section 17 of the Children Act 1989 so as to *require* a local authority to provide a home for a mother and her children.[622]
- Article 8 does not require the State to provide for gypsies and travellers an adequate number of sites on which to live.[623]

(b) Public authority landlords

12.184 **Introduction.** The HRA applies directly to local authorities, and registered social landlords have been held to be hybrid public authorities.[624] Article 8 therefore has important implications for housing management and housing allocation policies. It would be a breach of Article 8 in conjunction with Article 14, for example, to give preference to housing married couples; and it may well breach Article 8 to require applicants for council housing to disclose their criminal convictions, particularly if those convictions are spent under the Rehabilitation of Offenders Act.[625]

12.185 **Positive obligations.** Local authority landlords may be obliged to take positive steps[626] to protect their own tenants from noise,[627] fumes,[628] pollution[629] (which might extend to

---

[617] Ibid, para 19.

[618] Ibid, para 33.

[619] Ibid, para 43.

[620] *R (Morris) v London Borough of Newham* (2002) 27 EG 143.

[621] *Michalak v Wandsworth London Borough Council* [2003] 1 WLR 617.

[622] *R (W) v Lambeth London Borough Council* [2002] 2 FLR 327.

[623] *Chichester District Council v Secretary of State* [2005] 1 WLR 279, para 55.

[624] *Poplar Housing and Regeneration Community Association Ltd v Donoghue* [2002] QB 48, para 59.

[625] See s 1(1), s 4(1)(2) and s 5 of the Act.

[626] For positive obligations under Art 8 see generally, para 12.240ff below.

[627] *Arrondelle v United Kingdom* (1982) 26 DR 5, EComm HR; *Powell and Rayner v United Kingdom* (1990) 12 EHRR 394; contrast the position in domestic law where a tenant cannot make a claim for breach of the covenant of quiet enjoyment or nuisance: see *Southwark London Borough Council v Mills* [1999] 3 WLR 939.

[628] *Lopez Ostra v Spain* (1994) 20 EHRR 277.

[629] *Guerra v Italy* (1998) 26 EHRR 357.

matters such as vermin and cockroaches) and anti-social neighbours.[630] These positive obligations may mean that a local authority will be liable, for example, if it fails to take proper steps to protect its tenants from nuisance caused by other local authority tenants[631] or to sound-proof local authority flats.[632] Article 8 may also be breached by the failure of the local authority to take action under Parts VI and IX of the Housing Act 1985 in relation to unfit housing for private tenants as well as local authority tenants.[633] The question of whether a positive obligation arises in these cases will depend on the balance struck by the court between the general interest of the community and the rights of the individual.[634] In *Lee v Leeds City Council*,[635] the Court of Appeal accepted there may be cases in which property let by a local authority was in such poor condition that a failure to repair breached Article 8. However, the Court went on to hold that, on the facts, the condition did not reach such a level. Furthermore, the condition was not such as to require other legislation to be interpreted, in the light of Article 8, to alter the duty of a local authority landlord to undertake repairs.[636]

(c) Possession proceedings

Introduction.   The taking possession of a person's home is plainly a substantial interfer-   **12.186**
ence with their Article 8 rights which requires justification under Article 8(2). This, in turn, raises the issue as to whether the court requires to be satisfied, in the circumstances of each specific case, that the possession order is 'necessary in a democratic society' and proportionate. These issues have led to a substantial volume of case law.

Balancing interests in possession cases.   In general, it seems that Article 8 makes very   **12.187**
little practical difference to the way in which the Courts approach possession actions. This was the view of the Court of Appeal in the initial cases in which Article 8 issues were raised. Thus, in *Castle Vale Housing Action Trust v Gallagher*,[637] it was held that Article 8 would probably not make any difference to the way the court approached the question of the reasonableness of making a possession order in respect of residential property occupied under a secured tenancy. A similar conclusion was reached with regard to possession proceedings relating to a non-secure tenancy in *Sheffield City Council v Smart*.[638] It was held that the county court was held to be entitled to assume that the Housing Act itself struck the correct balance of interests pursuant to Article 8(2) unless something exceptional had occurred

---

[630] There is no implied covenant on a landlord to enforce a covenant not to commit a nuisance against a neighbour (see *O'Leary v Islington London Borough Council* (1983) 9 HLR 81); nor can the landlord be liable for the acts of the neighbour in nuisance: see *Smith v Scott* [1973] Ch 314; *Hussein v Lancaster City Council* [1999] 4 All ER 125.

[631] Requiring reconsideration of *Hussein v Lancaster City Council* (n 630 above).

[632] Requiring reconsideration of *Southwark London Borough Council v Mills* (n 627 above).

[633] A local authority cannot use the enforcement provisions of the Housing Act against itself: see *R v Cardiff City Council ex p Cross* (1981) 6 HLR 6.

[634] See para 6.178 ff above.

[635] [2002] 1 WLR 1488.

[636] For a critique of this decision, see P.F. Smith, 'Disrepair and Unfitness Revisited' [2003] Conveyancer and Property Lawyer 112–125.

[637] (2001) 33 HLR 72; see also *Lambeth LBC v Howard* (2001) 33 HLR 58.

[638] [2002] HLR 34; see also *R (McLellan) v Bracknell Forest Borough Council* [2002] QB 1129. See also Emma Laurie, 'The Compatibility of Introductory Tenancies with the Human Rights Act 1998' [2002] Conveyancer and Property Lawyer 414–420.

after the notice to quit was served. In *Sheffield City Council v Hopkins*,[639] the Court of Appeal stated that Article 8 merely reinforced the policy of Part IV of the Housing Act 1988, so that a court, when exercising its discretion under section 85 to suspend the execution of a warrant for possession, should only evict after a serious breach of the tenancy agreement, where it was reasonable to do so, or where the tenant had been proved to breach any condition of a suspended warrant. Finally, in *Poplar Housing and Regeneration Community Association Ltd v Donoghue*[640] the Court of Appeal held that the statutory provisions relating to possession orders made against assured shorthold tenant was necessary in a democratic society under Article 8(2).[641]

12.188 The issue was considered by the House of Lords in *Harrow London Borough Council v Qazi*.[642] The majority held that the local authority property which Mr Qazi occupied with his wife under a secure tenancy was his home for the purposes of Article 8. However, when Mr Qazi's wife left him and gave notice to quit, he had no defence under ordinary law to the subsequent possession proceedings. Lords Hope, Millett and Scott held that the possession order did not infringe the essence of Mr Qazi's right to respect for his home (which they considered purely to be an aspect of his right to privacy, as distinct from his right of possession) at all and that, accordingly, no question arose for consideration under Article 8(2).[643]

12.189 However, after the decision in *Qazi*, the Court of Human Rights handed down judgment in *Connors v United Kingdom*,[644] in which it held that the summary proceedings allowing a local authority to evict a family of gypsies from a local authority site did not provide the essential procedural safeguards necessary to make the interference with their Article 8 rights proportionate. The apparent inconsistency of this decision with the decision in Qazi was considered by the House of Lords in *Kay v Lambeth London Borough Council*.[645] The majority decision reflects a shift in reasoning as compared with *Qazi*, but is likely to have little different practical effect. In *Kay*, the local authority terminated leases granted to a housing trust and then sought possession orders against individual who had been living on the property under arrangements made with the housing trust. This case was considered with *Leeds City Council v Price*, in which the local authority sought possession orders against gypsies who had moved their caravans onto recreational ground owned by the local authority.

12.190 The House of Lords held that the reasoning in *Qazi* required modification. It was not the case that the enforcement of a right to possession in accordance with domestic law could never be incompatible with Article 8 as a matter of principle. A possession order against a

---

[639] [2002] HLR 12; and see *St Brice v Southwark LBC* [2002] 1 WLR 1537.
[640] [2002] QB 48.
[641] Ibid, paras 67–72.
[642] [2004] 1 AC 983.
[643] Ibid, paras 71 and 83–84 (per Lord Hope) and para 100 (per Lord Millet); for Lord Scott's more trenchant approach, see paras 127 and 130.
[644] (2005) 40 EHRR 9. See para 12.390 below.
[645] [2006] 2 AC 465.

person's home would indeed amount to an infringement of Article 8(1).[646] However, it was to be presumed that domestic law – whether common law or statute – struck the balance required by Article 8(2) and it was not for those seeking possession to plead and prove this. However, it was held that in exceptional cases a defendant to such proceedings could raise an Article 8 challenge in the county court.[647]

The majority of the House of Lords held that the exceptional circumstances which **12.191** could justify an Article 8 challenge were confined to challenges to the compatibility of the legislation with Article 8 and that it was not open to a defendant to rely on the particular circumstances of his case.[648] The minority, Lords Bingham, Nicholls and Walker, gave strong and persuasive dissenting judgments on this last point, holding that personal circumstances could form a basis for challenge; and this view is clearly in accordance with ordinary principles on the application of the proportionality test.[649] The approach of the majority in *Kay* was applied by the Court of Appeal in *Doherty v Birmingham City Council*[650] which held that:

> There are only two possible 'gateways' (our term) for a successful defence to summary judgment in such cases [where a public landowner has a right of possession under domestic law]:
> (a) a seriously arguable challenge under Article 8 to *the law* under which the possession is made, but only where it is possible (with the interpretative aids of the HRA) to adapt the domestic law to make it more compliant;
> (b) a seriously arguable challenge on conventional judicial review grounds (rather than under the HRA) to *the authority's decision* to recover possession . . .

The defendant in *Doherty* appealed to the House of Lords. After the hearing of the appeal, **12.192** the Court of Human Rights gave judgment in *McCann v United Kingdom*.[651] This restated the need for the courts to be able to consider the proportionality of particular cases on their own facts. The Court of Human Rights endorsed the reasoning of Lords Bingham, Nicholls and Walker in *Kay*, including the suggestion that 'it would only be in exceptional cases that an applicant would succeed in raising an arguable case which would require a court to examine the issue; in the great majority of cases, an order for possession could continue to be made in summary proceedings'.[651a] As a result, it was argued in *Doherty* that the approach of the majority in *Kay* could not longer stand. This argument was rejected by the House of Lords.[652] It reaffirmed that the basic rule was that interference with the right to respect for

---

[646] Ibid, paras 28 (Lord Bingham), 53 (Lord Nicholls), 107 (Lord Hope), 150 (Lord Scott), para 175 (Lord Walker agreeing with Lords Bingham and Nicholls), paras 179–180 (Baroness Hale), para 200 (Lord Brown).

[647] Ibid, paras 29 (Lord Bingham), 55–56 (Lord Nicholls), 108–109 (Lord Hope), para 168 (Lord Scott), para 175 (Lord Walker agreeing with Lords Bingham and Nicholls), paras 180–182 and 185 (Baroness Hale); paras 199–200 (Lord Brown—who took the view that this was only a 'theoretical possibility' and that the county court judge had to apply the domestic law).

[648] Ibid, para 110 (Lord Hope), para 172 (Lord Scott), para 192 (Baroness Hale); para 200 (Lord Borwn).

[649] Ibid, para 39 (Lord Bingham), para 59 (Lord Nicholls), paras 175 (Lord Walker, agreeing).

[650] [2007] HLR 32.

[651] (2008) 47 EHRR 40.

[651a] Ibid, para 50.

[652] *Doherty v Birmingham City Council* [2008] 3 WLR 636, see para 19 (Lord Hope—who said that this would have required a panel of 9 law lords); para 82 (Lord Scott—who said that *McCann* was based on a misunderstanding of English possession procedure); para 108 (Lord Walker—who expressed disquiet).

home which flowed from the application of legislation which gave an unqualified right to possession would not violate Article 8 unless the legislation itself could be attacked.[653] This is 'Gateway (a)' and has two parts: (i) rendering the legislation compatible by use of section 3; (ii) make a declaration of incompatibility.[654] The second possibility, 'Gateway (b)' is limited to 'conventional judicial review' of the decision to exercise the power to seek possession—the test being was the decision one which no reasonable person would consider justifiable.[655] As a result, it was said that County Court judges dealing with possession cases should continue to follow the guidance in *Kay*.[656] Although the exclusion of gipsies from the statutory protection provided under the Mobile Homes Act 1983 was incompatible with Article 8, this incompatibility had been remedied by statute so that a declaration of incompatibility was unnecessary. The decision to close a site on which the defendant gipsies had been resident for 17 years was remitted to the judge to consider the issue of reasonableness under 'Gateway (b)'.

12.193 **Suspended orders.** In some cases, at least, it is arguable that the court's power to suspend a possession order gives it the requisite scope to consider proportionality on the facts of each case. In *Smith v Evans*[657] the Court of Appeal held that an amendment to the Caravan Sites Act 1968, which allowed defendants to apply for the suspension of possession orders, dealt with the procedural concerns expressed in *Connors* because such an application would permit and require a judge to consider the merits of the case. There are similar provisions in respect of possession orders on some (though not all) grounds under section 85 of the Housing Act 1985, but this argument was not considered in the *McCann* judgment.

12.194 **Private landlords.** The *Kay* line of cases involved public authorities. It remains unclear whether similar challenges may be made to the legislation relied on by private landlords. However, save for the applicability of judicial review principles of reasonableness, it is suggested that the approach of the House of Lords would be equally applicable to possession claims brought by private landlords. County court judges have a general duty under section 3 of the HRA 1998 to interpret legislation compatibly with the Convention and are themselves public authorities under section 6. Moreover, several cases between private parties involving the loss of a home, decided both before and after the *Kay* case, have held that Article 8 is of relevance. In both *Barca v Mears*[658] and *Donohoe v Ingram*,[659] for instance, it was held that Article 8 might require the court to interpret broadly the terms 'exceptional circumstances' in section 335A of the Insolvency Act 1986, under which a trustee in bankruptcy may apply for an order for the sale of the bankrupt's home. In *Patel v Pirabakaran*,[660] the Court of Appeal did not need to rely on Article 8 to find that a property which was let

---

[653] Ibid, para 22 (Lord Hope).

[654] Ibid, para 46 (Lord Hope).

[655] Ibid, para 55 (Lord Hope).

[656] Ibid, para 56 (Lord Hope).

[657] [2008] 1 WLR 661, paras 60–61; This case was decided before the *McCann* decision, but there is no reason to think this would have affected the Court of Appeal's reasoning.

[658] [2005] 2 FLR 1 (the point proceeded on the basis the court was a public authority; there was no discussion as to whether a trustee in bankruptcy might be carrying out public functions).

[659] [2006] 2 FLR 1084.

[660] [2006] 1 WLR 3112.

partly as a business and partly as a dwelling attracted the procedural safeguards under section 2 of the Protection from Eviction Act 1977; however, it was held any other interpretation would have been incompatible with Article 8.[661]

(d) Confiscation orders relating to the home

The courts have power to make confiscation orders to recover monies held to have been **12.195** obtained as a result of criminal activity.[662] In assessing the amounts payable, the court has regard to the defendant's realisable assets, which will often include his home. The Court of Appeal has held that the confiscation regime as a whole is compliant with Article 8.[663] Indeed, it has been held that there is no interference with Article 8 in making an order because it does not necessarily follow that the family home will have to be sold; it is upon appointment of a receiver or an order for sale that Article 8 considerations, which may relate not just to the offender but to others who live in or have an interest in the property, apply.[664]

(e) Planning and environment law

Introduction. Planning law is another area in which the right to respect for 'home' in **12.196** Article 8 has had an impact. Article 8 only applies, however, if the 'home' is already established. The refusal of planning permission to allow a person to continue to live in a particular place is a *prima facie* breach of Article 8,[665] but the right does not extend to land on which a person plans to build a house.[666]

Taking Article 8 into account. Planning authorities have to take into account the poten- **12.197** tial impact of their decisions on the Article 8 rights of individuals. Before the coming into force of the HRA, personal circumstances were only relevant to planning decisions in exceptional circumstances.[667] However, the general approach of the Convention is that personal circumstances are put first[668] and any interference with those rights must be justified as 'necessary in a democratic society'. It has been suggested that this might require a fundamental change of approach:

> . . . the approach under the Convention is that interference with individual rights is unjustified unless public interest reasons are adduced which are of sufficient importance. In current planning policy, decisions are made in accordance with the public interest, with affected private rights being subsidiary.[669]

---

[661] Ibid, paras 44 and 55.

[662] Criminal Justice Act 1988, s 71.

[663] *R v Goodenough* [2004] EWCA Crim 2260, paras 29–30.

[664] Ibid, para 31; *R v Ahmed* [2005] 1 WLR 122, paras 11–12; see also *R v Richards* [2005] EWCA Crim 491.

[665] Cf *Buckley v United Kingdom* (1996) 23 EHRR 101; and see *Chesterfield Properties v Secretary of State for the Environment* [1998] JPL 568 where Laws J dealt with a *Wednesbury* challenge to a compulsory purchase order on the basis it involved a fundamental human right.

[666] See *Loizidou v Turkey* (1996) 23 EHRR 513.

[667] *Great Portland Estate v City of Westminster Council* [1985] AC 661.

[668] See the approach taken in *Britton v Secretary of State for the Environment* [1997] JPL 617.

[669] See T Corner, 'Planning, Environment and the European Convention on Human Rights' [1998] JPL 301, 312.

The Court of Appeal emphasized in *Lough v First Secretary of State*,[670] that Article 8 had to be 'an integral part' of the decision maker's approach to material considerations in planning decisions, and not, as happened in that case, a footnote. Pill LJ commented that the jurisprudence under Article 8, and the standards it sets, would sometimes be an important factor in considering the legality of a planning decision or process,[671] and that decision makers would thus have to engage in a proportionality analysis. Given this, it seems planning authorities will have to make clear, in the reasons for their decisions, that they have not acted incompatibly with Article 8 rights.[672] If the reasons given do not demonstrate that there is a 'Convention justification' for the interference, then the decision will be unlawful and liable to be quashed.[673]

12.198   It was held in *R (Clarke) v Secretary of State for Transport, Local Government and the Regions*[674] that, in deciding whether to grant planning permission for the use of certain land for stationing a caravan for residential use, the planning inspector should carry out a detailed examination of the applicant's objections to living in conventional housing (ie whether it was contrary to his and his family's cultural values or beliefs to live in conventional housing) in order to determine the extent to which Article 8 would be engaged in the planning decision. In that case, however, a refusal of planning permission to safeguard the Green Belt was held to comply with Article 8.

12.199   **Compulsory purchase.**   Compulsory purchase orders can be made by local authorities and development agencies under various statutes;[675] they are used to free up ineffectively used land for urban regeneration or for projects such as the 2012 Olympics in London. Such orders have been challenged in a number of cases. The courts have confirmed that the Article 8 rights of homeowners must be taken into account when deciding whether to grant the order.[676] However, it has been held that the Compensation Code applicable to compulsory purchase orders is compliant with Article 8, even though it was argued that homeowners were being compensated at levels much lower than market value.[677]

12.200   **Enforcement powers.**   The power of the police, pursuant to sections 61 and 62 of the Public Order Act 1994, to direct trespassers living on land to move, has been held to be compatible with Article 8.[678] Nevertheless, a public authority must not use its powers to

---

[670] [2004] 1 WLR 2557.

[671] Ibid, para 48.

[672] See *Britton v Secretary of State for the Environment* [1997] JPL 617; and contrast *R v Leicestershire County Council, ex p Blackfordby and Boothorope Action Group* [2001] Env LR 35.

[673] The absence of the word 'proportionality' from the reasons will not necessarily render the decision liable to be quashed. *Lough v First Secretary of State* [2004] 1 WLR 2557, para 50; this approach was subsequently confirmed by the approach of the House of Lords in *R(SB) v Deneigh High School* [2007] 1 AC 100; and see generally, para 6.94ff.

[674] [2002] JPL 1365.

[675] Made under legislation such as the Town and Country Planning Act 1990, the Regional Development Agencies Act 1998 or the Leasehold Reform, Housing and Urban Development Act 1993.

[676] *R (Pascoe) v First Secretary of State* [2007] 1 WLR 885; *R (Powell) v Secretary of State for Communities and Local Government* [2007] EWHC 2051 (Admin); *R (Smith) v Secretary of State for Trade and Industry* [2007] EWHC 1013 (Admin).

[677] *Pascoe*, ibid, para 88.

[678] *R (Fuller) v Chief Constable of Dorset Police* [2003] QB 480.

enforce compliance with planning controls in a way that is incompatible with the right to respect for the home. This is particularly important under Part VII of the Town and Country Planning Act 1990, which allows for the eviction of trespassing gypsies. Before the enactment of the HRA, the courts took account of the fundamental right to shelter when considering local authority decisions to evict gypsies.[679] Gypsies can now rely directly on Article 8 as a defence to possession proceedings.[680] In *Chapman v United Kingdom*, however, the Court of Human Rights held that such proceedings may not infringe Article 8 if they are pursued for the legitimate aim of protecting the rights of others through preserving the environment, and that the domestic authorities had a wide margin of appreciation concerning the planning considerations attaching to a particular site.[681] This principle was applied in *R (Ward) v London Borough of Hillingdon*,[682] where Stanley Burnton J held that the decision to evict gypsies from a caravan site was proportionate under Article 8(2). Similarly, in *Somerset County Council v Isaacs*,[683] Stanley Burnton, J decided that section 4(6) of the Caravan Sites Act 1968 and section 5 of the Mobile Homes Act 1983, which deal with local authority land used as 'exempted sites' for gypsies, would not inevitably infringe Article 8.

Injunctions to enforce planning decisions.   The scope of the court's discretion when making an injunction to enforce the planning decisions of a local authority[684] was considered by the House of Lords in *South Buckinghamshire DC v Porter*.[685] Local planning authorities applied under section 187B of the Town and Country Planning Act 1990 for injunctive relief against the defendants, who were gipsies, to prevent them from living in mobile homes and caravans on land acquired by them for that purpose but for which planning consent had been refused. Injunctive relief was refused. The House of Lords held found that the jurisdiction to grant injunctions was original and discretionary, and the court was not limited to considering issues which had not already been considered as part of the planning decision. When considering a request for an injunction, the court must undertake a proportionality analysis, in which it can weigh in the balance the hardship caused by the injunction, against the legitimate planning and environmental concerns

12.201

---

[679] See eg, *R v Lincolnshire County Council, ex p Atkinson* [1996] 160 JPLCL 580 and *R v Wolverhampton Metropolitan Borough Council, ex p Dunne* (1997) 29 HLR 754 in relation to the powers to deal with unauthorized encampments under the Criminal Justice and Public Order Act 1994; and *R v Kerrier District Council, ex p Uzell* [1996] 71 P & CR 566 in relation to a decision of a planning authority to take enforcement action against gypsies occupying a site in breach of planning control; and contrast the approach taken where a local authority commences summary proceedings for possession in *R v Brighton and Hove Council, ex p Marman* [1998] 2 PLR 48 and *R v Hillingdon Borough Council, ex p McDonagh*, The Times, 9 November 1998.

[680] Until the HRA came into force, gypsies were been obliged to apply to adjourn the possession proceedings so that judicial review proceedings could be brought to challenge the decision to commence the possession proceedings: see *Avon County Council v Buscott* [1988] QB 656.

[681] *Chapman v United Kingdom, Coster v United Kingdom, Beard v United Kingdom, Lee v United Kingdom* and *Smith v United Kingdom* (2001) 33 EHRR 18. See para 12.368 below.

[682] [2001] LGR 457.

[683] [2002] 25 EGCS 151.

[684] Under section 187B of the Town and Country Planning Act 1990.

[685] [2003] 2 AC 558. See, for the application of these principles. *Tonbridge and Malling BC v Davis* [2003] NPC 63; *South Cambridgeshire District Council v Flynn* [2007] BLGR 471 and *Cates v South Buckinghamshire District Council* [2004] EWCA Civ 1378.

of the local authority.[686] The House of Lords endorsed the conclusion of the Court of Appeal that:

> Proportionality requires not only that the injunction be appropriate and necessary for the attainment of the public interest objective sought—here the safeguarding of the environment—but also that it does not impose an excessive burden on the individual whose private interests—here the gipsy's private life and home and the retention of his ethnic identity—are at stake[687]

The court takes a similar approach when considering an application for judicial review of a decision to use the powers under section 178 of the 1990 Act to enter land and remove the caravans of families of gypsies and travellers.[688]

12.202 **Environmental cases.** In *Dennis v Ministry of Defence*[689] it was held that there was a violation of Article 8 where the claimants had suffered 'severe' and 'frightening' noise disturbance on a daily basis as the result of RAF Harrier jets overflying their property. In *Andrews v Reading Borough Council*[690] Calvert-Smith J held that a planning decision to divert traffic into a residential street caused environmental pollution of sufficient severity to breach Article 8, given that the Council had offered no compensation to residents.

(8) Other privacy rights in English law

(a) Introduction

12.203 English law gives little clear recognition to privacy rights outside the fields of misuse of information, surveillance and intrusion. However, the HRA has led the courts to take into account broader Article 8 rights, such as the right to personal autonomy and physical and moral integrity, in claims against public authorities and in the interpretation of legislation.

(b) Privacy and personal autonomy

12.204 **Introduction.** The right to private life under Article 8 guarantees, amongst other things, a right to personal autonomy. This encompasses the right to conduct one's life in a manner of one's own choosing, which includes choices concerning one's own body and control over one's physical and psychological integrity.[691]

12.205 **Sexual identity.** It has been suggested that a person has a right to his or her own sexual preferences and to determine his or her sexual identity and that this is an aspect of privacy rights. No such right is recognized at common law, and attempts by transsexuals to have their birth certificates changed to reflect their new sexual identities were therefore rejected by the English courts.[692] This was challenged several times under Article 8;[693] and the jurisprudence of the Court of Human Rights developed from a position where the United Kingdom's policy of refusing legal recognition of the acquired gender was regarded as

---

[686] See para 37 (per Lord Bingham) and para 58 (per Lord Steyn).
[687] [2002] 1 WLR 1359, para 41.
[688] *R (McCarthy) v Basildon DC* [2008] EWHC 987 (Admin).
[689] [2003] Env LR 34.
[690] [2005] EWHC 256 (QB).
[691] See paras 12.269ff below.
[692] See *Re P and G (Transsexuals)* [1996] 2 FLR 90.
[693] See para 12.250ff below.

falling within the margin of appreciation, to the decision in *Goodwin v United Kingdom*[694] in 2002 in which it was held that society had changed sufficiently to render such a refusal a breach of Article 8. This history was charted by Baroness Hale in *Chief Constable of West Yorkshire v A*,[695] in which a post-operative female transsexual challenged the rejection of her application to join the police force. The case was not decided under Article 8, as the facts that formed its basis occurred before the HRA was enacted, but it was clear that the right to privacy under Article 8 would be engaged by actions of public authorities when deal with transsexuals. As a result of *Goodwin*, the government enacted legislation giving full legal recognition to the acquired gender of post-operative transsexuals, including the right to marry in their acquired gender and to be given birth certificates that recognize the acquired gender.[696] Transsexual people are also able to obtain benefits as a person of their acquired gender.

Sexual orientation. Changes relating to sexual orientation discrimination have also **12.206** been brought about by decisions under Article 8. In *Lustig-Prean v United Kingdom*[697] and *Smith v United Kingdom*,[698] the applicants complained that investigations into their homosexuality and their subsequent discharge from the military on the sole ground that they were homosexual, in pursuance of the Ministry of Defence's absolute policy against homosexuals in the British armed forces, constituted a violation of their right to respect for their private lives protected by Article 8. The Court upheld their challenge, and homosexuals have been allowed to serve in the United Kingdom armed forces since 12 January 2000. The Government has since introduced the Employment Equality (Sexual Orientation) Regulations 2003[699] and the Equality Act (Sexual Orientation) Regulations 2007[700] which provide protection against discrimination on grounds of sexual orientation.

Self-fulfilment. In *R (Countryside Alliance) v Attorney-General*,[701] the House of Lords **12.207** held that there was no reasonable expectation of privacy in relation to hunting activities and that the ban on hunting with dogs under the Hunting Act 2004 was compatible with Article 8. This contention was rejected by all the members of the Judicial Committee after consideration of the extent to which Article 8 covered 'self-fulfilment' and social activities. Lord Rodger held that, but for the public spectacle, Article 8 would have been engaged, taking the view that:

> article 8(1) protects those features of a person's life which are integral to his identity.[702]

---

694 (2002) 35 EHRR 18. See para 12.251 below.
695 [2005] 1 AC 51 paras 37–40.
696 The Gender Recognition Act 2004, which came into force on 4 April 2005.
697 (1999) 29 EHRR 449.
698 (1999) 29 EHRR 493.
699 SI 2003/1661, see generally, para 17.92ff.
700 SI 2007/1263.
701 [2008] 1 AC 719.
702 Ibid, para 101; the public spectacle issue is discussed at paras 107–109.

This was, however, the minority view. Lord Bingham pointed out that the activity of fox hunting was 'a very public activity, carried out in daylight with considerable colour and noise, often attracting the attention of onlookers'[703] and was very remote from the values which Article 8 exists to protect. Lord Hope agreed, concluding out that the prohibition was directed at activities carried out in public which lay outside the private sphere of a person's existence.[704] Baroness Hale described Article 8 as protecting:

> the personal and psychological space within which each individual develops his own sense of self and relationships with other people.[705]

Lord Brown, for his part, regretted that Article 8 did not yet extend to cover activities such as fox hunting as a form of a 'wider concept of self-fulfilment'.[706] Despite this unanimity of view, there is a strong argument that the House of Lords failed properly to recognize the wide scope of the 'right to establish and develop relationships' established by the Strasbourg case law.[707]

12.208   In *Evans v Amicus Healthcare*[708] the claimant and her partner had begun the process of IVF treatment, but the partner then withdrew his consent for the fertilization of the embryos. Under the legislation, the fertilization could not then proceed. The claim was argued under the privacy, rather than family, element of Article 8. The Court of Appeal accepted a concession that there was an interference with the claimant's right to respect for her private life;[709] however, the bright line rule was justified and proportionate.[710] In *L v Human Fertilization & Embryology Authority*[711] it was held that the need for effective consent to storage in the United Kingdom of the sperm of the claimant's deceased husband for subsequent use in the United Kingdom was not incompatible with the claimant's Article 8 rights.

(c) Physical and moral integrity

12.209   **Introduction.**   An aspect of privacy which has developed in Convention jurisprudence is its use to guarantee the physical and moral integrity of the person.[712] Although English law has long recognized the importance of the physical integrity and physical liberty of the person through torts such as assault, battery and false imprisonment, the common law does not as such recognize the right to moral integrity.

12.210   **Medical treatment and mental health.**   The right to physical and moral integrity is particularly relevant to medical law. It arises in a number of circumstances, including

---

[703] Ibid, para 15.

[704] Ibid, para 55.

[705] Ibid, para 116, describing this as one of two fundamental values reflected by Art 8, the other being 'The inviolability of the home and personal communications from official snooping, entry and interference without a very good reason'.

[706] Ibid, para 139.

[707] See para 12.299 below.

[708] [2005] 1 Fam 1.

[709] Ibid, paras 60 and 108.

[710] Ibid, paras 69 and 110. The Grand Chamber took the same view in *Evans v United Kingdom* (2006) 43 EHRR 21.

[711] [2008] EWHC 2149 (Fam); applying the decision of the Grand Chamber in *Evans*.

[712] See para 12.269ff below.

questions surrounding a patient's consent to medical treatment which would otherwise constitute battery, false imprisonment or other torts.[713] The House of Lords has emphasized that even minor medical treatment may amount to an interference with Article 8 rights.[714] The Court of Appeal has held[715] that:

> Where a competent patient makes it clear that he does not wish to receive treatment which is, objectively, in his medical best interests, it is unlawful for doctors to administer that treatment. Personal autonomy or the right of self determination prevails.

At common law, the patient cannot properly consent to treatment unless he understands **12.211** in broad terms the nature of that treatment,[716] and the doctor is obliged to disclose the risks inherent in and the alternatives to the procedure. It is arguable, however, that Article 8 may impose a stricter duty on doctors to provide more detailed information to patients.

The importance of consent in this area led Holman J to hold that the Mental Health **12.212** Review Tribunal had no power to attach to the release of a patient from detention a condition that a patient undergo medical treatment, unless there was a proper basis for concluding that the patient did and would consent to the treatment.[717] Moreover, the Secretary of State could not lawfully recall such a patient merely because he refused to consent to that treatment on any particular occasion.

Where the patient does not have the capacity to consent, more difficult issues arise. In *R (B)* **12.213** *v S*,[718] the Court of Appeal emphasized the great importance attached by the common law to interference with physical integrity without consent.[719] However, when considering whether forcible treatment of a person who is deemed to lack the mental capacity to consent amounts to a breach of Article 8, an expressed lack of consent is not determinative.[720] The Court concluded that Article 8(2) would be satisfied in such a case if the treatment was in the best interests of the patient. This issue involves wider considerations that just the efficacy of the treatment, such as the availability of alternative (perhaps less effective) treatment and any need for the use of force.[721]

In *R (Munjaz) v Mersey NHS Trust*[722] the House of Lords held that the seclusion of **12.214** those detained in mental health hospitals is capable of breaching the Convention if improperly used.[723] However, Lord Bingham took the view that seclusion would not interfere with the right to respect for private life provided it was used for the shortest period necessary to

---

[713] See generally, I Kennedy and A Grubb, *Principles of Medical Law* (Oxford University Press, 1998), paras 3.86–3.100.

[714] *R (B) v Ashworth* [2005] 2 AC 278, para 36.

[715] In *R (Burke) v General Medical Council* [2006] QB 273, para 30.

[716] *Chatterton v Gerson* [1981] QB 432, 443; *Sidaway v Board of Governors of the Bethlem Royal Hospital and the Maudsley Hospital* [1984] 1 All ER 1018 (CA), 1026, per Sir John Donaldson MR and 1029 per Dunn LJ.

[717] *R (SH) v Mental Health Review Tribunal* [2007] EWHC 884 (Admin).

[718] [2006] 1 WLR 810.

[719] Ibid, para 31.

[720] Ibid, para 31.

[721] Ibid, paras 61 and 62.

[722] [2006] 2 AC 148.

[723] Ibid, para 32.

protect the safety of others[724] and that any such action would, in any event, be justified.[725] The majority of the House also held that a clear policy, even one which departed from the statutory Code, was enough to satisfy the requirement that any interference was in accordance with the law.[726]

12.215 Article 8 might also have an impact on the treatment of '*Gillick* competent'[727] or 16- or 17-year-old children.[728] At common law the court is not bound to implement the wishes of a *Gillick* competent[729] child or of the 16- or 17-year-old child.[730] However, under the HRA it will be arguable that the child's wishes should prevail over those of his or her parents or, indeed, medical advisers.

12.216 The withdrawal of treatment has also raised difficult issues under Article 8. In *R (Burke) v General Medical Council*[731] the Claimant sought to challenge the GMC's guidance on the withdrawal of artificial nutrition. The Court of Appeal held[732] that:

> the duty to keep a patient alive by administering [artificial nutrition and hydration] or other life-prolonging treatment is not absolute, [but] the exceptions have been restricted to the following situations: (1) where the competent patient refuses to receive ANH [artificial nutrition or hydration] and (2) where the patient is not competent and it is not considered to be in the best interests of the patient to be artificially kept alive. It is with the second exception that the law has had most difficulty. The courts have accepted that where life involves an extreme degree of pain, discomfort or indignity to a patient, who is sentient but not competent and who has manifested no wish to be kept alive, these circumstances may absolve the doctors of the positive duty to keep the patient alive. Equally the courts have recognized that there may be no duty to keep alive a patient who is in a persistent vegetative state. In each of these examples the facts of the individual case may make it difficult to decide whether the duty to keep the patient alive persists.

Since the claimant in that case was competent and had indicated his wish to be kept alive, there was no question of withdrawal of treatment being lawful.[733] This was not because a doctor has any obligation generally to provide treatment simply because a patient requests it, but because there is a common law duty to keep a patient alive.[734] The Court of Appeal refused to consider in the abstract the question of how the best interests of a non-competent patient would be determined in cases concerning the withdrawal of

---

[724] Ibid, paras 32 and 88–89.

[725] Ibid, para 90.

[726] Ibid, paras 34 and 92.

[727] A child can validly consent to medical treatment where he has sufficient understanding and intelligence to understand fully what is proposed: see *Gillick v West Norfolk and Wisbech Area Health Authority* [1986] AC 112, 169, 186, 188–189, 195, 201. See generally, Kennedy and Grubb (n 713 above) paras 4.62–68.

[728] Family Law Reform Act 1969, s 8.

[729] *In re R (A Minor)(Wardship: Consent to Treatment)* [1992] Fam 11; *In re W (A Minor)(Medical Treatment: Court's Jurisdiction)* [1993] Fam 64.

[730] *In re R (A Minor)(Wardship: Consent to Treatment)* (n 729 above); *In re W (A minor)(Medical Treatment: Court's Jurisdiction)* (n 729 above).

[731] [2006] QB 424 (a subsequent application to the ECtHR was inadmissible, *Burke v United Kingdom*, Decision of 11 July 2006).

[732] Ibid, para 33.

[733] Note, though, that this was based on a duty to keep a patient alive once he has been admitted into hospital: para; there is no general obligation on a doctor to provide treatment insisted upon by a patient if the doctor does not consider it to be clinically appropriate: ibid, para 50.

[734] Ibid, paras 31–32, 50, and 53.

artificial nutrition.[735] However, the Court rejected the assertion that the continuation of life would have to be 'intolerable' before such a step could lawfully be taken.[736]

In *R (E) v Bristol City Council*[737] Bennett J held that Article 8 required the local authority **12.217** to respect the wish of an individual with mental health problems not to have her sister involved in her care. In such a case, it would not be 'practicable' within the meaning of 11 of the Mental Health Act 1983 to consult with the claimant's nearest relative and the Council should not do so.

Physical and psychological integrity was unsuccessfully relied on in *R (M) v Nottinghamshire* **12.218** *Healthcare NHS Trust*,[738] a challenge to a decision that the claimant's psychopathy was not treatable in hospital and that he should be remitted to prison. The Court of Appeal found that the decisions complained of did not fall within the concept of respect for private life at all.[739]

Other areas. The right to personal and moral integrity can arise in many other contexts. **12.219** In *R (Gillan) v Commissioner of Police for the Metropolis*[740] the House of Lords held that interference with the right to physical integrity required a sufficient level of seriousness and that ordinary, superficial stops and searches would be unlikely to engage Article 8 rights.[741] Any search which was undertaken for genuine reasons and in accordance with the Code of Practice would be likely to be justified.[742]

In *S v Secretary of State for the Home Department*[743] the child of an asylum seeker developed **12.220** rickets while in detention. Wyn Williams J held that, in such circumstances, the State had a positive duty under Article 8 to take steps to ensure the welfare of detainees. The duty was engaged provided the risk was foreseeable and avoidable, as it was in this case.[744] The Secretary of State had failed in that duty and, accordingly, acted in breach of Article 8. However, it has been held that ordinarily, the State is under no obligation to provide welfare support unless the potential effects are serious enough to amount to inhuman or degrading treatment within the meaning of Article 3.[745]

In *R (MacKenzie) v Secretary of State for the Home Department*,[746] Collins J held that night **12.221** time inspections in a prison could in some cases amount to an interference with the right to respect for private life. However, there was no such interference in that case.

---

[735] The Court also cautioned against reliance on Munby J's efforts to do so in the first instance decision: Ibid, para 24.
[736] Ibid, paras 61–63.
[737] [2005] EWHC 74 (Admin).
[738] [2003] 1 All ER 784.
[739] Ibid, para 49.
[740] [2006] 2 AC 307.
[741] Ibid, para 28.
[742] Ibid, para 29.
[743] [2007] EWHC 1645 (Admin).
[744] Paras 90–92.
[745] *Anufrijeva v London Borough of Southwark* [2004] QB 1124; *A v Essex County Council* [2007] EWHC 1652 (QB); *R (A) v Secretary of State for Health* [2008] EWHC 855 (Admin).
[746] [2006] EWHC 1746 (Admin).

12.222   In *R (G) v Nottinghamshire healthcare NHS Trust*[747] the claimants who were mental patients in secure hospitals sought to quash a provision which would prevent smoking their rooms[748] as being incompatible with their rights under Article 8. The Divisional Court concluded that

> Preventing a person smoking does not, at any rate in the culture of the United Kingdom, generally involve such adverse effect upon the person's 'physical or moral integrity', or the other concepts cited above, as would amount to an interference with the right to respect for private or home life within the meaning of article 8. We do not accept the notion of an absolute right (subject to article 8(2)) to smoke wherever one is living.[749]

As a result, there was no interference with Article 8 rights. However, the Court was circumspect about whether that would be so if the ban were extended into private homes.[750]

12.223   Finally, the Privy Council held In *Whitefield v General Medical Council*[751] that a condition on the appellant doctor's registration requiring him to abstain from alcohol did not breach Article 8. The Privy Council acknowledged that a person's private life extends to social pastimes outside the home, but held that the ban on consuming alcohol was not, per se, an interference with the right to respect for his private life, as he was not prevented from going to his local public house or engaging in his social life while drinking non-alcoholic drinks.[752] The Privy Council held, in any event, that the conditions were justifiable under Article 8(2).[753]

(d) Immigration, asylum, and extradition cases

12.224   **Introduction.**   For the most part, those resisting deportation from the United Kingdom seek to rely on their right to respect for family life under Article 8.[754] In addition, a number of cases have raised issues involving private life. Article 8 can be engaged where the foreseeable consequences of deportation or extradition for health and welfare are not sufficiently serious to engage Article 3.[755] It is clear that reliance can be placed on the effect of removal on an applicant's health or physical and mental integrity.[756] Nevertheless, the domestic courts have been slower to find in applicants' favour than in cases involving 'family life'.[757]

12.225   **Deportation and Article 8.**   A person subject to removal who wishes to argue that this would be a disproportionate interference with his Article 8 rights does not have to

---

[747] [2008] HLR 42, para 101. The Court also held than any interference was justified in the particular case, which concerned the effect of the ban in mental health institutions (para 124).

[748] Regulation 10(3) of the Smoke-free (Exemption & Vehicles) Regulations 2007 (SI 2007/765).

[749] *R (G) v Nottinghamshire Healthcare Trust* (n 747 above), para 101 (nor was the claim 'within the ambit' of Art 8 for Art 14 purposes).

[750] Ibid, para 102.

[751] [2003] IRLR 39.

[752] Ibid, para 27.

[753] Ibid, paras 30–31.

[754] See para 13.71ff below.

[755] *R (Ullah) v Special Adjudicator* [2004] 2 AC 323.

[756] *R (Razgar) v Secretary of State for the Home Department* [2004] 2 AC 368, para 9.

[757] See I Macdonald and R Toal, *Immigration Law and Practice in the United Kingdom* (7th edn, LexisNexis, 2008), para 8.98.

establish 'exceptional circumstances'[758] Although it will in practice be exceptional for a claimant's Article 8 rights to outweigh the legitimate aim of immigration control, a breach of Article 8 does not depend on a finding that the case is exceptional.[759] In general, the requirements of immigration policy will be sufficient, without more, to justify an interference under Article 8(2).[760] However, a foreseeable breach of Article 8 in the country of removal will only preclude removal if it would be so serious as a flagrant breach of the right to respect for private and family life such as would completely deny or nullify the right.[761]

In *Jegatheeswaran v Secretary of State for the Home Department*[762] it was held that the removal **12.226** of a child with severe hearing loss and learning difficulties to Germany could breach Article 8 since he would be unable to communicate in any spoken language. In *B v Secretary of State for the Home Department*,[763] the Court of Appeal held that it would be disproportionate interference with the convicted claimant's Article 8 rights to deport him to his home country of Italy. Even though the offences of which he had been convicted were serious, the prospects of re-offending were small and his private life would be seriously disturbed given that he had lived in the UK since he had been a small child.

Extradition. Extradition carried out in accordance with the relevant extradition treaty **12.227** will be a proportionate interference with private life save in wholly exceptional circumstances. Thus, in *R (Bermingham) v Serious Fraud Office*,[764] the Divisional Court held that it was no breach of Article 8 to extradite to the United States individuals accused of conspiring with the directors of the oil company Enron to defraud a United Kingdom bank. The fact that extradition causes some risk to health does not mean that there is a breach of Article 8: question is whether risk is disproportionate.[765]

EU law. In *Chen v Secretary of State for the Home Department*[766] the European Court of **12.228** Justice held that the Chinese parents of a child with Irish nationality should be granted a long-term residence permit. The Court took Article 8 into account in holding that the child's right under European law to reside in the UK would be ineffective unless the permit was granted.

---

[758] See *Huang v Secretary of State for the Home Department* [2007] 2 AC 167 (in which it was held that such a principle was not established by the case of *Razgar v Secretary of State for the Home Department* [2004] 2 AC 368).

[759] *AG (Eritrea) v Secretary of State for the Home Department* [2008] 2 All ER 28; *JN (Uganda) v Secretary of State for the Home Department* [2007] EWCA Civ 802.

[760] *LK (Serbia) v Secretary of State for the Home Department* [2007] EWCA Civ 1554, para 8; *AG (Eritrea) v Secretary of State for Home Department* [2007] EWCA Civ 801, para 30; *RU (Sri Lanka) v Secretary of State for the Home Department* [2008] EWCA Civ 753.

[761] *R (Ullah) v Secretary of State for the Home Department* [2004] 2 AC 323; *EM (Lebanon) v Secretary of State for the Home Department* [2008] 3 WLR 931, HL (the removal of mother and child to the Lebanon where the abusive father would have custody would destroy family life and Art 8 precluded removal).

[762] [2005] EWHC 1131.

[763] [2006] EWCA Civ 922, para 35.

[764] [2007] QB 727, paras 118 and 128; see also *Hosseini v France* [2006] EWHC 1333 (Admin).

[765] *Taylor v Government of United States* [2007] EWHC 2527 (Admin) (risk moderated by appropriate measures).

[766] C-200/02 [2005] QB 326, para 94.

(e) Crime and prisons

12.229 **Criminal law.**   Article 8 has had little impact on the substantive approach to criminal law. However, in *Forbes v Secretary of State for the Home Department*,[767] the Court of Appeal accepted that a conviction of importing child pornography and a subsequent entry on the sex offender's register did interfere with the defendant's private life. The Court of Appeal went on to hold that the fact that the prosecution was not required to prove that the defendant was aware of the particular nature of the imported goods—it had to be shown that he was aware that they were prohibited, but not that they were specifically child pornography—was proportionate. In *R v Quayle*[768] the court rejected an argument that Article 8 required the defence of medical necessity be extended to cases in which cannabis had been used to relieve serious pain and suffering. In *R v G*,[769] the majority of the House of Lords reluctantly accepted that a prosecution of a 15 year old for the 'strict liability' offence of rape[770] in relation to consensual sex with girl under the age of 13 could engage Article 8 but held that the interference was justified.[771]

12.230 **Prisons.**   In the leading case of *R (Daly) v Secretary of State for the Home Department*[772] the House of Lords held that a policy of requiring a prisoner's absence whenever privileged legal correspondence held by him in his cells was examined, by giving rise to the possibility that an officer might improperly read it and to the inhibiting effect such possibility would have on the prisoner's willingness to communicate freely with his legal adviser was an unjustified interference with the prisoner's right to respect for his correspondence.

12.231 In *R (Taylor) v Governor of HMP Risley*,[773] a prisoner complained about a policy under which prisoners were allowed to telephone out to only 20 different telephone numbers, which were vetted by the prison. McCombe J held that this was a proportionate interference with the Claimant's Article 8 rights in the particular context, because the prison had a serious drugs problem and the policy was aimed at controlling it. However, the court warned that this should not be seen as a green light to other prisons. In *Woodin v Home Office*,[774] a prison officer mistakenly opened mail contrary to the Home Office policy; however, he realized that he had done so and did not read the contents of the letter. An apology was also issued to the prisoner in question. The court held that the opening of the mail was not in accordance with the law; however, it was held that the prisoner was not

---

[767] [2006] 1 WLR 3075; (the defence relied, inter alia, on the Canadian case of *R v Parker* (2000) 75 CRR (2d) 233).

[768] [2005] 1 WLR 3642.

[769] [2008] 1 WLR 1379 (Lord Hoffmann, Baroness Hale, and Lord Mance). The majority expressed strong views as to the merits of the Art 8 argument, Lord Hoffmann describing it as 'another example of the regrettable tendency to try to convert the whole system of justice into questions of human rights' (para 10).

[770] Contrary to section 5 of the Sexual Offences Act 2003.

[771] But see the dissenting speeches of Lords Hope and Carswell who were of the view that the prosecution was incompatible with the defendant's Art 8 rights; see also *H v R* [2007] EWCA Crim 2622, holding that a lifelong reporting requirement for a 16-year-old convicted of a serious sexual assault was justifiable.

[772] [2001] 2 AC 532.

[773] [2004] EWHC 2654 (Admin).

[774] Unrep, 31 July 2006.

a 'victim' within the meaning of section 7 of the HRA because of the immediate rectification and apology.[775]

Interferences with prisoner's correspondence has been held to be proportionate in a number of cases. In *R v Governor of HMP Whitemoor, ex p Ponting*[776] the complaint concerned the imposition of conditions on the use of a computer which had been supplied to a prisoner for the purposes of conducting litigation. The Court held that the conditions, including an obligation to print documents only in the presence of a prison officer, were proportionate. In *R (Szuluk) v Secretary of State for the Home Department*,[777] a high security prisoner's medical correspondence was opened to check it for authenticity. This policy was held to be proportionate in the particular circumstances.

12.232

The detention of children in prison engages Article 8 and must be justified. The content of Article 8 can be informed by the United Nations Convention on the Rights of the Child.[778] In *R (DT) v Secretary of State for the Home Department*,[779] it was held proportionate on the facts of the case to detain a 16-year-old to an adult prison.

12.233

C. The Law under the European Convention

(1) Introduction

Article 8 of the Convention provides:

12.234

(1) Everyone has the right to respect for his private and family life, his home and his correspondence.
(2) There shall be no interference by a public authority with the exercise of this right except such as is in accordance with the law and is necessary in a democratic society in the interests of national security, public safety or the economic well-being of the country, for the prevention of disorder or crime, for the protection of health or morals, or for the protection of the rights and freedoms of others.

The issues raised by Article 8(1) concern the scope and content of 'private life', home and correspondence and the obligation of the state to 'respect' those interests. They also concern the extent of the state's positive obligations to ensure that private life, home and correspondence are respected.[780]

Article 8 states that 'everyone' has the right to respect for his private and family life, home and correspondence. This clearly extends to all natural persons and may, in certain circumstances, be transferred to the estate after death.[781] It is now clear that companies,

12.235

---

[775] Ibid, para 34.
[776] [2002] EWCA Civ 224.
[777] [2004] EWCA Civ 1426.
[778] See *R (SR) v Nottingham* (2001) 166 JP 132, para 65, and see para 2.64ff above.
[779] [2004] EWHC 13 (Admin).
[780] See generally, D Feldman, 'The Developing Scope of Article 8 of the European Convention on Human Rights' [1997] EHRLR 265; N Moreham 'The Right to Respect for Private Life in the European Convention on Human Rights: A Re-Examination' [2008] EHRLR 44.
[781] Cf *Editions Plon v France* (2006) 42 EHRR 36, para 34.

as well as natural persons, enjoy a right to respect for aspects of their privacy, premises and correspondence.[782]

12.236 Article 8 concerns 'rights of central importance to the individual's identity, self-determination, physical and moral integrity, maintenance of relationships with others and a settled and secure place in the community'.[783] There are four areas which are expressly protected under Article 8(1): private life, home, correspondence and family life.[784] These areas overlap and interferences will often fall within two or more. For example, the tapping of a telephone will be interference with private life and correspondence.[785] The scope of each of the areas has been gradually extended by the case law under the Convention.

12.237 Article 8(1) sets out the scope of the protected rights and Article 8(2) the grounds on which interferences may be justified. As with all 'qualified rights' under the Convention, in each case when a violation is alleged, it is necessary to consider two questions: first, is there an interference with a right protected by Article has the state failed to 'respect' the privacy of individuals, and, if so, secondly, is that failure justified as being in accordance with the law, for a legitimate aim, and necessary in a democratic society? The final question involves considering whether there is a 'pressing social need' for the interference and whether the interference is proportionate to the legitimate aim of the measure. In addition, it is necessary to consider whether the State has provided an appropriate degree of 'procedural protection' in relation to the right in question. When considering the proportionality of the interference the state is afforded a 'margin of appreciation', the breadth of which will vary according the nature of the Article 8 in issue.

12.238 The object of Article 8 is essentially that of protecting the individual against arbitrary interference by the public authorities:[786] this is a 'primarily negative' undertaking. However, in addition, there are positive obligations upon states that are inherent in an effective 'respect' for Article 8 rights even in the sphere of the relations of individuals between themselves.

12.239 The right to 'family life' in Article 8, and the related Article 12 right to marry and found a family, will be discussed in Chapter 13. In this section we will begin by considering the nature of the positive obligations under Article 8. We will then consider the scope of the rights to respect for 'private life', 'home' and 'correspondence'. In the final section we will examine the justification of interferences with Article 8 rights including, in particular, the procedural protections required and the nature of the margin of appreciation afforded to the State.

---

[782] See para 22.22 below, and see *Wieser and Bicos Beteiligungen v Austria* (2008) 46 EHRR 54, para 67.
[783] *Connors v United Kingdom* (2005) 40 EHRR 9, para 82.
[784] The first three areas are dealt with in this chapter, the last in Chapter 13 below.
[785] See eg, *Halford v United Kingdom* (1997) 24 EHRR 523.
[786] *Belgian Linguistic (No 2)* (1968) 1 EHRR 252 para 7; cited in *Marckx v Belgium* (1979) 2 EHRR 330; *X and Y v Netherlands* (1985) 8 EHRR 235; *Abdulaziz, Cabales and Balkandali v United Kingdom* (1985) 7 EHRR 471; *Rees v United Kingdom* (1986) 9 EHRR 56; *Keegan v Ireland* (1994) 18 EHRR 342; *Hokkanen v Finland* (1994) 19 EHRR 139; *Kroon v Netherlands* (1994) 19 EHRR 263.

(2) Negative and positive obligations[787]

(a) Introduction

The original drafts of what became Article 8(1) of the Convention provided for 'freedom   **12.240**
from arbitrary interference'.[788] This was changed at a later stage of the drafting to the current
wording.[789] It is clear that, although the primary aim was to prevent state interference with
individual's rights, it was also recognized that the Article would extend to private persons.

The 'negative obligation' in Article 8 requires the state to justify interferences. The thresh-   **12.241**
old as to 'seriousness' required to engage Article 8 has never been fully examined in the
cases.[790] It is however, plain that activities such as searches of a person's home or opening of
correspondence by state officials require justification.

In addition to these 'negative' obligations it has been established since the Court's early case   **12.242**
law that:

> Article 8 does not merely compel the state to abstain from interference: in addition to this,
> there may be positive obligations inherent in an effective respect for private and family life
> even in the sphere of the relations of individuals between themselves.[791]

Member States may be held responsible for the actions of private bodies if they encourage,
connive in, or play an active part in activities which infringe Article 8.[792] However, the
Court has allowed a certain margin of appreciation[793] to states to determine whether
'respect' for Article 8 rights demands positive action in the circumstances.[794]

There is a distinction to be made between the assessment of the content of the right under   **12.243**
Article 8(1) and the justification process under Article 8(2). Under Article 8(1), 'in determining whether a positive obligation exists, a fair balance must be struck between the general interest of the community and the interests of the individual'.[795] In justifying an
interference under Article 8(2), the interests of the state are balanced against a right which
has already been established.

---

[787] For positive obligations generally see para 6.168 above and for a survey of the Art 8 case law see
A Mowbray, *The Development of Positive Obligations under the European Convention on Human Rights by the
European Court of Human Rights* (Hart, 2004), Chap 6.

[788] *Travaux Preparatoires*, Doc. AS (1), 77, p 204; DOC A833, p 3; note that although this provision was
based on Art 12 of the Universal Declaration it was decided at an early stage not to include the words 'nor to
attacks upon his honour and reputation'.

[789] Ibid, Doc CM/W 4(5) 19; the British Government had proposed a version which included the words
'Everyone shall have the right to freedom from government interference. . .'

[790] See para 12.328 below.

[791] *Marckx v Belgium* (1979) 2 EHRR 330, para, 31; *Airey v Ireland* (1979) 2 EHRR 305, para 32; *X and Y
v Netherlands* (1985) 8 EHRR 235, para 23; see also *Johnston v Ireland* (1986) 9 EHRR 203, para 55); *Powell
and Rayner v United Kingdom* (1986) 47 DR 5, 12.

[792] *MM v Netherlands* (2004) 39 EHRR 19; *Van Vondel v Netherlands* (2009) 48 EHRR 12; *Storck v
Germany* (2006) 43 EHRR 96, para 146.

[793] See generally, para 6.42ff above.

[794] See the comments made by the Grand Chamber in *Goodwin v United Kingdom* (2002) 35 EHRR 447
and *I v United Kingdom* (2003) 36 EHRR 53, para 52. See also *Lopez-Ostra v Spain* (1994) 20 EHRR 277,
para 51; *Cossey v United Kingdom* (1990) 13 EHRR 622.

[795] *Cossey v United Kingdom* (n 794 above) para 37: 'the search for which balance is inherent in the whole
of the Convention'.

12.244   In practice, the Court has not applied this distinction consistently.[796] It has found the applicable principles to be broadly similar, regardless of whether the issue is formulated as a 'positive duty on the state to take reasonable measures to secure the rights of the applicant under Article 8(1)', or as an 'interference by a public authority to be justified in accordance with paragraph 2'. The Court has stated that in both contexts regard must be had to the fair balance between the competing interests of the individual and of the community as a whole.[797] In striking the required balance in relation to the positive obligations flowing from Article 8(1), the aims under Article 8(2) will have some relevance.[798]

12.245   An issue arises as to whether the margin of appreciation will be different according to whether the dispute is a conflict between individual and state or one in which the state is exercising a duty of positive action in an essentially private dispute. Clapham has argued[799] that there should be a wider margin in the latter case, reflecting the greater complexity of questions which arise when the state is found to have a positive duty to intervene between individuals for the protection of human rights.

(b) Factors in deciding whether to recognize positive obligation

12.246   When considering whether a positive obligation under Article 8 arises in a particular case 'regard must be had to the fair balance that has to be struck between the general interest and the interests of the individual'[800] while the State has, in any event, a margin of appreciation. A positive obligation will not be imposed simply because an individual's everyday life is disrupted and disruption could be remedied by action on the part of the state.[801]

12.247   It has been said that Article 8 does not apply where what is in issue are 'interpersonal relations of such broad and indeterminate scope that there could be no conceivable direct link between the measures the State was urged to take and the applicant's private life'.[802] Thus, the Court has refused to impose positive obligations which would require a disabled person to obtain access to the beach[803] or to be provided with special equipment to allow the performance of ordinary motor functions.[804]

12.248   No clear test has been formulated in the cases but it has been suggested that positive obligations will only be imposed where there 'is a direct and immediate link between the

---

[796] See eg, C Warbrick, 'The Structure of Article 8' [1998] EHRLR 32.

[797] *Powell and Rayner v United Kingdom* (1990) 12 EHRR 355, paras 37–46; also *Lopez-Ostra v Spain* (n 794 above) paras 47–58: 'Whether the question is analysed in terms of a positive duty on the state—to take reasonable and appropriate measures to secure the applicant's rights under para 1 of Article 8—. . . or in terms of an 'interference by a public authority' to be justified in accordance with para 2, the applicable principles are broadly similar. In both contexts regard must be had to the fair balance between the competing interests of the individual and of the community as a whole, and in any case the state enjoys a certain margin of appreciation'.

[798] *Powell and Rayner v United Kingdom* (n 797 above) paras 37–46 (there was 'no violation of the Convention, however the claim was framed'); *Rees v United Kingdom* (1986) 9 EHRR 56, para 37.

[799] A Clapham, *Human Rights in the Private Sphere* (Clarendon Press, 1993), 211–22.

[800] *Nuutinen v Finland*, Judgment of 27 June 2000, para 127; *Šečić v Croatia*, Decision of 15 June 2006.

[801] *Sentges v Netherlands*, Decision of 8 July 2003.

[802] *Botta v Italy* (1998) 26 EHRR 241, para 35.

[803] Ibid.

[804] *Sentges v Netherlands* (n 801 above)(provision of robotic arm to a person suffering from muscular dystrophy).

measures sought by an applicant and the latter's private life'.[805] The matters to be taken into account include the following:

- The extent to which 'fundamental values' and 'essential aspects of private life'[806] or a 'vital interest' protected by the Convention are in issue.[807]
- The prejudice suffered by the applicant.[808]
- The breadth and clarity of the positive obligation sought to be imposed.[809]
- The extent of consensus on the issue among Council of Europe States or internationally.[810]

(c) Positive action where the applicant suffers directly from state inaction or refusal to act

Introduction. The Court have considered the question as to whether or not the state **12.249** should be required to provide positive protection to applicant who have suffered directly from its inaction in a range of cases. These include the following:

- Recognition of transsexuals
- Recognition of a choice of names
- Access to official information
- Provision of facilities for the disabled
- Provision of housing.

Transsexual cases. In a series of cases transsexuals have contended that the State has **12.250** caused them harm as a result of a failure to provide legal or administrative recognition of their new status as post-operative transsexuals. In none of these cases was the physical transformation of the individuals in issue; no state had prevented the treatment, and in the United Kingdom the public health system had provided it. The complaint was that the Government had failed to respect the private life of the applicants by refusing to alter their birth certificates to reflect the change in gender once the physical procedure had been undergone. The first four United Kingdom cases dealing with this issue failed because, in light of the lack of consensus among Member States the applicants' interest in having their birth certificates amended was not found to outweigh the fact that the certificate was intended to register the position at birth and the burden on the state if it altered the system.[811] In *B v France*,[812] on the other hand, the applicant succeeded because the French administrative system could be more easily changed than that of the British, and the need to rely frequently in practice on the certificate meant that a failure to rectify it would have more serious consequences for the applicants.

In 2002, the Grand Chamber reconsidered the position of transsexuals in the United **12.251** Kingdom, and overturned its previous findings. In *Goodwin v United Kingdom*[813] and *I v*

---

[805] *Botta v Italy* (n 802 above) para 34.
[806] *X & Y v Netherlands* (1985) 8 EHRR 235, para 27 (remedy for sexual abuse).
[807] *Gaskin v United Kingdom* (1989) 12 EHRR 36, para 49.
[808] See eg, *Stjerna v Finland* (1994) 24 EHRR 194, para 42.
[809] *Botta v Italy* (n 802 above) para 35.
[810] *Goodwin v United Kingdom* (2002) 35 EHRR 18 (GC), paras 84–85.
[811] *Rees v United Kingdom* (1986) 9 EHRR 56; *Cossey v United Kingdom* (1990) 13 EHRR 622; *X, Y and Z v United Kingdom* (1997) 24 EHRR 143 and *Sheffield and Horsham v United Kingdom* (1998) 27 EHRR 163.
[812] (1992) 16 EHRR 1.
[813] (2002) 35 EHRR 447.

United Kingdom[814] it held that, given the increasing sophistication of medical treatment and an emerging consensus within Contracting States to provide legal recognition following gender reassignment, that balance had shifted in favour of the positive obligation arising. It concluded that:

> In the twenty first century the right of transsexuals to personal development and to physical and moral security in the full sense enjoyed by others in society cannot be regarded as a matter of controversy requiring the lapse of time to cast clearer light on the issues involved . . .[The United Kingdom] can no longer claim that matter falls within their margin of appreciation, save as regards the appropriate means of achieving recognition of the right protected under the Convention. Since there are no significant factors of public interest to weigh against the interest of the individual applicant in obtaining legal recognition of her gender re-assignment, it reaches the conclusion that the fair balance that is inherent in the Convention now tilts decisively in favour of the applicant.[815]

12.252 **Recognition of a choice of name.** Not all regulation of names will give rise to Article 8 issues and the state has a wide margin of appreciation.[816] However, in a number of cases the Court has found that there is a positive obligation on the State to recognize an individual's choice of name. This was first established in *Burghartz v Switzerland*[817] in which the Swiss authorities had refused to recognize the applicants' joined names as their surname. The existence of the positive obligation was confirmed in *Stjerna v Finland*.[818] However, it was held that the restrictions on a person changing his name could be justified in the public interest and that the applicant's reasons for wishing to change his name were insufficient to give rise to a positive obligation. The positive obligation also applies to the recognition of forenames.[819] The following principles apply in relation to disputes concerning surnames and forenames:[820]

(a) Although the spelling of surnames and forenames concerns essentially the area of the individual's private and family life, it cannot be dissociated from the linguistic policy conducted by the State. . . . provided that the rights protected by the Convention are respected, each Contracting State is at liberty to impose and regulate the use of its official language or languages in identity papers and other official documents.

(b) A language is not in any sense an abstract value. It cannot be divorced from the way it is actually used by its speakers. . . . a measure intended to protect and promote a national language corresponds to the protection of the 'rights and freedoms of others', within the meaning of Article 8(2) of the Convention. Furthermore, the authorities, especially the national courts, are in principle in a better position than the international judge to give an opinion on the need for interference in such a sensitive area.

---

[814] (2003) 36 EHRR 53.

[815] *Goodwin* (n 810 above) paras 90–91.

[816] *Johansson v Finland* (2008) 47 EHRR 14, para 29.

[817] (1994) 18 EHRR 101.

[818] (1994) 24 EHRR 194.

[819] *Guillot v France*, Judgment of 24 October 1996 (no violation resulting from failure to register 'Fleur de Marie' as a forename because insufficient inconvenience caused by failure to register); *Salonen v Finland* (2003) 36 EHRR CD 238 (refusal to register 'The One and Only Marjaana' as name not unreasonable); *Johansson v Finland* (n 816 above) (failure to register 'Axl' a violation).

[820] See generally, *Bulgakov v Ukraine*, Judgment of 11 September 2007, para 43.

(c) The process whereby surnames and forenames are given, recognized and used is a domain in which national particularities are the strongest and in which there are virtually no points of convergence between the internal rules of the Contracting States. . . .

(d) The fact that a country finds itself in an isolated position as regards one aspect of its legislation does not necessarily imply that that aspect offends the Convention, particularly in a field which is so closely bound up with the cultural and historical traditions of each society.

Determination of paternity. There is a positive obligation to establish legal mechanisms **12.253** enabling a prompt determination of paternity.[821] Violations of this obligation have been found in a number of cases.[822] Although there is no obligation to compel DNA testing, Member States must have some means of establishing paternity swiftly, which may include legal presumptions[823] but such presumptions must not be permitted to obscure ascertainable biological reality and Article 8 might require the re-opening of a case on the basis of new evidence.[824] In *Znamenskaya v Russia*[825] the Court extended the principle so as to allow a mother accurately to record the paternity of her stillborn baby on his gravestone. However, in *Odièvre v France* the Grand Chamber held by a majority that the French system of allowing 'anonymous births' where requested by the mother, balanced the privacy interest of the child and the mother, father and other siblings in a way that fell within the margin of appreciation.[826]

Access to information. Although the Court has not yet recognized a general Convention **12.254** right to access to public information there are some circumstances such a right will arise as a positive obligation under Article 8. A positive obligation to provide information was recognized in *Gaskin v United Kingdom*[827] where the Court required the authorities take steps to release records of the applicant's foster care which were held to be of special importance to his private life. In *Guerra v Italy*[828] the Grand Chamber held that there was positive obligation to provide local residents with safety and environmental information concerning a local chemical plant with a bad record of pollution. In *McGinley and Egan v United Kingdom*[829] a complaint was made about the withholding of documents concerning the exposure of the applicants to radiation at Christmas Island. The Court took the view that where the government engages in hazardous activities with hidden consequences for health, respect for private and family life requires an effective and accessible procedure to ensure that all relevant and appropriate information is made available. A majority of the court concluded that such a procedure was available under domestic legislation. In contrast, in

---

[821] *Mikulic v Croatia* (2002) 11 BHRC 689.

[822] Ibid, (violation of Article 8 because judicial system failed properly to determine paternity). *Jäggi v Switzerland* (2008) 46 EHRR 30 (violation because of refusal to order a DNA test); *Phinikaridou v Cyprus*, Judgment of 20 December 2007 (violation because of inability to determine paternity due to statute of limitations).

[823] *Jeremovic v Serbia* (Judgment of 17 July 2007), paras 108–110.

[824] see *Tavli v Turkey* [2007] 1 FLR 1136, paras 35–36; *Mizzi v Malta* [2006] 1 FLR 1048; *Shofman v Russia* [2006] 1 FLR 680; *Różanski v Poland* [2006] 2 FLR 1163; see generally A Bainham, ' "Truth will out" Paternity in Europe' (2007) 66 CLJ 278.

[825] (2007) 44 EHRR 15.

[826] (2004) 38 EHRR 43, paras 40–49.

[827] (1989) 12 EHRR 36; but see *Willsher v United Kingdom* (1997) 23 EHRR CD 188 (complaint about lack of access rejected because applicant's sister had been offered access but had refused).

[828] (1998) 26 EHRR 357.

[829] (1998) 27 EHRR 1.

Roche v United Kingdom[830] in a case involving access to information concerning mustard nerve gas tests involving the applicant the Grand Chamber held that the positive obligation had not been fulfilled.

12.255 **Provision of facilities for the disabled.** Applications based on the contention that Article 8 includes a positive obligation to provide facilities for the disabled have, so far, proved unsuccessful. In *Botta v Italy*[831] it was held that respect for private life did not extend to giving a disabled person a right of access to the beach and sea which was distant from his normal holiday residence. Similarly, an application based on the contention that there was a positive obligation to provide a robotic arm to a person suffering from muscular dystrophy was unsuccessful.[832] In *Zehnalovà and Zehnal v Czech Republic*[833] it was held that there was no general obligation to provide disabled access to public buildings. But the case left open the possibility of imposing a positive obligation where a lack of access to public buildings interferes with the right to establish and develop relationships with other human beings and the outside world and suggests that an obligation would have been imposed if the applicant had shown a 'special link between the lack of access to the buildings in question and the particular needs of her private life'.

12.256 **Provision of housing.** It has been accepted that, in some circumstances, there might be a positive obligation to provide housing assistance to an individual suffering from a serious disease.[834] However, the Court has not to date found any breach of this obligation. In *Barreto v Portugal*[835] the Court held that respect for private and family life did not require the existence in national law of legal protection enabling each family to have a home for themselves or giving the landlord a right to recover possession of a rented house in any circumstances.

12.257 **Positive obligations in other areas.** The Court has considered the existence of positive obligations in a number of other areas:

- There may be an obligation to provide funding for healthcare provision—but there is a wide margin of appreciation as this involves the allocation of limited State resources.[836]
- There is no positive obligation to provide prisoners with the facilities to make telephone calls.[837]
- There is no positive obligation to provide access to documents which do not concern a person's identity or personal history.[838] There is a positive obligation to compensate individuals for injury to reputation caused by unlawful state action.[839]

---

[830] (2006) 42 EHRR 30 (GC).

[831] (1998) 26 EHRR 241, para 34ff.

[832] *Sentges v Netherlands*, Decision of 8 July 2003; see also *Maggiolini v Italy*, Decision of 13 January 2000 (access of a disabled person to properly adapted housing); *Mółka v Poland*, Decision of 11 April 2006 (access of a disabled person to polling stations).

[833] Decision of 15 May 2002.

[834] *Marzari v Italy*, Decision of 4 May 1999; *O'Rourke v United Kingdom*, Decision of 26 June 2001; see also *Chapman v United Kingdom* (2001) 33 EHRR 18, Joint Dissenting Opinion, para 7; see generally, P Kenna, 'Housing Rights Positive Duties and Enforceable Rights at the European Court of Human Rights' [2008] EHRLR 193.

[835] [1996] EHRLR 214; see also *Burton v United Kingdom* (1996) 22 EHRR CD 135 (no obligation to provide the applicant who was a gypsy suffering from cancer with accommodation in a caravan).

[836] *Pentiacova and Others v Moldova*, Decision of 4 January 2005.

[837] *AB v Netherlands*, Judgment of 29 January 2002, para 92.

[838] *Smith v United Kingdom*, Decision of 4 January 2007.

[839] *Kynakides v Cyprus*, Judgment of 16 October 2008, see also *Taliadorou Stylianou v Cyprus*, Judgment of 16 October 2008 to the same effect.

(d) Positive action to prevent interference by non-state bodies

Introduction.   States might also be obliged to take positive action to prevent or stop   **12.258**
another *individual* from interfering with private life. The argument that Article 8(2) refers
only to justification of interference by a 'public authority' has been rejected by the Court as
irrelevant to the question as to what rights are protected by Article 8(1). It is clear that in
appropriate cases the State may be required to take positive action to prevent interferences
with Article 8 rights by private bodies.

Environmental cases.[840]   The state has a positive obligation to protect individuals from   **12.259**
the effects of serious environmental pollution by private bodies. Such an obligation was recognized by the Court in a 1990 noise pollution case.[841] The first finding of breach of this
obligation was in the leading case of *Lopez-Ostra v Spain*.[842] The Court held that the Spanish
authorities had failed properly to protect the applicant and her family from noxious gases
produced by a waste reprocessing plant constructed by a private company 12 metres from her
home. Findings of breach of this positive obligation have been made in cases involving noise
from bars and discos in a residential area,[843] the discharge of sodium cyanide from a mining
operation,[844] severe atmospheric pollution caused by the operation of steel plants.[845]

Media cases.   In recent years the Court has given clear recognition to positive obligation   **12.260**
to protect individuals from media intrusion into their private lives in a series of cases
involving the publication of photographs and other material by non-state parties. The leading case is the decision in *Van Hannover v Germany*.[846] In that case Princess Caroline of
Monaco complained about the publication of photographs in the tabloid press. These
photographs typically showed her engaging in ordinary activities in a variety of public
places. The Court held that the State had a positive obligation to guarantee respect for
private life even in relations between individuals and to protect a person's picture 'against
abuse by others'[847] When considering this obligation a balance had to be struck between
privacy and freedom of expression: neither can neutralize the other, both 'must be implemented and survive in harmony through the necessary compromises, depending on the
facts of each particular case'.[848]

This approach has been followed in a number of subsequent cases.[849] In addition to the   **12.261**
obligation to protect private information the state also has a positive obligation to protect

---

[840] See the discussion of environmental cases at para 12.310 below.

[841] *Powell and Rayner v United Kingdom* (1990) 12 EHRR 355 (noise pollution from Heathrow airport,
no violation of Article 8); see also *Hatton v United Kingdom* (2003) 37 EHRR 28 (GC)(no violation as a result
of Heathrow noise pollution) and *Ashworth v United Kingdom* Decision of 20 January 2004.

[842] (1994) 20 EHRR 277; see also *Giacomelli v Italy* (2007) 45 EHRR 38 (plant for storage and treatment
of 'special waste').

[843] *Moreno Gomez v Spain* (2005) 41 EHRR 40.

[844] *Taşkin v Turkey* (2006) 42 EHRR 50.

[845] *Fadeyeva v Russia* (2007) 45 EHRR 10; *Ledyayeva v Russia* (Judgment of 26 October 2006).

[846] (2005) 40 EHRR 1.

[847] Ibid, para 57.

[848] *Lindon, Otchakovsky-Laurens and July v France* (2008) 46 EHRR 35, O-19 (Concurring Opinion of
Judge Loucaides); see generally Council of Europe, Parliamentary Assembly Resolution 1165 (1998), 'Right
to Privacy'.

[849] See eg, *Leempoel v Belgium*, Judgment of 9 November 2006. *Gourguenidze v Georgia*, Judgment of
17 October 2006 and the cases discussed at para 12.285ff below.

a person's Article 8 right to reputation by taking appropriate measures against the publishers of defamatory material. In *Pfeifer v Austria*[850] there was a breach of the state's positive obligation to protect the applicant's Article 8 right to his reputation as a result of the domestic courts having dismissed his defamation action. The finding of the domestic courts that the freedom of expression of the publisher outweighed the right of the applicant to have his reputation safeguarded was not convincing and, as a result, the Court held that the domestic courts failed to strike a fair balance between the competing interests involved.[851] There is also a positive obligation to provide effective protection against media publication of private information, including an obligation that effective sanctions are provided for breaches of the right to privacy.[851a]

12.262 Criminal cases. It is well established that the state is under a positive obligation to protect citizens from criminal acts by others. In *X & Y v Netherlands*[852] the state was held to have a duty to provide an effective criminal remedy to ensure deterrence in relation to a sexual assault on a mentally handicapped sixteen year old. In *MC v Bulgaria*[853] it was held that the failure of Bulgarian law and practice to provide effective protection against rape and sexual abuse was a violation of Article 8 (and Article 3). Whether or in what circumstances the positive obligation will extend to the criminalization of private acts remains unresolved.

(e) Positive obligation to require positive action by private persons

12.263 The obligation to provide 'respect' may impose a duty on the state to require positive action by private persons. States might be obliged to require that private data collection firms grant access to individuals to records kept about them or that the parent with custody of children allow access to the other parent or other relatives like grandparents.[854] In *Van Kuck v Germany*[855] the Court held that the state should have required a private health insurance company to pay for the applicant's medically-required gender reassignment surgery.

(3) Scope of 'private life'

(a) Introduction

12.264 Defining private life. The Court has not sought to provide a comprehensive definition of 'private life'. It has, however, given guidance in many cases about the meaning

---

[850] (2009) 48 EHRR 8; see also *KU v Finland*, Judgment of 2 December 2008 (failure to protect a child's right to respect for private life following an advertisement of a sexual nature being posted about him on an Internet dating site); contrast *White v Sweden* (2008) 46 EHRR 3 (although the state had a positive obligation to secure respect for the private life of a person accused by the press of murder there was no breach because a fair balance had been struck with the media's Article 10 rights).

[851] *Pfeifer* (n 850 above), paras 48–49; the case is discussed at para 12.302 below.

[851a] See *Armonas v Lithuania*, Judgment of 25 November 2008 (violation where domestic law limited non-pecuniary damages for publication of private information to €2, 896, the Court awarded €6,500 just satisfaction; see also, *Biriuk v Lithuania*, Judgment of 25 November 2008, to the same effect.

[852] (1985) 8 EHRR 235; *August v the United Kingdom* Decision of 21 January 2003; cf *Stubbings v United Kingdom* (1996) 23 EHRR 213, paras 62–64 (Art 8 does not require unlimited civil remedies where criminal sanctions are in operation).

[853] (2003) 15 BHRC 627; see also *Szula v United Kingdom*, Decision of 4 January 2007 (positive obligation also applies to serious sexual offences inflicted on children).

[854] See *Hokkanen v Finland* (1994) 19 EHRR 139, Com Rep, paras 129–146 which relates to family life.

[855] (2003) 37 EHRR 51.

of the term. It is clear that 'private life' it extends beyond 'the right to privacy, the right to live as far as one wishes, protected from publicity'.[856] In *Niemetz v Germany*[857] it was said that:

> The Court does not consider it possible or necessary to attempt an exhaustive definition of the notion of 'private life'. However, it would be too restrictive to limit the notion to an 'inner circle' in which an individual may choose to live his personal life as he chooses and to exclude entirely the outside world not encompassed within that circle. Respect for private life must also comprise to a certain degree the right to establish and develop relationships with other human beings.

There appears, furthermore, to be no reason in principle why this understanding of the notion of 'private life' should be taken to exclude the activities of a professional or business nature since it is, after all, in the course of their working lives that the majority of people have a significant, if not the greatest opportunity of developing relationships with the outside world.[858] The general test as to whether the right to private life in Article 8 is engaged is whether there is a 'reasonable' or 'legitimate' expectation of privacy.[859]

The term private life 'must not be interpreted restrictively' and encompasses the establishment and development of relationships with others, even in a public or business context.[860] Deportation can accordingly interfere with respect for private life as well as family life, although an individual has no Article 8 right to live in the country of his choice.[861] **12.265**

Personal autonomy. The notion of personal autonomy is an important principle underlying the interpretation of the guarantees of Article 8.[862] Such personal autonomy includes the right to conduct one's life in a manner of one's own choosing[863] and covers the pursuit of activities that are physically or morally harmful. Further, Article 8 requires respect for human dignity and quality of life.[864] The right to respect for private life and home must also not be looked at in isolation. Article 8 must be read in conjunction with freedom of religion under Article 9,[865] the right to receive and impart information and ideas under Article 10[866] and the right to education under Article 2 of the First Protocol.[867] **12.266**

---

[856] *X v Iceland* (1976) 5 DR 86.

[857] (1992) 16 EHRR 97 para 29; see also *Peck v United Kingdom* (2003) 36 EHRR 41, para 57; *PG v United Kingdom* (2008) 46 EHRR 51, para 56.

[858] The Court reiterated that the scope of 'private life' was broad enough to include professional and business activities in *Amann v Switzerland* (2000) 30 EHRR 843, para 65, and *Rotaru v Romania* (2000) 8 BHRC 449. A dismissal from employment on the basis of personal status—including former membership of the KGB—can interfere with Article 8 rights too: see *Rainys v Lithuania* (Judgment of 7 April 2005).

[859] See *Halford v United Kingdom* (1997) 24 EHRR 523, para 45; *PG v United Kingdom* (2008) 46 EHRR 51, para 57; *Von Hannover v Germany* (2005) 40 EHRR 1, para 51.

[860] *Von Vondel v Netherlands* (2009) 48 EHRR 12, para 48.

[861] *Kaya v Germany* (Judgment of 28 June 2007); *Uner v Netherlands* (2007) 45 EHRR 14 (GC); *Sisjeva v Latvia* (Judgment of 16 June 2005; the case went to the Grand Chamber, which gave a Judgment on 15 January 2007, but did not consider this issue on the ground that it had been resolved between the parties).

[862] *Pretty v United Kingdom* (2002) 35 EHRR 1, para 61.

[863] Ibid, para 62.

[864] See also *L v Lithuania* (2008) 46 EHRR 22, para 56.

[865] See para 14.87ff below.

[866] *Kjeldsen, Busk Madsen and Pedersen v Denmark* (1976) 1 EHRR 711; and see para 15.248ff below.

[867] See *Belgian Linguistics case (No 2)* (1968) 1 EHRR 252, para 7 which states that 'measures taken in the field of education may affect the right to respect for private and family life or derogate from it'; and see para 19.94ff below.

12.267 **Protection of private life.**   The state must take practice and effective measures to protect private life. The domestic legal framework must provided proper protection. This means not only a right to compensation for damage caused by unlawful interference but also effective protection 'to exclude the possibility' of interference occurring in the first place.[868]

12.268 **Specific areas of private life.**   The following specific areas have been considered by the Court to form part of 'private life' within the terms of Article 8:

- physical and psychological integrity;
- personal or private space and surveillance;
- collection and publication of personal information;
- personal identity;
- personal autonomy and sexuality;
- self development, relations with others and reputation.

(b) Physical and psychological integrity

12.269 **Introduction.**   'Private life' covers the physical and moral integrity of the person. It therefore includes freedom from physical or sexual assault,[869] corporal punishment,[870] a compulsory blood[871] or urine[872] test, medical treatment or procedures administered without consent,[873] and a general detriment to health and well-being caused by pollution.[874] The Court stressed in *Raninen v Finland*[875] that the right to physical and moral integrity guaranteed by Article 8 comes into play even though it is not so severe as to amount to inhuman treatment under Article 3.[876]

12.270 **Physical integrity.**   In *Costello-Roberts*,[877] the Court indicated that Article 8 could in some circumstances provide protection against school discipline; but found that the punishment of being hit with a slipper across the buttocks 'did not entail adverse effects sufficient to bring it within the scope of the prohibition contained in Article 8'. It is difficult to reconcile these views with other cases of slight physical intervention: except, perhaps, because the incident took place at school. The Court has more recently held[878] that:

> even a minor interference with the physical integrity of an individual must be regarded as an interference with the right to respect for private life under Article 8 if it is carried out against the individual's will.

---

[868] See *I v Finland*, Judgment of 17 July 2008, para 47 (unauthorized access to personal information).

[869] *X and Y v Netherlands* (1985) 8 EHRR 235, involved a sexual assault by a man on a mentally handicapped young woman: at para 22, the Court found that the facts concerned a matter of 'private life'. In *August v United Kingdom* (2003) 36 EHRR CD115, the Court held that Article 8 did not require the State to compensate the 13-year-old victim of unlawful sexual assault as if it were a crime of violence when the child in question was a willing and active participant, even though his consent was not a defence to the charge.

[870] *Costello-Roberts v United Kingdom* (1993) 19 EHRR 112, Com Rep para 49.

[871] *X v Austria* (1979) 18 DR 154, EComm HR.

[872] *Peters v Netherlands* (1994) 77–A DR 75, EComm HR.

[873] *Glass v United Kingdom* (2004) 39 EHRR 15, para 70; *Juhnke v Turkey*, Judgment of 13 May 2008.

[874] *Ledyayeva v Russia*, Judgment of 26 October 2006, para 100.

[875] (1997) 26 EHHR 563.

[876] See para 8.83ff above.

[877] See n 870 above.

[878] In *Storck v Germany* (2006) 43 EHRR 96, para 143.

The Court has recognized that the detention of prisoners necessitates some interference **12.271** with Article 8 rights. However, prisoners do not lose such rights and any interference with them must be justifiable. Accordingly, poor conditions[879] or excessive restrictions on the right to receive visits from family and friends[880] may be unlawful. Strip searching prison visitors will also interfere with their Article 8 rights and, though such invasive actions might be justifiable in particular circumstances, they must be carried out with scrupulous regard to procedures.[881]

Issues concerning pregnancy and abortion are likely to fall within the scope of Article 8. **12.272** In *Tysiac v Poland*,[882] the pregnant applicant could find only one doctor willing to certify that she met the requirements for a therapeutic abortion, while the legislation required two; several doctors took the view that there was an insufficiently serious risk to her health. Accordingly, she went through with the pregnancy but suffered damage to her eyesight as a result. The Court held that the applicant's physical integrity was at stake and this, taken with the inherently personal nature of pregnancy, meant that Article 8 was applicable. The Court also held that there were inadequate safeguards to deal with the medical dispute and that Article 8 had accordingly been breached.[883]

Moral integrity. Slights on an individual's moral integrity may also raise Article 8 issues. **12.273** In *Sanchez Cardenas v Norway*,[884] a family court recorded an official suspicion that an individual was suspected of child abuse but chose to make no finding on it. The Court held that this was a disproportionate interference with Article 8 rights: either the allegations were relevant and needed resolution or else they should not have been mentioned at all.[885] Article 8 has now been recognized as including the 'right to reputation'.[886]

(c) Personal or private space

Introduction. The infringement of private space, which is to be enjoyed free from unwel- **12.274** come interference, whether apparent or covert,[887] has been recognized in many cases. Before the judgment in *Von Hannover v Germany*,[888] the difficult question was whether 'private space' included anything beyond those places in which the applicant had exclusive rights of occupancy. The surveillance of an individual, whether by listening, watching or recording will constitute an infringement of the right to private life.

Public and private space. In *Friedl v Austria*[889] the Commission took the view **12.275** that police photography of the applicant participating in a 'sit-in' as part of a political

---

[879] *DG v Ireland* (2002) 35 EHRR 33.

[880] *Nowicka v Poland* [2003] 1 FLR 417; *Ciorap v Moldova* (Judgment of 19 June 2007); *Ostrovar v Moldova* (2007) 44 EHRR 19.

[881] *Wainwright v United Kingdom* (2007) 44 EHRR 40, paras 43–44.

[882] (2007) 45 EHRR 42.

[883] This judgment seems to go behind the Polish legislative scheme requiring two doctors to certify the abortion and to require the State to adjudicate on differing medical views.

[884] Judgment of 4 October 2007, para 33.

[885] Ibid, para 37.

[886] See para 12.301ff below.

[887] D Harris, M O'Boyle, and C Warbrick, *Law of the European Convention on Human Rights* (Butterworths, 1995), 308.

[888] (2005) 40 EHRR 1.

[889] (1996) 21 EHRR 83, Com Rep, paras 48 and 51.

demonstration did not violate Article 8, giving weight to the fact that the photograph was taken and retained as a record of the demonstration and no action had been taken to identify the persons photographed on that occasion by means of data processing.[890] By comparison, in *Murray v United Kingdom*[891] a photograph which was taken at an army centre was held to be an interference with the applicant's right to privacy. A core, though not necessarily determinative, question seems to be whether the applicant had a reasonable expectation of privacy, which involves issues such as whether the photographs relate to private matters or public incidents and whether the material obtained is envisaged for a limited use or is likely to be made available to the general public.[892] In *Halford v United Kingdom*,[893] the Court decided that a telephone call made from a private telephone line in an office came within the scope of Article 8(1) because the applicant had a reasonable expectation of privacy.[894]

12.276   The Court has increasingly recognized that Article 8 protects a 'zone of interaction' of a person with others, even in a public context[895] which is relatively narrow in the case of well known figures and wider for an 'ordinary person'.[896] It is clear that the making a visual record of a public scene can give rise to 'private life' considerations.[897] In *Peck v United Kingdom*,[898] for example, the Court held that the release to the media of unobscured CCTV images of the applicant, who had subsequently tried to commit suicide, infringed his right to privacy under Article 8. In *PG v United Kingdom*[899] the Court said that:

> Since there are occasions when people knowingly or intentionally involves themselves in activities which are or may be recorded or reported in a public manner, a person's reasonable expectations as to privacy may be a significant, although not necessarily conclusive factor. A person who walks down the street, will inevitably, be visible to any member of the public is also present. Monitoring by technological means of the same public scene (for example, a security guard viewing through closed circuit television) is of a similar character. Private life considerations may arise, however, once any systematic or permanent record comes into existence of such material from the public domain.

12.277   The high watermark of this development is *Von Hannover v Germany*,[900] in which the Court held that Princess Caroline of Monaco was entitled to protection from the taking and publication of photographs of her engaging in ordinary activities in a variety of public places. The Court had no doubt that the publication of photographs of the applicant in her

---

[890]   Ibid, paras 51–52.
[891]   (1994) 19 EHRR 193.
[892]   *Friedl v Austria* (1996) 21 EHRR 83, paras 49–52.
[893]   (1997) 24 EHRR 523.
[894]   Ibid, para 45.
[895]   *Von Hannover v Germany* (2005) 40 EHRR 1, para 50; *Petrina v Roumania* Judgment of 14 October 2008, para 27.
[896]   *Sciacca v Italy* (2006) 43 EHRR 20, para 29 (it is not narrowed when a person is subject to criminal proceedings).
[897]   Ibid, para 57. See also *Peck v United Kingdom* (2003) 36 EHRR 41, para 58.
[898]   (2003) 36 EHRR 41.
[899]   (2008) 46 EHRR 51, para 57 (in the context of considering the use of listening devices at a police station where Art 8 was held to be engaged); see also *Peck v United Kingdom* (n 898 above); *Perry v United Kingdom* (2004) 39 EHRR 3 (cover photography of the applicant in a custody suite).
[900]   (2005) 40 EHRR 1.

daily life fell within the scope Article 8,[901] and explicitly stated that the public did not have a legitimate interest in knowing where the applicant was and how she behaved generally in her private life, even if she appeared in non-secluded places and despite the fact that she was well known.[902] Given the photographs showed non-official activities of a purely private nature, their publication was held not contribute to public debate, and was thus not afforded a high degree of protection under Article 10.[903]

The Court in *Von Hannover* criticized the use of the criterion of 'spatial isolation' to define **12.278** privacy as being too vague and difficult to apply in practice[904] and it appears that Article 8 will now be engaged in relation to the taking of photographs for publication in the media in public places, unless the subject is performing 'public functions'.[905] The position is less clear in relation to the taking of the photographs in public places when there is no actual or threatened publication. It is submitted that when this is done by state agencies then Article 8 will be engaged[906] but that a positive obligation in relation to private bodies will not arise unless there are special circumstances of intrusion involving intimate, traumatic or embarrassing events or some other special circumstances in which a person can reasonable expect that they will not be photographed in public.

Surveillance. It will be an interference with the right to private life in Article 8 to inter- **12.279** cept telephone calls to a person's home[907] or workplace[908] or to install a listening device in a home[909] or prison cell.[910] In *PG v United Kingdom*,[911] the Court found that the recording of a suspect in his police cell interfered with his right to respect for private life.[912] In the course of its judgment, the Court considered in detail the instances when capturing personal information, even when it is public, may engage the right to private life. The Court commented that, on the occasions when people knowingly or intentionally involve themselves in activities which are or may be recorded or reported in a public manner, a person's reasonable expectations as to privacy may be a significant factor as to whether the right is engaged:

> A person who walks down the street will, inevitably, be visible to any member of the public who is also present. Monitoring by technological means of the same public scene (eg a security guard viewing through close circuit television) is of a similar character. Private life

---

[901] Ibid, paras 52–53.
[902] Ibid, para 77.
[903] Ibid, para 59.
[904] Ibid, paras 69–75.
[905] See the cases discussed at para 12.285 below.
[906] See eg, *Martin v United Kingdom*, Judgment of 19 February 2004 (FSett)(Agreed payment of £4,000 for covert CCTV filming outside front of applicant's home) see Decision of 27 March 2003.
[907] *Huvig v France* (1990) 12 EHRR 528, para 25 (interference with right to respect for private life and correspondence).
[908] *Halford v United Kingdom* (1997) 24 EHRR 523, para 52.
[909] *Lewis v United Kingdom* (2004) 39 EHRR 9, para 18; *Khan v United Kingdom* (2001) 31 EHRR 45, para 25; *Elahi v United Kingdom* (2007) 44 EHRR 30.
[910] *Allan v United Kingdom* (2003) 36 EHRR 12, para 35.
[911] (2008) 46 EHRR 51; see also *Perry v United Kingdom* (2004) 39 EHRR 3.
[912] Similar practices were considered in *Khan v United Kingdom* (2001) 31 EHRR 45; *Allan v United Kingdom* (2003) 36 EHRR 12 and *Wood v United Kingdom*, Judgment of 16 November 2004, all of which found the UK in breach of Article 8.

considerations may arise however once any systematic or permanent record comes into existence of such material from the public domain. It is for this reason that files gathered by security services on a particular individual fall within the scope of Article 8 even where the information has not been gathered by any intrusive or covert method.[913]

It will also be an interference with Article 8 to make a video recording of a person in a prison cell[914] or in a police custody suite.[915]

12.280   The Court has imposed strict requirements of precision and accessibility on the law governing surveillance and the collection of personal information, especially when such activity is covert.[916] However, it has been acknowledged that the law cannot sensibly permit an individual to foresee covert surveillance to the extent that he could modify his conduct so as to thwart it.[917] These points are considered under the heading of 'justification'.

(d) Collection, storage, and publication of personal information

12.281   **Collection and storage of personal information.**   The collection and storage of personal information by state authorities without consent is a violation of private life. This is most obvious where the collection is surreptitious, by activities such as telephone tapping or interception of post. Article 8 can be engaged when a private individual collects the data, if a public authority makes a decisive contribution by, for example, conniving in the process or providing equipment.[918] In *Z v Finland*[919] the Court emphasized that the protection of personal data, not least medical data, is of fundamental importance to a person's enjoyment of his right to respect for privacy and family life; and that there must be appropriate safeguards to prevent communication or disclosure of personal health data.

12.282   There is also a *prima facie* breach of the right to respect for private life where personal information is collated by an official census,[920] fingerprinting and photography by the police,[921] a compulsory medical examination[922] and the maintenance of medical records.[923] The storing of information about a person on a card in a file was found by the Grand Chamber to be an interference with private life, even though it contained no sensitive information and had probably never been consulted.[924] Proof that the information is used to the detriment of the applicant is unnecessary, so long as the compilation and retention of such a

---

[913] See (n 911 above) para 56. The Court has since confirmed that photographs taken by persons unconnected with the State of individuals in public places may interfere with the right to private life: *Von Hannover v Germany* (2005) 40 EHRR 1, paras 50–51.

[914] *Allan v United Kingdom* (n 910 above).

[915] *Perry v United Kingdom* (n 911 above).

[916] See *Association for European Integration and Human Rights v Bulgaria* (Judgment of 28 June 2007), paras 75–93; *Volokh v Ukraine* (Judgment of 2 November 2006); *Liberty v United Kingdom* (2009) 48 EHRR 1.

[917] *Malone v United Kingdom* (1984) 7 EHRR 14.

[918] *MM v Netherlands* (2004) 39 EHRR 19, paras 36–40; *Van Vondel v Netherlands* (2009) 48 EHRR 12.

[919] (1997) 25 EHRR 371.

[920] *X v United Kingdom* (1982) 30 DR 239, EComm HR.

[921] *Murray v United Kingdom* (1994) 19 EHRR 193, para 85; *McVeigh v United Kingdom* (1981) 25 DR 15, 49.

[922] *X v Austria* (1979) 18 DR 154.

[923] *Chave v France* (1991) 71 DR 141, 155, EComm HR.

[924] *Amann v Switzerland* (2000) 30 EHRR 834, paras 65–67.

dossier is adequately shown.[925] The retention of fingerprints. DNA samples, and cellular samples taken in the course of criminal investigations constitutes an interference.[925a] Even personal information which is already in the public domain may fall within the scope of private life where it is systematically collected and stored in files held by the authorities.[926] This is particularly so where such information concerns a person's distant past; and the storage of that kind of information is less likely to be proportionate.[927]

However, the Commission has held that an obligation to carry an identity card and to show **12.283** it on request was not a breach of private life.[928] Further, a security check on a potential employee is not of itself a violation of private life unless it involves the collection of information about his private affairs.[929] Employees will normally have a reasonable expectation of privacy in relation to telephone, email and internet activity carried out in the workplace,[930] although a clear policy or warning about the monitoring of employees might remove that expectation of privacy.[931] Absent such a policy, any monitoring or surveillance by public employers of activities of this nature will need to be in accordance with the law and proportionate.

Disclosure of information. In *Roche v United Kingdom*[932] the Court found a breach of **12.284** Article 8 as a result of the failure to operate an effective and accessible procedure allowing the applicant access to all relevant and appropriate information about his participation in medical tests concerned with the effects of chemical weapons However, in *Segerstedt v Sweden*,[933] the Court held that the security services were entitled not to disclose information which they considered would jeopardize national security or the prevention of terrorism, despite the fact that some of the information which *had* been released was held to have been kept in contravention of Article 8. The Court held that there were sufficient safeguards in national law, though it is not clear from the judgment whether the Court viewed and reached a conclusion on the undisclosed material itself.

---

[925] Ibid, 118.

[925a] *S and Marper v United Kingdom*, Judgment of 4 December 2008 (CG), paras 66 to 86.

[926] *Rotaru v Romania* (2000) 8 BHRC 449, para 43; *Segerstedt v Sweden* (2007) 44 EHRR 2; see also *Cemalettin Canli v Turkey*, Judgment of 18 November 2008, paras 33 to 34 (information as to suspected previous criminal offences was within scope of Art 8).

[927] *Segerstedt* (n 926 above) paras 90–91, in which the Court held that it was disproportionate to store information about an individual's advocacy of violent resistance to police control of demonstrations, or about their former membership of a political party which advocated armed opposition (paras 90–91). The existence of information had been disclosed to the applicants by the security services. Paradoxically, the Court held that the refusal of the security services to disclose the rest of the applicants' files was *not* disproportionate and there is no sign in the Judgment that those files had been disclosed to the Court either (paras 102 and 14).

[928] *Filip Reyntjens v Belgium* (1992) 73 DR 136.

[929] *Hilton v United Kingdom* (1988) 57 DR 108, 117. However, the concept of private information in this context has been widely interpreted so as to include, for example, information about participation in demonstrations and about bomb threats made against the individual in question: *Segerstedt v Sweden* (n 926 above).

[930] *Copland v United Kingdom* (2007) 45 EHRR 37, paras 41 and 44. In *Peev v Bulgaria* (Judgment of 26 July 2007), para 39, the Court confirmed that the test is whether the employee has a reasonable expectation of privacy. It held that and employee did have a reasonable expectation that his own filing cabinet and desk were private, although this might not extend to the rest of the office.

[931] *Peev* (n 930 above) para 39; *Copland* (n 930 above) para 42.

[932] Decision of 23 May 2002.

[933] (2007) 44 EHRR 2, paras 99–104.

12.285 **Publication of personal information.**   Over the past five years, the Court has recognized the state's positive obligation to protect individuals from media intrusion into their private lives in a series of cases involving the publication of photographs and other material by non-state parties. The positive Article 8 obligation was found to be engaged in each of the following cases:[934]

- In *Schüssel v Austria*,[935] where the applicant, the Deputy Prime Minister of Austria, complained about the use of his photograph on stickers, alongside a photograph of the right-wing politician Jörg Haider, with the slogan 'The social security slashers and the education snatchers share a common face'.
- The well-known *Von Hannover*[936] case, which concerned a series of photographs taken of the applicant, Princess Caroline of Monaco, going about her everyday (private) affairs in public places.
- In *Anguelov v Bulgaria*,[937] where the applicant politician complained of a single photograph taken of him in the course of a criminal trial and published in the press.
- The case of *Minelli v Switzerland*,[938] which concerned the publication in a magazine of a photograph of the applicant, who was a public figure, taken during a televized event in which he had taken part.
- In *Sciacca v Italy*,[939] where the press published an identity photograph taken by the police of a person who was subject to criminal investigation for revenue offences.
- In *Gourguenidze v Georgia*[940] which concerned a photograph of the applicant emerging from a police station after being interviewed.
- The case of *Leempoel v Belgium*,[941] which concerned the contents of a confidential file submitted to a parliamentary inquiry into the judicial conduct of a high profile criminal investigation.
- In *Hachette Filipacchi v France*[942] the complaint concerned the publication of a previously published photograph of the body of the deceased Prefect of Corsica lying in the street after his assassination.

12.286 In each of these cases, the Court considered the balance between the Article 10 rights of those who had published (or wished to publish) the photographs or information and the Article 8 rights of the person photographed or the subject of the information. The Court has held that:

> the decisive factor in balancing the protection of private life against freedom of expression should lie in the contribution that the published photos and articles make to a debate of general interest.[943]

---

[934] See also *Reklos and Davourlis v Greece* (Decision of 6 September 2007) which concerned two photographs of newborn baby taken in a hospital and not published. The application was held to be admissible on the basis that Art 8 was applicable.

[935] Decision of 21 February 2002.

[936] (2004) 40 EHRR 1.

[937] Decision of 14 December 2004.

[938] Decision of 14 June 2005.

[939] (2006) 43 EHRR 20.

[940] Judgment of 17 October 2006.

[941] Judgment of 9 November 2006.

[942] Judgment of 14 June 2007 (this was an Article 10 complaint by a magazine publisher which had been the subject of an adverse judgment arising out of the publication).

[943] See *Von Hannover* (n 936) at para 76; see also *Gourguenidze* (n 940) at para 59.

Furthermore, the Court has made it clear on a number of occasions that:

> the publication of the photos and articles in question, of which the sole purpose was to satisfy the curiosity of a particular readership regarding the details of the applicant's private life, cannot be deemed to contribute to any debate of general interest to society despite the applicant being known to the public.[944]

As a result the Court has found violations of Article 8 in *Von Hannover*,[945] *Sciacca*,[946] *Gourguenidze*,[947] and *Leempoel*[948] cases. In the *Hachette Filipacchi*[949] case it was held that the domestic judgment against the publisher in was not a breach of Article 10, because the Article 8 rights of the family prevailed. However, in *Schüssel*,[950] *Minelli*[951] and *Anguelov*,[952] the applications were 'manifestly ill founded'. Each application was rejected as inadmissible. They concerned politicians or public figures and the publication of information in clear 'public interest' contexts.

The balance between Articles 8 and 10 was also considered in *Craxi v Italy (No.2)*.[953] This **12.287** was a complaint by the former Italian prime minister concerning the publication of transcripts of his private telephone calls, parts (but not all) of which had been read in open court in the presence of the press in the course of a criminal hearing. The Court said that:

> public figures are entitled to the enjoyment of the guarantees set out in Article 8 . . . on the same basis as every other person. In particular, the public interest in receiving information only covers facts which are connected with the criminal charges brought against the accused. This must be borne in mind by journalists when reporting on pending criminal proceedings and the press should abstain from publishing information which are likely to prejudice, whether intentionally or not, the right to respect for the private life and correspondence of the accused persons.[954]

It was held that the publication of this material—which did not relate to the criminal charges—was a violation of Article 8 for which the state was responsible.

(e) Personal identity

Introduction. At the heart of private life is the capacity of the individual to formulate a **12.288** perception of himself and to choose his personal identity. An individual therefore has the *prima facie* right to choose his own name[955] and the names of his children[956] He may also be entitled to information about his identity, such as the records of his upbringing in public

---

[944] See *Von Hannover* (n 936) at para 65; see also *Leempoel* (n 941) at para 68.

[945] See n 936 above.

[946] See n 939 above.

[947] See n 940 above.

[948] See n 941 above.

[949] Note that this was a majority decision, with Judges Loucaides and Vajić dissenting.

[950] See n 935 above.

[951] See n 938 above.

[952] See n 937 above.

[953] (2004) 38 EHRR 47.

[954] Ibid, para 65.

[955] *Burghartz v Switzerland* (1994) 18 EHRR 101; *Stjerna v Finland* (1994) 24 EHRR 194; *Konstandinis v Stadt Altensteigstandsamt* [1993] ECR-I 1191, ECJ. However, in *Bulgakov v Ukraine* (Judgment of 11 September 2007), the Court found no breach of Article 8 when an individual did not at first object to the official use of the Ukrainian rather than Russian version of his surname and refused to utilize the national procedures for name changes when, several years later, he decided he wanted to revert to his 'real' name.

[956] *Johansson v Finland* (2008) 47 EHRR 14 (some regulation of children's names, to avoid the ridiculous or whimsical, for example, or to promote a national language, is permissible: see paras 29 and 36); see also

foster care[957] or his paternity[958] if it is significant to the development or determination of his personal identity.[959] Identity also involves the manner in which an individual presents himself to the state and to others.[960] An individual's choice as to how he should dress also engages Article 8.[961]

12.289 **Information about identity.** The right to personal development includes a vital interest in obtaining information necessary to discover the truth concerning important aspects of one's personal identity.[962] Indeed, some judges have commented that the right to an identity lies within the 'inner core' of right to respect for private life.[963] In some circumstances, therefore, Article 8 can give rise to a right of access to personal information, although it is doubtful whether it gives rise to a general right of access to personal data and information.[964] The Court has held that information concerning highly personal aspects of birth,[965] childhood, development and history[966] relate to private life in such a way that the question of access to such information comes within the scope of Article 8.[967]

12.290 The state may, in some circumstances, have a positive obligation to require a DNA test to enable a person to establish his parentage.[968] However, in *Odièvre v France* the Grand Chamber held by a majority that the French system of allowing 'anonymous births' where requested by the mother, balanced the privacy interest of the child and the mother, father and other siblings in a way that fell within the margin of appreciation.[969]

12.291 **Transsexuals.** A number of cases have considered the position of transsexuals. Initially, the Court rejected claims that a failure to amend a birth certificate to reflect the applicant's change of identity engaged Article 8,[970] although a similar complaint did succeed in *B v France*[971] primarily because of its specific impact on the applicant's social and professional life. The Court also found there was no breach of Article 8 where the United Kingdom failed to recognize a transsexual as the father of a child born after artificial insemination from a donor.[972] However, the position dramatically changed when the Grand

---

Heidecker-Tiemann v Germany (2008) 47 EHRR SE8 (refusal to register a compound surname not a lack of respect for private life).

[957] *Gaskin v United Kingdom* (1989) 12 EHRR 36, paras 36–37.

[958] See *Rasmussen v Denmark* (1984) 7 EHRR 371, para 33; *MB v United Kingdom* (1994) 77–A DR 108, 114–116, EComm HR and generally, para 12.253 above.

[959] See also *Odièvre v France* (2004) 38 EHRR 43, paras 29 and 44–49.

[960] On names, see para 12.252 above.

[961] See *McFeeley v United Kingdom* (1980) 20 DR 44, 91, EComm HR (prison dress).

[962] *Odièvre v France* (2004) 38 EHRR 43.

[963] Ibid, Joint Dissenting Opinion of Judges Wildhaber, Bratza, Bonello, Loucaides, Cabral Barreto, Tulkens, and Pellonpää, para 11.

[964] *Gaskin v United Kingdom* (1989) 12 EHRR 36 and *Odièvre v France* (n 959 above).

[965] *Odièvre v France* (n 959 above) para 12.

[966] *Gaskin v United Kingdom* (n 964 above) para 36.

[967] See also *MG v United Kingdom* (2003) 36 EHRR 3.

[968] *Jäggi v Switzerland* (2008) 46 EHRR 30 (violation because of refusal to order a DNA test).

[969] (2004) 38 EHRR 43, paras 40–49.

[970] *Sheffield and Horsham v United Kingdom* (1998) 27 EHRR 163; see, also *Rees v United Kingdom* (1986) 9 EHRR 56 and *Cossey v United Kingdom* (1990) 13 EHRR 622.

[971] (1993) 16 EHRR I, paras 55–62.

[972] *X, Y and Z v United Kingdom* (1997) 24 EHRR 143.

Chamber considered the cases of *Goodwin v United Kingdom*[973] and *I v United Kingdom*,[974] and held that the failure legally to recognize gender reassignment breached Article 8.[975] The Grand Chamber found that social norms had changed and that to oblige post-operative transsexuals to live in an intermediate zone as not quite one gender or the other was no longer acceptable.[976] It therefore held that failure to recognize transsexuals' new gender identity interfered with their Article 8(1) rights to personal development and to physical and moral security in the full sense enjoyed by others in society. Several further cases have reaffirmed the principle, and the Court has held that the application of the principle could not be delayed because of the need to implement the necessary legislation.[977]

A failure to facilitate gender reassignment surgery may in some circumstances contravene **12.292** Article 8. In *Van Kuck v Germany*[978] the Court held that the state's questioning of the necessity of gender reassignment for medical reasons without obtaining supplementary medical information contravened her Article 8 rights.[979] The Court held that, in not requiring a private health insurance company to pay for the applicant's surgery, the state had failed to strike a fair balance between the interests of the insurance company and the applicant's interests.[980] In *L v Lithuania*,[981] a gap in the national legislation meant that, though full gender reassignment was permissible and recognized, the surgical procedures were unregulated. As a result, though the applicant was able to undergo partial surgery, no available medical facilities could carry out the complete procedure. The Court held that there had been a breach of Article 8.[982]

(f) Personal autonomy and sexuality

Introduction. The notion of personal autonomy is an important principle underlying **12.293** the interpretation of Article 8.[983] Private life includes 'the ability to conduct one's life in a manner of one's own choosing': even including activities perceived to be physically or morally harmful.[984] The Court has said that:

> The right to maintain sexual relations derives from the right to do as one chooses with one's body which is an integral part of the notion of personal autonomy.[985]

---

[973] (2002) 35 EHRR 447.

[974] (2003) 36 EHRR 53.

[975] Thus overturning *Rees v United Kingdom* (1986) 9 EHRR 56, *Cossey v United Kingdom* (1990) 13 EHRR 622 and *Sheffield and Horsham v United Kingdom* (1998) 27 EHRR 163.

[976] *Goodwin* (n 973 above) paras 77 and 90; *I v UK* (n 974 above) paras 57 and 70. See para 13.128 below.

[977] *Grant v United Kingdom* (2007) 44 EHRR 1.

[978] (2003) 37 EHRR 51.

[979] Ibid, paras 78–80. The three dissenting judges held that transsexuals' Article 8 rights do not prevent courts from investigating whether reassignment surgery was medically necessary, even if that required a painful and intrusive analysis of the applicant's case history. Dissenting Opinion, paras 12 and 16.

[980] Ibid, para 86.

[981] (2008) 46 EHRR 23.

[982] Ibid, paras 57–60.

[983] *Pretty v United Kingdom* (2002) 35 EHRR 1, para 61.

[984] Ibid, para 62.

[985] *KA and AD v Belgium* Judgment of 17 February 2005, para 83.

The right to make decisions about sexuality and sexual activity is central to private life. The notion of autonomy has also been held to cover decisions are to the way in which life is lived (and ended) and about whether or not to start a family.

12.294 **Sexuality.**   Sexual activity and sexual orientation are important components of the personal domain protected by Article 8.[986] In *Dudgeon v United Kingdom*[987] the Court described sexual activity as 'a most intimate aspect of private life'. Interferences by the State with the area of sexuality require particularly serious reasons.[988]

12.295 It has been suggested that some aspects of private sexual conduct may not be protected by Article 8. In *Laskey, Jaggard and Brown v United Kingdom*[989] the Court expressed doubt as to whether sado-masochistic encounters between the applicants and 44 others involving, inter alia, the recruitment of new 'members', the provision of specially equipped chambers and the taking of video film fell entirely within the notion of private life. However, in *KA and AD v Belgium*[990] the Court dealt with charges relating to sado-masochistic practices and incitement to prostitution as falling within the protection of Article 8. The Court held that the applicants' convictions were not disproportionate, as the practices had continued after the victim had withdrawn consent, there had been an increasing degree of violence and the applicants themselves had admitted that they had not known where it would end.

12.296 Most of the cases in this area deal with homosexuality and are sometimes decided under Article 14 taken with Article 8. It is clear that adult, consenting homosexual activity is now universally accepted in Member states.[991] In *ADT v United Kingdom*[992] it was held that the criminalization of homosexual acts in private where more than two people were present was an interference with 'private life', and the Court rejected the Government's argument that because a number of individuals were present and the activities were videotaped the activities were not 'private'. In *Lustig-Prean v United Kingdom*[993] and *Smith v United Kingdom*,[994] the Court confirmed that only weighty and convincing evidence could justify interfering with private life by investigating and dismissing members of the armed forces on grounds of their homosexuality.[995]

---

[986] Ibid, para 78.

[987] (1981) 4 EHRR 149, para 52.

[988] *KA and AD* (n 985 above), para 84.

[989] (1997) 24 EHRR 39, para 36 (the Court nevertheless considered the case under Art 8 as its applicability was not disputed by the State).

[990] See n 985 above; see also *ADT v United Kingdom* (2001) 31 EHRR 33 (sexual activities between 5 consenting males in applicant's home which were video taped were 'private') also *Pay v United Kingdom* (2009) 48 EHRR SE2 (sado-masochistic acts shown in anonymized internet photos and performances in BDSM clubs, court prepared to assume Art 8 applicable).

[991] *Dudgeon v United Kingdom* (1981) 4 EHRR 149, para 52; consensual homosexual acts between adult men in private; also *Norris v Ireland* (1988) 13 EHRR 186; *Modinos v Cyprus* (1993) 16 EHRR 485.

[992] (2001) 31 EHRR 33.

[993] (1999) 29 EHRR 449.

[994] (1999) 29 EHRR 493.

[995] See also *Brown v United Kingdom* (Decision of 4 June 2002) and *Brown v United Kingdom (Friendly Settlement)* (Judgment of 29 July 2003).

The age of consent for homosexual relations was considered in *GL and AV v Austria*[996] and **12.297**
SL v Austria,[997] which concerned legislation providing that males over 19 years of age, who had a sexual relationship with another male aged between 14 and 18, committed a criminal offence and risked being imprisoned for between six months and five years. This offence was regularly prosecuted, with an average of 60 criminal proceedings being opened each year. The Court held that differences based on sexual orientation require particularly justi-fication, which the impugned legislation clearly lacked. The Court recognized an ever-growing European consensus to apply equal ages of consent for heterosexual, lesbian and homosexual relations,[998] and found that impugned law embodied a predisposed bias on the part of a heterosexual majority against a homosexual minority.[999]

Other cases.   Criminal penalties for assisted suicide which had the effect of preventing a   **12.298**
person suffering from exercising her choice to avoid an undignified and distressing end to her life are within the scope of Article 8.[1000] In *Evans v United Kingdom*,[1001] the applicant sought the implantation in her uterus of embryos which had previously been artificially fertilized with the sperm of her then partner. However, he had since withdrawn his consent for the continuation of the IVF treatment and the UK legislation prohibited ongoing IVF treatment in the absence of the consent of both parties. The applicant thereby lost her opportunity to conceive a child. The Grand Chamber held that the concept of private life encompasses the right to become—and not to become—a parent, including specifically a parent in the genetic sense.[1002] However, by a majority of 13 to 4, it was held that it was within the United Kingdom's margin of appreciation to adopt a clear and bright-line approach to the difficult balancing act between the competing rights.[1003]

(g) Self-development, relations with others, and reputation

Introduction.   The Court has consistently stated that the right to respect for private life   **12.299**
includes the 'right to establish and develop relationships with other human beings'.[1004] Article 8 protects a 'zone of interaction' of a person with others, even in a public context[1005] which is relatively narrow in the case of well known figures and wider for an 'ordinary person'.[1006] Private life embraces self-determination, maintenance of relationships with others and a settled and secure place in the community.[1007] As a result, it includes 'the totality

---

[996] (2003) 36 EHRR.
[997] (2003) 37 EHRR. There have been a number of subsequent cases against Austria, including *RH v Austria* (Judgment of 19 January 2006); *HG v Austria* (Judgment of 2 June 2005); *Wolfmeyer v Austria* (Judgment of 26 May 2005), which confirmed that Article 8 was breached even though the applicant was acquitted of the offence on the basis that it was unconstitutional.
[998] *GL and AV v Austria* (n 996 above) paras 49–50; *SL v Austria* (n 997 above) paras 41–42.
[999] *GL and AV v Austria* (n 996 above) para 52; *SL v Austria* (n 997 above) para 44.
[1000] *Pretty v United Kingdom* (2002) 35 EHRR 1, para 67 (the interference was held to be justified).
[1001] [2007] 1 FLR 1990.
[1002] Ibid, paras 71–72.
[1003] Ibid, para 89.
[1004] See eg, *X v Iceland* (1976) 5 DR 86, 97; *Niemietz v Germany* (1992) 16 EHRR 97, para 29.
[1005] *Von Hannover v Germany* (2005) 40 EHRR 1, para 50.
[1006] *Sciacca v Italy* (2006) 43 EHRR 20, para 29 (it is not narrowed when a person is subject to criminal proceedings).
[1007] See *Connors v United Kingdom* (2005) 40 EHRR 9, para 82.

of social ties' between a person and the community in which they are living.[1008] The limits of this 'social dimension' of Article 8 have not yet been fully worked out in the case law. Two specific areas have been considered: rights in relation to employment and the right to reputation.

12.300 **Employment.** The Convention does not contain any right to employment or right to work. However, a far-reaching ban on taking up private employment has been held to affect 'private life' because it affected the applicants' ability to develop relationships with the outside world to a very significant degree.[1009] Similar considerations applied where the applicants had been dismissed from their jobs because of employment restrictions.[1010]

12.301 **Reputation.** Although the Convention provides no express 'right to reputation'[1011] such a right has now been recognized in the case law as being an aspect of the right to respect for private life in Article 8.[1012] The Article 8 'right to protection of reputation' was combined with the positive obligations of the state in the application in *White v Sweden*.[1013] The applicant had brought criminal proceedings against newspapers which alleged that he had murdered the Swedish Prime Minister in 1986. The press were acquitted on the basis that the newspapers had had a reasonable basis for the published information. The applicant complained that his Article 8 rights had been breached, since the Swedish courts had failed to provide due protection for his name and reputation. The Court accepted that Article 8 was engaged and that as a result:

> The Court must therefore assess whether the domestic courts struck a fair balance between the two conflicting values guaranteed by the Convention, namely the protection of the applicant's reputation as part of his right to respect for his private life and the newspapers' freedom of expression. In that respect, it needs to be ascertained whether the courts applied standards which were in conformity with the principles embodied in arts 8 and 10 of the Convention.[1014]

The Court concluded that the domestic courts were, in the circumstances, justified in finding that the public interest in publishing the information in question outweighed the applicant's right to the protection of his reputation.

12.302 The Court found a violation of the positive obligation to protect reputation in *Pfeifer v Austria*.[1015] A professor committed suicide following the collapse of defamation proceedings

---

[1008] See *Üner v Netherlands* (2007) 45 EHRR 14 (GC), para 59.

[1009] *Sidabras and Džiautas v Lithuania* (2006) 42 EHRR 6, paras 47 to 48; *Albanese v Italy*, Judgment of 23 March 2006 (entry in bankruptcy register preventing applicants from carrying out professional or commercial activities) and see J-P Marguénaud and J Mouly, 'Le droit de gagner sa vie par le travail devant la Cour européenne des droits de l'homme', *Recueil Dalloz*, 16 February 2006, 477.

[1010] *Rainys and Gasparavičius v Lithuania*, Judgment of 7 April 2005.

[1011] Contrast, the International Covenant on Civil and Political Rights, which provides by Art 17(1) that 'No one shall be subjected to . . . unlawful attacks on his honour and reputation' and by Art 17(2) that 'Everyone has the right to the protection of the law against such interference or attacks'. As mentioned above, it was decided not to include this right in the Convention, see para 12.240 n 788 above.

[1012] See *Chauvy v France* (2005) 41 EHRR 610, para 70; *Cumpănă and Mazăre v Romania* (2005) 41 EHRR 200 para 91.

[1013] (2008) 46 EHRR 3.

[1014] Ibid, para 26.

[1015] Judgment of 15 November 2007; see also *Petrina v Roumania*, Judgment of 14 October 2008 (violation of Art 8 when domestic claim for defamation unsuccessful).

over an article, written by the applicant, which criticized the professor for alleging that the Jews had declared war on Germany in 1933 and trivializing the crimes of the Nazi regime. The applicant was accused, in a later publication, of having unleashed a manhunt which had led to the death of the professor and having been a member of a 'hunting society' which had chased him to his death. The applicant's defamation action in the Austrian Courts failed and he complained that Austria had failed in its positive obligation to protect his Article 8 right to reputation. The issue was whether the State, in the context of its positive obligations under Article 8, had achieved a fair balance between the applicant's right to protection of his reputation, as an element of his 'private life', and the other party's right to freedom of expression guaranteed by Article 10 of the Convention.[1016] The majority said the publication sued on claimed that the applicant had caused the professor's death by ultimately driving him to commit suicide. No proof had been offered for the alleged causal link between the applicant's article and the professor's death. The publishers had overstepped acceptable limits, because they accused the applicant of acts tantamount to criminal behaviour Even if the statements were value judgments, the Court held that they lacked sufficient factual basis. As a result, the Court was not convinced that the reasons advanced by the domestic courts for protecting freedom of expression outweighed the right of the applicant to have his reputation safeguarded. There had accordingly been a violation of Article 8.[1017]

(4) 'Home'

(a) Introduction

In addition to protecting 'private life', Article 8 requires respect for the home and correspondence. These concepts clearly overlap; and some actions, such as searches and seizures or monitoring of telephone conversations in the home, may constitute an interference with Article 8 rights in two or more senses. In *Miailhe v France*,[1018] for example, the Court found it unnecessary to examine whether the searches involved the 'home', as it was sufficient to base the interference on the 'private life' and 'correspondence' provisions. **12.303**

Article 8 creates a right of 'respect for the home'. In general, the failure to provide a home does not breach Article 8[1019] although, such a right may arise in some limited circumstances.[1020] Respect for 'home' involves more than the integrity of home life; what is at stake is the physical security of a person's living quarters and possessions.[1021] It includes the ability (facilitated by the state) to live freely in the home and to enjoy it, not merely as a property right.[1022] In *Buckley v United Kingdom*[1023] the Court rejected the argument that **12.304**

[1016] Ibid, para 38.

[1017] Ibid, paras 47–49.

[1018] (1993) 16 EHRR 332.

[1019] *X v Germany* (1956) 1 YB 202. *Burton v United Kingdom* (1996) 22 EHRR CD 135.

[1020] See *Marzari v Italy*, Decision of 4 May 1999 and see generally, para 12.256 above, note that there is no case to date in which it has been held that the State was, in fact, under an obligation to provide a home.

[1021] Ibid, *Gillow v United Kingdom* (1986) 11 EHRR 335; see also *Selcuk and Asker v Turkey* (1998) 26 EHRR 477 (burning the applicant's property constituted a grave and unjustified interference).

[1022] *Howard v United Kingdom* (1987) 52 DR 198, EComm HR.

[1023] (1996) 23 EHRR 101, paras 52–55; see also, for example, *Tuleshov v Russia* (Judgment of 24 May 2007), in which the applicants purchased a home which had already been bought by somebody else.

Article 8 only protected a home which was lawfully established; and went on to find that a gypsy who had continuously occupied land for five years without planning permission was nevertheless entitled to respect for the home.

(b) Scope of term 'home'

12.305 'Home' has been given a broad interpretation.[1024] In general, the term is taken to mean the place where a person lives on a settled basis.[1025] The Court has described a 'home' in these terms:

> the place, the physically defined area, where private and family life develops. The individual has a right to respect for his home, meaning not just the right to the actual physical area, but also to the quiet enjoyment of that area. Breaches of the right to respect for the home are not confined to concrete or physical breaches, such as unauthorized entry into a person's home, but also include those that are not concrete or physical, such as noise, emissions, smells or other forms of interference.[1026]

12.306 The concept of 'home' can include a holiday home,[1027] or a place of intended, rather than actual, residence.[1028] The 'home' of a professional person or private businessman also includes his business premises; this approach is consistent with the use of 'domicile' in the French text of the Convention.[1029] A search of a person's car will also engage Article 8.[1030] A person may have more than one 'home'.[1031] The concept of 'home' is not confined to a residence which is lawfully occupied. Thus a caravan being used on a particular plot of land in breach of planning laws has been held to be a 'home'.[1032]

12.307 The concept of a 'home' does not extend to premises in which an individual has not lived for ten years;[1033] nor does it extend to a home which is to be built in the future.[1034] Further, though premises occupied under a lease can plainly be a home, the fact that a Tenant's Union has power to negotiate the rent payable by an individual tenant is not an interference with his right to a home.[1035] Premises which are not used for private purposes may fall outside the Article 8 meaning of 'home'.[1036]

[1024] *Niemetz v Germany* (1992) 16 EHRR 97.

[1025] *Murray v United Kingdom* (1994) 19 EHRR 193, paras 84–96.

[1026] *Borysiewicz v Poland*, Judgment of 1 July 2008, para 48; *Giaconelli v Italy*, Judgment of 2 November 2006, para 76.

[1027] *Kanthak v Germany* (1988) 58 DR 94 (raises the question as to whether a camper van could be 'home').

[1028] *Gillow v United Kingdom* (1986) 11 EHRR 335; (the applicants had lived in several places around the world and had houses in England and Guernsey; the Court accepted that although they had been long absent from it, they had always intended to return to Guernsey and held that they had a right to re-establish home life in that particular house).

[1029] *Niemetz v Germany* (1992) 16 EHRR 97, para 30; *Wieser and Bicos Beteiligungen v Austria* (2008) 46 EHRR 54, para 43; *Buck v Germany* (2006) 42 EHRR 21, paras 31–32; *Société Colas v France* (2004) 39 EHRR 17 (competition warrant in relation to a company, violation of Art 8).

[1030] *Ernst v Belgium* (2004) 39 EHRR 35, para 110; *Steeg and Wenger v Germany* (2008) 47 EHRR SE 16, at 207.

[1031] *Demades v Turkey*, Judgment of 31 July 2003, para 33; *Fägerskiöld v Sweden*, Decision of 26 February 2008.

[1032] *Buckley v United Kingdom* (1996) 23 EHRR 101, para 24; *Turner v United Kingdom* (1997) 23 EHRR CD 181; *Chapman v United Kingdom* (2001) 33 EHRR 19 GC).

[1033] *Iordanou v Turkey* (Decision of 25 June 2002).

[1034] *Loizidou v Turkey* (1996) 23 EHRR 513, para 66.

[1035] *Langborger v Sweden* (1990) 12 EHRR 416.

[1036] *Pentidis v Greece* (1997) 24 EHRR CD 1, CD7 (room used for Jehovah's witnesses meetings).

(c) Interference with home

An interference with the home arises where there is a direct infringement (such as a forcible **12.308** search by executing a seizure order[1037] or searching of a lawyer's office[1038]) or where the home itself is threatened (by, for example, a compulsory purchase order).[1039] The protection of 'respect for home' implies a right of access and occupation,[1040] and a right not to be displaced or prevented from the physical possibility of returning to the home.[1041]

The right of access and occupation may be difficult to distinguish from the right to enjoy- **12.309** ment of property protected by Article 1 of Protocol 1, and certain government measures might interfere with both Article 8 and the Protocol. In *Cyprus and Turkey*,[1042] for example, the Grand Chamber found that the failure to allow Greek Cypriots to return to their homes in the north of Cyprus was a breach of Article 8. The taking and occupation of their houses and land by Cypriot and mainland Turks, both civilian and military, was also held to be a continuing violation of Article 1 of Protocol 1.[1043] Physical removal of persons from their homes and the taking, occupation or destruction of possessions[1044] might each be considered a violation of the Article 8 right to respect for the home; and, even if this is done by private individuals, the State may be implicated by connivance or inactivity and might have a positive obligation to investigate and assist by providing compensation or alternative accommodation.[1045] The Court has found breaches in several cases on the basis that the State has breached a positive obligation to provide adequate assistance to persons who have lost their homes, at least when that has been as a result of the actions of public authorities.[1046]

(d) Environment

Home and environment.   Damage to the environment, of itself, will not engage **12.310** Article 8—it must affect the applicant's home or private life.[1047] Blights on the environment[1048] such as noise,[1049] emissions[1050] or smells may interfere with the home if the individual is prevented from enjoying the amenities of his home.[1051] Severe environmental

---

[1037] *Chappell v United Kingdom* (1989) 12 EHRR 1; *Gutu v Moldova* (Judgment of 7 June 2007); *Smirnov v Russia* (Judgment of 7 June 2007).

[1038] *Niemetz v Germany* (n 1029 above); *Sallinen v Finland* (2007) 44 EHRR 18.

[1039] *Howard v United Kingdom* (1987) 52 DR 198, EComm HR.

[1040] *Wiggins v United Kingdom* (1978) 13 DR 40, EComm HR; *Gillow v United Kingdom* (1986) 11 EHRR 335.

[1041] *Cyprus v Turkey* (1976) 4 EHRR 482, 519–520, EComm HR; *Cyprus v Turkey* (1983) 72 DR 5, 41–43, EComm HR.

[1042] (2002) 35 EHRR 30, paras 172–175.

[1043] Ibid, para 188.

[1044] See also *Mentes v Turkey* (1997) 26 EHRR 595 where the homes of the applicants were burnt down.

[1045] *Moldovan v Romania* (Judgment of 12 July 2005).

[1046] See, for example. *Tulsehov v Russia* (Judgment of 24 May 2007), para 53; *Novotseletskiy v Ukraine* (2006) 43 EHRR 53.

[1047] *Kyratos v Greece* (2005) 40 EHRR 16, paras 51–53; *Hamer v Belgium,* Judgment of 27 November 2007, para 79.

[1048] See generally M McMereux, 'Deriving Environmental Rights from the European Convention on Human Rights and Fundamental Freedoms, (2001) 21 OJLS 521.

[1049] *Powell and Rayner v United Kingdom* (1990) 12 EHRR 355; *Hatton v United Kingdom* (2003) 37 EHRR 28; *Giacomelli v Italy* (2007) 45 EHRR 38.

[1050] *Guerra v Italy* (1998) 26 EHRR 375.

[1051] *Giacomelli,* (n 1049 above) para 76.

pollution may affect individuals' well-being and prevent them from enjoying their homes in such a way as would affect their private and family life adversely, without seriously endangering their health in any identifiable way.[1052] Article 8 may apply in such cases if the pollution is directly caused by the State and the State may also have a positive obligation to regulate private industry.[1053]

12.311 In *Powell and Rayner v United Kingdom*[1054] the Court rejected a complaint that the noise disturbance created by Heathrow Airport breached Article 8. It stressed that a fair balance had to be struck between the competing interests of the individual and the community as a whole; and held that the operation of a major international airport pursued a legitimate aim and that the steps taken by the Government to control, abate and compensate for airport noise did not exceed its margin of appreciation. A similar conclusion was reached by the Grand Chamber in *Hatton v United Kingdom*,[1055] a case about disturbance caused by night flights from Heathrow. Reversing the decision of the Chamber[1056] the Grand Chamber found that a fair balance had been struck between the United Kingdom's economic well-being and the applicants' effective enjoyment of their right to respect for their homes and their private and family lives.[1057] Similarly, levels of noise from wind turbines which were below World Health Organization recommendations were not so serious as to reach the high threshold established in cases dealing with environmental issues.[1058]

12.312 **Breaches in environmental cases.**   The Court has allowed a wide margin of appreciation in environmental cases, but has found breaches of Article 8 on a number of occasions. In *Lopez Ostra v Spain*[1059] the applicant complained about the failure of the local authority to use its powers to prevent a waste treatment plant releasing fumes and smells. The Court again stated that regard must be had to the fair balance to be struck between the competing interests of the individual and the community as a whole; and decided that Article 8 had been breached. In *Guerra v Italy*,[1060] the Court also ruled that a failure of the authorities to reduce the risk of pollution from a chemical factory violated Article 8. In *Fadeyeva v Russia*[1061] the Court recognized that environmental pollution was a matter of growing public concern, but still held that the Court's role was a 'subsidiary' one: provided that national authorities had adopted a fair decision-making process and had due regard to individual interests, the Court would interfere only in exceptional circumstances. However,

---

[1052] See *Lopez-Ostra v Spain* (1994) 20 EHRR 277; *Guerra v Italy* (n 1050 above); *Ledyayeva v Russia* (Judgment of 26 October 2006).

[1053] *Hatton v United Kingdom* (2003) 37 EHRR 28 para 98; *Giacomelli* (n 1049 above), para 78; see generally, para 12.259 above.

[1054] (1990) 12 EHRR 355; see also *Arrondelle v United Kingdom* (1982) 26 DR 5 (F Sett), EComm HR and *Baggs v United Kingdom* (1987) 52 DR 29, EComm HR.

[1055] (2003) 37 EHRR 28; see also *Ashworth v United Kingdom,* Decision of 20 January 2004.

[1056] (2002) 34 EHRR 1. See G Jones and J Pike, 'Proportionality and Planning: A Difficult and Nice Point' [2002] JPL 908.

[1057] For an evaluation of the Court's reasoning, see Jeremy Hyam, '*Hatton v United Kingdom* in the Grand Chamber: One Step Forward, Two Steps Back' [2003] EHRLR 631.

[1058] *Fägerskiöld v Sweden,* Decision of 26 February 2008.

[1059] (1994) 20 EHRR 277; and see generally, P Sands, 'Human Rights, Environment and the *Lopez-Ostra* Case' [1996] EHRLR 597.

[1060] (1998) 26 EHHR 375.

[1061] (2007) 45 EHRR 10, paras 104–105.

the Court did find a breach of Article 8 on the facts of the case: Russia had, for instance, failed to enforce its own protected zone around a steel plant, and had failed to offer the applicant any effective solution to enable her to move out of that zone.[1062] Breaches have also been found in cases where severe chemical pollution affected the well-being of the neighbouring population[1063] and where high noise levels from bars and discos caused health problems.[1064]

(5) 'Correspondence'

(a) Introduction

The right to respect for correspondence in Article 8 has mainly been considered in relation **12.313** to interference with postal delivery, search and seizures of written documents and the interception of telephone conversations. It is clear that the right to respect for correspondence also covers electronic documents.[1065]

(b) Postal correspondence

The cases concerning interference with correspondence have usually been brought by pris- **12.314** oners. Control over prisoners' correspondence is not of itself incompatible with the Convention.[1066] It is not clear whether this implies a threshold of permissible control that does not violate Article 8 or that some supervision of correspondence, while an interference, is justifiable under the second paragraph. It is suggested that the second is the preferable analysis.[1067] The nature and extent of the interference will be taken into account, but absent compliance with a clear and precise set of rules[1068] or a regime of control, any interference is unlikely to be in accordance with the law.

The Court has been particularly strict in controlling interference with legal correspond- **12.315** ence to and from prisoners. Preventing a prisoner from initiating correspondence with his solicitor was held to be the most far-reaching form of interference with the exercise of the right to respect for correspondence.[1069] In *Campbell v United Kingdom*[1070] correspondence between the applicant and his solicitor was opened and read in accordance with the Prison rules. The Court held in favour of the applicant who alleged that he was restricted from

---

[1062] Ibid, paras 132–134.
[1063] *Taşkin v Turkey* (2006) 42 EHRR 50 (sodium cyanide leeching from gold mine); see also *Giacomelli v Italy* (2007) 45 *EHRR* 38 (plant for treatment of hazardous waste).
[1064] *Moreno Gómez v Spain* (2005) 41 EHRR 40.
[1065] *Wieser and Bicos Beteiligungen v Austria* (2008) 46 EHRR 54, para 45.
[1066] See *Silver v United Kingdom* (1983) 5 EHRR 347; also *Boyle and Rice v United Kingdom* (1988) 10 EHRR 425: although the prisoner had previously benefited from a more liberal regime, he was nevertheless required to serve his time at his then current place of detention on the same terms and conditions as the other prisoners there.
[1067] See *De Wilde, Ooms and Versyp v Belgium (No 1)* (1971) 1 EHRR 373, in which supervision of correspondence 'to a certain extent' during detention was held unquestionably to constitute an 'interference by a public authority with the exercise of the right enshrined in para 1 of Article 8'; and see *Herczegfalvy v Austria* (1992) 15 EHRR 437.
[1068] See, for example, *Volokh v Ukraine* (Judgment of 2 November 2006), para 51; *Ostrovar v Moldova* (Judgment of 13 September 2005), paras 100–101. A failure to comply with an existing regime will also render an interference in breach of Article 8: see *Ciorap v Moldova* (Judgment of 19 June 2007).
[1069] *Golder v United Kingdom* (1975) 1 EHRR 524.
[1070] (1992) 15 EHRR 137.

communications with his solicitor 'because he knew his letters would be read'.[1071] Similarly, in *Campbell and Fell v United Kingdom*,[1072] in which only one letter from the adviser to the applicant was stopped, the 'prior ventilation rule' was found to amount to an interference with Article 8 because it, in effect, prevented all correspondence between the applicants and their advisers concerning proposed litigation until the internal inquiry in question had been completed. However, if there are compelling reasons to think that correspondence to or from a lawyer contains illicit disclosures, it may be checked, provided there are sufficient guarantees.[1073]

12.316 The Court takes an even stricter view of correspondence between individuals and the Convention organs or domestic courts. In several cases, it has suggested that opening, reading, stopping and/or censoring such correspondence can never be justified.[1074]

12.317 The Court has not been tolerant of blanket prohibitions,[1075] or indiscriminate checking, even in cases where prisoners have been convicted on charges involving serious dishonesty.[1076] In *McCallum v United Kingdom*[1077] the Court held that stopping letters, withholding copies of letters and a 28-day restriction on correspondence imposed by a prison disciplinary award violated Article 8. In *Puzinas v Lithuania*[1078] it was held that opening and censoring a prisoner's correspondence with his wife and international institutions was not justified and breached Article 8. The onus was on the authorities to show that they had discharged their obligation to deliver a prisoner's correspondence, and that provision by the state of a record of a prisoner's incoming mail was not sufficient proof that the items reached their destination.[1079]

12.318 The Court has found interference with respect for correspondence in a number of other situations:

- where 64 letters were stopped or delayed;[1080]
- where the investigating judge deleted certain passages from the applicant's letter;[1081] and
- where the authorities failed to forward the applicant's letter to the addressee.[1082]

12.319 However, the Court has permitted some targeted interference with correspondence. It was held to be legitimate to restrict the number of letters which a prisoner was permitted to send to two to three per week.[1083] Further, a restriction on receiving parcels or small packets

---

[1071] The Court rejected the Government's argument that the applicant had not made out his claim because he had not proved that a specific letter related to the pending proceedings had been opened.

[1072] (1984) 7 EHRR 165.

[1073] *Drozdowski v Poland* (Judgment of 6 December 2005), para 28.

[1074] See *AB v Netherlands* (2003) 37 EHRR 48; *Drozdowski v Poland* (n 1073 above); *Wasilewski v Poland* (2004) 38 EHRR 10; *Karalevicius v Lithuania* (Judgment of 7 July 2005); *Piuzinas (No 2) v Lithuania* (Judgment of 23 May 2007), para 33.

[1075] *AB v Netherlands* (2003) 27 EHRR 48.

[1076] *Jankauskas v Lithuania* (Judgment of 6 July 2005), para 22.

[1077] (1990) 13 EHRR 596.

[1078] Judgment of 14 March 2002.

[1079] *Messina v Italy* Series A No 257-H (1993).

[1080] *Silver v United Kingdom* (1983) 5 EHRR 347.

[1081] *Pfeifer and Plankl v Austria* (1992) 14 EHRR 692.

[1082] *Schönenberger and Durmaz v Switzerland* (1988) 11 EHRR 202; *Faulkner v United Kingdom* (2002) 35 EHRR 686.

[1083] *AB v Netherlands* (n 1075 above).

to one every six weeks, in order that the parcels could be checked by prison staff, was found to strike a proper balance between the interests of security and respect for the right of inmates to maintain contact with the outside world.[1084] In *Messina v Italy (No.2)*[1085] the Court found that the interferences with correspondence and family visits which had been placed on a prisoner charged and convicted of Mafia-style activities were proportionate. Further, in *Puzinas v Lithuania*,[1086] the Court held that, if the authorities impose a lawful system of screening letters, it is permissible to impose a proportionate penalty on prisoners for failing to comply with its rules: in that case, the prisoner was lawfully prohibited from receiving a package at his next personal visit.

(c) Searches and seizures

The Court has taken the view that house searches and seizures raise issues in connection **12.320** with all the rights secured in Article 8(1), with the exception of the right to respect for family life.[1087] Searches and seizures are not restricted to certain types of 'correspondence'.[1088] Where a warrant issued by a court ordered a search and seizure of 'documents' resulting in the examination of four cabinets containing client data and six individual files, the operations were found to be covered by 'correspondence' and the material was regarded as such for Article 8 purposes.[1089] Furthermore, correspondence does not have to be 'personal' in nature. In the leading case of *Niemietz v Germany*[1090] it was not suggested that Article 8 might be inapplicable on the ground that correspondence with a lawyer was of a professional nature.[1091] Electronic data is also protected.[1092]

(d) Telephone tapping

Although telephone conversations are not expressly mentioned in Article 8(1), the Court **12.321** has made it clear that they are covered by the notion of 'private life' and 'correspondence'.[1093] As a result the interception of telephone calls by State bodies constitutes an interference with Article 8 rights. The mere existence of legislation permitting surveillance constitutes an interference that:

> strikes at the freedom of communication between users of the . . . telecommunication services and . . . with the exercise of the applicants' right to respect for private and family life and correspondence.[1094]

[1084] *Dankevich v Ukraine* (2004) 38 EHRR 25, paras 163–166.
[1085] Judgment of 28 September 2000.
[1086] Judgment of 23 May 2007.
[1087] *Funke v France* (1993) 16 EHRR 297; *Crémieux v France* (1993) 16 EHRR 357; *Miailhe v France* (1993) 16 EHRR 332.
[1088] *Niemetz v Germany* (1992) 16 EHRR 97; *Buck v Germany* (2006) 42 EHRR 21.
[1089] Ibid.
[1090] (1992) 16 EHRR 97.
[1091] Ibid. See also *Tamosius v United Kingdom* (2002) 35 EHRR CD323; *Sallinen v Finland* (2007) 44 EHRR 18.
[1092] *Iliya Stefanov v Bulgaria* (Judgment of 22 May 2008), para 34.
[1093] Telephone conversations between family members are covered by both 'family life' and 'correspondence' under Art 8: *Andersson v Sweden* (1992) 14 EHRR 615; see also *Kopp v Switzerland* (1998) 27 EHRR 91 (telephone calls to and from business premises covered by 'private life' and 'correspondence'); *Lüdi v Switzerland* (1992) 15 EHRR 173 (interception of telephone calls was interference with 'private life' and 'correspondence').
[1094] *Klass v Germany* (1978) 2 EHRR 214.

In *Malone v United Kingdom*[1095] interception of only one call could be proved.[1096] Nevertheless, the Court found that, because the system established in England and Wales for the surveillance of communications itself amounted to an 'interference', it was unnecessary to inquire into the claims of the applicant that the interceptions had spanned a number of years.[1097] The broad approach taken by the Court was confirmed in *Halford v United Kingdom*,[1098] where it held that respect for correspondence extended to private telephone calls at work on a personal line.

12.322 In *Amann v Switzerland*[1099] the Grand Chamber held that the interception and recording of the applicant's telephone conversation by the Public Prosecutor's Office interfered with his right to private life and correspondence under Article 8. The consequent creation and storage of an index card in the name of the defendant were also both held to interfere with his right to private life. In *PG v United Kingdom*[1100] the Court held that telephone metering (ie obtaining information concerning the numbers called on a telephone) was an interference with Article 8.[1101] In *Greuter v Netherlands*[1102] a telephone tap of the partner of a suspect in a criminal investigation was found to be justified for the purpose of Article 8.

12.323 If public authorities are sufficiently involved in telephone tapping undertaken by private individuals, for instance by encouraging the surveillance or by providing or installing equipment, there will be an interference with Article 8 rights.[1103] The same principle applies to other aspects of Article 8.[1104] To permit otherwise would be tantamount to allowing investigating authorities to evade their Convention responsibilities by the use of private agents.[1105]

(6) Justification under Article 8(2)

(a) Introduction

12.324 Under Article 8(2) interference by a public authority must be justified as being in accordance with the law and necessary in a democratic society in support of one of the following legitimate aims:

- national security;
- public safety;

[1095] (1984) 7 EHRR 14.

[1096] The Government declined to disclose to what extent, if at all, the telephone calls of the applicant had been otherwise intercepted on behalf of the police.

[1097] See also *Huvig v France* (1990) 12 EHRR 528; which followed *Klass* and *Malone* in holding that telephone-tapping amounted to an 'interference by a public authority' with the exercise of the right to respect for 'correspondence' and 'private life'; *Kruslin v France* (1990) 12 EHRR 547: where a police wire-tap of a telephone line of one party resulted in the recording of several conversations of the applicant, leading to proceedings taken against him, the Government did not deny that there had been an 'interference'; and see *Valenzuela Contreras v Spain* (1998) 28 EHRR 483.

[1098] (1997) 24 EHRR 523, paras 53–58.

[1099] (2000) 30 EHRR 843 (GC).

[1100] (2008) 46 EHRR 51, paras 42–51.

[1101] The interference was justified under Art 8(2).

[1102] Decision of 19 March 2002.

[1103] See *MM v Netherlands* (2004) 39 EHRR 19; *Van Vondel v Netherlands* (2009) 48 EHRR 12.

[1104] see *Storck v Germany* (2006) 43 EHRR 96, para 146 (State responsible for treatment in private mental clinic because police brought the applicant back by force).

[1105] *MM v Netherlands* (n 1103 above), para 40.

- the economic well-being of the country;
- the prevention of disorder or crime;
- the protection of health or morals; and
- the protection of the rights and freedoms of others.

We will consider the nature of interference required under Article 8(1), the requirement **12.325** that interference be 'in accordance with law' and 'necessary in a democratic society'. We will then deal with the implied procedural protections and safeguards under Article 8. Finally, we will consider the case law on justification in relation to each of the 'legitimate aims' in Article 8(2).

(b) 'Interference by a public authority'

Introduction.   The first stage in an Article 8 claim is the establishment of an interfer- **12.326** ence.[1106] In many cases the question of whether a governmental act constitutes an interference is not contested by the state. The Court has therefore placed little emphasis on defining interference, focusing instead on its justification once it is determined that there is a protected right.

Government acts which have been found to constitute interference include 'supervision' of **12.327** correspondence,[1107] stopping, delaying or failing to forward letters to the applicant,[1108] impeding a person from even initiating correspondence,[1109] 'secret surveillance' measures[1110] including interception of telephone conversations,[1111] house searches and seizures,[1112] the imposition of a fine on the applicant for failing to obtain a licence to live in his own home,[1113] the generation of airport noise pollution[1114] and the storage and release of personal information on the applicant.[1115]

Threshold for interference.   The court has not attempted to define a 'minimum thresh- **12.328** old' for the engagement of Article 8. It has been said that, in the context of expulsion, that 'not every act or measure which adversely affects moral or physical integrity will interfere

---

[1106] *Campbell v United Kingdom* (1992) 15 EHRR 137 para 32; and see generally, para 6.213ff above.

[1107] *De Wilde, Ooms and Versyp v Belgium (No 1)* (1971) 1 EHRR 373.

[1108] *Silver v United Kingdom* (1983) 5 EHRR 347; *Campbell and Fell v United Kingdom* (1984) 7 EHRR 165; *Schönenberger and Durmaz v Switzerland* (1988) 11 EHRR 202; *McCallum v United Kingdom* (1990) 13 EHRR 596; *Herczegfalvy v Austria* (1992) 15 EHRR 437.

[1109] *Golder v United Kingdom* (1975) 1 EHRR 524.

[1110] *Klass v Germany* (1978) 2 EHRR 214.

[1111] *Malone v United Kingdom* (1984) 7 EHRR 14; *Huvig v France* (1990) 12 EHRR 528; *Kruslin v France* (1990) 12 EHRR 547; *Lüdi v Switzerland* (1992) 15 EHRR 173; *A v France* (1993) 17 EHRR 462.

[1112] *Funke v France* (1993) 16 EHRR 297; *Crémieux v France* (1993) 16 EHRR 297; *Miailhe v France* (1993) 16 EHRR 332; *Murray v United Kingdom* (1994) 19 EHRR 193; *Chappell v United Kingdom* (1989) 12 EHRR 1; *Niemetz v Germany* (1992) 16 EHRR 97.

[1113] *Gillow v United Kingdom* (1986) 11 EHRR 335.

[1114] In *Powell and Rayner v United Kingdom* (1990) 12 EHRR 355, the Court stated that the quality of the private life of the applicant and enjoyment of amenities of his home were 'adversely affected'; see also *Lopez Ostra v Spain* (1994) 20 EHRR 277.

[1115] *Leander v Sweden* (1987) 9 EHRR 433, where the storage and release of information was coupled with a refusal to allow the complainant to refute the information.

with the right to respect for private life'[1116] but these words do not state any general principle and it is submitted that state action resulting in 'adverse affect' will, ordinarily, be sufficient to engage Article 8. The position is different where the complaint is about 'inaction'.
Where a 'positive obligation' is relied on Article 'cannot be considered applicable each time
an individual's everyday life is disrupted'[1117] and additional factors must be identified to
justify the imposition of such an obligation.[1118]

12.329 **Failure to act.**   A failure to act will not constitute an interference with a negative obligation.[1119] Where the substance of the complaint is not that the state has acted, but has failed
or refused to act, it cannot normally be said to have 'interfered'.[1120] However, the position
is different where the 'respect' required by Article 8(1) compels the Member State to take
positive action: a failure then to take that action will be an 'interference' with the right to
respect which will require justification.[1121]

12.330 **Direct affect on applicant.**   An interference can sometimes be established even where
there are no measures directly affecting the complainant. In these circumstances a 'victim'
test has been employed: in other words, even when the alleged government acts cannot be
proved the Court might nevertheless make a finding of interference on grounds that the
existence of a legislative or administrative system may be sufficient in itself to constitute an
interference with the Article 8 rights of the applicant. In several different contexts, the
Court has held that a complainant may be victimized by an established system or legal
regime if it is one which facilitates infringement, and which *might* be applied to him,
whether or not an intrusion can be proven on the facts.[1122] The 'victim' test[1123] means that
the applicant need only establish a sufficient threat or risk to the effective enjoyment of his
rights, whether the potential impact is a material one or has only a psychological effect.

12.331 Thus, legislation which criminalized homosexual activity was found to be a 'continuing
interference' with private life, even though the risk of proceedings against consenting adult
male homosexuals was not great.[1124] The applicant had, however, been investigated and the
threat of prosecution was found not to be 'illusory or theoretical'. In this context it was held
that the legislation affected the private life of male homosexuals, including the applicant.
Similar reasoning was used by the Court in *Norris v Ireland*,[1125] although there had been no
criminal investigation into the homosexual activities of the applicant and in spite of arguments that the existence of the legislation posed no threat to his lifestyle.

[1116] *Bensaid v United Kingdom* (2001) 33 EHRR 205, para 46; see also *Nnyanzi v United Kingdom* (2008)
47 EHRR 18, para 73.

[1117] *Šečić v Croatia* Decision of 15 June 2006.

[1118] See the discussion at para 12.232 above.

[1119] See the discussion at para 6.100 above.

[1120] *Airey v Ireland* (1979) 2 EHRR 305.

[1121] See para 12.243ff above.

[1122] See para 22.42ff below.

[1123] For comment on this see P Duffy, 'The Protection of Privacy, Family Life and Other Rights Under
Article 8 of the European Convention on Human Rights' (1982) 2 YEL 191.

[1124] *Dudgeon v United Kingdom* (1981) 4 EHRR 149, para 40.

[1125] (1988) 13 EHRR 186, para 37.

In other areas of 'private life' and 'correspondence', a system which facilitates surreptitious **12.332** interception of telephone conversations has been found to create a 'menace of surveillance', even where applicants could not prove actual interception.[1126] The existence in England and Wales of laws and practices which permitted and established a system for effecting secret surveillance of communications amounted in itself to an 'interference', whether or not any measures were actually taken against the applicant.[1127] It was enough in the *Malone* case that the complainant, who was suspected of receiving stolen goods, was a member of a class of persons against whom measures of postal and telephone interception, were liable to be employed.

A similar approach has been taken where there was a general policy of supervision of corre- **12.333** spondence of prisoners,[1128] whether or not correspondence is actually interfered with. Although in *Campbell and Fell v United Kingdom*[1129] it was proved that one letter had been stopped, the Court noted that the effect of the established 'prior ventilation rule' was to prevent all correspondence between the applicants and their advisers concerning the proposed litigation until an internal inquiry had been completed.

(c) 'In accordance with the law'

Justification of an interference under Article 8(2) requires that the measures in question be **12.334** imposed 'in accordance with law'. The Court has identified a number of requirements as flowing from that phrase[1130] and these are examined in detail in Chapter 6.[1131]

First, the acts being challenged must have a basis in domestic law.[1132] Clearly 'in accordance **12.335** with law' refers to national law,[1133] which includes statute,[1134] other non-statutory enact-ments[1135] and common law,[1136] as the Court has interpreted 'law' in its substantive rather than its formal sense.[1137] It does not, however, merely refer to the existence of domestic law, but to the quality of the law, requiring it to be compatible with the rule of law, which is

---

[1126] *Klass v Germany* (1978) 2 EHRR 214.

[1127] *Malone v United Kingdom* (1984) 7 EHRR 14.

[1128] Supervision has been held to be 'unquestionably' an interference by a public authority with the exer-cise of Art 8 rights: *De Wilde, Ooms and Versyp v Belgium (No 1)* (1971) 1 EHRR 373; *Silver v United Kingdom* (1983) 5 EHRR 347 in which 64 letters were stopped or delayed.

[1129] (1984) 7 EHRR 165.

[1130] See *Olsson v Sweden (No 1)* (1988) 11 EHRR 259 in which the Court itemizes them.

[1131] See para 6.215ff above.

[1132] *Leander v Sweden* (1987) 9 EHRR 433 para 50; *Chappell v United Kingdom* (1989) 12 EHRR 1 para 52; *Margareta and Roger Andersson v Sweden* (1992) 14 EHRR 615; *A v France* (1993) 17 EHRR 462 para 38; *Murray v United Kingdom* (1994) 19 EHRR 193, para 88.

[1133] *Campbell and Fell v United Kingdom* (1984) 7 EHRR 165, para 37.

[1134] *Norris v Ireland* (n 1125 above) para 40: the interference was plainly 'in accordance with the law' since it arose from the very existence of the impugned legislation.

[1135] *De Wilde, Ooms and Versyp v Belgium (No 1)* (1971) 1 EHRR 373, para 93; *Golder v United Kingdom* (1975) 1 EHRR 524, para 45 (involving Prison Rules 1964).

[1136] See *Dudgeon v United Kingdom* (1981) 4 EHRR 149, para 44; *Kruslin v France* (1990) 12 EHRR 547, para 29; *Huvig v France* (1990) 12 EHRR 528, para 28; *Herczegfalvy v Austria* (1992) 15 EHRR 437, para 91: the provisions in question did not offer the minimum degree of protection against arbitrariness required by the rule of law and there was no case law to remedy the situation; *Murray v United Kingdom* , n 1132 above the taking and retention of a photograph of the applicant without her consent had no statutory basis but was lawful under the common law.

[1137] *Kruslin v France* (1990) 12 EHRR 547, para 29; *Huvig v France* (1990) 12 EHRR 258, para 28.

expressly mentioned in the preamble to the Convention.[1138] 'In accordance with law' thus implies that the interfering measures must be accompanied by adequate and effective safeguards in the domestic law to protect against arbitrary interferences by authorities with the rights guaranteed by Article 8(1).[1139] In light of the necessity of determining that measures are rooted in national law, the Court has reiterated on several occasions that its role is not to interpret and apply domestic law: this is primarily the task of the national courts.[1140] The role of the Court in reviewing compliance with domestic law is relatively limited.[1141]

12.336 Secondly, the law must be accessible and foreseeable. It must be accessible to the persons concerned, and formulated with sufficient precision to enable the citizen to foresee, to a reasonable degree, the consequences which a given action may entail.[1142] In determining whether this criterion has been met, the Court must take into account that absolute precision is unattainable and that, in order to avoid excessive rigidity and to keep pace with changing circumstances, many laws will inevitably be couched in terms which are to some extent vague.[1143] The degree of precision required of the 'law' will depend upon the particular subject matter.[1144] Thus, a prisoner who was unable to read unpublished regulations succeeded in establishing that the procedure was not in accordance with the law.[1145]

12.337 In the special context of secret surveillance,[1146] the Convention requirement of foreseeability cannot be exactly the same as it is where the law seeks to restrict the conduct of individuals. Foreseeability cannot mean that an individual should be able to foresee when the authorities are likely to intercept his communications so that he can adapt his conduct accordingly[1147] However, especially where the power is exercised in secret the risks of arbitrariness are evident:

> It is therefore essential to have clear, detailed rules on interception of telephone conversations, especially as the technology available for use is continually becoming more sophisticated. . .

[1138] *Malone v United Kingdom* (1984) 7 EHRR 14, para 67; *Silver v United Kingdom* (1983) 5 EHRR 347, para 90; *Golder v United Kingdom* (1975) 1 EHRR 524, para 34.

[1139] *Malone v United Kingdom* (n 1138 above) para 67; *Herczegfalvy v Austria* (1992) 15 EHRR 437, para 91; *Rieme v Sweden* (1992) 16 EHRR 155, para 60: (although a basis in Swedish law was undisputed, the applicant argued unsuccessfully that the law in question did not afford him adequate protection against arbitrary interference); *Chappell v United Kingdom* (1989) 12 EHRR 1, para 56 ('search orders' in United Kingdom law and their associated dangers which necessitate accompanying provisions safeguarding against arbitrary interference and abuse); see also *Eriksson v Sweden* (1989) 12 EHRR 183, para 60 and *Olsson v Sweden (No 1)* (1988) 11 EHRR 259, para 62 (safeguards in relation to taking children into public care: 'preparatory work' providing guidance as to the exercise of the discretion conferred, and administrative review at several levels).

[1140] *Olsson v Sweden (No 2)* (1992) 17 EHRR 134, para 79; *Andersson v Sweden* (1992) 14 EHRR 615, para 82; *Kruslin v France* (1990) 12 EHRR 547, para 29; *Eriksson v Sweden* (1989) 12 EHRR 183, para 62; *Chappell v United Kingdom* (1989) 12 EHRR 1, para 54; *Campbell v United Kingdom* (1992) 15 EHRR 137, para 37: it is not for the Court to examine the validity of secondary legislation.

[1141] *Eriksson v Sweden* (1989) 12 EHRR 183, para 62.

[1142] *Olsson v Sweden (No 1)* (n 1139 above) para 61.

[1143] *Silver v United Kingdom* (n 1138 above) para 88; *Olsson v Sweden (No 1)* (n 1139 above); see also *Sunday Times v United Kingdom (No 1)* (1979) 2 EHRR 245, para 49.

[1144] *Sunday Times v United Kingdom* (n 1143 above) para 49; *Malone v United Kingdom* (n 1138 above) para 67.

[1145] *Silver v United Kingdom* (n 1138 above); *Petra v Roumania*, Judgment of 23 September 1998.

[1146] *Malone v United Kingdom* (n 1138 above) para 79; *Hewitt and Harman v United Kingdom* (1989) 67 DR 88, 99, EComm HR; *N v United Kingdom* (1989) 67 DR 123, 132, EComm HR; *Kruslin v France* (1990) 12 EHRR 547, para 17; and see generally, para 6.228 above.

[1147] *Leander v Sweden* (1987) 9 EHRR 433, para 51.

The domestic law must be sufficiently clear in its terms to give citizens an adequate indication as to the circumstances in which and the conditions on which public authorities are empowered to resort to any such measures. . . . Moreover, since the implementation in practice of measures of secret surveillance of communications is not open to scrutiny by the individuals concerned or the public at large, it would be contrary to the rule of law for the legal discretion granted to the executive or to a judge to be expressed in terms of an unfettered power. Consequently, the law must indicate the scope of any such discretion conferred on the competent authorities and the manner of its exercise with sufficient clarity to give the individual adequate protection against arbitrary interference.[1148]

The following minimum safeguards, which should be set out in statute law to avoid abuses **12.338** of power, apply in secret surveillance cases:

- the nature of the offences which may give rise to an interception order;
- a definition of the categories of people liable to have their telephones tapped;
- a limit on the duration of telephone tapping;
- the procedure to be followed for examining, using and storing the data obtained;
- the precautions to be taken when communicating the data to other parties; and
- the circumstances in which recordings may or must be erased or the tapes destroyed.[1149]

These safeguards apply to both 'targeted' measures and generalized 'strategic monitoring'.[1150]

Thirdly, a law which confers a discretion is not in itself inconsistent with the requirement **12.339** of foreseeability, provided that the scope of the discretion and the manner of its exercise are indicated with sufficient clarity, having regard to the legitimate aim of the measure in question, to give the individual adequate protection against arbitrary interference.[1151] A related issue is the extent to which the necessary detail must itself be contained in the substantive law, as opposed to accompanying administrative practice and associated directives.[1152] This point was considered in the *Silver*[1153] case in which the Court stated that although the scope of the discretion must be indicated in the law, it is not necessary that the detailed procedures be contained in rules of substantive law. In that case administrative directives nonetheless constituted an established practice that was to be followed save in exceptional circumstances, rather than one that varied with each individual case. On the other hand, where the practice applied in a particular case conflicted with the administrative safeguards in place, the applicant succeeded in proving that the authorities had not acted in accordance with the law.[1154]

[1148] See *Weber and Saravia v Germany*, Decision of 29 June 2006, paras 93 and 94 (citations omitted), see also *Association for European Integration and Human Rights v Bulgaria*, Judgment of 28 June 2007, paras 75–76 and *Liberty v United Kingdom* (2009) 48 EHRR 1, para 62.

[1149] See *Weber and Saravia* (n 1148 above) para 95; *Liberty* (n 1148 above) para 62.

[1150] *Liberty* (n 1148 above) para 63.

[1151] *Malone v United Kingdom* (1984) 7 EHRR 14 para 67; *Gillow v United Kingdom* (1986) 11 EHRR 335, para 51; *Olsson v Sweden (No 1)* (1988) 11 EHRR 259, para 61; *Kruslin v France* (1990) 12 EHRR 547; *Andersson v Sweden* (1992) 14 EHRR 615; *Eriksson v Sweden* (1989) 12 EHRR 183, para 60.

[1152] *Malone v United Kingdom* (n 1151 above) para 68; *Silver v United Kingdom* (1983) 5 EHRR 347, paras 88–90.

[1153] n 1152 above.

[1154] *Kopp v Switzerland* (1998) 27 EHRR 91.

12.340 Following the decision in *Malone v United Kingdom*[1155] that there was no legal basis in the United Kingdom for the interception of telephone conversations,[1156] Parliament enacted the Interception of Communications Act 1985 which provided a statutory foundation for telephone-tapping which met the substantive as well as formal requirements of 'law'.[1157] This Act has since been replaced by the more comprehensive Regulation of Investigatory Powers Act 2000. Similarly, the Security Services Act of 1989 remedied the lack of foundation for secret surveillance indicated in *Hewitt and Harman v United Kingdom*.[1158] In France, the law that 'the investigating judge shall, in accordance with the law, take all investigative measures which he deems useful for establishing the truth',[1159] and case law to the effect that such measures included telephone-tapping did not provide sufficient safeguards against abuse of the power to render it in accordance with 'law' under Article 8. Furthermore, where a court rejected a complaint about illegal surveillance on the ground that the telephone line that was tapped belonged to a third party, the Court held there was a breach of Article 8.[1160] The law of telephone-tapping in Luxembourg, on the other hand, exhibited the necessary detail and provision for control of the use of the discretion so as to be in accordance with 'law.'[1161]

(d) 'Necessary in a democratic society' for a legitimate aim

12.341 The state must identify at least one of the 'legitimate aims' listed in Article 8(2) as a basis for its claim that its interference with privacy is necessary in a democratic society. The legitimate aims are similar to those set out in Articles 9 to 11 of the Convention, with the distinction that Article 8(2) permits interference in the interests of 'the economic well-being of the country'.[1162]

12.342 The Court has dealt with the meaning of the phrase 'necessary in a democratic society', the nature of the functions of the Court in the examination of issues turning on that phrase, and the manner in which it performs those functions on many occasions.[1163] The relevant principles are discussed in Chapter 6.[1164] The following general points can be made:

- The term 'necessary' is not synonymous with 'indispensable' but does not have the flexibility of such expressions as 'admissible', 'ordinary', 'useful', 'reasonable' or 'desirable'.[1165]

[1155] (1984) 7 EHRR 14.

[1156] Ibid, paras 69–80.

[1157] *Christie v United Kingdom* (1993) 78–A DR 119, 133, EComm HR: the Commission declared inadmissible an application claiming that the legislation was not sufficient protection against abuse of the power to issue warrants.

[1158] (1989) 67 DR 88: for comment see I Leigh and L Lustgarten (1989) 52 MLR 801. The enactment of the Intelligence Services Act 1994 provides further statutory foundation for secret surveillance procedures: for comment see J Wadham, 'The Intelligence Services Act 1994' (1994) 57 MLR 916.

[1159] Code of Criminal Procedure, Art 81.

[1160] *Lambert v France* (2000) 30 EHRR 346.

[1161] *Mersch v Luxembourg* (1985) 43 DR 34, 94, 114, EComm HR (the Commission acknowledged the presence of the ultimate safeguard: the Convention was directly applicable in Luxembourg law).

[1162] See generally, para 6.248 above.

[1163] See *Dudgeon v United Kingdom* (1981) 4 EHRR 149, paras 50–54, 60; *Silver v United Kingdom* (1983) 5 EHRR 347, paras 97–98.

[1164] See para 6.251ff above.

[1165] *Handyside v United Kingdom* (1976) 1 EHRR 737, para 48; cited in *Silver v United Kingdom* (1983) 5 EHRR 347, para 97; and see generally, para 6.68 above.

- 'Necessary in a democratic society', in the context of Article 8, as in connection with other Convention interests, requires the state to demonstrate that the interference corresponds to a 'pressing social need' and that it is 'proportionate' to the legitimate aim.[1166]
- It is for the authorities of Member States to make the initial assessment as to necessity: a certain margin of appreciation[1167] is left to them, subject to review by the Court.

The exceptions under Article 8(2) are to be interpreted narrowly and the need for them in **12.343** a given case must be convincingly established.[1168] There is no scope for implying limitations to Article 8.[1169] Furthermore, as the Court emphasized in *Dudgeon v United Kingdom*,[1170] where the restrictions concern a most intimate part of an individual's private life, there must be particularly serious reasons to satisfy the requirements of justifying Article 8(2). The detailed factual analysis which should be undertaken is illustrated in the cases of *Lustig-Prean v United Kingdom*[1171] and *Smith and Grady v United Kingdom*;[1172] in which the Government failed to show that the investigations into the applicants' sexual orientation (once they had confirmed their homosexuality) and subsequent dismissal were sufficiently convincing and weighty to comply with Article 8(2).

(e) Procedural requirements and safeguards under Article 8

Introduction. Although Article 8 contains no explicit procedural requirements, it has **12.344** long been established that there are 'implicit' procedural safeguards.[1173] The case law in relation to these safeguards was originally concerned with decisions impacting on the right to respect for family life[1174] but the implicit procedural protection extends all the rights protected by Article 8. As the Court said in *Tysiac v Poland*:[1175]

> the Convention is intended to guarantee not rights that are theoretical or illusory but rights that are practical and effective. . . .Whilst Article 8 contains no explicit procedural requirements,

---

[1166] *Handyside v United Kingdom* (1976) 1 EHRR 737, para 48; *Dudgeon v United Kingdom* (1981) 4 EHRR 149, para 51; *Silver v United Kingdom* (1983) 5 EHRR 347, para 97; *Gillow v United Kingdom* (1986) 11 EHRR 335, para 55; *Leander v Sweden* (1987) 9 EHRR 433, para 58; *Olsson v Sweden (No 1)* (1988) 11 EHRR 259, para 67; *Schönenberger and Durmaz v Switzerland* (1988) 11 EHRR 202, para 27; *Berrehab v Netherlands* (1988) 11 EHRR 322 para 28; *Moustaquim v Belgium* (1991) 13 EHRR 802, para 43 (as to family life); *Campbell v United Kingdom* (1992) 15 EHRR 137, paras 44, 53; *Beldjoudi v France* (1992) 14 EHRR 801, para 74; *A v United Kingdom* (2003) 36 EHRR 51, para 102 and see generally, para 6.67ff above.

[1167] See generally, para 6.42ff above.

[1168] See eg, *Klass v Germany* (1978) 2 EHRR 214, para 42; *Silver v United Kingdom* (1983) 5 EHRR 347, para 97; *Funke v France* (1993) 16 EHRR 297, para 55.

[1169] See *Golder v United Kingdom* (1975) 1 EHRR 524, para 44; and see para 6.204 above.

[1170] (1981) 4 EHRR 149, para 52.

[1171] (1999) 29 EHRR 449, paras 83–104.

[1172] (2000) 29 EHRR 493, paras 90–111.

[1173] See *Moser v Austria* [2006] 3 FCR 107, para 67; and see generally P van Dijk, F van Hoof, A van Rijn and L Zwaak, *Theory and Practice of the European Convention on Human Rights* (4th edn, Intersentia, 2006), 745–747.

[1174] See eg, *B v United Kingdom* (1988) 10 EHRR 87; *McMichael v United Kingdom* (1995) 20 EHRR 205, para 87.

[1175] (2007) 45 EHRR 42, para 13 (references omitted); see also *Buckley v United Kingdom*(1996) 23 EHHR 101, para 76 (case concerning planning permission for caravan); *Blečić v Croatia* (2004) 41 EHRR 185, para 68 (the Chamber judgment in a case concerning housing, the point was not dealt with in Grand Chamber which dismissed the application as incompatible *ratione temporis* with the provisions of the Convention); *Turek v Slovakia*, Judgment of 14 February 2006, para 113 (a case concerning personal information); *Shtukaturov v Russia*, Judgment of 27 March 2008, para 89 (a case concerning mental health).

it is important for the effective enjoyment of the rights guaranteed by this provision that the relevant decision-making process is fair and such as to afford due respect to the interests safeguarded by it. What has to be determined is whether, having regard to the particular circumstances of the case and notably the nature of the decisions to be taken, an individual has been involved in the decision-making process, seen as a whole, to a degree sufficient to provide her or him with the requisite protection of their interests.

The extent of the State's margin of appreciation depends on the quality of the decision making process.[1176]

12.345 **The nature of the safeguards.**   Where there is a direct interference with a 'core' Article 8 rights then the 'legislation and practice' must afford individuals 'adequate and effective safeguards against abuse'.[1177] This is of particular importance in cases of eviction,[1178] search and seizure and secret surveillance.[1179] If individuals are to be protected from arbitrary interference by the authorities with Article 8 rights, the reasons given to justify such measures must be 'relevant and sufficient' and there must be a legal framework and very strict limits on the powers it confers.[1180] We suggest that analogous safeguards should also be available when other serious interferences with Article 8 rights take place.

12.346 When the Court is concerned with a search it will consider:

- Whether it was based on a warrant issued by a judge and based on reasonable suspicion.
- Whether the scope of the warrant was reasonably limited.
- The impact on the work and reputation of the persons affected by the search.[1181]
- Where the search is of a lawyer's office, whether it was carried out in the presence of an independent observer in order to ensure that privileged material was not removed.[1182]

12.347 **Safeguards and communications with lawyers.**   In relation to the last point, it is clear that Article 8 protects confidential communications between lawyers and clients. In *Campbell v United Kingdom*[1183] the Court said that:

> It is clearly in the general interest that any person who wishes to consult a lawyer should be free to do so under conditions which favour full and inhibited discussion. It is for this reason that the lawyer-client relationship is, in principle, privileged.

[1176] *Shtukaturov v Russia* (n 1175 above) para 89; *Connors v United Kingdom* (2005) 40 EHRR 9 (GC), para 83.

[1177] See eg, *Funke v France* (1993) 16 EHRR 297, para 56; *Miailhe v France* (1993) 16 EHRR 332, para 37; *Crémieux v France* (1993) A 256-B, para 39; *Camenzind v Switzerland* (1998) 28 EHRR 458, para 45.

[1178] See *Connors v United Kingdom* (n 1176); *McCann v United Kingdom* (2008) 47 EHRR 40.

[1179] *Rotaru v Romania* (2000) 8 BHRC 449 (GC), paras 55 and 59.

[1180] *Camenzind* (n 1177 above) para 45.

[1181] Ibid, para 45; *Smirnov v Russia*, Judgment of 7 June 2007, para 44.

[1182] *Wieser and Bicos Beteiligungen v Austria* (2008) 46 EHRR 54, para 57 (violation because safeguards not observed in relation to electronic data); *Mancevschi v Moldova*, Judgment of 7 October 2008 (violation where warrant in broad terms and no safeguards for legal privilege).

[1183] (1992) 15 EHRR 137, 160, para 46.

In *Niemietz v Germany*[1184] in holding that a search of a lawyer's office was a breach of his Article 8 rights, the Court specifically relied on the fact that:

> where a lawyer is involved, an encroachment on professional secrecy may have repercussions on the proper administration of justice and hence on the rights guaranteed by Article 6 of the Convention.[1185]

However, Article 8 does not provide absolute protection for privileged material.[1186] In **12.348** *Foxley v United Kingdom*[1187] the Court recognized that if the privilege was being abused or there were other exceptional circumstances this might justify an interference with privileged communications. Nevertheless, searches which include privileged material must be subject to strong safeguards, including the presence of an independent observer.[1188] In a number of cases, warrants to search legal offices have been found to be accompanied by sufficient procedural safeguards.[1189]

Investigative Obligation. In some circumstances, Article 8 may give rise to an implied **12.349** investigative obligation at least in relation to criminal offences which seriously impact on an individual's physical integrity. Such an obligation has been held to arise in relation to the investigation of rape.[1190] An investigative obligation may also arise in relation to the actions of state agents or third parties which constitute serious violations of the right to respect for home.[1191]

(f) Justification in relation to particular 'legitimate aims'

National security and public safety. The justification of interferences which have as their **12.350** objective the protection of national security and public safety is usually straightforward. This is particularly true in the context of secret surveillance. While in most cases search and seizure will be carried out under criminal law procedures and require at least judicial authorization by warrant,[1192] where the state can show that there are 'exceptional conditions', surreptitious measures of surveillance will be justified. For example, sophisticated tech-

---

[1184] (1992) 16 EHRR 97.

[1185] Ibid, para 37.

[1186] See eg, *Sallinen v Finland* (2007) 44 EHRR 18 (the court considered whether such a seizure could be justified under Art 8(2), finding that it was not justified because not 'in accordance with law'); and see *B R v Germany* Decision of 23 October 1997 (warrant was limited to specific documents and, as a result, the obtaining of such documents, from a lawyer's office was justified under Article 8(2)).

[1187] (2001) 35 EHRR 637, para 44.

[1188] *Wieser and Bicos Beteiligungen v Austria* (n 1182 above) para 57; *Iliya Stefanov v Bulgaria,* Judgment of 22 May 2008, para 38.

[1189] *Botka and Paya v Austria,* Decision of 29 March 1993; *Tamosius v United Kingdom* (2002) 35 EHRR CD323.

[1190] *MC v Bulgaria* (2003) 15 BHRC 627, paras 152–153; see also *Baláž v Slovakia,* Decision of 28 November 2006 and *Szula v United Kingdom,* Decision of 4 January 2007.

[1191] See *Gergely v Roumania,* Decision of 9 December 2003 (in which a complaint as to a lack of effective investigation into the destruction of the applicant's home by communal violence was held to be admissible under Article 8—the case was later struck out of the list following a unilateral declaration by the government, Judgment of 26 April 2007).

[1192] See eg, *Funke v France* (1993) 16 EHRR 297, (lack of prior judicial authorisation was determinative in regard to a search of the applicant's house resulting in seizure of documents and collection of information as to his foreign assets); even a warrant may not be sufficient: see *Niemetz v Germany* (1992) 16 EHRR 97 (search for documents was found disproportionate to the aim of prevention of crime and protection of rights of others, even though a warrant had been procured.

niques of foreign espionage in *Klass v Germany*[1193] justified exceptional telephone tapping counteraction measures, and internal terrorist activity in *Leander v Sweden*[1194] amounted to a serious threat to national security which justified the collection of information and maintenance of secret files on candidates for sensitive employment positions. In *Segerstedt v Sweden*,[1195] although the Court held that 'powers of secret surveillance of citizens are tolerable under the Convention only in so far as strictly necessary for safeguarding democratic institutions',[1196] the Court appeared willing to defer to the judgments of the national courts as to the national security justification for refusing to disclose files held by the secret services.[1197]

12.351   **The economic well-being of the country.**   The unusual ground of the 'economic well-being of the country' has been found to justify a wide variety of government activities: a licensing scheme for the occupation of premises;[1198] immigration control policy;[1199] the operation of an international airport;[1200] the running of a polluting steel plant;[1201] customs investigation procedures;[1202] and disclosure of medical records for the purpose of assessing a social security claim.[1203]

12.352   In *Gillow v United Kingdom*,[1204] as a consequence of a change in the law the applicants, who had lost their 'residence qualifications' and were refused the required licence to live in their house in Guernsey, were convicted and fined for unlawful occupation of the premises. The Court held that it was legitimate for the authorities to try to maintain the population within limits that would permit the balanced economic development of the island. It was also legitimate for them to discriminate in the granting of licences in favour of persons who had strong attachments to the island, or who were engaged in an employment essential to the community. However, there was a breach in the application of the legislation of the facts.

12.353   The existence of large international airports, even in densely populated urban areas, and the increasing use of jet aircraft have also become necessary in the interests of a country's economic well-being. The Court in *Powell and Rayner*[1205] found that Heathrow Airport occupies a position of central importance in international trade and communications and in the economy of the United Kingdom. The applicants conceded that the Government had pursued a legitimate aim, and that the negative impact on the environment which resulted could not be entirely eliminated. Similarly, in deciding whether a scheme regulat-

---

[1193] (1978) 2 EHRR 214, para 56: the aim of the legislation for monitoring communications (the G10 Act) is to safeguard national security and/or prevent disorder or crime; see also *Weber and Saravia v Germany*, Decision of 29 June 2006 (new version of G10 act justified in the interests of national security and for the prevention of crime).

[1194] (1987) 9 EHRR 433, para 60.

[1195] (2007) 44 EHRR 2.

[1196] Ibid, para 88.

[1197] Ibid, paras 99–104; the Court did, however, hold that the retention of some old material on the applicants' activities was disproportionate (paras 90–91).

[1198] *Gillow v United Kingdom* (1986) 11 EHRR 335.

[1199] *Berrehab v Netherlands* (1988) 11 EHRR 322.

[1200] *Powell and Rayner v United Kingdom* (1990) 12 EHRR 355.

[1201] *Fadeyeva v Russia* (2007) 45 EHRR 10, paras 98–100.

[1202] *Funke v France* (1993) 16 EHRR 297.

[1203] *MS v Sweden* (1999) 28 EHRR 313.

[1204] (1986) 11 EHRR 335.

[1205] *Powell and Rayner v United Kingdom* (1990) 12 EHRR 355.

ing night flights from Heathrow was justified, the Grand Chamber in *Hatton v United Kingdom*[1206] accepted that the government was safeguarding an important economic interest,[1207] and that a system based on noise quotas struck the right balance between the interests of those living close to Heathrow and the economic importance of night flights.

Customs investigations leading to seizure of information about assets abroad and documents concerning foreign bank accounts in connection with customs offences under French law, though 'perhaps also for the prevention of crime' as held by the Commission, were primarily in the interests of the economic well-being of the country.[1208]   **12.354**

In *MS v Sweden*[1209] the applicant had injured her back in an accident while at work. When, a number of years later, she made a claim for compensation under the Industrial Injury Insurance Act, it was discovered that copies of her confidential medical records had been submitted by the clinic to the Social Insurance Office, in breach of professional secrecy contrary to the Secrecy Act 1980. The Court decided that the interference was justified as all the information disclosed was necessary and relevant for the determination of the applicant's claim for compensation; and it was necessary for the economic well-being of the country to ensure that public funds were only allocated to deserving claimants.   **12.355**

For the prevention of disorder or crime.   Measures interfering with Article 8(1) rights which have been found to be for the legitimate aim of the prevention of disorder and crime include the supervision of prisoners' correspondence[1210] telephone interception and other forms of secret surveillance,[1211] immigration control policy,[1212] medical examinations[1213] and searches for and seizure of documents and other physical evidence in connection with alleged offences.   **12.356**

When considering whether searches and seizures for the prevention of disorder and crime are necessary, the Court will look at the seriousness of the interference, the nature of the crime involved and the presence or absence of judicial warrant. But judicial authority will not necessarily be enough. The search of the office of a lawyer who was accused of insulting and imposing pressure on a judge was found to be disproportionate to its aim[1214] on grounds that the warrant was a broadly framed order for seizure of 'documents' without limitation, and unduly infringed professional secrecy.[1215]   **12.357**

In *Funke v France*[1216] the Court agreed that measures including house searches and seizures (which 'might' be for the prevention of crime but were undoubtedly in the interests of the   **12.358**

[1206] Ibid, paras 127–129.

[1207] (2003) 37 EHRR 28, para 126.

[1208] *Funke v France* (1993) 16 EHRR 297; also *Crémieux v France* (1993) 16 EHRR 357; and *Miailhe v France* (1993) 16 EHRR 332.

[1209] n 1203 above.

[1210] *De Wilde, Ooms and Versyp v Belgium (No 1)* (1971) 1 EHRR 373; *Schönenberger and Durmaz v Switzerland* (1988) 11 EHRR 202; *Pfeifer and Plankl v Austria* (1992) 14 EHRR 692; *Campbell v United Kingdom* (1992) 15 EHRR 137.

[1211] *Lüdi v Switzerland* (1992) 15 EHRR 173; *Klass v Germany* (1978) 2 EHRR 214.

[1212] *Beldjoudi v France* (1992) 14 EHRR 801.

[1213] *Junkhe v Turkey* (Judgment of 22 May 2008), at least in principle: paras 72 and 81.

[1214] *Niemietz v Germany* (1992) 16 EHRR 97; (the interference pursued aims that were legitimate under Art 8(2), namely the prevention of crime and protection of the rights of others, that is the honour of the judge).

[1215] See *Stefanov v Bulgaria* (Judgment of 22 May 2008).

[1216] (1993) 16 EHRR 297; *Miailhe v France* (1993) 16 EHRR 332; *Crémieux v France* (1993) A 256-B.

economic well-being of the country) were necessary in order to obtain physical evidence of exchange-control offences and to prevent outflow of capital and tax evasion, but nevertheless held that the legislation did not provide adequate safeguards against abuse of the wide powers available to customs authorities. The Court also emphasized that in the absence of the requirement of a judicial warrant, conditions and restrictions on the law were too lax to ensure that interferences with the rights of the applicant were proportionate to the aim pursued.[1217] In *McLeod v United Kingdom*[1218] the entry of police officers into the applicant's home to prevent a breach of the peace was disproportionate to the legitimate aim of the prevention of disorder.

12.359   On the other hand, in *Camenzind v Switzerland*[1219] the specific procedures in place and the limited scope of the search were a proportionate interference with the right of respect for the home. Similarly, in *Murray v United Kingdom*[1220] entry and search of the Murray family home by military authorities in Northern Ireland was not disproportionate to the aim of arresting Mrs Murray, who was reasonably suspected of terrorist-linked crime. The Court noted that special precautions were justified as a means to that end, given the 'conditions of extreme tension' under which such arrests in Northern Ireland had to be carried out.

12.360   The significance of the particular applicant's interest emerges clearly from the cases involving interference with prisoners' correspondence. Although some measure of control of prisoners' correspondence is not incompatible with the Convention,[1221] the Court has given high priority in this context to protecting the right of prisoners to communicate with their legal advisers. In *Golder v United Kingdom*[1222] the Court rejected the Government's argument that a refusal of the authorities to transmit a letter from prisoner to solicitor regarding the prospect of action against a prison official was necessary to prevent disorder. In *Campbell v United Kingdom*[1223] the introduction of Standing Orders for English and Scottish prisons which allowed the opening and reading of letters regarding prospective legal proceedings, but not those already in progress, was held to infringe Article 8. As no useful distinction could be made between instituted and contemplated proceedings and the privilege attached to all such letters was upheld, requiring that the government show reasonable cause for suspecting that the correspondence contains illicit material before opening it. The Court has held that there can be no justification for screening letters to and from the Strasbourg institutions or the domestic courts.[1224]

12.361   Correspondence in general does not require the same degree of confidentiality as lawyer-client or litigation-related communications, but powers of supervision, interception and scrutiny must not be exercised under general terms which would expose the contents of

---

[1217] See also *Crémieux v France* (n 1216 above); and *Miailhe v France* (n 1216 above).

[1218] (1998) 27 EHRR 493; for the domestic decision see *McLeod v Commissioner of Police of the Metropolis* [1994] 4 All ER 553.

[1219] (1998) 28 EHRR 458, paras 45–47.

[1220] (1994) 19 EHRR 193.

[1221] See eg, *Pfeifer and Plankl v Austria* (1992) 14 EHRR 692, para 46.

[1222] (1975) 1 EHRR 524, para 45.

[1223] (1992) 15 EHRR 137; see also *Foxley v United Kingdom* (2001) 31 EHRR 25 (letters from a bankrupt to his legal advisers).

[1224] *AB v Netherlands* (2003) 37; EHRR 48; *Drozdowski v Poland* (Judgment of 6 December 2005); *Wasilewski v Poland* (Judgment of 6 December 2005); *Karalevicius v Lithuania* (Judgment of 7 July 2005); *Piuzinas (No 2) v Lithuania* (Judgment of 23 May 2007), para 33.

unobjectionable letters, but must relate to some specific objection.[1225] However, in *Schönen-berger and Durmaz v Switzerland*[1226] the Court accepted that preventing disorder or crime may justify wider measures of interference for convicted prisoners than individuals who are at liberty. Nevertheless, measures such as stopping letters which hold the prison authorities up to contempt, or deleting passages of private letters may be disproportionate to the aim of ensuring the protection of the rights of others or the prevention of crime.[1227] Telephone surveillance measures have been justified on grounds of prevention of disorder and crime as well as national security. The tapping of a telephone can be necessary for the prevention of crime, and lawful, even if the telephone is that of the partner of a suspect rather than the suspect himself.[1228]

The prevention of crime can justify the disclosure of confidential information. In *Z v Finland*[1229] **12.362** the Court considered the balance between the confidentiality of information about a person's HIV infection against the interests of the public in investigating and prosecuting crime and having public court proceedings; and stressed that interference with Article 8 could only be justified by an overriding requirement of the public interest. The seizure and use of the applicant's medical records and an order requiring her medical advisers to give evidence were justified but the decision to make transcripts of the trial public after a 10 year period and the disclosure of the applicant's name were not supported by sufficient reasons and were, therefore, violations of Article 8. A police power to retain fingerprints, DNA samples, and cellular samples of suspected but unconvicted persons had the legitimate aim of the prevention of crime. However, the power was blanket and indiscriminate and did not strike a fair balance between the competing public and private interests with the result that there was a breach of Article 8.[1229a]

For the protection of health or morals. Interferences justified on grounds of the protection **12.363** of health alone usually involve the taking of children into care by public authorities[1230] and impact not on private life, home or correspondence but on family life.[1231] However, the protection of health can arise in private life cases. The Court has held, for instance, that a ban on assisting suicide, which interfered with the right to personal integrity and autonomy, was justified as it protected the life and health of others, in particular of those who might not be able to make informed decisions about ending their life.[1232] It has also held that, where a parent refuses to consent to medical treatment for a child, the court may authorize the treatment.[1233]

The 'protection of morals and of the rights and freedoms of others'[1234] or the 'protection of **12.364** health and morals'[1235] have also been claimed as the basis for interference with prisoners'

[1225] See *De Wilde, Ooms and Versyp v Belgium (No 1)* (1971) 1 EHRR 373; *Jankauskas v Lithuania* (Judgment of 6 July 2005).

[1226] (1988) 11 EHRR 202.

[1227] *Pfeifer and Plankl v Austria* (1992) 14 EHRR 692.

[1228] *Greuter v Netherlands* (Decision of 19 March 2002) (claim inadmissible).

[1229] (1997) 25 EHRR 371.

[1229a] *S and Marper v United Kingdom*, Judgment of 4 December 2008 (GC), paras 87 to 126.

[1230] See *W v United Kingdom* (1987) 10 EHRR 29; *B v United Kingdom* (1987) 10 EHRR 87; *R v United Kingdom* (1987) 10 EHRR 74.

[1231] See para 13.169ff below.

[1232] *Pretty v United Kingdom* (2002) 35 EHRR 1.

[1233] *Glass v United Kingdom* (2004) 39 EHRR 15.

[1234] *Silver v United Kingdom* (1983) 5 EHRR 347.

[1235] *De Wilde, Ooms and Versyp v Belgium (No 1)* (n 1225 above).

correspondence; and the 'protection of morals' alone has been asserted most often in conjunction with restrictions on sexual activity. This is an area in which the Court has required particularly substantial and current reasons to justify the interference. So, for example, the existence of legislation criminalizing homosexuality in Northern Ireland dating back to 1861 and 1885[1236] nevertheless contravened the Article 8 rights of the applicant to his private life.[1237] The decision of the Court was taken in the face of a contrary assessment by the United Kingdom and wide support for the existing position in Northern Ireland; it relied instead on the developing European consensus towards eliminating criminal sanctions and the absence of evidence to show that the failure of Northern Ireland authorities to implement the law had reduced moral standards. The Court affirmed the qualities of broadmindedness and tolerance as features of a democratic society and held that the shock factor of homosexual practices was not sufficient justification for criminalizing them.[1238]

12.365 **For the protection of the rights and freedoms of others.** The protection of rights and freedoms of others is generally coupled with other bases for justification under Article 8(2) and has most often been cited in connection with cases involving 'family'[1239] rather than 'private' life. However, the rights of others under Article 10 in particular are often relied on in cases involving publication of private information by the media and other bodies.[1240] In the *Vagrancy* case[1241] the aim of restrictions in connection with the supervision of prisoners' correspondence was not discussed or questioned before the Court, but the Commission had considered whether each interference was necessary for one of the purposes pleaded by the Government: protection of morals or protection of the rights and freedoms of others.

12.366 In other contexts, the protection of the 'honour' of a judge, coupled with prevention of crime, was not sufficient justification for a blanket warrant to search a lawyer's office for 'documents'.[1242] A search of the home of a video dealer being sued in breach of copyright was, however, justified as a legitimate means of protecting the rights of others in that it served to defend the plaintiffs' copyright against unauthorized infringement.[1243] The proceedings were civil and a seizure order (formerly an *Anton Piller* order) was employed in order to keep the evidence from 'disappearing'; even though the invasion of privacy was 'disturbing, unfortunate and regrettable' the order was not disproportionate to that end.[1244]

[1236] The scope of the legislation had been restricted in England, Scotland, and Wales, but remained unchanged in Northern Ireland.

[1237] *Dudgeon v United Kingdom* (1981) 4 EHRR 149.

[1238] *Norris v Ireland* (1988) 13 EHRR 186.

[1239] *W v United Kingdom* (1987) 10 EHRR 29; *B v United Kingdom* (1987) 10 EHRR 87; *R v United Kingdom* (1987) 10 EHRR 74; *Olsson v Sweden (No 1)* (1988) 11 EHRR 259 (decision to take children into care had legitimate aims of protecting health and morals and protecting the rights and freedoms of others); see also *Olsson v Sweden (No 2)* (1992) 17 EHRR 134; *Andersson v Sweden* (1992) 14 EHRR 615; *Keegan v Ireland* (1994) 18 EHRR 342; *Hokkanen v Finland* (1994) 19 EHRR 139; *Eriksson v Sweden* (1989) 12 EHRR 183 (legitimate aim of protecting the health and rights of the child).

[1240] See, for example, *Von Hannover v Germany* (2005) 40 EHRR 1; *Schussel v Austria* (Decision of 21 February 2002).

[1241] *De Wilde, Ooms and Versyp v Belgium (No 1)* (1971) 1 EHRR 373.

[1242] *Niemetz v Germany* (1992) 16 EHRR 97.

[1243] *Chappell v United Kingdom* (1989) 12 EHRR 1.

[1244] Ibid, paras 65–66.

The retention and use of personal information collected about an individual may require justi-   **12.367**
fication separate and apart from that of the collection itself. If information is used for a purpose
other than that for which it was legitimately collected, this may constitute an interference. For
example, in *TV v Finland*[1245] the fact that a prisoner was HIV-positive was disclosed to prison
staff directly involved in his custody; they were themselves subject to rules of confidentiality
and the disclosure of the information was found to be justified in 'the interests of others'.

The Court has also held that steps taken to safeguard the environment can be relied upon   **12.368**
as protecting the rights and freedoms of others. In *Chapman v United Kingdom*,[1246] the
Court held that the eviction of gypsies from land occupied by them in breach of planning
decisions pursued the legitimate aim of protecting the rights of others through preserving
the environment. The planning inspectors had identified strong environmental factors
relating to the applicants' use of land which outweighed their individual interest. In the
circumstances, the enforcement proceedings were proportionate. In *Connors v United
Kingdom*,[1247] however, the Court held that the summary eviction of a family of gypsies
from a local authority site did not fall within the margin of appreciation afforded states in
determining whether the action was necessary for the prevention of anti-social behaviour.
Under the summary proceedings, the local authority was not required to establish any substantive justification for evicting the applicant, and judicial review did not provide any
opportunity for an examination of the facts in dispute. As a result, the essential procedural
safeguards necessary to make the interference proportionate were found to be lacking.[1248]

A possession order against a tenant will serve the legitimate aim of protecting the rights and   **12.369**
freedoms of the landlord. However, in order for the interference of an eviction to be 'necessary in a democratic society' the tenant must have the opportunity to have the proportionality of the measure determined by an independent tribunal in the light of Article 8.[1249] The
fact that, as a matter of domestic property law, the tenancy has come to an end is not decisive: proportionality must still be examined.[1250] As a result, in *McCann v United Kingdom*[1251]
the fact that the possession order could not be resisted on 'proportionality' grounds meant
that there was a violation of Article 8.

Appendix 1: United Kingdom Cases under Article 8

(1) Introduction

A large number of United Kingdom applications based on Article 8 have come before the   **12.370**
Commission and the Court. The United Kingdom has been found to have violated the

---

[1245] (1994) 76A DR 140, EComm HR.
[1246] (2001) 33 EHRR 18.
[1247] (2005) 40 EHRR 9.
[1248] Ibid, paras 93–95.
[1249] *McCann v United Kingdom* (2008) 47 EHRR 40, para 50.
[1250] See *Connors v United Kingdom* (n 1247 above) and *Blečić v Croatia* (2004) 41 EHRR 185 (the
Chamber judgment, the point was not dealt with in Grand Chamber which dismissed the application as
incompatible *ratione temporis* with the provisions of the Convention).
[1251] See n 1249 above, for discussion of this case by the English courts see para 12.192 above.

right to respect for private life, home and correspondence on 45 occasions to date.[1252] A substantial proportion of the Article 8 cases against the United Kingdom have fallen under three general heads: prisoners' privacy rights, surveillance and telephone tapping, and complaints concerning privacy and sexual relationships. However, several other important issues have also been considered.

(2) Prisoners' rights

(a) Correspondence

12.371 A number of important cases have considered the right of prisoners to respect for their correspondence. In *Golder v United Kingdom*[1253] the letters of the applicant to his MP were stopped and he was refused permission to consult a solicitor. The Court held that these constituted the most far-reaching interference with the applicant's right to respect for correspondence. In *Silver v United Kingdom*[1254] the applicants complained of letters being stopped because of a 'prior ventilation' rule and the Court found that the majority of them had not been legitimately stopped.[1255] The case of *Campbell v United Kingdom*[1256] concerned the regular opening and screening of a prisoner's letters to his solicitor. This was again held to be an unjustified interference with his Article 8 rights. However, a prisoner's right to respect for his correspondence can be legitimately restricted in accordance with Article 8(2) in appropriate circumstances. Thus, the practices of reading prisoners' letters[1257] and restricting the numbers of letters which prisoners may send[1258] have been upheld.

[1252] *Golder v United Kingdom* (1975) 1 EHRR 524; *Dudgeon v United Kingdom* (1981) 4 EHRR 149; *Silver v United Kingdom* (1983) 5 EHRR 347; *Campbell and Fell v United Kingdom* (1984) 7 EHRR 165; *Malone v United Kingdom* (1984) 7 EHRR 14; *Gillow v United Kingdom* (1986) 11 EHRR 335; *Boyle and Rice v United Kingdom* (1988) 10 EHRR 425; *Gaskin v United Kingdom* (1989) 12 EHRR 36; *McCallum v United Kingdom* (1990) 13 EHRR 596; *Campbell v United Kingdom* (1992) 15 EHRR 137; *Halford v United Kingdom* (1997) 24 EHRR 523; *McLeod v United Kingdom* (1998) 27 EHRR 493; *Lustig-Prean v United Kingdom* (1999) 29 EHRR 449; *Smith and Grady v United Kingdom* (2000) 29 EHRR 493; *Khan v United Kingdom* (2001) 31 EHRR 45; *Foxley v United Kingdom* (2001) 31 EHRR 25; *ADT v United Kingdom* (2001) 31 EHRR 33; *Goodwin v United Kingdom* (2002) 35 EHRR 447; *I v United Kingdom* (2003) 36 EHRR 53; *Faulkner v United Kingdom* (2002) 35 EHRR 686; *PG v United Kingdom* (2008) 46 EHRR 51; *Taylor-Sabori v United Kingdom* (2003) 36 EHRR 17; *Beck, Copp and Bazeley v United Kingdom* (Judgment of 22 October 2002); *Perkins and R v United Kingdom* (Judgment of 22 October 2002); *MG v United Kingdom* (2003) 36 EHRR 3; *Allan v United Kingdom* (2003) 36 EHRR 12; *Armstrong v United Kingdom* (2003) 36 EHRR 30; *Peck v United Kingdom* (2003) 36 EHRR 41; *Chalkley v United Kingdom* (2003) 37 EHRR 30; *Hewitson v United Kingdom* (2003) 37 EHRR 31; *Perry v United Kingdom* (2004) 39 EHRR 3; *Glass v United Kingdom* (2004) 39 EHRR 15; *Wood v United Kingdom* (Judgment of 16 November 2004); *Lewis v United Kingdom* (2004) 39 EHRR 9; *Connors v United Kingdom* (2005) 40 EHRR 9; *Roche v United Kingdom* (2006) 42 EHRR 30; *Wainwright v United Kingdom* (2007) 44 EHRR 40; *Grant v United Kingdom* (2007) 44 EHRR 1; *Keegan v United Kingdom* (2007) 44 EHRR 33; *Elahi v United Kingdom* (2007) 44 EHRR 30; *Copland v United Kingdom* (2007) 45 EHRR 37; *Dickson v United Kingdom* (2008) 46 EHRR 41 (GC); *McCann v United Kingdom* (2008) 47 EHRR 40; and *Liberty v United Kingdom* (2009) 48 EHRR 1; *S and Marper v United Kingdom*; Judgment of 4 December 2008 (GC).

[1253] (1975) 1 EHRR 524.

[1254] (1983) 5 EHRR 347; and see also *McCallum v United Kingdom* (1990) 13 EHRR 596.

[1255] See also *Campbell and Fell v United Kingdom* (1984) 7 EHRR 165; and *Faulkner v United Kingdom* (2002) 35 EHRR 686 (letter stopped without explanation).

[1256] (1992) 15 EHRR 137.

[1257] *Boyle and Rice v United Kingdom* (1988) 10 EHRR 425.

[1258] See *Chester v United Kingdom* (1990) 60 DR 65.

(b) Other Article 8 prisoner cases

In *Galloway v United Kingdom*[1259] the Commission rejected a complaint that mandatory **12.372** drug tests in prisons breached Article 8. A failure to introduce needle exchange programmes in prison was not a breach of the Article 8 rights of a prisoner who was an intravenous drug user.[1260] An order in the course of a drug search that a prisoner remove an item inserted in his anus was justified under Article 8.[1261] The Court was prepared to assume that the transfer of a prisoner from a hospital back to prison was within the scope of Article 8 but held that it was a justified interference.[1262]

In *Dickson v United Kingdom*[1263] the Grand Chamber found a violation in respect of the **12.373** refusal to grant artificial insemination facilities to a prisoner. A prisoner did not lose his Article 8 rights simply because of his detention. Although the state was entitled to take steps to maintain public confidence in the system a requirement that the applicants should demonstrate that their case was exceptional before they would be permitted to use artificial insemination was too high a threshold. The policy adopted by the United Kingdom did not permit the required proportionality assessment to be made in an individual case.

(3) Telephone tapping and surveillance[1264]

(a) Telephone tapping

In *Malone v United Kingdom*[1265] the applicant complained that the police had tapped his **12.374** telephone. The Court held that the regulation of telephone tapping by administrative practice was not regulation 'in accordance with the law'. This case resulted in the enactment of the Interception of Communications Act 1985 ('the 1985 Act'), which was held to satisfy the requirements of Article 8 in respect of domestic telephone communications.[1266] However, in relation to external communications from the United Kingdom, the Act allowed the executive an extremely broad discretion as to the communications intercepted and those listened to or read. The absence of published information as to these arrangements in a form accessible to the public meant that the interception of communications between Britain and Ireland was not 'in accordance with law'.[1267]

The 1985 Act did not apply to tapping of calls on internal communications systems. As a **12.375** result, in *Halford v United Kingdom*[1268] the interception of office telephone calls was held

---

[1259] (1998) 27 EHRR CD 241; see also; see also *Young v United Kingdom*, Decision of 11 October 2005 (no breach by requirement that cerebral palsy sufferer provide a urine sample in prison).

[1260] *Shelley v United Kingdom*, Decision of 4 January 2008.

[1261] *Black v United Kingdom*, Decision of 27 September 2005.

[1262] *Morley v United Kingdom*, Decision of 5 October 2004.

[1263] (2008) 46 EHRR 41 (GC).

[1264] See generally, David Ormerod 'ECHR and the Exclusion of Evidence: Trial Remedies for Article 8 Breaches' (2003) Criminal Law Review 61–80.

[1265] (1984) 7 EHRR 14.

[1266] *Christie v United Kingdom* (1994) 78-A DR 119, EComm HR; but note that in *Liberty v United Kingdom* (2009) 48 EHRR 1, para 63 the Court stated that its 'approach to the foreseeability requirement in [surveillance] field has, therefore, evolved since the Commission considered the United Kingdom's surveillance scheme in *Christie*.'

[1267] *Liberty v United Kingdom* (2009) 48 EHRR 1 (communications between British and Irish civil liberties organizations—applicants were persons to whom powers of interception might have been applied)

[1268] (1997) 24 EHRR 523.

to constitute a breach of Article 8. In *Taylor-Sabori v United Kingdom*,[1269] the interception of messages sent by pager was held not to be in accordance with the law. The United Kingdom has since enacted the Regulation of Investigatory Powers Act 2000, which extends the 1985 Act so as to regulate, among other things, the interception of internal communications systems.

(b) Other forms of surveillance

12.376 Complaints have also been made about other forms of surveillance by the police. The Commission and the Court have dealt on several occasions with cases in which the police, acting under Home Office Guidelines, placed listening devices in applicants' houses. In *Govell v United Kingdom*[1270] the Commission held that such surveillance amounted to an interference with Article 8 rights and, as there was no statutory system to regulate the use of covert recording devices by the police at the relevant time, the interference was not 'in accordance with the law' as required by Article 8(2). The Court followed this in *Armstrong v United Kingdom*[1271] and *Chalkley v United Kingdom*.[1272] In *Hewitson v United Kingdom*[1273] and *Lewis v United Kingdom*,[1274] the government conceded that the installation of listening devices in the workplace and home respectively were not in accordance with the law. In *Copland v United Kingdom*,[1275] the Court confirmed that similar principles applied to the monitoring of employees by public employers. The use of the telephone, emails and the internet in the workplace were held to be private, though the Court suggested that the existence of a clear employment policy stating otherwise might have removed the reasonable expectation of privacy. Since the Telecommunications (Lawful Business Practice) Regulations 2000 were not in force at the time, the surveillance was not in accordance with the law.

12.377 An application concerning covert video surveillance of the applicant's home to obtain evidence of anti-social behaviour was held to be admissible in *Martin v United Kingdom*,[1276] but the Court did not rule on the matter as the parties reached a friendly settlement.[1277]

(c) Secret listening devices

12.378 There has also been a series of cases dealing with the use of secret listening devices in police stations. In *Khan v United Kingdom*[1278] the Court held that, in the absence of a scheme of statutory regulation,[1279] the use of such a device was not 'in accordance with the law'. As a result, the interference with the applicant's rights under Article 8 could not be justified. A similar result was reached in *PG v United Kingdom*,[1280] which concerned the covert

---

[1269] (2003) 36 EHRR 17.
[1270] (1999) EHRLR 101; See also the case comment in [1999] EHRLR 121–123.
[1271] (2003) 36 EHRR 30.
[1272] (2003) 37 EHRR 30.
[1273] (2003) 37 EHRR 31.
[1274] (2004) 39 EHRR 9.
[1275] (2007) 45 EHRR 37.
[1276] (2003) 37 EHRR CD91.
[1277] *The Times*, 26 February 2004.
[1278] (2001) 31 EHRR 45; see also *Taylor-Sabori v United Kingdom* (2003) 36 EHRR 17; *Hewitson v United Kingdom* (2003) 37 EHRR 1 and *Elahi v United Kingdom* (2007) 44 EHRR 30.
[1279] The use of such devices is now regulated by the Police Act 1997, see para 12.157ff above.
[1280] (2008) 46 EHRR 51.

recording of conversations with police members in order to obtain voice samples of the applicants. Again, the Court confirmed that the general powers of the police to collect evidence, coupled with the existence of Home Office Guidelines, was not in these circumstances sufficient to render the interference 'in accordance with the law.[1281] In *Allan v United Kingdom*[1282] a cell and the prison visiting area had been 'bugged' using audio and video technology, and a police informer had been the placed in the applicant's cell in order to elicit information. At the time the measures were implemented in 1995, they also fell foul of not having a basis 'in law'.[1283] In *Perry v United Kingdom*,[1284] the government argued that the video-taping of the applicant in a police station was no interference with his private life at all, on the basis that the police station was a public place and that video-cameras were visible. This argument was rejected and, again, justification could not be made out because of the absence of sufficient legal framework. In *Wood v United Kingdom*,[1285] the UK government accepted that the bugging of a police cell amounted to an infringement.

(d) Surveillance by the security services

Applications have also been brought in relation to surveillance by the security services. The **12.379** Commission held that a security check was not, of itself, objectionable; but could be where it was based on information about a person's private life.[1286] In *Hewitt and Harman (No 1) v United Kingdom*[1287] the applicants were both employed by the National Council for Civil Liberties and complained that they had been placed under secret surveillance by the security service. The Commission ruled the complaint to be admissible on the basis that the interference with the private life of the applicant was not 'in accordance with the law'. A friendly settlement was reached with the applicants and the Security Service was placed on a statutory basis by the Security Services Act 1989.[1288] In *Esbester v United Kingdom*[1289] the Commission held that the Security Services Act meant that secret surveillance by the Security Service was 'in accordance with the law'. A similar challenge to the activities of the security services was rejected by the Commission in *Hewitt and Harman (No 2) v United Kingdom*[1290] in which the Commission dismissed the application as 'manifestly ill-founded'.

(4) Privacy and sexual relationships

(a) Privacy and sexual orientation

Complaints about interference with private life by legislation regulating sexual orientation **12.380** have frequently been made. In *X v United Kingdom*[1291] the applicant had been found guilty of buggery of two 18-year-old males. The Commission took the view that the higher age of

---

[1281] Ibid, paras 62–63.
[1282] (2003) 36 EHRR 12.
[1283] Ibid, para 35.
[1284] (2004) 39 EHRR 3.
[1285] Judgment of 16 November 2004.
[1286] *Hilton v United Kingdom* (1988) 57 DR 108, EComm HR; and *N v United Kingdom* (1989) 67 DR 123 (these decisions should now be read with the approach taken in *Segerstadt v Sweden* (2007) 44 EHRR 2 as to what kind of information may relate to private life).
[1287] (1991) 14 EHRR 657.
[1288] See para 12.175ff above.
[1289] (1994) 18 EHRR CD 72.
[1290] (1991) 47 DR 88.
[1291] (1978) 3 EHRR 63.

consent of 21 for homosexuals was an interference with the applicant's private life under Article 8 but was 'justified as being necessary in a democratic society for the protection of the rights of others'. Things have moved on since then. In *BB v United Kingdom*,[1292] an attempt to prosecute the applicant under the then existing legislation, which set the age of consent for homosexuals at 18 and for heterosexuals at 16, was held to violate Article 14 taken with Article 8. The fact that the government had since introduced the Sexual Offences (Amendment) Act 2000, which equalized the ages of consent, did not assuage the breach. In *Sutherland v United Kingdom*,[1293] however, the applicant (who had not been prosecuted) consented to his case being struck out as a result of that legislative amendment.,

12.381 The most important case in this area is the Northern Ireland case of *Dudgeon v United Kingdom*.[1294] The applicant complained that the laws restricting homosexual conduct were an interference with his private life. The Court agreed, holding that, even though the applicant had not in fact been prosecuted, the very existence of the legislation continuously and directly affected his private life. It also rejected the Government's contention that the legislation was 'necessary in a democratic society', noting that it differed from the position in the large majority of Council of Europe states. This case led to the Homosexual Offences (NI) Order 1982 which brought the law in Northern Ireland into line with the rest of the United Kingdom. It was followed in cases relating to Ireland[1295] and Cyprus[1296] and it is now clear that legislation criminalizing any type of homosexual activity is contrary to Article 8.[1297] In *ADT v United Kingdom*,[1298] for instance, the Court confirmed that the offence of gross indecency between men in private was a violation of Article 8. Nevertheless, such criminalization has been held not to be a sufficiently serious breach of Article 8 to prevent the deportation of a failed asylum seeker to a country in which homosexuality was criminalized.[1299]

12.382 A series of cases were also brought challenging the absolute policy of the Ministry of Defence against the presence of homosexuals in the armed forces. The cases of *Lustig-Prean v United Kingdom*[1300] and *Perkins and R v United Kingdom*[1301] concerned investigation of the applicants' sexual orientation, and their discharge by the Royal Navy. The cases of *Smith and Grady v United Kingdom*[1302] and *Beck, Copp and Bazeley v United Kingdom* concerned investigation and discharge from the Royal Air Force.[1303] The applicants in each case were interviewed and asked questions of an intimate sexual nature, and were discharged despite exemplary service records. The leading decision by the Court was given in *Lustig-Prean* and

---

[1292] (2004) 39 EHRR 30.
[1293] [1997] EHRLR 117 (the Commission held by 14 votes to 4 that the fixing of a minimum age for lawful homosexual activities at 18 rather than 16 was in violation of Art 8 of the Convention).
[1294] (1981) 4 EHRR 149.
[1295] *Norris v Ireland* (1988) 13 EHRR 186.
[1296] *Modinos v Cyprus* (1993) 16 EHRR 485.
[1297] See generally, R Wintemute, *Sexual Orientation and Human Rights* (Clarendon Press, 1995), Chap 4.
[1298] (2001) 31 EHRR 33.
[1299] *F v United Kingdom* (2004) 39 EHRR SE20.
[1300] (1999) 29 EHRR 449.
[1301] Judgment of 22 October 2002.
[1302] (2000) 29 EHRR 493.
[1303] Judgment of 22 October 2002.

Smith, which were heard together. It was held that both the investigations into the applicants' homosexuality and their consequent administrative discharge on the sole ground of their sexual orientation constituted an interference with their right to respect for their private lives.[1304] The Government's attempt to justify the infringement under Article 8(2) also failed, despite the Court recognizing that a margin of appreciation must be allowed to the State to organize its own system of military discipline, and that it is open to the State to impose restrictions on an individual's right to respect for his private life where there is a real threat to the armed forces' operational effectiveness.[1305] The Court held that the argument that the presence of open or suspected homosexuals in the armed forces would have a substantial and negative effect on morale and, consequently, on the fighting power and operational effectiveness of the armed forces was not persuasive, particularly if it was founded solely upon the negative attitudes of heterosexual personnel towards those of homosexual orientation.[1306]

(b) Privacy and transgender issues

Seven applications have been brought by transsexuals contending that the refusal of the **12.383** United Kingdom authorities to change the sex indicated on the register of births constituted a breach of their rights under Article 8. In the first four applications, the claim was rejected.[1307] The Court held that the mere refusal to alter the register of births could not constitute an 'interference' under Article 8 and that the positive obligations to protect privacy rights did not extend as far as making arrangements to assist transsexuals. Nevertheless, the Court repeatedly noted that the lack of legal recognition of transsexuals' new gender faced them with serious problems, and stressed the importance of keeping the need for appropriate legal measures in this area under review.[1308] When the matter came before the Grand Chamber in 2002 in *Goodwin v United Kingdom*[1309] and *I v United Kingdom*,[1310] it acknowledged that social conditions in both the United Kingdom and other European countries had changed sufficiently to warrant departing from the Court's previous jurisprudence.[1311] The Grand Chamber pointed to the illogicality of the government authorizing and financing the treatment and surgery alleviating gender dysphoria, but then refusing to recognize the legal implications of the result to which the treatment lead.[1312] Although the Grand Chamber acknowledged the administrative burden occasioned by the full recognition of gender reassignment, it found that the problems were not insuperable, and that society could 'reasonably be expected to tolerate a certain inconvenience to enable individuals to live in dignity and worth in accordance with the sexual identity chosen by

---

[1304] *Lustig-Prean* (n 1300 above) para 64; *Smith* (n 1302 above) para 71.

[1305] *Lustig-Prean* (n 1300 above) para 82; *Smith* (n 1302 above) para 89.

[1306] *Lustig-Prean* (n 1300 above) para 89; *Smith* (n 1302 above) para 96.

[1307] The position of a female to male transsexual was considered in *Rees v United Kingdom* (1986) 9 EHRR 56. *Cossey v United Kingdom* (1990) 13 EHRR 622, *X, Y and Z v United Kingdom* (1997) 24 EHRR 143 and *Sheffield and Horsham v United Kingdom*, (1998) 27 EHRR 163 concerned male to female transsexuals.

[1308] *Rees v United Kingdom*, para 47; *Cossey v United Kingdom*, para 42 and *Sheffield and Horsham v United Kingdom*, para 60.

[1309] (2002) 35 EHRR 447.

[1310] (2003) 36 EHRR 53.

[1311] *Goodwin* (n 1309 above) para 90, *I v UK* (n 1310 above) para 70.

[1312] *Goodwin* (n 1309 above) para 78, *I v UK* (n 1310 above) para 58.

them at great personal cost'.[1313] It therefore held that the United Kingdom's failure to give legal recognition to gender re-assignment breached Article 8. The United Kingdom subsequently conceded the similar case of *Grant*.[1314]

(c) Other privacy and sexuality cases

12.384 In *Laskey, Jaggard and Brown v United Kingdom*[1315] the applicants had engaged in sadomasochistic acts and were convicted of assault occasioning actual bodily harm. The applicants' argument that this constituted an unjustified interference with their right to private life was rejected by the Court. It was common ground that the interference pursued the legitimate aim of the 'protection of health or morals' and the Court held that the interference was 'necessary in a democratic society'. In *Pay v United Kingdom*[1316] the applicant had been dismissed from the Probation Service because of his involvement in a company providing bondage, domination and sadomasochism products and his involvement in domination performances at nightclubs. The Court was prepared to assume that these activities fell within the scope of Article 8 but found that, bearing in mind the duty of loyalty owed by an employee and his work with sex offenders, his dismissal was not disproportionate. The application was inadmissible.

(5) Other applications

(a) Personal information

12.385 The Court has considered several important cases involving the right to obtain personal information. In *Gaskin v United Kingdom*[1317] it held that the applicant had a vital interest, protected by the Convention, in receiving information necessary to know and understand his childhood, early development and history, and access to such personal information thus came within the scope of Article 8. Similarly, in *MG v United Kingdom*[1318] the state's limitation of the applicant's right of access to social service records, containing the principal source of information about significant periods of his formative years, was found to breach Article 8. The Court did, however, comment that once the Data Protection Act 1998 entered into force on 1 March 2000, the appeal process under the statutory scheme would fulfil the state's positive obligation under Article 8.[1319] In *McGinley and Egan v United Kingdom*[1320] it held that withholding documents concerning the exposure of the applicants to radiation at Christmas Island was a breach of Article 8. Finally, in *Roche v United Kingdom*,[1321] the Court held that an individual who took part in tests into the effects of chemical weapons at Porton Down was entitled to all relevant and appropriate information about those tests. However, there is no positive obligation to provide access to documents which do not concern a person's identity or personal history.[1322]

[1313] *Goodwin* (n 1309 above) para 91, *I v UK* (n 1310 above) para 71.
[1314] (2007) 44 EHRR 1.
[1315] (1997) 24 EHRR 39.
[1316] (2009) 48 EHRR SE2.
[1317] (1989) 12 EHRR 36.
[1318] (2003) 36 EHRR 3.
[1319] Ibid, para 33.
[1320] (1998) 27 EHRR 1.
[1321] (2006) 42 EHRR 305.
[1322] *Smith v United Kingdom*, Decision of 4 January 2007.

In the important case of *S and Marper v United Kingdom*[1322a] the Grand Chamber decided   **12.385A**
that the retention under section 64(1A) of DNA and cellular samples of persons who had
been arrested but not convicted constituted an interference with their Article 8 rights. This
retention could not be justified for the prevention of crime as it was a blanket and indiscriminate power and no justification had been provided for treating arrested persons differently from other unconvicted people.

However, the Commission has dismissed a number of applications where individuals have   **12.386**
claimed access to personal information. In *Martin v United Kingdom*[1323] the Commission
decided that a fair balance had been struck between the applicant and the state where access
to medical records was denied to a person suffering from catatonic schizophrenia on the
ground that it protected his medical health. In *Wiltshire v United Kingdom*[1324] the
Commission held that there was no breach of Article 8 where the applicant's files were
edited to protect third parties.

(b) Right to respect for home

General.   In *Gillow v United Kingdom*,[1325] the applicants complained about the refusal of   **12.387**
the Guernsey authorities to allow them to occupy their house. It was held that the refusal
of a licence to occupy was disproportionate to the legitimate aim of promoting the economic well being of the island; and constituted a violation of Article 8.

In a number of cases the Commission and the Court have considered complaints by former   **12.388**
joint tenants of local authority property after the joint tenancy had come to an end. In
many the Commission found these applications to be manifestly ill-founded.[1326] However,
in *McCann v United Kingdom*[1327] the Court found there was a violation of Article 8 because
the summary procedures available to landlords where one joint tenant served a notice to
quit meant that the proportionality of the possession order could not be determined by an
independent tribunal. The applicant had been deprived of his home in circumstances in
which there was a lack of adequate procedural safeguards.

Entry by police.   In *McLeod v United Kingdom*[1328] the applicant complained that the   **12.389**
police had entered her house at the request of her ex-husband. The Court held that the
power to enter premises to prevent a breach of the peace was 'in accordance with the law'[1329]
and was for the legitimate aim of 'the prevention of crime or disorder'. However, on the
facts, the entry of the police into the applicant's home was disproportionate as it did not
strike a fair balance between her right to respect for home and the prevention of crime and
disorder.[1330] In *Keegan v United Kingdom*[1331] the Court held that a lack of malice on the part

---

[1322a] Judgment of 4 December 2008 (GC).
[1323]   (1996) 21 EHRR CD 112.
[1324]   (1997) 23 EHRR CD 188.
[1325]   (1986) 11 EHRR 335.
[1326]   See *S v United Kingdom* (1986) 47 DR 274; *DP v United Kingdom* (1986) 51 DR 195; *Ure v United Kingdom*, Decision of 27 November 1996; *Wood v United Kingdom*, Decision of 2 July 1997.
[1327]   (2008) 47 EHRR 40; for a discussion of this case by the House of Lords see *Doherty v Birmingham City Council* [2008] 3 WLR 636.
[1328]   (1998) 27 EHRR 493.
[1329]   Ibid, paras 38–45.
[1330]   Ibid, paras 49–58.
[1331]   (2007) 44 EHRR 33.

of police could not excuse an entry into the applicant's home under the authority of a search warrant when the police had failed to carry out reasonable investigations to verify the connection between the address and the suspected offences prior to seeking the warrant. Although the police could not be held liable under domestic law absent malice, this was not a necessary ingredient for a breach of Article 8.

12.390   **Gypsy cases.** The rights of gypsies and travellers to sites for their caravans has led to a number of applications. In *Buckley v United Kingdom*,[1332] the refusal to grant the applicant gypsy planning permission to keep caravans on her own land did not breach Article 8. The planning restrictions in question pursued the legitimate aims of public safety, economic well-being, the protection of health and the protection of the rights of others. Similarly, in *Chapman v United Kingdom*,[1333] the Court confirmed that the State was under no obligation to provide a sufficient number of gypsy sites and held that the enforcement of planning decisions was, in that case, justified for the protection of the environment. However, a breach was established in *Connors v United Kingdom*,[1334] in which the Court observed that there is some positive obligation upon Contracting States to facilitate the gypsy way of life.[1335] The court held that there were insufficient procedural safeguards in the summary eviction procedure to satisfy Article 8 in this context, since the facts could not adequately be determined and considered.

(c) Environmental cases

12.391   The case of *Powell and Rayner v United Kingdom*[1336] concerned a complaint by applicants living near Heathrow Airport that excessive aircraft noise was interfering with their private life and home. Such interference was established in one case but was held to be 'necessary in the interests of the economic well-being of the country'. In a number of other cases involving aircraft noise, friendly settlements have been reached following Commission admissibility decisions in favour of the applicants.[1337]

12.392   The case of *Hatton v United Kingdom*[1338] considered the issue of noise disturbance from night flights into and out of Heathrow, and the Court held that there was a breach of the applicants' Article 8 rights as not enough was being done to reduce noise levels. This decision was, however, overturned by a majority of the Grand Chamber, which held that the scheme adopted by the Government was within its margin of appreciation. The scheme was regularly reviewed and had been preceded by a series of investigations and studies carried out over a long period of time and announced to the public by way of a Consultation Paper.[1339] The Grand Chamber also noted that house prices had not been adversely affected

---

[1332] (1996) 23 EHRR 101; see also two Commission decisions involving gypsies: *Turner v United Kingdom* (1997) 23 EHRR (CD) 181 and *Webb v United Kingdom* [1997] EHRLR 680.
[1333] (2001) 33 EHRR 18.
[1334] (2005) 40 EHRR 9.
[1335] Ibid, para 84.
[1336] (1990) 12 EHRR 355.
[1337] *Arrondelle v United Kingdom* (1980) 19 DR 186; (1982) 26 DR 5, EComm HR: payment of £7,500 made re noise at Gatwick; *Baggs v United Kingdom* (1985) 44 DR 13; (1987) 52 DR 29, EComm HR: noise at Heathrow; see also *Vearncombe v United Kingdom and Germany* (1989) 59 DR 186, EComm HR: noise from a military shooting range not intolerable; application inadmissible.
[1338] (2002) 34 EHRR 1.
[1339] Ibid, paras 128–130.

by the night noise, thus giving the applicants the opportunity to move elsewhere without financial loss.[1340]

Conversely, in *Chapman v United Kingdom*,[1341] the Court held that protection of the environment was capable of *justifying* interferences with Article 8 rights, since it involved protecting the rights and freedoms of others. **12.393**

(d) Personal privacy

In *Winer v United Kingdom*[1342] the Commission found that there had been no failure to respect the private life of the applicant even though it considered that the only domestic remedies for damage to reputation were those available in defamation in respect of untrue statements. In *Earl and Countess Spencer v United Kingdom*[1343] the Commission rejected a claim that the absence of a right to privacy in English law breached Article 8 on the basis that the applicant had failed to exhaust domestic remedies: a claim for breach of confidence might have covered his particular complaint. In *Stewart-Brady v United Kingdom*[1344] the Commission rejected the allegation that the state had breached its positive obligations under Article 8 because the Press Complaints Commission had dismissed the applicant's complaint that the publication of his photograph in the *Sun* newspaper breached his right to privacy under its Code of Practice. The Court's subsequent decision in *Von Hannover v Germany*[1345] confirmed that there is a positive obligation to protect privacy rights which encompasses the reporting of accurate information: accordingly, the reasoning in *Winer* at least, cannot stand. However, the widening of the tort of breach of confidence so as to take into account certain Article 8 rights[1346] is likely in most cases of this sort to satisfy that positive obligation. **12.394**

In *Tamosius v United Kingdom*,[1347] the Court held that the procedure for the issue and execution of a warrant for the seizure of documents relating to suspected tax fraud from a solicitor's office had sufficient safegaurds for the purposes of Article 8. The warrant was issued by a judge and the seizure was supervised by counsel, who was tasked with identifying documents covered by legal professional privilege, which were not seized. **12.395**

In *Peck v United Kingdom*,[1348] the police were able to intervene and save a man from a suicide attempt after observing CCTV footage showing him in the street with a large knife, though the cameras did not record the actual suicide attempt. The local council subsequently released the footage they did have to the media, as an example of the benefits of CCTV. The Court held that this was serious breach of Article 8. Even though the applicant was in a public place and he did not complain about the existence of the CCTV footage as such, this degree of exposure was for beyond what a reasonable person would expect. Further, there had been no effort to obscure the man's identity or to obtain his consent for the transmission of the images. **12.396**

1340 Ibid, para 127.
1341 (2001) 33 EHRR 18.
1342 (1986) 48 DR 154, 170–171, EComm HR.
1343 (1998) 25 EHRR CD 105.
1344 (1998) 27 EHRR CD 284.
1345 (2005) 40 EHRR 1.
1346 See generally, para 12.24 above.
1347 (2002) 35 EHRR CD323.
1348 (2003) 36 EHRR 41.

(e) Personal autonomy

12.397 In *Pretty v United Kingdom*[1349] the Court held that the legal restriction which prevented Mrs Pretty from exercising her choice to avoid an undignified and distressing death from an assisted suicide interfered with her rights to physical and psychological integrity. The Court declined to follow the approach of the House of Lords in *R (Pretty) v DPP*[1350] which had held that Article 8 was directed at the protection of personal autonomy while an individual was alive but did not confer the right to decide how or when to die. Nevertheless, the Court held that the interference created by a ban on assisting suicide was justified under Article 8(2) as it protected the life and health of others, in particular of those who might not be able to make informed decisions about ending their life.

12.398 In *Glass v United Kingdom*,[1351] the Court confirmed that administering medical treatment to a child in defiance of his parent's wishes interfered with the child's right to physical integrity. The hospital should have sought the intervention of the High Court, even in an emergency situation. The failure to do so resulted in a breach of Article 8

Appendix 2: Scottish Cases on Privacy and the Home

(1) Introduction

12.399 There is no remedy for invasion of privacy in Scottish private law. However, the Data Protection Act 1998 applies in Scotland. Article 8 issues have been raised before the Scottish Courts in a wide range of cases. These will be considered under the following headings:

- Information issues: personal information, employment and media
- Intrusion into the home and business: entry, search and seizure
- Photography, surveillance, covert tracking and telephone tapping
- Housing Law and Respect for the Home
- Prevention of anti-social behaviour and sex offences
- Other Article 8 issues

(2) Information issues: personal information, employment and media

(a) Misuse of personal information

12.400 In *HM Advocate v Murray (Gavin Mitchell)*[1352] the accused had previously been sentenced to detention for eight years for assault to severe injury and danger of life. The original offence had involved him striking a young boy with a hammer and burying him in a shallow grave. As part of his probation plan he had a meeting with two social workers. In his conversations with the social workers he stated that he was in possession of a hammer and threatened to sexually assault and murder a child but that would commit his next crime more efficiently by digging a deeper grave and committing the crime outwith his local area. He was charged with breach of the peace in relation to these conversations but sought to

---

[1349] (2002) 35 EHRR 1.
[1350] [2002] 1 AC 800; see also *R (Purdy) v DPP* [2008] EWHC 2565 (Admin).
[1351] (2004) 39 EHRR 15.
[1352] 2007 SCCR 271.

argue that by bringing a prosecution in respect of things said by him to social workers in the context of a treatment programme, the Crown was acting incompatibly with his rights under the Article 8. In rejecting this contention the sheriff held that the accused had volunteered the information in question, and the prosecutor had therefore not acted in a manner incompatible with Article 8.

(b) Confidentiality and employment

The case of *Lord Advocate v Scotsman Publications Ltd*[1353] was a pre-HRA and Scotland Act **12.401**
House of Lords decision, in effect the Scottish *Spycatcher* case, in which their Lordships confirmed that a third party (the Scotsman newspaper) which came into information from a former Crown servant (which it was conceded could not be said to be damaging to national security) could not be restrained from publishing it in Scotland notwithstanding the existence of an injunction against publication of the same material by the *Sunday Times* in England.

(c) Privacy and the media

In *Nicol v Caledonian Newspapers Ltd*[1354] the Lord Ordinary held that in principle the **12.402**
defence of qualified privilege available in defamation actions at common law was not incompatible with the requirements of Article 8. In *X v BBC*[1355] the pursuer who was 17 obtained an injunction to prevent the broadcast of a documentary showing her outside court, taking pills and drinking. The broadcast also revealed information about her background. Although the pursuer had signed a 'contributors agreement' it was contended that she lack the capacity to contract or consent. The judge considered section 12(3) of the HRA and decided that the Article 8 rights of the pursuer outweighed the Article 10 rights of the broadcaster.

(3) Intrusion into the home and business: entry, search and seizure

(a) Civil procedure

One area of civil litigation in which Article 8 considerations definitely do apply is in rela- **12.403**
tion to applications under Section 1 of the Administration of Justice (Scotland) Act 1972 for the seizure and recovery of evidence without warning and prior to the raising of litigation, the so called 'dawn raid procedure'. The rules of the Court of Session governing this procedure have been amended to ensure the Convention compatibility of the Scottish procedure in the light of the decision of the European Court of Human Rights in *Chappell v United Kingdom*[1356] and subsequent cases.

(b) Criminal procedure

In *Birse (Gordon Dickson) v HM Advocate*,[1357] the Court of Criminal Appeals upheld the **12.404**
Article 8 compatibility of the summary procedure for the issuing by a justice to the police

---

[1353] 1989 SC (HL) 122.
[1354] 2002 SC 493.
[1355] 2005 SCLR 740.
[1356] *Chappell v United Kingdom* (1990) 12 EHRR 1. See also Case C–94/00, *Roquette Frères v Director General of Competition* [2002] ECR I–9011 at paras 51–52, 79–84, a decision of the European Court of Justice in the dawn raid procedure of the European Commission in investigations into anti-competitive behaviour.
[1357] 2000 JC 503.

of a search warrant of a private home in which illegal drug use was suspected.[1358] In *Calder v Frame*[1359] the *ex parte* procedure whereby a sheriff pronounced an order allowing evidence of illegal drug use which had been obtained by police in Scotland upon an issued search warrant of a private house to be forwarded to the US Department of Justice was upheld as Convention compatible, the High Court of Justiciary noting as follows:

> we accept that the requirement of lawfulness expressed in Articles 8 and Article 1 [of the First Protocol] demands more than compliance with the relevant provisions of domestic law. The rule of law is inherent in these and other articles of the Convention, and to be lawful an interference with Convention rights must also be compatible with the rule of law. The provisions of the domestic law must therefore be sufficiently precise and foreseeable in effect. There must be a measure of legal protection against arbitrary interference by public authorities with Convention rights. The scope of any discretion must be adequately defined. Measures affecting fundamental rights must be accompanied by appropriate procedural safeguards.[1360]

(4) Photography, surveillance, covert tracking, and telephone tapping

(a) Covertly obtained evidence in civil proofs

12.405 The case of *Martin v McGuiness*[1361] was an action for damages for injuries sustained in a road accident in which the pursuer also sought a declarator that the conduct of private investigators who had come to his house and spoken to his wife, under the pretence of being a former army colleague of the pursuer was unlawful as contrary to Article 8 in that it was designed to obtain private information about the pursuer from the most intimate family member by deception, and that the surveillance intruded on his private life and property and was carried out covertly. The pursuer sought an order from the court excluding any evidence thereby obtained from the proof. He also sought HRA damages for the infringement of his Convention right to respect for his privacy. The court rejected the pursuer's submissions holding that admission of the evidence would not be contrary to the pursuer's Article 8 rights on the basis that he was bound to anticipate that his conduct might be scrutinized and such inquiries and surveillance could conceivably be proved as having been reasonable and proportionate steps to be taken on the defender's behalf to protect his rights in terms of Article 8(2) and as a contribution to the protection of the wider rights of the community. Further the claim for HRA damages was misconceived as the defender was not a public authority.

12.406 In *McGowan v Scottish Water*[1362] the appellant had been subjected to covert surveillance by his employer who suspected him of falsifying his time-sheets. The employee worked at a water treatment plant and lived in a nearby tied house. The employer's covert surveillance included the filming of the employee coming and going from his house. As a result of their

---

[1358] See, too, *Ormiston v HM Advocate* unreported decision of High Court of Justiciary (Appeal) 19 September 2000 where the court confirmed the validity of search warrants of an individual's house granted by the justices on the basis of sworn evidence from a police officer that information had been received from an unnamed informer that a controlled substance, heroin, was present in the house.

[1359] 2007 JC 4.

[1360] Ibid, para 32.

[1361] 2003 SLT 1424.

[1362] [2005] IRLR 167, EAT.

investigation the employee was subject to a disciplinary procedure and was dismissed. He complained to the Employment Tribunal of unfair dismissal which in dismissing his claim ruled held that there had been no breach of the employee's rights under Article 8(1) and that the evidence relied upon by the employer could not be said to have been unlawfully, unreasonably or illegally obtained. In dismissing the appeal from this decision, the Employment Appeal Tribunal held that while at first sight, covert surveillance of a person's home unbeknown to him raised a presumption that his rights under Article 8 to have his private life respected was being invaded, in fact in the circumstances of the case the employer's measures had been proportionate and so justified under Article 8(2). The employer had considered how best to deal with the matter and had concluded that inserting cameras in the workplace would be impractical and ineffective. The aim of the surveillance was to see how many times the employee left the house to go to the plant since it was that issue which bore directly on the accuracy or otherwise of the employee's timesheets. Thus the surveillance was not undertaken for external reasons but instead went to the essence of the obligations and rights of the employer, a public corporation, to protect public assets and as such it was not disproportionate.

(b) Irregularly obtained evidence in criminal trials

In *Hoekstra v HM Advocate (No.7)*[1363] four Dutch nationals appealed against their conviction for being concerned in the importation of three tonnes of cannabis resin. They argued inter alia that the use of a tracking device attached to a ship on which they had allegedly carried the drugs to a rendezvous point with a second ship, was illegal and contrary Article 8 and any evidence flowing from it was inadmissible. In dismissing the appeal the court proceeded on the assumption that the tracking device had been planted deliberately, and noted that that would weigh heavily against the admission of any evidence arising from its use. However, the device had played a very limited role in the proceedings and no evidence directly derived from it had been relied on against the accused and so the irregularity could be excused. **12.407**

In *Connors v HM Advocate*[1364] the Court rejected a claim that the police operation involving the systematic surveillance of his home during which some people entering and leaving the building were detained and questioned, and their identity and other observations noted contravened his rights to privacy and respect for his home guaranteed under Article 8. **12.408**

The case of *McGibbon (David) v HM Advocate*[1365] was an appeal against conviction for drugs offences. The indictment resulted from an undercover operation and at the trial the entire evidence consisted of eyewitness evidence of undercover officers and covert video and audio recordings. The Crown conceded that there had been a breach of Article 8 in the obtaining of the covert evidence but nonetheless insisted on leading the evidence on the basis that this was compatible with the accuser's rights to a fair trial both at common law and under reference to Article 6. The sheriff accepted the Crown's concession on Article 8 and upheld their submissions on Article 6. The Criminal Appeal Court upheld the Sheriff's **12.409**

[1363] 2002 SLT 599.
[1364] 2003 JC 255.
[1365] 2004 JC 60.

decision while remitting the matter back to the sheriff to allow him to submit a further report on the allegations made at the trial of entrapment.

12.410 In *Gilchrist v HM Advocate*,[1366] the Court of Criminal Appeal held that observations covertly made in public place by the police as a result of a tip–off did not enter into the sphere of Article 8 and that, notwithstanding the failure on the part of the police to obtain a valid authorization for directed surveillance operations under and in terms of Regulation of Investigatory Powers (Scotland) Act 2000, the evidence obtained was admissible and Convention compatible.

12.411 In *Henderson v HM Advocate*,[1367] the Court of Criminal Appeals relying on the *McGibbon* decision noted above again found that a failure by the police in inserting a covert recording device on a telephone and recording thereby evidence corroborative of misconduct to follow the procedures laid down by the Regulation of Investigatory Powers (Scotland) Act 2000 did not prevent the Crown from relying upon this evidence, even if obtained in breach of the requirements of Article 8, provided that the reliance was compatible with the accused fair trial rights.

12.412 The decision in *HM Advocate v Higgins*[1368] concerned a trial within a trial in which the accused stated their objections to the admissibility of evidence which the Crown intended to elicit from police officers about the contents of conversations between one accused and his co-accused which the officers had overheard and recorded after being posted specifically to listen outside the adjacent police cells in which the accused's had each been placed after being arrested but before being charged. In upholding the accused's objections to the admissibility of this evidence the court held that the methods used by the police could only be described as entrapment. The police had failed to observe the requirements of the Regulation of Investigatory Powers (Scotland) Act 2000 and the surveillance was therefore unlawful and so constituted a breach of Article 8.

(c) Telephone tapping: civil proceedings

12.413 In *Potter v Scottish Ministers*,[1369] the petitioner prisoner petitioned for judicial review of a policy of the respondent Scottish Prison Service and/or the prison governor that a prerecorded message be attached to all outgoing telephone calls, informing the recipient that the call was coming from a prison. The Scottish Prison Service accepted that the inclusion of the message constituted an interference by a public authority with the exercise of a right protected by Article 8 and the issue raised by the petition was whether that interference was justified in terms of Article 8(2). At first instance the Lord Ordinary found that the respondent had failed to show that their admitted interference with the petitioner's article 8 right has sufficiently ground in domestic regulation as to be regarded for Convention purposes as being 'in accordance with the law' for the purposes of Article 8(2). This finding was reversed on appeal to the Inner House.[1370]

[1366] 2005 JC 34.
[1367] 2005 JC 301.
[1368] 2006 SLT 946.
[1369] 2007 SLT 363, OH.
[1370] 2007 SLT 1019, IH.

(d) Telephone tapping: criminal trials

In *Dudley (Fiona Jacqueline) v HM Advocate*[1371] the Court of Criminal Appeals rejected a **12.414** claim to the effect that the requirements of Article 8 prevented the admission of evidence in her trial for attempting to smuggle heroin into prison of the terms of an intercepted telephone call between the accused and a prison inmate. The suggestion that Article 8 required a warning that there be a warning that the call was likely to be monitored and recorded was dismissed by the court.

(5) Housing law and respect for the home

In *HM Advocate v Burns (Thomas Fowler) (Sentencing)*[1372] the Crown applied under Section **12.415** 1 of the Proceeds of Crime (Scotland) Act 1995 for a confiscation order against the accused, who had been convicted of drug trafficking offences and sentenced to two years' imprisonment. The accused's former wife entered the process and relied upon her rights under Article 8 and Article 1 Protocol 1 to seek an order excluding her property from the scope of any confiscation order made. The Crown alleged that the former wife held items of property (including her home, her car and funds in a bank account) which fell to be treated as implicative gifts from ex-husband and hence potentially realisable in settlement of any confiscation order. The order was granted by the court over the wife's objections.

In *Glasgow City Council v Al-Abassi*[1373] the local authority landlord sought recovery of pos- **12.416** session of a top floor flat occupied by the defender, a single mother with language, cultural and mental health difficulties, and her children. There had been a series of incidents which the council considered to be antisocial including the deliberate flooding of her neighbours living in flats below and the storage of rubbish which was flung from windows. It was argued on behalf of the defender that her eviction would contravene her rights under Article 8 and that the local authority were acting unreasonably in refusing to offer her alternative accommodation and rendering her homeless. In granting decree the sheriff held that against the background of the rent arrears, the flooding of neighbours and the anti-social behaviour of the defender her children were in cumulo sufficient to establish grounds for recovery of possession of the property under Housing (Scotland) Act 1987 and consistently with Article 8(2) and given the degree of culpability of the defender for the behaviour resulting in her eviction that it had not been unreasonable in all the circumstances for the local authority to refuse to offer alternative accommodation.

In *Cannell v Scottish Ministers*[1374] the Inner House rejected the claim that statutory provi- **12.417** sion which failed to provide for recovery of expenses (costs) from the respondents incurred by the petitioner in the course of his ultimately successful appeal against a listed building enforcement notice requiring him to restore certain panels to his private house, a listed building, was contrary to Article 8. The Court held that the decision by the respondents to refuse to reimburse him for his costs did not impose on the petitioner an excessive burden disproportionate to any aim legitimate for the state to seek to achieve and his rights under

---

[1371] 2003 JC 53.
[1372] 2001 JC 1.
[1373] 2001 Hous. L.R. 23.
[1374] 2003 SC 404.

Article 1 of the First Protocol and Article 8 of the Convention were accordingly not infringed.

12.418 In *MacLeod's Trustee v MacLeod*[1375] the Sheriff upheld the contention of the permanent trustee on the sequestrated estate of a debtor in an action against his wife for the division and sale of heritable subjects of which the debtor and his wife were joint proprietors, and for warrant to have the debtor, his wife and family (a son, a daughter and her partner and their 20 month old child) ejected from the property. The sheriff held that the public interest in completing sequestrations within a reasonable period justified the interference with their Convention rights to respect for their home (Article 8) and property (Article 1 Protocol 1) and that the remedy of division and sale was in the circumstances compliant with the Convention.

(6) Prevention of anti-social behaviour and sex offences

12.419 In *M v Chief Constable of Strathclyde*[1376] the pursuer, who obtained employment in a kitchen and restaurant at a centre frequented by children, sought to interdict the Chief Constable from disclosing information to his employer third parties to the effect that he had been questioned by police and subsequently charged with offences involving illegal sexual conduct with three young girls. He argued among other grounds, that he was not employed in circumstances in which children were exposed to risk and that informing his employer of the charges which had not yet been determined as he awaited trial on them would constitute a disproportionate and hence unjustifiable interference with his Article 8 right to respect for his privacy. The Chief Constable countered that there would have been no need to write a letter if the pursuer had sought employment where he was not likely to be involved with young children. In refusing the application for declarator and interdict and for leave to reclaim the Lord Ordinary held that it was not unreasonable for the Chief Constable in the circumstances to have decided to inform the employer having regard to the material before him which suggested the risks that existed towards other children, provided that the letter made it plain that the information was provided in the strictest confidence and should not be disclosed further and that the employer should contact the local divisional commander first if it felt it was necessary to make any further disclosure to protect any individual.

12.420 In *Application by the Superintendent of Fife Constabulary*[1377] the sheriff upheld the validity of the provisions of the Antisocial Behaviour etc (Scotland) Act 2004 which empower a senior police officer to authorize the service of a closure notice prohibiting access to premises by any person other than the person who habitually resides in the premises with a view to preventing significant and persistent disorder, or significant, persistent and serious nuisance to members of the public.

[1375] 2007 Hous. L.R. 34.

[1376] 2003 SLT 1007.

[1377] Unrep, 12 October 2007 (Sheriff William Holligan, Kirkcaldy). See also *Application by the Superintendent of Fife Constabulary*, 2005 SLT (Sh Ct) 2.

In *A v Scottish Ministers*[1378] the petitioner sought judicial review of the imposition on him **12.421** of an indefinite period of notification on the Sex Offenders' Register, without provision for review. He had been sentenced to four years' detention in 1995 for crimes including assault with intent to rape, which were committed when he was 14. Given that the order was imposed in terms of the Sex Offenders Act 1997, as amended by the Sexual Offences Act 2003 the petitioner accepted that interference with his rights under Article 8 was in accordance with the law. He contended however that the measures imposed conflicted with the principle of proportionality as reflected in the need for such interference to be necessary in a democratic society. The petitioner sought declarator that the continued application of s 81 and s 82 of the 2003 Act, without the possibility of any review to consider the variation or ending of his obligation to comply with the notification requirement was incompatible with his right to respect for private and family life under Article 8. He also sought declarator that continued application was incompatible with his right of access to the court for proper determination of his civil rights under Article 6 and was incompatible with his right to enjoy Convention rights and freedoms without discrimination under Article 14. The Lord Ordinary rejected the petitioner's arguments holding the provisions of the Sex Offenders Register as applied to the petitioner to be compatible with due respect for his Convention rights.

In *Chief Constable of Tayside v Basterfield*[1379] the Sheriff granted as compatible with the **12.422** individual's Convention rights a sexual offences prevention order under section 105(1) of the Sexual Offences Act 2003 which sought to prevent the defender from being alone or remaining in the company of any lone female and from approaching, accosting, following or communicating in person with any lone female, for a minimum period of 5 years. The individual in question was said to exhibit a schizotypal personality disorder, and tended not to abide by normal social boundaries but displayed strong psychopathic trends. He had been previously convicted of breach of the peace and placed on the Sex Offenders Register as a result of an incident whereby he followed a woman home and entered her property as a result of which he was made the subject of a probation order lasting three years. And in February 2006 while he was on bail, the defender approached another lone female, continually touched her and followed her.

(7) Other Article 8 issues

(a) Sexual identity

In *MacDonald v Ministry of Defence*[1380] it was argued that the Sex Discrimination Act pro- **12.423** hibition of discrimination on ground of sex, could and should—if properly interpreted in line with Articles 8 and 14—be read so as to apply to employment discrimination ostensibly on grounds of sexual orientation—but in reality, so the argument went, if one maintained the identity (including gender) of the person to whom an attraction was admitted, the acceptability of the admission of sexual attraction varied depending on the gender of the person making this admission). The argument was unsuccessful before the House of

---

[1378] *A v Scottish Ministers*, 2008 SLT 412, OH.
[1379] 2007 SLT (Sh Ct) 129.
[1380] [2003] ICR 937.

Lords on the grounds, inter alia, that Parliament had by the time the case was argued before the House made specific provision in respect of discrimination on grounds of sexual orientation (namely the Employment Equality (Sexual Orientation) Regulations 2003) and so it would run contrary to the intention of Parliament to read the existing Sex Discrimination Act in the manner contended for.

(b) Right to the name of one's choice

12.424 In *Baron of Ardgowan v Lord Lyon King of Arms*[1381] the heritable proprietor of the land and barony of Ardgowan successfully relied inter alia upon his rights under Article 8 to obtain reduction of a decision of the Lord Lyon King of Arms refusing to officially recognize him in the surname 'Kerr of Ardgowan'. The court also granted an order ordaining the Lord Lyon to recognize the name in the warrant and letters patent to follow thereon matriculating in the name of the petitioner his said ensigns armorial with baronial additaments. The court held that by the law of Scotland, a person might call himself by whatever name he chose and the Lord Lyon's function in relation thereto was to give official recognition to a name which had already been changed, not to authorize the change of name itself and as a result, the Lord Lyon had no jurisdiction to impose a restriction on a change of name which he had been asked to recognize and had no power to require, in the case of a territorial designation, that there be a substantial nexus between the applicant and the lands in question. On the facts of the case it appeared that the Lord Lyon had not taken into account the petitioner's right to respect for his private and family life and thereafter carried out the necessary balancing exercise when he refused to recognize the change of name. None of the materials presented indicated that the Lord Lyon had expressly considered Article 8: no reference was made to it at any point, and a Convention right could not be considered subconsciously by a decision-maker.

(c) Involuntary medical treatment

12.425 In *M v Cook*[1382] the Lord Ordinary dismissed a claim that Article 8 was breached in the case of an individual who had been detained in a psychiatric hospital under the Mental Health (Scotland) Act 1984 s 26 and who sought judicial review of a decision to administer anti psychotic medication to him despite his refusal to give his consent to such treatment. It was held that on the facts of the case the clear violation of the individual's right to autonomy—including refusal of medical treatment—was proportionate and justified in terms of Article 8(2).

(d) Criminal injuries compensation

12.426 In *S v Criminal Injuries Compensation Board* the Inner House rejected a claim that the denial of criminal injuries compensation to parties living under the same roof (*in casu* compensation was sought in respect of sexual abuse inflicted by the claimants father between 1968 and 1971, when she was aged between four and seven years old) was incompatible with the requirements of Article 8, observing:

> [T]he core content of the article is the creation of protection for private and family life against factors which would assail the values protected, emanating from outside the family.

[1381] 2008 SLT 251, OH.
[1382] 2003 SC 52, OH.

That, of course, is not what was involved in the origins of this case. Furthermore, the 1996 Scheme was a means of providing financial compensation in certain circumstances to victims of criminal activity, a mechanism which is itself not directly concerned with the maintenance of the core values of Article 8. We cannot regard that Scheme as having more than, at best, a tenuous link with those core values.[1383]

(e) Hunting

In *Friend v Lord Advocate*,[1384] the House of Lords held that the Scottish Parliament's ban **12.427** on hunting with dogs in Scotland did not engage or violate Article 8 on the basis that the activity in question did not involve issues of personal autonomy; it was carried on in public and had social aspects involving the wider community. The right to establish and develop relationships with other human beings was said to be only protected to a degree and Art. 8 could not be extended to a generalized right of respect for minority community activities.

(f) Immigration, asylum, and extradition cases

In *Abdadou v Secretary of State for the Home Department*[1385] Lord Eassie in upholding a **12.428** judicial review challenge to a decision to deport an Algerian national who had entered the country illegally in 1992 and had contracted a marriage four years later held that the Secretary of State had failed to take any proper notice of the fact of the marriage had taken place binding himself instead to his understanding of a Home Office policy to disregard and discount any marriage had lasted for less than two years at the time of an enforcement action being taken. The Lord Ordinary observed that although Article 8 provides States with a wide discretion in the formulation of immigration rules, a decision could be so disproportionate that it fell outwith the margins within which national law could operate and that this was, in the circumstances then pertaining in Algeria, such a decision. A similar approach was taken by the Inner House in *Saini v Secretary of State for the Home Department*[1386] which observed that if there was any material risk that the petitioner would be permanently separated from his wife and child, the rights conferred by Article 8 would be very much in point.[1387] In *Aslam v Secretary of State for the Home Department*[1388] the decision to deport was upheld as Convention compatible in similar factual circumstances (of illegal entry followed by marriage of less than 2 years' duration at the time of enforcement action) on the basis that it was not unreasonable for the applicant's wife to move with him to Pakistan and maintain their family life there.

[1383] 2007 SC 748, para 83.

[1384] 2007 SLT 1209, HL.

[1385] 1998 SC 504, OH.

[1386] 2001 SC 951.

[1387] Compare the decisions to reject Article 8 based claims in, among others: *Singh v Secretary of State for the Home Department (Leave to Remain)* Lord Bonomy, OH 11 November 1999; *Ahmed (Nisar) v Secretary of State for the Home Department* 2000 SCLR 761, OH; *Ahmed (Nasim) v Secretary of State for the Home Department* 2001 SC 705, OH; *Ahmed (Saleem) v Secretary of State for the Home Department* 2001 SLT 1347, OH; *Akhtar v Secretary of State for the Home Department* 2001 SLT 1239, OH; *Nwokoye v Secretary of State for the Home Department*, 2002 SLT 128.

[1388] 2005 SC 10.

12.429 In *Wright v Scottish Ministers (No.2)*,[1389] the Inner House rejected a challenge based on consideration of *inter alia* Article 8 for the extradition to Estonia of a domiciled Scot to stand trial there on drugs related charges. The court noted that there were both domestic and foreign aspects to the alleged interference with the petitioner's Article 8 rights. They considered that the Lord Ordinary had fully considered the domestic aspects of the interference, namely the potential effects on the petitioner's health and family contact caused by extradition. It noted that, in respect of the foreign aspects of Article 8 interference, an extremely high threshold had to be overcome, and the petitioner would have to show that if extradited there would be a flagrant denial or gross violation of his rights, which he had not made out.[1390]

12.430 In *Brian Howes, Kerry Anne Shanks, Petitioners*[1391] the petitioners challenged their extradition to the United States of America to face trial in Arizona in relation to charges of conspiring to and unlawfully importing into and distributing into the United States chemicals that are used to manufacture methamphetamine. They argued that their extradition would deprive of them of any meaningful access to their four children in the United Kingdom. The Sheriff did not consider on the facts that their proposed extradition (which was properly based in the procedures of the domestic law of the sending state and the relevant bilateral treaty) would constitute be flagrant denial or gross violation of the parents' Article 8 right to family life.

(g) Prisons

12.431 In *Napier v Scottish Ministers*[1392] the Lord Ordinary, Lord Bonomy, founded that the conditions for the detention of remand prisoners in HM Barlinnie suffered from the triple vices (of over-crowding, lack of in-cell sanitation and an inadequate out-of-cell regime) were of such severity as to be in breach of the requirements of Article 3 prohibiting the subjecting of individuals to inhuman or degrading treatment. Even had these conditions not be sufficient to reach the severity of a breach of Article 3, they were also found to be in contravention of the respect for individual dignity implicitly conferred by Article 8(1); and that the decision to detain the petitioner in these squalid conditions of detention involving the practice of slopping out was found not to be in the circumstances a proportionate response to the problem of requiring to securely detain for the purpose of appearance in court. As a result detention in these conditions could not be said to be 'necessary in a democratic society'. This finding was not challenged on appeal.[1393]

(h) Incapacity and compulsory treatment measures

12.432 In *Muldoon, Applicant*[1394] the applicant sought an order under Section 57 of the Adults with Incapacity (Scotland) Act 2000 to be appointed as guardian to his 77-year-old mother who suffered who suffered from severe vascular dementia and had been admitted to acute

---

[1389] 2005 SC 453.
[1390] See similarly *Goatley (Stephen Maurice) v HM Advocate*, 2008 JC 1 and *La Torre (Antonio) v HM Advocate*, 2008 JC 23.
[1391] Sh Ct (Lothian), 3 April 2008.
[1392] 2005 SC 229 OH.
[1393] See *Napier v Scottish Ministers*, 2005 SC 307, IH.
[1394] 2005 SLT (Sh Ct) 52.

medical and rehabilitative care where her needs were assessed as being nursing home care. She was considered to be no longer capable of independent living or of managing her own affairs. In terms of specific powers relating to the welfare, property and financial affairs of his mother, the applicant specifically sought the power to decide where she should live, to have access to confidential documents, and to consent to, or withhold consent to, medical treatment. In granting the order sought the sheriff held that notwithstanding that the mother was currently 'compliant' with her current nursing and care regime, she was legally incapable of consenting to or disagreeing with it, and consequently could be said to be being deprived of her liberty Article 5. Accordingly in order to avoid a legal vacuum by placing her care on a lawful footing, the least restrictive option was one which granted statutory powers of guardianship (as sought by her son). This would allow issues such as payment of fees from her estate for her care, consent to possible medical intervention and access to otherwise confidential documents also to be dealt with on a proper legal basis and consistently with her rights under Article 8.

(i) Contaminated land and Article 8

In *Magnohard Ltd and others v United Kingdom Atomic Energy Authority*[1395] the pursuers, **12.433** who were owners variously of fishing rights and of land abutting a beach which lay adjacent to Dounreay nuclear power station, sought a declarator that the defender was in breach of its duties under Section 7 of the Nuclear Installations Act 1965 after particles of nuclear matter had been found on the beach. The pursuer claimed that their property had been materially damaged as a result of the inadequacies in the defenders the current monitoring and particle removal programme which was carried out under the auspices of the Scottish Environmental Protection Agency and that they as individuals had suffered stress and anxiety caused by the deposit of the particles which they claimed had given rise to various risks to health. In granting the requested declarator the Lord Ordinary held that there remained a possible case to answer in respect of breaches of Article 8 and Article 1 Protocol 1.

(j) Recovery of documents in civil court proceedings

The Convention compatibility of the previously accepted procedures for the recovery of **12.434** documentation in civil proceedings in Scotland remain debatable. In *Narden Services Ltd v Inverness Retail & Business Park Ltd*[1396] it was argued that the procedures under the Act of Sederunt (Rules of the Court of Session) 1994 for recovery of documents was unsound and incompatible with their rights under Article 8 unless the question as to whether they were entitled to claim and maintain confidentiality were to be determined by a Commissioner or judge. The court accepted that the rules for recovery of documents insofar as confidential documents could be applied only insofar as compatible with Article 8. While in *Somerville v Scottish Ministers*[1397] the House of Lords took the view that the upholding of by the lower courts in Scotland of a claim for Public Interest Immunity taken by the Ministers without any judicial inspection of the documentation which the Ministers

---

[1395] 2004 SC 247.
[1396] 2006 SLT 338.
[1397] [2007] 1 WLR 2734.

sought to protect was an unsatisfactory procedure and arguably in breach of the petitioners' Article 6 fair trial rights.

Appendix 3: The Canadian Charter of Rights

(1) Introduction

12.435 The Canadian Charter of Rights and Freedoms does not contain a general provision for the constitutional protection of privacy; Charter protection of the right to privacy primarily relates to restricting the ability of governmental authorities to invade the privacy of Canadians in the criminal law context.[1398] However, the Federal Privacy Act provides extensive protection for this right in ordinary domestic law and some provinces have also enacted general privacy legislation.[1399] More recently, the federal and some provincial governments have passed statutes protecting personal information. This legislation is more specific than the general privacy legislation and applies to both the public and private sectors.[1400]

(2) Privacy decisions beyond the Charter

12.436 Section 5 of the Québec Charter of Human Rights and Freedoms provides that '[e]very person has a right to respect for his private life'.[1401] Two important cases have considered the impact of the right to privacy under section 5 of the Quebec Charter of Human Rights and Freedoms.

12.437 In *Godbout v Longueil*,[1402] the Supreme Court took a liberal view of the concept of privacy and said that its purpose was to protect a sphere of individual autonomy for all decisions relating to choices which are of a fundamentally private or inherently personal nature. The city of Longueil had adopted a resolution which required all permanent employees to reside within its boundaries, and the plaintiff had signed a declaration agreeing that her employment would be terminated if she moved outside the city. She moved out of the city, was dismissed, and brought an action for damages and reinstatement. The Supreme Court decided that the residence requirement deprived the plaintiff of the right to privacy: it deprived her of the ability to choose where to establish her home.

12.438 In *Aubry v Les Editions Vice-Versa*,[1403] the Supreme Court had to consider the extent to which 'privacy' rights would protect material gathered in a public place. A photograph was

---

[1398] See generally, M Russell, 'The Impact of the Charter on Privacy and Freedom of Expression in Canada', in M Colvin (ed), *Developing Key Privacy Rights* (Hart Publishing, 2002); see also, M Hayes, 'Privacy Law in Canada' in C Wolf (ed), *Proskauer on Privacy: A Guide to Privacy and Data Security Law in the Information Age* (Practising Law Institute, 2000).

[1399] *Privacy Act*, R.S.C. 1985, c.P-21. For a survey, see J Craig and N Nolte, 'Privacy and Free Speech in Germany and Canada: Lessons for an English Privacy Tort' [1998] EHRLR 162.

[1400] *Personal Information Protection and Electronic Documents Act*, S.C. 2000, c. 5.

[1401] The Québec Charter is often referred to as a 'quasi-constitutional' document, but it is a regular provincial statute and is subject to amendment and repeal. In terms of its legislative status, it is akin to the Human Rights Codes enacted in the common law provinces.

[1402] [1997] 3 SCR 844.

[1403] [1998] 1 SCR 591.

taken of a young woman sitting on a step in front of a building and was published without her consent by a magazine. She then brought proceedings against the magazine. The Supreme Court took the view that the right to individual autonomy included the ability to control the use made of one's image; and that this right was infringed when the image was published without consent, enabling an individual to be identified.[1404] However, the right to privacy had to be balanced against the right to freedom of expression. The majority of the Supreme Court held that the balance depends both on the nature of the information and the situation of those concerned, concluding that in these circumstances, the plaintiff's right to protection of her image was more important than the artist's right to publish a photograph of her without first obtaining her consent. The majority of the Supreme Court found that there was insufficient justification for the violation of the plaintiffs' fundamental right to privacy; it had not been shown that the public's interest in publication of the photograph was predominant.

The conflict between the right to privacy and freedom of expression has been considered in **12.439** a number of other cases.[1405] In *Silber v BCTV*[1406] a television company decided to make a film about a long and bitter strike at the plaintiff's company. A television crew were attempting to film from the parking lot because the plaintiff had been uncooperative and a scuffle ensued which was broadcast on television. When the plaintiff sought damages under the provincial privacy legislation, the television company relied on a public interest defence. It succeeded on the grounds that the filming of the struggle took place in a parking lot, where the plaintiff had no reasonable expectation to privacy given that anyone walking by could have observed what happened, and that the strike was a newsworthy matter of public interest and the plaintiff's conduct was part of that context. By comparison, in *Valiquette v The Gazette*,[1407] a teacher recovered damages for violation of his privacy rights under the Quebec Charter when a newspaper disclosed the fact he had AIDs. The public interest defence was rejected because the plaintiff was not himself a public figure, and his position did not warrant disclosure of his condition.

(3) Section 8 of the Charter[1408]

The right to privacy has been embraced by the Supreme Court as the rationale for the guar- **12.440** antee against unreasonable search and seizure under section 8 of the Charter.[1409] Under the common law police and government authorities are precluded from entering private property

---

[1404] Notably, the Supreme Court held that the right to privacy was violated when the photograph was published, not the fact that it was taken. There was an infringement of privacy even though the photograph was not defamatory, insulting or offensive.

[1405] See eg, in relation to Quebec, *Field v United Amusements* [1971] SC 283; *Rebeiro v Shawningan Chemicals* [1973] SC 389; and in relation to British Columbia, *Pierre v Pacific Press* (1994) 113 DLR (4th) 511 BCCA; *Hollinsworth v BCTV* (1996) 34 CCLT (2d) 95 BCSC aff'd by (1998) 44 CCLT (2d) 83 BCCA; and see generally, Craig and Nolte (n 1399 above).

[1406] (1986) 25 DLR (4th) 345 BCSC.

[1407] (1992) 8 CCLT (2d) 302 varied [1997] RJQ 30 QCA (on the issue of exemplary damages).

[1408] See generally, J Fontana, *The Law of Search and Seizure in Canada* (5th edn, Butterworths, 2002) and P Hogg, *Constitutional Law of Canada* (5th edn, Carswell, 2007), para 48.

[1409] Section 8 of the Charter guarantees that 'Everyone has the right to be secure against unreasonable search or seizure'.

without authorization of law to search for and seize evidence of crime. The common law authorized search and seizure of evidence in two circumstances: (1) without warrant if incidental to a lawful arrest, and (2) with judicial warrant on sworn evidence of a strong basis for belief that stolen goods were concealed in the place to be searched. The common law against unreasonable search and seizure was founded on the protection of property rights rather than privacy. Entry onto private premises was trespass and removal of goods or paper amounted to conversion. Outside of the law regarding invasion of property rights, there was no prohibition against the use of evidence derived from what state officials might see or hear. Moreover, some of the common law safeguards, such as warrants, have been overridden in Canadian jurisdictions by enactment of statutory powers of search and seizure which omit them.[1410]

12.441   However, the Charter now applies to all search and seizures by government agents, whether authorized by the common law, statute or not at all. A search or seizure is reasonable within the meaning of section 8 'if it is authorized by law, if the law itself is reasonable and if the manner in which the search is carried out is reasonable.'[1411] Consequently, a search or seizure that was not authorized by statute or common law is not reasonable and will violate section 8. For example, where the police took hair samples, buccal swabs, and teeth impressions from a 17-year-old arrested for a brutal murder but failed to seize them in accordance with statutory or common law powers, the seizure was held to be highly intrusive and in breach of section 8.[1412]

12.442   The value protected by the law of search and seizure has now shifted from property rights to privacy. In its first case interpreting section 8, the Supreme Court of Canada held in *Hunter v Southam*[1413] that the Charter guarantee against unreasonable search and seizure protected a 'reasonable expectation of privacy'. In doing so, it followed the American decision in *Katz v United States*,[1414] which involved police placement of an electronic listening device on the outside of a public telephone booth to record the accused's end of a telephone conversation. In the absence of police trespass onto private property, the US Supreme Court found that the 'bug' was an infringement of the Fourth Amendment which prohibits 'unreasonable searches and seizures', on grounds that there had been an invasion of the 'reasonable expectation of privacy' relied upon by the accused in using the telephone booth. The Supreme Court of Canada in *Hunter v Southam* adopted the 'reasonable expectation of privacy' rationale even though the case involved actual entry onto the premises of a corporation for the purposes of a combines investigation. It also found that a corporation has the same constitutionally protected expectation of privacy as an individual, and, because the purpose of section 8 is to 'protect individuals from unjustified state intrusions upon their privacy', an *ex post facto* determination as to the reasonableness of the search would

---

[1410] The common law regarding authorization of search and seizure still applies in common law provinces unless overridden by statute.

[1411] *R. v Collins* [1987] 1 SCR 265.

[1412] *R v Stillman* [1997] 1 SCR 607.

[1413] [1984] 2 SCR 145.

[1414] (1967) 389 US 347; cf *Minnesota v Carter* (1998) 5 BHRC 457 (in which the majority of the US Supreme Court took a restrictive approach to this case).

not suffice. It held that the purpose of the section 'requires a means of preventing unjustifiable searches before they happen, not simply of determining, after the fact, whether they ought to have occurred in the first place'.

The basic principles which apply to the right to be secure against unreasonable search or **12.443** seizure under section 8 were summarized in *R v Edwards*:[1415]

- A claim for relief under section 24(2) of the Charter can be made only by the person whose Charter rights have been infringed.[1416]
- Like all Charter rights, section 8 is a personal right; it protects people, not places.[1417]
- The right to challenge the legality of a search depends upon the accused establishing that his personal rights to privacy have been violated.[1418]
- As a general rule, two distinct inquiries must be made in relation to section 8. The first is whether the accused had a reasonable expectation of privacy; the second, if such an expectation is present, is whether the police search was conducted reasonably.[1419]
- A reasonable expectation of privacy is to be determined on the basis of the totality of the circumstances.[1420]
- The factors to be considered in assessing the totality of the circumstances may include, but are not restricted to, the following:
  (a) presence at the time of the search;
  (b) possession or control of the property or place searched;
  (c) ownership of the property or place;
  (d) historical use of the property or item;
  (e) the ability to regulate access, including the right to admit or exclude others from the place;
  (f) the existence of a subjective expectation of privacy; and
  (g) the objective reasonableness of the expectation.

(4) A personal right

The essence of section 8 protection is that it is a personal privacy right.[1421] The right alleg- **12.444** edly infringed must, therefore, be that of the person, most often the accused, who makes the challenge.

A personal right of privacy is not coterminous with a possessory or property interest in **12.445** premises or articles,[1422] although possession or ownership might properly be considered evidence of that personal right.[1423] For example, as the applicant in *Pugliese*[1424] was unable

---

[1415] [1996] 1 SCR 128.
[1416] *R v Rahey* [1987] 1 SCR 588, 619.
[1417] *Hunter v Southam*, [1984] 2 SCR 145, citing Stewart J in *Katz v United States* (1967) 389 US 347.
[1418] *R v Pugliese* (1992) 71 CCC (3d) 295 Ont CA.
[1419] *Rawlings v Kentucky* (1980) 448 US 98.
[1420] *R v Colarusso* [1994] 1 SCR 20; *R v Wong* [1990] 3 SCR 36.
[1421] *R v Edwards* ([1996] 1 SCR 128); *R v Pugliese* (n 1418 above).
[1422] Dickson J in *Hunter v Southam* ([1984] 2 SCR 145) emphatically rejected any requirement of a connection between the section 8 right and a property interest in the premises searched.
[1423] *R v Edwards* (n 1421 above) quoting Finlayson JA in *R v Pugliese* (n 1418 above).
[1424] n 1418 above.

to advance any ground for an expectation of privacy beyond ownership of the building in question, the Court concluded that he had no expectation of privacy in a leased apartment in a building or the portion of it from which drugs were seized. Neither did possession of a driver's licence in *R v Hufsky*[1425] give its owner any right to withhold it when demanded by a police officer. The Supreme Court of Canada held that the requirement to produce the driver's licence 'did not constitute an intrusion on a reasonable expectation of privacy' as there can be no such intrusion 'where a person is required to produce a licence or permit or other documentary evidence of a status or compliance with some legal requirement that is a lawful condition of the exercise of a right or privilege.' Instead, the Supreme Court has indicated that a key element in privacy is the right to be free from intrusion or interference. This element could not be established in *Edwards*, where the Court found that the accused had been no more than a 'privileged guest' in the home of his girlfriend. Particularly relevant was the fact that it was not the accused but his girlfriend who had the authority to regulate access to, and exclude others from, the premises.[1426]

12.446 It is possible, in some circumstances, to establish an expectation of privacy in goods themselves. Such was the case in relation to the records of a business proprietorship in *Thomson Newspapers*[1427] which were subject to an order for production under the federal Combines Investigation Act. The accused in *R v Plant*,[1428] on the other hand, failed to establish a right of privacy in his electricity bills. The accused in *Edwards* also attempted to argue that an interest in seized drugs created a reasonable expectation of privacy.[1429]

12.447 The expectation of privacy by third parties will only be relevant to the disposition of an application under section 8 in 'somewhat rare circumstances'.[1430] In *R v Edwards*, the police conducted a drug search of the premises of the girlfriend of the accused, who was persuaded to allow them access without a warrant, in the absence of her boyfriend. The majority held the search to be constitutional as the accused had no reasonable expectation of privacy in the apartment. The rights of the accused's girlfriend were not considered by the Court, although it was acknowledged that the intrusion of the search on third parties might have been relevant to the reasonableness of the search in the second stage of the analysis, had it been necessary to go that far.[1431] 'A potentially massive invasion of the privacy of persons . . . cannot be ignored simply because it is not brought to the attention of the court by one of those persons.' But the majority held that any such invasion of third-party privacy rights is not determinative of the reasonableness of the search; in any authorization of a search or seizure there is a possibility of an invasion of privacy of innocent third parties. Contrary to the view

---

[1425] [1988] 1 SCR 621.

[1426] *R v Edwards* [1996] 1 SCR 128.

[1427] *Thomson Newspapers Ltd v Canada* [1990] (Director of Investigation and Research, Restrictive Trade Practices Commission) 1 SCR 425.

[1428] *R v Plant* [1993] 3 SCR 281, followed in *R v Tessling* [2004] 3 SCR 432, discussed further below.

[1429] In *R v Edwards* (n 1426 above) the appellant sought unsuccessfully to assert a right in the drugs seized, after having maintained in the Ontario Court of Appeal that they did not belong to him. The SCC precluded him from changing his position so as to raise a fresh defence. See also *R v Sandhu* (1993) 82 CCC (3d) 236 BCCA in which the question of privacy in a suitcase of drugs arose.

[1430] *R v Edwards* (n 1426 above).

[1431] Ibid, for the two stages see para 12.448.

of the majority, La Forest J felt that section 8 protects a right enuring to all the public to security from intrusion by unwarranted police searches; it is a right of citizens, and not just the accused. Accordingly, the expectation of privacy of the girlfriend ought to have been taken into account.

(5) Section 8 analysis: a two-step process

(a) Introduction

The determination as to whether section 8 has been infringed is a two stage process.[1432] The **12.448** expectation of privacy is relevant to each stage. First, the presence (or absence) of a reasonable expectation of privacy is relevant as to whether the activity in question constitutes a search or seizure within the meaning of section 8.[1433] Secondly, once a search or seizure has been established, the court must assess its reasonableness; and presumes the search or seizure is reasonable unless the contrary is proved. Where a reasonable expectation exists, but in a diminished form, the threshold will be lowered and the presumption of reasonableness more easily rebutted. The two stages must be considered separately. Whether a reasonable expectation of privacy exists is to be ascertained without reference to the police conduct during the search or to the seriousness of the alleged offences. Whether the search constitutes an unreasonable intrusion on that right to privacy is a distinct question from whether such a right exists.

(b) First stage: the existence of a 'search' or 'seizure'

Electronic surveillance. The Supreme Court of Canada has followed the American deci- **12.449** sion in *Katz*[1434] and held that electronic surveillance is a search or seizure under section 8 of the Charter.[1435] A reasonable expectation of privacy is violated when a telephone conversation is intercepted without the knowledge or consent of the participants.[1436] The Criminal Code of Canada provides for electronic interception of private telephone conversations under judicial warrant, and when the statutory procedure is complied with, a wiretap is both lawful and reasonable under section 8.[1437]

The Supreme Court has, however, refused to distinguish between 'participant electronic **12.450** surveillance', in which one party to a conversation or interaction consents to its surreptitious electronic recording, and 'third-party electronic surveillance', in which none of the parties consent. In *R v Duarte*[1438] the police obtained the cooperation of an informer to enable them to install audio-visual equipment on his premises and to record his drug transaction with the accused. In *R v Wiggins*[1439] the informer consented to wear a microphone which transmitted his conversations with the accused about drug dealings to the police. In each of these cases, the surreptitious recording was found to invade a reasonable expectation

---

[1432] Ibid.
[1433] Where there is no expectation of privacy, then there is no search or seizure within the meaning of section 8 and no requirement of reasonableness.
[1434] *Katz v United States* (1967) 389 US 347.
[1435] *R v Duarte* [1990] 1 SCR 30.
[1436] *R v Thompson* [1990] 2 SCR 1111.
[1437] *R v Garofoli* [1990] 2 SCR 1421.
[1438] n 1435 above.
[1439] [1990] 1 SCR 62.

of privacy and be unreasonable under section 8. The difficulty with this approach is that the breaching of confidence is not an invasion of privacy and disclosure of a private conversation by one of the parties is therefore admissible evidence. As a result, evidence from informers is admissible whereas the electronic recording of the very same conversation is not.[1440] Another problem is that if the recording is an invasion of privacy, it is so whether or not it is tendered as evidence, and thus police are prohibited from using recording devices even as a means of protection of undercover officers or informers.[1441]

12.451   In spite of these difficulties, the Supreme Court of Canada has maintained the view that a participant does not accept the risk of disclosure by another participant. It has extended the finding of a reasonable expectation of privacy from private telephone conversations to illegal gambling activities in a crowded hotel room. In *R v Wong*[1442] the hotel consented to the installation of a hidden camera, and although few of the guests knew one another, the Court found that the video-recording of illegal gambling activities in the room invaded their reasonable expectation of privacy, in violation of the Charter.

12.452   As a result of these decisions, the police in Canada can lawfully use participant electronic surveillance techniques without a warrant only where there is no reasonable expectation of privacy, such as a conversation or transaction taking place on the street or in a public venue, or where there are exceptional circumstances.[1443] The Charter would not apply to a recording initiated by a private individual, but, if for example a shop proprietor installed a video camera at the suggestion of the police, he might be deemed an agent of the police.[1444]

12.453   **The collection of evidence.**   The collection of evidence, even in the absence of a search, may also amount to a 'seizure' on the basis of a reasonable expectation of privacy. In *R v*

[1440] Evidence obtained in breach of the Charter is generally not admissible, unless it can be shown that the police were unaware that they had violated the Charter and were acting in good faith. See P Hogg (n 1408 above) para 41. See also *R v Fiss* [2002] 1 SCR 535 where an undercover police officer obtained a warrant to wear a body pack and record a conversation with a murder suspect. At trial, the judge determined that the warrant should not have been issued and, following *Duarte*, he ruled that the transcript of the recording was inadmissible. Of course, the police officer was free to testify to his recollection of the conversation and was free to refresh his recollection with the transcript. The police officer read verbatim from the excluded transcript at trial. On appeal, a majority of the Supreme Court held that the trial judge should not have permitted the police officer to read verbatim from the transcript, and it constituted a violation of section 8, but upheld the conviction. The concurring minority found that the reading of the transcript was not a violation of section 8, and it was a trivial error not affecting the outcome or fairness of the trial.

[1441] The Criminal Code of Canada has been amended to provide for state-initiated participant surveillance where police officers obtain prior judicial authorization on reasonable grounds: S.C. 1993, C. 40, s 4. This provision of the Criminal Code was upheld as in compliance with section 8 in *R v Pires* [2005] 3 SCR 343. Additionally, a police officer may resort to participant surveillance without prior judicial authorization in exceptional circumstances, where it is believed on reasonable grounds that the urgency of the situation is such and authorization could not be obtained with 'reasonable diligence', or where the agent of the state 'believes on reasonable grounds that there is risk of bodily harm to the persons who consented to the interception' and the 'purpose of the interception is to prevent bodily harm.' Evidence obtained in the latter manner is only admissible 'for the purposes of proceedings in which actual, attempted or threatened bodily harm is alleged' and any other evidence must be destroyed. This is clearly aimed at protecting informers and undercover police officers.

[1442] *R v Wong* [1990] 3 SCR 36.

[1443] See n 1441 above.

[1444] *R v Broyles* [1991] 3 SCR 595 where a friend of a suspect visiting the suspect in prison at the suggestion of the police, and recording their conversation, was a police agent.

Dyment[1445] a doctor collected blood from the wound of an unconscious traffic accident victim for medical purposes, but then delivered it to a police officer for analysis, resulting in charges of impaired driving against the victim. Although section 8 did not apply to the private act of the doctor collecting the sample, the Supreme Court of Canada found that the receipt of the sample by the police officer, without a warrant and without the consent of the accused, was an unreasonable 'seizure' violating the reasonable expectation of privacy of the accused in the blood and infringing section 8. The Court used the concept of an expectation of privacy to distinguish a 'gathering' of evidence from that of an unconstitutional 'seizure', citing the example of police collection of blood from the seat of a car driven by an accused, where the individual would be considered to have 'abandoned' the blood, retaining no reasonable expectation of privacy in regard to it.

In *R v Dersch*,[1446] the Supreme Court of Canada held that the disclosure of hospital records, **12.454** including the results of a blood alcohol test performed for medical reasons, to police was a breach of the accused's reasonable expectation of privacy in those records, which he was justified in assuming would be kept confidential by the hospital.

In *R v Arp*,[1447] the Supreme Court of Canada held that providing consent to bodily samples **12.455** being taken for the purposes of analyzing DNA for one murder investigation also authorized the use of those samples for a subsequent murder investigation, absent express prior restriction on their use for collateral purposes. The accused lost any reasonable expectation of privacy in the bodily samples once he provided informed consent for the initial collection.

A 'seizure' may also occur where police recover lost or stolen property; it does not necessar- **12.456** ily support an inference that the owner voluntarily relinquished the property or no longer has an expectation of privacy in it. In *R v Law*,[1448] the police recovered a stolen safe that had been abandoned by the thieves. Before returning the safe to its owners, a police officer unconnected with the theft investigation, but who suspected the owners of violating tax laws, photocopied financial documents found in the safe. The documents indicated that the owners had not been fully reporting and remitting taxes. The Supreme Court of Canada held that there had been a violation of the right to privacy. Despite the fact that the owners had reported the theft of the property and implicitly agreed to police possession of the safe for the duration of the investigation of the theft, they retained 'a residual, but limited, reasonable expectation of privacy in the contents' and the expectation of a police inspection was limited to what was necessary in the circumstances.

The Supreme Court of Canada found that there was a reasonable expectation of privacy over **12.457** the contents of a rented bus locker in *R v Buhay*.[1449] Private security guards at a bus station opened a locker after they smelled marijuana. After finding drugs within, they replaced the drugs in the locker, re-locked it and called the police, who seized the drugs without a warrant.

[1445] [1988] 2 SCR 417.
[1446] [1993] 3 SCR 768.
[1447] [1998] 3 SCR 339.
[1448] [2002] SCC 10.
[1449] [2003] 1 SCR 631; see also *R v Kang-Brown*, 2008 SCC 18 (sniffer dog search of a back pack at a bus station was an unlawful search).

The Court found that the initial search by the security guards did not trigger section 8, as they were not acting as agents of the state, but the police should have obtained a warrant to search the locker. The accused's reasonable expectation of privacy was not destroyed by the security guards' invasion of that privacy prior to the police or the fact that the management of the bus station had a master key which could be used access the locker; it only reduced rather than negated the expectation of privacy. School students have a reasonable expectation that their back packs would not be subject to random and speculative scrutiny by the police.[1449a]

12.458 **Collection of documents.** Where there is a reasonable expectation of privacy in relation to documents, an order for their production may constitute a 'search' or 'seizure' under section 8.

12.459 In *R v Hufsky*[1450] a demand by a police officer that a driver produce a driver's licence and vehicle insurance certificate was found not to be a 'search' under the section because it did not intrude on a reasonable expectation of privacy. It was clear that there could be no such intrusion on any reasonable expectation of privacy by way of a request for evidence of compliance with a requirement that is a lawful condition of the exercise of a right or privilege.[1451]

12.460 While there is no reasonable expectation of privacy in regard to a motor vehicle licence, such expectation does exist in regard to business records. In order for constitutional protection to be extended to documents, the information seized must be of a 'personal and confidential nature'; this would include information revealing intimate details of the lifestyle of its owner. The computerized records of electricity consumption were found in *Plant*[1452] to reflect a purely commercial relationship between appellant and utility, because they revealed little personal information of the occupant of the residence, and were available to the public. By contrast, in *Thomson Newspapers v Canada*[1453] the records of a business proprietor were characterized as confidential communications. There, the order under the federal Combines Investigation Act to produce the documents was found to be a 'seizure', even though there was no entry or search of premises on grounds that there was 'little difference between taking a thing and forcing a person to give it up'.[1454]

12.461 **Disclosure of information.** In *R v Plant*,[1455] police arrested the accused for cultivation of marijuana after they searched electrical utility records and determined that his house consumed four times as much electricity as similar residences. There had been no entry onto the accused's property and no inspection of the accused's documents; the electrical utility had agreed to give the police access to it records. The Supreme Court of Canada held that an individual has a reasonable expectation of privacy to information that is 'personal and confidential', but the majority found that the accused did not have a reasonable

---

[1449a] *R v AM* 2008 SCC 19 (sniffer dog search of student back pack breach of s 8).
[1450] [1988] 1 SCR 621; followed by *R v Ladouceur* [1990] 1 SCR 1257.
[1451] *R v Hufsky* [1988] 1 SCR 621, 638.
[1452] *R v Plant* ([1993] 3 SCR 281).
[1453] [1990] 1 SCR 425.
[1454] Note, though, that ultimately the seizure was found to be a reasonable one, in spite of the fact that it had been authorized by the investigating agency, rather than a court, on grounds that a demand to produce documents is far less intrusive upon privacy than an actual search of premises.
[1455] n 1452 above.

expectation of privacy in relation to the electricity records as they only revealed the pattern of electricity consumption in the residence and not any intimate details of the accused's life. The minority adopted the view that the information was not public and a reasonable person would have concluded that the records should only be used for the purposes for which they were made (billing of electricity) and not divulged to government authorities without proper authorization.

Similarly, in *R v Tessling*,[1456] another case involving charges of cultivation of marijuana, the **12.462** Supreme Court of Canada found that the use of an infra-red camera to thermally scan properties owned by the accused for heat, and the use of the information derived from that, in order to obtain a search warrant for the accused home, was not a violation of section 8. The Court characterized the thermal scan as external surveillance of the residence and not equivalent to entry. The technology utilized information from the exterior of the building and in that sense, only records information available to the public, albeit not visible to the naked eye, over which the accused could not have a reasonable expectation of privacy. Additionally, the thermal scan did not reveal any intimate, personal details about the accused and did not infringe his dignity, integrity or autonomy.

In *Smith v Canada*,[1457] no breach of section 8 was found when a customs declaration was **12.463** disclosed to unemployment authorities that showed the appellant had been on holiday outside Canada while receiving unemployment benefits, which was prohibited. Canada Customs had an agreement with the Employment Insurance Commission to disclosure this information, and the appellant was ordered to repay two weeks of benefits. Although the appellant claimed that she did not expect information in her customs declaration form to be used by the government for other purposes, the Supreme Court of Canada held that any expectation of privacy in the information was outweighed by the public interest in ensuring compliance with the unemployment insurance scheme.

(c) Second stage: the reasonableness of the search or seizure

The expectation of privacy will also, to some extent, be relevant in the assessment of the **12.464** reasonableness of the search or seizure. The test for reasonableness of a search or seizure was established by unanimous decision of the Supreme Court of Canada in *Hunter v Southam*:[1458] it is reasonable if it is authorized by law, if the law itself is reasonable and if the manner in which the search or seizure is carried out is reasonable. In *Hunter v Southam*, the power of search and seizure in the Combines Investigation Act was found to infringe section 8 of the Charter because it authorized 'unreasonable' searches and seizures. The Court held that generally there must be a mechanism for prior authorization, where feasible; warrantless searches are presumed to be unreasonable. It was acknowledged that it would not always be feasible to satisfy the prescribed criteria, and therefore, a search without a warrant might be justified if a presumption of unreasonableness could be rebutted.

[1456] [2004] 3 SCR 432.
[1457] [2001] SCC 88.
[1458] *Hunter v Southam* ([1984] 2 SCR 145) the Court said that a search was reasonable only if it was authorized by statute which stipulated three conditions: a prior warrant or other authorization; issued by a person 'capable of acting judicially'; and on oath that there are 'reasonable and probable grounds' for believing that an offence has been committed and that evidence is located in the place to be searched.

12.465 The presumption of unreasonableness of a warrantless search may be rebutted where the search or seizure is not significantly intrusive, or where the expectation of privacy itself is diminished, or both. The order for production of documents in *Thomson Newspapers*, for example, was considered minimally intrusive, in comparison with the imposition of an actual search, upon the undiminished expectation of privacy in the documents. As a result, the order for production, though issued under non-judicial authorization, resulted in a reasonable 'seizure' when held up to a reduced standard or threshold of reasonableness in the circumstances. In *R v Plant*,[1459] on the other hand, the Supreme Court of Canada held that a perimeter search of premises was unreasonable, despite a minimal level of intrusion, as there was no evidence of any circumstances that justified a search without a warrant under the Narcotics Control Act.

12.466 Statutory schemes that provide for warrantless searches may also be reasonable where there are 'exigent circumstances'. In *R v Grant*,[1460] the Supreme Court 'read down' a provision of the federal Narcotic Control Act that provided for warrantless searches to limit it to 'situations in which exigent circumstances render obtaining a warrant impracticable', such as 'where there exists an imminent danger of the loss, removal, destruction or disappearance of the evidence sought in a narcotics investigation if the search or seizure is delayed in order to obtain a warrant.'

12.467 A lower expectation of privacy will reduce the standard of reasonableness so as not to require fulfilment of the warrant requirements of *Hunter v Southam*. This will occur, for example: in the prison context, where inmates, while having some expectation of privacy, are subject to random or routine searches of their person and their cells;[1461] where an individual has been convicted of multiple serious offences and remains in custody, he or she must submit to a DNA sample for a data bank;[1462] in a school context, it has been held reasonable for a teacher to search a student without warrant for possession of drugs;[1463] at an international border, where the absence of a warrant requirement for a strip search authorized by the Customs Act was found to be reasonable;[1464] at public buildings that involve screening procedures, the expectation of privacy is diminished and warrantless searches are reasonable;[1465] or during travel in an automobile.[1466] The expectation of privacy will also be less if the activity in question is regulated. Administrative inspections of commercial premises, or even private homes, in order to check for compliance with building standards, zoning rules, public health and safety requirements are not unreasonable searches[1467] and

---

[1459] [1993] 3 SCR 281.

[1460] [1993] 3 SCR 223.

[1461] *Weatherall v Canada* [1993] 2 SCR 872.

[1462] *R v Rodgers* [2006] 1 SCR 554.

[1463] *R v JMG* (1986) 56 OR (2d) 705 CA; *R v M(MR)* [1998] 3 SCR 393.

[1464] *R v Simmons* [1988] 2 SCR 495.

[1465] *R v Campanella* (2005) 75 OR (3d) 342 CA.

[1466] *R v Wise* [1992] 1 SCR 527: the expectation of privacy in automobile travel is markedly decreased relative to the expectation of privacy in one's home or office; in *R v Belnavis* [1997] 3 SCR 341 the Supreme Court held that the reasonable expectation depends on the totality of the circumstances.

[1467] See *Re Belgoma Transportation* (1985) 51 OR (2d) 509 CA: employment standards; *R v Quesnel* (1985) 53 OR (2d) 338 CA: marketing board inspection; *R v Bichel* (1986) 33 DLR (4th) 254 BCCA: building

confiscation of an illegal or dangerous or diseased thing without a warrant in such circumstances is not an unreasonable seizure.[1468]

A forced 'bedpan vigil' by customs officers of a detainee suspected to have ingested pellets of drugs was held to be a reasonable search in *R v Monney*.[1469]   **12.468**

A strip search of an arrested suspect was held to be unreasonable in the circumstances in *R v Golden*,[1470] as it took place in a restaurant (out of view of customers) and the Supreme Court put restrictions on the use and manner of this form of search. The majority of the court stated that the fact that the police had reasonable and probable grounds to carry out an arrest did not confer on them the automatic authority to carry out a strip search, even where the strip search met the definition of being 'incident to lawful arrest'. In addition to reasonable and probable grounds justifying the arrest, the police must establish reasonable and probable grounds justifying the strip search.   **12.469**

Police may not search for evidence without a warrant, beyond conducting a pat-down search for potentially dangerous weapons, during detention of a suspect for the purposes of investigation (without making an arrest). In *R v Mann*,[1471] police had stopped an individual who fit the description of a suspect, and detained him for investigative purposes. They conducted a pat-down search for weapons, and in doing so, discovered drugs. The Supreme Court of Canada found that the police officer, in reaching into the suspect's pocket after feeling something soft, went beyond the permissible search for weapons; the evidence was obtained in breach of section 8.   **12.470**

Where there is an increased expectation of privacy, such as in a lawyer's office, the threshold of what constitutes a reasonable search will, accordingly, also be increased. In *Lavallee*,[1472] the Supreme Court of Canada considered the validity of Criminal Code provisions for searches of law offices, and found the legislative scheme to be unconstitutional. The legislation purportedly included elements to safeguard solicitor-client privilege, and allowed an opportunity for a lawyer to assert a claim of privilege over documents, which would then, following review by a Court, potentially be excluded from the search warrant. The majority of the Court stressed the importance and sanctity of solicitor-client privilege and held that any legislative scheme that inferred with that privilege more than 'absolutely necessary' would be unreasonable. After the statutory provisions for searches of law offices were struck down in *Lavallee*, the Supreme Court of Canada had to consider the constitutionality of a search conducted under a warrant obtained through the common law procedure in *Maranda v Richer*.[1473] The Court found the search to have been unreasonable on the basis   **12.471**

---

inspection of private home; *Ontario Chrysler (1997) Ltd v Ontario* (1990) 72 OR (2d) 106 CA: business practices inspection.

[1468] *R v Bertram S Miller* [1986] 3 FC 291 CA: (confiscation and destruction of diseased plants); *Re Ozubko* (1986) 33 DLR (4th) 714 Man CA: (confiscation of illegal syringe); *Re Milton* (1986) 37 DLR (4th) 694: (confiscation of illegal fishing nets).

[1469] [1999] 1 SCR 652.

[1470] [2001] 3 SCR 679.

[1471] [2004] 3 SCR 59.

[1472] *Lavallee, Rackel & Heintz v Canada* [2002] 3 SCR 209.

[1473] [2003] 3 SCR 193.

that the warrant was issued without evidence that there was no alternative method for obtaining the information sought, (the lower court had found as a fact that at least half the information could have been obtained from other sources) and that advance notice of the search had not been provided to the lawyer, preventing him from asserting a claim of privilege at the outset.

Appendix 4: The New Zealand Bill of Rights Act

(1) Introduction: the common law

12.472 Like the Canadian Charter of Rights and Freedoms, the New Zealand Bill of Rights Act 1990 makes no express provision for the guarantee of respect to privacy. Nevertheless, the law of New Zealand protects privacy in a number of ways including legislation in relation to harassment, data protection and covert filming of persons in intimate situations.[1474]

12.473 In the case of *Hosking v Runting*[1475] by a majority of 3 to 2, the New Zealand Court of Appeal recognized the existence of a common law tort of breach of privacy. The elements of the tort are:

- the existence of facts in respect of which there was a reasonable expectation of privacy
- publicity given to those private facts that would be considered highly offensive to an objective reasonable person.[1476]

There is a defence if the publication can be justified by a legitimate public concern in the information. It has been held that there is no reasonable expectation of privacy in relation to a video reconstruction of a murder and an interview with the suspect which were to be broadcast after his acquittal.[1477]

12.474 Before the decision in *Hosking v Runting* a number of breach of privacy claims had been successful at first instance. Thus, in *P v D*[1478] a journalist informed a public figure that he was preparing a newspaper article concerning his treatment at a psychiatric hospital and an injunction was sought to prevent publication. Although the claim for breach of confidence failed, Nicholson J held the tort of breach of privacy was established by public disclosure of private facts which are highly offensive and objectionable to a person of reasonable sensibilities subject to the nature and extent of legitimate interest in the public disclosure of the information. Such factors had to be balanced against the right to freedom of expression under section 14 of the New Zealand Bill of Rights Act. In *L v G*[1479] it was held that the

---

[1474] For a general survey see New Zealand Law Commission, *Privacy Concepts and Issues* (Study Paper 19, January 2008) and see also, generally, R Tobin, 'Privacy and Freedom of Expression in New Zealand', in M Colvin (ed), *Developing Key Privacy Rights* (Hart Publishing, 2002).

[1475] *Hosking v Runting* [2005] 1 NZLR 1 (CA). (the case concerned the taking of photographs of children in a public street which, it was held, did not constitute a breach of privacy): see generally, John Burrows 'Invasion of Privacy—Hosking and Beyond' [2006] NZ Law Rev 389, 390.

[1476] Ibid, 32 (Gault P and Blanchard J).

[1477] *Television New Zealand v Rogers* [2008] 2 NZLR 277 (SC).

[1478] [2000] 2 NZLR 591.

[1479] [2002] DCR 234.

publication of sexually explicit photographs of the claimant was an invasion of her privacy, despite the fact that she could not be identified. Damages of NZ$2,500 were awarded for invasion of privacy. More recently in *Brown v Attorney-General*[1480] an award of NZ$25,000 was made to a parolee, who had been convicted of kidnapping and indecently assaulting a young boy, in respect of a flyer distributed to residents of his neighbourhood alerting them to his presence and attaching a photograph of him.

(2) New Zealand Bill of Rights Act

(a) Introduction

12.475 The New Zealand Bill of Rights Act protects privacy in the area of search and seizure. Section 21 provides that:

> **Unreasonable search and seizure**
> Everyone has the right to be secure against unreasonable search or seizure, whether of the person, property or correspondence or otherwise.

The final words reflect the Fourth Amendment in the American Bill of Rights and have some similarity to the Article 8 of the Convention.

12.476 The New Zealand approach to reasonableness of search and seizure places less emphasis on the protection of privacy than does that of the Canadian courts. Whether a search or seizure has been unreasonable and evidence unfairly or improperly obtained is determined by balancing all of the relevant interests in the circumstances, including, but not focusing exclusively on an 'expectation of privacy'. In *R v Holford*,[1481] for example, the court admitted evidence which had been illegally obtained by private investigators who were trespassers, as its admission did not result in unfairness.

12.477 The Court of Appeal first considered the relationship of privacy to search and seizure in *R v Jeffries*,[1482] in which the police, believing the accused and his companions to be fleeing an armed robbery, stopped and searched the vehicle they were driving for weapons and stolen goods. The search, conducted without warrant, would have been lawful under the Arms Act had they identified themselves properly and advised the suspects of the section of the Act under which the search was to take place; they did not so comply with the statute and the search of the boot of the car revealed not arms but $30,000 worth of cannabis. The issue before the Court of Appeal was whether the search was reasonable under the New Zealand Bill of Rights Act. Five of the seven judges agreed that a search may be 'unlawful' and yet reasonable under the Bill of Rights Act; four found that although the search was unlawful it had not been rendered unreasonable. Two judges held that the search was lawful and reasonable; one judge in dissent held the unlawful search was *ipso facto* unreasonable. The cannabis was admitted as evidence in the trial of the accused.

[1480] [2006] NZAR 552.
[1481] [2001] 1 NZLR 385.
[1482] [1994] 1 NZLR 290.

12.478   After consideration of the Canadian position on the relationship of privacy to the reasonableness of a search,[1483] Richardson J stated that an analysis of section 21 would emphasize four considerations:

(i)   rights of the citizen reflect an amalgam of values: property, personal freedom, privacy and dignity. A search of premises or the person is an invasion of property rights, a restraint on individual liberty, an intrusion on privacy and an affront to dignity.

(ii)   neither the Bill of Rights Act nor the International Covenant provides a general guarantee of privacy, and New Zealand did not have a general privacy law. There is no one privacy value that applies in all cases; rather, the nature and significance of a privacy value depends on the circumstances in which it arises.

(iii)   a section 21 inquiry is an exercise in balancing competing values and interests; in particular, the legitimate state interests in detection and prosecution of offending against the immunity of citizens from arbitrary and unlawful searches of their property and persons. Whether the intrusion is 'unreasonable' involves weighing all relevant public interest considerations and their application in the particular case.

(iv)   protection against unreasonable search or seizure must be distinguished from a 'reasonable expectation of privacy'. The two would be the same if one could ignore the interests of society as a whole or the interests of anyone other than the person whose privacy is affected, but rights are never absolute and individual freedoms are necessarily limited by membership of society.

A section 21 assessment must start with the presumption that any search is a significant invasion of individual freedom. How significant it is will depend on the particular circumstances and the other values and interests including law enforcement considerations which weigh in the particular case.

12.479   The intrusiveness of the search and the extent of the violation of individual rights vary according to the subject-matter of the search and the manner in which it is carried out. Thus, frisking an individual is less intrusive than a search of body cavities; the home is more a sanctuary than the office. Reasonable expectations of privacy are lower in public places than within private property. While in a mobile society the privacy of one's motor vehicle is highly valued and may be perceived as a projection of the privacy of the home, road safety and the legitimate protection of other users of the roads justify extensive rules governing the use of vehicles and allowing surveillance and supervision of vehicles, drivers and passengers. The expectation of privacy may be less where the property searched belongs to a third party, particularly where that person purports to consent to the search, and the complainant is a guest or family member or shares the use of the property. The manner in which a search is carried out will also affect the degree of any intrusion on private rights. It follows that in assessing the reasonableness of a search or seizure it is important to consider 'both the subject-matter and the time, place and circumstance'.

[1483] In particular *Hunter v Southam* (1984) 14 CCC 3d 97 and the US case of *Katz v United States* 389 US 347.

(b) Section 21 cases

Introduction.   Since 1994, the New Zealand Court of Appeal has been inundated with   **12.480**
section 21 cases.[1484] The Court has preferred the 'amalgam of values' approach taken in
Jeffries to the 'expectation of privacy' perspective of the American and Canadian jurisprudence. The test of unreasonableness of a search or seizure involves an assessment of all of the
circumstances: the relevant values and public interest considerations and their application
in the particular case.[1485]

While *Jeffries* established that lawfulness does not always determine reasonableness, or vice   **12.481**
versa, the unlawfulness of a search and seizure is highly relevant to reasonableness.[1486] If a
warrant is readily obtainable, that will tell strongly against the reasonableness of an unauthorized search.[1487] Only in rare cases will an unlawful search and seizure be reasonable.[1488]
So for example, in *R v H* where the police deliberately decided to refrain from obtaining a
search warrant readily available under the Summary Proceedings Act, the search of the
premises of an accountant and seizure of the company records was found to be
unreasonable.

The *Grayson* principles.   The principles were restated by the Court of Appeal in *R v*   **12.482**
Grayson and Taylor.[1489] In that case, the police observed suspicious activity, including the
construction of an electric fence and erection of shadecloth on the appellants' kiwi fruit
orchard. Believing that they did not have enough evidence to obtain a search warrant, the
police entered the property for the purposes of corroborating the information they had
received. The entry involved negotiating electric fences and thick underbrush, but was not
forceful. During their five minutes on the property, the officers observed rows of cannabis
plants growing between the kiwifruit vines. A search warrant was subsequently obtained
and surveillance videos taken, plants seized and appellants charged with cultivation of cannabis. The trial judge found the initial search unlawful but not unreasonable. The Court of
Appeal dismissed the appeal and held that in all the circumstances, entry onto the property
was reasonable and the evidence admissible.

The Court of Appeal in *Grayson* set out a number of statutory and common law principles   **12.483**
relevant to a challenge to the admissibility of evidence on grounds of breach of section 21.

[1484]   See eg, *R v A* [1994] 1 NZLR 429; *R v H* [1994] 2 NZLR 143; *R v Ririnui* [1994] 2 NZLR 439; *R v
Pratt* [1994] 3 NZLR 21; *Simpson v A-G (Baigent's case)* [1994] 3 NZLR 667; *Auckland Unemployed Workers'
Rights Centre Inc v A-G* [1994] 3 NZLR 720; *R v McNicol* [1995] 1 NZLR 576; *R v Kahu* [1995] 2 NZLR 3; *R
v Stockdale* [1995] 2 NZLR 129; *Television New Zealand Ltd v A-G* [1995] 2 NZLR 641; *R v Reuben* [1995] 3
NZLR 165; *R v Wojcik* (1994) 11 CRNZ 463; *Campbell v Police* [1994] 3 NZLR 260; *R v Wong-Tung* (1995)
13 CRNZ 422; *R v Smith* (1996) 13 CRNZ 481; *R v Barlow* (1995) 14 CRNZ 9; *R v Faasipa* (1995) 2 HRNZ
50; *Queen Street Backpackers Ltd v Commerce Commission* (1994) 2 HRNZ 94; *R v Dodgson* (1995) 2 HRNZ
300. See generally, A & P Butler, *The New Zealand Bill of Rights Act: A Commentary* (LexisNexis, 2005),
Chap 18.
[1485]   *R v A* [1994] 1 NZLR 429; *R v Pratt* [1994] 3 NZLR 21, 24: the test is 'whether the circumstances
giving rise to it make the search itself unreasonable or if a search that is otherwise reasonable is carried out in
an unreasonable manner'.
[1486]   See *R v H* [1994] 2 NZLR 143, 148.
[1487]   Ibid, 148.
[1488]   *R v Pratt* [1994] 3 NZLR 21, 24.
[1489]   [1997] 1 NZLR 399.

It was pointed out that entry and search of private property by state officials, without permission, is an actionable trespass,[1490] but that evidence obtained by illegal searches is admissible, subject only to a discretion to exclude it on the ground of unfairness to the accused.[1491] This basis for a challenge to admissibility is not affected by section 21. The Court noted that section 21 is a restraint on governmental action that does not confer any positive power[1492] on the state to conduct a 'reasonable search'.

12.484 The Court of Appeal went on to hold that:

> A search is unreasonable if the circumstances giving rise to it make the search itself unreasonable or if a search which would otherwise be reasonable is carried out in an unreasonable manner. So too seizure. Whether a police search or seizure is unreasonable depends on both the subject-matter and the particular time, place and circumstance.[1493]

A prime purpose of section 21 is to ensure that governmental power is not exercised unreasonably. A section 21 enquiry is an exercise in balancing legitimate state interests against any intrusions on individual interests. It requires weighing relevant values and public interests.[1494] The guarantee under section 21 to be free from unreasonable search and seizure reflects an amalgam of values. A search of premises is an invasion of property rights and an intrusion on privacy. It may also involve a restraint on individual liberty and an affront to dignity. Any search is a significant invasion of individual freedom. How significant it will be depends on the circumstances.[1495]

12.485 The Court gave express consideration to the role of 'privacy' in connection with the reasonableness of searches under section 21:

> Contemporary society attaches a high value to privacy and to the security of personal privacy against arbitrary intrusions by those in authority. Privacy values underlying the section 21 guarantee are those held by the community at large. They are not merely the subjective expectations of privacy which a particular owner or occupier may have and may demonstrate by signs or barricades. Reasonable expectations of privacy are lower in public places than on private property. They are higher for the home than for the surrounding land and for land not used for residential purposes. And the nature of the activities carried on, particularly if involving public engagement or governmental oversight, may affect reasonable expectations of privacy. An assessment of the seriousness of the particular intrusion involves considerations of fact and degree, not taking absolutist stances. In that regard, and unlike the thrust of the American Fourth Amendment jurisprudence, the object of section 21 is vindication of individual rights rather than deterrence and disciplining of police misconduct.[1496]

Taking these matters into account, illegality was not the touchstone of unreasonableness. In terms of section 21, what is unlawful is not necessarily unreasonable. The lawfulness

---

[1490] Ibid, Principle 1, 406.
[1491] Ibid, Principle 2, 407.
[1492] Ibid, Principle 3, 407.
[1493] Ibid, Principle 4.
[1494] Ibid, Principle 5.
[1495] Ibid, Principle 6.
[1496] Ibid, Principle 6.

or unlawfulness of a search will always be highly relevant but will not be determinative either way.[1497]

After considering the specific provisions of New Zealand law in relation to search warrants, **12.486** the Court summarized the position in relation to the Bill of Rights Act as follows:

> The Bill of Rights is not a technical document. It has to be applied in our society in a realistic way. The application and interpretation of the Bill must also be true to its purposes as set out in its title of affirming, protecting and promoting human rights and fundamental freedoms in New Zealand, and affirming New Zealand's commitment to the International Covenant on Civil and Political Rights. The crucial question is whether what was done constituted an unreasonable search or seizure in the particular circumstances. Anyone complaining of a breach must invest the complaint with an air of reality and must lay a foundation for the complaint before the trial Court by explicit challenge or cross-examination or evidence.[1498]

In *R v Kappely*[1499] the Court of Appeal reiterated that, when considering the reasonableness **12.487** of a search under a warrant, neither validity nor legality were the sole determinant. The search in that case was unreasonable under section 21 and the evidence inadmissible because:

- the warrant was not validly issued (because there was no adequate evidential basis);
- the warrant was not validly executed as it did not authorize the search of the particular premises; and
- it would have been practical for the officers to observe the premises while a new warrant was obtained which correctly identified the address.

The current approach. The most recent exposition of the concept of 'unreasonable **12.488** search' in section 21 is found in the decision of the Court of Appeal in *R v Williams*.[1500] The Court made clear that an unlawful search will necessarily be an unreasonable one, transferring the wider *Grayson and Taylor* factors to the balancing phase when admissibility is being considered.[1501] This will not, however, apply to 'minor or technical breaches' – although this concept should not be given an expansive interpretation.[1502] It remains possible for a lawful search to be an unreasonable one – although this will be rare.[1503] The *Williams* case also contains a detailed exposition of the general principles which apply in relation to the issuing of warrants and the contents of applications in support.[1504]

Commercial regulatory cases. Section 21 protects companies as well as individuals. **12.489** As the Court of Appeal said *Tranz Rail Ltd v Wellington District Court*:[1505]

[1497] Ibid, Principle 7.
[1498] Ibid, Principle 10, 409.
[1499] [2001] 1 NZLR 7; See also *R v Thompson* [2001] 1 NZLR 129.
[1500] [2007] 3 NZLR 207 (CA).
[1501] Ibid, paras 16–17; (for 'balancing' see *R v Shaheed* [2002] 2 NZLR 377, discussed at para 12.490 below).
[1502] Ibid, paras 21–23.
[1503] Ibid, para 24 (for examples, see *R v Pratt* [1994] 3 NZLR 21 and *R v H* [1994] 2 NZLR 143).
[1504] See generally, ibid, para 209.
[1505] [2002] 3 NZLR 780 (CA); see also *Commerce Commission v Koppers Arch Wood Protection (NZ) Ltd* [2007] 2 NZLR 805, and *A Firm of Solicitors v District Court at Auckland* [2006] 1 NZLR 586.

Although expectations of privacy may not be as great in the commercial world as they are in the domestic sphere, corporations as well as human beings do have legitimate privacy expectations.

The Court went on to hold that the warrant was invalid because there was a reasonable alternative to the use of a warrant and the warrant was expressed in too general terms.

(c) Admissibility of evidence

12.490 There are a large number of the decisions dealing with admissibility of evidence obtained under searches which breach section 21. The Courts developed a *prima facie* exclusion rule under which evidence obtained in breach of section 21 was inadmissible except where there was good reason to admit it. In practice this became an automatic exclusion rule. The law was definitively stated by a seven judge Court of Appeal in *R v Shaheed*.[1506] It was held that the admissibility of evidence obtained in breach of a right guaranteed by the New Zealand Bill of Rights Act 1990 was to be determined by means of the Judge conducting a balancing exercise to decide whether, exclusion of the evidence was in the circumstances a proportionate response to the breach. A number of matters were identified as relevant to the balancing exercise including:

- the value which the right protected and the seriousness of the intrusion upon it;
- whether the breach had been deliberate or arose through gross carelessness;
- whether other investigatory techniques, not involving any breach of rights, were known to be available and not used;
- the nature and quality of the disputed evidence;
- the centrality of the evidence to the prosecution's case; and
- in cases where a conviction would not lead to a sentence of imprisonment, the availability of an alternative remedy or remedies

These principles have been applied by the New Zealand courts a number of subsequent cases and were re-stated by the Court of Appeal in *R v Williams*[1507] In that case the Court departed from its previous jurisprudence and held that a search or seizure that is illegal is to be regarded as unreasonable for the purposes of section 21 of the Bill of Rights Act. To the extent there are other considerations affecting the desirability of admitting illegally obtained evidence they can be taken into account as part of the admissibility process governed by s 30 of the Evidence Act 2006 ('improperly obtained evidence').

(3) Electronic surveillance

(a) Non-participant surveillance

12.491 In *R v Fraser*[1508] the police video-taped an accused drug dealer apparently concealing items in the garden of an address where he was not a resident. The surveillance took place from outside the private property without a warrant. Under the Summary Proceedings Act, the police could have obtained a warrant to 'enter' and search for 'things', but the Court found

---

[1506] [2002] 2 NZLR 377.
[1507] n 1500 above.
[1508] [1997] 2 NZLR 442.

that no such warrant was necessary to conduct a video-recording in the open area outside a private residence. The search was lawful, as there was no statutory or common law prohibition against observing or video-taping the open area surrounding a residential property.

Nevertheless, the search was not necessarily reasonable under the Bill of Rights Act; this **12.492** depended on what the accused might reasonably be subjected to in the circumstances, having regard to standards of the community concerning respect for privacy. It was necessary to consider all the circumstances prevailing at the time the search was undertaken and to balance the legitimate interests of the individual to a reasonable expectation of privacy with those of the state in the detection and prosecution of criminal activities. The Court found no evidence that the accused could have expected not to be observed in the area covered by the video camera. A similar result was reached in *R v Peita*[1509] where cannabis was discovered growing on the appellant's farm by a police spotter plane. It was held that the conduct of the aerial surveillance was not unreasonable and that evidence discovered as a result of that activity was admissible.

(b) Participant recording

In relation to 'participant recording' or 'participant surveillance' the New Zealand Court **12.493** has followed the United States rather than the Canadian approach and held that such surveillance is not unreasonable under the Act. The Court in *R v A*[1510] provided four reasons for this position:

- It is not unlawful for any participant in a conversation to record a discussion surreptitiously. There is no basis in parliamentary consideration of electronic surveillance for the courts to conclude that public policy requires treatment of participant recording as inherently destructive of basic values.

- Advances in information technology have advantages as well as risks. The social answer to the problem turns on an examination of all of the circumstances rather than on an impossible quest for universally agreed moral absolutes. It is a matter of time, place and circumstance.

- The expectation of privacy, while important, is not the only consideration in determining whether a search or seizure is unreasonable.

- Characterizing participant recording as always constituting unreasonable search and seizure would have significant consequences contrary to the public interest. First, if such recording is a breach of section 21 it would, *prima facie*, be excluded from evidence, while the intrusion on privacy would have occurred in any event. Secondly, it would necessarily inhibit the police from wiring a police officer for safety reasons.

In *R v Smith*[1511] the evidence of an informer fitted with a video camera was held admissible against a suspected drugs trafficker.

[1509] (1999) 5 HRNZ 250.
[1510] [1994] 1 NZLR 429.
[1511] [2000] 3 NZLR 456.

Appendix 5: South African Constitutional Cases

(a) Introduction

12.494 The Constitution of South Africa provides:

> (14) Everyone has the right to privacy, which includes the right not to have
>   (a) their person or home searched;
>   (b) their property searched;
>   (c) their possessions seized; or
>   (d) the privacy of their communications infringed.[1512]

In common with the Convention, and in contradistinction to the US and German Constitutions, this clause overtly links the general guarantee of privacy with specific protection of the home and communications.

(b) The nature of the right

12.495 The 'richest and most comprehensive interpretation of the right'[1513] was provided in *Bernstein v Bester*,[1514] in which the applicants challenged the constitutionality of provisions of the Companies Acts[1515] providing for the summoning and examination of persons in relation to the affairs of a company being wound up. It was contended that the examination mechanism infringed, *inter alia*, rights to privacy. These arguments were rejected by the Court. Ackermann J said that:

> The truism that no right is to be considered absolute, implies that from the outset of interpretation each right is always already limited by every other right accruing to another citizen. In the context of privacy this would mean that it is only the inner sanctum of a person, such as his/her family life, sexual preference and home environment, which is shielded from erosion by conflicting rights of the community. This implies that community rights and the rights of fellow members place a corresponding obligation on a citizen, thereby shaping the abstract notion of individualism towards identifying a concrete member of civil society. Privacy is acknowledged in the truly personal realm, but as a person moves into communal relations and activities such as business and social interaction, the scope of personal space shrinks accordingly.[1516]

12.496 Ackerman J set out that the right comprises two elements:

(1) a subjective expectation of privacy
(2) that society has recognized as objectively reasonable.[1517]

Where communal relations and activities are involved, any subjective expectation of privacy starts to become less likely to be objectively reasonable.

[1512] See generally, S Woolman, T Roux, J Klaaren, A Stein, M Chaskalson, and M Bishop (eds) *Constitutional Law of South Africa* (2nd edn, Juta, 2006) Part 2, 'Privacy'—David Mc Quoid-Mason.
[1513] I Currie and J De Waal *Bill of Rights Handbook* (5th edn, 2005) 317.
[1514] 1996 (4) BCLR 449, CC, paras 65 and 67.
[1515] ss 417 and 418; analogous to Insolvency Act 1986, s 236.
[1516] *Bernstein* (n 1514 above) para 67; cf the discussion of the South African common law of privacy at para 68ff.
[1517] Ibid, para 75.

In *National Council for Gay and Lesbian Equality v Ministry of Justice*[1518] the Constitutional **12.497**
Court held that the common law offence of sodomy and number of related statutory
offences were unconstitutional and invalid. The applicants' arguments were based primarily on the right to equality[1519] but the Court stressed that the right to privacy was also
infringed:

> Privacy recognizes that we all have a right to a sphere of private intimacy and autonomy
> which allows us to establish and nurture human relationships without interference from the
> outside community. The way in which we give expression to our sexuality is at the core of this
> area of private intimacy. . . . The fact that a law prohibiting forms of sexual conduct is dis-
> criminatory, does not, however, prevent it at the same time being an improper invasion of the
> intimate sphere of human life to which protection is given by the Constitution in section 14.
> We should not deny the importance of a right to privacy in our new constitutional order,
> even while we acknowledge the importance of equality.[1520]

In his concurring judgment, Sachs J drew attention to the misleading nature of spatial **12.498**
metaphors (such as 'inner sanctum' or 'personal sphere'), which suggest that privacy is a
space or a place.[1521] He emphasized that the fact that conduct takes place in a person's home
is not decisive of whether it merits the protection of the privacy right. This was further
explored in the thought-provoking minority decision of Sachs J and O'Regan J in *S v
Jordaan*,[1522] which concerned an unsuccessful challenge to the statutory prohibition of
prostitution.

In *Case v Minister of Safety and Security*,[1523] the majority of the Constitutional Court **12.499**
observed that the possession of 'indecent or obscene' material could be subjected to limitation, even in the privacy of one's own home.[1524] The constitutional challenge in issue, however, was successful. The case concerned section 2(1) of the Indecent or Obscene
Photographic Matter Act 1967, which prohibited the possession of indecent or obscene
photographic matter. The Court held that the invasion of privacy occasioned by the prohibition was aggravated by the very broad definition of 'indecent or obscene photographic
matter' contained in the Act, which had the effect of sanctioning an unwarranted invasion
of the privacy right regardless of the nature of the material possessed.

The statute at issue in *Case* was repealed and replaced by the Films and Publications **12.500**
Act 1996, which criminalized the knowing creation, production, importation or possession of 'a publication which contains a visual presentation of child pornography'. This was
challenged in *De Reuck v Director of Public Prosecutions, Witwatersrand Local Division*[1525]

[1518] 1998 (12) BCLR 1517 (CC).
[1519] See s 9 of the Constitution.
[1520] *National Council for Gay and Lesbian Equality* (n 1518 above) para 32 (per Ackerman J); see also Sachs J
concurring at paras 108 to 119 for an important analysis of the relationship between equality and privacy rights.
[1521] Ibid, para 116.
[1522] 2002 (11) BCLR 1117 (CC).
[1523] 1996 (5) BCLR 608 (CC) (the Court was dealing with the Interim Constitution, s 13 of which is in
materially identical terms).
[1524] See Langa J, para 99; Madala J, paras 103–107. Didcott J took the opposite view, commenting at
para 91 that 'what erotic material I may choose to keep within the privacy of my home, and only for my
personal use there, is nobody's business but mine'.
[1525] 2003 (12) BCLR 1333 (CC).

on the basis that the legislation failed to provide for a defence of legitimate purpose or public interest where such material was possessed or imported for the creation of a bona fide documentary, research work, drama or work of art. The Constitutional Court observed that the definition of child pornography in the legislation was in several respects narrower than the primary dictionary meaning of the word, and that a common core of the definition of child pornography was the notion of stimulation of erotic rather than aesthetic feeling.[1526] The Court held unanimously that the limitation of privacy occasioned by the offence was necessary and justified, as the sexual abuse and degradation of children through such pornography was a serious harm. The legislation also served three legitimate objectives: protecting the dignity of children; stamping out the market for photographs made by abusing children and preventing a reasonable risk that images would be used to harm children. These objectives remained valid in relation to film-makers or researchers, so the argument for a defence was rejected.[1527]

(c) Search and seizure

12.501 The case of *Investigating Directorate: Serious Economic Offences v Hyundai Motor Distributors Ltd*[1528] concerned the search of business premises under broad search and seizure powers in the National Prosecuting Authority Act 1998. The Constitutional Court held that juristic persons could have privacy rights, although they could never be 'as intense as those of human beings', because of the link between privacy and the protection of human dignity.[1529] The Court found that the search and seizure powers under scrutiny did limit the right to privacy, but held that limitation was justified, as the impugned provision could be interpreted to include significant safeguards: a judicial officer could only issue a search warrant where there was a reasonable suspicion that an offence had been committed; that there were reasonable grounds to believe that objects connected with an investigation into that suspected offence might be found on the relevant premises, and in the exercise of his or her discretion, the judicial officer considered it appropriate to issue a search warrant.[1530]

12.502 A search and seizure by competition authorities was held to have breached constitutional privacy rights in *Pretoria Portland Cement Co v Competition Commission*.[1531] The Supreme Court of Appeal found that the appellants had been hampered in their efforts to have the search warrant set aside. The court also relied on the impropriety of the Competition Commission officials in inviting television cameras surreptitiously to enter the premises being searched.[1532] The Constitutional Court has also found that a statute regulating gambling amounted to a breach of the right to privacy, to the extent that it authorized warrantless searches of premises which were not licensed.[1533] The objectives of such searches could

---

[1526] Ibid, paras 21–38.
[1527] Ibid, para 74.
[1528] 2000 (10) BCLR 1079 (CC).
[1529] Ibid, para 18.
[1530] Ibid, para 52.
[1531] 2003 (2) SA 385 (SCA).
[1532] Ibid, para 60ff.
[1533] *Magajane v Chairperson, North West Gambling Board and Others* 2006 (10) BCLR 1133 (CC).

have been achieved by requiring warrants, which would have been less invasive of the right to privacy.[1534]

In contrast, in *Zuma v National Director of Public Prosecutions*[1535] the Constitutional Court **12.503** upheld the validity of searches and seizures carried out under various warrants issued in a corruption investigation in relation to a prominent politician. The Court accepted that:

> The privacy of the individual is no less important. Section 14 of the Constitution entrenches everyone's right to privacy, including the right not to have one's person, home, or property searched, possessions seized or the privacy of his or her communications infringed. These rights flow from the value placed on human dignity by the Constitution. The courts therefore jealously guard them by scrutinising search warrants 'with rigour and exactitude'.[1536]

The Court went on to hold that the State had demonstrated the need for the search and seizure warrants which were not overbroad and that the duty of utmost good faith had been complied with.

(d) Informational privacy

The informational aspect of the right to privacy was considered by the Constitutional **12.504** Court in *Mistry v Interim National Medical and Dental Council of South Africa*,[1537] which concerned a challenge to search and seizure powers under the Medicines and Related Substances Control Act 1965. A patient of the applicant had provided the Medical Council with information about his possible violation of the law. This information was provided by the Council to an official who had statutory powers to inspect premises for the purpose of protecting public health. The Constitutional Court held that this did not breach of the right to privacy. It considered various factors important in determining the informational aspect of the privacy challenge: whether the information had been obtained in an intrusive manner; whether it was about intimate aspects of the applicant's personal life; whether it involved data provided by the applicant for one purpose which was then used for another; whether it was disseminated to the press or the general public or persons from whom the applicant could reasonably expect such private information would be withheld.[1538]

(e) Privacy and the media

The balancing of privacy rights and the right to freedom of expression of the media has **12.505** been considered on a number of occasions in South Africa.[1539] In *Independent Newspaper Holdings v Suliman*[1540] a defamation and privacy claim was made arising out of the publication of a report and photograph of the claimant which suggested that the claimant had been arrested on suspicion of responsibility for a bomb attack. The defamation claim succeeded but the privacy claim failed on the grounds that the case did not involve private facts

---

[1534] For an interesting discussion of the admissibility of improperly obtained evidence see Woolman et al (n 1512 above) and Currie and De Waal (n 1513 above) at 329–332.

[1535] [2008] ZACC 13.

[1536] Ibid, para 75 (citations omitted).

[1537] 1998 (7) BCLR 880 (CC).

[1538] Ibid, para 44.

[1539] See generally the illuminating discussion in D Milo, *Defamation and Freedom of Speech* (Oxford University Press, 2007), esp 126–128.

[1540] 2005 (7) BCLR 641 (SCA).

and damage to the claimant's dignity was compensated by the defamation award. In *NM v Smith*[1541] the applicants were three HIV positive women who had participated in clinical trials who complained that their names and HIV status was disclosed in the authorized biography of a public figure. The Constitutional Court held that this constituted a wrongful disclosure of a private fact and violated the dignity and psychological integrity of the applicants. Their expectation of privacy in relation to private facts had not been overridden by any compelling public interest. In *Tshabala-Msimang v Makhanya*[1542] the applicant, the Minister of Health, brought claim against a newspapers which had obtained copies of her medical records which were alleged to show consumption of alcohol in hospital. The Court held that section 14 of the Constitution envisaged a right to privacy which would entitle the applicant not to have her private medical information disclosed publicly without consent. The newspaper was ordered to return the medical records but the judge refused to restrain the publication of further comment about them on matters in the public domain.

Appendix 6: Human Rights Cases in Other Jurisdictions

(1) Introduction

12.506 The right to privacy is protected under the civil and criminal law of most European states. In France, Article 9 of the Civil Code was introduced in 1970 and provides for the right to 'respect for privacy'. This has now been recognized as a 'constitutional right'.[1543] The German courts have developed a general 'right to personality' which has enabled them to protect a range of privacy rights.[1544] In *Re C*[1545] the German Constitutional Court held that the publication of three photographs of Princess Caroline of Monaco with her children taken in publicly accessible places was a breach of her privacy rights. It was said that the decisive criterion for differentiating between the private and the public sphere was whether the individual was in a situation where he reasonably believed that he could not be observed by the public. The protection of privacy rights in Italy has also been a matter for judge made law.[1546]

12.507 In many common law jurisdictions the right to privacy is now the subject of statutory protection.[1547] The right has, however, been the subject of sustained consideration in the constitutional context in the American courts where the right has been recognized as covering

---

[1541] 2007 (7) BCLR 751 (CC).

[1542] [2008] 4 LRC 1003.

[1543] See generally, E Picard, 'The Right to Privacy in French Law', in B Markesinis (ed), *Protecting Privacy* (Oxford University Press, 1999).

[1544] See generally, P Quint, 'Free Speech and Private Law in German Constitutional Theory' (1989) 48 Maryland L Rev 247–346; B Markesinis, 'Privacy, Freedom of Expression and the Horizontal Effect of the Human Rights Bill: Lessons from Germany' (1999) 115 LQR 47; H Stoll, 'General Rights to Personality in German Law' in Markesinis (n 1543 above); and see, J Craig and N Nolte, 'Privacy and Free Speech in Germany and Canada: Lessons for an English Privacy Tort' [1998] EHRLR 162; R English, 'Protection of Privacy and Freedom of Speech in Germany', in M Colvin (ed), *Developing Key Privacy Rights* (Hart Publishing, 2002).

[1545] (2001) 10 BHRC 131.

[1546] See G Alpa, 'Protection of Privacy in Italian Law' in Markesinis (n 1543 above).

[1547] See for example the Privacy Act 1988 (Australia).

both the interest in avoiding the disclosure of personal information and the 'interest in independence in making certain kinds of important decisions'.[1548] This right has been used to provide constitutional protection for the use of contraception,[1549] the distribution of contraceptives to unmarried persons[1550] and abortion.[1551] The right has not, however, been extended to sexual privacy generally, the Supreme Court refusing to strike down statutes criminalizing sodomy.[1552] Furthermore, the right to privacy is subject to freedom of expression rights, and the publication of false private information will only be actionable if malicious.[1553]

The Fourth Amendment to the US Constitution affirms the right of the people to be secure **12.508** 'in their persons, houses, papers and effects, against unreasonable searches and seizures'. This provision embodies the principle of respect for privacy of the home,[1554] but not a general right of privacy.[1555] It also protects persons on office premises[1556] overnight guests in hostels[1557] or houses[1558] but does not extend to 'open fields'[1559] or to a visitor to a house.[1560] It also covers the use of hidden microphones and telephone tapping,[1561] but not aerial inspection of a garden.[1562] Government officials are not permitted to undertake searches or seizures without an 'individualized suspicion' unless it was based on 'special needs' beyond the normal requirements of law enforcement.[1563] In *Kyllo v United States*[1564] the Supreme Court held that the Fourth Amendment was violated when the Government used, without warrant, a thermal imaging device to explore details of a private home. The use of this device was a 'warrantless search'.

[1548] *Whalen v Roe* (1977) 429 US 589, 599–600 per Stevens J; a full discussion is outside the scope of this book but see generally, L Tribe, *American Constitutional Law* (2nd edn, Foundation Press, 1988) Chap 15, E Chemerinsky, *Constitutional Law: Principles and Policies* (3rd edn, Aspen, 2006), para 10.6, 855ff, and also D Anderson, 'The Failure of American Privacy Law' in Markesinis (n 1543 above).

[1549] *Griswold v Connecticut* (1965) 381 US 479 (criminal law prohibiting the use of contraceptive unconstitutional).

[1550] *Eisenstad v Baird* (1972) 405 US 438.

[1551] *Roe v Wade* (1973) 410 US 113 (law prohibiting abortion unconstitutional); this was, of course, one of the most controversial decisions of modern times, see generally, Tribe (n 1548 above) para 15–10 and also *Planned Parenthood v Casey* (1992) 505 US 833. See also *Stenberg v Carhart* (2000) 120 Sup Ct 2597.

[1552] *Bowers v Hardwick* (1986) 478 US 186; but see *Romer v Evans* (1996) 517 US 620 (Colorado constitutional amendment prohibiting action designed to protect homosexuals from discrimination unconstitutional under Fourteenth Amendment 'Equal Protection' provisions); see generally, Tribe (n 1548 above) paras 15–21 and R Wintemute, *Sexual Orientation and Human Rights* (Clarendon Press, 1995), Chaps 2 and 3.

[1553] *Time Inc v Hill* (1967) 385 US 374.

[1554] *Wilson v Layne* (1999) 7 BHRC 274 ('media ride alongs' unconstitutional).

[1555] *Katz v United States* (1967) 389 US 347, 350.

[1556] *Gouled v United States* (1921) 255 US 298.

[1557] *Lustig v United States* (1949) 338 US 74.

[1558] *Minnesota v Olson* (1990) 495 US 91.

[1559] *Oliver v United States* (1984) 466 US 170.

[1560] *Minnesotav v Carter* (1998) 5 BHRC 457.

[1561] *Katz v United States* (n 1555 above; *United States v United States District Court for Eastern District of Michigan* (1972) 407 US 297.

[1562] *California v Ciraolo* (1986) 476 US 207; *Florida v Riley* (1989) 488 US 445.

[1563] *Chandler v Miller* (1997) 3 BHRC 234 (drug testing programme for candidates for state office unconstitutional); contrast the drug testing programmes approved in *National Treasury Employees Union v Von Raab* (1989) 489 US 109 (customs officials) and *Vernonia School District 47J v Acton* (1995) 515 US 646 (high school students engaged in athletic competitions).

[1564] (2001) 533 US 27.

(2) Australia[1565]

12.509 There is no constitutional protection of privacy in Australia. The Privacy Act 1988 (Cth) regulates the handling of an individual's personal information and a number of corresponding state statutes.[1566] The development of privacy law has been regarded as restricted by the decision in *Victoria Park Racing and Recreation Grounds Co Ltd v Taylor*[1567] where the High Court expressly rejected, in dicta, the recognition of a tort based on invasion of privacy.

12.510 However, in *Lenah Game Meats v Australian Broadcasting Corporation*[1568] the High Court opened the door to the possible development of a tort of invasion of privacy. In that case the claimant sought an injunction to restrain the broadcast of video film which had been obtained by trespassers in a meat processing plant. The High Court refused to grant an injunction. The majority held that the claimant had no cause of action. The judges who considered whether there was a developing tort of invasion of privacy in Australian law held that, even if there was, it would not avail a corporation.[1569] Since this decision some claims for invasion privacy have succeeded[1570] whilst others have failed on the basis that the cause of action is not recognized.[1571]

(3) Fiji

12.511 Section 37 of the Constitution of Fiji provides:

> Every person has the right to personal privacy including the right to privacy of personal communication.

12.512 In *McCoskar v State*[1572] the Fiji High Court held that a statutory offence proscribing homosexual conduct in private by consenting adults was not consistent with this constitutional right. The right to privacy included 'the positive right to establish and nurture human relationships free of criminal or indeed community sanction'.[1573] The provisions were also in breach of the constitutional right to equality.

(4) Hong Kong

12.513 Evidence obtained in breach of the right to privacy is not automatically inadmissible, the court still retains a discretion and must balance the importance of the right against the

---

[1565] For a study of privacy issues in one State see New South Wales Law Reform Commission *Invasion of Privacy* (NSWLRC CP1, Sydney, 2007).

[1566] See ibid, paras 2.2 to 2.15 for the position in the Commonwealth and New South Wales.

[1567] (1937) 58 CLR 479.

[1568] (2001) 185 ALR 1.

[1569] See D Lindsay, 'Freedom of Expression, Privacy and the Media in Australia', in M Colvin (ed), *Developing Key Privacy Rights* (Hart Publishing, 2002).

[1570] *Grosse v Purvis* [2003] QDC 151; *Jane Doe v Australian Broadcasting Corporation* [2007] VCC 281.

[1571] See *Giller v Procopets* [2004] VSC 113. *Milne v Haynes* [2005] NSWSC 1107; *Kalaba v Commonwealth of Australia* [2004] FCA 763 (cause of action for privacy does not currently exist in Australia).

[1572] [2005] FJHC 252.

[1573] Ibid, para 75.

interest in the detection of crime.[1574] The Hong Kong Law Reform Commission has published a series of reports on privacy issues.[1575]

(5) Human Rights Committee[1576]

Article 17 of the International Covenant on Civil and Political Rights provides that: **12.514**

(1) No one shall be subjected to arbitrary or unlawful interference with his privacy home or correspondence, nor to unlawful attacks on his honour and reputation.
(2) Everyone has the right to the protection of the law against such interferences or attacks.

This provision does not, unlike other Articles, specify the grounds on which a state party may interfere with privacy.

An interference will be 'unlawful' unless it is authorized by a domestic law which itself **12.515** complies with 'the provisions, aims and objectives of the Covenant'.[1577] An interference can be arbitrary even if it is lawful. The concept of arbitrariness is intended to guarantee that an interference is 'reasonable' in the circumstances.[1578] Article 17 is the subject matter of General Comment 16, in which it was stated that:

the competent public authorities should only be able to call for such information relating to an individual's private life the knowledge of which is essential in the interests of society as understood under the Covenant.[1579]

In *Toonen v Australia*[1580] the Committee took the view that the requirement of **12.516** 'reasonableness' implied that 'any interference with privacy must be proportional to the end sought and be necessary in the circumstances of any given case'. It was held that laws in Tasmania prohibiting sex between men were an arbitrary interference with privacy.[1581]

(6) India

Article 21 of the Constitution of India provides that: **12.517**

No person shall be deprived of his life or personal liberty except according to procedure established by law.

[1574] *HKSAR v Li Man Tak* [2006] HKC 293; *HKSAR v Chan Kau-tai* [2006] 1 HKLRD 400, 443ff

[1575] See in particular *Privacy: The Regulation of Cover Surveillance* (March 2006) and *Privacy and Media Intrusion* (December 2004), *Civil Liability for Invasion of Privacy* (August 1999) available on <www.hkreform. gov.uk>.

[1576] See generally, J Michael, 'Privacy' in D Harris and S Joseph (eds), *The International Covenant on Civil and Political Rights and United Kingdom Law* (Clarendon Press, 1995), 333–354.

[1577] General Comment 16, para 3.

[1578] Ibid, paras 4 and 8.3.

[1579] Ibid, para 7.

[1580] 488/1992, 31 Mar 1994, UNHRC.

[1581] Cf the discussion in R Wintemute, *Sexual Orientation and Human Rights* (Clarendon Press, 1995), 143–149.

The Supreme Court has held that a right to privacy is implicit in this provision.[1582] In *Rajagopal v State of Tamil Nadu*[1583] BP Jeevan Reddy J summarized the position in relation to this implicit right as follows:

> This is a 'right to be let alone'. A citizen has a right to safeguard the privacy of his own, his family, marriage, procreation, motherhood, child-bearing and education among other matters. None can publish anything concerning the above matters without his consent—whether truthful or otherwise or whether laudatory or critical. If he did so, he would be violating the right to privacy of the person concerned . . .[1584]

There are, however, exceptions in relation to the publication of information based on public records and the right to privacy is not available if public officials are acting in the course of their official duties unless, in the latter case, the publication is made with reckless disregard for the truth.[1585]

12.518 In *People's Union for Civil Liberties v Union of India*[1586] it was held that telephone tapping infringed Article 21 which had to be interpreted in accordance with Article 17 of the International Covenant on Civil and Political Rights.[1587] Although there were statutory restrictions on the power to intercept messages or conversations, these had to be backed by procedural safeguards to ensure that the power was exercised in a fair and reasonable manner.[1588] It was held that, as the Government had laid down no procedural safeguards it was necessary for the Court to do so. The Court specified who should authorize telephone tapping, the duration and scope of authorizations, the records which should be maintained and the limits on the use of intercepted material.

(7) Ireland[1589]

12.519 The Irish Constitution does not make express provision for any right to privacy. In the 1980s the courts rejected a number of attempts to establish such a right.[1590] However, the right was finally recognized in the 'telephone tapping' case of *Kennedy v Ireland*.[1591] It was held that:

> although not specifically guaranteed by the Constitution, the right to privacy is one of the fundamental personal rights of the citizen which flow from the Christian and democratic nature of the State. It is not an unqualified right. Its exercise may be restricted by the constitutional rights of others, or by the requirements of the common good, and it is subject to the requirements of public order and morality.

[1582] *Kharak Singh v State of UP* [1964] 1 SCR 332; *Gobind v State of MP* (1975) 2 SCC 148; *Rajagopal v State of Tamil Nadu* [1995] 3 LRC 566.
[1583] Ibid, 581e.
[1584] Ibid, 581d–f.
[1585] Ibid, 581f–582b.
[1586] [1999] 2 LRC 1.
[1587] See App J in Vol 2. It was also held that telephone tapping infringed rights of freedom of expression under Art 19 of the Constitution, see para 15.539ff below.
[1588] Applying *Maneka Ghandi v Union of India* (1978) 1 SCC 248.
[1589] See generally, JM Kelly, *The Irish Constitution* (4th edn, Butterworths, 2003), 7.3.115ff.
[1590] *Norris v A-G* [1984] IR 36 (in relation to criminal laws penalising homosexuality); *Madigan v A-G* [1986] IRLM 136 (in relation to laws requiring disclosure of income).
[1591] [1987] IR 587.

As a result, it was held that the unjustifiable tapping of the plaintiffs' telephones by the state was a breach of their rights to privacy. In one case,[1592] the Supreme Court was prepared to assume, for the purpose of argument, that there might be a right to privacy in a public street. However, police surveillance was justified in that case and in a case in which a person in police custody was kept under observation.[1593] In *Redmond v Mr Justice Flood*[1594] the applicant complained that public hearings of a statutory tribunal relating to certain planning matters were an interference with his right to privacy. The Supreme Court dismissed the application holding that the constitutional right to privacy was not an absolute one and could be outweighed by the exigencies of the common good. The inquiry in question had to be held in public for the purpose of allaying the public disquiet that led to its appointment. In *Re Ansbacher (Cayman) Ltd*[1595] an applicant in legal proceedings who sought to keep secret his name in those proceedings was unsuccessful. The court held that the right to a public trial outweighed in that case the rights to privacy or confidentiality.

(8) Malta

In *Ellul v Advocate General*[1596] the Constitutional Court held that identity documents of a **12.520** transsexual other than the birth certificate should be amended. The court accepted that there was a breach of Article 8 of the European Convention on Human Rights, and that any documents issued by the state or any state authority identifying the applicant, with the exception of birth certificates, such as identity cards and passports should indicate the applicant's new gender. Birth certificates, however, were intended to record a historic fact and the state was right to keep their contents as objective and determinate as possible. Although the birth certificate should not be changed, a document should be attached to it stating that all of the applicant's other documents have been modified to reflect her new sex and name.

[1592] *Kane v Governor of Mountjoy Prison* [1988] IR 757.
[1593] *DPP v Kenny* [1992] 2 IR 141.
[1594] [1999] 1 IRLM 241.
[1595] [2002] IEHC 27.
[1596] (2002) 3 CHRLD 335.

15

FREEDOM OF EXPRESSION

A. The Nature of the Right	15.01	(3) The licensing power	15.262	
B. The Right in English Law	15.06	(4) 'Interference' with the right to freedom of expression	15.267	
(1) Introduction	15.06	(5) Justifying interferences with freedom of expression: general considerations	15.273	
(2) Prior restraint	15.25			
(3) Protection of reputation and private life	15.49	(6) Justifying interferences with media expression	15.310	
(4) Comment on court proceedings: contempt of court	15.80	(7) Justifying interferences with expression for specific legitimate aims	15.359	
(5) Orders that restrict court reporting	15.103	Appendix 1: United Kingdom Article 10 Cases in Strasbourg	15.386	
(6) Protection of journalistic sources	15.145			
(7) Obscenity and indecency	15.153	Appendix 2: Human Rights Cases in Scotland	15.412	
(8) Media regulation and censorship	15.170			
(9) Freedom of expression and the criminal law	15.188	Appendix 3: The Canadian Charter of Rights	15.426	
(10) Expression and government secrecy	15.212	Appendix 4: The New Zealand Bill of Rights Act	15.467	
(11) Freedom of expression in other areas	15.219			
(12) Freedom of expression in Community law	15.234	Appendix 5: Human Rights Cases in South Africa	15.499	
C. The Law under the European Convention	15.236	Appendix 6: Human Rights Cases from Other Jurisdictions	15.514	
(1) Introduction	15.236			
(2) Scope of the right	15.241			

A. The Nature of the Right

Freedom of expression is often said to be essential to the operation of democracy.[1] It is **15.01** sometimes claimed that freedom of expression establishes a market place of ideas[2] which promotes the search for truth;[3] or that free speech ensures individual development and self fulfilment[4] and is, for example, to be derived from the right to human dignity and to

---

[1] The philosophical underpinnings of the right have been much discussed; see E Barendt, *Freedom of Speech* (2nd edn, Oxford University Press, 2005); F Schauer, *Free Speech: A Philosophical Enquiry* (Cambridge University Press, 1982).

[2] See eg, the famous dissenting judgment of Holmes J in *Abrams v United States* 250 US 616 (1919) at 630; see para 15.515 below.

[3] See eg, J Milton, 'Areopagitica: A Speech for Licensed Printing' in *Prose Writings* (Everyman, 1958); JS Mill, *On Liberty* (Cambridge University Press, 1989), Chap 2.

[4] Schauer (see n 1 above) Chaps 4 and 5.

equality of concern and respect.[5] However, the most persuasive vindication of freedom of expression is that it secures the right of the citizen to participate in the democratic process.[6] The House of Lords[7] have said that expression enjoys protection on all three grounds. Freedom of expression has been described as 'the primary right in a democracy', one without which 'an effective rule of law is not possible'.[8]

15.02 One of the earliest and most well-known constitutional rights provisions is the First Amendment to the Constitution of the United States which provides that:

> Congress shall make no law. . .abridging the freedom of speech, or of the press . . .

This has given rise to one of the most highly developed areas of human rights jurisprudence in the world.[9] All of the major international human rights instruments protect the right to freedom of expression. Article 19 of the International Covenant on Civil and Political Rights, for example, states:

(1) Everyone has the right to freedom of opinion and

(2) Everyone shall have the right to freedom of expression; this right shall include freedom to seek, receive and impart information and ideas of all kinds, regardless of frontiers, either orally, in writing or in print, in the form of art, or through any other media of his choice.

(3) The exercise of the right provided for in paragraph 2 of this Article carries with it special duties and responsibilities. It may, therefore, be subject to certain restrictions, but these shall only be

  (a) For respect of the rights or reputations of others;

  (b) For the protection of national security or of public order, or public health or morals.[10]

15.03 The major rights instruments and constitutions nevertheless treat the right of expression very differently. Some, like the First Amendment, express it in unqualified terms.[11] Typically, however, human rights instruments expressly define the limitations on freedom of expression.[12] Article 10 of the Convention defines the right in language which is weaker than that of Article 19 of the Covenant and circumscribes the right by provision of a full list of exceptions.[13]

---

[5] R Dworkin, *Taking Rights Seriously* (Duckworth, 1977), Chap 12.

[6] See eg, Brandeis J in *Whitney v California* (1927) 274 US 357, 375; see para 15.515 below.

[7] *R v Secretary of State for the Home Department, ex p Simms* [2000] 2 AC 115, 126 per Lord Steyn: see para 15.00 below.

[8] *McCartan Turkington Breen v Times Newspapers* [2001] 2 AC 277 at 297 (Lord Steyn); see statements to the same effect in the Supreme Court of Canada: *Irwin Toy v Quebec* [1989] 1 SCR 927, 976 per Dickson CJ, Lamer and Wilson J; *R v Keegstra* [1990] 3 SCR 697, 762, 763 per Dickson CJ.

[9] For an overview, see Barendt (see n 1 above); see generally, eg, L Tribe, *American Constitutional Law* (2nd edn, Foundation Press, 1988) *Cg the First Amendment* (Hart Publishing, 1998); and see para 15.515ff below.

[10] See also Universal Declaration, Art 19; the text is reproduced at App H in Vol 2.

[11] For a fuller treatment, see eg, Tribe (see n 9 above) Chap 12.

[12] See eg, the Inter-American Convention, Art 13(2), which excludes from protection prior censorship.

[13] See generally, A Lester, 'Freedom of Expression', in R St J Macdonald, F Matscher, and H Petzold (eds), *The European System for the Protection of Human Rights* (Kluwer, 1983), 465–468.

The freedom of expression must be weighed against other public and private interests. **15.04** Expressions of opinion and the publication of information in the mass media can violate other rights and freedoms and have a clear and direct impact on the political process. As a result, they are subject to close governmental scrutiny. Regulation of the press and broadcasting raises questions as to the extent of control that national authorities ought to maintain over the production and distribution of information, and the justifiable bases for such interference.

The relationship between freedom of expression and the various limitations to which it **15.05** may be subject is the subject of serious debate in a number of areas. Five areas can be highlighted:

Prior restraint: an issue of immediate importance concerns the circumstances in which injunctions will be granted by the courts to restrain publication of material which is allegedly defamatory, or otherwise in breach of private or public law. Such injunctions are severely restrictive of freedom of expression but their refusal may lead to irreparable damage to more important interests.

Reputation and privacy: the restriction of expression in order to protect reputation and privacy involves complex questions of the 'balancing' of competing rights particularly where public figures are involved.

Reporting on court proceedings: the curtailment of expression in the interests of the administration of justice has been particularly controversial in England where there are strict rules concerning the reporting of pending proceedings.

Blasphemy, obscenity and hate speech: the censorship and regulation of media content on grounds of public morality is an area in which the balance has to be struck between freedom of expression and other important rights and values such as respect for religion and the protection of children. The regulation of 'hate speech' involves a particularly direct conflict of values and has been intensely disputed over recent decades.

Regulation of the media: government regulation of the mass media has also been a focus of 'freedom of expression' debates in a number of jurisdictions.[14] These issues have been given new impetus by the growth of new media such as the Internet which are outside the traditional regulatory regimes.[15]

B. The Right in English Law

(1) Introduction

(a) Freedom of expression and the common law

Freedom of expression, like other fundamental freedoms in the common law, has tradition- **15.06** ally been considered to be merely residual in character.[16] Over recent decades, however,

---

[14] For the position in the United States see E Barendt, 'The First Amendment and the Media' in I Loveland (ed), *Importing the First Amendment* (Hart Publishing, 1998); and see generally, T Gibbons, *Regulating the Media* (2nd edn, Sweet & Maxwell, 1998).

[15] Cf *Reno v ACLU* (1997) 2 BHRC 405 (provisions regulating publication of indecent material on the Internet struck down by Supreme Court).

[16] Dicey did not refer to freedom of expression in his discussion of personal liberties, describing it instead in the context of wrongs and libel: see A Dicey, *An Introduction to the Study of the Law of the Constitution*

the right has increasingly been recognized as a common law, or even 'quasi-constitutional' principle[17] to be invoked by the judiciary in the interpretation of statutes, to limit or balance other public interests[18] and as a basis for refusing some types of relief.[19] This shift in the common law was influenced by Article 10 of the Convention, so that to some extent domestic law was already consistent with its requirements when the Human Rights Act 1998 ('the HRA') came into force.[20] In *McCartan Turkington Breen v Times Newspapers*[21] Lord Steyn said that even before the HRA came into force, principle of freedom of expression attained the status of a constitutional right with attendant high normative force. Lord Bingham has described free expression as 'a fundamental right which has been recognized at common law for very many years'.[22] He went on to say:

> The reasons why the right to free expression is regarded as fundamental are familiar, but merit brief restatement in the present context. Modern democratic government means government of the people by the people for the people. But there can be no government by the people if they are ignorant of the issues to be resolved, the arguments for and against different solutions and the facts underlying those arguments. The business of government is not an activity about which only those professionally engaged are entitled to receive information and express opinions. It is, or should be, a participatory process. But there can be no assurance that government is carried out for the people unless the facts are made known, the issues publicly ventilated. Sometimes, inevitably, those involved in the conduct of government, as in any other walk of life, are guilty of error, incompetence, misbehaviour, dereliction of duty, even dishonesty and malpractice. Those concerned may very strongly wish that the facts relating to such matters are not made public. Publicity may reflect discredit on them or their predecessors. It may embarrass the authorities. It may impede the process of administration. Experience however shows, in this country and elsewhere, that publicity is a powerful disinfectant. Where abuses are exposed, they can be remedied. Even where abuses have already been remedied, the public may be entitled to know that they occurred. The role of the press in exposing abuses and miscarriages of justice has been a potent and honourable one. But the press cannot expose that of which it is denied knowledge.

15.07 Some types of speech in English law enjoy protection in positive terms. Debate and proceedings in Parliament are absolutely privileged against impeachment or question in any

---

(8th edn, Macmillan, 1915), Chap 6 'The Right to Freedom of Discussion'; and see also A Boyle, 'Freedom of Expression as a Public Interest in English Law' [1992] PL 574.

[17] See E Barendt, 'Libel and Freedom of Expression in English Law' [1993] PL 449, 450; at 459–460, Barendt suggests that freedom of expression may be a positive right. Boyle (see n 16 above), suggests that freedom of expression as a public interest exists in addition to the residual categorization which remains an important sense in which 'rights' exist in English law; see also T Allan, *Law, Liberty and Justice* (Clarendon Press, 1993) Chap 6; and for a discussion of positive rights in English law, see para 1.40ff above.

[18] See in regard to defamation: *Derbyshire County Council v Times Newspapers Ltd* [1993] AC 534; in connection with contempt of court and the defence of public interest disclosure to actions for breach of confidence see *A-G v Guardian Newspapers Ltd (No 2)* [1990] 1 AC 109.

[19] The prior restraint approach is exemplified by the rule in *Bonnard v Perryman* [1891] 2 Ch 269 which precluded an interim injunction in a libel action, where the defendant raised a defence of justification or fair comment; see generally, P Milmo and W Rogers (eds), *Gatley on Libel and Slander* (11th edn, Sweet & Maxwell, 2008) Chap 27.

[20] See para 2.16ff above.

[21] [2001] 2 AC 277, 297.

[22] *R v Shayler* [2003] 1 AC 247, para 21; see also per Lord Steyn, *R v Secretary of State for the Home Department, ex p Simms* [2000] 2 AC 115, 126.

court or place out of Parliament.[23] Media and journalists reporting on parliamentary proceedings are subject to absolute privilege. Reports of court[24] proceedings are also privileged against actions in defamation, so long as their publication is fair, accurate and not actuated by malice. Parliamentary papers and their publishers also receive statutory protection.

English law also imposes statutory duties on certain public bodies to facilitate freedom of **15.08** speech. For example, free postal communications and broadcast time must be made available prior to parliamentary or European Assembly elections,[25] educational institutions must ensure freedom of speech for members, students, employees and visiting speakers,[26] and individuals who make disclosures of information about their employers are given some protection.[27] Outside these clearly defined areas, the protection of freedom of expression has traditionally been limited to preventing prior restraint of damaging material.[28] In particular, reputation was given greater importance than the right to freedom of expression.[29]

However, the established exceptions to the freedom of expression are widely drawn and **15.09** often not clearly defined. The following are the most important:

- the law of *defamation* which restricts expression which damages individual reputations or provokes public disorder;
- the law of *contempt of court* which requires that certain expression be curtailed in the interests of the administration of justice;
- the law of *obscenity and indecency* which gives rise to censorship and the regulation of media content on grounds of public morality;
- the *criminal law* which also prohibits certain forms of expression as likely to provoke public disorder or racial hatred, be offensive to the Christian religion or incite persons to violence against the state;
- the law relating to the *regulation and censorship* of broadcast media, film and video;
- civil and criminal law restraints on speech which discloses Government secrets or confidential information in the interests of *national security*.

In practice, the rules governing the lawfulness of a particular 'item of expression' can be **15.10** extremely complex. It may be made by one of a number of public or private parties, through a variety of media and may be challenged under more than one head, each subject to various defences. The position is further confused because 'freedom of the press' is not treated consistently: sometimes the press are in the same position as ordinary 'publishers' and

---

[23] Bill of Rights 1689, Art 9; and see generally; para 11.74ff above.
[24] See the Defamation Act 1952, s 7, extending heads of qualified privilege; also the Contempt of Court Act 1981, ss 5 and 10.
[25] Representation of the People Act 1983, ss 95–97, as amended by the Representation of the People Act 1985.
[26] Education (No 2) Act 1986, s 43; E Barendt, 'Freedom of Speech in the Universities' [1987] PL 344 refers to these as 'bizarre' provisions.
[27] Public Interest Disclosure Act 1998 amending the Employment Rights Act 1996.
[28] See para 15.25ff below.
[29] It is regarded by Blackstone as part of the 'right of personal security', the first of the 'absolute rights of man', *Blackstone's Commentaries* (17th edn, 1830) Book I, Chap 1.

sometimes they are given special protection. As a result, the role which any positive principle of 'freedom of expression' will play in a decision is difficult to predict.

(b) Freedom of expression and the Human Rights Act 1998[30]

15.11   The HRA reinforces and gives greater weight to the protection of freedom of expression which was already established at common law.[31] It is a 'constitutional' measure which buttresses freedom of expression so that any curtailment of it must be convincingly established by compelling countervailing considerations, and the means employed must be proportionate to the end sought to be achieved.[32]

15.12   The extent to which Article 10 requires specific 'justification' of an interference on the facts of each case remains controversial. In *Ashdown v Telegraph Group*[33] Morritt V-C rejected the argument that where Article 10 was engaged, the facts of each case have to be considered to determine whether a restriction goes further than is necessary in a democratic society. In contrast, in *Loutchansky v Times Newspapers*[34] the Court of Appeal held that it was necessary to consider the application of general principles to the facts of each case in order to determine whether a particular interference with freedom of expression was justified under Article 10(2). We suggest that the approach in *Loutchansky* reflects the Strasbourg jurisprudence and is to prefered.

15.13   It has often been said that, as a result of the HRA, restrictions on freedom of expression in the public interest must be 'strictly proved'.[35] A dictum of Munby J said in *Kelly v BBC*[36] is regularly cited:

> . . . if those who seek to bring themselves within paragraph 2 of article 10 are to establish 'convincingly' that they are—and that is what they have to establish—they cannot do so by mere assertion, however eminent the person making the assertion, nor by simply inviting the court to make assumptions; what is required . . . is proper evidence . . .

15.14   However, this approach has not always been followed in practice. Despite the 'high constitutional importance' of the right to freedom of expression, the courts have continued to accord a substantial margin of discretion to the executive in freedom of expression cases and have not rigorously imposed the requirement of 'convincing evidence'. Thus, in the surprising case of *R (Farrakhan) v Secretary of State for the Home Department*,[37] the Court of Appeal accepted that one reason for the decision of the Home Secretary to exclude the claimant from the United Kingdom was to prevent him from exercising his right to freedom of expression and that, as a result, the restriction had to justified under Article 10(2).[38]

---

[30] For a comprehensive and closely argued discussion of the HRA and the media see, H Fenwick and G Phillipson, *Media Freedom under the Human Rights Act* (Oxford University Press, 2006).

[31] See *Venables v News Group* [2001] Fam 430, para 36.

[32] *McCartan Turkington Breen v Times Newspapers* [2001] 2 AC 277, 300.

[33] [2002] QB 546, paras 15–18.

[34] [2002] QB 321, para 46, after considering *Sunday Times v United Kingdom* (1979) 2 EHRR 245, para 65.

[35] *R v Secretary of Health, ex p Wagstaff* [2001] 1 WLR 292, 300.

[36] [2001] Fam 59, 67, See also *Venables v News Group* [2001] Fam 430 and *Re X (a child)* [2001] 1 FCR 541. Contrast the views expressed by Dyson LJ in *R (Samaroo) v Home Secretary* [2001] UKHRR 1150, discussed at para 6.103 above.

[37] [2002] QB 1391.

[38] The matter could also have been approached on the basis of an interference with the right of the claimant's United Kingdom followers to 'receive information' (see, for example, *Benjamin v Minister of Information and Broadcasting* [2001] 1 WLR 1040, see para 15.228 above.

The court then held that the exclusion on the ground that the claimant's visit 'might provide a catalyst for disorder' was a proportionate restriction of freedom of expression despite the absence of any 'convincing evidence' of a significant risk of disorder. The decision was, effectively, upheld on the traditional *Wednesbury* basis that it was within the Home Secretary's 'margin of discretion'. Although the House of Lords refused permission to appeal, it is suggested that the Court of Appeal's judgment does not embody the correct approach to the review of decisions which interfere with the right to freedom of expression.

(c) Section 12 of the Human Rights Act

Introduction. The HRA contains makes contains a specific provision relating to freedom **15.15** of expression. Section 12 is headed 'Freedom of Expression'. It was introduced at the Committee stage by the Government to meet concerns raised about press freedom and the conflict with the right to privacy.[39] The Home Secretary explained the purpose of section 12 during the Committee stage:[40]

> So far as we are able in a manner consistent with the Convention and its jurisprudence, we are saying to the court that wherever there is a clash between article 8 and article 10 rights, they must pay particular attention to the article 10 rights.

In fact, section 12 has rather broader implications. It provides as follows: **15.16**

(1) This section applies if a court is considering whether to grant any relief which, if granted, might affect the exercise of the Convention right to freedom of expression.

(2) If the person against whom the application for relief is made ('the respondent') is neitherpresentnorrepresented,nosuchreliefistobegrantedunlessthecourtissatisfied-

    (a) that the applicant has taken all practicable steps to notify the respondent; or

    (b) that there are compelling reasons why the respondent should not be notified.

(3) No such relief is to be granted so as to restrain publication before trial unless the court is satisfied that the applicant is likely to establish that publication should not be allowed.

(4) The court must have particular regard to the importance of the Convention right to freedom of expression and, where the proceedings relate to material which the respondent claims, or which appears to the court, to be journalistic, literary or artistic material (or to conduct connected with such material), to -

    (a) the extent to which—

        (i) the material has, or is about to, become available to the public; or

        (ii) it is, or would be, in the public interest for the material to be published;

    (b) any relevant privacy code.

(5) In this section—

    'court' includes tribunal;

    'relief' includes any remedy or order (other than in criminal proceedings).

---

[39] See HC Deb, 2 Jul 1998, Col 538 ff: The Home Secretary. For *Hansard* extracts on s 12, see J Wadham, H Mountfield, A Edmundson and C Gallagher, *Blackstone's Guide to the Human Rights Act 1998* (4th edn, Oxford University Press, 2007), 347–350; for a discussion of this provision see J Beatson, S Grosz, T Hickman, and R Singh, *Human Rights: Judicial Protection in the United Kingdom* (Sweet & Maxwell, 2008), para 4.255ff.

[40] *Hansard* HC 2 Jul 1998, col 543 (Jack Straw MP).

It is submitted that these provisions should be construed 'generously'[41] and in accordance with the principle of 'practical effectiveness'.[42] Each sub-section merits specific consideration.

15.17 **Section 12(1).** Section 12(1) establishes the scope of application of the section. First, it is clear that what is being protected is not any English law right, but 'the Convention right to freedom of expression'. This means that the section encompasses the same wide range of 'forms of expression' as is covered by Article 10 of the Convention.[43]

15.18 Secondly, section 12 will apply with respect to 'any relief' which, if granted, 'might affect' the exercise of the Convention right. Therefore, although the section was contemplated to 'safeguard press freedom',[44] it clearly extends beyond court orders which might affect publication of material by the media. Injunctions granted, for example, in actions for breach of confidence, contract or copyright 'might affect' the exercise of the right to freedom of expression. An injunction in a matter of private and public nuisance might similarly be affected if its purpose was to restrain demonstrations. Furthermore, the distinction between 'speech' and 'conduct' is not a clear one[45] and section 12 may have a wider impact than is initially apparent.

15.19 Furthermore, the words 'any relief' are not restricted to 'injunctive' relief. Relief which 'might affect' the exercise of the freedom must include awards of damages in civil actions.[46] As a result of section 12(5), tribunals[47] as well as courts must apply its principles. However, it is clear from section 12(5) that the criminal courts are outside the scope of the section. This means that the provision will not need to be considered when, for example, the court is making reporting restrictions during criminal trials.[48]

15.20 **Section 12(2).** Section 12(2) restricts the circumstances in which an injunction may be granted in the absence of the defendant. It resembles the statutory restrictions on granting interim injunctions in industrial relations disputes;[49] and would appear to apply whenever it is genuinely claimed that relief might affect the right to expression *regardless* of whether the claim might succeed.[50] Section 12 gives no indication that it does not also apply to final orders. If the defendant is not present at the trial, the court can only grant a final injunction or award of damages if the claimant shows that he has taken 'all practicable steps to notify the respondent'. This is a stronger test than that presently applied but is likely to be of limited practical importance.

---

[41] See generally, para 3.105ff above.
[42] See para 6.39ff above.
[43] See para 15.241 below.
[44] See n 39 above.
[45] See E Barendt, *Freedom of Speech* (2nd edn, Oxford University Press, 2005), 78–88.
[46] See *Tolstoy Miloslavsky v United Kingdom* (1995) 20 EHRR 442.
[47] Defined in s 21(1) of the HRA as 'any tribunal in which legal proceedings may be brought'; the meaning of the phrase is discussed at para 5.55 above.
[48] See para 15.114ff above.
[49] Trade Union and Labour Relations (Consolidation) Act 1992, s 222(1).
[50] See *Gouriet v Union of Post Office Workers* [1978] AC 435 in relation to s 221(1).

Section 12(3).   The effect of section 12(3) appears to be raise the threshold test for the   **15.21**
restraint of expression: to require the claimant to establish a stronger *prima facie* case.[51] The
principal purpose of this provision is to buttress the protection afforded to freedom of
speech at the interim stage by setting a higher threshold for the grant of interim injunctions
against the media than the previous test of a 'real prospect of succeeding at trial in the claim
for a permanent injunction'.[52] However, 'likely' in section 12(3) cannot be construed as
meaning 'more likely than not' in all situations because this would be to set the test too
high. There could be no single rigid standard governing all applications for interim relief.
The House of Lords summarized the position as follows:

> on its proper construction the effect of section 12(3) is that the court is not to make an
> interim restraint order unless satisfied the applicant's prospects of success at the trial are suffi-
> ciently favourable to justify such an order being made in the particular circumstances of the
> case. As to what degree of likelihood makes the prospects of success 'sufficiently favourable',
> the general approach should be that courts will be exceedingly slow to make interim restraint
> orders where the applicant has not satisfied the court he will probably ('more likely than not')
> succeed at the trial. In general, that should be the threshold an applicant must cross before
> the court embarks on exercising its discretion, duly taking into account the relevant jurispru-
> dence on article 10 and any countervailing Convention rights. But there will be cases where
> it is necessary for a court to depart from this general approach and a lesser degree of likelihood
> will suffice as a prerequisite. Circumstances where this may be so include those mentioned
> above: where the potential adverse consequences of disclosure are particularly grave, or where
> a short-lived injunction is needed to enable the court to hear and give proper consideration
> to an application for interim relief pending the trial or any relevant appeal.[53]

Section 12(3) has been applied in a number of cases[54] but does not appear, in practice, to
have altered the approach taken by the courts to the grant of interim relief. In the leading
case of *Cream Holdings v Bannerjee*[55] the House of Lords discharged the injunction granted
by Lloyd J and the Court of Appeal on the facts when applying both the flexible standard
under section 12(3) and the common law an injunction should have been refused.[56]

Section 12(4).   Section 12(4) provides that the court 'must have particular regard to' the   **15.22**
importance of the right to freedom of expression when granting relief. It has been said that
this provision 'puts beyond question the direct applicability of at least one article of the
Convention as between one private party to litigation and another'.[57] Where the proceedings relate to material which the respondent claims, or which appears to the court, to be
journalistic, literary or artistic material (or to conduct connected with such material), the
court must also have regard to the extent of the current or pending availability of the
material to the public; or interest of the public in having it published; and to any relevant

---

[51] See *Hansard* HC 2 Jul 1998, col 562.
[52] *Cream Holdings v Bannerjee* [2005] 1 AC 253, para 15.
[53] Ibid, para 22; see also see *Douglas v Hello! Ltd* [2001] QB 967, 1008, para 150, per Keene LJ.
[54] See eg, *Douglas v Hello! Ltd* (n 53 above); *Imutran Ltd v Uncaged Campaigns Ltd* [2001] 2 All ER 385;
Theakston v MGN Ltd [2002] EMLR 398; *A v B plc* [2003] QB 195.
[55] n 52 above.
[56] Because there was a strongly arguable 'public interest' defence in a breach of confidence claim, see generally H
Rogers and H Tomlinson 'Privacy and Expression: Convention Rights and Interim Injunctions' [2003] EHRLR
Privacy Special Issue 37, 47; and see also *Northern Rock plc v Financial Times* [2007] EWHC 2677 (QB).
[57] *Douglas v Hello! Ltd* [2001] QB 967, para 133 (Sedley LJ).

privacy code. The reference to 'conduct connected with such material' appears to be intended to cover journalistic enquiries which suggest the presence of a story without the support of existing material.[58] It appears that this sub-section was intended to 'tip the balance' in favour of expression in applications for injunctions to restrain breaches of privacy. However, the effect of section 12(4) is not to make freedom of expression a 'trump card'[59] or to give it 'presumptive priority' over other Convention rights.[60] The extent to which material has become available to the public is a relevant factor but is not determinative.[61]

15.23 Where an order is sought seeking to restrain publication of information which is alleged to be private the following principles are now applied:[62]

- No Convention right has, as such, precedence over another;
- Where a conflict arises between the values safeguarded under different convention rights an 'intense focus' is necessary upon the comparative importance of the specific rights being claimed in the individual case.
- The Court must take into account the justification for interfering with or restricting each right.
- The proportionality test must be applied to each Convention right.

15.24 **Section 12(5).**   Section 12(5) defines relief to include any remedy or order but specifically excludes orders made in criminal proceedings. This means that the section does not apply to the making of reporting restriction orders in the criminal courts. The Consolidated Criminal Practice Direction does not require the media to be given notice of applications for such orders.[63]

(2) Prior restraint

(a) Introduction

15.25 The power of the courts to *prevent* publication is the most stringent form of restriction upon freedom of expression. Prior restraint has always been approached with particular caution; as Blackstone said:

> The liberty of the press is indeed essential to the nature of a free state; but this consists in laying no *previous* restraints upon publications and not in freedom from censure for criminal matter when published. Every freeman has an undoubted right to lay what sentiments he pleases before the public: to forbid this, is to destroy the freedom of the press; but if he publishes what is improper, mischievous or illegal, he must take the consequence of his own temerity.[64]

---

[58] See *Hansard* HC 2 Jul 1998, col 540 (Jack Straw MP).

[59] *Douglas v Hello! Ltd* (see n 53 above) para 136 (Sedley LJ).

[60] *Re S (a child) (Identification: Restriction on Publication)* [2005] 1 AC 593, para 17; *British Broadcasting Company v Rochdale Metropolitan Borough Council* [2007] 1 FLR 101, paras 42–43.

[61] See *R X, Y (Children)* [2004] EMLR 29; *Mosley v News Group Newspapers* [2008] EMLR 20.

[62] See eg, *Lord Browne of Madingley v Associated Newspapers* [2008] QB 103; *CC v AB* [2007] EMLR 11, Eady J; *Mosley v News Group Newspapers* (see n 61 above), Eady J, para 28.

[63] Paragraph I.3.2 says only that there is 'nothing which precludes the court from hearing a representative of the press. Indeed it is likely that the court will wish to do so'. Crown Courts frequently make s 4 and s 11 Orders (see para 15.117ff below) without hearing from the press.

[64] *Blackstone's Commentaries*, (17th edn, 1830) Book IV, 151–2; quoted in *Holley v Smyth* [1998] QB 726, 737.

This statement of principle appears to have had a significant influence on the development of the law in the United States.[65] The basic principle and its affinity with the provisions of Article 10 of the Convention has been acknowledged in a number of cases. As Laws J put it:

> there is a general principle in our law that the expression of opinion and the conveyance of information will not be restrained by the courts save on pressing grounds. Freedom of expression is as much a sinew of the common law as it is of the European Convention. . .[66]

The Court of Human Rights has, in turn, made it clear that prior restraints 'call for the most careful scrutiny', particularly when the press is concerned.[67]

(b) Defamation cases

Rule in *Bonnard v Perryman*.   It has long been recognized that freedom of expression is   **15.26** an important consideration in determining whether an interim injunction ought to be granted to restrain the publication of material which is alleged to be defamatory. In such cases, an injunction will not be granted if the defendant asserts a defence of justification on grounds that the words complained of are *true*. The fundamental approach was described in *Bonnard v Perryman*:[68]

> The right of free speech is one which it is for the public interest that individuals should possess and, indeed, that they should exercise without impediment, so long as no wrongful act is done; and unless an alleged libel is untrue there is no wrong committed. . .

This principle has been affirmed in a large number of cases.[69] Provided that the defendant advances some evidence to support a proposed plea of justification, an injunction will be granted only in the extremely rare case in which the claimant can satisfy the court than the plea of justification is bound to fail.[70] Furthermore, the rule in *Bonnard v Perryman* applies irrespective of motive or the manner in which publication is threatened. For example, a court refused an injunction even where a defendant sought to extract money from the plaintiffs on threat of publication of what he said were damaging but true allegations about them.[71]

In *Greene v Associated Newspapers*[72] the Court of Appeal rejected the argument that the rule   **15.27** in *Bonnard v Perryman* had been changed by the HRA. It held that Parliament could not

---

[65] See *Schering Chemicals Ltd v Falkman Ltd* [1982] 1 QB 1, 17C–H; see generally, L Levy, *The Emergence of a Free Press* (Oxford University Press, 1985); and see also L Tribe, *American Constitutional Law* (2nd edn, Foundation Press, 1988), 785ff; and E Chemerinsky, *Constitutional Law: Principles and Policies* (3rd edn, Aspen, 2006), para 11.2.3.

[66] *R v Advertising Standards Authority Ltd, ex p Vernons Organization Ltd* [1992] 1 WLR 1289, 1293A.

[67] *Observer v United Kingdom* (1992) 14 EHRR 153, para 60, for prior restraint and Art 10 see para 15.268ff below.

[68] [1891] 2 Ch 269, 284.

[69] See eg, *Fraser v Evans* [1969] 1 QB 349, 360; *Bestobell Paints v Bigg* [1975] FSR 421; *Crest Homes v Ascott* [1980] FSR 396; *Khasshoggi v IPC Magazines Ltd* [1986] 1 WLR 1412; see generally the survey of the law in *Greene v Associated Newspapers* [2005] QB 972, paras 42–57.

[70] See generally, P Milmo and W Rogers (eds), *Gatley on Libel and Slander* (11th edn, Sweet & Maxwell, 2008), para 27.6.

[71] See *Holley v Smyth* [1998] QB 726.

[72] n 69 above.

be interpreted as having abrogated the rule by a 'side wind'.[73] The Court of Appeal accepted that the right to reputation was among the rights guaranteed by Article 8[74] but held that the rule continued to apply. According to Brooke LJ

> If a claimant were able to stop a defendant from exercising its Article 10 right merely by arguing on paper-based evidence that it was more likely than not that the defendant could not show that what it wished to say about the claimant was true, it would seriously weaken the effect of Article 10.[75]

He went on to say that 'one cannot speak sensibly of the violation of the right [to a fair reputation] until it is established at the trial'.[76]

15.28 The analysis of in the *Greene* case is unsatisfactory and is inconsistent with the modern jurisprudence of the Court of Human rights. Once it is accepted that there is an Article 8 right to reputation the court must carry out a proper 'parallel analysis' in every case in which interim relief is sought.[77] The fact that the defendant says it will prove the truth of the allegations made is only one relevant factor and cannot be a 'trump card'. As a result, the rule in *Bonnard v Perryman* must give way to a proper proportionality analysis.[78]

15.29 **Other causes of action.** The courts have, however, refused to allow the rule *Bonnard v Perryman* to be evaded by dressing up libel claims as other causes of action. The application for injunction in *Femis-Bank (Anguilla) Ltd v Lazar*[79] was unsuccessful on the basis that, whatever the cause of action, freedom of speech was an important factor to be taken into account in the exercise of the discretion of the court. Even though the rule in *Bonnard v Perryman* does not apply to trademark infringement[80] or breach of copyright, the courts will not allow such a claim to be used as a 'vehicle' for what is, in essence, a claim for defamation.[81] In a claim for breach of a contract 'not to publish', demonstration by the claimant of a good arguable case will not be sufficient grounds for a grant of interim injunction: the court should be able to assess the relative strengths of the parties' cases.[82]

(c) Breach of confidence

15.30 **Introduction.** At common law the rule in *Bonnard v Perryman* preventing prior restraint in defamation cases also extends to trade libel, injurious falsehood and related claims.[83] It does not, however, provide a defence against the imposition of interim injunctions sought on the basis of *other* causes of action. A claimant attempting to restrain the publication of

---

[73] Ibid, paras 61–64.

[74] Ibid, para 68, for 'reputation' as an Article 8 right, see para 12.301 above and para 15.341 below.

[75] Ibid, para 74.

[76] Ibid, para 76.

[77] For 'parallel analysis' see para 12.41ff.

[78] See also the discussion in *Gatley* (n 70 above) para 27.14ff and see the discussion of the rule by the High Court of Australia in *Australian Broadcasting Corp v O'Neill* (2006) 22 BHRC 305, especially the dissenting judgments of Kirby and Heydon JJ; and see also *SHG v Baines* [2006] EWHC 2359 (QB), para 16ff.

[79] [1991] Ch 391.

[80] *Boehringer Ingelheim v Vetplus* [2007] FSR 29, para 56; see para 15.42 below.

[81] Cf *Service Corporation v Channel Four Television*, [1999] EMLR 83, Lightman J.

[82] See *Cambridge Nutrition Ltd v British Broadcasting Corporation* [1990] 3 All ER 523.

[83] *Lord Brabourne v Hough* [1981] FSR 79, 85.

material which he believes to be damaging will therefore often seek to do so on other grounds: conspiracy to injure, breach of copyright, and, most importantly, breach of confidence.

Breach of confidence and the *Spycatcher* case.   The most important basis upon which a   **15.31** claimant may obtain 'prior restraint' of publication is that of a claim of *breach of confidence*. The rule in *Bonnard v Perryman* does not apply to prevent interim injunctions from being granted in such cases. Proceedings for confidential information are in a special category, because

> if, pending the trial, the court allows publication, there is no point in having a trial since the cloak of confidentiality can never be restored. Confidential information is like an ice cube. . . Give it to the party who has no refrigerator or will not agree to keep it in one, and by the time of the trial you just have a pool of water.[84]

As a result, before the HRA the claimant only needed to show an arguable claim and that the 'balance of convenience' was in favour of granting the order.[85]

The availability of interim injunctions to restrain breaches of confidence has been a serious   **15.32** threat to freedom of expression.[86] The most important example of such restraint was in the *Spycatcher* litigation, in which the British Government sought to restrain the publication of a book by a former intelligence officer, Peter Wright. The book had been written in breach of the Official Secrets Act and of the duty of confidentiality of the author. In June 1986, a number of British newspapers published articles containing allegations made by Mr Wright concerning the Security Service which the British Government was seeking to restrain in court proceedings in Australia.[87] On 27 June 1986, the Attorney-General obtained *ex parte* injunctions to restrain further publication. On 11 July 1986 these injunctions were continued in modified form by Millett J. The injunctions were upheld by the Court of Appeal. The application for an injunction before the Australian courts by the British Government was unsuccessful.

On 11 July 1987, the book was published in the United States. As a result, after hearing a   **15.33** preliminary issue in July 1987, Sir Nicholas Browne-Wilkinson V-C discharged the interlocutory injunctions.[88] Although the Judge accepted that the 'ice cube' of the confidential information needed to be preserved, he took the view that:

> It has been put in the refrigerator, but the American publication is as though somebody had turned off the refrigerator. . .[89]

---

[84] Per Sir John Donaldson MR in *A-G v Newspaper Publishing plc* [1988] Ch 333, quoted in *A-G v Guardian Newspapers Ltd (No 1)* [1987] 1 WLR 1248, 1259F–H.

[85] In accordance with the principles in *American Cyanamid Company v Ethicon Ltd* [1975] AC 396; however it must be possible to frame an interim injunction in clear terms: cf *Times Newspapers Ltd v MGN Ltd* [1993] EMLR 442 in which an injunction was refused on this ground.

[86] Concerns in relation to this were one reason for the addition of s 12 of the Human Rights Act; see para 15.155ff below.

[87] Mr Wright was resident in Australia and was proposing to publish a book there.

[88] *A-G v Guardian Newspapers Ltd (No 1)* [1987] 1 WLR 1248.

[89] Ibid, 1268B–C.

The Court of Appeal nevertheless allowed in part the Attorney-General's appeal and granted a modified interlocutory injunction. This injunction was upheld by the House of Lords on 30 July 1987 on the ground that there was an arguable case for the protection of an important public interest, namely the maintenance of the secrecy of the Security Service.[90] However, Lords Bridge and Oliver dissented; and Lord Bridge was particularly critical:[91]

> I have had confidence in the capacity of the common law to safeguard the fundamental freedoms essential to a free society including the right to freedom of speech which is specifically safeguarded by Article 10 of the Convention. My confidence is seriously undermined by your Lordships' decision . . . The maintenance of the ban, as more and more copies of the book *Spycatcher* enter this country and circulate here, will seem more and more ridiculous. If the Government are determined to fight to maintain the ban to the end, they will face inevitable condemnation and humiliation by the European Court of Human Rights in Strasbourg. Long before that they will have been condemned at the bar of public opinion in the free world.[92]

Lord Templeman and the other members of the majority took the view that the restraints imposed were necessary in accordance with Article 10 of the Convention.[93]

15.34 The newspapers applied to the Court of Human Rights. In *The Observer and The Guardian v United Kingdom*[94] the Court accepted the argument of the Government that the injunctions had the legitimate aim of 'maintaining the authority of the judiciary' and safeguarding the operation of the security services. Nevertheless, the majority took the view that, the confidentiality of the material having been destroyed by its publication, there was no sufficient reason for the continuation of the injunction after 30 July 1987.[95]

15.35 **Breach of confidence and section 12(3).**   The position has been altered by section 12(3) of the HRA.[96] A claimant who seeks to prevent the publication of confidential information must now show that the prospects of success are sufficiently favourable to justify such an order being made in the particular circumstances of the case. This will usually mean that the claimant has to show that it is more likely that not that he will succeed in obtaining an injunction at trial.[97]

(d) Publication of private information

15.36 **Introduction.**   The Court has power to grant an interim injunction to restrain the publication of private information.[98] The Court must carry out a 'a parallel analysis', looking at

---

[90] Ibid.

[91] The majority comprised Lords Brandon, Templeman, and Ackner.

[92] Ibid, 1286C–H; when the case was heard before the Court of Human Rights, it held the injunction breached freedom of expression under Art 10: see *The Observer and The Guardian v United Kingdom* (1991) 14 EHRR 153.

[93] Ibid, 1296F–1299G.

[94] n 92 above.

[95] Ibid, para 68.

[96] See para 15.21 above.

[97] *Cream Holdings v Bannerjee* [2005] 1 AC 253.

[98] For misuse of private information see generally, para 12.21ff above.

the matter from the point of view of Articles 8 and 10 in turn, with neither taking precedence.[99] In other words, the court must determine:[100]

- whether Article 8 is engaged—whether in respect of the disclosed facts the claimant has
  a reasonable expectation of privacy—although the nature of the relationship between the
  claimant and the discloser is of central importance it is not determinative;[101]
- whether Article 10 is engaged and the 'value' of the threatened expression—does it concern matters of 'public interest';[102]
- whether the claimant had shown that he was more likely than not to succeed at the trial
  in establishing that publication should not be allowed.

15.37 The Court has a general jurisdiction to restrain the publication of information in relation
to which the claimant has a reasonable expectation of privacy.[103] Applications under this
jurisdiction are regularly brought in relation to threatened publication of private information in the media.[104] In addition, the Court can grant injunctions to restrain other interferences with Article 8 rights [105] and can, in appropriate cases, grant injunctions anonymising
court proceedings[106] or orders binding the whole world (orders "*contra mundum*").[107] This
latter jurisdiction is not confined to information concerning children and vulnerable adults
[108] although most applications relate to people in these categories.

15.38 In *Venables v News Group*[109] an injunction was granted in favour of two claimants who had
been convicted of a notorious child murder and were about to be released. There was a
'strong possibility' that if the claimants were identified their lives would be at risk.[110] The
injunction prevented the publication of information which might lead to their identification.[111] The Court held that there was jurisdiction to grant an injunction for breach of confidence against the whole world. This injunction would now be granted under the court's
jurisdiction deriving from the HRA to prevent interference with Convention rights.

15.39 In *Leeds City Council v Channel 4 Television*[112] Munby J refused an application for an
injunction to restrain the broadcast of film which had been surreptitiously taken in a school

---

[99] *In Re S (A Child) (Identification: Restrictions on Publication)* [2005] 1 AC 593, para 17; *McKennitt v Ash*
[2008] QB 73, paras 46–48; *Lord Browne of Madingley v Associated Newspapers* [2008] QB 103, para 39.

[100] *Lord Browne* (see n 99 above), para 23.

[101] Ibid, paras 24–37.

[102] Ibid.

[103] See generally, para 12.27ff above.

[104] See generally, para 12.109 above

[105] *In Re S (A Child) (Identification: Restrictions on Publication)*(see n 99 above).

[106] See para 15128ff below.

[107] See para 12.116 below.

[108] For the former approach see *A Local Authority (Inquiry: Restraint on Publication)* [2004] Fam 96
(injunction was granted to restrain the publication of a report on an inquiry into child fostering to protect
children and vulnerable adults who were referred to but no jurisdiction to protect adult of full capacity).

[109] [2001] Fam 430.

[110] Ibid, para 94.

[111] See also *X, A Woman Formerly known as Mary Bell v O'Brien* [2003] EMLR 37; see also *Maxine Carr v
News Group Newspapers* [2005] EWHC 971 (QB) (injunction under Art 8), see para 12.116 above.

[112] [2007] 1 FLR 678 (the defendant had agreed to obscure the faces of the children); see also *E v Channel
Four Television* [2005] EMLR 30 (injunction refused to retrain broadcast of film about an adult who suffered
from dissociative identity disorder).

as part of an investigation into disruptive behaviour. However, an injunction was granted in *T v BBC*[113] to prevent the identification of a vulnerable mother in programme about adoption: she did have the capacity to consent and the material to be broadcast constituted a 'massive invasion of her privacy and autonomy'.[114]

(e) Other causes of action

15.40 **Introduction.** Interim injunctions which impact on freedom of expression can be obtained in a number of different kinds of cases. Prior to the HRA coming into force, different criteria were sometimes applied, depending on the type of claim being brought. However, all such claims are now subject to the provisions of section 12 of the HRA and, as a result, interim injunctions should not be granted unless the claimant can show that the claim is likely to succeed at trial. We will deal with five causes of action: conspiracy to injure, trademark infringement, harassment.

15.41 **Conspiracy.** A claim for an interlocutory injunction on the basis of an alleged conspiracy to injure was, successful in *Gulf Oil (Great Britain) Ltd v Page*,[115] where the plaintiff obtained an injunction to restrain the defendant from displaying a defamatory airborne sign. In *Gate Gourmet v Transport and General Workers Union*[116] an employer sought an injunction to restrain picketing of its premises. The Court took into account the Article 10 (and Article 11) rights of the workers in granting an interim injunction to limit the number of pickets to six.

15.42 **Trade mark infringement.** An application for an injunction by the owner of a trade mark who is seeking to restrain comparative advertising engages Article 10. The rule in *Bonnard v Perryman*[117] does not apply but section 12(3) of the HRA means that an applicant must show that it was more likely than not that it would succeed at trial.[118] Applying this test, the Court has refused to grant interim injunctions to restrain comparative advertising in two recent cases.[119] However it has been held that section 12(3) does not apply to trade mark cases outside the realm of comparative advertising as the mere use of a trade mark is not the expression of thoughts or opinions.[120]

15.43 **Harassment.** Injunctions under the Protection from Harassment Act 1997 can involve serious interference with the Article 10 rights of defendants. Such injunctions are often granted against protestors to prevent them from communicating with employees of organizations whose activities they find objectionable. In *Heathrow Airport Ltd v Garman*[121] taking into account Article 10 rights, the court refused to grant an injunction in harassment against protestors at Heathrow Airport.

---

[113] [2008] 1 FLR 281.
[114] Ibid, para 16.
[115] [1987] Ch 327.
[116] [2005] IRLR 881.
[117] [1891] 2 Ch 269, See para 15.26 above.
[118] *Boehringer Ingelheim Ltd v Vetplus Ltd* [2007] FSR 29.
[119] Ibid, *Red Dot Technologies v Apollo Fire Detectors* [2007] EWHC 1166 (Ch).
[120] See *Oven Clean v Gilbert* [2007] EWHC 3483 (Ch).
[121] [2007] EWHC 1957 (QB).

It is, however, clear that the exercise of the right to free speech could fall within the concept **15.44** of harassment provided that other necessary ingredients such as unreasonable and oppressive conduct were present.[122] A claim for harassment can engage both Article 8 and Article 10 rights and, as a result, a balancing exercise has to be carried out.[123] An injunction was granted to restrain 'aerial harassment' and surveillance of the claimant.[124]

(f) Contempt proceedings

Introduction. The court has jurisdiction to grant an injunction to restrain the publication **15.45** of any material which may constitute a 'criminal' contempt.[125] Although only the Attorney-General may institute proceedings for criminal contempt[126] it appears that anyone with a sufficiently proximate interest may also apply.[127]

Circumstances in which orders granted. Because the prior restraint of a publication is a **15.46** very serious interference with press freedom, an injunction on grounds of contempt will only be granted where the publication would, manifestly, be a contempt of court.[128] It has to be shown, to the criminal standard, that publication will create a real risk of prejudice to the administration of justice and that the Defendants will publish that material with a specific intent of causing that risk.[129] As a result, applications for injunction have been refused in a number of cases.[130]

It is clear, however, that an application to restrain a manifestly contemptuous publication **15.47** will not be refused simply because the defendant seeks to justify. The position was summarized by Sir John Donaldson MR as follows:

> In practice, I think that the rule in *Bonnard v Perryman* will be decisive unless and until the strict liability rule is invoked. Once it is invoked it will prevail, because, in the form in which it survives in 1981, if strictly construed and applied, the balance must always come down on the side of protecting the right to justice.[131]

It was, however, emphasized that section 5 of the Contempt Act would protect general discussion of topics with which forthcoming trials were incidentally concerned.[132] An injunction was granted in *Ex Parte HTV (Cymru) Wales Ltd*[133] in the course of a murder trial

---

[122] *Thomas v Hughes* [2002] EMLR 4.

[123] *Howlett v Holding* [2006] EWHC 41 (QB).

[124] Ibid.

[125] For the distinction between 'civil' and 'criminal' contempts see para 15.81 below.

[126] Contempt of Court Act 1981, s 7.

[127] See *Peacock v London Weekend Television* (1985) 150 JP 71 (Police Federation granted injunction to restrain TV programme on grounds that it would prejudice a pending inquest) and *Leary v BBC*, unreported, 29 Sep1989, CA; but see *Pickering v Liverpool Daily Post and Echo Newspapers plc* [1991] 2 AC 370, 425 where Lord Bridge expressed doubt on this point; see generally, *Arlidge, Eady and Smith on Contempt* (3rd edn, Sweet & Maxwell, 2005), paras 6-22 to 6-29.

[128] *A-G v British Broadcasting Corporation* [1981] AC 303, 311, 362.

[129] *Coe v Central Television* [1994] EMLR 433; see also *Chief Constable of Greater Manchester Police v Channel 5* [2005] Pol LR 183 (Auld LJ expressing doubts about the appropriateness of the criminal standard).

[130] See eg, *Schering Chemicals Ltd v Falkman Ltd* [1982] 1 QB 1 (an injunction was granted to restrain breach of confidence); *A-G v News Group Newspapers Ltd* (Botham libel case) [1987] QB 1.

[131] *A-G v News Group Newspapers Ltd* (see n 130 above) 14.

[132] Ibid, 14–15.

[133] [2002] EMLR 11; see also *Chief Constable of Greater Manchester Police* (n 129 above)(injunction to restrain broadcast which might prejudice a criminal investigation refused).

to restrain a television company from interviewing a witness who had given evidence. The Judge held that there was a substantial risk that the course of justice in the trial would be seriously impeded or prejudiced.

15.48 **Advance clearance.** When a newspaper had given undertakings not to publish confidential material derived from a former member of the security services, it was entitled to a variation excluding information in the public domain. It was not necessary for it to obtain clearance from the Attorney-General before publishing.[134] When an injunction is granted to restrain the publication of allegedly confidential material pending trial a third party who, with knowledge of the order, publishes the information commits a contempt of court because the purpose of making the order was intentionally frustrated.[135] However, the court could not render it a criminal offence for a newspaper to fail to obtain clearance from the Attorney-General before publishing material to which there could manifestly not be the slightest ground of objection. The contrary conclusion would be a breach of Article 10.[136]

(3) Protection of reputation and private life

(a) Introduction

15.49 The English law of defamation protects the reputation of every person from defamatory statements about him made to third parties without lawful justification. Although many defamation cases refer to the importance of freedom of expression, the common law has always placed great emphasis on the right to reputation. As the Court of Appeal said in *Kiam v Neill*:[137]

> The right to protection of the law against attacks on honour and reputation are as important in a democratic society as the right to freedom of the press. History discloses examples which show that undermining the reputation of a political opponent of an arbitrary domineering or oppressive regime can be one of the first weapons deployed by the despot.

The effect of this emphasis is that the common law provides no special protection or defence to the press: press publications are subject to the same rules of law as apply to publications by private individuals.

15.50 The right to reputation has now been recognized by the Court of Human Rights as being one aspect of the right to respect for private life under Article 8.[138] The right to freedom of expression is subject to interference from both the torts of defamation (which protects reputation) and of misuse of private information (which protects other aspects of private life). These claims will be both considered in this section.

---

[134] *Attorney-General v Times Newspapers* [2001] 1 WLR 885.

[135] See *Attorney-General v Times Newspapers* [1992] 1 AC 191.

[136] See *Attorney-General v Punch Ltd* [2003] 1 AC 1046, para 108.

[137] *The Times*, 29 July 1996; see also *Reynolds v Times Newspapers Ltd* [2001] 2 AC 127, 201 (per Lord Nicholls).

[138] See generally, para 12.301 above.

(b) The meaning of 'defamatory'

A statement is defamatory if it tends to lower the claimant in the estimation of right think-   **15.51**
ing members of society generally.[139] The statement does not have to have any actual effect
on reputation: the law looks at its 'tendency'.[140] The court considers the 'natural and
ordinary meaning' of the words used rather than the literal meaning: it can include any
implication or inference which a reasonable reader would draw from the words.[141] In addition, a statement may be defamatory on the basis of extrinsic facts known to some readers:
this is known as an innuendo.[142] The meaning of a particular statement and whether or not
it is defamatory are matters for a jury[143] but the question of whether the words are 'capable'
of being defamatory is decided by the judge.[144] The prominent role of the jury introduces
a considerable degree of uncertainty: it is often difficult to predict with any accuracy
whether a jury is likely to find particular words defamatory.

The law of defamation presumes that defamatory imputations are false[145] and that the per-   **15.52**
son defamed is of good reputation. The claimant is not required to prove actual damage to
reputation or any other loss. The burden of establishing the truth of the words used, or any
other defences, is on the publisher of the words. This burden is, inevitably, a considerable
restriction on freedom of expression. When a defamatory statement is published in permanent form, the tort of *libel* is committed, and:

> the law presumes that *some* damage will flow in the ordinary course of things from the mere
> invasion of his absolute right to reputation.[146]

Defamation that is expressed orally or in a less than permanent form constitutes the tort of   **15.53**
slander. Slander is, in general, only actionable at common law if actual damage can be
proved. There are, however, a number of forms of slander which are actionable without
proof of damage.[147] Once a cause of action in slander is established, damages are 'at large'.

(c) Who can bring a defamation action?

General.   An action for defamation can be brought by a natural person or by a company.   **15.54**
A trading corporation can sue for damage to its trading reputation[148] and a non-trading

---

[139] Per Lord Atkin, *Sim v Stretch* (1936) 52 TLR 669; generally, *Gatley on Libel and Slander* (11th edn,
Sweet & Maxwell, 2008), Chap 2.

[140] See *Hough v London Express Newspapers Ltd* [1940] 2 KB 507, 515.

[141] *Lewis v Daily Telegraph* [1964] AC 234, 258; *Jones v Skelton* [1963] 1 WLR 1362, 1370; *Gatley on Libel
and Slander* (see n 139 above) para 3.16ff. Note that an 'inferred' imputation is sometimes called a 'popular'
or 'false' innuendo (*Lewis*, 280).

[142] This is a 'true innuendo', see generally, *Gatley on Libel and Slander* (see n 139 above) para 3.20ff.

[143] There remains a right to trial by jury in libel actions under the Supreme Court Act 1981, s 69(1). This
right may be lost if the case involves prolonged examination of documents or accounts: see *Aitken v Guardian
Newspapers* [1997] EMLR 415.

[144] See eg, *Gillick v BBC* [1996] EMLR 267; and *Gatley on Libel and Slander* (see n 139 above) para 32.2ff.

[145] *Gatley on Libel and Slander* (see n 139 above) para 11.3.

[146] *Ratcliffe v Evans* [1892] 2 QB 524, 528.

[147] These are: an imputation of a criminal offence punishable by imprisonment, an imputation of a con-
tagious disease, an imputation of unchastity against a woman under the Slander of Women Act 1891, and
words calculated to disparage a person in any office, calling, trade or business.

[148] *Gatley on Libel and Slander* (see n 139 above) para 8.16ff; this applies to a foreign trading corporation
which conducts no business in the jurisdiction but has a trading reputation, see *Jameel v Wall Street Journal*
[2007] 1 AC 359 (rule upheld by HL, 3-2).

corporation can bring an action in respect of imputations which are damaging to its property or finances.[149] A trade union cannot, however, sue for libel because it is not a body corporate.[150]

15.55 **Public authorities.** It is now clear that a local government corporation cannot sue for libel. The point arose in *Derbyshire County Council v Times Newspapers*,[151] in which the Court of Appeal, placing considerable reliance on Article 10 of the Convention,[152] denied a local authority the right to sue for libel. This decision was upheld by the House of Lords on the basis of the common law, without any reliance upon the Convention. Lord Keith was of the view that it was:

> of the highest public importance that a democratically elected governmental body, or indeed any governmental body, should be open to uninhibited public criticism.[153]

As a result, he concluded that:

> not only is there no public interest favouring the right of organs of government whether central or local, to sue for libel, but . . . it is contrary to the public interest that they should have it. It is contrary to the public interest because to admit such actions would place an undesirable fetter on freedom of speech.[154]

This principle has been applied to governmental bodies[155] and to political parties.[156] It does not, however, extend to individually elected officials, public employees or members of political parties.

(d) Defences to an action for defamation

15.56 **Introduction.** The most important defences[157] to actions for defamation are 'justification' on grounds of truth, fair comment on a matter of public interest, absolute privilege and qualified privilege. The 1996 Defamation Act has also introduced a defence of an offer to make amends[158] where a defendant makes an offer to apologize and to pay damages assessed by a judge.[159]

---

[149] *Gatley on Libel and Slander* (see n 139 above) para 8.19.

[150] *Electrical, Electronic, Telecommunications and Plumbing Union v Times Newspapers Ltd* [1980] QB 585.

[151] [1992] QB 770, CA; [1993] AC 534, HL.

[152] See para 2.16 above.

[153] [1993] AC 534, 547F–G.

[154] Ibid, 549; it should be noted that this approach is stricter than that taken under the Convention.

[155] *British Coal Corporation v NUM*, unreported, 28 Jun 1996.

[156] *Goldsmith v Bhoyrul* [1998] QB 459.

[157] See generally, *Gatley on Libel and Slander* (see n 139 above) Pt 2, Chaps 10 to 19.

[158] See s 3(5); the defence of 'offer to make amends' replaces the statutory defence of unintentional defamation contained in the 1952 Act, s 4.

[159] Acceptance of such an offer does not create contractual rights but a court would only permit a party to resile on a traditional contractual ground—there was no interference with Art 10 rights since a defendant who had made an offer could repeat the words complained of: see *Warren v Random House Group* [2008] EWCA Civ 834.

Justification. 'Justification' or proof of the substantial truth of a defamatory imputation is **15.57** a complete defence. The defendant carries the burden of proving the truth of the defamatory imputations which the words bear:

> When a plea of justification is pleaded, it involves the justification of every injurious imputation which a jury may think is to be found in the alleged libel.[160]

The operation of the defence of justification in the modern law of libel is highly technical. The following points should be noted:

- the claimant must set out the 'sting' of the libel on which he relies in his Particulars of Claim;[161]
- the claimant can 'pick and choose' from a publication containing more than one defamatory imputation, basing his claim on only some of the imputations;[162]
- the defendant must justify either the 'sting' relied on by the claimant or a 'lesser' defamatory meaning which he says the words bear;[163]
- if the claimant picks one defamatory imputation, the defendant cannot justify another separate and distinct imputation in the same publication;[164]
- if the claimant complains that the publication contains several defamatory imputations, the defence of justification does not fail only because the truth of every charge is not proved, *if* the untrue words 'do not materially injure the claimant's reputation' having regard to the remaining charges.[165]

The burden on a defendant is a high one. Uncertainty results from the fact that the jury determines the meaning of the words used and is obliged to find a single meaning.[166] The result is that a defendant who can prove the truth of almost everything in a long publication could still be successfully sued if the jury finds that the publication contains one defamatory imputation the truth of which the defendant cannot prove.

It has been held that the requirement that the defendant bears the burden of proving the **15.58** truth of the sting of the libel (rather than justifying some lesser allegation) is consistent with Article 10:

> To require a defendant . . . to be able to justify not a diminished version of a damaging assault on a claimant's reputation but the essence or substance or sting of that assault is not in our judgment a disproportionate invasion of the right of free expression. It meets the legitimate purpose, recognized by Article 10(2), of protecting people from the publication of damaging and unjustified falsehoods.[167]

---

[160] *Digby v Financial News* [1907] 1 KB 502.
[161] See *Lucas-Box v News Group Newspapers Ltd* [1986] 1 WLR 147, 151–152.
[162] *Cruise v Express Newspapers* [1999] QB 931.
[163] This must be specifically set out in the defence and is known as a 'Lucas-Box' meaning, see *Lucas-Box v News Group Newspapers Ltd* (see n 161 above).
[164] *Cruise v Express Newspapers* (see n 162 above); *Polly Peck (Holdings) plc v Trelford* [1986] QB 1000.
[165] Defamation Act 1952, s 5.
[166] See *Charleston v News Group Newspapers Ltd* [1995] 2 AC 65.
[167] *Berezovsky v Forbes* [2001] EMLR 1030, para 12.

The Court of Appeal rejected the argument that the decision in *Bergens Tidende v Norway*[168] had altered the course of Convention jurisprudence on this subject. The principles relating to justifying an allegation of 'reasonable grounds for suspicion' have been held to be compatible with Article 10.[169]

15.59 **Fair comment.** Another defence that may be established by the defendant to an action in defamation is that the words used were fair comment[170] on a matter of public interest. The law recognizes that it is important not to require publishers to prove the truth of value judgments.[171] There are five stages in proving fair comment. First, the defendant must show that the words used were 'comment', rather than assertions of fact: this can include not just statements of opinion but also 'inferences'.[172] The test is 'how the words would be understood by an ordinary reader'.[173] In practice, the line between comment and factual assertion is difficult to draw.[174] Secondly, the facts on which the comment is based must be 'sufficiently indicated' by the words used—it is not necessary for them to be stated when the comment is made.[175] Thirdly, these facts must be shown to be true.[176] The defence will not fail, however, solely for lack of proof of the truth of every allegation of fact, if the defendant can show that the expression of opinion is fair comment, having regard to the facts which are proved.[177] Fourthly, the defendant must show that the comment was 'fair'. This is the least onerous requirement because 'fair', in this context, simply means 'capable of being honestly held'. As Diplock J said to the jury in *Silkin v Beaverbrook Newspapers Ltd*:[178]

> do not apply the test of whether you agree with it. If juries did that, freedom of speech, the right of the crank to say what he likes, would go. Would a fair minded man holding strong views, obstinate views, prejudiced views, have been capable of making this comment? If the answer to that is yes then [the defence succeeds].

Fifthly, it must be shown that the comment was on a matter of public interest. This is not confined within narrow limits.[179] It will cover the conduct of anyone who ventures into

---

[168] (2001) 31 EHRR 16, see para 15.337 below.

[169] *Chase v News Group Newspapers* [2003] EMLR 218)(the requirements that the defence should focus upon some conduct of the individual claimant that in itself gave rise to suspicion, that hearsay evidence was not permitted and that post publication material could not be relied on were justified restrictions on freedom of expression).

[170] The defence is more accurately described as 'honest comment', per Lord Nicholls, *Reynolds v Times Newspapers Ltd* [2001] 2 AC 127, 193.

[171] See *Keays v Guardian Newspapers* [2003] EWHC 1565, para 30 (referring to *Nilsen & Johnsen v Norway* (2000) 30 EHRR 878 and see *Branson v Bower* [2002] QB 737 at para 27.

[172] See *Branson v Bower* [2001] EMLR 32.

[173] *Slim v Daily Telegraph Ltd* [1968] 2 QB 157.

[174] See generally, *Gatley on Libel and Slander* (11th edn, Sweet & Maxwell, 2008), para 12.6ff.

[175] This can be by stating the facts in the article, referring to them or because the facts are 'general knowledge', see generally *Lowe v Associated Newspapers* [2007] 1 QB 580 and see also the decision of the High Court of Australia in *Channel Seven v Manock* (2007) 241 ALR 468 (especially paras 52–55 criticizing *Lowe* for expressing the test too broadly), and see also *WIC Radio Ltd v Simpson* 2008 SCC 40.

[176] See *Broadway Approvals Ltd v Odhams Press Ltd* [1964] 2 QB 683.

[177] Defamation Act 1952, s 6.

[178] [1958] 1 WLR 743.

[179] See *London Artists Ltd v Littler* [1969] QB 375, 391.

public life,[180] every kind of artistic production placed before the public and anything which might fairly be said to 'invite comment' or challenge public attention.[181]

The defence of fair comment can be rebutted by proof that the defendant was actuated by malice.[182] In order to rebut the defence of fair comment a claimant must show that the defendant did not have a genuine belief in what he said. In contrast to the position in relation to qualified privilege, it is not sufficient to show that the defendant was actuated by spite, animosity, intent to cause injury or other ulterior motive.[183] **15.60**

Absolute privilege. The public interest requires that individuals be permitted in certain circumstances to express themselves with complete freedom. Certain speech is therefore protected against actions in defamation or 'privileged'. Privilege may be absolute or qualified. Absolute privilege is a complete defence, no matter how damaging or defamatory the statements may be, providing a complete defence to an action in defamation. The most important heads of 'absolute privilege' are: **15.61**

- Statements made by witnesses, advocates or judges in the course of litigation.[184] This privilege extends to witness statements,[185] court documents and to any statement made as part of the process of investigating crime[186] and a complaint of criminal conduct to a regulatory body.[187] It does not, however, extend to fabricating evidence.[188]
- Statements made in the debates or proceedings in Parliament, and evidence given by witnesses to select committees.[189] The fact that proceedings in Parliament cannot be 'questioned' means that a party cannot rely, in an action, on anything said in Parliament.[190] A member of Parliament may, however, waive the privilege for the purposes of defamation proceedings.[191]
- Fair and accurate reports of court proceedings if they are published contemporaneously with the proceedings.[192]

---

[180] See *Branson v Bower* [2002] QB 735, 747.

[181] See generally, *Gatley on Libel and Slander* (see n 174 above) paras 12.27ff.

[182] For malice, see para 15.64 below.

[183] *Cheng Albert v Tse Wai Chun Paul* (2001) 10 BHRC 525 (Hong Kong Court of Final Appeal)(Lord Nicholls); applied in England in *Branson v Bower (No.2)* [2002] QB 737, Eady J, para 11, see also *Panday v Gordon* [2006] 3 LRC 252 (PC), para 12.

[184] *Munster v Lamb* (1883) 11 QBD 588, 607; see *Gatley on Libel and Slander* (n 174 above) para 13.5ff.

[185] *Watson v M'Ewan* [1905] AC 480; including written (*Buckley v Dalziel* [2007] 1 WLR 2933) and oral statements by the complainant *Westcott v Westcott* [2009] EMLR 2.

[186] *Taylor v Director of the Serious Fraud Office* [1999] 2 AC 177.

[187] *Mahon v Rahn (No.2)* [2000] 1 WLR 2150.

[188] *Darker v Chief Constable of West Midlands Police* [2001] 1 AC 435.

[189] Bill of Rights 1688, Art 9.

[190] *Prebble v Television New Zealand* [1995] 1 AC 321; see generally, para 11.76 above.

[191] Defamation Act 1996, s 13(1); *Gatley on Libel and Slander* (see n 174 above) para 13.32; and see *Hamilton v Al-Fayed* [1999] 1 WLR 1569.

[192] Defamation Act 1996, s 14: the privilege extends to reports of proceedings before the European Court of Justice, the European Court of Human Rights, and defined international criminal tribunals.

The courts are cautious about extending the categories of absolute privilege,[193] but the categories are not closed.[194]

15.62 **Qualified privilege.** Words spoken in good faith on other occasions may also be subject to privilege, albeit of a qualified nature. There is now statutory provision for qualified privilege which protects the publication of reports or statements from across a wide range of subject matter,[195] so long as they are 'fair and accurate'.[196] These include fair and accurate reports of the proceedings of foreign legislatures, courts, public commission inquiries, public meetings and local authorities or local authority committees and public meetings.[197] The reference in the statute to 'public meeting' had to be interpreted in a manner which gave effect to the intention of the legislature in the social and other conditions which obtain today to include a press conference.[198]

15.63 Qualified privilege protects communications where there is a legal, moral, or social duty on the person to communicate a statement, and a corresponding interest or duty on the person who receives the publication. It is helpful to distinguish two categories of this type of privilege: where there is an existing and established relationship and where the communication is between strangers.[199] The privilege is more readily established in the first case than in the second which requires particularly cogent justification. The privilege covers matters such as 'reply to attack'[200] and ordinary business communications. The categories of qualified privilege are not closed: they are no more than applications, in particular circumstances, of an underlying principle of public policy to the effect that both the maker and the recipient of the statement must have a 'duty or interest' in making or receiving it.[201] However:

> The essence of this defence lies in the law's recognition of the need, in the public interest, for a particular recipient to receive frank and uninhibited communication of particular information from a particular source.[202]

In determining whether an occasion is subject to qualified privilege, the court has regard to all the circumstances.[203] The question in each case is whether the publishee is entitled to know the particular information: this 'duty-interest' test cannot be carried out in isolation

---

[193] *Royal Aquarium and Summer and Winter Garden Society Ltd v Parkinson* [1892] 1 QB 431, 451; *S v Newham Borough Council* [1999] EMLR 583.
[194] See *Merricks v Nott-Bower* [1965] 1 QB 57, 73; and cf *Hasselblad (GB) Ltd v Orbinson* [1985] QB 475.
[195] See Defamation Act 1996, s 15 and Sch 1.
[196] For the case law on this phrase, see *Gatley on Libel and Slander* (11th edn, Sweet & Maxwell, 2008), para 15.4.
[197] *Gatley on Libel and Slander* (see n 196 above), Chap 16.
[198] *McCartan Turkington Breen v Times Newspapers* [2001] 2 AC 277; for a discussion of this case, see I Loveland, 'Freedom of Political Expression: Who Needs the Human Rights Act?' [2001] PL 233.
[199] *Kearns v General Council of the Bar* [2003] 1 WLR 1357, 1369.
[200] *Adam v Ward* [1917] AC 309.
[201] Ibid, 334.
[202] Per Lord Nicholls, *Reynolds v Times Newspapers Ltd* [2001] 2 AC 127, 1017F–G.
[203] *London Association for the Protection of Trade v Greenlands Ltd* [1916] 2 AC 15, 23.

from factors such as the nature, status and source of the material and the circumstances of the publication[204] but there is no separate 'circumstantial test'.[205]

15.64 Once the defendant has established qualified privilege, his good faith is presumed. The onus then shifts to the claimant to rebut the defence by showing that the publication was actuated by express malice. 'Express malice' entails either that the defendant had some improper motive for publication, such as injuring the claimant, or that he knew the words were false or was reckless as to whether they were true or false.[206] The burden imposed is a heavy one, and, if the evidence at trial is equally consistent with malice or its absence, there will be no case for the defendant to answer and the claim may be dismissed without hearing the defendant's evidence.[207]

15.65 **Media publication.** One important issue that arises is the extent to which qualified privilege protects publications by the media or by non-media publishers to the public generally. Qualified privilege might apply because the media arguably have a duty to supply and the public have an interest in receiving information as to issues of contemporary importance. In *Reynolds v Times Newspapers Ltd*[208] the House of Lords rejected the argument that there should be a new category of qualified privilege for 'political information'[209] on the basis that such a privilege would not provide adequate protection for reputation and that it would be unsound in principle to distinguish 'political expression' from other matters of serious public concern. Lord Hobhouse commented that, to allow for such a privilege:

> would be handing to what are essentially commercial entities a power which would deprive the subjects of such publications of the protection against damaging misinformation. Such persons and the public are entitled to the disinterested and objective involvement of the law. It is for the publisher to establish to the satisfaction of the law that the publication was privileged.[210]

---

[204] For a list of 'illustrative' circumstances relevant to publication to the whole world, see per Lord Nicholls, *Reynolds v Times Newspapers Ltd* (n 202 above) 205 and see further para 15.65ff below.

[205] See *Reynolds v Times Newspapers* (see n 202 above) 197, disapproving the approach of the Court of Appeal in that case.

[206] See *Horrocks v Lowe* [1975] AC 135; and *Gatley on Libel and Slander* (n 196 above) Chap 16, see also *Lillie & Reed v Newcastle City Council* ([2002] EWHC 1600 (QB) para 1370 in which Eady J found malice despite a finding of honest belief in the truth of the facts published because the defendants were not 'acting in good faith'.

[207] See *Telnikoff v Matusevitch* [1991] 1 QB 102, 121: overruled, but not on this point [1992] 2 AC 343; and *Gatley on Libel and Slander* (see n 196 above) para 34.18.

[208] See n 202 above; for discussions of *Reynolds*, see I Loveland, '*Reynolds v Times Newspapers* in the House of Lords' [2001] PL 351 and 'A New Legal Landscape: Libel Law and Freedom of Political Expression in the United Kingdom' [2000] EHRLR 476; K Williams, 'Defaming Politicians: The Not So Common Law' (2000) 63 MLR 748; F Trindade, 'Defamatory Statements and Political Discussion' (2000) 116 LQR 185; R Milne, 'Press Freedom and Qualified Privilege' (2000) 5 Comms L 124; K Rimel, 'A New Public Interest Defence For the Media' (2000) 11 Ent LR 36; K Schilling, 'The Americanization of English Libel Laws' (2000) 11 Ent LR 48.

[209] The House of Lords were not persuaded to follow US and Commonwealth cases which recognized, in various degrees, a 'public figure' defence: see *Sullivan v New York Times* (1964) 376 US 254; *Rajagopal v State of Tamil Nadu* JT 1994 6 SC 524; *Lange v Australian Broadcasting Corporation* (1997) 189 CLR 520; *Lange v Atkinson and Australian Consolidated Press NZ Ltd* [1998] 3 NZLR 424.

[210] n 202 above, 239.

Nevertheless, it was recognized that the 'powerful arguments in favour of the constitutional right of free speech' meant that, 'where politicians are involved, the interest and duty tests are likely to be satisfied in most cases without too much difficulty'.[211] Although the case was decided before the HRA came into force, the approach of the House of Lords was strongly influenced by the Convention case law.[212]

15.66 The operation of the media qualified privilege defence in practice has been controversial. In the years following the *Reynolds* decision, the defence was relied on by the media in many cases but was rarely successful.[213] The defence was re-considered by the House of Lords in *Jameel v Wall Street Journal*.[214] The majority were of the view that the defence was best analysed in terms of the traditional 'duty/interest test'.[215] That duty/interest test can be satisfied if the public is entitled to know the particular information being published. This is, in turn, subject to two 'essential prerequisites':[216]

> The first is that the article as a whole must be in the public interest. What engages the interest of the public, as in the example given by Baroness Hale, the most 'vapid tittle tattle about the activities of footballers' wives and girlfriends', may not be material which truly engages the public interest.
>
> Responsible journalism is the second prerequisite. Whether the article is of value of the public depends upon its quality as well as its subject matter and the value of the article to the public must be tested against a standard of responsible journalism. Responsible journalism is the point at which a fair balance can be held between freedom of expression on matters of public concern and the reputation of the individual harmed by that disclosure, the vital balance between article 10 and article 8 of the European Convention.

It has also been emphasized that due weight must be given to editorial judgment and that the necessity of the interference must be judged in the circumstances of each case, taking

---

[211] Ibid, 235, per Lord Hope.

[212] In *McCartan Turkington Breen v Times Newspapers* [2001] 2 AC 277, Lord Cooke said that the opinions in *Reynolds* were intended to ensure that the common law of England harmonized with human rights jurisprudence in general and the European Convention on Human Rights in particular.

[213] See, in particular, *Grobelaar v News Group Newspapers* [2001] 2 All ER 437; *Baldwin v Rusbridger* [2001] EMLR 1062, (Eady J); *English v Hastie* 21 January 2002 (Gray J); *Field v Local Sunday Newspapers* [2002] EWHC 336 (QB); *Loutchansky v Times Newspapers (Nos 2 to 5)* [2002] QB 783; *Henry v BBC* [2005] EWHC 2787 (QB); *Miller v Associated Newspapers* [2003] EWHC 2799 (QB); *Howlett v Holding* [2003] EWHC 286 (QB); *Galloway v Telegraph Group* [2006] EMLR 221 (Eady J and CA); the only cases in the period between *Reynolds* and *Jameel* in which the defence was successful were *GKR Karate v Yorkshire Post Newspapers* [2000] EMLR 410; *Lukowiak v Unidad Editorial SA*,) [2001] EMLR 1043; *Al-Fagih v H H Saudi Research* [2002] EMLR 13; *Bonnick v Morris* [2003] 1 AC 300 and *Roberts v Gable* [2006] EMLR 23.

[214] [2007] 1 AC 359; for discussions of this case see D Hooper, 'The Importance of the Jameel Case,' (2007) 18 Ent LR 62; K Beattie 'New Life for the *Reynolds* 'Public Interest Defence" [2007] EHRLR 81; J Rowbottom, 'Libel and the Public Interest' (2007) 66 CLJ 8; and for a US perspective see M Scordato, 'The International Legal Environment for Serious Political Reporting Has Fundamentally Changed: Understanding the Revolutionary New Era of English Defamation Law' (2007) 40 Connecticut LR 165.

[215] *Jameel* (n 214 above), Lord Bingham (para 30), Lord Hope (para 105) and Lord Scott (para 133), but note that Lord Hoffmann preferred to call it the *'Reynolds* public interest defence' (para 46) and Baroness Hale preferred 'a defence of publication in the public interest' (para 146).

[216] *Roberts v Gable* [2008] QB 502, para 32, (2) and (3) (per Ward LJ, summarizing the effect of *Jameel*), see also *Charman v Orion Publishing* [2008] 1 All ER 750, para 66 for another summary of the position by the same judge.

into the 'ten indicative factors' given by Lord Nicholls in *Reynolds*.[217] In *Jameel* the House of Lords overturned the findings of the Judge and the Court of Appeal in favour of the claimant and held that the defence had been made out. The subsequent case law has shown some liberalizing of the approach of the courts[218] and it seems likely that, in the future, it will be easier for the media to establish that the 'right to know' test is satisfied.

The *Reynolds* qualified privilege defence will also be available when the media is engaged in **15.67** 'reportage': when they are reporting not the truth of statements but the fact that they were made.[219] In these circumstances if the media report the statements in a fair, neutral and disinterested way they are absolved from the responsibility to verify their truth.[220]

The defence is not just available to the print and broadcast media and book publishers[221] **15.68** but also extends to any publications made by any person who published material of public interest in any medium to the public generally so long as the conditions applicable to 'responsible journalism' are satisfied.[222]

(e) Remedies in defamation

Damages. The primary remedy for defamation is damages. The amount of the award has **15.69** traditionally been in the sole province of the jury; judges and counsel were not permitted to influence the decision of the jury by mentioning specific figures that might be appropriate.[223] The powers of intervention of the Court of Appeal were limited to ordering a re-trial if the award was 'divorced from reality'.[224] As a result, jury awards varied over an enormous range. Jury awards were first scrutinized in Convention terms by the Court of Appeal in *Rantzen v Mirror Group Newspapers*[225] which held that the power of the Court to order a new trial or to substitute a different damage award[226] should be applied consistently with Article 10. In *John v MGN Ltd*,[227] it was held that the reasonableness of jury awards could be tempered by directing the jury to the level of damages in personal injury cases. In practice, both the judiciary and counsel are now permitted to mention figures to the jury.

---

[217] Ibid, para 32 (7) and (8), for Lord Nicholls's 'factors', see *Reynolds* (see n 202 above) 205. It was emphasized in *Jameel* that these should not be treated as 'hurdles' which the defendant has to surmount, para 33 (Lord Bingham), para 56 (Lord Hoffmann).

[218] The defence was upheld in the Court of Appeal in *Roberts v Gable* (see n 216 above) and in *Charman v Orion* (see n 216 above) but failed in *Malik v News Post* [2007] EWHC 3063 (QB) *Prince Radu of Hohenzollern v Houston* [2008] EWCA Civ 921and *Seaga v Harper* [2008] 3 WLR 478 (PC).

[219] *Roberts v Gable* (see n 216 above), para 61(3).

[220] Ibid; see also *Al-Fagih v H H Saudi Marketing* (see n 213 above) and *Charman v Orion* (see n 216 above), paras 48–57.

[221] See *Charman v Orion* (see n 216 above).

[222] *Seaga v Harper* (see n 218 above).

[223] See *Ward v James* [1966] 1 QB 273; see also *Sutcliffe v Pressdram Ltd* [1991] QB 153.

[224] See *McCarey v Associated Newspapers (No 2)* [1965] 2 QB 86, 111; see generally, *Gatley on Libel and Slander* (11th edn, Sweet & Maxwell, 2008), para 9.4ff.

[225] [1994] QB 670.

[226] Under the Courts and Legal Services Act 1990, s 8.

[227] [1997] QB 586; see also *Campbell v New Group* [2002] EMLR 43 (jury award of £350,000 reduced to £30,000); *Purnell v Business Magazine* [2007] EWCA Civ 744 (no reduction in damages to take into account vindication deriving from judgment striking out defence), but see *Gleaner v Abrahams* [2004] 1 AC 628 (PC)(Jury award of the equivalent of £533,000 upheld).

15.70 The effect of *Rantzen* and of *John* has been to depress the value of damages awards and settlements in libel cases although a 'tariff' of Court of Appeal approved awards has been slow
to develop.[228] The value of settlements in cases against newspapers, in particular, has been
substantially reduced. It has been recognized that exorbitant awards of damages have
a 'chilling effect' on the exercise of the right of freedom of expression.[229] In practice,
the 'ceiling' on libel awards—for the most serious libels such as allegations of serious
criminality—is now of the order of £200,000.[230] Although exemplary damages are available in libel actions if it can be shown that the defendant published calculating that the benefit would outweigh the likely award of damages,[231] such awards are rare in practice.[232]

15.71 If the defendant uses the 'offer of amends' procedure[233] then compensation is determined
by the judge 'on the same principles as damages in defamation proceedings'.[234] The courts
have adopted a 'two-stage' procedure: assessing the sum which a jury would have been
likely to award at the conclusion of a trial and then applying a 'discount' to reflect the fact
that the defendant has mitigated the damage by using the offer of amends procedure.[235]

15.72 **Injunctions.** The courts also have power to award permanent injunctions if a claim in
defamation is established at trial. An injunction will be granted if there is any reason to
believe that the defendant is likely to publish the same or similar defamatory words. Such
injunction may also affect the position of third parties who publish the defamatory
imputations. Although, where an interim injunction has been granted, a third party will be
in contempt of court if his publication is likely to interfere with the course of justice between
the claimant and the defendant[236] this is not the position in the case of permanent injunctions which are binding only on the parties.[237] It seems unlikely that, in the absence of a
specific intention to interfere with the course of justice, the publication of the libel by a
third party would constitute a breach of a final injunction against a defendant.[238]

---

[228] For such awards, see the Appendix of Court of Appeal 'Approved Libel Awards' in *Gatley on Libel and Slander* (see n 224 above), A3.1–A3.516.

[229] *Skrine v Euromoney* [2001] EMLR 434, 443, para 36 (Morland J) and see *Tolstoy v United Kingdom* (1995) 20 EHRR 442, see also *Gleaner v Abrahams* (see n 227 above) (libel damages should have a deterrent element and a chilling effect on poor journalistic conduct was not undesirable).

[230] Reflecting the top end of the scale for libel damages, see *Lillie v Reed* [2002] EWHC 1600 (QB) (£200,000 awarded in a judge alone case in relation to allegations of child abuse); *Veliu v Mazrekaj* [2007] 1 WLR 495 (£175,000 awarded in a judge alone case in relation to allegations of involvement in London 7/7 bombings), and see generally, *Gatley on Libel and Slander* (n 224 above) para 9.4ff.

[231] See Lord Devlin's 'third category' in *Rookes v Barnard* [1964] AC 1129.

[232] But see *John v MGN* (see n 227 above) (jury award of £275,000 exemplary damages reduced to £50,000 by CA).

[233] Under ss 2–4 of the Defamation Act 1996; see generally, *Gatley on Libel and Slander* (see n 224 above), para 19.1ff.

[234] See s 3(5), Defamation Act 1996.

[235] See *Nail v News Group Newspapers* [2005] 1 All ER 1040 (discount of 50%); *Campbell-Jones v Guardian* [2005] EMLR 24 (discount 35% to reflect the defendant's attitude to publication of apology); *Turner v News Group* [2006] 1 WLR 3469 (discount of 40%).

[236] *A-G v News Group Newspapers Ltd* [1987] QB 1.

[237] See *Jockey Club v Buffham* [2003] QB 462.

[238] In contrast to the position in breach of confidence, where the purpose of the injunction is to restrain the publication of particular items of confidential information.

Remedies on summary judgment. Under the summary procedure provided for in sections **15.73** 8 to 10 of the Defamation Act 1996 the Court may make a declaration that the statement complained of was false and defamatory of the claimant.[239] The Court may also order that the defendant publish a suitable correction or apology.[240]

Other remedies. At common law, the Court cannot make a declaration of falsity at **15.74** the conclusion of a libel action.[241] As already mentioned there is, however, statutory jurisdiction to make such a declaration on the 'summary disposal' of a libel action.[242] In *W v Westminster City Council*.[243] Tugendhat J said

> it is possible, in an appropriate case, that a court might, in a claim under s 7 of the HRA, be willing to investigate the truth or falsity of words complained of, and to grant some declaration, even if the claim is clearly one to which a defence of privilege would be available, if brought in libel.

At a subsequent hearing the judge granted a declaration that the defendant had interfered with the claimant's Article 8 rights by making disclosure of false information on a privileged occasion.[244] It is submitted that, the positive obligation of the state to protect the Article 8 right to reputation[245] requires this remedy to be extended to claims between private parties. Furthermore, the right to reputation is a Convention right which is, therefore, a civil right under Article 6[246] and it is arguable that the right of access to court requires the availability of a remedy to vindicate reputation even where a 'privilege' defence bars the right to damages. The fact that privilege provides a defence to a defamation claim would not, of itself, prevent the court granting declaratory relief as the jurisdiction to such relief at common law is not confined to matters where the claimant has a 'legal right'.[247]

(f) Defamation and Article 10

Article 10 has only had a limited impact on the law of defamation. Before the HRA came **15.75** into force three significant changes were strongly influenced by the Convention: the rule that public authorities cannot sue for libel,[248] the change of approach in relation to damages[249] and development of the *Reynolds* qualified privilege defence.[250]

---

[239] See s 9(1)(a).
[240] See s 9(1)(b).
[241] See *Jameel v Dow Jones* [2005] QB 946, para 67; see also *Loutchansky v Times Newspapers* [2002] EMLR 44 (permission refused to amend to add a claim for a declaration of falsity in a *Reynolds* qualified privilege case).
[242] See para 15.73 above.
[243] *W v Westminster City Council* [2005] 1 FLR 816, para 103; see also *H v Tomlinson* [2008] EWCA Civ (application to amend to add declaration of breach of Art 8 right to reputation refused because no damage to reputation).
[244] [2005] EWHC 102 (QB).
[245] See para 12.299 above.
[246] See para 11.335ff above.
[247] See H Woolf and J Woolf, *The Declaratory Judgment* (3rd edn, Sweet & Maxwell, 2002), para 3.136.
[248] See para 15.49ff above.
[249] See para 15.69 above, this was, in turn, influenced by the decision of the ECtHR in *Tolstoy Miloslavsky v United Kingdom* (1995) 20 EHRR 442, see para 15.356 below.
[250] See para 15.65 above.

15.76 Since October 2000 the only successful challenge to the common law of defamation on Article 10 grounds was *O'Shea v MGN*[251] in which Morland J held that the principle of strict liability in unintentional defamation cases did not apply to 'look alike' photographs, as it would constitute an unjustifiable interference with the freedom of expression disproportionate to the legitimate aim of protecting the reputations of 'look alikes'. In *Culnane v Morris*[252] it was held that it was not compatible with Article 10 to construe section 10 of the Defamation Act 1952[253] as having the effect of precluding a candidate at a local election from relying on a qualified privilege defence

15.77 The Courts have considered a wide range of other challenges to defamation based on Article 10 and have held that established principles are consistent with the Convention.[254] This accords with the approach of the Strasbourg court which has rejected attacks on the English law of defamation on a number of occasions.[255]

(g) Misuse of private information

15.78 The HRA has led to a profound change in the approach of the courts to cases involving the publication of private information. The values enshrined in Article 8 have been absorbed into the cause of action for breach of confidence to provide protection against the misuse of private information, with the claim being renamed 'misuse of private information'.[256]

15.79 When a claim for misuse of private information is made the matter is approached in two stages. At the first stage the court considers whether the claimant has a reasonable expectation of privacy in respect of the disclosed facts in all the circumstances. If so there is a *prima facie* right to protection of the information. Once this has been established, the second stage must be considered. The Court must look at the Article 8(2) justifications for interference with the claimant's privacy rights. If another Convention right (for example Article 10) is in play the court must carry out what has been referred to as 'ultimate balancing' or 'parallel analysis': looking at the position under Article 8 and Article 10 in turn, considering the justification under each article in parallel on the basis of presumptive parity.[257] The factors to be considered include the 'value' of the expression in question and the nature of the 'privacy interests' which are engaged. The case law on the

---

[251] [2001] EMLR 40.

[252] [2006] 1 WLR 2880.

[253] Which provides that 'A defamatory statement published by or on behalf of a candidate in any election to a local government authority or to Parliament shall not be deemed to be published on a privileged occasion on the ground that it is material to a question in issue in the election, whether or not the person by whom it is published is qualified to vote at the election.'

[254] See *Berezovsky v Forbes (No 2)* [2001] EMLR 45 (presumption of falsity, see para 15.57 above); *Chase v News Group Newspapers* [2003] EMLR 218 (rules as to pleading justification, see para 15.537 below); *Jameel v Wall Street Journal* [2007] 1 AC 359 (presumption of damage, see para 15.52 below); *Roberts v Gable* [2008] 2 WLR 129 (*Reynolds* qualified privilege, see para 15.65ff below).

[255] See para 15.396ff below.

[256] *Campbell v MGN* [2004] AC 457, para 17, per Lord Nicholls; *A v B plc* [2003] QB 195 para 11, per Lord Woolf CJ, see para 12.24ff below, and see *Gatley and Libel and Slander* (n 228 above), Chap 12.

[257] *A Local Authority v W* [2006] 1 FLR 1, para 53.

'ultimate balance' between Article 8 and Article 10 where both are engaged is considered in Chapter 12.[258]

(4) Comment on court proceedings: contempt of court

(a) Introduction

'Contempt of court' means interference with the due administration of justice.[259] Its pur- **15.80**
pose is to ensure respect for the administration of justice as a whole and for the remedies
ordered by the court.[260] Nevertheless, the law of contempt has historically been seriously
restrictive of freedom of expression, which the courts have traditionally treated as having
secondary importance.[261] It is also open to criticism in its summary trial procedures [262] and
its uncertain scope.

The classification of contempt at common law is not straightforward. 'Civil' contempts **15.81**
such as non-compliance with court orders or undertakings [263] in civil proceedings are generally [264] are distinguished from 'criminal'[265] contempts. The latter can be divided into at
least three categories:

- 'contempt in the face of the court' (which refers to conduct of persons in the
  courtroom);
- 'scandalizing the court' (which involves publications which undermine public confidence in the judicial system or otherwise interfere with the course of justice as a continuing process); and
- 'prejudicing active legal proceedings' under the '*sub judice* rule' (which prohibits publication of material tending to prejudice or impede specific civil or criminal proceedings
  before the courts).

The law of contempt applies only to 'courts of justice properly so-called'.[266] These include **15.82**
Mental Health Tribunals [267] and Employment Tribunals.[268] The authorities were reviewed

---

[258] See para 12.26ff.
[259] See eg, *A-G v Times Newspapers Ltd* [1974] AC 273, 322.
[260] See eg, *Morris v Crown Office* [1970] 2 QB 114.
[261] See generally, G Robertson and A Nicol, *Media Law* (5th edn, Sweet & Maxwell, 2007), paras 7.001
to 7.005.
[262] Contempt involves a serious criminal charge triable without a jury. The summary trial procedures used
in contempt cases may lack the elements of procedural fairness that are normally required for criminal trials,
see generally *Arlidge, Eady and Smith on Contempt* (3rd edn, Sweet & Maxwell, 2005), paras 2-17 to 2-25; and
see, generally, 11.220 above.
[263] These can include injunctions or orders restricting or postponing reporting of trials when the administration of justice may be affected. Such restrictions may be imposed when trials are held in private, when
reporting might prejudice the fairness of proceedings, when children, rape or blackmail are involved, or in
regard to material disclosed on discovery.
[264] Except in Scotland.
[265] For discussion of the technical distinction between civil and criminal contempt see *Arlidge, Eady and
Smith on Contempt* (3rd edn, Sweet & Maxwell, 2005), Chap 3; see also the judgments of the Australian High
Court in *Witham v Holloway* (1995) 183 CLR 525, 530–49.
[266] *Badry v DPP* [1983] 2 AC 297, 307; cf Contempt of Court Act 1981, s 19: 'court' includes 'any tribunal or body exercising the judicial power of the state'.
[267] *Pickering v Liverpool Daily Post and Echo Newspapers plc* [1991] 2 AC 270.
[268] *Peach Grey and Company v Sommers* [1995] 1 ICR 549.

by the Court of Appeal in *General Medical Council v British Broadcasting Corporation*[269] which decided that the Professional Conduct Committee of the General Medical Council is not a 'court' for the purposes of the law of contempt. There may be jurisdiction to restrain grave and obvious interference with proceedings before non-curial tribunals but no such order has ever been made.[270]

15.83   The contempts most likely to be committed by the press or broadcasting media are the criminal contempts of publication of material which prejudices active proceedings or scandalizes the court and breaches of civil undertakings or court orders which prohibit media publication.

(b) Prejudicing or impeding proceedings

15.84   **Introduction.**   At common law, this type of contempt restricted the media from discussing or reporting on issues being addressed in civil and criminal proceedings on the basis that those proceedings might be prejudiced. The time before and after the trial when a publication was *sub judice* started from the point at which proceedings were 'imminent'.[271] However, the test was criticized for being broad and vague. The *actus reus* involved creating a *real risk* of prejudice to proceedings even if no detriment was suffered. Although it was essential to prove *intent to publish*[272] it was not necessary to show that the contemnor intended that the publication should interfere with the course of justice and, as a result, liability was strict.

15.85   The House of Lords in the *Sunday Times* case[273] held that a risk of prejudice to proceedings might be brought about by a publication which 'prejudged' the matter at trial, on the basis of policy arguments against 'trial by newspaper' or 'trial by television'. The case involved an attempt to prevent the publication of an article in the *Sunday Times* newspaper which was potentially prejudicial to civil proceedings against the manufacturer of the drug thalidomide. Distillers Limited had manufactured and marketed the drug in the United Kingdom from 1958 to 1961 which, when prescribed to treat nausea in pregnant women, resulted in appalling deformities in hundreds of babies. During Distillers' negotiations to establish a trust fund for the children, the *Sunday Times* published an article which criticized the company's proposals and announced that a further article, in relation to the history of the tragedy, would be forthcoming. Distillers' complaint to the Attorney-General resulted in an injunction, which was later overturned by the Court of Appeal, to prevent publication of the second article. The House of Lords reinstated it on the basis that the proposed article would 'prejudge' the negligence issue and thereby interfere with the administration of justice. In effect, the House of Lords held that any 'prejudgment' would amount to contempt, whether or not it had a direct effect on the litigant. Previously, only a 'real risk' of influence upon the tribunal, witnesses or parties would amount to contempt, and it had been assumed

---

[269] [1998] 1 WLR 1573.
[270] *A-G v British Broadcasting Corporation* [1981] AC 303, 344; see *General Medical Council v British Broadcasting Corporation* (see n 269 above); and see generally, *Arlidge and Eady* (n 262 above) para 13.70ff.
[271] *R v Savundranayagan* [1968] 1 WLR 1761; [1968] 3 All ER 439.
[272] *R v Thompson Newspapers Ltd, ex p A-G* [1968] 1 WLR 1.
[273] *A-G v Times Newspapers Ltd* [1974] AC 273.

that this would not normally be found in the absence of a jury trial.[274] The decision imposed greater limitations on the media without any greater certainty as to what was publishable.

In 1974, in light of the *Sunday Times* case, the Phillimore Committee was established to **15.86** address the need for reform. Although the Committee stressed the desirability of avoiding trial by media, it criticized the prejudgment test of the House of Lords. The Phillimore Committee recommended that this type of contempt remain governed by strict liability.[275] Its report, together with the decision of the Court of Human Rights in the *Sunday Times* case,[276] was the impetus for the enactment of the Contempt of Court Act 1981.

Contempt of Court Act 1981.   The Act does not codify the common law of contempt: it **15.87** addresses only publications which may prejudice active legal proceedings, with the aim of bringing the law into line with the European Convention. The Act was intended to be a 'liberalizing measure'.[277] It establishes a rule of strict liability, as recommended by the Phillimore Committee, which changes the common law on three important respects: it defines contempt more narrowly, it requires active proceedings and it provides for a public interest defence. Any ambiguity in the Act is presumed to have been intended to avoid future conflict between the law of contempt of court and the obligations of the United Kingdom under the Convention.[278] The statutory purpose of the Act

> was to effect a permanent shift in the balance of public interest away from the protection of the administration of justice and in favour of freedom of speech.[279]

When considering whether or not a particular publication is in contempt, the court will, in each case, look at the 'localized balance' between freedom of speech and the right to a fair trial, looking at the significance of the interference in each case.[280]

First, publications[281] which tend to interfere with the course of justice generally (and legal **15.88** proceedings in particular), are subject to strict liability under section 1 of the Act, regardless of intent. The principles were summarized in *A-G v MGN Ltd*.[282] The test is whether the publication will create a 'substantial risk'[283] that the course of justice in the 'proceedings in

---

[274] In the *Sunday Times* case the Divisional Court applied the principle that a deliberate attempt to influence the settlement of pending proceedings by bringing public pressure to bear on a party amounted to a contempt of court: see [1973] QB 710.

[275] See generally, *Arlidge, Eady & Smith on Contempt* (see n 262 above), para 1-86 and App 4 (summarizing its recommendations).

[276] *Sunday Times v United Kingdom* (1979) 2 EHRR 245. The ECtHR disagreed with the prejudgment test, and found that the restriction on freedom of expression was not founded on a sufficiently pressing social need to justify it in a democratic society.

[277] See *Arlidge, Eady and Smith on Contempt* (n 262 above) para 1–115.

[278] *Re Lonrho plc* [1990] 2 AC 154, 208.

[279] Per Lloyd LJ, *A-G v Newspaper Publishing plc* [1988] Ch 333, 382.

[280] Per Sedley LJ, *A-G v Guardian Newspapers* [1999] EMLR 904.

[281] Defined to include speech or writing or whatever form addressed to the public at large or any section of the public: see s 2(1).

[282] [1997] 1 All ER 456; see generally, *Arlidge, Eady and Smith on Contempt* (n 262 above) para 4–84ff; and see H Fenwick and G Phillipson, *Media Freedom under the Human Rights Act* (Oxford University Press, 2006), 259–279.

[283] Contempt of Court Act 1981, s 2(2); *A-G v MGN Ltd* (see n 282 above) 461, Principle 4; 'substantial' means that the risk of influence is 'more than remote', for any risk that is more than remote must be 'substantial' (see *A-G v English* [1983] 1 AC 116, 141F–G); it has been suggested that, under the HRA, 'substantial' should

question'[284] will be seriously impeded or prejudiced.[285] This test is difficult to apply in practice.

15.89 In relation to a trial by jury a publication will be in contempt if there is a serious risk of it causing such prejudice as would justify a discharge of the jury, the stay of the prosecution or a successful appeal against conviction.[286] Concern has been expressed that the courts have taken a robust attitude when considering applications for the stay of criminal proceedings or appeals based on prejudicial publicity[287] but have been more sensitive when dealing with contempt.[288] It has been suggested that this is because section 2(2) postulates a lesser degree of prejudice than is required to make good an appeal against conviction.[289] However, the better view appears to be that there is a single standard which operates differently in the two contexts.[290] It has been held the provision of section 2(2) are compatible with Article 10[291] but the point has not considered by the Courts since the HRA came into force.[292]

15.90 In relation to civil trials by judge alone or appeals of any kind it is highly unlikely that a publication will be found to be in contempt under the strict liability rule as professional judges should not be influenced by media comment.[293] Thus in the remarkable case of *Re Lonhro and Observer*[294] the publishers of the 'Observer' were acquitted of contempt for publishing a copy of a unpublished report which was the subject of pending proceedings before the House of Lords to, inter alia, four members of the committee hearing the case. A differently constituted committee held that the possibility of a professional judge being influenced by anything he read about the case was remote.

15.91 Secondly, this rule of strict liability applies only to proceedings which are 'active' at the time of publication, as defined by the Act. Criminal proceedings are considered to be active from the time of arrest without warrant or the issue of warrant or summons.[295] Civil proceedings, on the other hand, are active from the time that 'arrangements for trial are made'.[296]

---

be interpreted in accordance with the Convention case law (see para 15.385 below) to mean 'likelihood' see H Fenwick and G Phillipson (n 282 above) 276–279.

[284] *A-G v MGN Ltd* (see n 282 above) 461, Principle 5; it is noteworthy that the provision does not protect the administration of justice generally.

[285] See also *A-G v Independent Television News Ltd* [1995] 2 All ER 370.

[286] See, eg, *A-G v Guardian Newspapers* [1999] EMLR 904; *A-G v Guardian Newspapers (No 3)* [1992] 1 WLR 874.

[287] See, especially *Montgomery v HM Advocate* [2003] 1 AC 641; *R v Abu Hamza* [2007] QB 659.

[288] *A-G v Birmingham Post and Mail* [1999] 1 WLR 361 DC; *A-G v Unger* [1998] 1 Cr App Rep 308.

[289] As was suggested by Simon Brown LJ in *A-G v Birmingham Post and Mail* [1999] 1 WLR 361, 369H.

[290] See *A-G v Unger* (see n 288 above) and *A-G v Guardian Newspapers*, [1999] EMLR 904, DC.

[291] *A-G v Guardian Newspapers* (n 290 above).

[292] See H Fenwick and G Phillipson (n 282 above) 270–272.

[293] See, *R v Duffy, ex p Nash* [1960] 2 QB 188, 198; but see *A-G v BBC* [1981] AC 303, 335 and see *Kelly v O'Nell and Brady* [2000] IR 354 and generally *Arlidge, Eady and Smith on Contempt* (3rd edn, Sweet & Maxwell, 2005), paras 4.118 to 4.128.

[294] [1990] 2 AC 154.

[295] Sch 1, para 4.

[296] Sch 1, para 13. Under the CPR, there is no procedure for 'setting down'.

This was the date of 'setting down' but, under the CPR, is likely to be an earlier date.[297] The Act creates a defence of 'innocent publication and distribution'.[298] This is available to a publisher who, having taken all reasonable care, either:

* does not know and has no reason to suspect that relevant legal proceedings are active;[299] or
* does not know and has no reason to suspect that the publication contains matter to which the strict liability rule applies.[300]

The innocent publication defence is only available in respect of prosecutions under the 'strict liability' rule.[301] Furthermore, it does not alter the general common law principle that publishing offending material by mistake is no defence.[302]

Thirdly, section 5 of the Act states that: **15.92**

> A publication made as or as part of a discussion in good faith of public affairs, or other matters of general public interest is not to be treated as a contempt of court under the strict liability rule if the risk of impediment or prejudice to particular legal proceedings is merely incidental to the discussion.

Strictly speaking, the provision of section 5 is not a 'defence' at all: the burden is on the prosecution to show that the publication does not fall within the section.[303] The House of Lords in *A-G v English*[304] held that the only question raised by section 5 is whether the risk of prejudice is 'merely incidental' to the main theme of the publication. The publication complained of in *English* did not refer to any actual proceedings, but it would seem that even if an accused is mentioned by name, section 5 may apply.[305] It has been pointed out that section 5 does not allow the courts to apply a proportionality test in order to enable the seriousness of the prejudice to be balanced against the significance of the speech and that there is a strong argument in favour of using section 3 of the HRA to read words into this provision.[306]

Intentional contempt. Since the enactment of the Contempt of Court Act, it has   **15.93** been uncertain whether publications that intentionally threaten to prejudice pending

---

[297] The date on which the trial date is fixed under CPR, r 29.2(2).

[298] Contrast the common law position: neither ignorance of the proceedings (*R v Odhams Press Ltd, ex p A-G* [1957] 1 QB 73) nor the content of imported publications (*R v Griffiths, ex p A-G* [1957] 2 QB 192) was a defence.

[299] See s 3(1).

[300] See s 3(2).

[301] N Lowe and B Sufrin, *Borrie and Lowe: The Law of Contempt* (3rd edn, Butterworths, 1996), 398–400.

[302] See *R v Evening Standard Company Ltd* [1954] 1 QB 578 (editor had every reason to believe that the case report was accurate); *R v Thomson Newspapers Ltd, ex p A-G* [1968] 1 WLR 1 (editor had established a proper system to avoid prejudicial publication).

[303] *A-G v English* [1983] 1 AC 116.

[304] Ibid.

[305] See *A-G v Times Newspapers Ltd* (the *Fagan* case), *The Times*, 12 February 1983; also *A-G v Guardian Newspapers* [1992] 3 All ER 38 and *A-G v TVS Television*, *The Times*, 7 July 1989 see also *A-G v Guardian Newspapers* [1999] EMLR 904 (no s 5 defence when discussion about the defendant's actions which had led to the criminal trial).

[306] See H Fenwick and G Phillipson (n 282 above) 282–283.

proceedings[307] might be prosecuted at common law to circumvent the more stringent requirements of the Act. The 1981 Act itself, in section 6(c), preserves liability for intentional contempt at common law.[308]

15.94 It appears that a common law contempt will be committed if material which is published is designed to prejudice criminal proceedings which are 'pending or imminent'. A finding of contempt was made on this basis in *A-G v News Group Newspapers*[309] after the 'Sun' published an article attacking a doctor when it had already agreed to finance a private prosecution of him. This doctrine, with its uncertain limits, has a continuing chilling effect on investigative journalism. It appears that where it is established that the defendant intended to prejudice processing, it is not necessary to show that proceedings are imminent, provided that they are in contemplation.[310]

15.95 Lord Donaldson suggested in the *Spycatcher* case[311] that 'intention' requires a 'specific intent to interfere with the administration of justice'; and that 'recklessness' is therefore not a sufficient basis for liability under section 6. The necessary intent might, however, be inferred from the foreseeability of the consequences of the conduct. In that case, foresight on the part of the editor of the *Independent* that publication would prejudice the action of the Attorney-General against the *Guardian* and the *Observer* could support an inference of intention to prejudice the administration of justice amounting to contempt under the common law. The decision was followed in *A-G v Observer Ltd*[312] which found that libraries which innocently made copies of *Spycatcher* available to the public pending the trial of the action must have had sufficient knowledge of the circumstances to infer intention for the purposes of contempt. Because proof of intention is required, honest mistake is a defence to an allegation of intentional contempt.[313]

15.96 Intention to prejudice proceedings was also established where the defendants sought to bring improper pressure to bear on the other party.[314] In *A-G v Hislop*[315] the defendants published material in *Private Eye* which, it was held, was intended to persuade Sonia Sutcliffe, the wife of the 'Yorkshire Ripper', to discontinue her defamation action[316] against the publication. There was a substantial risk that the articles might have prejudiced the

---

[307] Among other reforms, the Report of the Phillimore Committee, at Cmnd 5794, published Dec 1974, recommended that intentional contempt should be dealt with through proper criminal rather than summary procedures, and that contempt in the absence of intention ought to be more narrowly defined.

[308] See s 6(3) states that nothing in the previous sections of the Act 'restricts liability for contempt of court in respect of conduct *intended* to impede or prejudice the administration of justice'.

[309] [1987] QB 1; see also *A-G v Sport Newspapers* [1991] 1 WLR 1194 (Hodgson J expressing some doubt as to whether the intention was to retain this common law liability); see generally, *Arlidge, Eady and Smith on Contempt* (3rd edn, Sweet & Maxwell, 2005), paras 5-67 to 5-95.

[310] *A-G v News Group Newspapers* (n 309 above) and see *A-G v Sport Newspapers* [1991] 1 WLR 1194 in which Bingham LJ agreed with this approach but Hodgson J considered that proceedings that to be 'pending', which he interpreted as being synonymous with 'active'; see generally *Arlidge, Eady and Smith* (n 309 above) paras 5–96 to 5–99 and H Fenwick and G Phillipson 284–289.

[311] See *A-G v Guardian Newspapers Ltd (No 2)* [1988] Ch 333, 374–375.

[312] [1988] 1 All ER 385; see also *A-G v News Group Newspapers plc* [1989] QB 110.

[313] See eg, *Dobson v Hastings* [1992] Ch 394.

[314] *A-G v Hislop* [1991] 1 QB 514.

[315] Ibid.

[316] The magazine was also guilty of statutory contempt.

course of justice because Mrs Sutcliffe might have been deterred from having her complaint tried before a court.

(c) Scandalizing the court

'Scandalizing the court' is a form of contempt that developed to protect the judicial system **15.97** from media criticism. It has been defined as 'any act done or writing published calculated to bring a court or a judge into contempt or to lower his authority. . .'[317] Scandalizing the court is not affected by the Contempt of Court Act 1981, as there are generally no active proceedings which might be prejudiced. Even if the publication occurred when proceedings were active, the effect of any abuse of a court or judge is likely to create a risk of prejudice to the administration of justice in general rather than a risk to particular proceedings. The *actus reus* of the offence may be fulfilled in two ways: by a scurrilous attack on a court or judge, or by an attempt to impute bias to a judge.

The leading case is *R v Gray*,[318] in which Darling J, in an obscenity trial, directed the press **15.98** to refrain from publishing an account of the trial, lest they too be prosecuted for obscenity. Following the trial, Gray published a newspaper article attacking Darling J in a vitriolic fashion, insulting him personally and decrying his warning to the media and his capacity to act as a judge of the court. The article was held to be a grave contempt. Other cases have since stressed that criticism consisting of 'respectful, even though outspoken, comments of ordinary men' must not be considered to be contempt.[319] No offence is committed in such cases provided there is no imputation of improper motives to the judge.[320]

However, a publication which imputes bias to a judge, even if expressed moderately may **15.99** scandalize the court. The last successful prosecution of a contempt of this type was in the *Colsey* case[321] where an article implied that a judge might have been biased when construing a statute because he had earlier been involved in initiating the legislation as Solicitor General. Prosecutions for scandalizing the court are now very rare. It has been suggested that the offence should be abolished, since the notion of undermining public confidence in the administration of justice is so vague[322] and that suppressing expression is likely to cause resentment and suspicion.[323] Nevertheless, it has been held that the offence is compatible with constitutional guarantees of freedom of expression, it being noted that the offence is

---

[317] *R v Gray* [1900] 2 QB 36, 40 per Lord Russell; see generally, *Arlidge, Eady and Smith on Contempt* (n 309 above), paras 5-204–5-274.

[318] See n 317 above.

[319] *R v Metropolitan Police Commissioner, ex p Blackburn (No 2)* [1968] QB 150; see also *Ambard v A-G for Trinidad and Tobago* [1936] AC 322.

[320] *Ambard v A-G for Trinidad and Tobago* (see n 319 above) 335.

[321] *The Times*, 9 May 1931; see also *R v Editor of New Statesman, ex p DPP* (1928) 44 TLR 301 (article doubting whether Marie Stopes would receive a fair trial from a Catholic judge); Arlidge, Eady and Smith point out that judges have brought a number of successful libel actions against newspapers in relation to allegations of incompetence or bias (*Arlidge, Eady and Smith on Contempt* (see n 309 above) para 5-208).

[322] See N Lowe and B Sufrin, *Borrie and Lowe: The Law of Contempt* (3rd edn, Butterworths, 1996), 243; Law Commission, *Offences Relating to Interference with the Course of Justice* (Law Com No 96) 67–68.

[323] Cf the American position where this form of contempt is almost extinct following the case of *Bridges v California* (1941), 314 US 252 in which it was held that a display of disrespect for the judiciary should not be averted by enforced silence.

narrowly defined and that there was a defence based on the right to criticize, in good faith, the public acts done in the courts.[324] Most commentators have recognized that there is a residual need for the protection afforded by this offence and the Law Commission has recommended a statutory offence of knowingly publishing false allegations that a court is corrupt.[325]

15.100 It is not contempt to engage in reasoned criticism of the judicial system or of the judiciary as individuals or a whole, even if it was expressed in robust, insulting or vulgar language.[326]

(d) Disclosing jury deliberations

15.101 By section 8 of the Contempt of Court Act 1981 it is a contempt of court to obtain, disclose or solicit any information concerning the deliberations of a jury in the course of any proceedings.[327] It has been held that this covers both direct and indirect disclosure to the media.[328] Section 8 sets out a blanket restriction on the freedom of expression and it had been suggested that it was incompatible with Articles 6 and 10 of the Convention.[329] It should, however, be noted that the section only relates to 'deliberations' and does not prevent jurors from expressing views on the desirability of a prosecution, the conduct of the lawyers or the sentence of the court.[330]

15.102 In *R v Mirza*[331] the House of Lords considered whether section 8(1) was compatible with Article 6. It was held that the section did not apply to the Court itself but only to third parties. The common law rule protecting the confidentiality of jury deliberations promoted candour and to guarantee the full and frank discussion and was legitimate to protect the proper functioning of the jury process. The rule was compatible without modification with a defendant's right to a fair trial without modification. The compatibility of section 8 with Article 10 was considered in *A-G v Scotcher*.[332] The appellant was a juror who had written to defendant's mother after the trial and told her that the jury had not weighed the evidence properly. His conviction for contempt under section 8 was upheld by the House of Lords which rejected the defence argument that a 'defence' should be read into section 8 where the juror motivated by a desire to expose a miscarriage of justice. It was held that no such

---

[324] See *Ahnee v DPP of Mauritius* [1999] 2 AC 294, 306, but see the criticism of this decision in G Robertson and A Nicol, *Media Law* (5th edn, Sweet & Maxwell, 2007), 451–452.

[325] *Offences Relating to Interference with the Court of Justice* (see n 322 above) 213.

[326] *Attorney-General v H* [2001] 2 FLR 895.

[327] See generally, *Arlidge, Eady and Smith on Contempt* (3rd edn, Sweet & Maxwell, 2005), para 11-354ff; G Robertson and A Nicol (n 324 above) para 7-056ff and H Fenwick and G Phillipson, *Media Freedom under the Human Rights Act* (Oxford University Press, 2006), 228–245.

[328] *A-G v Associated Newspapers* [1994] 2 AC 238.

[329] See eg, Sir Robin Auld, *Review of the Criminal Courts of England and Wales* (2001), Chap 5, para 98.

[330] See G Robertson and A Nicol (n 324 above), 445, citing comments of the Attorney-General during the debate on the Contempt of Court Bill, *Hansard HC Debs,* 1981, Vol 9, col 426.

[331] [2004] 1 AC 1118 (4:1, Lord Steyn dissenting); see also *R v Smith* [2005] 1 WLR 704; and see generally, para 11.268 above.

[332] [2005] 1 WLR 1867.

defence was necessary as the juror would not have been in breach of section 8 if he had written to the Court to expose a miscarriage of justice.[333]

(5) Orders that restrict court reporting[334]

(a) Introduction

The principle of 'open justice' is a fundamental one which is deeply rooted in the common law and which is subject only to narrow exceptions.[335] The reasons for the principle have often been stated. As Lord Diplock put it in *Attorney General v Leveller Magazine Limited*[336]   **15.103**

> If the way that courts behave cannot be hidden from the public ear and eye, this provides a safeguard against judicial arbitrariness or idiosyncrasy and maintains the public confidence in the administration of justice. The application of this principle of open justice has two aspects: as respects proceedings in the court itself, it requires that they should be held in open court to which the press and public are admitted and that, in criminal cases at any rate, all evidence communicated to the court is communicated publicly.

The principle has been reinforced by Articles 6[337] and 10 of the Convention. As Lord Steyn said in the case of *In Re S (A Child) (Identification: Restrictions on Publication)*[338]

> under the ECHR there is a general and strong rule in favour of unrestricted publicity of any proceedings in a criminal trial . . . the common law has long adopted a similar approach

The principle applies to both civil and criminal proceedings, although the 'public policy' justifications for openness and for restricting public access are different in the two areas. The principle also applies to tribunals and inquiries. Thus, the decision to hold in private an inquiry following the convictions of Dr Shipman for 15 murders was held to be irrational.[339]   **15.104**

(b) Civil proceedings

In civil cases, the general rule is now that hearings are to be in public.[340] However, this general rule does not require the court to make special arrangements for accommodating members of the public.[341]   **15.105**

Under the CPR 39.2 a hearing, or any part of it, may be in private if: **15.106**

- publicity would defeat the object of the hearing;
- it involves matters relating to national security;
- it involves confidential information and publicity would damage that confidentiality;

---

333 For criticism of this decision see H Fenwick and G Phillipson (n 327 above) 233–243.
334 See generally, *Arlidge, Eady and Smith on Contempt* (n 327 above) Chaps 7and 8; G Robertson and A Nicol (n 324 above), Chaps 8 and 9 and H Fenwick and G Phillipson (n 327 above) Part II.
335 See generally, *Scott v Scott* [1913] AC 417.
336 [1979] AC 440 at 450A to C.
337 See para 11.474ff above.
338 [2005] 1 AC 593, para 15, citing *Scott v Scott* (see n 335 above) and *Attorney General v Leveller* (see n 336 above).
339 *R v Secretary of State, ex p Wagstaff and Associated Newspapers* [2001] 1 WLR 292.
340 CPR, r 39.2(1).
341 CPR, r 39.2(2).

- a private hearing is necessary to protect the interest of any child or patient;
- it is a hearing without notice and it would be unjust to any respondent for there to be a public hearing;
- it involves uncontentious matters arising out of the administration of trusts or estates; or
- the court considers it necessary in the interests of justice.[342]

The court may order that the identity of a party or witness must not be disclosed if it considers non-disclosure necessary in order to protect the interests of that party or witness.[343] 'Private' under the CPR means the same as 'secret' or 'in camera' under the former procedure.[344]

15.107   Under section 97(2) of the Children Act 1989, it is provided that no person shall publish to the public at large any material likely to identify any child involved in proceedings under the Act. This prohibition comes to an end when the proceedings are concluded.[345] However, by section 97(4), the Court may dispense with the requirements of section 97(2) if satisfied that the welfare of the child requires it. This provision has to be read in a Convention compliant way to permit the court to dispense with section 97(2) where the right to free expression under Article 10 or other Convention rights required it.[346] The judge has to adopt the same 'parallel analysis' leading to the same 'ultimate balancing test' as that which is applicable in deciding whether to relax or enhance reporting restrictions. The rule under section 97(2) is properly to be regarded simply as a 'default provision' but not as a provision indicating some heavy presumption in favour of privacy. The rule has to be read, construed and applied compatibly with the Convention, 'balancing' all the various interests and not giving any special pre-eminence to the claim to privacy.[347]

15.108   The fact that proceedings are held in private does not mean that they are secret. By section 12(1) of the Administration of Justice Act 1960 ('the AJA'):

> The publication of information relating to proceedings before any court sitting in private shall not of itself be contempt of court except in the following cases, that is to say—
>
> (a) Where the proceedings—
>
>   (i) relate to the exercise of the inherent jurisdiction of the High Court with respect to minors;
>
>   (ii) are brought under the Children Act 1989 (or the Adoption and Children Act 2002); or
>
>   (iii) otherwise relate wholly or mainly to the maintenance or upbringing of a minor.

---

[342] CPR, r 39.2(3).

[343] CPR, r 39.2(4).

[344] *Economic Department of the City of Moscow v Bankers Trust Co* [2005] QB 207.

[345] *Clayton v Clayton* [2006] Fam 83.

[346] See *Re Webster; Norfolk County Council v Webster* [2007] EMLR 199.

[347] Ibid, para 77 (in that case, taking into account previous publicity, the claim that the case involved a miscarriage of justice and the speculative nature of the alleged risks to the child an order was made allowing the media to attend the hearing and report the names of the parents and the child).

(b) Where the proceedings are brought under Part VIII of the Mental Health Act 1959 or under any provision of that Act authorising an application or reference to be made to a Mental Health Review Tribunal or to a county court;

(c) Where the court sits in private for reasons of national security during that part of the proceedings about which the information in question is published;

(d) Where the information relates to a secret process, discovery or invention which is in issue in the proceedings;

(e) Where the court (having power to do so) expressly prohibits the publication of all information relating to the proceedings or of information of the description which is published.

There was previously some debate as to the precise meaning of 'publication' under section 12.[348] The better view was that this took place whenever the law of defamation would treat there as being publication—in other words, whenever there was disclosure to any third party.[349] An amendment was subsequently made to make it clear that there would not be publication if disclosure was authorized by rules of court.[350] Disclosure is now authorized to specific persons including MPs and Peers.   **15.109**

The restriction on publication of information falling under section 12(1)(a)–(d) of the AJA continues after the conclusion of the proceedings.[351] However, the Court can give permission for the publication of information concerning such a hearing.[352] It relation to hearings involving children the court must conduct a balancing exercise between the Article 8 rights of the child and the Article 10 rights of the media and a parent who wishes to give publicity to some aspect of the proceedings.[353]   **15.110**

It is not a contempt to publish the following information in relation to such hearings:[354]   **15.111**

- details as to the date, time or place of the proceedings;[355]
- a summary of the nature of the dispute (although not the evidence);[356]
- the identity of an individual as having given evidence;[357]
- the order made (unless this is expressly prohibited);[358]

---

[348] For a full discussion see *Arlidge, Eady and Smith on Contempt* (3rd edn, Sweet & Maxwell, 2005), para 8-102ff.

[349] See *Re B (A Child) (Disclosure)* [2004] FLR 142 and *Re G (Litigants in Person)* [2003] 2 FLR 963.

[350] By s 62 of the Children Act 2004, adding the words '(and in particular where the publication is not so punishable by reason of being authorized by rules of court)' in s 12(4). Other statutory provisions have been amended, see *Arlidge, Eady and Smith* (see n 348 above), para 8-107 n 42.

[351] See *Clayton v Clayton* (see n 345 above).

[352] *Re R (MJ) (Publication of Transcripts)* [1975] 2 All ER 749.

[353] *Clayton v Clayton* (see n 345 above) (the father's proposal to make a film with the child was a disproportionate interference with the child's Art 8 rights).

[354] See generally, *X v Dempster* [1999] 1 FLR 894.

[355] *P v Liverpool Daily Post and Echo* [1991] 2 AC 270, 423.

[356] *Re B (A Child: Disclosure)* [2004] 1 FLR 142, para 79.

[357] Ibid, para 76.

[358] *Forbes v Smith* [1998] 1 All ER 973; *Hodgson v Imperial Tobacco* [1998] 1 WLR 1056; the court should, even in cases involving children, permit the publication of at least an anonymized summary of the order, *Re G (Minors) (Celebrities: Publicity)* [1999] 1 FLR 409.

- anything seen or heard by a person conducting himself lawfully in the public parts of the court building.[359]

In addition, it will not be a contempt to publish material from a private hearing if the publisher was not aware of this fact.[360]

15.112 In a case which does not fall under section 12(1)(a)–(d) of the AJA then, in the absence of a specific order (which the court has power to make) the publication of information relating to the proceedings will not be a contempt of court, even though an order has been made under CPR 39.2.[361] An order will not be made under section 12(e) simply to save litigants embarrassment[362] but only after weighing the Article 10 rights of press and public against the Article 8 rights of the party seeking the restriction.[363]

(c) Criminal proceedings

15.113 The principle of open justice is of particular importance in the criminal context. As Lord Steyn put it:[364]

> A criminal trial is a public event. The principle of open justice puts, as has often been said, the judge and all who participate in the trial under intense scrutiny. The glare of contemporaneous publicity ensures that trials are properly conducted. It is a valuable check on the criminal process. Moreover, the public interest may be as much involved in the circumstances of a remarkable acquittal as in a surprising conviction. Informed public debate is necessary about all such matters. Full contemporaneous reporting of criminal trials in progress promotes public confidence in the administration of justice. It promotes the values of the rule of law.

In *Re Trinity Mirror plc*[365] the President of the Queen's Bench Division, giving the judgment of a seven judge Court of Appeal expressed the point as follows:

> In our judgment it is impossible to over-emphasize the importance to be attached to the ability of the media to report criminal trials. In simple terms this represents the embodiment of the principle of open justice in a free country. An important aspect of the public interest in the administration of criminal justice is that the identity of those convicted and sentenced for criminal offices should not be concealed. Uncomfortable though it may frequently be for the defendant that is a normal consequence of his crime. Moreover the principle protects his interests too, by helping to secure the fair trial which, in Lord Bingham of Cornhill's memorable epithet, is the defendant's 'birthright'.

---

[359] *Re W* [1989] 1 FLR 246, 257 G–H.

[360] *BBC v Rochdale MBC* [2006] EMLR 6; see generally *Arlidge, Eady and Smith* (see n 348 above) paras 8-129 to 8-140.

[361] See *AF Noonan (Architectural Practice) Ltd v Bournemouth & Boscombe Athletic Community Football Club Ltd* [2007] 1 WLR 2614.

[362] *Trustor AB v Smallbone* [2000] 1 All ER 811.

[363] *Clibbery v Allan* [2001] 2 FLR 819 (Munby J) and [2002] Fam 261 (CA).

[364] *In Re S (A Child) (Identification: Restrictions on Publication)* [2005] 1 AC 593, para 31.

[365] [2008] QB 770, para 32.

(d) Orders restricting publication

Introduction. The general rule is that reporting restrictions will only be imposed where **15.114** there is express statutory provision and where 'the absolute necessity' for making the order has been established.[366]

There are a number of types of orders a court might make to restrict the media from report- **15.115** ing upon court proceedings. The three most important are:

- the power to 'postpone' the reporting of proceedings;
- the power to prevent the publication of the names of parties or of other information relating to the proceedings; and
- the power to make restrictions on the publication of information relating to children.[367]

Courts are also permitted to restrict reporting of: indecent matters,[368] the identity of the victims of rape and certain other sexual offences[369] and committal proceedings before magistrates' courts.[370]

A person aggrieved by orders restricting or preventing reports or restricting public access in **15.116** relation to a trial in the Crown Court can appeal to the Court of Appeal.[371] This right of appeal is subject to a requirement of permission being granted.[372] There is no further appeal to the House of Lords. Where orders are made by magistrates' courts they can be challenged by an application for judicial review.

Orders for postponement of trial reporting. Under section 4(2) of the 1981 Act, a court **15.117** may order the postponement of the publication of material until the conclusion of a trial or series of trials[373] in order to avoid a risk of prejudice to the administration of justice in those proceedings. The section provides that in any legal proceedings held in public:

> the court may, where it appears to be necessary for avoiding a substantial risk of prejudice to the administration of the justice in those proceedings, or in any other proceedings pending or imminent, order that the publication or any report of the proceedings, or any part of the proceedings, be postponed for such period as the court thinks necessary for that purpose.

The risk to the administration of justice must be 'substantial', and the courts have determined that 'blanket bans' on reporting are likely to be inappropriate.[374] Section 4(2) is designed to enable the court to prevent the publication of a report of proceedings where the

---

[366] Ibid.

[367] For a full discussion of these and other powers see *Arlidge, Eady and Smith on Contempt* (3rd edn, Sweet & Maxwell, 2005), Chaps 6–8.

[368] Judicial Proceedings (Regulation of Reports) Act 1926.

[369] Sexual Offences (Amendment) Act 1976.

[370] Magistrates' Court Act 1980, s 8.

[371] Criminal Justice Act 1981, s 159; after the decision in *R v Central Criminal Court, ex p Crook, The Times*, 8 November 1984 and following the application of the journalist to the European Court of Human Rights; see also G Robertson and A Nicol, *Media Law* (5th edn, Sweet & Maxwell, 2007), para 8-086.

[372] Which is determined without a hearing, this provision was held to be *intra vires* in *R v Guardian Newspapers Ltd* [1994] Crim LR 912, see generally, *Arlidge, Eady and Smith on Contempt* (see 367 above) para 7–266.

[373] *Arlidge, Eady and Smith* (see n 367 above), paras 7-111 to 7-279; Robertson and Nicol (see n 371 above) 8-076 to 8-80.

[374] *R v Horsham Justices, ex p Farquarhson* [1982] QB 762.

publication would prejudice the conduct of those proceedings or specific pending proceedings and the need for the postponement cannot subsist beyond the end of the proceedings in question.[375]

15.118 In assessing the necessity of a section 4(2) order, the court must consider the alternatives and should not lightly interfere with the freedom of the press.[376] The test is a three stage one:[377]

- is there a substantial risk of prejudice[378] to the administration of justice?
- is an order necessary?
- should the court exercise its discretion in favour of making an order?

The operation of these tests is illustrated by the case of *Ex parte Central Television plc*.[379] A jury was required to stay overnight in a hotel and the judge, in order to insulate the jurors from the media, ordered that reporting of the trial be postponed until the next day. The Court of Appeal held that there was little evidence that reports would have been anything but fair and accurate and that the risk to the administration of justice was therefore minimal. Even if there had been a substantial risk, the order would not have been automatic, as alternative methods of preventing exposure of the jurors to the media may have been available.[380]

15.119 Orders made under section 4(2) must be formulated in precise terms and committed to writing.[381] It has been suggested that copies of all section 4 orders should be faxed by the court to the Press Association.[382] Unless the order is varied or set aside on appeal, a breach will render the press liable to be committed for contempt.[383]

15.120 An employment tribunal also has a power to make a restricted reporting order at any stage until its decision is promulgated in any cases involving allegations of sexual misconduct[384] or in a disability discrimination case where evidence of a personal nature is likely to be heard.[385] In *R v London (North) Industrial Tribunal, ex p Associated Newspapers Ltd*[386] it was emphasized that because of the principle of the freedom of the press to report court hearings fully and contemporaneously, the power to make an order should be interpreted narrowly.

---

[375] *Re Times Newspapers Ltd* [2008] 1 All ER 343.

[376] *Ex p Central Television plc* [1991] 1 WLR 4; for the test to be applied when making a s 4(2) order see, *Arlidge, Eady and Smith on Contempt* (see n 367 above) paras 7-163 to 7-202.

[377] *MGN Pension Trustees Ltd v Bank of America National Trust and Savings Association* [1995] 2 All ER 355; also *R v Sherwood, ex p Telegraph Group* [2001] EWCA Crim 1075.

[378] Note that, in contrast to the position under the Contempt of Court Act 1981, s 2(2) there is no requirement that the prejudice be 'serious'.

[379] [1991] 1 WLR 4.

[380] See also *A-G v Guardian Newspapers (No 3)* [1992] 1 WLR 874; *Ex parte The Telegraph plc* [1993] 2 All ER 971; *R v Beck, ex p Daily Telegraph plc* [1993] 2 All ER 177.

[381] *Practice Direction (Contempt: Reporting Restrictions)* [1982] 1 WLR 1475.

[382] *A-G v Guardian Newspapers Ltd (No 3)* (see n 380 above).

[383] Ibid, 884H–885A.

[384] Employment Tribunal Act 1996, s 11.

[385] Ibid, s 12.

[386] [1998] ICR 1212; see also *Leicester University v A* [1999] IRLR 352.

Orders to prevent publication of the 'name or other matter'. Under section 11 of the **15.121**
Contempt of Court Act 1981, the court has limited powers to restrict the publication of
material in relation to hearings which are held in private [387] and to prohibit the reporting
of material, including names of participants, mentioned in open court. The section provides that:

> In any case where a court (having power to do so) allows a name or other matter to be with-
> held from the public in proceedings before the court, the court may give such directions pro-
> hibiting the publication of that name or matter in connection with the proceedings as appear
> to the court to be necessary for the purpose for which it was so withheld.

No order can be made under section 11 unless the court has first decided to allow 'a name
or other matter to be withheld from the public'. Unless this is done then there is no jurisdiction to make an order under section 11. [388]

Section 11 does not confer any additional powers on the court, but simply regulates the **15.122**
exercise of existing powers [389] such as the well-established common law power to withhold
the identity of witnesses in blackmail cases since their disclosure would prejudice the
administration of justice by discouraging witnesses from coming forward in the future. [390]
These policy considerations apply whether or not the accused is subsequently acquitted.
Once section 11 orders are made they appear to be binding on everyone who is aware of
them. [391] 'Publication' in this section is not understood in the broad sense in which it is used
in the law of libel but in its ordinary sense of 'made available to the public'. [392]

The purpose of section 11 is to give a court power to 'prohibit publication'. [393] There was **15.123**
no such power at common law [394]—but the court had a common law power to give directions relating to the control of its proceedings. For example, a court could direct in the
course of a hearing that a name or a particular piece of evidence be withheld. A breach of
such a direction may constitute a contempt of court even without an express direction to
the media. [395]

Like the power to sit in private, the common law power to impose restrictions on the **15.124**
reporting of court proceedings is a broad one which is not circumscribed by any inflexible
rules. This is because

> there are an immense variety of situations in which it is appropriate to restrict the general
> rule. These situations depend very much on their individual circumstances [396]

---

[387] *Scott v Scott* [1913] AC 417.
[388] *R v Arundel JJ, ex p Westminster Press Limited* [1985] 1 WLR 708, 710 and 711B–C; see also *R v Z* [2005] 2 AC 467, para 2.
[389] See N Lowe and B Sufrin, *Borrie and Lowe: The Law of Contempt* (3rd edn, Butterworths, 1996), 299; G Robertson and A Nicol, *Media Law* (5th edn, Sweet & Maxwell, 2007), para 8-071.
[390] See *R v Socialist Worker Printers and Publishers Ltd, ex p A-G* [1975] QB 637.
[391] *A-G v Leveller Magazine Ltd* [1979] AC 440.
[392] *Borrie and Lowe* (see n 389 above) 85.
[393] See *Independent Publishing v A-G of Trinidad and Tobago* [2005] 1 AC 190, para 51.
[394] Ibid, para 67.
[395] See *A-G v Leveller* (see n 391 above), 452A–B; 458C–D.
[396] *R v Legal Aid Board, ex p Kaim Todner* [1999] QB 966, 977A.

In deciding whether or not to make an order it is appropriate for the Court to take into account the extent of the interference—it is less objectionable if it relates only to identity and does not involve proceedings being conducted behind closed doors.[397]

15.125 There is a general power to withhold names in civil[398] or criminal proceedings.[399] This power includes a power to prevent identification in other ways—for example, by the publication of addresses, or sketches or photographs.[400] The power to withhold addresses is regularly exercised in relation to witnesses who, in criminal proceedings, are no longer required to disclose their addresses in court.[401] A section 11 order can be made where evidence given in camera is accidentally repeated in open court.[402]

15.126 The circumstances in which the court can make an order for anonymity or an order restricting publicity, in favour of a defendant have not been exhaustively defined in the cases. It is clear that an anonymity order cannot be made 'for the benefit of the comfort or feelings of defendants'[403] However, the position is obviously different where the material is revealed in a criminal trial is such that the defendant could suffer substantial harm. For example, in *R v Tower Bridge Magistrates, ex p Osborne*[404] the further publication of highly sensitive material which the magistrates had wrongly heard in open court (including the defendant's address) was restricted by an injunction. Similarly, an order restricting publicity can be made where the defendant's safety is at risk from third parties.[405] Such orders fall within the established exceptions to the openness principle because the administration of justice might be endangered if those facing prosecution were harmed by third parties—this might deter the authorities from prosecuting future cases[406] and the administration of justice would be brought into disrepute if defendants in sensitive cases were exposed to attacks by third parties.

---

[397] Ibid, 978B–C.

[398] *R v Westminster City Council, ex p Castelli* ([1996] 1 FLR 534.

[399] See *R v Evesham JJ, ex p McDonagh* ([1988] 1 QB 553, 561C. See also *R v Dover JJ, ex p Dover DC* (1991) 156 JP 433 and *R v Reigate JJ, ex p Argus Newspapers* (1983) 5 Cr App R (S) 181.

[400] In *A-G v Leveller* (see n 391 above) the House of Lords proceeded on the basis that the court could have directed that the 'identifying information' (which was ultimately used to name 'Colonel B') should not be published.

[401] As to the making of such an order in relation to a defendant see *R v Tower Bridge Magistrates, ex p Osborne* (1987) 88 Cr App Rep 28, 31.

[402] *Re Times Newspapers Ltd* [2008] 1 All ER 343 (alternatively, the court could make it clear that the evidence was a breach of an 'in camera direction' and that to publish it would be a contempt as it would frustrate a lawful order of the court).

[403] See the *Evesham JJ* case (see n 399 above), at 562B; *R v Newtonabbey Magistrates' Court ex parte Belfast Telegraph Newspapers Limited* [1997] NI 309 (justices wrong to grant anonymity to a defendant charged with indecent assault who feared attack, it likely that this case would be decided differently today taking Arts 3 and 8 into account); *Dover JJ ex p Dover DC* (see n 399 above) (justices wrong to grant anonymity to a restaurant charged with food hygiene offences on the ground on possible damage to its business).

[404] See n 401 above.

[405] See *R v Reigate JJ, ex p Argus Newspapers* (see n 399 above) where it was held that an anonymity order could have been made to protect a person who was at risk of being identified as a supergrass).

[406] cf the discussion of why 'national security' is an exception to the openness principle in *A-G v Leveller* (see n 391 above) at 471 (Lord Scarman).

More generally, the issue can be said to be one of fairness.[407] When considering this **15.127** issue concerns other than actual risks should be considered: the court can consider subjective fears that are not well-founded.[408] It is unfair and wrong for witnesses to be avoidably subjected to fears arising from giving evidence. When considering the position at common law the court must balance the extent to which the witness's fears and the grounds giving rise to them will be alleviated by an anonymity order against the adverse consequences for the fairness of the proceedings of granting such an order.[409] This kind of 'balancing' is, however, not appropriate when there is an 'immediate risk' to life such as to engage Article 2 of the Convention[410] to which we will now turn.

Reporting restrictions under the HRA: Articles 2 and 3. The positive obligation to protect **15.128** life under Article 2 (or to protect a witness from degrading or inhuman treatment under Article 3) may arise when witnesses are called to give evidence by a court or tribunal. The same approach applies whether the individual concerned is a witness or a defendant.[411] The principles to be applied were explained by the House of Lords in *Re Officer L*[412] and can be summarized as follows:[413]

- The substantive obligation under Article 2 is engaged where there is a real and immediate risk to life; in other words, a risk that is objectively verified and is present and continuing.[414]
- The subjective fears of a witness count only as evidence in favour of a real and immediate risk. Subjective fear is neither necessary nor sufficient to establish a real and immediate risk.
- Against this risk must be balanced the reasonableness of the steps or precautions proposed. Public interest factors, such as the credibility of a hearing, may be relevant are relevant considerations in carrying out an assessment of reasonableness.

It was said that the question of witness immunity should be approached from the point of **15.129** view of the common law test of fairness 'with an excursion if the facts require it into the territory of Article 2'.[415] It would only be necessary to consider Article 2 if it was found that, viewed objectively, a risk to a witness's life would be created or materially increased if no order was made for anonymity.[416] If such a risk would be created or material increased, then

---

[407] *Re Officer L* [2007] 1 WLR 2135.

[408] Ibid, para 22.

[409] Ibid.

[410] Ibid, para 29.

[411] See *Times Newspapers v Soldiers A-F* [2008] EWCA Crim 2559 (in which such orders were made to anonymize defendants).

[412] [2007] 1 WLR 2135.

[413] Ibid, paras 20–21.

[414] This is described by Lord Carswell (ibid, para 20) in as 'a high threshold' but note the qualification in *Van colle v Chief Constable of Hertfordshire* [2008] 3 WLR 593 Lord Bingham at para 30 ('the test . . . is clear and calls for no judicial exegesis'), and Lord Hope at para 66 (describing Lord Carswell's words as 'no more than a comment . . . not a qualification or gloss').

[415] *Re Officer L* (see n 407 above) para 29.

[416] Ibid, para 29; differing from the approach of the Court of Appeal in *R v Lord Saville of Newdigate* [2002] 1 WLR 1249 and *R (A) v HM Coroner for Inner South London* [2005] UKHRR 44.

anonymity would be required by Article 2. If so, the tribunal should then consider whether the increased risk would amount to a real and immediate risk to life.

15.130 Anonymity has been granted to soldiers who were called as witnesses at the 'Bloody Sunday' inquiry[417] and to police officers in respect of an inquest into the death of a suspect shot by one of the officers.[418] In *Times Newspapers v Soldiers A–F*[419] an order was made granting anonymity to five defendants in a Court-Martial on the grounds of immediate risk to life.

15.131 **Reporting restrictions under the HRA: Article 8.** At common law the court had no general power to restrict the reporting of proceedings to protect the private lives or witnesses. There was, however, an inherent jurisdiction to restrict the publication of information concerning children. This power was considered in *Re S (A Child) (Identification: Restriction on Publication).*[420] The House of Lords held that the foundation of the jurisdiction to restrain publicity to protect a child's private and family life was now derived from the Convention rights rather than the inherent jurisdiction. In that case an application was made for an order, under the inherent jurisdiction of the court, restricting publicity of a criminal trial to protect a child of the accused. The House refused an order. What was in issue was the child's 'qualified' Convention right to respect for private life (under Article 8 of the Convention) which had to be balanced against the right to freedom of expression (under Article 10 of the Convention). Lord Steyn summarized the applicable principles as follows:

> First, neither article has *as such* precedence over the other. Secondly, where the values under the two articles are in conflict, an intense focus on the comparative importance of the specific rights being claimed in the individual case is necessary. Thirdly, the justifications for interfering with or restricting each right must be taken into account. Finally, the proportionality test must be applied to each. For convenience I will call this the ultimate balancing test.[421]

Under Article 10 the court had to take into account the fact that the freedom of the press to report the progress of a criminal trial was of the highest importance. In the circumstances, the Article 10 rights of the press prevailed.

15.132 The approach which the Court takes to making reporting restriction orders under the HRA is the same as that taken when considering whether or not to grant an interim injunction to restrain the misuse of private information.[422] Once it is established that Article 8 is engaged—because publication would interfere with the private life of a party or witness, the Court must consider the position under Article 8 and 10 in turn. It must bear in mind that:

> each article propounds a fundamental right which there is a pressing social need to protect. Equally, each article qualifies the right it propounds so far as it may be lawful, necessary and proportionate to do so in order to accommodate the other. The exercise to be performed is

---

[417] *R v Lord Saville, ex p A* [2000] 1 WLR 1855 CA and see also the decision as to the venue for the hearing of evidence in the same case which involved similar considerations, *R (A) v Lord Saville of Newdigate* (n 416 above).

[418] *R (A) v HM Coroner for Inner South London* (n 416 above).

[419] See n 411 above.

[420] [2005] 1 AC 593.

[421] Ibid, para 17.

[422] See generally, para 12.24ff above.

one of parallel analysis in which the starting point is presumptive parity, in that neither article has precedence over or 'trumps' the other. The exercise of parallel analysis requires the court to examine the justification for interfering with each right and the issue of proportionality is to be considered in respect of each. It is not a mechanical exercise to be decided upon the basis of rival generalities. An intense focus on the comparative importance of the specific rights being claimed in the individual case is necessary before the ultimate balancing test in terms of proportionality is carried out.[423]

The Court's jurisdiction to make reporting restriction orders to protect the Article 8 rights **15.133** of parties, witnesses or victims[424] extends to adults as well as children. In *R v J*[425] the Court of Appeal held that a defendant should be anonymous on the hearing of an appeal because of risks to his mental health resulting from publicity. Anonymity orders have been made to protect the Article 8 rights of an individual subject to control order proceedings and his family.[426] However, orders can only be made by a court which has the jurisdiction to grant injunctive relief: in particular, they cannot be made by the Crown Court.[427]

Applications for such orders are closely scrutinized by the Courts and have in general, been **15.134** unsuccessful. In order to justify the exceptional step of making an order which has the effect of granting anonymity there must be something more than distress, upset or embarrassment: there must be evidence of a risk of 'real and substantial damage' to Article 8 rights.[428] For example, in *A Local Authority v PD*[429] the Court refused to make an order restricting reporting of the identity of the father of a six-year old girl, whose mother had been murdered by the father in gruesome circumstances. A number of applications have been refused in circumstances in which there has been media comment and discussion on controversial family proceedings.[430] In *Re Trinity Mirror plc*[431] the Court of Appeal noted that the fact that families of those convicted of crime would suffer adverse consequences was not sufficient to make an order under this jurisdiction and that such an order could not be contemplated unless the circumstances could truly be described as 'exceptional'.

Reporting restrictions relating to a child may be discharged if the child is sufficiently mature **15.135** and wishes to exercise Article 10 rights. Thus, in the case of *Torbay BC v News Group Newspapers*[432] a newspaper sought the variation of an injunction prohibiting the publication

---

[423] *A Local Authority v W* [2006] 1 FLR 1, para 53 (Potter P).

[424] See *Re S (A Child) (Identification: Restriction on Publication)* [2005] 1 AC 593, and see above, para 15.125ff.

[425] [2003] EWCA Crim 3268; this was a preliminary application in a reference by the Criminal Cases Review Commission, the appeal was subsequently allowed, *R v J* [2003] EWCA Crim 3309; see also *Carr v News Group Newspapers* [2005] EWHC 971 (QB) (a *contra mundum* injunction to protect identity of claimant on Art 8 grounds).

[426] *Times Newspapers Ltd v Secretary of State for the Home Department* [2008] EWHC 2455 (Admin).

[427] *Re Trinity Mirror* [2008] QB 770, para 30.

[428] See *Re LM (Reporting Restrictions: Coroner's Inquest)* [2008] 1 FLR 1360, para 33(3).

[429] [2005] EMLR 35.

[430] *BBC v Rochdale MBC* [2005] EMLR 6 (application to restrain the publication of the names of expert witnesses in wardship proceedings was also refused); such anonymity will only be granted in highly exceptional circumstances, *Re W (Children) (Care Proceedings: Witness Anonymity)* [2003] 1 FLR 329; *Medway Council v G* [2008] 2 FLR 687 (agreed summary of facts relating to care proceedings released, this was sufficient for the media's purposes and full publication of judgments given in private was unnecessary).

[431] See n 427 above, para 33.

[432] [2004] EMLR 8.

of the identity of Angela Roddy, who had become pregnant when she was 12 and who had been the subject of care orders which were later discharged. She offered her story to the press but the local authority sought to prevent publication of information which could identify her baby. The application was allowed as Ms Roddy had sufficient understanding and maturity to decide for herself what should remain private, and the court had a duty to protect her right to make a choice and her Article 10 right to tell her story.

15.136 Injunctions have, however, been was granted in a number of cases in which there has been serious interferences with Article 8 rights without strong countervailing Article 10 considerations. In *A Local Authority v W*[433] the identification of the defendant awaiting sentence in criminal proceedings would have disclosed that her children were HIV positive and rendered them liable them to harassment and abuse. An order was made to restrain publication of the identity of the accused and the victim in a criminal trial to protect their children.

15.137 **Statutory reporting restrictions in relation to Children:** Restrictions on publications which identify children may be effected by way of an order under section 39 of the Children and Young Persons Act 1933.[434] That section provides:

(1) In relation to any proceedings in any court . . . the court may direct that . . .

   (a) no newspaper report of the proceedings shall reveal the name, address, or school, or include any particulars calculated to lead to the identification of any child or young person concerned in the proceedings, either as being the person [by or against] or in respect of whom the proceedings are taken, or being a witness therein;

   (b) no picture shall be published in any newspaper as being or including a picture of any child or young person so concerned in the proceedings as aforesaid;

except in so far (if at all) as may be permitted by the direction of the court.

Such orders, although discretionary, are routinely made in criminal, family[435] and education cases; they normally should be made if a child or young person is before the court.[436] The power applies only to a person 'concerned in the proceedings', that is a party or a witness and do not cover victims or relatives of parties.

15.138 An 'anonymity' order under section 39 of the Children and Young Persons Act will only be justified if Article 10 is met—the restriction must fulfil the tests in Article 10(2). Such orders constitute a significant curtailment of press freedom and 'the courts must be vigilant to see that they were justified and made in clear and unambiguous terms'. However, if the order is properly made then its enforcement will not violate Article 10.[437] When considering whether to make such an order in proceedings for an anti-social behaviour order each

---

[433] [2006] 1 FLR 1; see also *Re LM (Reporting Restrictions: Coroner's Inquest)* (see n 428 above) (the court refused to make orders in relation to the identity of the parents and family members in an inquest but made an order preventing the publication of the name of the child).

[434] This is due to be replaced, for criminal courts, by s 45 of the Youth Justice and Criminal Evidence Act 1999 which has not yet been brought into force.

[435] See *Re X County Council v A* (the Mary Bell case) [1985] 1 All ER 53.

[436] *R v Leicester Crown Court, ex p S (A Minor)* [1992] 2 All ER 659, 662.

[437] See *Briffet v DPP* [2002] EMLR 203.

case must be considered on its merits but evidence as to the effects on members of the offender's family is not, prima facie, relevant.[438]

Section 39 does not confer an express power to order that publication of the name of **15.139** the defendant is to be restricted.[439] Nevertheless, the provision is wide enough to enable the court to prevent the publication of everything concerning the proceedings, including the fact that the order has been made. The Court of Appeal has, however, recognized difficulties with orders of this type and has approved the practice of the release of a summary of the court decision by the Official Solicitor.[440]

In the Youth Courts there is a presumption in favour of anonymity.[441] The power to **15.140** dispense with such anonymity has to be exercised with great caution.[442] If the child is a defendant in a criminal case and is convicted then the conviction may lead to the order being discharged, although this is not automatic.[443]

Other statutory reporting restrictions. In 1976, the recommendation of the Heilbron **15.141** Report[444] was implemented to given anonymity to the complainant in rape cases. This has now been extended to the complainants in a wide range of sexual offences.[445] The complainant may, however, consent to being identified[446] and the court can allow the complainant to be named if anonymity would impose a 'substantial and unreasonable restriction on the reporting of the proceedings at the trial and it is in the public interest to relax the restriction'.[447] It is an offence to publish material 'likely to identify' the complainant. It has been held that these provisions are compatible with Art.10. Although the offence is one of strict liability, it was sufficiently clear to enable an individual to regulate his conduct and was necessary in a democratic society.[448]

By section 46 of the Youth Justice and Criminal Evidence Act 1999 the Court has a power **15.142** to prohibit the identification of witnesses over 18 whose evidence or co-operation was likely to be diminished because of the witness's fear or distress at the prospect of being publicly identified as a witness. This does not extend to the defendant.

Restrictions on reporting material made available on disclosure. Documents which are **15.143** the subject of disclosure between parties to proceedings cannot be used for any purpose other than the conduct of the litigation and cannot be supplied to the media. This is

---

[438] *R (T) v Crown Court at St Albans* [2002] EWHC Admin 1129.

[439] *R v Crown Court at Southwark, ex p Godwin* [1992] QB 190; see also *R v Teesside Crown Court, ex p Gazette Media* [2005] EWCA Crim 1983.

[440] *Re G (Minors) (Celebrities: Publicity), The Times*, 28 October 1998; and see also *Re R (A Minor) (Wardship: Restrictions on Publication)* [1994] Fam 254 (if order relates to criminal proceedings it should be made by the judge hearing those proceedings, not in wardship proceedings).

[441] *R v Central Criminal Court, ex p W, B and C* [2001] 1 Cr App R 7.

[442] See generally, *McKerry v Teesdale and Wear Valley Justices* [2001] EMLR 127.

[443] See *R v Inner London Crown Court, ex p B* [1996] COD 17; *R v Central Criminal Court, ex p S and P* [1999] Crim LR 159.

[444] Advisory Group on the Law of Rape (1975) Cmnd 6352.

[445] Sexual Offences (Amendment) Act 1992, s 2.

[446] Ibid, s 5.

[447] Ibid, s 3(2).

[448] *O'Riordan v DPP, The Times*, 31 May 2005.

because disclosure constitutes a serious invasion of privacy and confidentiality.[449] The obligation is imposed by law[450] and applies in criminal proceedings as well as civil.[451]

15.144   The issue has arisen as to whether, once a disclosed document has been read in court, the parties are entitled to supply copies of it to journalists. In *Home Office v Harman*[452] the House of Lords held that they were not. In that case, 800 pages of documents relating to Home Office prison policy had been read in open court and copies were subsequently supplied by the plaintiffs' solicitor to a journalist. It was held that this constituted a contempt of court. The European Commission on Human Rights held that there had been a violation of Article 10.[453] A friendly settlement was reached and as a result the Rules of the Supreme Court were changed.[454] The rule provides that the implied undertaking of confidentiality ceases to apply after a document has been 'read to or by the court or referred to in open court'. This includes documents pre-read by the court, referred to in a skeleton argument or referred to in open court by counsel or the court but not read.[455] However, this rule has been given a restrictive interpretation, allowing the party to make the contents of the document known, but to use it for no other purpose.[456] The position is now governed by CPR 31.22(1) which provides that a disclosed document can only be used for the purposes of the proceedings except where it has been read to or by the court, referred to at a hearing in open court or if the court or the disclosing party gives permission.

(6) Protection of journalistic sources[457]

(a) Introduction

15.145   The common law provided limited protection for journalistic sources. In libel cases, disclosure of sources was governed by the so-called 'newspaper rule' which meant that newspapers could not be forced to disclose sources of information before trial.[458] In other cases, however, the 'newspaper rule' did not apply.[459] The perceived need to protect journalistic sources more generally led to the enactment of section 10 of the Contempt of Court Act.[460] That section provides:

> No court may require a person to disclose, nor is any person guilty of contempt of court for refusing to disclose, the source of information contained in a publication for which he is

---

[449] *Home Office v Harman* [1983] 1 AC 280, 308.

[450] *Prudential Assurance v Fountain Page Ltd* [1991] 1 WLR 756, 764; in civil proceedings it is now expressly imposed by CPR 31.22.

[451] *Taylor v Director of the Serious Fraud Office* [1998] 1 WLR 1040.

[452] Ibid; see generally, I Eagles, 'Disclosure of Material Obtained on Discovery' (1984) 47 MLR 284; N Lowe and B Sufrin *Borrie and Lowe: The Law of Contempt* (3rd edn, Butterworths, 1996), 594–596; G Robertson and A Nicol, *Media Law* (5th edn, Sweet & Maxwell, 2007), paras 8-106 to 8-109.

[453] *Harman v United Kingdom* (1985) 7 EHRR 146, EComm HR.

[454] RSC Ord 24, r14A was introduced (and is now CPR, r 31.22).

[455] *Derby v Weldon (No 2)*, The Times, 19 October 1988; *Smithkline Beecham Biologicals SA v Connaught Laboratories Inc* [1999] 4 All ER 498; and see also *GIO Personal Investment Services v Liverpool and London Steamship Protection and Indemnity Association* [1999] 1 WLR 984.

[456] *Singh v Christie*, The Times, 11 November 1993; see also the comments of Lord Hoffmann in *Taylor v Director of the Serious Fraud Office* [1998] 1 WLR 1040, 1051.

[457] See generally, *Arlidge, Eady and Smith on Contempt* (3rd edn, Sweet & Maxwell, 2005), Chap 9 and H Fenwick and G Phillipson, *Media Freedom under the Human Rights Act* (Oxford University Press, 2006), 311–382.

[458] *Gatley on Libel and Slander* (11th edn, Sweet & Maxwell, 2008), para 33.32.

[459] *British Steel Corporation v Granada Television Ltd* [1981] AC 1096.

[460] *Arlidge, Eady and Smith on Contempt* (n 457 above) para 9-52.

responsible,[461] unless it be established to the satisfaction of the court that disclosure is necessary in the interests of justice or national security or for the prevention of disorder or crime.

Section 10 applies not only to a direct disclosure of the identity of a source but to the disclosure of documents which might reveal the identity of the source.[462] Although the section refers to 'the source of information contained in a publication' it appears that the protection only extends to 'confidential journalistic sources'.[463]

(b) Section 10 exceptions

Section 10 recognizes that the protection of sources is a matter of 'high public importance'[464] and effectively creates a presumption in favour of journalists who wish to protect their sources. The presumption is, however, subject to four wide exceptions where disclosure of the source is a matter of necessity: **15.146**

- in the interests of justice;
- in the interests of national security;
- for the prevention of disorder; or
- for the prevention of crime.

The word 'necessary' has a meaning somewhere between 'indispensable' and 'useful' or expedient, the nearest paraphrase being 'really needed'.[465]

In relation to 'national security' and 'the prevention of disorder or crime', the courts have said that: **15.147**

> These two public interests are of such overriding importance that once it is shown that disclosure will serve one of those interests, the necessity of disclosure follows almost automatically.[466]

In *Secretary of State for Defence v Guardian Newspapers Ltd*[467] the House of Lords decided that the *Guardian* should disclose a photocopy of a memorandum, dealing with the arrival in the United Kingdom of cruise missiles, which had been supplied by an anonymous source, despite the absence of clear evidence of the sensitivity and urgency of the subject matter.[468] A similar result was reached in the case of *In re An Inquiry under the Company Securities (Insider Dealing) Act 1985*[469] in which it was held to be sufficient to show that

---

[461] The section applies to information received for the purposes of publication, even though it is never in fact published: see *X Ltd v Morgan-Grampian (Publishers) Ltd* [1991] 1 AC 1, 40F, in which the point was conceded.

[462] *Secretary of State for Defence v Guardian Newspapers* [1985] AC 339, 347.

[463] See, for example, the discussion in *Goodwin v United Kingdom* (1996) 22 EHRR 123.

[464] *X v Morgan-Grampian* (see n 461 above) 41E.

[465] *In re An Inquiry under the Company Securities (Insider Dealing) Act 1985* [1988] AC 660, 704.

[466] *X Ltd v Morgan-Grampian (Publishers) Ltd* (see n 461 above) 43B (although not if the crime was of a 'trivial nature').

[467] See n 462 above.

[468] *Borrie and Lowe* (see n 452 above) 54; G Robertson and A Nicol, *Media Law* (5th edn, Sweet & Maxwell, 2007), 5-066.

[469] [1988] AC 660.

disclosure could assist in the prosecution of a crime already committed.[470] Such an application was, however, refused where a health authority sought disclosure of the identity of doctors who were practising despite having contracted AIDS: the prevention of crime was not the task of the plaintiff health authority and criminal investigation was unlikely.[471]

(c) 'Necessary in the interests of justice'

15.148 The question as to whether disclosure is 'necessary in the interests of justice' has given rise to considerable difficulty. The courts have construed 'interests of justice' as being wider than 'the administration of justice'. It covers the interest of the public

> in the maintenance of the system of law, within the framework of which every citizen has the ability and the freedom to exercise his legal right to remedy a wrong done to him or to prevent it being done. . .[472]

In the *Morgan-Grampian* case Lord Bridge set out a number of factors which were relevant when balancing the interests of justice against the policy of protection from disclosure underlying section 10, stating that:

> if it appears that the information was obtained illegally, this will diminish the importance of protecting the source unless, of course, this factor is counter-balanced by a clear public interest in publication of the information.[473]

15.149 In the case itself it was found 'necessary in the interests of justice' that the court should order the disclosure of the source of financial confidential information concerning the claimant's business even though the dissemination of the confidential information had been restrained by injunction. The journalist applied to the Court of Human Rights. In *Goodwin v United Kingdom*[474] the Court held that, insofar as the disclosure order served to reinforce the injunction, the additional restriction on freedom of expression was not justified under Article 10(2). Furthermore, the Court took the view that the interest of the plaintiff in eliminating the residual threat of damage through dissemination of confidential information and in unmasking a disloyal employee was not sufficient to outweigh the public interest in protecting the journalist's source.

15.150 When the issue again arose before the English courts in *Camelot Group plc v Centaur Communications Ltd*[475] the Court of Appeal said that 'the tests which the ECHR and the House of Lords applied were substantially the same'. There was no public interest in protecting the source of the draft accounts of the plaintiff and the Court upheld an order

---

[470] Rejecting the view of Hoffmann J that it was necessary to show that, in the absence of disclosure, it was likely that further crimes would be committed.

[471] *X v Y* [1988] 2 All ER 648; and see *Handmade Films v Express Newspapers* [1986] FSR 463 (no order for disclosure of source of photographs taken on a film set as no serious damage threatened).

[472] *X Ltd v Morgan-Grampian (Publishers) Ltd* (n 461 above) 54C. See also *Ashworth Hospital Authority v MGN* [2001] 1 WLR 515 (interests of justice did not cover just narrow purposes of administration of justice but all interests which were justiciable).

[473] See n 461 above, 44.

[474] (1996) 22 EHRR 123 (by an 11:7 majority).

[475] [1999] QB 124; see also *O'Mara Books Ltd v Express Newspapers plc*, 3 March 1998, Neuberger J: following *Camelot*, disclosure ordered.

for disclosure. This decision can be contrasted with that in *Saunders v Punch Ltd*[476] where Lindsay J refused to order the disclosure of sources of information concerning a DTI inquiry[477]—despite the fact that some of the disclosed information appeared to have been protected by legal professional privilege. He said that an injunction already granted to restrain the use of the information meant that the interests of justice were not so pressing as to require that the ban on 'statutory privilege against disclosure' be overridden.[478] This approach was approved by the Court of Appeal in *John v Express Newspapers*[479] which held that before overriding the public interest in protecting confidential sources, the minimum requirement was that other ways of obtaining the information had to have been explored.

In *Ashworth Hospital Authority v MGN*[480] the issue was whether the newspaper should **15.151** reveal the source of extracts from the medical records of a patient in a secure hospital. The Court of Appeal took the view that the disclosure of medical records was serious misconduct and the need to protect patient confidentiality meant that disclosure was necessary. This decision of the Court of Appeal was upheld by the House of Lords[481] on the basis that while the exercise of the jurisdiction to require a third party who was involved in wrongdoing, in this case a journalist, to identify the wrongdoer was subject to Article 10, in the exceptional circumstances of the case itself the order to disclose was justifiable. The newspaper disclosed that it had obtained the records via an intermediary, Mr Ackroyd. The subsequent application for a source disclosure order against him was unsuccessful.[482] The Judge held that the the position was very different from that when the first set of proceedings had been taken against the newspaper and, in particular, it was now clear that the source was not seeking payment but was acting in a misguided belief that disclosure was in the public interest. As a result, an order for disclosure was not proportionate.

(d) Source disclosure and proportionality

The 'new methodology' of balancing Article 8 and Article 10 rights is now applied in the **15.152** context of the protection of sources.[483] As a result, it is wrong to speak of a 'presumption' in favour of free speech: rather it cannot be determined whether an encroachment on the confidentiality of a source is necessary and proportionate in a given case without balancing

---

[476] [1998] 1 WLR 986; see also *Chief Constable of Leicestershire v Garavelli* [1997] EMLR 543: disclosure not necessary.

[477] The DTI inquiry concerned Mr Ernest Saunders who was ultimately convicted for his role in the Guinness take over.

[478] Saunders (n 476 above) at 250b–d.

[479] [2000] 1 WLR 1931, para 27 and see also *Ashworth Hospital Authority v MGN Ltd* [2002] 1 WLR 2003, para 61 where Lord Woolf said that the court will 'normally protect journalists' sources'.

[480] [2001] 1 WLR 515 (CA).

[481] [2002] 1 WLR 2033 (HL); see also *Interbrew SA v Financial Times* [2002] 1 Lloyd's Rep 542 in which exceptional circumstances existed so as to require a journalist to identify a source (upheld by the Court of Appeal [2002] EMLR 24 ; but see the comments of Lord Woolf on this decision in *Ashworth Hospital Authority v MGN*, paras 50 to 58).

[482] *Mersey Care NHS Trust v Ackroyd (No 2)* (2006) 88 BMLR 1 (Tugendhat J) and [2008] EMLR 1 (CA).

[483] See *Mersey Care NHS Trust v Ackroyd (No 2)* (n 482 above); *Assistant Deputy Coroner for Inner West London v Channel 4 Television* [2008] 1 WLR 945, para 25; for the arguments in favour of this approach see H Fenwick and G Phillipson, *Media Freedom under the Human Rights Act* (Oxford University Press, 2006), 352–370.

the competing interests.[484] The court will, in each case, consider the 'public interest' value of the disclosure and balance that against the 'confidentiality' rights of the person whose information has been disclosed.

(7) Obscenity and indecency

(a) Introduction

15.153   English law restricts freedom of expression by regulating content and prohibiting the publication of material which obscene or indecent.[485] The extent to which the display or publication of such material ought to be criminalized and the content of film, theatre and telecommunications broadcasts ought to be suppressed or regulated remains highly contentious. The Court of Human Rights has taken a cautious approach in this area[486] and its case law has had little impact on the approach of the domestic courts.

(b) The Obscene Publications Acts

15.154   **Introduction.**   The moral and legal debate concerning obscenity focuses on whether obscenity falls within the realm of protected expression at all;[487] and if so, whether there are justifiable bases for its restriction.[488] In practice, Parliament and the courts have had difficulty devising a test of obscenity which adequately distinguishes between expression which is defensible and expression which is not.[489]

15.155   The Obscene Publications Acts of 1959 and 1964[490] supersede but do not abolish the common law. They were a response to a number of prosecutions of serious literature during the 1950s followed by deliberations of a Parliamentary Committee and the recommendations of the 'Society of Authors' chaired by Sir Alan Herbert.[491] The Acts prohibit anyone from publishing an obscene article, whether for gain or not, unless it can be shown that the publication is justified as being for the common good[492] or that it can be shown

---

[484] *Assistant Deputy Coroner for Inner West London* (see n 483 above) para 25.

[485] For a fuller discussion, see G Robertson and A Nicol, *Media Law* (5th edn, Sweet & Maxwell, 2007), Chap 4; see also, H Fenwick and G Phillipson, (n 483 above) Chap 8.

[486] See para 15.387ff below.

[487] See discussion in E Barendt, *Freedom of Speech* (2nd edn, Oxford University Press, 2005), 355ff.

[488] See J Bakan, [1984] Ottawa L Re, 1; E Barendt, *Freedom of Speech* (see n 463 above) Chap X discusses the three main grounds: specific harm to individuals, impact on the moral tone of society (community standards), and the offensiveness principle.

[489] See eg, proposals in *Pornography: The Longford Report* (1972); *The Pollution of the Mind; New Proposals to Control Public Indecency and Obscenity*, The Society of Conservative Lawyers (1972); *The Obscenity Laws: Report of Arts Council Working Party* (1969); also proposals put forward by the Defence of Literature and the Arts Society (1978) 12 NLJ 423.

[490] See also: Children and Young Persons (Harmful Publications) Act 1955; Indecent Displays (Control) Act 1981; Criminal Justice Act 1988, s 160 in relation to offence of possession of indecent photograph of child; Theatres Act 1968; Post Office Act 1953, s 11; Customs Consolidation Act 1876, s 42 in relation to controls on importation of indecent or obscene articles; Judicial Proceedings (Regulation of Reports) Act 1926, s 1(1)(a) in relation to indecent details of legal proceedings.

[491] See C H Rolph, *Books in the Dock* (Andre Deutsch, 1969), 93; G Robertson, *Obscenity* (Weidenfeld and Nicholson, 1979), Chap 2; G Robertson and A Nicol, *Media Law* (5th edn, Sweet & Maxwell, 2007), 4-003ff; also *R v Martin Secker and Warburg Ltd* [1954] 1 WLR 1178, per Stable, J.

[492] See s 4 of the 1959 Act provides that there should be no conviction or forfeiture if it is proved that the article in question is justified as being for the common good on the ground that it is in the interests of science, literature, art, or learning.

that the publisher was ignorant of the nature of the article.[493] The legislation also provides powers of search and seizure, and for forfeiture of obscene articles upon conviction. The restrictions imposed by these Acts are likely to be held to be compatible with Article 10.[494]

Definition of obscenity. The statutory definition of obscenity provides that an article is **15.156** 'obscene' if its effect tends to:

> deprave and corrupt persons who are likely, having regard to all relevant circumstances, to read, see or hear the matter contained or embodied in it.[495]

This is the common law *Hicklin*[496] test, modified (to redefine the class of persons liable to be depraved) so as to include those to whom the material is likely to be distributed, circulated or offered for sale.[497] The result is that, for example, material intended for adults will not be 'obscene' merely because it would tend to corrupt a young person, to whom it would not normally be made available. In addition, there is authority for the suggestion that 'persons' means a 'significant proportion' of the likely readers,[498] and that 'likely readers' will only be excluded from consideration if they are negligible in number.[499] The provision protects not only the innocent, but also those whose morals are already in a state of corruption because it is fallacious to assume that they cannot be further depraved.[500]

The phrase 'deprave and corrupt' refers to the mental and moral corruption originally pro- **15.157** pounded by Lord Cockburn CJ in *R v Hicklin*.[501] Depravity is not confined to sexual matters;[502] and sexual explicitness does not necessarily amount to obscenity.[503] Even the fact that an article is 'filthy' or 'lewd' may not be sufficient: it is a defence to assert that the article is so disgusting that, far from corrupting the individual, it would cause him to revolt from the activity it describes.[504] The decision in *R v Calder and Boyars Ltd*[505] suggests that the number of readers susceptible, the strength of the tendency to corrupt and deprave, and

---

[493] See s 2(5) of the 1959 Act provides that 'a person shall not be convicted of an offence against this section if he proves that he had not examined the article in respect of which he is charged and had no reasonable cause to suspect that it was such that *his publication* of it would make him liable to be convicted of an offence against this section'. The 1964 Act, s 1(3), amends the 1959 reference to 'his publication' of the article to read 'his having of it'.

[494] The only direct challenge was in *R v Perrin* ([2002] EWCA Crim 747) where it was held that Parliament was 'entitled to conclude' that restrictions on the publication of obscene material was necessary in a democratic society; on the basis of a very general 'balancing' test, see also *Perrin v United Kingdom*, Decision of 18 October 2005 (inadmissible), see para 15.391 below.

[495] Obscene Publications Act 1959, s 1(1).

[496] *R v Hicklin* (1868) LR 3 QB 360, 371. The old test was 'whether the tendency of the matter charged as obscenity is to deprave and corrupt those whose minds are open to such immoral influences and into whose hands such a publication might fall'.

[497] As suggested by *R v Martin Secker and Warburg Ltd* [1954] 1 WLR 1138.

[498] *R v Calder and Boyars Ltd* [1969] 1 QB 151.

[499] *DPP v Whyte* [1972] AC 849.

[500] Ibid.

[501] (1868) LR 3 QB 360.

[502] *John Calder (Publications) Ltd v Powell* [1965] 1 QB 509.

[503] *R v Stanley* [1965] 2 QB 327; *Darbo v DPP* [1992] Crim LR 56.

[504] *R v Anderson* [1972] 1 QB 304.

[505] [1969] 1 QB 151.

the nature of the corruption or depravity are all elements which should be considered.[506] The purpose or intention of the publisher is, however, irrelevant, for the test for obscenity depends on the article itself.[507]

15.158 **The offences.** It is an offence to publish an obscene article [508] or to have an obscene article for publication for gain.[509] The maximum penalty is three years' imprisonment on trial on indictment. An 'article' includes anything 'containing or embodying matter to be read or looked at or both, any sound record and any film or other record of a picture or pictures'.[510] This includes photographic negatives[511] video cassettes[512] and images on computer disc in digitised form.[513] 'Publication' is given a wide definition[514] and includes giving or lending. It is committed by a photographic developer who develops film sent by customers depicting obscene acts, makes prints and sends them to the customers[515] and when material is downloaded onto a computer.[516] However, mere possession of obscene material is not publication

15.159 **Seizure and forfeiture.** By section 3 of the Obscene Publications Act 1959 a justice of the peace can issue a warrant for the search and seizure of obscene articles kept for publication for gain. The articles must be brought before the justice who may issue a summons to the occupier to show cause why the articles should not be forfeited.[517] This provision also applies to articles kept for publication abroad.[518] This procedure is often used by the police to avoid having to prove obscenity offences at a jury trial.[519]

15.160 **Defence of public good.** Section 4 of the Obscene Publications Act 1959 provides that there should be no conviction or forfeiture:

> if it is proved that publication of the article in question is justified as being for the common good on the ground that it is in the interests of science, literature, art or learning or of other objects of general concern.

---

[506] See also *Hoare v United Kingdom* [1997] EHRLR 678 (the applicant had engaged in publication and distribution of pornographic videotapes by post: a brochure describing the contents of the videos was provided to those who responded to an advertisement in a Sunday paper, and the videos distributed thereafter, upon request. The applicant was convicted, and given a 30-month prison sentence. His argument that the videos could not deprave or corrupt since only those who shared his interests would have purchased them from the brochure was rejected by the EComm HR).

[507] *R v Shaw* [1962] AC 220: affirmed on other grounds, [1962] AC 237; followed in *Knuller (Publishing, Printing and Promotions) Ltd v DPP* [1973] AC 435.

[508] Obscene Publications Act 1959, s 2(1).

[509] Obscene Publications Act 1964, s 1(2) a person is deemed to have an article for publication for gain if, with a 'view to publication', he has it in his ownership, possession or control.

[510] Obscene Publications Act 1959, s 1(2).

[511] Publications Act 1964, s 2(1).

[512] *A-G's Reference (No 5 of 1980)* [1981] 1 WLR 88.

[513] *R v Fellows* [1997] 2 All ER 548.

[514] Obscene Publications Act 1959, s 1(3).

[515] *R v Taylor (Alan)* [1995] 1 Cr App R 131.

[516] *R v Waddon*, 6 April 2000, CA.

[517] See *Olympia, Press v Hollis* [1973] 1 WLR 1520, see also R Stone, 'Obscene Publications: The Problems Persist' [1986] Crim PR 139.

[518] *Gold Star Publications Ltd v DPP* [1981] 1 WLR 732.

[519] See the criticism by G Robertson and A Nicol, *Media Law* (5th edn, Sweet & Maxwell, 2007), 4-036.

The defence will only be considered once it is established that an article is obscene,[520] and may be assisted by expert evidence concerning the literary or other merits[521] of the material in question.[522] 'Learning' means the 'product of scholarship'[523] and, as a result, a publication used for the purposes of teaching cannot be defended under section 4.

(c) Other obscenity and indecency offences

Common law. The Obscene Publications Act 1959 was intended to protect defendants **15.161** against prosecution for obscene libel. Thus, section 2(4) provides that an article shall not be proceeded against at common law 'where it is of the essence of the offence that the matter is obscene'. However, this does not prevent prosecutions being brought at common law on the basis that the essence of the offence is 'indecency'. This is not confined to sexual indecency but covers any conduct which an ordinary person would find to be 'shocking, disgusting or revolting'.[524] The result is that the defence of 'public good' is not available. Moreover, the common law offences of conspiracy to corrupt public morals[525] and of outraging public decency[526] are unaffected by the legislation.[527]

Statutory indecency offences. It is an offence publicly to display 'indecent matter'.[528] It **15.162** appears that material can be 'indecent' for these purposes without being obscene.[529] A public place does not include a place to which the public only have access on payment or a shop to which the public can only gain access by passing a warning sign.[530]

By section 85 of the Postal Services Act 2000 it is an offence to enclose in a postal packet **15.163** 'any indecent or obscene print, painting, photograph, lithograph, engraving, cinematograph film book and written communication or any indecent or obscene article. . .' The case of *R v Kirk*[531] concerned an anti vivisection campaigner who was convicted of this offence after sending sent graphic images of animal experiments to various individuals through the post. It was held that section 85 was compatible with Article 10: it was

---

[520] *R v Calder and Boyars Ltd* [1969] 1 QB 151; *DPP v Jordan* [1977] AC 699.

[521] In *John Calder Publications v Powell* [1965] 1 QB 509 it was held that a court is entitled to reject even favourable evidence and hold that the publication is not justified as being for the public good.

[522] s 4(2).

[523] *A-G's Reference (No 3 of 1977)* [1978] 1 WLR 1123.

[524] *Knuller v DPP* [1973] AC 435, 458; and see also *R v Stanley* [1965] 2 QB 327 ('offending against recognized standards of propriety at the lower end of the scale').

[525] This would not entail the publication of the obscenity, but an agreement to do an act of a kind that may corrupt. See *Shaw v DPP* [1962] AC 220, regarding publication of a magazine offering the services of prostitutes; *Knuller v DPP* (see n 524 above).

[526] See *R v Gibson* [1990] 2 QB 619; the criminal offence of outraging public decency, which prohibits the public display of offensive material, is aimed at protecting individuals from the shock or offence of exposure to certain material, rather than protecting public morals—it is not necessary to prove an intention to outrage decency; see also cases on conspiracy to corrupt public morals: *Shaw v DPP* (n 525 above) and *Knuller v DPP* (n 524 above) ; for criticism of this decision see H Fenwick and G Phillipson, *Media Freedom under the Human Rights Act* (Oxford University Press, 2006), 474–477.

[527] See generally, G Robertson and A Nicol (see n 519 above) 4-61-4-64.

[528] Indecent Displays (Control) Act 1981, s 1.

[529] Cf *R v Stanley* (see n 524 above).

[530] Indecent Displays (Control) Act 1981, s 1(3).

[531] [2006] Crim LR 850.

proportionate to restrict the transmission of indecent and obscene material through the post. Unfortunately, the Court did not consider whether the restriction was justified on facts of the case, basing itself on the erroneous approach that if the legislation was, in general, compatible then any prosecution brought under it would not breach Article 10.

15.164 **Protection of children.** Under the Protection of Children Act 1978 it is an offence to take or make or permit to be taken or made any indecent photograph of a child (that is, a person under 16),[532] to distribute or show such photographs,[533] to possess them with a view to distribution,[534] or to publish an advertisement likely to be understood as conveying that the advertiser distributes or shows such indecent photographs.[535] The offence covers the downloading of images from the internet or printing them off.[536] 'Indecent photographs' include films, film negatives, and video recordings. The only defence to the offence of taking a photograph is that it is not 'indecent'. The motive for taking the photograph is irrelevant.[537] This means that, for example, taking a photograph for medical purposes would involve the commission of the offence. It is also an offence to possess an indecent picture of a child.[538] It is a defence to show a legitimate reason for possessing the photograph.

15.165 In *R v Smethurst*[539] it was held that the offence of making indecent photographs of children contrary to section 1(1)(a) of the Protection of Children Act 1978 did not contravene Article 10. The offence was 'there for the prevention of crime, for the protection of morals and, in particular, for the protection of children from being exploited' which, the court said, 'is undoubtedly a matter which is necessary in a democratic society'. The court did not go on to analyse the proportionality of the sanctions.

15.166 **Malicious communications.** By section 1 of the Malicious Communications Act 1988 it is an offence to send to another person a letter or article which conveys a threat, or information which is known to be false or any other article 'which is, in whole or part, of an indecent or grossly offensive nature' if the purpose of the communication is to cause distress or anxiety. In *Connolly v DPP*[540] it was held that the conviction under this provision of an anti-abortion campaigner who sent photographs of an aborted foetuses to chemists stocking the morning after pill was justified under Article 10. The Court held that the Act should be interpreted compatibly with Article 10, either by giving a heightened meaning to the requirement that the communication be 'grossly offensive' or 'indecent' or by reading in a provision that the section would not apply where to create an offence would breach Convention rights. The prosecution was for the legitimate aim of protecting the rights of others to be protected from receiving such material and, in the circumstances, it was necessary in a democratic society.

---

[532] See s 1(1)(a).
[533] See s 1(1)(b).
[534] See s 1(1)(c).
[535] See s 1(1)(d).
[536] *R v Bowden* [2001] 1 QB 88.
[537] *R v Graham-Kerr* [1988] 1 WLR 1098.
[538] Criminal Justice Act 1988, s 160.
[539] [2002] 2 Cr App R 6; this area was the subject of a careful and detailed analysis by the Supreme Court of Canada in *R v Sharpe* [2001] 1 SCR 45, see para 15.449 below.
[540] [2007] 2 All ER 1012.

By section 127(1)(a) of the Communications Act 2003 a person is guilty of an offence if he **15.167** sends by means of a public electronic communications network a message or other matter that was grossly offensive or of an indecent, obscene or menacing character. The purpose of this provision is to prohibit the use of a public service for the transmission of communications which contravene the basic standards of our society.[541] Under this provision the very act of sending the message over the public communications network constitutes the offence. This provision is compatible with Article 10. It is prescribed by law, is directed to the legitimate aim of preventing the use of a public electronic communications network for attacking the reputations and rights of others and goes no further than is necessary in a democratic society to achieve that end.[542]

Import of indecent material. The import into the United Kingdom of 'indecent or obscene **15.168** prints, paintings, photographs, books, cards, lithographic or other engravings or any other indecent or obscene articles' is prohibited.[543] The test of 'indecency' is much less strict than that under the Obscene Publications Act. However, it was held that insofar as this prohibition related to indecent articles imported from the EC it was in breach of Article 36[544] of the Treaty of European Union[545] and the Customs no longer seize material solely on the ground that it is 'indecent'. When considering a claim for forfeiture by the Customs, the court can order forfeiture if the material is 'obscene' within the definition in section 1 of the Obscene Publications Act 1959. The court does not have to go on to consider whether a section 4 'public good' defence might be available.[546]

(d) Licensing sex establishments

In recent times, the emphasis has been less on prosecuting those who distribute obscene **15.169** material and more on licensing their activities.[547] These licensing activities engage the Article 10 rights of includes the right to use particular premises to distribute pornographic books, videos and other articles but it is likely to be relatively easy to justify restrictions as pornography is low in the hierarchy of protected speech.[548] The requirement that video recordings with a classification of R18 could only be supplied from a licensed sex shop is a justified restriction under Article 10(2).[549]

---

[541] See *DPP v Collins* [2006] 1 WLR 2223 (racist telephone messages to an MP, the fact that the MP and his staff did not find the messages grossly offensive was irrelevant, HL overturned magistrates' view that the communications were not 'grossly offensive'); see the discussion of this case in G Robertson and A Nicol, *Media Law* (5th edn, Sweet & Maxwell, 2007), 4-058.

[542] Ibid, para 14.

[543] Customs Consolidation Act 1876, s 42; see generally, Robertson and Nicol (see n 541 above) 4-059.

[544] Formerly, Art 30 of the Treaty of Rome.

[545] *Conegate Ltd v HM Customs and Excise* [1987] QB 254.

[546] *R v Bow Street Metropolitan Stipendiary Magistrates, ex p Noncyp Ltd* [1990] 1 QB 123.

[547] See the comments of Lord Hoffmann in *Belfast City Council v Miss Behavin' Ltd* [2007] 1 WLR 1420, paras 1 and 2.

[548] Ibid, para 38 (Baroness Hale).

[549] *Interfact Ltd and Pabo Ltd v Liverpool City Council* [2005] EWHC 995 (Admin).

(8) Media regulation and censorship

(a) Introduction [550]

15.170 The regulation of broadcasting, theatre, film and video has evolved in Britain over a long period of time and reflects an ambiguous attitude towards the media, which has been seen as both providing important public benefits and as a source of potential harm. It raises issues concerning the independence of radio and television from government, political impartiality and the standards to be applied when regulating the content of broadcasts.

(b) Broadcasting regulation [551]

15.171 **Introduction.** In the 1950s, there was a movement from regulation by means of the criminal law to direct statutory regulation. This change coincided with the introduction of commercial television. In contrast to the absence of direct government regulation of news-papers, there was a perceived need for careful monitoring of television by a public body.

15.172 The Independent Broadcasting Authority ('IBA') was established in 1954 to ensure that nothing in independent television programming would offend against good taste, decency or public feeling or would be likely to encourage or incite to crime or to lead to disorder; that news was presented with accuracy and impartiality; and that impartiality of presenta-tion was preserved with respect to matters of political or industrial controversy or relating to current public policy.[552] The Board of Governors of the British Broadcasting Corporation ('BBC') in 1964 voluntarily undertook[553] to comply in general terms with the statutory duties imposed on independent television, so that in effect all broadcasting, both public and independent, was subjected to the same standards. In 1990 the Broadcasting Act replaced with the IBA with the Independent Television Commission and the Radio Authority.

15.173 **Ofcom.** The Communications Act 2003 merged, the Broadcasting Standards Commission ('the BSC') (which regulated all television and radio services provided by the BBC and other television and radio companies in the United Kingdom) and the Independent Television Commission (which regulated all non-BBC television) into a single regulator known as Ofcom. This is responsible for the licensing of broadcasters and its decisions as to whether or not licences are granted engage Article 10 although in practice, if the

---

[550] For a fuller treatment, see for example T Gibbons, *Regulating the Media* (2nd edn, Sweet & Maxwell, 1998); R Craufurd Smith, *Broadcasting Law and Fundamental Rights* (Clarendon Press, 1997); for a discus-sion of the impact of the HRA see H Fenwick and G Phillipson, *Media Freedom under the Human Rights Act* (Oxford University Press, 2006), Chaps 10 to 12.

[551] See eg, A Briggs, *The History of Broadcasting in the UK, Vol I: The Birth of Broadcasting* (Oxford University Press 1961); *Vol II: The Golden Age of Wireless* (Oxford University Press 1965); *Vol IV: Sound and Vision* (1979); B Sendall, *Independent Television in Britain; Origin and Foundations 1946–62* (Macmillan, 1982); R Negrine (ed), *Cable Television and the Future of Broadcasting* (Croom Helm, 1985); T Hollins, *Beyond Broadcasting to the Cable Age* (BFI, 1984).

[552] See Broadcasting Act 1981, s 4.

[553] Letter from Lord Normanbrook, Chairman of the BBC to the Postmaster-General 19 June 1964: 'The Board accept that so far as possible the programmes for which they are responsible should not offend against good taste or decency, or be likely to encourage crime or disorder, or be offensive to public feeling. In judging what is suitable for inclusion in programmes, they will pay special regard to the need to ensure that broadcasts designed to stimulate thought do not so far depart from their intention as to give general offence.'

provisions of the 2003 Act in relation to licensing are complied with challenges under the Convention are most unlikely to succeed.[554]

The 2003 Act requires Ofcom to draw up a code for television and radio, covering stand-**15.174** ards in programmes, sponsorship, fairness and privacy. This Code is known as the Ofcom Broadcasting Code ('the Ofcom Code'), the latest edition of which is dated October 2008. Ofcom must secure the standards objectives set out in the 2003 Act. This not only involves setting minimum standards but also such other standards as may be appropriate.[555] Independent broadcasters are directly bound by the code[556] and the BBC's Agreement with the Government now contains an obligation to comply with the codes, save in relation to impartiality and accuracy, elections and sponsorship and commercial references in which areas the BBC retains responsibility.[557]

The Ofcom Code covers ten specific areas,[558] including protection of the under-18s, harm **15.175** and offence, crime, religion, due impartiality and due accuracy, elections, fairness, privacy,[559] sponsorship and commercial references. By section 237 of the 2003 Act Ofcom has powers to impose sanctions on broadcasters who breach the code, including fines or the withdrawal of the licences of independent broadcasters.

Review by the courts. The courts have, in general, been reluctant to interfere with the **15.176** decisions of broadcasters and specialist regulators. In the leading case of *R (Prolife Alliance) v British Broadcasting Corporation*[560] the applicants sought to overturn a decision by the BBC to refuse to broadcast a party election broadcast on the ground that it contained offensive material. The broadcast contained graphic images of abortion and the BBC took the view that it did not comply with the BBC's producer's guidelines or the ITC programme code regarding taste and decency. The Court of Appeal held that the broadcasters' refusal to transmit the broadcast failed to give sufficient weight to the importance of free speech in the political arena. This decision was overturned by the House of Lords on the ground that the Court, in the exercise of its supervisory role, should not interfere with the broadcasters' decision that material was offensive. The broadcasters' application of the statutory criteria could not be faulted. It was held that the Court of Appeal was wrong to carry out its own balancing exercise between the requirements of freedom of political speech and the protection of the public from the broadcasting of offensive material. It is suggested that the House of Lords wrongly failed to subject to the decision of the BBC to strict scrutiny (as required by Article 10); and that the result in the Court of Appeal (although not all of its reasoning) is to be preferred.[561]

---

[554] See eg, *R (Wildman) v Ofcom* [2005] EWHC 1573 (Admin).

[555] See 2003 Act, s 3(1)(a) and (b), (2)(e) and (f) and (4)(b)(g)(h)(j)(k) and (l), 319, 320, 321, 325, and 326 and s 107(1) of the Broadcasting Act 1996 Act.

[556] Communications Act 2003, s 326.

[557] G Robertson and A Nicol, *Media Law* (5th edn, Sweet & Maxwell, 2007), para 16-019.

[558] For a detailed consideration of the provisions of the Code see ibid, paras 16-020 to 16-060.

[559] For the provisions of the Ofcom Code relating to privacy see para 12.99ff above.

[560] [2004] 1 AC 185; See generally, H Fenwick and G Phillipson, *Media Freedom under the Human Rights Act* (Oxford University Press, 2006), 577–592.

[561] See H Fenwick and G Phillipson (n 560 above), 586–592 and I Hare 'Debating Abortion – the Right to Offend Gratuitously', (2003) 62 CLJ 525 but see A Geddis 'If Thy Right Eye Offend Thee Pluck it Out'

15.177 **Political advertising.** Political advertising is prohibited by section 321(2) of the 2003 Act.[562] This includes 'an advertisement which is inserted by or on behalf of a body whose objects are wholly or mainly of a political nature'. When the 2003 Act was before Parliament the Government indicated that it was not sure that this prohibition was compatible with the Convention.[563] In the case of *R (Animal Defenders) v Secretary of State for Culture, Media and Sport*[564] a non-profit-making company the aims of which included the suppression, by lawful means, of all forms of cruelty to animals sought a declaration of incompatibility under section 4 of the HRA.[565] This application was dismissed by the House of Lords that the interference was necessary in a democratic society to protect the rights of others under Article 10(2). Lord Bingham (with whom the other members of the Judicial Committee agreed) said that although debate was fundamental to the democratic process:

> it is highly desirable that the playing field of debate should be so far as practicable level. This is achieved where, in public discussion, differing views are expressed, contradicted, answered and debated. It is the duty of broadcasters to achieve this object in an impartial way by presenting balanced programmes in which all lawful views may be ventilated. It is not achieved if political parties can, in proportion to their resources, buy unlimited opportunities to advertise in the most effective media, so that elections become little more than an auction. Nor is it achieved if well-endowed interests which are not political parties are able to use the power of the purse to give enhanced prominence to views which may be true or false, attractive to progressive minds or unattractive, beneficial or injurious. The risk is that objects which are essentially political may come to be accepted by the public not because they are shown in public debate to be right but because, by dint of constant repetition, the public has been conditioned to accept them. The rights of others which a restriction on the exercise of the right to free expression may properly be designed to protect must, in my judgment, include a right to be protected against the potential mischief of partial political advertising.[566]

(c) The DA Notice system [567]

15.178 The Defence Press and Broadcasting Advisory Committee ('DPBAC') is a joint committee of the Ministry of Defence, publishers and broadcasters. It offers informal advice to the press on the content of proposed publications and broadcasts, in the interests of and for the protection of national security. The DPBAC acts as a cooperative consultative and negotiating body between the media and the Ministry: it has no judicial function and participation by the press in the DA Notice system is entirely voluntary.

(2003) 66 MLR 885 defending the House of Lords' approach.

[562] See generally, Robertson and Nicol (see n 557 above), paras 16-062 to 16-063.

[563] As a result of decision of the Court of Human Rights in *VgT Verein gegen Tierfabriken v Switzerland* (2001) 34 EHRR 159 that such a blanket ban was a violation of Art 10, see para 15.375A below.

[564] [2008] 2 WLR 781.

[565] See para 4.68ff above.

[566] Ibid, para 28.

[567] See D Fairley, 'D Notices, Official Secrets and the Law' (1990) 10 OJLS 430 ('D Notices' were renamed 'Defence Advisory Notices' or 'DA Notices' in 1993) and P Sadler 'Still keeping secrets? The DA-Notice system post 9/11' (2007) 12 Comms L 205.

The function of the DPBAC, as broadly defined by the Ministry of Defence, is to review **15.179** proposed publications to identify information that the Government considers it necessary to keep secret. There are five 'standing' DA Notices:[568]

- DA-Notice 01: Military Operations, Plans & Capabilities
- DA-Notice 02: Nuclear & Non-Nuclear Weapons & Equipment
- DA-Notice 03: Ciphers & Secure Communications
- DA-Notice 04: Sensitive Installations & Home Addresses
- DA-Notice 05: United Kingdom Security & Intelligence Services and Special Service

A publisher or broadcaster may itself approach the Committee to ask its advice on a pro- **15.180** posed publication. The Committee may on, the other hand, initiate contact.[569] If the DPBAC concludes that the contents of a publication threaten national security in one of its areas of responsibility, it will suggest that changes are made. If the advice is not accepted, it will issue a DA Notice.

The DA Notice serves solely as a warning device. The fact that a DA Notice has no legal **15.181** force has both positive and negative implications: the media can be assured that it will not be prosecuted merely for defying the advice of the Committee; on the other hand, the DPBAC has no power to provide security clearance and provides a publisher with no defence or justification should the Government seek to restrain the publication under the Official Secrets Act [570] or on grounds of breach of confidence.[571]

(d) Theatre, film, and video censorship

Theatres. The Theatres Act 1968 removed the official censorship of theatrical productions **15.182** so that theatre performances are now only subject to the criminal law. By section 2(4) of the Act, proceedings at common law cannot be brought in respect of a performance of a play where it is of the essence of the offence that it was obscene, indecent, offensive, disgusting or injurious to morality.[572] These have been replaced by a new offence of 'obscenity in a play'.

Film and video censorship. Film censorship continues to be governed by the Cinemas **15.183** Act 1985 which establishes a licensing requirement for premises used for film exhibitions.

---

[568] See <http://www.dnotice.org.uk>.

[569] If a publisher does not normally participate in the DA Notice system, the DPBAC will send it a copy of the relevant DA Notice and a guide to the system called the *General Introduction to the DA Notices*.

[570] There is, however, substantial overlap between the contents of a DA Notice and the relevant Government legislation in the area. DA Notice 5 in relation to United Kingdom Security and Intelligence Services, for example, requests that the media refrain from publishing references to an extensive list of specific matters that comes close to comprehensive coverage of the matters that could be caught by the Official Secrets Act.

[571] For example, when the BBC approached the DPBAC in regard to a radio series exploring aspects of national security in the wake of the *Spycatcher* litigation, it was told that advice was not necessary: neverthe-less, the Government sought and obtained injunctions restraining the broadcasts on grounds of breach of confidence. Although the Government eventually acknowledged that the programmes were not a threat and the injunctions were lifted, the BBC delayed their broadcast.

[572] For a discussion of this provision, see *R (Green) v City of Westminster Magistrates Court* [2008] EMLR 15, paras 18 to 23.

The Act also imposes a duty on the licensing authority[573] to define regulations and conditions for the admission of children to such exhibitions. Furthermore, the Act authorizes the licensing body to make regulations for the 'safety', 'health', and 'welfare' of children attending film exhibitions.

15.184 In 1912, the British Board of Film Censors was established by the film industry to provide guidance to local authorities which had been given licensing powers under the Cinematograph Act 1909.[574] The decisions and classification criteria of the non-statutory body were well accepted and the objective of the BBFC largely achieved. Although there has been controversy over specific films, most councils have generally been happy to rely upon the judgment of the BBFC. The Board, renamed the British Board of Film Classification, is also the authority designated by the Home Secretary to deal with the arrangements for certifying videos under section 4(1) of the Video Recordings Act 1984 as:

> the authority responsible for making arrangements
>
> (a) for determining, for the purposes of [the] Act whether or not video works are suitable for classification certificates to be issued in respect of them, having special regard to the likelihood of video works in respect of which such certificates have been issued being viewed in the home,
>
> (b) in the case of works which are determined in accordance with the arrangements to be so suitable
>
> > (i) for making such other determinations as are required for the issue of classification certificates, and
> >
> > (ii) for issuing such certificates. . .

15.185 The Video Recordings Act 1984 gives rise to a number of problems. First, it requires classification of almost all video recordings,[575] whether or not they have already been broadcast on television. The BBFC will censor videos containing a wide range of material including cruelty to animals, drug use, violence, sexual violence and blasphemy.[576] Decisions regarding classification may be appealed to the Video Appeals Committee,[577] which is selected by the BBFC. The decision of the Video Appeals Committee to certify the film, called 'Visions of Ecstasy', on the ground of blasphemy resulted in an unsuccessful application to the Court of Human Rights in *Wingrove v United Kingdom*.[578]

---

[573] The licensing authorities are now London boroughs and district councils across the country: see Cinemas Act 1985, ss 3(10), 21.

[574] See G Robertson and A Nicol, *Media Law* (5th edn, Sweet & Maxwell, 2007), 15-003ff.

[575] For exemptions, see Cinemas Act 1985, s 2.

[576] See Robertson and Nicol (see n 574 above) 15-011ff.

[577] See eg, *R v Video Appeals Committee of the British Board of Film Classification ex p British Board of Film Classification*, [2000] EMLR 850; *R (British Board of Film Classification) v Video Appeals Committee* [2008] 1 WLR 1658.

[578] (1996) 24 EHRR 1, see para 15.390 below.

The BBFC now classifies films and videos in accordance with its published guidelines.[579] It **15.186** often makes distribution under a particular classification conditional upon cuts being made to the film.

The power of local authorities to license cinemas is contained in the Cinemas Act 1985. It **15.187** is an offence to use unlicensed premises for film exhibition.[580] Conditions, which usually require compliance with BBFC classifications, may be attached to licences.[581] Local authorities can, however, prohibit the showing of films which the BBFC have certified for viewing.[582] Local authorities also have licensing powers under which they regulate sex cinemas.[583]

(9) Freedom of expression and the criminal law

(a) Introduction

The criminal law has traditionally placed significant restrictions on freedom of expression. **15.188** At common law there were four related offences: obscene libel, blasphemous libel, seditious libel and defamatory or criminal libel. The first of these has been codified by statute. This is dealt with in section 7 above.[584] The common law offence of blasphemous libel was abolished by section 79 of the Criminal Justice and Immigration Act 2008.[585] In addition, the common law powers of the police in relation to breach of the peace can restrict freedom of expression. There are a large number of statutory offences which affect expression. Finally, there are statutory restrictions on police powers to seize 'journalistic material' for the purposes of investigation of criminal offences. Offences restricting the disclosure of official information are considered in Part 10 below.

When a court is considering a criminal prosecution when the defendant's Article 10 rights **15.189** are engaged it should approach the matter in three stages:[586]

- *Is the defendant liable under ordinary principles of criminal law?* If not, then there is no need for the court to consider Article 10 at all, if so then is necessary to go to the second stage.
- *Is the conviction and punishment of the defendant justified under Article 10(2)?* The Court must consider whether, on the facts, the conviction and sentence of the defendant is a prescribed by law, for a legitimate aim and 'necessary in a democratic society', that is, a proportionate interference with his Article 10 rights. If the answer to this question is 'yes'

---

[579] U (universal); Uc (universal and suitable for young children); PG (parental guidance required); 12 (passed only for persons 12 years and over); 15 (passed only for persons 15 years and over); 18 (passed only for persons 18 years and over); R18 (restricted 18: passed only for distribution through specially licensed cinemas or sex shops to which no one under 18 is admitted).

[580] See s 10; licences are not required for exhibitions which are not for private gain.

[581] See s 1(3).

[582] Notorious examples include 'Ulysses' and 'The Life of Brian' which were banned in many local authority areas; see generally, G Robertson and A Nicol, *Media Law* (5th edn, Sweet & Maxwell, 2007), 15-006.

[583] Local Government (Miscellaneous Provisions) Act 1982, Sch 3.

[584] See para 15.153ff above.

[585] This provision came into effect on 8 July 2008; see generally, para 14.18ff above.

[586] See generally the illuminating article by S Turenne, 'The compatibility of criminal liability with freedom of expression' [2007] Crim LR 866 to which this discussion is indebted.

then the Court can convict the defendant. If the answer is 'no' then it must consider the third question.

- *Can the statute under which the defendant was convicted be read and given effect in a way which is compatible with the defendant's Article 10 rights?* In other words, the court must apply section 3 of the HRA.[587] If it is not possible to read and give effect to the statute in a way which is compatible with Article 10 then the court should consider making a declaration of incompatibility.[588]

This approach has not been consistently applied in the post-HRA criminal cases.

(b) Common law

15.190 **Seditious libel.** It is a common law offence to publish words with a seditious intention. The words may be written or spoken. In *R v Chief Metropolitan Stipendiary Magistrate, ex p Choudhury*[589] the offence was confined to

> an intention to incite to violence or create public disturbance or disorder against His Majesty or the institutions of government. Proof of an intention to promote feelings of ill-will and hostility between different classes of subjects does not alone establish a seditious intention. Not only must there be proof of an incitement to violence in this connection but it must be violence or resistance or defiance for the purpose of disturbing constituted authority.[590]

Seditious libel involves demonstration of a more restrictive 'mental element' than other common law libel offences. It seems, however, that the Divisional Court has extended the offence by the reference to the 'disturbance of constituted authority'[591] but the precise scope of the offence is uncertain.

15.191 Prosecutions for seditious libel are very rare, with only one prosecution in the past 80 years. This was the 1947 case of *R v Caunt*[592] which concerned an article attacking British Jews. The editor was acquitted. On the analysis of the offence put forward in *Ex parte Choudhury*,[593] it would appear that the judge was wrong to hold that the offence could extend to the stirring up of racial hatred or class violence. In *R (Green) v City of Westminster Magistrates Court*[594] the Administrative Court described the offence as 'obsolete' and said that it was difficult, if not impossible, to envisage circumstances in which a prosecution for seditious libel would be appropriate.

15.192 **Defamatory or criminal libel.**[595] The common law offence of 'defamatory' libel is the most common of the common law libel offences and is often known as 'criminal libel'. The

---

[587] See para 4.05ff above.

[588] See para 4.68ff above.

[589] [1991] 1 QB 429.

[590] Ibid, 453.

[591] See D Feldman, *Civil Liberties and Human Rights in England and Wales* (2nd edn, Oxford University Press, 2002), 900.

[592] Noted in (1947) 64 LQR 203; but see *R v Aldred* (1909) 22 Cox CC 1 (published statements that political assassination in the cause of Indian independence were not murder constituted the offence).

[593] See n 589 above.

[594] [2008] EMLR 15, para 22.

[595] See Law Commission, *Report on Criminal Libel* (Law Com No 149, Cmnd 9618, 1985) and *Gatley on Libel and Slander* (11th edn, Sweet & Maxwell, 2008), Chap 24.

publication must be in permanent form and the words must tend to vilify a person and to bring them into hatred, contempt and ridicule.[596] Furthermore, the words must constitute a 'serious' and not a trivial libel.[597] It is no longer necessary, however, that the libel relates to a public figure or that it should have a tendency to provoke the person defamed to commit a breach of the peace.[598] The mental element of the offence is not clear. It may be that all that is required is an intention to publish the words[599] or perhaps to prove an intention to defame.[600]

Although the principles of law applicable to civil and criminal libels are for the most part similar,[601] there are some important differences. First, it appears that whereas in civil cases, the burden of establishing defences is on the defendant, once a defence to criminal libel is raised the burden is on the prosecution to negative it.[602] Second, while a civil action requires publication of the statement to a third person, it appears that publication to the defamed person alone will sustain a prosecution in criminal libel.[603] Third, no civil action lies against a dead person, but if the libel was intended or tends to damage living persons or to cause a breach of the peace, it may be criminally prosecuted. Fourth, no civil action for libel can be aimed at a group or class of people; but such defamation will be subject to the criminal law if it tends to excite public hatred against the class.[604] Finally, the truth of a defamatory statement has always been an absolute defence to an action under the civil law; while in the criminal law this was not so at common law. There is, however, a statutory defence of truth to an action in criminal libel, if publication is for the public benefit.[605] **15.193**

Section 8 of the Law of Libel Amendment Act 1888 requires that leave must be obtained before bringing a prosecution for criminal libel against a proprietor, publisher, editor or any other person responsible for publishing a newspaper. It has been held that section 8 does not apply to prosecutions of individual journalists.[606] However, there is a strong argument that the section should now be construed in the light of Article 10 to require leave in such cases.[607] A judge should not give leave unless there is a clear *prima facie* case and the public interest requires the institution of criminal proceedings.[608] **15.194**

---

[596] This is the traditional definition of libel and continues to apply in the criminal law: see *Goldsmith v Pressdram* [1977] QB 83, 87.

[597] See *Gleaves v Deakin* [1980] AC 477, 487, 495; see generally, *Gatley on Libel and Slander* (n 595 above), para 24.2.

[598] *R v Wicks* [1936] 1 All ER 384, 386; *Gleaves v Deakin* (see n 597 above) 498g.

[599] *R v Wicks* (see n 598 above).

[600] *Gatley on Libel and Slander* (see n 595 above) para 22.3.

[601] For example, where an occasion is privileged at common law it will be privileged in criminal cases, see *Gatley on Libel and Slander* (see n 595 above), para 24.8.

[602] See the discussion in *Worme v Commissioner of Police* [2004] 2 AC 430, paras 24 to 30, applying the decision of Hunt J in *Spautz v Williams* [1983] 2 NSWLR 506.

[603] Although *Gatley on Libel and Slander* (see n 595 above) suggests that this is no longer the case, see para 24.5.

[604] See *R v Williams* (1822) 5 B & Ald 595.

[605] Libel Act 1843, s 6.

[606] See *Desmond v Thorne* [1983] 1 WLR 163; *Gleaves v Insall* [1999] EMLR 779 and see *Gatley on Libel and Slander* (n 595 above) para 24.10.

[607] See the discussion in G Robertson and A Nicol, *Media Law* (5th edn, Sweet & Maxwell, 2007), para 3-083.

[608] See *Goldsmith v Pressdram* [1977] QB 83, 89; and *Desmond v Thorne* (see n 606 above).

15.195 In *Worme v Commissioner of Police*[609] the Privy Council considered whether the crime of criminal libel was consistent with the right to freedom of expression in the Constitution of Grenada. It held that the offence had a legitimate objective and was rationally connected to it. Taking into account the fact that criminal libel in one form or another was found in the law of England, Canada and Australia, it was held that the crime was a justifiable part of the law of Grenada.[610]

15.196 **Breach of the peace.** At common law all police officers and citizens can seek to prevent, by arrest or action short of arrest, any breach of the peace occurring in their presence, or which they reasonably believed was about to occur. This can involved, for example, detaining those involved in public protests. However, the Article 10 and 11 rights of protestors must be taken into account and the police he police cannot take whatever action short of arrest they reasonably judged to be reasonable to prevent a breach of the peace which was not sufficiently imminent to justify arrest.[611] The action of the police in stopping a coach on the way to a protest was disproportionate restriction on the claimant's rights under Articles 10 and 11.[612]

(c) Public order offences

15.197 **Introduction.** The Public Order Act 1986 ('POA') contains a number of offences which potentially impact on freedom of expression. It criminalizes the use of threatening, abusive or insulting words or behaviour which is likely to cause, in general terms, public disorder. In some circumstances these provisions may be applicable to racially motivated actions. Section 4 provides that it is an offence to use threatening, abusive or insulting words or behaviour or to distribute or display such writing, signs or other visible representation, with intent to cause a person to believe that immediate unlawful violence will be used against him or to provoke him to use violence. Section 4A makes it an offence to cause harassment, alarm or distress with intent. Section 5 prohibits disorderly behaviour which is causes harassment, alarm or distress. A criminal offence will be committed under that section if words or behaviour that are threatening, abusive or insulting are used or any such material displayed 'within the hearing of a person likely to be caused harassment, alarm or distress'.[613]

15.198 These provisions must be construed in a way which is consistent with Article 10. Thus in *Percy v DPP*[614] the appellant was a protester against US military policy who had defaced the American flag. She was convicted of using threatening, abusive and insulting words or behaviour likely to cause distress contrary to section 5 of the Public Order Act 1986. The Administrative Court overturned the conviction, holding that it was incompatible with Article 10 of the Convention. The behaviour had been insulting but there had been no risk of disorder and a high threshold had to be overcome before interference with an individual's

---

[609] See n 602 above.

[610] Particular reliance was placed on the Canadian case of *R v Lucas* [1998] 1 SCR 439, see para 15.436 below.

[611] *R (Laporte) v Chief Constable of Gloucestershire Constabulary* [2007] 2 AC 105.

[612] Ibid, (Lord Bingham, Lord Rodger, Lord Carswell, and Lord Mance).

[613] Animal rights demonstrators using signs designed to shock have been charged with these offences.

[614] [1995] 1 WLR 1382; see also *Hutchinson v Newbury Magistrates*, 9 October 2000, DC.

Article 10 rights was permitted. The restriction was not 'strictly necessary'. In *Dehal v DPP*[615] the Administrative Court quashed the conviction of a defendant who had posted a notice in the Sikh Temple describing the president of the Temple as a hypocrite on the ground that it was not necessary to prevent public disorder under Article 10(2).

In contrast, in the case of *Norwood v DPP*[616] the applicant had displayed a poster saying **15.199** 'Islam out of Britain'. His conviction for displaying an insulting sign under section 5 of the POA was upheld on the ground that this was necessary to protect the rights of others.[617] A similar result was reached in *Hammond v DPP*[618] where the Divisional Court upheld the section 5 conviction of an evangelical Christian who had held up a sign saying 'Stop Immorality, Stop Homosexuality' whilst preaching. The court rejected the argument that a criminal conviction was a disproportionate restriction on the defendant's Article 10 rights. It is submitted that this case is wrongly decided. The fact that religious expression may be insulting to a particular section of the community cannot, of itself, provide a sufficient justification for interference with it.

Racial hatred.   Incitement to racial hatred was first criminalized under the Race Relations **15.200** Act of 1965. Part III of the POA contains a number of offences which restrict freedom of expression. The POA defines racial hatred as:

> hatred against a group of persons in Great Britain defined by reference to colour, race, nationality (including citizenship) or ethnic or national origins.[619]

It therefore does not include hatred based on grounds of religion which is now the subject of a separate statutory offence.[620]

The POA creates three main offences relating to the incitement of racial hatred. Each **15.201** requires that the accused acts either with the intention of stirring up racial hatred, or in circumstances in which there is a likelihood that racial hatred will be stirred up.[621] First, it is an offence to use threatening or abusive or insulting words or behaviour[622] or to display abusive or insulting written material. The same prohibition applies to the publication or distribution of written material,[623] the presentation or direction of public performances of

---

[615] (2005) 169 JP 581.

[616] [2003] EWHC 1564 (Admin).

[617] But see the applicant's unsuccessful application to the ECtHR, *Norwood v UK* (2004) 40 EHRR SE 111) in which the ECtHR took the view that, by virtue of Art 17, no Art 10(2) exercise was required, for criticism of this decision, see S Turenne (see n 586 above) 873–874.

[618] (2004) 168 JP 601, DC; for discussions of this case see A Geddis 'Free Speech Martyrs or Unreasonable Threat to Social Peace? Insulting Expression and Section 5 of the Public Order Act 1986' [2004] PL 853; S Foster 'Free speech, insulting words or behaviour and Article 10 of the European Convention on Human Rights' (2004) 168 JP 277 and D Tausz [2004] Crim LR 85. An attempt by Mr Hammond's daughter to challenge his conviction before the ECtHR after his death failed due to her lack of status as a 'victim': see *Fairfield v United Kingdom*, Decision of 8 March 2005.

[619] See s 17.

[620] See s 29A (inserted by the Racial and Religious Hatred Act 2006), the offence includes a 'freedom of expression' defence, see s 29J; this is discussed at para 14.22 above.

[621] See s 18.

[622] Ibid.

[623] See s 19.

plays,[624] the distribution or presentation of visual images or sounds [625] and the provision or production of a programme or programme service containing such material.[626] Finally, it is an offence to be in possession of written material or recordings of images or sounds which is threatening, abusive or insulting with a view to its being displayed or published.[627]

15.202 The racial hatred provisions of the POA have been criticized as not providing a solution to the problem of racially motivated demonstrations or marches. Although section 18 is likely to be applied in relation to processions and assemblies, it may be ineffective in protecting racial groups against intimidatory marches, which are not intended to stir up racial hatred; furthermore, public or private meetings held in a 'dwelling' are not covered.[628]

(d) Other criminal offences restricting expression

15.203 There are a large number of other criminal offences which, potentially impact on the Article 10 rights of defendants. In such cases, the 'justification' for the interference will usually be the prevention of disorder or crime under Article 10(2). Four particular areas have can be mentioned.

15.204 The Protection from Harassment Act 1977 creates a criminal offence of harassment which can restrict freedom of expression.[628a] A restraining order can be made under section 5 to prevent a defendant from communicating with one or more people. Such an order must be justified under Article 10(2).[629]

15.205 Under section 75(1) of the Representation of the People Act 1987 it is an offence for a third party to incur election expenses which are not authorized by election agent. It has been held that this is a proportionate restriction on Article 10 rights.[630]

15.206 By 132 of the Serious Organized Crime and Police Act 2005 a demonstration in a designated area requires advance authorization by the police and it is an offence to organize or take part in a demonstration where no authorization is sought. It has been held that this requirement for prior authorization is not, of itself, incompatible with Article 10 (or Article 11).[631]

15.207 The offence of 'glorifying terrorism' was created by s.1(1) of the Terrorism Act 2006.[632] The section applies

> to a statement that is likely to be understood by some or all of the members of the public to whom it is published as direct or indirect encouragement or other inducement to them to the commission, preparation or instigation of acts of terrorism . . .

---

[624] See s 20.

[625] See s 21.

[626] See s 22.

[627] See s 23.

[628] See s 18(2); hence there is no protection against attacks on racial groups meeting in the context of a pub or restaurant; but note that which is not an incitement to racial hatred under ss 18 through 23 may breach s 4 or s 5 if it is threatening to a particular racial group.

[628a] See generally, *Thomas v News Group* [2002] EMLR 2 and *Howlett v Holding* [2006] EWHC 41 (QB).

[629] See *R v Delnath* [2006] 2 Cr App Rep (S) 169.

[630] *R v Holding* [2005] EWCA Crim 3185 (construing the statute using s 3 of the HRA to allow the expenditure by third parties of permitted sums under the provision to s 75).

[631] *Blum v DPP* [2006] EWHC 3209 (Admin).

[632] For a discussion of this offence, see H Fenwick and G Phillipson, *Media Freedom under the Human Rights Act* (Oxford University Press, 2006), 527–533,

These include statements which 'glorify' the commission of such acts or offences.[633] The person publishing the statement or disseminating the publication has to

> intend members of the public to be directly or indirectly encouraged or otherwise induced by the statement to commit, prepare or instigate acts of or terrorism . . .[634]

It is sufficient if the defendant is reckless as to these consequences. It is, however, a defence of 'innocent publication': to show the statement did not express his views or have his endorsement.[635] Considerable reservations have been expressed about the breadth and vagueness of these provisions.[636]

(e) Police powers to seize journalistic material

Material which is acquired or created for the purposes of journalism is specially protected against search and seizure by the police. By section 8 of the Police and Criminal Evidence Act 1984, a Justice of the Peace can authorize entry and search only where the material sought does not consist of or include 'journalistic material'.[637] A constable who wishes to obtain access to excluded material or special procedure material for the purposes of a criminal investigation may make an application to the circuit judge under section 9 of the Police and Criminal Evidence Act 1984 for a production order or a search warrant under and in accordance with Schedule 1. No order can be made for the production of journalistic material held in confidence[638] unless such an order could have been made under the previous law.[639] **15.208**

A circuit judge can only make a production order for other journalistic material if he is sat- **15.209** isfied that a number of 'access conditions' are fulfilled.[640] There must be reasonable grounds for believing that:

- a serious arrestable offence has been committed;
- the material is likely to be of substantial value to the investigation and is likely to be relevant evidence; and
- other methods of obtaining the material have failed or appear to be bound to fail.

More importantly, it must be in the public interest to make an order, having regard to the benefit likely to accrue to the investigation if the material is obtained and to the circumstances under which the person in possession of the material holds it.[641]

---

[633] Terrorism Act 2006, s 1(3); glorification 'includes any form of praise or celebration'.

[634] Ibid, s 1(2)(b)(i).

[635] Ibid, s 1(6).

[636] See, Joint Committee on Human Rights, Third Report of 2005-2006, 'Counter-Terrorism Policy and Human Rights: Terrorism Bill and related matters' HL 75/HC 561; see also HRC 'Concluding Observations on the United Kingdom's Report under Article 40 of the Covenant' CCPR/C/GBR/CO/6, 30 July 2008, para 26 which suggests that the United Kingdom should consider amending s 1 to avoid a disproportionate interference with freedom of expression.

[637] Defined by Police and Criminal Evidence Act 1984, s 13.

[638] As defined by ibid, s 11(3).

[639] This covers a limited range of circumstances, for example, if the material was stolen.

[640] Police and Criminal Evidence Act 1984, Sch 1, para 1.

[641] Ibid, Sch 1, para 2(c).

15.210 The effect of these provisions in relation to journalistic material was considered in *Chief Constable of Avon and Somerset Constabulary v Bristol United Press*.[642] The judge ordered the production of photographs of public disorders taken for 'journalistic purposes'. Although the mere assertion that the material would be of substantial value was insufficient, the court was entitled to draw inferences; but the respondent could produce evidence to the court, without the police seeing it, to show that the material was not of substantial value. It was held that, to fulfil paragraph 2(a) of the access conditions in Schedule 1, it was not necessary for the material sought to relate to some particular criminal offence. The judge was prepared to draw the inference, in the absence of contrary evidence, that photographers would take pictures of assaults and acts of violence and that their material would, therefore, be likely to provide evidence of 'serious arrestable offences'. The judge was of the view that the public interest in the 'impartiality and independence of the press' would not be undermined by making the order. Even if it was undermined in some people's eyes 'that could not outweigh the great public interest in the conviction of those guilty of serious crime'. An application for judicial review of this decision was refused.[643]

15.211 The court in the *Bristol United Press* case did not directly consider the impact of 'freedom of expression'. However, in *Re an application under Police and Criminal Evidence Act*[644] it was held that the 'public interest' condition was not satisfied. The judge decided that interference with the public interest in press freedom had to be 'convincingly established'. The assertion that the material was needed for the detection and prosecution of crime was not, of itself, sufficient for this purpose and the police had to avoid treating these applications as routine.

(10) Expression and government secrecy

(a) Introduction

15.212 Restrictions upon freedom of expression are often justified because they protect the national security interests of the state. The laws safeguarding secrecy include the law of confidence [645] and the Official Secrets Acts of 1911 to 1989. The Official Secrets Acts cover everything from serious national security offences to unauthorized releases of public information and involve serious restrictions on freedom of expression.[646]

(b) Official secrets and the criminal law

15.213 The Official Secrets Act 1911 was passed through Parliament in one day in an atmosphere of panic and was subjected to intensive criticism over many years.[647] The catch-all

---

[642] *The Independent*, 4 November 1986 (Stuart-Smith J, sitting as a circuit judge).

[643] *R v Bristol Crown Court, ex p Bristol Press and Picture Agency Ltd* (1986) 85 Cr App R 190.

[644] 2 July 1999, Central Criminal Court, HHJ Pownall; see also *R v Central Criminal Court ex p Bright*, [2001] 1 WLR 662 and *R (Malik) v Manchester Crown Court* [2008] 4 All ER 803.

[645] See para 12.22ff above.

[646] See generally, G Robertson and A Nicol, *Media Law* (5th edn, Sweet & Maxwell, 2007), Chap 11 'Reporting Executive Government' and H Fenwick and G Phillipson, *Media Freedom under the Human Rights Act* (Oxford University Press, 2006), Chap 19 'Official Secrets, Access to Information and the Media'.

[647] See eg, *Report of the Franks Committee on Section 2 of the Official Secrets Act 1911* (1972) Cmnd 5104; and see P Birkinshaw, *Reforming the Secret State* (Hull University Press, 1990).

provision of section 2 has now been repealed, but the 'espionage' provision of section 1 remains in force.

Section 1 of the Official Secrets Act 1911 provides that an offence is committed where   **15.214**

> any person for any purpose prejudicial to the safety or interests of the State. . .communicates to any other person any secret official code word, or pass word, or any sketch plan, model, article, note, or other document or information which is calculated to be or might be or is intended to be directly useful to an enemy.[648]

'Enemy' in this section includes 'potential enemy'.[649] In *Chandler v DPP*[650] the House of Lords held that 'the interests of the state' meant such interests according to the policies of the state as they in fact were, not as it might be argued they ought to be.

Section 2 of the Official Secrets Act 1911 created a very wide offence of 'disclosure of any   **15.215** official information, without authority'. The disclosure of the information did not have to be harmful.[651] This section was repealed by the Official Secrets Act 1989 ('the 1989 Act') and replaced by a number of more specific restrictions on various types of disclosure of information.[652] These include:

- disclosure of information relating to security or intelligence by members and former members of the security and intelligence services;[653]
- damaging disclosure[654] of security or intelligence information by other Crown servants or Government contractors;[655]
- damaging disclosure[656] of information relating to defence by Crown servants or Government contractors;[657]
- damaging disclosure[658] of information relating to international relations or confidential information obtained from another state by Crown servants or Government contractors;[659]
- disclosure of information obtained as a result of warrants issued under the Interception of Communications Act 1985 or the Security Service Act 1989.[660]

---

[648] See s 1(1).

[649] *R v Parrott* (1913) 8 Cr App R 186.

[650] [1964] AC 763; an argument to the contrary was rejected by the trial judge in *R v Ponting* [1985] Crim LR 318—but the jury acquitted in any event, effectively rejecting the direction of the judge on this point, see generally, C Ponting, *The Right to Know* (Sphere Books, 1985).

[651] See *R v Crisp and Homewood* (1919) 83 JP 121 (army clothing contracts).

[652] For general discussion of the 1989 Act, see S Palmer 'Tightening Secrecy Law' [1990] PL 243 and A Bailin, 'The Last Cold War Statute' [2008] Crim LR 625.

[653] See s 1(1), there is no requirement under this subsection that the information is 'damaging'. The House of Lords held in *A-G v Blake* [2001] 1 AC 268, that where an intelligence officer published an autobiography which breached s 1, the Crown was entitled to confiscate his profits by obtaining an order for an account based upon his breach of contract; see also *Blake v United Kingdom* (2007) 44 EHRR 29.

[654] As defined by s 1(4).

[655] See s 1(3).

[656] As defined by s 2(2).

[657] See s 2(1).

[658] As defined by s 3(2).

[659] See s 3(1).

[660] See s 4(1), (3); there is no requirement under this subsection that the information is 'damaging'.

It is also an offence to disclose information which has been disclosed by Crown servants or Government contractors without lawful authority or on terms requiring it to be held in confidence.[661] The 1989 Act makes no provision for a defence of 'public interest' or 'prior publication' in relation to any type of disclosure.

15.216 In the case of *R v Shayler*[662] the defendant contended that, on a proper construction of the 1989 Act he was entitled to a 'public interest defence' and, if not, the relevant parts of the Act were incompatible with his rights under Article 10. This argument was rejected by the trial judge, the Court of Appeal and the House of Lords. It was held that, on a proper construction of section 1(1), section 4(1) and section 4(3) of the 1989 Act, a defendant was not entitled to be acquitted if he showed that it was, or that he believed that it was, in the public or national interest to make the disclosure in question. Lord Bingham considered that the thrust of the Strasbourg cases on the need to preserve the secrecy of official information

> has not been to discount or disparage the need for strict and enforceable rules but to insist on adequate safeguards to ensure that the restriction does not exceed what is necessary to achieve the end in question. The acid test is whether, in all the circumstances, the interference with the individual's Convention right prescribed by national law is greater than is required to meet the legitimate object which the state seeks to achieve.[663]

He then considered in detail the safeguards available under the 1989 Act and concluded that

> The crux of this case is whether the safeguards built into the [1989 Act] are sufficient to ensure that unlawfulness and irregularity can be reported to those with the power and duty to take effective action, that the power to withhold authorization to publish is not abused and that proper disclosures are not stifled. In my opinion the procedures discussed above, properly applied, provide sufficient and effective safeguards.[664]

As a result, there was no incompatibility with Article 10. Lord Hope was more sceptical of the scheme of the 1989 Act, pointing out that it was not sensitive to the facts of each case but ultimately concurred in the result. Mr Shayler was subsequently convicted and sentenced to 6 months imprisonment. The decision in *Shayler* has been strongly criticized[665] and the operation of the 1989 Act continues to be controversial. There are, however, no plans to amend the Act to introduce a public interest defence.

(c) Official secrets and breach of confidence

15.217 The Government has often relied on civil remedies against the media to prevent publication of allegedly secret material, particularly breach of confidence.[666] In the 'Crossman Diaries' case[667] the Attorney-General sought an injunction to restrain publication of the diaries, on the ground that disclosure of Cabinet discussions was contrary to the

---

[661] See s 5.
[662] [2003] 1 AC 247 (for discussion of this case see A T H Smith, 'Security Services, Leaks and the Public Interest' (2002) 61 CLJ 514).
[663] Ibid, para 26.
[664] Ibid, para 36.
[665] See eg, H Fenwick and G Phillipson (n 646 above), 939–948.
[666] See generally, para 12.22ff above.
[667] *A-G v Jonathan Cape Ltd* [1976] 1 QB 752.

public interest. The defendants' argument that the private law doctrine of 'breach of confidence' did not apply to Cabinet discussions was rejected; Lord Widgery CJ denied that the courts should be powerless to restrain the publication of public secrets.[668] He held, however, that, in order to obtain an injunction, the Attorney-General had to show:

- that such publication would be a breach of confidence;
- that the public interest requires that publication be restrained; and
- that there are no other facets of the public interest contradictory to and more compelling than that relied upon.

Moreover, the court, when asked to restrain a publication, must examine the extent to which relief is necessary to ensure that restrictions are not imposed beyond the strict requirement of public need.[669] As much of the material was 10-years-old and three general elections had since been held, there was, on the facts no sufficient public interest in restraining publication and an injunction was refused.[670]

This principle was invoked most significantly in the *Spycatcher* litigation.[671] The House of **15.218**
Lords in *A-G v Guardian Newspapers Ltd (No 2)*[672] held that members and former members of the security service owed a lifelong duty of confidence to the Crown. Lord Goff, however, made clear that, in the case of Government secrets:

> it is incumbent on the Crown, in order to restrain disclosure of Government secrets, not only to show that the information is confidential, but also to show that it is not in the public interest that it should be published.[673]

In *A-G v Times Newspapers*[674] an injunction was sought to restrain the serialization of a book by a former MI6 officer about his experiences. The parties agreed that the injunction should not cover material which had only been published, whether inside or outside the jurisdiction. The Attorney General contended that the defendants had to demonstrate that this was the case and thus had to obtain prior clearance before publishing. It was held that the Attorney-General had to demonstrate a public interest in restraining publication and that a requirement of prior clearance should not be imposed

(11) Freedom of expression in other areas

(a) Introduction

The English Courts have considered the right to freedom of expression in a variety of other **15.219**
contexts. After the coming into force of the HRA, the Courts have consistently approached the issue as to whether restrictions on freedom of expression are justified by considering the application of a proportionality test in accordance with Article 10(2). In this section we will deal with six specific areas: prisoners, restrictions on advertising, regulation of conduct

---

[668] Ibid, 769G–H.
[669] Ibid, 770G–771A.
[670] See also *Commonwealth of Australia v John Fairfax and Sons Ltd* (1980) 147 CLR 39.
[671] See para 15.31ff above.
[672] [1990] 1 AC 109.
[673] Per Lord Goff, *A-G v Guardian Newspapers Ltd (No 2)*; see also *Lord Advocate v The Scotsman Publications Ltd* [1990] 1 AC 812.
[674] [2001] EMLR 19

of public officials, access to information, the operation of conditional fee arrangements and copyright law.

(b) Prisoners

15.220　The rights of prisoners to communicate with journalists have been considered in a number of cases.[675] In the leading case of *R v Secretary of State for the Home Department, ex p Simms*[676] the House of Lords held that a blanket ban on prisoners communicating with journalists unless the latter signed an undertaking to use material without the permission of the Governor was unlawful. Lord Steyn emphasized the fact that prisoners wished to communicate with journalists to order to challenge what they claimed were wrongful convictions:

> The value of free speech in a particular case must be measured in specifics. Not all types of speech have an equal value. For example, no prisoner would ever be permitted to have interviews with journalists to publish pornographic material or to give vent to so-called hate speech. Given the purpose of a sentence of imprisonment, a prisoner can also not claim to join in a debate on the economy or on political issues by way of interviews with journalists. In these respects the prisoner's right to fee speech is outweighed by deprivation of liberty by the sentence of a court and the need for discipline and control in prisons. But the free speech at stake in the present case is qualitatively of a different order. The prisoners are in prison because they are presumed to have been properly convicted. They wish to challenge the safety of their convictions. In principle it is not easy to conceive of a more important function which free speech might fulfil.[677]

15.221　In *R (Hirst) v Secretary of State for Home Department*[678] the applicant wished to give pre-recorded interviews on matters of public interest, subject to approval by the prison authorities of the content. The decision of the Governor to refuse him permission was quashed. Elias J held that restrictions on access to the media did not constitute an integral part of the sentence of imprisonment. He granted a declaration that a blanket policy denying contact with the media by telephone was unlawful. However, a blanket policy restricting telephone calls by prisoners to certain 'enabled numbers' is not unlawful.[679] It was also lawful for the Secretary of State to prevent a notorious murderer from publishing an autobiography whilst serving his prison sentence: such a restriction was not a disproportionate restriction the prisoner's Article 10 rights.[680]

15.222　There was no breach of Article 10 when the Secretary of State laid down requirements for the monitoring of journalists' interviews with asylum seekers detained as suspected terrorists. The requirements were justified by the need to safeguard national security and to safeguard good order and discipline at the prisons where the suspected terrorists were held.[681]

---

[675] See generally, T Owen, S Livingstone, and A Macdonald, *Prison Law* (4th edn, Oxford University Press, 2008), paras 7.43 to 7.52.
[676] [2000] 2 AC 115.
[677] Ibid, 127.
[678] [2002] UKHRR 758.
[679] *R (Taylor) v Governor of HM Prison Risley* [2004] EWHC 2654 (Admin).
[680] *R (Nielsen) v Secretary of State for the Home Department* [2005] 1 WLR 1028.
[681] *R (A) v Secretary of State for the Home Department* [2004] HRLR 12.

(c) Restrictions on advertising

The regulation of advertising engages Article 10. The Advertising Standards Authority has **15.223** been treated as a public body for judicial review purposes. It has been held that that the adjudications of the Authority published under the Codes were 'prescribed by law' for the purposes of Article 10(2) and were for legitimate aims.[682] The courts have consistently refused to grant interim injunctions to restrain the publication of the adjudications of the Authority.[683]

In *R (British and American Tobacco) v Secretary of State for Health*[684] the applicants sought **15.224** to challenge the Tobacco Advertising and Promotion (Point of Sale) Regulations 2004 on the grounds that the restrictions were in breach of Article 10. The Court held that the proportionality of the Regulations had to be judged in the context that the protection of health was a far reaching social policy, that restrictions on the right to commercial expression had to be justified and that the need to restrict tobacco advertising was not challenged. The objective of the Regulations was sufficiently important to justify limiting a fundamental right.

(d) Regulation of conduct in public life

The Standards Board for England was established under the Local Government Act 2000 **15.225** and must have regard to the need to promote and maintain high standards of conduct by members of relevant authorities in England.[685] A model of Code of Conduct governs the activities of local authority members and employees and includes a number of provisions which can impact on freedom of expression. Complaints of breaches of the Code are dealt with by the Adjudication Panel for England. In *Sanders v Kingston*[686] it was held the code of conduct was sufficiently precise to comply with the Article 10(2) 'prescribed by law' requirement and that the suspension of the claimant for insensitive, angry and abusive statements was a justified interference with his Article 10 rights. However, the Tribunal has been wrong to disqualify him and a period of suspension for one year was substituted.

The case of *Livingstone v Adjudication Panel for England*[687] concerned a remark made the **15.226** then Mayor of London to a Jewish journalist that he was 'just like a concentration camp guard'. The Adjudication Panel found that the Mayor had brought his office into disrepute and suspended him for four weeks. This suspension was overturned by the Administrative Court. Collins J emphasis the need for justification of an interference with freedom of expression under Article 10(2) and held that

> the tribunal misdirected itself in deciding that it was proportionate for the Code to extend as far as it did on the tribunal's construction. The restraint was not in my judgment shown to be necessary in a democratic society even though the higher level of protection appropriate for the expression of political opinion was not engaged.[688]

---

[682] *R (Matthias Rath BV) v Advertising Standards Authority* [2001] HRLR 22.

[683] *R v Advertising Standards Authority, ex p Vernons* [1992] 1 WLR 1289; *R (J) v Advertising Standards Authority* [2005] EWHC 2609 (Admin); *R (Direct Free Direct) v Advertising Standards Authority* [2007] EWHC 1337 (Admin).

[684] [2004] EWHC 2493 (Admin).

[685] Local Government Act 2000, s 57(4).

[686] [2005] BLGR 719.

[687] [2006] EWHC 2533 (Admin).

[688] Ibid, para 39.

(e) Access to information

15.227   The Freedom of Information Act 2000 now gives a wide right of rights of access to information held by a large number of public authorities.[689] Additional rights of access cannot be derived from Article 10 which the Court of Human Rights has consistently held does not include a general right to receive information in the absence of willingness to impart the information.[690]

15.228   It was held in *R v Secretary of State for Health, ex p Wagstaff and Associated Newspapers*,[691] in relation to the inquiry into the murders carried out by Dr Shipman, that given the right to receive information provided by Article 10, it was irrational to hold that inquiry in private without sufficient justification. In *Wagstaff* the court was of the view that there is a presumption in favour of a public inquiry. However, this view was rejected by the court in *Persey v Secretary of State for Environment, Food and Rural Affairs*.[692] In *Persey* the claimants sought an order that the government carry out a public inquiry into the handling of the foot and mouth outbreak. The Administrative Court held that the decision to hold the inquiry in private was not irrational and that Article 10 of the Convention was not engaged by such a decision. Article 10 prohibited interference with freedom of expression but imposed no positive obligation on government to provide an open forum to achieve the wider dissemination of information. The claimants did not have any right under Article 10 to require a public authority to gather information which they would have an interest in receiving, still less to require the public authority to gather that information in any particular form or manner, ie by public rather than private inquiry. Furthermore, even if the decision constituted a restriction on the claimants' or media's right to freedom of expression it was capable of being justified under Art 10(2). The government's decision was one which was open to it to take and it could not be impugned as irrational or otherwise unlawful.[693]

(f) Conditional fee agreements

15.229   Many actions against the media are now brought with the benefit of conditional fee agreements ('CFAs') which provide for 'success fees' of up to 100%, thus doubling the cost liability of an unsuccessful media defendant. In *Campbell v MGN (No. 2)*[694] the defendant newspaper, which had been unsuccessful in a House of Lords appeal claimed that the success fee was a disproportionate restriction on its Article 10 rights. The House of Lords held that the provision of legal assistance in actions for defamation and the like was a legitimate objective. The purpose of a 'success fee' was to require losing defendants to contribute to the funds which would enable lawyers to take on other cases. This was a proportionate measure to provide those other litigants with access to justice and it had been open to the legislature to choose to fund access to justice by CFAs.

---

[689] For a discussion of the provisions of the Act, see P Coppel, *Information Law* (2nd edn, Sweet & Maxwell, 2008).

[690] *R v Bow County Court, ex p Pelling* [2001] 1 UKHRR 165, para 36.

[691] [2001] 1 WLR 292.

[692] [2003] QB 794.

[693] See also *R (Howard) v Secretary of State for Health* [2003] QB 830.

[694] [2005] 4 All ER 793; note that MGN has an outstanding application to the ECtHR: *MGN v United Kingdom*, App No 39401/04 .

(g) Copyright law[695]

Copyright has its origins in the common law but now derives from the provisions of the **15.230**
Copyright Designs and Patents Act 1988 ('the 1988 Act'). Copyright is a property right
which subsists in original dramatic, musical or artistic works, sound recordings, films,
broadcasts and the typographical arrangement of published editions.[696] The copyright
owner has the exclusive right to copy the work, to issue copies, to rent or lend the work to
the public, to perform, show or play the work in public, communicate the work to the
public or to make an adaptation of the work.[697] This covers the whole of the work or a
'substantial part' of it.[698]

Copyright only protects the *form* of the work, it does not normally prevent the publication **15.231**
of the *information* conveyed by the work. Nevertheless, it is clear that freedom of
expression protects the right both to publish information and to receive it. As a result, there
will be occasions when the public will have an Article 10 right to know the very words used
by a person, notwithstanding that the author enjoys copyright in them.[699]

These provisions obviously restrict the freedom of expression of non-owners. The extent **15.232**
of this interference is limited by the various 'permitted acts' under 1988 Act: there are 42
circumstances in which copying material does not infringe copyright.[700] Nevertheless, in
Ashdown v Telegraph Group[701] the Court of Appeal accepted that

> rare circumstances can arise where the right of freedom of expression will come into conflict
> with the protection afforded by the [HRA] notwithstanding the express exceptions to be
> found in the Act.

It seems unlikely that this 'defence' will be of practical significance and it has not been suc- **15.233**
cessfully invoked in any subsequent case.

(12) Freedom of expression in Community law

Freedom of expression as embodied in Article 10 is among the general principles of law the **15.234**
observance of which is ensured by the Court of Justice.[702] The Court of First Instance has
also referred to the guarantee of freedom of expression in Article 11 of the Charter of
Fundamental Rights.[703] The maintenance of cultural pluralism is connected with freedom

---

[695] See generally, E Barendt, *Freedom of Speech* (2nd edn, Oxford University Press, 2005), Chap 7; H
Fenwick and G Phillipson, *Media Freedom under the Human Rights Act* (Oxford University Press, 2006), Part
V 'Copyright and Media Freedom'.

[696] 1988 Act, s 1(1).

[697] Ibid, s 16(1).

[698] Ibid, s 16(3).

[699] See *Ashdown v Telegraph Group* [2002] 1 Ch 149 (CA), para 43, relying on *Fressoz and Roire v
France* (1999) 31 EHRR 28, para 54.

[700] See *Ashdown v Telegraph Group* [2001] Ch 685, 694 (Sir Andrew Morritt V-C).

[701] See n 699 above, para 45; see also *HRH Prince of Wales v Associated Newspapers* [2008] Ch 57. For criticism of the decision see H Fenwick and G Phillipson, (n 695 above) 910–915.

[702] See, for example, *Ter Voort* [1992] ECR I-5495, para 35; *Commission v Netherlands* [1991] ECR I-
4069, para 30; Case C-274/99, *Connolly v Commission* [2001] ECR I-1611, Case C-340/00, *Commission v
Kwik* [2001] ECR I-10269.

[703] Case T-309/04, *TV2/Danmark v Commission,* 22 October 2008, para 118.

of expression.[704] The general principle of freedom of expression includes commercial expression.[705]

15.235 Restrictions on the freedom of expression on the ground of protection of health are permitted in the Community legal order. Thus restrictions on the advertising of alcoholic beverages to consumers under Swedish law were justified on this ground.[706] In a field as 'complex and fluctuating' as that of advertising, review of measures which limit freedom of expression is limited to an examination of reasonableness and proportionality.[707] As a result a measure prohibiting tobacco advertising in the press and radio advertising of tobacco productsdid not exceed the limits of the discretion of the Community legislature and was not disproportionate.[708] The Copyright Directive is not a disproportionate interference with the on right to right information because it is justified in the light of the need to protect intellectual property rights.[709]

C. The Law under the European Convention

(1) Introduction

(a) Article 10 of the Convention

15.236 Article 10 of the Convention provides:

(1) Everyone has the right to freedom of expression. This right shall include freedom to hold opinions and to receive and impart information and ideas without interference by public authority and regardless of frontiers. This Article shall not prevent States from requiring the licensing of broadcasting, television or cinema enterprises.

(2) The exercise of these freedoms, since it carries with it duties and responsibilities, may be subject to such formalities, conditions, restrictions or penalties as are prescribed by law and are necessary in a democratic society, in the interests of national security, territorial integrity or public safety, for the prevention of disorder or crime, for the protection of health or morals, for the protection of the reputation or rights of others, for preventing the disclosure of information received in confidence, or for maintaining the authority and impartiality of the judiciary.

15.237 The Convention was the first human rights instrument to make express provision for limitations on the freedom of expression.[710] Article 10 specifically acknowledges that freedom

---

[704] Case C-250/06. *United Pan-Europe Communications Belgium SA and Others v Belgian State* [2007] ECR I-11135; see also Case C-288/89 *Collectieve Antennevoorziening Gouda* [1991] ECR I4007, para 23; Case C-148/91 *Veronica Omroep Organisatie* [1993] ECR I487, para 10.

[705] *R v Secretary of State for Health, ex p Imperial Tobacco Ltd* [2000] All ER (EC) 769, Opinion of Advocate General, paras 153–154.

[706] *Konsumentombudsmannen (KO) v Gourmet International Products AB* [2001] All ER (EC) 308.

[707] *Re Tobacco Advertising Directive 2003/33: Germany v Council of the European Union (Spain and Others, intervening)* (Case C-380/03) [2007] 2 CMLR 1, para 155; see also *Herbert Karner Industrie-Auktionen GmbH v Troostwijk GmbH* (Case C-71/02) [2004] 2 CMLR 5 (restriction on advertising goods of insolvent companies justified, paras 51–52).

[708] *Re Tobacco Advertising* (see n 707 above), paras 157–158.

[709] *Laserdisken ApS v Kulturministeriet* [2007] 1 CMLR 6, para 65.

[710] Contrast Art 19 of the Universal Declaration, see App H in Vol 2.

of expression has the potential to damage the interests of others or the public interest. The tension between the right of expression and the need to protect other rights has been at the heart of the Convention jurisprudence under Article 10.

(b) 'Everyone'

The right to freedom of expression in Article 10 is available to 'everyone'. This includes **15.238** natural and legal persons:[711] Article 10 protects expressive activity of all kinds by private individuals and corporations. The most important area in practice is expression in the media. Article 10 protects writers, journalist and editors as well as media corporations.[712] It also protects the freedom of expression of state owned media corporations.[713] In addition, Article 10 can be relied on by civil servants[714] including members of the police[715] and the armed forces and members of the judiciary.[716]

(c) Fundamental principles

The Court of Human Rights has emphasized in many cases that the right to freedom of **15.239** expression is an 'essential foundation of a democratic society' and a 'basic condition for its progress and for the development of every man'.[717] The fundamental principles have been explained in terms such as the following in many cases:

(i) Freedom of expression constitutes one of the essential foundations of a democratic society and one of the basic conditions for its progress and for each individual's self-fulfilment. Subject to paragraph 2 of Article 10, it is applicable not only to 'information' or 'ideas' that are favourably received or regarded as inoffensive or as a matter of indifference, but also to those that offend, shock or disturb. Such are the demands of pluralism, tolerance and broadmindedness without which there is no 'democratic society'. As set forth in Article 10, this freedom is subject to exceptions, which. . .must, however, be construed strictly, and the need for any restrictions must be established convincingly.

(ii) The adjective 'necessary', within the meaning of Article 10(2), implies the existence of a 'pressing social need'. The Contracting States have a certain margin of appreciation in assessing whether such a need exists, but it goes hand in hand with European supervision, embracing both the legislation and the decisions applying it, even those given by an

---

[711] *Autronic AG v Switzerland* (1990) 12 EHRR 485, para 47.

[712] See eg, *Sunday Times v United Kingdom (No 1)* (1979) 2 EHRR 245; however, a journalist's trade union cannot complain of violation of Article 10 in relation to a specific publication: *see Hodgson and Woolf v United Kingdom* (1987) 51 DR 136.

[713] See, eg *Radio France v France* (2005) 40 EHRR 29; *Österreichischer Rundfunk v Austria,* Judgment of 7 December 2006, see also *British Broadcasting Corporation v United Kingdom*, Decision of 18 January 1996 (applicability of Art 10 to BBC left open).

[714] See *Vogt v Germany* (1995) 21 EHRR 205 (teachers); *Ahmed v United Kingdom* (2000) 29 EHRR 1 (local government officers).

[715] See eg, *Rekvényi v Hungary* (2000) 30 EHRR 519.

[716] See eg, *Wille v Liechtenstein* (2000) 30 EHRR 558.

[717] This formulation consistently appears in the cases over a period of more than three decades, for example, *Handyside v United Kingdom* (1976) 1 EHRR 737, para 49 and *Lindon, Otchakovsky-Laurens and July v France* (2008) 46 EHRR 35 (GC), para 45.

independent court. The Court is therefore empowered to give the final ruling on whether a 'restriction' is reconcilable with freedom of expression as protected by Article 10.

(iii) The Court's task, in exercising its supervisory jurisdiction, is not to take the place of the competent national authorities but rather to review under Article 10 the decisions they delivered pursuant to their power of appreciation. This does not mean that the supervision is limited to ascertaining whether the respondent State exercised its discretion reasonably, carefully and in good faith; what the Court has to do is to look at the interference complained of in the light of the case as a whole and determine whether it was 'proportionate to the legitimate aim pursued' and whether the reasons adduced by the national authorities to justify it are 'relevant and sufficient'. . .In doing so, the Court has to satisfy itself that the national authorities applied standards which were in conformity with the principles embodied in Article 10 and, moreover, that they relied on an acceptable assessment of the relevant facts.[718]

(d) Contents of this Section

15.240 In this Section we will begin by discussing a number of issues arising under Article 10(1). First, we will examine the general scope of the right to freedom of expression. Secondly, we will deal with the subject of the licensing and regulation of the media which is specifically mentioned in Article 10(1). Thirdly, we will then consider the nature of 'interferences' under Article 10 and the general principles which are applied. In particular, we will consider the different approaches adopted by the Court in relation to different types of 'expression'. Fourthly, we will look at the principles developed by the court in its extensive case law in relation to interferences with the freedom of expression of the media. Finally, we will consider the case law in relation to justification in other types of Article 10 cases.

(2) Scope of the right

(a) Introduction

15.241 **General.** 'Expression' has been interpreted broadly to include communications of any kind or subject matter: spoken or written words, television programmes[719] and broadcasting,[720] film,[721] video,[722] pictures,[723] dress,[724] graffiti[725] and images.[726] Furthermore, the concept of 'expression' covers conduct such as acts of protest (even where they involve physically

---

[718] See *Lindon, Otchakovsky-Laurens and July v France* (see n 717 above), para 45; and see *Jersild v Denmark* (1994) 19 EHRR 1, para 31; *Hertel v Switzerland*, (1999) 28 EHRR 534, para 46; and *Steel and Morris v United Kingdom* (2005) 41 EHRR 22, para 87; *Guja v Moldova*, Judgment of 12 February 2008 (GC), para 69.

[719] See eg, *Hodgson v United Kingdom* (1987) 51 DR 136, EComm HR.

[720] See eg, *Autronic AG v Switzerland* (1990) 12 EHRR 485 (where the Court acknowledged that the public have a right to receive broadcasts).

[721] See eg, *Otto-Preminger-Institute v Austria* (1994) 19 EHRR 34.

[722] See eg, *Wingrove v United Kingdom* (1996) 24 EHRR 1.

[723] *Müller v Switzerland* (1988) 13 EHRR 212.

[724] *Stevens v United Kingdom* (1986) 46 DR 245, EComm HR; *Vajnai v Hungary*, Judgment of 8 July 2008 (criminal conviction for wearing a 5-pointed red star on a jacket, violation).

[725] *N v Switzerland* (1983) 34 DR 208.

[726] *Chorherr v Austria* (1993) 17 EHRR 358.

interfering with the activity protested against),[727] the physical expression of feelings[728] performances by street musicians[729] and the wearing of a beard[730]. Freedom of expression also includes the right not to speak.[731] It does not, however, extend to linguistic freedom[732] or the right to vote or stand for election.[733]

Content of expression. In general, no form of expression is excluded from the protection of Article 10 on the basis of its *content* (although the Court has occasionally suggested that 'valueless' expression might not be protected).[734] This means, for example, that 'expression' is applicable to ideas that 'offend, shock or disturb'.[735] Thus, in *Jersild v Denmark*[736] the Court held that convicting a journalist for aiding and abetting racist insults in a television programme was disproportionate to the need to protect those whom he had insulted. Similarly, in *Lehideux v France*[737] the Court held that convictions for portraying Marshall Petain positively in a false light were disproportionate interferences with freedom of expression. However, in some older cases the Commission applied a low standard of review when considering whether Article 10 has been breached in cases arising from racist literature[738] or support for terrorist activities.[739]

15.242

Furthermore, the fact that views are expressed in polemical language does not take them outside the scope of Article 10. Thus, in *De Haes and Gijsels v Belgium*,[740] journalists who personally insulted certain members of the judiciary for their handling of child abuse and incest proceedings when writing critical articles nevertheless were entitled to rely on Article 10.

15.243

---

[727] *Steel v United Kingdom* (1998) 28 EHRR 603 para 92; *Chorherr v Austria* (see n 726 above); *Hashman and Harrup v United Kingdom* (2000) 30 EHRR 241, para 28; see also *Nicol and Selvanayagam v United Kingdom* (Decision of 11 January 2001).

[728] *X v United Kingdom* (1978) 3 EHRR 63, EComm HR (homosexual activity).

[729] *H & K v United Kingdom* (1983) 34 DR 218.

[730] *Tig v Turkey,* Decision of 24 May 2005 (the point was accepted as being arguable).

[731] *Young, James and Webster v United Kingdom* (1982) 4 EHRR 38, para 57; *K v Austria* (1993) Series A No 255-B, para 46.

[732] See the Belgian linguistics cases: *23 Inhabitants of Alsemberg and Beersel v Belgium* (1963) 6 YB 332; *X v Belgium,* (1963) 6 YB 444, in which it was held that the applicant had no freedom of choice as to the language of instruction for his children.

[733] *Liberal Party, Mrs R and Mr P v United Kingdom* (1982) 4 EHRR 106.

[734] *Otto-Preminger-Institute v Austria* (1994) 19 EHRR 34, para 49 addressed 'abusive or inflammatory words'; *Groppera Radio AG v Switzerland* (1990) 12 EHRR 321, per Judge Matscher and Judge Valticos, found that light music was mere entertainment and not 'information and ideas'.

[735] See *Lehideux and Isornia v France* (2000) 30 EHRR 665, para 55.

[736] (1994) 19 EHRR 1.

[737] n 735 above; see also *Orban v France*, Judgment of 15 January 2009.

[738] See eg, *Glimmerveen and Hagenbeek v Netherlands* (1979) 18 DR 187, EComm HR (racist leaflets); *X v Germany* (1982) 29 DR 194, EComm HR (Nazi leaflets); *T v Belgium* (1983) 34 DR 158 (Nazi leaflet); *Kuhnen v Germany* (1988) 56 DR 205, EComm HR (Nazi leaflet); *H, W, P and K v Austria* (1989) 62 DR 216, EComm HR (Nazi activities), *Hennicke v Germany,* Decision of 21 May 1997.

[739] See eg, *Purcell v Ireland* (1991) 70 DR 262, EComm HR (political support for terrorists); *Brind v United Kingdom* (1994) 18 EHRR CD 76, EComm HR (restrictions on broadcasting interviews with supporters of terrorism); *Gerry Adams v United Kingdom* [1997] EHRLR 293 (exclusion order preventing Gerry Adams speaking at House of Commons).

[740] (1997) 25 EHRR 1; *Jersild v Denmark* (1994) 19 EHRR 1.

15.244 **Hate speech.**   There are, however, some 'limit cases' in which, statements directed against the Convention's underlying values, have been held not to quality for protection under Article 10. Freedom of expression cannot be invoked in a sense contrary to Article 17 of the Convention.[741] There is a category of 'clearly established historical facts…whose negation or revision is removed from the protection of Article 10 by Article 17'.[742] An example would be the justification of a pro-Nazi policy.[743]

15.245 This principle was, applied in the case of *Norwood v United Kingdom*[744] to an applicant who had displayed a poster stating 'Islam out of Britain—Protect the British People' with a photograph of the Twin Towers in flames. It is difficult to see how Article 17 was properly applicable in that case which should, rather, have been dealt with under Article 10(2). This case can be contrasted with the judgment in *Müslüm Gündüz v Turkey*[745] in which it was held that, although Sharia law was contrary to Convention values, the conviction of the applicant for defending sharia in a television interview was a breach of Article 10. The mere fact of advocating sharia, without calling for violence to achieve it, did not constitute 'hate speech'.

15.246 **Expression by employees.**   Article 10 extends to expression by employees but is subject to restriction under Article 10(2).[746] However, there are some types of employment which, by their nature, involve restrictions on freedom of expression.[747] Furthermore, it is sometimes said that an employee can contract out of his right to freedom of expression, but this is open to question; and the better view is that, although the right to freedom of expression of employees can be restricted by contract, this is always subject to the scrutiny of the courts on 'public policy' grounds.[748]

15.247 **Facts and values.**   The distinction in Article 10 between information and ideas makes it clear that 'expression' is not restricted to statements of fact.[749] It encompasses opinions, criticism and speculation, whether or not they are objectively 'true'. In *Thorgeirson v*

---

[741] For Art 17 see para 6.197ff above.

[742] *Chauvy v France*, (2005) 41 EHRR 29, para 69 (the example given is the Holocaust).

[743] See *Lehideux and Isornia v France* (2000) 30 EHRR 665, para 53; *Chauvy v France*, (2005) 41 EHRR 29; see also *Garaudy v France*, Decision of 24 June 2003 (Art 10 complaint concerning prosecution for book questioning holocaust inadmissible as incompatible *ratione materiae*); *WP v Poland* (2005) 40 EHRR SE1 and also *Glimmerveen and Hagenbeek v Netherlands* (1982) 4 EHRR 260.

[744] (2005) 40 EHRR SE11; for criticism of this decision see S Foster 'Racist Speech and Articles 10 and 17 of the European Convention on Human Rights' (2005) 10 Cov LJ 91.

[745] Judgment of 4 December 2003, para 51.

[746] See generally, *Vogt v Germany* (1995) 21 EHRR 205; cf *Volkmer v Germany* (Decision of 22 November 2001) which held that dismissal of a teacher for political activity, in the former East Germany which was an abuse of authority was not a breach of Article 10 and *Petersen v Germany*, (Decision of 22 November 2001) in which it was held that the dismissal of a professor of modern history from East Germany for lack of professional qualifications was not a breach and *Guja v Moldova*, Judgment of 12 February 2008 (GC) (disclosure of documents to the press by Head of Press Department of Prosecutor General's Office, violation).

[747] See eg, *Morissens v Belgium* (1988) 56 DR 127, EComm HR (no breach by disciplining a teacher for criticizing her superiors in a TV broadcast); see also *Ahmed v United Kingdom* (1998) 5 BHRC 111; *Rekvényi v Hungary* (2000) 30 EHRR 519. (police officers); *Wille v Liechtenstein* (2000) 30 EHRR 558 (members of the judiciary).

[748] *Vereiniging Rechtswinkels Utrecht v Netherlands* (1986) 46 DR 200, EComm HR; *Rommelfanger v Germany* (1989) 62 DR 151, EComm HR; and see generally, para 6.264ff above.

[749] *Lingens v Austria* (1986) 8 EHRR 103; see generally, para 15.316ff below.

Iceland[750] the Court considered that an obligation on the applicant to prove the truth of his opinions was an interference with freedom of expression.

(b) The right to hold opinions and to impart information

Article 10 expressly includes the right to 'impart information and ideas'. The freedoms to   **15.248**
'receive' and 'impart' information and ideas are not mere corollaries of one another: they are two independent rights.[751] Thus, a speaker has a right to express opinions and a willing hearer has the right to receive the communication. The state must not stand between the speaker and his audience and thus defeat the purpose for which the protection of expression is realized.[752] In *Groppera Radio AG v Switzerland*[753] the Court declined to give a precise definition of 'information and ideas'. Nonetheless, a right to impart ideas means, for example, that organizing an exhibition of paintings was an exercise of freedom of expression on the part of the organizers.[754]

However, the right to receive information under Article 10 does *not* entail a corresponding   **15.249**
right of access to information (or an obligation on the Government to provide it), even when it is necessary for the purposes of forming an opinion or effectively exercising other freedoms. In *Leander v Sweden*[755] the applicant sought confidential Government information so he could bring a claim arising out of an unsuccessful job application. In dismissing the Article 10 claim, it was said:[756]

> The Court observes that the right of freedom to receive information basically prohibits a Government from restricting a person from receiving information that others wish or may be willing to impart to them. Article 10 does not, in the circumstances such as those of the present case, confer on an individual a right of access to a register containing information about his personal position, nor does it embody an obligation on the Government to impart such information to the individual.

In *Open Door Counselling v Ireland*[757] the court found that an injunction restraining the imparting of information to pregnant women by abortion clinics was a breach of both the clinic's right to impart information and the women's right to receive it. However, in the cases where the Court has accepted that there is a right of access to information, it has done so by reference to Article 8. Thus, in *Gaskin v United Kingdom*,[758] the Court decided the case under Article 8 and expressly denied that Article 10 embodied an obligation on the state to impart the information in question to the individual.

---

[750] (1992) 14 EHRR 843.
[751] *Sunday Times v United Kingdom (No 1)* (1979) 2 EHRR 245, paras 65–66.
[752] *Groppera Radio AG v Switzerland* (1990) 12 EHRR 321, para 53; *Casado Coca v Spain* (1994) 18 EHRR 1 para 59.
[753] See n 752 above, para 55.
[754] *Müller v Switzerland* (1988) 13 EHRR 212.
[755] (1987) 9 EHRR 433.
[756] Ibid, para 74; see also *Guerra v Italy* (1998) 26 EHRR 357, para 53; *Roche v United Kingdom* (2006) 42 EHRR 30 (GC), para 172 and *Stoll v Switzerland* (2008) 47 EHRR 59 (GC).
[757] (1992) 15 EHRR 244; see also *Cyprus v Turkey* (2002) 35 EHRR 30, paras 248–254 (violation of right to receive and impart information in respect of Greek Cypriots living in northern Cyprus resulting from the censorship of schoolbooks).
[758] (1989) 12 EHRR 36, paras 37, 52; see also *McGinley and Egan v United Kingdom* (1998) 27 EHRR 1; and see generally, para 12.254 above.

15.250 However, this approach of the Court is not consistent with the trend of international human rights jurisprudence which has recognized the importance of freedom of information and has found it in provisions relating to the "freedom to receive information".[759] It should also be noted that the Consultative (Parliamentary) Assembly of the Council of Europe has resolved that the right to freedom of expression involves a:

> corresponding duty for the public authorities to make available information on matters of public interest within reasonable limits and a duty for mass communication media to give complete and general information on public affairs.[760]

Although this resolution does not have binding effect, it indicates a trend in legal opinion within Contracting States.[761]

15.251 Similarly, Article 10 does not provide a general right to broadcast time or to advertise on television.[762] However, it may in exceptional circumstances create a right to 'access to broadcast time' such as where one political party is excluded from broadcasting when others are not.[763] But the inability of an independent candidate to make a party political broadcast did not breach Article 10.[764] Nor does Article 10 create a right to be granted a commercial radio licence.[765] However, where the state provides assistance to particular information providers, this must be done in an even-handed way.[766]

15.252 Where the information is otherwise available the state must not obstruct access to it.[767] In *Autronic v Switzerland*[768] the Court held that the refusal of the Swiss authorities to allow a company to receive, without Soviet consent, a satellite broadcast of a Soviet television programme for showing at an exhibition in Zurich, amounted to a violation of its right to receive information 'without interference by public authority and regardless of frontiers'.

(c) Freedom of the press and mass media

15.253 Although the Convention makes no specific reference to press or media freedom great importance has been attached to the role of the press and the mass media.[769] The press plays an essential role in a democratic society,[770] in particular, the 'vital role of public watchdog'.[771] The press has a duty on the press to impart information and ideas on political

---

[759] See, in particular, the important decision of the Inter-American Court of Human Rights in *Claude Reyes v Chile* (C/151) 19 September 2006 (in which it was concluded that the 'freedom of expression' provision of the Inter American Convention, Art 13, included an implied right of general access to government held information).

[760] Res 428 (1970), 21st Ordinary Session (Third Part), 22–30 Jan 1970, *Texts Adopted*.

[761] See P van Dijk, F van Hoof, A van Rijn, and L Zwaak eds, *Theory and Practice of the European Convention on Human Rights* (4th edn, Intersentia, 2006), 787–788.

[762] *X and Association Z v United Kingdom* (1971) 38 CD 86, EComm HR.

[763] *Haider v Austria* (1995) 85 DR 66, EComm HR.

[764] *Huggett v United Kingdom* [1996] ERHLR 84.

[765] *X v United Kingdom* (1972) 40 CD 29, EComm HR.

[766] *Vereinigung Demokratischer Soldaten Osterreichs and Gubi v Austria* (1994) 20 EHRR 55.

[767] *Z v Austria* (1988) 56 DR 13, EComm HR.

[768] *Autronic AG v Switzerland* (1990) 12 EHRR 485.

[769] See *Bladet Tromsø and Stensaas v Norway* (2000) 29 EHRR 125, para 59 and *Bergens Tidende v Norway* (2001) 31 EHRR 16, para 48.

[770] *Perna v Italy* (2004) 39 EHRR 28.

[771] *The Observer and The Guardian v United Kingdom* (1991) 14 EHRR 153, para 59; *Goodwin v United Kingdom* (1996) 22 EHRR 123, para 39; *Thorgeir Thorgeirson v Iceland* (see n 750 above) para 63, and *Bladet*

issues and on other areas of public interest;[772] and the public have a right to receive them.[773] As a result, the Court has emphasised that:

> Where . . . measures taken by the national authorities are capable of discouraging the press from disseminating information on matters of legitimate public concern, careful scrutiny of the proportionality of the measures on the part of the Court is called for.[774]

The overwhelming majority of Article 10 cases which come before the Court concern criminal or civil action taken against the media. The Article 10 issues which arise in relation to the press and mass media are dealt with in more detail below.[775]

Journalistic freedom means that the media can have recourse to exaggeration or even provocation.[776] Article 10 provides a safeguard to journalists in relation to reporting on issues of general interest, provided that they are acting in good faith in order to provide accurate and reliable information in accordance with the ethics of journalism.[777] Freedom of expression carries with it 'duties and responsibilities' which are of particular significance when the media attacks the reputation of a named individual.[778] The position of the media is discussed in detail at Section 6 below. **15.254**

(d) Article 10 and positive obligations

In some circumstances Article 10 creates positive obligations on the state to take action to protect the freedom of expression of private individuals.[779] This can extend to protecting the rights of freedom of expression against threats by private persons, including, for example, private employers[780] requiring the enactment of legislation to protect or facilitate freedom of expression[781] or taking measures to ensure access to information.[781a] In *Özgür Gündem v Turkey*[782] the Court held that genuine effective exercise of freedom of expression: **15.255**

> does not depend merely on the State's duty not to interfere, but may require positive measures of protection, even in the sphere of relations between individuals.

Tromsø and Stensaas v Norway (see n 769 above) para 62.

[772] *Lingens v Austria* (1986) 8 EHRR 103, para 26; *Oberschlick v Austria (No 1)* (1991) 19 EHRR 389 para 58; *Castells v Spain* (1992) 14 EHRR 445, para 43; *Thorgeirson v Iceland* (n 750 above); *Jersild v Denmark* (1994) 19 EHRR 1, para 31.

[773] *Sunday Times v United Kingdom* (1979) 2 EHRR 245, para 65; *Fressoz and Roire v France* (2001) 31 EHRR 2, para 51.

[774] *Bergens Tidende* (see n 769 above) para 52.

[775] See para 15.314ff below.

[776] *Prager and Oberschlick v Austria* (1995) 21 EHRR 1, para 38; *Thoma v Luxembourg* (2003) 36 EHRR 21, paras 45 and 46.

[777] *Goodwin v United Kingdom* (see n 771 above), para 39; *Bladet Tromsø and Stensaas* (see n 771 above) para 65; *Pedersen and Baadsgaard v Denmark* (2006) 42 EHRR 24 (GC), para 78.

[778] *Lindon, Otchakovsky-Laurens and July v France* (2008) 46 EHRR 35 (GC), para 67.

[779] For the distinction between negative and positive obligations, see para 6.166ff above; for positive obligations under Art 10 see P van Dijk, F van Hoof, A van Rijn, and L Zwaak eds, *Theory and Practice of the European Convention on Human Rights* (4th edn, Intersentia, 2006), 784–788.

[780] *Fuentes Bobo v Spain* (2001) 31 EHRR 50, para 38; see also *Khurshid Mustafa v Sweden*, Judgment of 16 December 2008, para 32 (landlord and tenant dispute).

[781] See *Vgt Verein gegen Tierfabriken v Switzerland* (2002) 34 EHRR 4, paras 46–48.

[781a] *Khurshid Mustafa v Sweden*, Judgment of 16 December 2008 (access to satellite broadcasts by Iraqis resident in Sweden).

[782] (2000) 31 EHRR 49, para 43.

In determining whether or not a positive obligation exists, regard must be had to the fair balance that has to be struck between the general interest of the community and the interests of the individual. The obligation must not be interpreted in such a way as to impose an impossible or disproportionate burden on the state.[783] In the *Özgür Gündem* case the state was found to be in breach of this positive obligation.[783a]

15.256   It is also arguable that States have a positive obligation to provide a right of reply or rectification for those criticized in the press.[784] In *Melnychuk v Ukraine*[785] the Court pointed out that the media must retain an editorial discretion as to whether to publish replies but that there may be exceptional circumstances in which a newspaper may legitimately be required to publish, for example, a retraction, an apology or a judgment in a defamation case. It went on to say that in that case

> a positive obligation arose for the State to protect the applicant's right to freedom of expression by ensuring, firstly, that he had a reasonable opportunity to exercise his right of reply by submitting a response to the newspaper for publication and, secondly, that he had an opportunity to contest the newspaper's refusal.

This was based on a provision in domestic law providing for a qualified right to reply and it is arguable that there is a positive obligation for States to make such a provision in their domestic law.[786]

(e)   The relationship between Article 10 and other Convention rights

15.257   Article 10 is often invoked in conjunction with complaints about breaches of other Convention rights. In *K v Austria*[787] the Commission decided that passing a sentence of imprisonment on the applicant for refusing to testify against himself was a breach of Article 10 and did not require further consideration as a breach of Article 6.[788] Freedom of expression (and, in particular, the right to hold an opinion) is also closely connected to freedom of thought under Article 9.[789] However, it seems that Article 10 has wider scope than Article 9. Whereas Article 9 only applies if the opinion reflects the conviction of the person who puts it forward,[790] Article 10 contemplates the protection of *any* expression of opinion.

---

[783]   Ibid; see also *Appleby v United Kingdom* (2003) 37 EHRR 38, para 40.

[783a] A breach was aslo found in the *Khurshid Mustafa* case (n 781a above) on the basis of a failure to protect against eviction from a flat for using a satellite dish.

[784]   See P van Dijk, F van Hoof, A van Rijn, and L Zwaak eds, *Theory and Practice of the European Convention on Human Rights* (4th edn, Intersentia, 2006), 786; see also Resolution (74) 26 of the Committee of Ministers of the Council of Europe on the rights of reply.

[785]   Decision of 5 July 2005; see also *Melnitchouk v Ukraine,* Decision of 5 July 2005 (to the same effect); and see *Vitrenko v Ukraine,* Decision of 15 December 2008 (which refers to the positive obligation 'to ensure that persons subjected to defamation have a reasonable opportunity to exercise their right to reply by submitting a response to defamatory information, in the same manner as it was disseminated); and see the discussion in K Reid, *A Practitioner's Guide to the European Convention on Human Rights* (3rd edn, Thomson, 2007), IIB-061.

[786]   Furthermore, such an obligation might be derived from the positive obligation of the state to protect reputation under Art 8, see eg, *Pfeifer v Austria* (2009) 48 EHRR 8 and see generally, para 12.261 above.

[787]   (1993) Series A No 255–B.

[788]   That is, of the privilege against self incrimination: see para 11.435ff above.

[789]   See para 14.87ff above.

[790]   *Arrowsmith v United Kingdom* (1980) 19 DR 5, EComm HR.

Complaints about freedom of expression frequently involve violations of freedom of assem- **15.258** bly under Article 11.[791] In *Ezelin v France*[792] the Court said that a disciplinary penalty against a lawyer for participating in a demonstration should be examined as a potential breach of freedom of association under Article 11. However, in *Steel v United Kingdom*[793] the Court accepted that arrests for breach of the peace when exercising a right of protest (even where the protests were not peaceful) could amount to an interference with Article 10(1).[794] In *Vogt v Germany*[795] a teacher was dismissed because of her political activities as a Communist and alleged that both Article 10 and 11 had been breached. The Court based its decision on Article 11 by examining the arguments put forward under Article 10.

On the other hand, where restrictions on expression are an unintended consequence of a **15.259** state's decision, the Court has been reluctant to consider the complaint under Article 10. For example, where interference with freedom of expression was incidental to the expulsion of an alien, no violation was found.[796]

The Court has taken a similar (and more controversial) approach[797] where public service **15.260** employees protest about restrictions on their freedom of expression. In *Glasenapp v Germany*[798] the applicant was dismissed from his post for expressing views contrary to the German Constitution. He alleged that his Article 10 rights had been breached. The Court took the view that the claimant, who held only a temporary position, was seeking access to public employment (rather than freedom of expression); and that access to public employment was not a right protected by the Convention.[799] By contrast, in *Vogt v Germany*[800] the Court decided that the dismissal of a teacher because of her membership of the Communist Party violated Article 10. The Court distinguished *Glasenapp* and *Kosiek* on the basis that in the earlier cases, the authorities had refused to grant temporary employees access to the civil service because they lacked one of the necessary qualifications.[801] Public officials serving in the judiciary are expected to show restraint in exercising freedom of expression in cases where the authority and impartiality of the judiciary are likely to be called into question.[802]

---

[791] See generally, para 16.76ff below.
[792] (1991) 14 EHRR 362.
[793] (1998) 28 EHRR 603.
[794] Ibid, para 92.
[795] (1995) 21 EHRR 205.
[796] *Agee v United Kingdom* (1976) 7 DR 164, EComm HR; but not if the purpose of the expulsion is the restriction of freedom of expression, *Piermont v France* (1995) 20 EHRR 301.
[797] Contrast with the Commission which decided in *Glasenapp* and *Kosiek* that legislation which required an obligation of loyalty and allegiance to the Constitution as a condition of employment directly interfered with freedom of expression under Art 10(1). It has been argued that the Court should have followed the opinion of the Commission (P van Dijk, F van Hoof, A van Rijn, and L Zwaak eds, *Theory and Practice of the European Convention on Human Rights* (4th edn, Intersentia, 2006), 776–778). Lester suggests that the dissenting Court judgment of Judge Spielam in *Glasenapp* is to be preferred: see A Lester, 'Freedom of Expression' in R St John Macdonald, F Matscher and H Petzold (eds), *The European System for the Protection of Human Rights* (Kluwer, 1993).
[798] (1987) 9 EHRR 25; see also *Kosiek v Germany* (1986) 9 EHRR 328.
[799] See also *Wille v Liechtenstein* (2000) 30 EHRR 558, para 41.
[800] (1995) 21 EHRR 205; see also *Sidabras and Džiautas v Lithuania* (2004) 42 EHRR 104 (Art 10 not engaged by ban on employment of former KGB officers).
[801] Ibid, para 44.
[802] *Wille v Liechtenstein* (see n 799 above) para 64.

15.261 However, an interference with the freedom of expression of a judge calls for close scrutiny.[803] A statement by the Head of State that a judge would not be reappointed to public office as a result of views expressed in a lecture violated the judge's freedom of expression.[804]

(3) The licensing power

(a) Introduction

15.262 The third sentence of Article 10(1) provides that it does not prevent states from requiring the licensing of broadcasting, television or cinema enterprises. The Court in *Groppera Radio AG v Switzerland*[805] said:

> . . .the purpose of the third sentence of Article 10(1) of the Convention is to make it clear that states are permitted to control by a licensing system the way in which broadcasting is organised in their territories, particularly in its technical aspects. It does not, however, provide that licensing measures shall not otherwise be subject to the requirements of Article 10(2), for that would lead to a result contrary to the object and purpose of Article 10 taken as a whole.

This view curtails the licensing power substantially, confining it to restrictions that can be construed as part of the licensing function as such.

(b) Scope of the licensing power

15.263 The scope of the 'licensing power' is not clear. It entitles a state to establish technical and financial criteria for issuing licences to operate radio, television or cinematic facilities; and permits the taking of enforcement action against unlicensed operators[806] provided the proceedings do not include interference with reception of programmes.[807] The state has a relatively wide margin of appreciation in relation to licensing decisions.[808] The grant of a licence may also be made conditional on such matters as the nature and objectives of a proposed station, its potential audience at national, regional or local level, the rights and needs of a specific audience and the obligations deriving from international legal instruments. However, the compatibility of such interferences must be assessed under Article 10(2).[809]

15.264 In *United Christian Broadcasters Ltd v United Kingdom*[810] a complaint that a statutory provision[811] prohibited religious or political bodies from holding national radio licences was held to be inadmissible. The purpose of the restriction was to avoid discrimination between religions and could not be said to be arbitrary. The Court also took into account the

---

[803] Ibid.

[804] Ibid, paras 67–70.

[805] (1990) 12 EHRR 321, para 61.

[806] See *Groppera Radio AG v Switzerland* (1990) 12 EHRR 321.

[807] *Radio X, S, W and A v Switzerland* (1984) 37 DR 236, EComm HR; *Groppera Radio AG v Switzerland* (see n 760 above) para 61; and see *Autronic AG v Switzerland* (1990) 12 EHRR 485.

[808] See *Skyradio AG v Switerland*, Decision of 27 September 2001.

[809] See *United Christian Broadcasters Ltd v United Kingdom*, Decision of 7 November 2000; and *Demuth v Switzerland*, (2004) 38 EHRR 20, paras 33–35; *Glas Nadezhda EOOD and Elenkov v Bulgaria* (2008) 24 BHRC 239, para 42.

[810] Decision of 7 November 2000.

[811] Paragraph 2(7) of Part 11 of Schedule 2 to the Broadcasting Act 1990.

fact that religious groups were not restricted from applying for licences for local radio broadcasting. In *Brook v United Kingdom*[812] the applicant's complaint about a failure to grant him a short-wave radio licence was held to be inadmissible as the requirements of Article 10(2) were satisfied. The proportionality test was met because the applicant had the alternative of applying for an AM or FM licence. In *Demuth v Switzerland*[813] it was held that the refusal of a licence to broadcast a TV programme about cars and road traffic for cable television was justified. The programme was primarily commercial and, as a result, standards of scrutiny were less severe.

A refusal to grant a broadcasting licence is an interference with the freedom to impart **15.265** information and ideas,[814] whether a specific application is refused or the applicant is unsuccessful in a tender process.[815] When a tender is rejected without reasons being given the interference will not be 'in accordance with law' because there is no legal protection against arbitrary interference with freedom of expression.[816]

(c) State monopoly on broadcasting

The question of whether a state monopoly on broadcasting breaches Article 10 has to be **15.266** considered under Article 10(2) rather than 10(1).[817] At one time the maintenance of public monopolies on broadcasting was considered by the Commission to be compatible with the Convention.[818] However, the Commission subsequently changed its view.[819] It is now clear that a public broadcasting monopoly is a breach of Article 10 as it involves a restriction which cannot be justified as being 'necessary in a democratic society'.[820] The restriction of private broadcasters to cable television broadcasting whilst the state broadcasting company had a monopoly over terrestrial broadcasting was a justifiable restriction in circumstances in which almost all households could receive cable.[821]

(4) 'Interference' with the right to freedom of expression

(a) Introduction

In contrast to the position under some other Articles of the Convention, the question as to **15.267** whether there has been an interference with an Article 10 rights will usually be straightforward. Interferences with the right to freedom of expression can take a wide variety of forms and the Court has, generally considered that anything which impedes, sanctions, restricts or deters expression constitutes an interference. Interferences can be considered under three heads: prior restraint, post-expression sanctions and other interferences.

---

[812] [2001] EHRLR 106.

[813] See n 809 above.

[814] *Glas Nadezhda EOOD and Elenkov v Bulgaria* (see n 809 above) para 42.

[815] *Meltex Ltd and Mesrop Movsesyan v Armenia,* Judgment of 17 June 2008, para 74.

[816] Ibid, para 82; *Glas Nadezhda EOOD and Elenkov v Bulgaria* (see n 809 above) para 51.

[817] *Informationsverein Lentia v Austria* (1993) 17 EHRR 93.

[818] See *X v Sweden* (1968) 26 CD 71, EComm HR; *Sacchi v Italy* (1976) 5 DR 435, EComm HR.

[819] See *Nydahl v Sweden* (1993) 16 EHRR CD 15.

[820] See *Informationsverein Lentia v Austria* (see n 817 above) and *Radio ABC v Austria* (1997) 25 EHRR 185; see also *Radio ABC v Austria* (1998) 25 EHRR 185.

[821] *Tele 1 Privatfernsehgesellschaft mbH v Austria* (2002) 34 EHRR 5.

(b) Prior restraint

15.268   There will be an interference with freedom of expression if a person is prevented from publishing material by an injunction or other court order, whether this is interim or final.[822] Pre-publication interferences can also include the banning of the distribution of a particular work[823] or the licensing of journalists.[824]

15.269   Prior restraint on publication in the media is not *as such* incompatible with Article 10.[825] However, it requires very close scrutiny: even if the restraints are temporary, they may deprive the information of interest because news is a perishable commodity.[826] The burden of establishing the necessity of pre-publication measures, such as licensing schemes or court injunctions, is therefore a heavy one.[827]

(c) Post-expression sanctions

15.270   There will also be an interference if a person is subject to sanctions a result of something which has been written, published or broadcast. Post-publication sanctions can include matters such as civil and criminal actions, forfeiture of property,[828] upholding of complaints against broadcasters[829] or disciplinary penalties.[830] Post publication sanctions may have a 'chilling effect' by acting as a deterrent to future publication of other information and materials.[831]

15.271   There will be an interference even if the 'sanction' does not involve the imposition of any criminal or financial penalty. For example, an order that there be a right of reply will be an interference which requires justification under Article 10(2)[832] as will orders that future publications should contain certain information[833] or that a summary of the court's judgment should be published.[834] An 'administrative warning' will also be an interference.[835]

---

[822] See *Sunday Times v United Kingdom (No 2)* (1991) 14 EHRR 229; *The Observer and The Guardian v United Kingdom* (1991) 14 EHRR 153, para 59; *Editions Plon v France* (2006) 42 EHRR 36; *Ferihumer v Austria* (2008) 47 EHRR 42.

[823] See eg, *Wingrove v United Kingdom* (1996) 24 EHRR 1 ('blasphemous' video).

[824] *De Becker v Belgium* (1962) 1 EHRR 43.

[825] Interim injunctions were not in breach of Art 10 in 'confidence' cases such as *Editions Plon v France* (2006) 42 EHRR 36, para 48 and *The Observer and The Guardian v United Kingdom* (see n 822 above), para 65; see generally C Munro, 'Prior restraint of the Media and Human Rights Law' [2002] Juridical Review 1–34.

[826] *The Observer and The Guardian v United Kingdom* (see n 822 above) para 60; *Sunday Times v United Kingdom (No 2)* (n 822 above) para 51; *Ekin v France* (2002) 35 EHRR 35 (blanket executive power to ban foreign books unjustified) but see *Wingrove v United Kingdom* (n 823 above).

[827] *The Observer and The Guardian Newspapers v United Kingdom* (see n 822 above) para 60; and see *De Becker v Belgium* (1962) 1 EHRR 43 (regarding licensing of outlets or journalists); and *Dzhavdov v Russia*, Judgment of 27 September 2007 (refusal to register a newspaper).

[828] See eg, *Müller v Switzerland* (1988) 13 EHRR 212; and *Moldovy v Moldova*, Judgment of 9 January 2007 (closure of a newspaper).

[829] *Monnat v Switzerland*, Judgment of 21 September 2006.

[830] See eg, *Casado Coco v Spain* (1994) 18 EHRR 1; *Fuentes Bobo v Spain* (2001) 31 EHRR 50; *Schmidt v Austria*, Judgment of 17 July 2008 (reprimand to a lawyer for statement made in court).

[831] *Barthold v Germany* (1985) 7 EHRR 383, para 58; *Lingens v Austria* (1986) 8 EHRR 103, para 44; *Jersild v Denmark* (1994) 19 EHRR 1, para 44.

[832] See *Ediciones Tiempo SA v Spain* (1989) 62 DR 247.

[833] *Hertel v Switzerland* (1999) 28 EHRR 534 (prohibition from stating that microwave ovens were a danger to health).

[834] *Hachette Filipacchi Associés v France*, Judgment of 14 June 2007.

[835] *Balsytė-Lideikienė v Lithuania*, Judgment of 4 November 2008.

(d) Other interferences

The Court has held that a variety of other actions have constituted 'interferences' for the purposes of Article 10. These have included: **15.272**

- The refusal to grant broadcasting licences[836] or to accept a tender for such a licence.[837]
- Confiscation of the applicant's cassettes, paperbacks, diary and map.[838]
- A refusal of the State to register a new periodical.[839]
- A conviction for failure to lodge a copy of a press statement with public prosecutor's office.[840]
- The early termination of compulsory military service as a result of membership of a particular political party.[841]

(5) Justifying interferences with freedom of expression: general considerations

(a) Introduction

Where there has been an interference with freedom of expression, it will be justified under Article 10(2) if: **15.273**

- the interference is prescribed by law;
- the interference furthers a 'legitimate aim' (as there set out); and
- the interference is necessary in a democratic society.

The 'legitimate aims' which can, potentially justify restrictions on the freedom of expression are: **15.274**

- the interests of national security;
- the interests of territorial integrity or public safety;
- for the prevention of disorder or crime;
- for the protection of health or morals;
- for the protection of the reputation or the rights of others;
- for preventing the disclosure of information received in confidence; or
- for maintaining the authority and impartiality of the judiciary.

When the Court assesses the question of justification under Article 10(2), it is essential to be clear whether its decision is based on the ground that the interference is a disproportionate restriction which is not 'necessary in a democratic society'; or whether it has decided that the interference is within a state's margin of appreciation. These doctrines are discussed in detail in Chapter 6. The principle of proportionality is a standard of judicial review.[842] On the other hand, the doctrine of the 'margin of appreciation' involves an interpretative **15.275**

---

[836] See eg, *Autronic AG v Switzerland* (1990) 12 EHRR 485; *Radio ABC v Austria* (1997) 25 EHRR 185.

[837] *Glas Nadezhda EOOD and Elenkov v Bulgaria* (2008) 24 BHRC 239.

[838] *Foka v Turkey*, Judgment of 24 June 2008.

[839] *Gawęda v Poland* (2004) 39 EHRR 4.

[840] *Karademirci v Turkey* (2007) 44 EHRR 44.

[841] *Erdel v Germany* (2007) 44 EHRR SE23; *Lahr v Germany* (2008) 47 EHRR SE22.

[842] See generally, para 6.67ff above.

obligation on an international human rights court to respect domestic cultural traditions and values.[843]

15.276 The potential justifications for interfering with freedom of expression under Article 10(2) must be narrowly interpreted: the 'necessity' for any restrictions must be 'convincingly established'.[844] The necessity of a restriction depends on the character of the expression, the duties and responsibilities of those exercising freedom of expression, the means of the communication, the audience to which it is directed, the significance of the interference and the purpose for which the restraint is imposed.

15.277 The doctrine of margin of appreciation has played an important and controversial role in the Article 10 jurisprudence. The Court has used a number of different approaches when applying the margin of appreciation to freedom of expression cases;[845] and it is strongly arguable that excessive use of the concept has seriously eroded the protection given by Article 10.[846]

15.278 The Court's approach to the issue of 'justification' is most highly developed in cases involving the mass media where 'necessity in a democratic society' is often the only contentious issue and involves a fact sensitive investigation of the circumstances of and justification for the interference. Media cases will be considered in the next section.[847]

(b) Duties and responsibilities

15.279 Article 10(2) states that the exercise of the freedoms in Article 10(1) carries with it 'duties and responsibilities'. The phrase implies that, in determining the necessity of restrictions, these duties and responsibilities must not be overlooked.[848] This consideration might legitimize discriminatory distinctions between people in different positions; and could also serve to justify restrictions upon 'irresponsible' expression. It is, however, unclear how the notion of 'duties and responsibilities' is to be applied. In some cases it has justified a broad interpretation of a limitation, while in other cases it has had the opposite effect.[849] In *Handyside*,[850] which concerned an obscene publication intended for children, the Court emphasized the responsibilities of publishers and upheld a restriction. In *Lingens*,[851] on the other hand, the right of a journalist to criticize a politician was upheld when the press was found to have a duty and responsibility in a democratic society to 'impart information and

---

[843] See para 6.42ff above.

[844] See generally, the principles restated in *Lindon, Otchakovsky-Laurens and July v France* (2008) 46 EHRR 35 (GC), para 45, see para 15.239 above.

[845] N Lavender, 'The Problem of the Margin of Appreciation' [1997] EHRLR 380.

[846] See for example A Lester 'Freedom of Expression' in R St J Macdonald, F Matscher, and H Petzold (eds), *The European System for the Protection of Human Rights* (1993, Kluwer); and see P Mahoney, 'Universality Versus Subsidiarity in the Strasbourg Case Law on Free Speech: Explaining Some Recent Judgments' [1997] EHRLR 364 and Lord Lester, 'Universality Versus Subsidiarity: A Reply' [1998] EHRLR 73.

[847] See para 15.310ff below.

[848] *Handyside v United Kingdom* (1976) 1 EHRR 737, para 49.

[849] See A Robertson and J Merrills, *Human Rights in Europe: A Study of the European Convention on Human Rights* (Manchester University Press, 1993), 151.

[850] *Handyside v United Kingdom* (see n 848 above) para 49.

[851] *Lingens v Austria* (1986) 8 EHRR 103; but a more restrictive view of 'duties and responsibilities' was taken in *Prager and Oberschlick v Austria* (1995) 21 EHRR 1 where it was found that a journalist had failed to prove that he had applied the necessary diligence in his research.

ideas on political issues'; and in *Castells v Spain*[852] a politician enjoyed the advantage of protection of his special position.

In particular, the phrase 'duties and responsibilities' has been used to justify interfering **15.280** with freedom of expression on grounds of status. Thus, the duties and responsibilities of soldiers,[853] civil servants[854] or teachers[855] were said to justify interferences with Article 10. However, the phrase has not played a prominent role in recent cases[856] and it now appears to have only minor significance as a further source of justification for interference with freedom of expression.

(c) Types of expression

Introduction. When considering 'justification' issues under Article 10(2), the Court **15.281** takes into account the 'type' of expression involved.[857] Whether or not a particular interference is 'prescribed by law' or 'necessary in a democratic society' may depend on the type of expression involved. The Court has distinguished three general 'types' of expression:

- political expression;
- artistic expression; and
- commercial expression.

The Court consistently attaches great importance to political expression; and applies rather less rigorous principles to artistic and commercial expression.

Political expression. The most important category of expression is what is usually described **15.282** as 'political expression'—although, perhaps more accurately, could be called expression on matters of public interest and debate. Political expression has been said to be central to a democratic system which requires that even ideas that 'offend, shock and disturb' be published.[858] Freedom of political debate and the press gives the public one of the best means of discovering and forming an opinion about the ideas and attitudes of political leaders and is a core concept of a democratic society.[859] While the electoral process is not itself protected by Article 10, expression during the course of an election is given specific protection.[860]

---

[852] (1992) 14 EHHR 445.

[853] *Engel v Netherlands (No 2)* (1976) 1 EHRR 706, para 100; but see *Vereinigung Demokratischer Soldaten Osterreichs and Gubi v Austria* (1994) 20 EHRR 55, para 27 where the Court expressed the view that freedom of expression under Art 10(1) applies to servicemen just as much as to others.

[854] *B v United Kingdom* (1985) 45 41, EComm HR.

[855] *X v United Kingdom* (1979) 16 DR 101, EComm HR; *Morissens v Belgium* (1988) 56 DR 127, EComm HR.

[856] Cf *Otto-Preminger-Institute v Austria* (1994) 19 EHRR 34, para 49 where the Court suggested that those who criticized the religious views of others had an obligation to avoid so far as possible remarks which were gratuitously offensive.

[857] See generally, H Fenwick, and G Phillipson, *Media Freedom under the Human Rights Act* (Oxford University Press, 2006), 51–72.

[858] *Handyside v United Kingdom* (1976) 1 EHRR 737, para 49.

[859] *Lingens v Austria* (1986) 8 EHRR 103, para 42.

[860] See *Bowman v United Kingdom* (1998) 26 EHRR 1, para 42 (restrictions on election expenses a violation of Art 10).

15.283 As a result, there is little scope for restricting political speech or debate on matters of public interest.[861] Interference with the expression of politicians and, in particular, the views of the opposition, must be given the 'closest scrutiny'.[862] Politicians must be tolerant of sharp criticism of themselves, in the same democratic interest.[863] In particular, the Court has distinguished between facts and value judgments when considering the validity of criticisms made against politicians. Value judgments are not susceptible to proof and, consequently, a requirement that a publisher must prove the truth of an opinion is impossible and is therefore unjustifiable under Article 10(2).[864]

15.284 The concept of political expression is broadly interpreted. In *Thorgeirson v Iceland*[865] the Court considered a complaint about defamation of the police; and said that its jurisprudence did not warrant a distinction between political discussion and discussion of other matters of public concern. A journalist's allegations of bias against a court where two of its lay judges were employed by local government was party to proceedings before it was treated as political expression.[866] Press statements made by a veterinary surgeon about the inadequacies of an emergency veterinary service [867] and advertising on television by an animal welfare group[868] have also been treated as political expression.

15.285 Furthermore, the Court has recognized that criticism of other public figures may attract some additional protection under Article 10:

> the limits of acceptable criticism are wider with regard to businessmen actively involved in the affairs of large public companies than with regard to private individuals.[869]

When statements are published as part of a 'general interest' debate concerning matters such as public health they may also be accorded greater protection.[870] An individual may be a public figure, even if his appearance is not known to the public. Thus it was held that the publication of a photograph of a politician, accused of impropriety, was protected by Article 10 even if his appearance was not widely known.[871] But, the 'general interest' does not extend to the discussion of the private lives of individuals who exercise no official functions.[872]

15.286 Publication concerning civil servants will not always fall within the highest category of 'political expression' as:

---

[861] *Wingrove v United Kingdom* (1996) 24 EHRR 1, para 58.
[862] *Castells v Spain* (1992) 14 EHRR 445, para 42.
[863] *Lingens v Austria* (1986) 8 EHRR 103; *Oberschlick v Austria (No 1)* (1991) 19 EHRR 389; *Schwabe v Austria* (1992) Series A No 242–B.
[864] *Lingens v Austria* (see n 863 above) para 46.
[865] *Thorgeirson v Iceland* (1992) 14 EHRR 843, para 62.
[866] *Barfod v Denmark* (1989) 13 EHRR 493.
[867] *Barthold v Germany* (1985) 7 EHRR 383.
[868] *Vgt Verein gegen Tierfabriken v Switzerland* (2002) 34 EHRR 4.
[869] *Fayed v United Kingdom* (1994) 18 EHRR 393, para 75; see also *Steel and Morris v United Kingdom* (2005) 41 EHRR 22, para 94; *Timpul Info-Magazin and Anghel v Moldova*, Judgment of 27 November 2007, para 33.
[870] See *Hertel v Switzerland* (1999) 28 EHRR 534.
[871] See *Krone Verlag GmBH v Austria* (2003) 36 EHRR 57 (publication of a photograph of a politician).
[872] See *Von Hannover v Germany* (2005) 40 EHRR 1, para 76; but see *Nikowitz v Austria* [2007] EMLR 8 (which suggests that society's attitude towards a sports star is a matter of 'general interest'—it is difficult to see how this is consistent with *Von Hannover*).

it may be necessary to protect public servants from offensive, abusive and defamatory attacks which are calculated to affect them in the performance of their duties and damage public confidence in the offices they hold.[873]

However, interference with freedom of expression can only be justified where there is a real threat to the performance of public duties or to public confidence.[874] Moreover, this principle does not extend to all persons employed by state owned companies.[875]

Artistic expression. The term 'artistic expression' covers activities such as painting, **15.287** exhibiting and giving an artist the opportunity to show his works in public and is an indisputable exercise of freedom of expression under Article 10.[876] But where artistic expression offends or shocks, the Court long took a cautious position. In *Müller v Switzerland*[877] paintings depicting activities involving homosexuality and bestiality were on public display without warnings. The Court held that the duties and responsibilities of the artist imposed on him special considerations of restraint rather than opportunities of freedom.

The *Müller* case was applied in *Otto-Preminger-Institute v Austria*.[878] A film was seized and **15.288** forfeited because its showing created 'justified indignation' among a local population on religious grounds. However, the Court's decision has been much criticized. The reasoning adopted was very broad; the outrage of people who knew the nature of the film but had not seen it justified state interference with expression; and the reaction of persons in a small geographic area was a sufficient justification for a national ban on the film. The decision of the Court was by a majority (6:3), the majority having had to rely on their own assessment of the lack of merit of the film, an approach which was inconsistent with basic principles of freedom of expression. It is therefore submitted that the reasoning in the case is limited to its own particular facts and should not be treated as being of general application.

In the more recent case of *Vereinigung Bildender Künstler v Austria*[879] the Court emphasized **15.289** that

> Those who create, perform, distribute or exhibit works of art contribute to the exchange of ideas and opinions which is essential for a democratic society.[880]

It went on to hold injunction forbidding artists from exhibiting collage showing photographs of well known figures on painted bodies of engaged in sexual activities on basis that politician's public standing was debased was violation of Art 10: the portrayal was artistic and satirical in nature and unlimited injunction disproportionate.[881]

---

[873] See *Busuioc v Moldova* (2006) 42 EHRR 14, para 64 and see *Janowski v Poland* (2000) 29 EHRR 705 and *Nikula v Finland* (2004) 38 EHRR 45, para 48.

[874] *Yankov v Bulgaria* (2005) 40 EHRR 36, para 142 (breach when a prisoner was disciplined for criticizing prison staff in a private manuscript).

[875] See *Busuioc* (see n 873 above).

[876] See *Müller v Switzerland* (1988) 13 EHRR 212, para 27.

[877] Ibid.

[878] (1994) 19 EHRR 34; for critical comment on this case see D Pannick, 'Religious Feelings and the European Court', [1995] PL 7.

[879] (2008) 47 EHRR 5.

[880] Ibid, para 26.

[881] But note that the decision was by a bare majority of 4:3, see in particular the joint dissenting opinion of Judges Spielmann and Jebens (Ibid, O-II9-13) which is based on the need to respect 'human dignity'.

15.290 **Commercial expression.**[882]   The paradigm form of commercial expression is advertising: which was the first type of commercial expression considered in Strasbourg.[883] However, 'commercial expression' would appear to cover other areas such as 'celebrity journalism' and pornography, which have a low degree of protection under Article 10.

15.291 Commercial expression has been protected on grounds that Article 10 does not apply 'solely to certain types of information or ideas or forms of expression'.[884] In *Markt Intern and Beermann v Germany*[885] the applicant published a trade magazine which contained an article describing the experience of a chemist who was dissatisfied with a mail order firm and sought a refund; the article also described the response of the firm to its own inquiries. Although the statements in the article were true, an injunction was granted, restraining *'Markt Intern'* from repeating the allegations on the basis that it had acted contrary to honest practices in breach of the Unfair Competition Act. The Court regarded the article as information of a commercial nature which was protected under Article 10, although on the facts the interference was justified. Similarly, in *Casado Coca v Spain*[886] the Court rejected an argument that professional advertising was not protected by Article 10.

15.292 Restrictions on commercial expression will generally be subject to less strict scrutiny on the basis that what is being served is a private, rather than a public, interest. Thus a wide margin of appreciation will be extended where the speech interfered with is found to have an essentially competitive purpose.[887] However, in *Barthold v Germany*[888] the Court distinguished commercial advertising from public discussion of a matter of general interest when considering the conviction of a veterinary surgeon who made comments to the press about the lack of public provision in his field. His conviction in proceedings brought by fellow vets for 'instigating or tolerating publicity on his own behalf' was unjustified; the newspaper article in question was not viewed by the Court as commercial expression but as involving political expression.

15.293 Commercial expression is treated as being of less importance than either political or artistic expression. Statements made for the purpose of competition fall outside the basic nucleus protected by freedom of expression and receive a lower standard of protection than other ideas or information.[889] Thus, in the *Markt Intern* case[890] the Court upheld an injunction against a trade magazine which prohibited it from publishing. The Court took the view that, as commercial speech, the magazine was subject to different standards. Even if statements in the publication were true, they could, nevertheless, be prohibited because of a duty to respect the privacy of others or the confidentiality of certain commercial information.

---

[882] See generally, M Randall 'Commercial Speech under the European Convention on Human Rights: subordinate or equal?' (2006) HRL Rev 53 and R Shiner, *Freedom of Commercial Expression* (Oxford University Press, 2003), 95–100.

[883] *X and Church of Scientology v Sweden* (1979) 16 DR 68.

[884] *Markt Intern and Beermann v Germany* (1989) 12 EHRR 161, paras 25–26.

[885] Ibid.

[886] (1994) 18 EHRR 1, paras 35–36.

[887] *Jacubowski v Germany* (1994) 19 EHRR 64, para 28 (but note the dissenting opinions of Judges Walsh, Macdonald, and Wildhaber).

[888] (1985) 7 EHRR 383, para 50.

[889] *Markt Intern and Beermann v Germany* (see n 884 above) para 32.

[890] Ibid, the Court was split 9–9 and the case was decided on the casting vote of the President.

However, the decisive factor in the Court's reasoning was the wide margin of appreciation it gave to the national courts.[891] By contrast, in *Hertel v Switzerland*[892] where the submission of a research paper to a scientific journal resulted in a criminal conviction, the Court took a much more restrictive approach to the margin of appreciation. It held that the conviction was a disproportionate interference with freedom of expression.

The close regulation of professional advertising in some European countries has resulted in decisions holding that the national authorities have a wide margin of appreciation when interfering with an advertiser's expression. In *Colman v United Kingdom*,[893] the Commission decided that restrictions on advertising by doctors was justified. This approach was followed in *Casado Coca v Spain*[894] where it was held that, in the absence of a common European standard, the regulation of advertising by barristers did not fall outside the wide margin of appreciation which states had on the matter. A complaint concerned prohibitions on the mentioning of fee scales in publicity was inadmissible. The special position of lawyers in the administration of justice was noted and the Court also relied on the EU case law which describes the area of unfair completion as 'complex and fluctuating'.[895]

15.294

Restrictions on advertising by medical professionals have, however, been subject to stricter scrutiny. Thus, in *Stambuk v Germany*[896] a violation was found when a doctor complained was disciplined for co-operating with a newspaper article which appeared to advertise his practice. It was said that the rules of conduct in relation to advertising by medical practitioners had to be balanced against the legitimate interest of the public in information and should be limited to those necessary to preserve the well-functioning of the profession as a whole.[897]

15.295

The Court has accepted that pornography is a form of freedom of expression which is protected under Article 10.[898] It has been said that

15.296

> Where no adult is confronted unintentionally or against his will with filmed matter, there must be particularly compelling reasons to justify an interference.[899]

However, in a case where no artistic merit is claimed for the films, the fact that it could not be said with certainty that minors would not have access to them meant that an interference was justified. In general, it will not be difficult to justify interference with obscene material under Article 10(2).

Summary. The Court has not produced any rigid typology of forms of expression and, indeed, this would be contrary to the 'fact sensitive' approach which it takes to justification issues. Nevertheless, the 'value' of the expression in question is an important consideration

15.297

---

[891] Ibid, paras 33–38.
[892] (1999) 28 EHRR 534.
[893] (1993) 18 EHRR 119; the case was the subject of a friendly settlement.
[894] (1994) 18 EHRR 1.
[895] *Brzank v Germany*, Decision of 23 October 2007; see also *Heimann v Germany*, Decision of 23 October 2007 (description as a 'specialist lawyer').
[896] (2003) 37 EHRR 42.
[897] Ibid, para 41.
[898] See eg, *Scherer v Switzerland* (1994) 18 EHRR 276 Comm Rep, para 62; *Hoare v United Kingdom* [1997] EHRLR 678.
[899] *Hoare* (see n 898 above).

in the justification exercise. We would tentatively suggest that in Article 10 cases, the following hierarchy of types of expression, beginning with the most valuable and going to the least valuable can be derived from the case law discussed in this section:

- Political expression concerning the conduct of politicians in public office, including statements made at elections.
- Other expression concerning matters of public interest, including the private conduct of politicians and the conduct of large corporations and other powerful bodies.
- Artistic expression, including writing of all forms, painting, film and video.
- Statements concerning the activities of civil servants.
- Statements concerning the conduct of private individuals.
- Statements made for commercial purposes, including advertising and 'entertainment journalism'.
- Pornography and expression which undermines the rights of others such as direct attacks on religious sensibilities.
- Speech which promotes or intended to provoke violence or attacks on the democratic order.

15.298 This 'hierarchy' of types of expression can be a useful guide, provided it is not rigidly applied and account is taken of the fact that many publications or actions will fall into one or more of theses categories. Interferences with 'political expression' will be the most difficult to justify and interferences with speech promoting violence or attacking the democratic order will be very easy to justify. Justification of interferences with other 'types of speech' will be increasingly easy as the 'hierarchy' is descended but will be fact sensitive.

(d) 'Prescribed by law'

15.299 **Introduction.** An interference with freedom of expression will be prescribed by law where:

- the interference in question has some basis in domestic law;
- the law is adequately accessible; and
- the law is formulated so that it is sufficiently foreseeable.

The principle applies to a number of qualified Convention rights and is examined in detail in Chapter 6.[900] There have, however, been a number of important cases which have considered its impact on Article 10.

15.300 **General.** Restrictions on the freedom of expression must be authorized by national law. Identification of the law or rule [901] in question has not, in general, been a source of difficulty in Article 10 cases. Whether or not the law is adequately accessible is also usually straightforward. The law must be formulated with sufficient precision to enable the citizen to regulate his conduct. He must be able—if need be with appropriate advice—to foresee, to a degree that is reasonable in the circumstances, the consequences which a given action may

---

[900] See para 6.215ff above.

[901] It is accepted that rules made by professional or other bodies constitute 'laws' where rule-making power has been delegated to those authorities; see *Barthold v Germany* (1985) 7 EHRR 383; *Casado Coca v Spain* (1994) 18 EHRR 1.

entail.[902] Absolute precision is not achievable, and flexibility is necessary where the circumstances are constantly changing.[903]

Common law. The Court has considered on several occasions whether the common law is **15.301** sufficiently foreseeable. In *Sunday Times v United Kingdom*[904] the Court accepted that a reformulation of the principles of contempt of court by the House of Lords[905] was still sufficiently foreseeable. In *Tolstoy Miloslavsky v United Kingdom*[906] it held that libel awards by juries were not too uncertain to be sufficiently foreseeable. The Court decided in *Steel v United Kingdom*[907] that the common law concept of breach of the peace was formulated with sufficient precision to be sufficiently foreseeable. In *Goodwin v United Kingdom*[908] the Court held that section 10 of the Contempt of Court Act 1981 was sufficiently precise to be foreseeable. On the other hand, in *Hashman and Harrup v United Kingdom*[909] the Court took the view that ordering a bind over on the basis that the applicant's conduct was *contra bonos mores* (that is, 'conduct which is wrong rather than right in the judgment of the majority of contemporary fellow citizens')[910] did not provide sufficient guidance about what sort of conduct would breach the order.

Commercial expression cases. The Court has taken a broad view of the accessibility **15.302** requirement in commercial expression cases. In *Barthold v Germany*[911] the Court acknowledged a wide discretion to control unfair competition and said that absolute precision is especially difficult in regulating competition. In *Markt Intern and Beermann v Germany*[912] the requirement of honest practices in German competition law was acceptable because absolute precision could not be achieved in a competitive environment which was constantly changing because of developments in the market and in the communications field. The state was entitled to rely on the norms of public international law to prove that its domestic law was sufficiently accessible in *Groppera Radio AG v Switzerland*[913] and in *Autronic AG v Switzerland*.[914]

---

[902] *Sunday Times v United Kingdom* (1979) 2 EHRR 245, paras 48, 49; see also *Grigoriades v Greece* (1997) 27 EHRR 464, para 37.

[903] In *Markt Intern and Beermann v Germany* (1989) 12 EHRR 161, a law requiring 'honest practices' was sufficiently foreseeable in the sphere of competition where changes in the market and in communication precluded absolute precision; see also *Müller v Switzerland* (1988) 13 EHRR 212 in which the Court referred to 'the need to avoid excessive rigidity and to keep pace with changing circumstances'; the language comes from *Sunday Times v United Kingdom* (n 902 above) in which the Court held that a development in the common law of contempt of court was an application of a general principle which might have been anticipated by the applicants and was thus 'reasonable in the circumstances'.

[904] (1979) 2 EHRR 245.

[905] Whereas in *A-G v Times Newspapers Ltd* [1973] QB 710 the Divisional Court applied the principle that a deliberate attempt to influence the settlement of pending proceedings by bringing public pressure to bear on a party amounted to a contempt of court, the House of Lords seemed to prefer the view that it is a contempt to publish material which prejudges pending litigation: see [1974] AC 273.

[906] (1995) 20 EHRR 442.

[907] (1998) 26 EHRR 603, paras 25–28, 55.

[908] (1997) 22 EHRR 123.

[909] (2000) 30 EHRR 241, paras 36–41.

[910] *Hughes v Holley* (1986) 86 Cr App R 130.

[911] (1985) 7 EHRR 383, para 47.

[912] (1989) 12 EHHR 161, para 30.

[913] (1990) 12 EHRR 321.

[914] (1990) 12 EHRR 485.

15.303   **Cases in which 'prescribed by law' requirement was not met.**   The Court has found that the 'prescribed by law' requirement was not met in a number of Article 10 cases. In *Gawęda v Poland*[915] the applicant was unable to register a new periodical because the title 'was in conflict with reality'. It was held that this was a violation because the domestic law not formulated with sufficient precision. A similar result was reached in *Karademirci v Turkey*[916] where the applicant had been convicted for a failure to lodge a copy of a press statement with public prosecutor's office. There was a violation because the domestic law did not satisfy requirement of foreseeability. When a protestor who had gathered signatures for a petition and held up placards was unlawfully arrested there was also a violation of Article 10 on the ground that the interference was not 'prescribed by law'.[917]

15.304   The 'prescribed by law' requirement has been extended in cases involving the application for broadcasting licences to include procedural guarantees. Thus, *Glas Nadezhda EOOD and Elenkov v Bulgaria*[918] the Court held that, although the criteria applied by the domestic authorities were sufficiently accessible and precise, the lack of reasons for the decision to refuse the applicant tender for a licence 'denied the applicants legal protection against arbitrary interferences with their freedom of expression' and, as a result, the convention requirement of lawfulness was not met.[919] These cases are difficult to follow and it is suggested that the requirement to give reasons should, properly, have been dealt with as an aspect of 'necessity in democratic society'.

(e) Legitimate aim

15.305   An interference will only be justified if it was for one or more of the 'legitimate aims' listed in Article 10(2). In practice, very few disputes arise about whether an interference falls within the broad scope of one or more of the listed aims. However, the aim of the interference will be relevant to the question as to whether an interference is necessary in a democratic society. In particular, the 'margin of appreciation' applied by the Court will differ depending on the aim of the interference.

(f) 'Necessary in a democratic society'

15.306   **General.**   The general principles which the Court applies when deciding whether an interference is necessary in a democratic society[920] are discussed in Chapter 6. The adjective 'necessary' does not mean 'indispensable' but does not have the flexibility of expressions such as 'admissible', 'ordinary', 'useful', 'reasonable or desirable'.[921] The Court must consider whether the interference complained of corresponded to a pressing social need, whether it was proportionate to the legitimate aim pursued and whether the reasons given by the national authority to justify it are relevant and sufficient under Article 10(2).[922]

---

[915] (2004) 39 EHRR 4; see also *Dzhavdov v Russia,* Judgment of 27 September 2007.
[916] (2007) 44 EHRR 44.
[917] *Kandzhov v Bulgaria,* Judgment of 6 November 2008, para 72.
[918] (2008) 24 BHRC 239.
[919] Ibid, paras 50–52; see also *Meltex Ltd and Mesrop Movsesyan v Armenia,* Judgment of 17 June 2008.
[920] See para 6.251ff above.
[921] See *Handyside v United Kingdom* (1976) 1 EHRR 737, para 46.
[922] See *Sunday Times v United Kingdom* (1979) 2 EHRR 245, para 62.

These principles have been reaffirmed in many subsequent cases.[923] In practice, the Court considers a variety of factors including:

- the value of the type of expression,[924]
- the medium of expression;
- the audience or target of the expression;
- the objective of the interference;
- the nature of the interference, in particular the nature of the sanctions imposed.

Council of Europe Standards.   The Parliamentary Assembly and the Committee of   **15.307** Ministers of the Council of Europe have, from time to time, made recommendations or passed resolutions relating to freedom of expression which can be taken into account when considering whether an interference is necessary in a democratic society. These recommendations and resolutions have covered a wide range of topics including the provision of information in relation to criminal proceedings,[925] investigative journalism,[926] the right of journalists not to disclose sources,[927] the right to privacy,[928] the freedom of political debate in the media[929] and the ethics of journalism.[930] A full list can be found on the Council of Europe Website.[931]

Margin of appreciation.   In considering whether an interference is justified the Court will   **15.308** accord a certain 'margin of appreciation' to the national authorities.[932] The 'width' of this margin will depend on matters such as the 'type' of expression involved and on the extent to which there is common ground between different Member States. The court has recognized that where an interference is based on the protection of morality it should accord particular respect for different national approaches.[933]

In the remainder of this section we shall first discuss the general approach taken by the   **15.309** Court in deciding whether an interference with media expression is necessary in a democratic society. We then consider the case law relating to each of the specific legitimate aims under Article 10(2).

---

[923] See eg, *Lindon, Otchakovsky-Laurens and July v France* (2008) 46 EHRR 35 (GC), para 45.

[924] See para 15.281ff above.

[925] Committee of Ministers, 'Recommendation No. R (2003) 13 on the provision of information through the media in relation to criminal proceedings'; see also the 'Declaration on the provision of information through the media in relation to criminal proceedings adopted on 10 July 2003'.

[926] See Declaration by the Committee of Ministers on the protection and promotion of investigative journalism, adopted on 26 September 2007.

[927] Committee of Ministers, 'Recommendation No. R (2000) 7 on the right of journalists not to disclose their sources of information and its Explanatory Memorandum'.

[928] Parliamentary Assembly Resolution 1165 (1998) on the right to privacy and Resolution 428, containing a Declaration on Mass Communication Media and Human Rights adopted on 23 January 1970.

[929] Committee of Ministers 'Declaration on the freedom of political debate in the media adopted on 12 February 2004'.

[930] Parliamentary Assembly, Recommendation 1215 (1993) on the ethics of journalism and Resolution 1003 (1993) on the ethics of journalism.

[931] <http://www.coe.int/t/dghl/standardsetting/media/>.

[932] See generally, para 6.42ff above.

[933] See eg, *Handyside v United Kingdom* (1979–80) 1 EHRR 737, para 48.

(6) Justifying interferences with media expression

(a) Introduction

15.310   Article 10 cases involving the media usually involve civil or criminal sanctions which have been imposed to 'protect the rights of others'—typically the right to reputation of the subject of the publication. Other legitimate aims such as national security,[934] the prevention of crime and disorder[935] and the protection of health or morals[936] are sometimes relied on to justify the interference. In such cases there will be a clear interference which has a legitimate aim under Article 10(2). In most cases the interference will be 'prescribed by law' in the sense that the applicant has been sanctioned after proceedings in which the domestic courts have applied the criminal or civil law of defamation. The central issue is usually whether or not the interference can be justified as being 'necessary in a democratic society'. As already mentioned, this exercise is fact sensitive and the justification for the interference must be considered in the circumstances of each case. Nevertheless, the Court has, on many occasions recognized the special position of the media in a democratic society and has set out general principles which guide the 'justification' exercise. We will begin by considering the position of the media. We will then deal with the principles that can be derived from the Article 10 media cases. Finally, we will consider their application in the case law under a number of headings.

15.311   *(b) The role of the media in a democratic society*

Although the Convention does not specifically refer to the press, the Court has consistently recognized the 'essential function the press fulfils in a democratic society'. The special role of the media in a democratic society has been recognized in many cases, particularly in reporting 'information and ideas on political issues and other matters of general interest'.[937] The Court has repeatedly emphasized stated that it is incumbent on the press

> to impart information and ideas on matters of public interest. Not only does the press have the task of imparting such information and ideas: the public also has a right to receive them. Were it otherwise, the press would be unable to play its vital role of 'public watchdog'.[938]

As a result, 'the safeguards to be afforded to the press are of particular importance'.[939] Journalistic freedom also covers possible recourse to a degree of exaggeration, or even provocation.[940] Similar protection is extended to NGOs which seek to keep the public informed on public interest matters.[941]

---

[934] See para 15.360ff below.

[935] See para 15.365ff below.

[936] See para 15.369ff below.

[937] See, among many other cases, *De Haes and Gijsels v Belgium*, (1998) 25 EHRR 1, para 37.

[938] *Observer and Guardian v United Kingdom* (1992) 14 EHRR 153, para 59(b).

[939] *Goodwin v United Kingdom* (1996) 22 EHRR 123, para 39; *Thoma v Luxembourg*, (2003) 36 EHRR 21, para 45; *Cumpănă and Mazăre v Romania* (2005) 41 EHRR 14, para 93.

[940] *Prager and Oberschlick v Austria* (1996) 21 EHRR 1, para 38, *Bladet Tromsø and Stensaas v Norway* (2000) 29 EHRR 125, para 59.

[941] See *Vides Aizsardzības Klubs v Latvia*, Judgment of 27 May 2004, para 42; also *Steel and Morris v United Kingdom* (2005) 41 EHRR 22, para 89 (protection extends to small and informal campaign groups).

Nevertheless, the press 'must not overstep certain bounds', in particular 'in respect of the reputation and rights of others'[942] and 'the need to prevent the disclosure of confidential information'.[943] This means that **15.312**

> By reason of the 'duties and responsibilities' inherent in the exercise of the freedom of expression, the safeguard afforded by Article 10 to journalists in relation to reporting on issues of general interest is subject to the proviso that they are acting in good faith in order to provide accurate and reliable information in accordance with the ethics of journalism.[944]

In general, there is an obligation on the media to verify factual allegations before they are made and

> special grounds were required before a newspaper could be dispensed from its ordinary obligation to verify factual statements that were defamatory of private individuals. The question whether such grounds existed depended in particular on the nature and degree of the defamation in question and the extent to which the newspaper could reasonably regard its sources as reliable with respect to the allegations.[945]

The Court has, in general, taken a generous approach towards the media in Article 10 cases, applying strict scrutiny to the decisions of the domestic courts and finding violations in a large percentage of cases. However, in recent years the recognition of an Article 8 right to reputation[946] which must be balanced against the right to freedom of expression has led to a number of judges expressing concern about 'media abuses'. In his concurring opinion in the case of *Lindon, Otchakovsky-Laurens and July v France*[947] Judge Loucaides said that the: **15.313**

> The main argument in favour of protecting freedom of expression, even in cases of inaccurate defamatory statements, is the encouragement of uninhibited debate on public issues. But the opposite argument is equally strong: the suppression of untrue defamatory statements, apart from protecting the dignity of individuals, discourages false speech and improves the overall quality of public debate through a chilling effect on irresponsible journalism. Moreover, such debates may be suppressed if the potential participants know that they will have no remedy in the event that false defamatory accusations are made against them. The prohibition of defamatory speech also eliminates misinformation in the mass media and effectively protects the right of the public to truthful information. Furthermore, false accusations concerning public officials, including candidates for public office, may drive capable persons away from government service, thus frustrating rather than furthering the political process.

In a number of recent cases the Court has held that the Article 10 rights of the media are outweighed by the Article 8 rights of a person who has been defamed.[948]

---

[942] *Cumpănă and Mazăre v Romania* (see n 939 above) para 93.

[943] *Selistö v Finland* (2006) 42 EHRR 8, para 48.

[944] *Bladet Tromsø and Stensaas* (see n 940 above) para 65.

[945] Ibid, para 66; *McVicar v United Kingdom* (2002) 35 EHRR 22, para 84.

[946] See para 12.301ff above.

[947] (2008) 46 EHRR 35 (GC), Concurring Opinion, O-I11; see, also *Von Hannover v Germany* (2005) 40 EHRR 1, O-II3 the concurring opinion of Judge Zupančič 'the courts have to some extent and under American influence made a fetish of the freedom of the press'.

[948] *Pfeifer v Austria* (2009) 48 EHRR 8; *Petrina v Roumania*, Judgment of 14 October 2008.

(c) The principles

15.314 The Court has on many occasions stated 'general propositions' which it applies when a violation of Article 10 is alleged.[949] No comparable exercise has been carried out in 'media cases'. We suggest that a number of principles relevant to media cases can be derived from the case law:

- The most important factor in considering 'justification' is the type of expression involved. There is little scope for restrictions on political expression or debate on matters of public interest[950] but scrutiny will be less strict where the publications in question do not contribute to a debate of general interest.[951]

- The identity of the persons who are being discussed is also important. The limits of acceptable criticism of a politician are wider than in relation to a private individual.[952] Political invective often spills over into the private sphere and is one of the hazards of politics.[953] The limits of permissible criticism are also wider in relation to other individuals involved in public life.[954] However, the court will take into account whether the publication concerned private life or behaviour in an official capacity.[955] If direct accusations are made against named public officials then there must be a sufficient factual basis for the assertions.[956]

- If the publications complained of consist of 'value judgments' then interference will not usually be justified. A sanction based on a failure to prove the truth of a value judgment will be a violation of Article 10.[957] The concept of 'value judgment' has been widely construed including, for example, an allegation of lying.[958] Nevertheless, a value judgment must have a factual basis to support it.[959]

- If the publications complained of are factual in nature then the media must be permitted to demonstrate their truth[960] and, if they do so, then no interference will be justified.

- If the publications complained of are factual in nature and false then an interference will not be justified if the media has acted in good faith in order to provide accurate and

---

[949] See, para 15.239 above.

[950] *Surek v Turkey* (1999) 7 BHRC 339, para 61; *Kulis v Poland*, Judgment of 18 March 2008, para 37.

[951] Where, for example, the publications concern a person's private life then interferences may be easier to justify (see eg, *Von Hannover v Germany* (2005) 40 EHRR 1).

[952] *Lingens v Austria*, (1986) 8 EHRR 407, para 54; *Incal v Turkey* (2000) 29 EHRR 449, para 54.

[953] *Kulis v Poland* (see n 950 above) para 52; *Lopes Gomes da Silva v Portugal* (2002) 34 EHRR 56, para 34.

[954] See eg, *Urbino Rodrigues v Portugal*, Judgment of 29 November 2005 (one journalist attacking another, limits of acceptable criticism wider).

[955] *Dalban v Romania* (2001) 31 EHRR 39 (GC), para 50; see eg, *Tammer v Estonia* (2003) 37 EHRR 43.

[956] *Cumpănă and Mazăre* (see n 939 above), para 101.

[957] *Grinberg v Russia* (2006) 43 EHRR 30–31.

[958] *Kulis v Poland* (see n 950 above) para 51; *Almedia Azevedo v Portugal*, Judgment of 23 January 2007, para 30 ; see also *Sokolowski v Poland*, Judgment of 29 March 2005 (allegation of improper appointment to election commissions was a value judgment).

[959] See *Turhan v Turkey*, Judgment of 19 May 2005, para 24; *Jerusalem v Austria* (2003) 37 EHRR 43; however this is not a high hurdle, see eg, *Dichand v Austria*, Judgment of 26 February 2002.

[960] *Castells v Spain* (1992) 14 EHHR 445; *Colombani v France*, Judgment of 25 June 2002, para 66.

reliable information in accordance with the 'ethics of journalism'.[961] The Court will take into account factors such as:[962]

- the nature the defamatory allegations made;
- the extent to which the media could have reasonably regarded sources as reliable with regard to the allegations:[963] this involves considering matters such as the authority of the source[964] and the amount of research conducted before publication;[965]
- whether the media presented the story in a reasonably balanced manner;[966]
- and whether the media gave the persons defamed the opportunity to defend themselves;[967]
- it is also relevant that individuals have a right to be presumed innocent of criminal offences until proved guilty.[968]

- Freedom of press requires the protection of confidential journalistic sources[969] and the duty to provide a sound factual basis for the allegations does not require the disclosure of the names of confidential sources.[970]
- The reporting of allegations made by others whether in the form of interviews or otherwise is essential to the function of the media[971] and a journalist is not required formally to distance himself from reported allegations.[972]
- The nature and severity of the penalty imposed on the media in relation to a particular publication will be taken into account when assessing the proportionality of the interference.[973] Measures or sanctions which dissuade the press from taking part in the discussion of matters of legitimate public concern will be closely scrutinized.[974] Criminal sanctions against the media will always be difficult to justify.[975]

It should be emphasized that (with the exception of the principles relating to 'reportage' and to sources) these are all maters which can arise in all Article 10 cases, but they have been most extensively analysed and developed in the context of media cases.

---

[961] *Cumpănă and Mazăre v Romania* (2005) 41 EHRR 4 (GC), para 102; *Radio France and others v France* (2005) 40 EHRR 29, para 37; *McVicar v United Kingdom* (2002) 35 EHRR 22, paras 83–86.

[962] See generally, *Alithia Publishing Company Ltd and Constantinides v Cyprus*, Judgment of 22 May 2008, para 49.

[963] *Bladet Tromsø and Stensaas v Norway* (2000) 29 EHRR 125, para 66.

[964] Ibid.

[965] *Prager and Oberschlick v Austria* (1995) 21 EHRR 1, para 37.

[966] *Bergens Tidende v Norway* (2001) 31 EHRR 16, para 57.

[967] Ibid, 58.

[968] *Pedersen v Denmark* (2006) 42 EHRR 24 (GC), para 78.

[969] See *Goodwin v United Kingdom* (1996) 22 EHRR 123, para 39, and *Roemen and Schmit v Luxembourg*, Judgment of 25 February 2003, para 57; and see generally 'Recommendation No R(2000) 7 of the Committee of Ministers on the right of journalists not to disclose their sources of information'.

[970] *Cumpănă and Mazăre* (see n 961 above) para 106.

[971] *Kulis v Poland* (see n 950 above) para 38; *Pedersen v Denmark* (see n 968 above) para 77.

[972] *Thoma v Luxembourg* (2003) 36 EHRR 21.

[973] *Cumpănă and Mazăre* (see n 961 above) para 111; see *Ceylan v Turkey* (2000) 30 EHRR 73, para 37; *Tammer v Estonia*, (2003) 37 EHRR 43, para 69; *Skałka v Poland*, Judgment of 27 May 2003, paras 41–42.

[974] See *Jersild v Denmark* (1994) 19 EHRR 1, para 35.

[975] A prison sentence in a media case will only be compatible with Article 10 in exceptional circumstances, eg, see *Katrami v Greece*, Judgment of 6 December 2007, para 39.

15.315   The issues which arise in relation to these principles will be considered under five heads: (i) facts and value judgments, (ii) cases involving politicians, (iii) other defamation cases, (iv) journalistic sources and (v) sanctions.

(d) Facts and value judgments

15.316   A crucial consideration in relation to proportionality is whether the statements being made are statements of fact or value judgments. Because the truth of value judgments is not susceptible to proof, restrictions on their publication are very difficult to justify under Article 10(2). This point has been considered in many cases. In *Feldek v Slovakia*[976] the applicant had been sued for libel by a government minister who he had accused of having a fascist past. The Court found that the statement was a value judgment, the truth of which was not susceptible proof. It rejected the argument that a value judgment could only be considered as such if it was accompanied by the facts on which the judgment was based. As a result, it was held that the Slovak court

> did not convincingly establish any pressing social need for putting the protection of the personal rights of a public figure above the applicant's right to freedom of expression and the general interest of promoting this freedom when issues of public interest are concerned.[977]

15.317   In *Perna v Italy*[978] the applicant journalist had suggested that a judge who was a member of the Communist Party had sworn a judicial oath to God, the law and Communist Party headquarters. This was a critical opinion couched in provocative language but with a factual basis, namely the judge's political militancy. A finding of aggravated defamation was a breach of Article 10. However, there was no violation in relation to sanctions imposed in relation to allegations concerning the complainant's participation in a plan to gain control of public prosecutors' offices as this was an allegation of fact. In *Dichand v Austria*[979] the fact that the applicants published harsh criticism of a politician in strong and polemical language on a slim factual basis did not mean that they lost the protection of Article 10 which protects information or idea which offend, shock or disturb.

15.318   The Court has regularly found that criticism of politicians, often in very strong terms, in reality consisted of 'value judgments' (or what might better be described as 'comment and criticism') and that, as a result, no interference was permissible. Some of these cases clearly fall on the 'value judgment' side of the line. Thus in *Grinberg v Russia*[980] a defamation award in respect of an article complaining that a politician was waging war against the press and had no shame or scruples was found to be a violation on this basis. In *Ukrainian Media Group v Ukraine*[981] a defamation award and an order to print correction in relation to articles about politicians were violations of Article 10: although the publications were 'in strong, polemical, sarcastic language',[982] politicians laid themselves open to robust criticism and scrutiny; and the articles were, in substance, 'value judgments'. Similarly, a violation

---

[976] Judgment of 12 July 2001, para 86.
[977] Ibid, para 87.
[978] (2004) 39 EHRR 28.
[979] Judgment of 26 February 2002.
[980] (2006) 43 EHRR 45.
[981] (2006) 43 EHRR 25.
[982] Ibid, para 67.

was found in *Chemodurov v Russia*[983] where a journalist had described a governor as abnormal'.

However, the concept of 'value judgment' has been broadly interpreted, particularly in cases involved political expression.[984] It has been held that the description of a person as a 'liar' is 'value judgment'.[985] In *Scharsach and News Verlagsgesellschaft v Austria*[986] the allegation was made that politician was a 'closet Nazi' was held to be a value judgment. As this allegation had a sufficient factual basis the imposition of sanctions was unjustified. In *Flux & Samson v Moldova*[987] it was held that an article which stated that a former Minister of Construction had "become rich off the back of the misery of others" consisted of value judgments supported by a sufficient factual basis.

15.319

Even where a statement amounts to a value judgment, the proportionality of an interference may depend on whether there exists a sufficient factual basis for the impugned statement, since even a value judgment may be excessive where there is no factual basis to support it.[988] Thus, the characterization of the right wing French politician Jean Marie le Pen as 'the chief of a gang of killers' was found to be excessive.[989]

15.320

(e) Defamation cases involving politicians or matters of public interest

Politicians and criminal libel. Proceedings for criminal libel in relation to statements about politicians are subject to very close scrutiny by the Court. Criminal convictions for defamation of politicians have been found to be in breach of Article 10 on many occasions and will rarely be justified.[990] In the leading case of *Lingens v Austria*[991] the conviction of a journalist for making allegations concerning Chancellor Kreisky's views on Nazism was held to have breached Article 10. Similarly, in *Castells v Spain*[992] a member of the Basque nationalist party alleged that the police were responsible for murdering Basque activists and had been protected from prosecution. He was convicted of serious insults to the Government. The Court found that the national courts had denied him the opportunity

15.321

---

[983] (2008) 47 EHRR 9.

[984] See eg, *Arbeiter v Austria*, Judgment of 25 January 2007 (statement that an expert appointed to advise on the future development of hospitals 'smashes our good health system in order take over hospitals with his company' was a value judgment).

[985] See *Almeida Azevedo v Portugal*, Judgment of 23 January 2007, para 30; *Kuliś v Poland*, Judgment of 18 March 2008, para 51.

[986] (2005) 40 EHRR 22; see also *Karman v Russia*, Judgment of 14 December 2006 (term 'local neo-fascist', value judgment) and *I Avgi Publishing and Press Agency SA and Karis v Greece*, Judgment of 5 June 2008 ('notorious crazy nationalist' value judgment); but contrast *Wabl v Austria* (2001) 31 EHRR 51 (injunction restraining use of expression 'Nazi journalism' justified).

[987] Judgment of 23 October 2007 (the court took into account the balanced tone of the article, as it presented both parties' views); see also *Standard Verlags GmbH v Austria* (2008) 47 EHRR 58 (allegation that a politician knew about fraudulent practices and received relevant documents was a value judgment).

[988] See eg, *Jerusalem v Austria* (2003) 37 EHRR 25, para 43; *Turhan v Turkey*, Judgment of 19 May 2005, para 24.

[989] *Lindon, Otchakovsky-Laurens and July v France* (2008) 46 EHRR 35 (GC), para 66. see also *Wabl v Austria* (n 986 above)(apparently decided on the basis that an accusation of 'Nazi journalism' lacked a factual basis) and *Krutil v Germany*, Decision of 20 March 2003 (defamation award for comparing a journalist to Goebbels was justified).

[990] For sanctions, see para 15.355 below.

[991] (1986) 8 EHRR 407.

[992] (1992) 14 EHHR 445.

to prove the truth of his allegations, and that it was not necessary to punish him for the publication of factual assertions which were or might be true. One concurring judge regarded Castell's claims as 'matters of opinion' which were not susceptible to being proved, while another said that as his comments were of 'general interest' the truth of them was irrelevant.

15.322   The same approach was taken in *Oberschlick v Austria (No 1)*,[993] *Thorgeirson v Iceland*,[994] and *Schwabe v Austria*[995] where criminal convictions were also held to have violated Article 10. The Court has, however, criticized journalists for not carrying out adequate research and suggested that, in the case of serious allegations, the journalist may be obliged to give the person concerned a right to comment.[996] In *Lepojić v Serbia*[997] the applicant was found guilty of criminal libel after alleging that a politician was suspected of criminal offences and was engaged in 'near insane spending of money belong to citizens'. It was held by a majority of 5:2 that this conviction and an order for compensation were unjustified even though the article contained untrue factual allegations which the applicant did not reasonably believe to be true. Another case which was close to the line was *Malisiewicz-Gasior v Poland*[998] where the applicant's conviction for defamation for alleging during an election campaign that a politician had orchestrated his arrest and detention was held to be a violation on the basis that it was 'not a gratuitous personal attack but were part of a political debate'. It is difficult to see how, in this case, adequate protection was being given to the reputation of the politician.

15.323   **Politicians and private life.**   The more recent case law of Court has shown greater sensitivity to the right to private life, including the right to reputation[999] of politicians. There is a need to make 'a fundamental distinction' between reporting facts capable of contributing to a debate in a democratic society and making 'tawdry allegations about an individual's private life.'[999a] Thus, in *Tammer v Estonia*[1000] the applicant was a journalist who had made insulting remarks about the wife of a former prime minister of Estonia who had held public positions. The applicant was convicted of the criminal offence of 'insult' and fined. The Court accepted that the words used were value judgments but said that they could have been formulated without resort to insulting expressions. It was held that, taking into account the margin of appreciation, domestic authorities were entitled to interfere with the exercise of the applicant's rights.

15.324   The case of *Editions Plon v France*[1001] concerned a book by the late President Mitterand's doctor dealing with his medical history. It was held that an interim injunction restraining the publication of the book was a justified interference with the Article 10 rights of the

---

[993] (1991) 19 EHRR 389, para 63 (conviction for publishing complaint that politician's views on immigration reflected philosophy and aims of Nazis).

[994] (1992) 14 EHRR 843, para 65 (defamation of the police).

[995] (1992) Series A No 242–B (conviction of politician for publishing spent conviction of another politician).

[996] *Prager and Oberschlick v Austria* (1995) 21 EHRR 1, para 37.

[997] (2008) 47 EHRR 56.

[998] (2007) 45 EHRR 21.

[999] See para 12.301ff above.

[999a] *Armonas v Lithuania*, Judgment 25 November 2008, para 39.

[1000] (2003) 37 EHRR 43.

[1001] (2006) 42 EHRR 3.

publishers but that the final injunction, some 9 months later, was not. The Court took into account the fact that the book had been widely circulated in any event and the length of time since the President's death.[1002] In *Hachette Filipacchi Associés v France*[1003] Paris Match published a photograph of the dead body of the Prefect of Corsica taken immediately after his murder by terrorists. His family brought a successful claim in the domestic courts alleging interference with their privacy. The applicant was ordered to publish an apology in the next edition. The Court held that the publication of thephotograph was an attack on their right to respect for their private life and the order to publish the statement was the sanction which imposed the most modest restriction on the Article 10 rights of the applicant. In the circumstances, there was no violation of Article 10.

These cases can be contrasted with *News Verlags v Austria*[1004] in which an injunction pro-   **15.325** hibiting the publication of a photograph of a right wing politician who was accused of sending letter bombs in the context of reporting criminal proceedings. It was held that the injunction was a disproportionate interference. Similarly, in *Verlagsgruppe News GmbH v Austria (No 2)*[1005] an injunction restraining the publication of a photograph of a well known businessman which had accompanied an article about a tax evasion investigation was an unjustified interference. The businessman was a public figure and the article reported on a matter of public interest. The publication of the photograph contributed to a public debate and the Article 10 rights of the applicant outweighed the Article 8 rights of the business-man. A similar result was reached in *Karhuvaara v Finland*[1006] which concerned a domestic finding of infringement of privacy in respect of articles concerning a criminal trial involving the husband of a Member of the Finnish Parliament. The MP brought proceedings for infringement of privacy and defamation. The Court noted that no details of her private life had been mentioned save that she was married to the defendant, which was already public knowledge. As a result, there was a breach of Article 10.

Politicians and defamation.   If defamatory factual allegations are made against politicians,   **15.326** then the court will require the media to prove their truth or, at the very least, to demonstrate that proper attempts have been made to verify the allegations in question. However, if the media rely in good faith on official reports they do not have a duty to conduct independent research.[1007] The Court has upheld domestic defamation awards in a number of cases in which false factual allegations have not been properly investigated or verified.

[1002] But note that the Court did not find that the award of damages was a violation, see ibid, para 57.

[1003] Judgment of 14 June 2007. See also *'Wirtschafts-Trend' Zeitschriften-Verlagsgesellschaft GmbH (No 2) v Austria* (2003) 36 EHRR CD 71 (an order for the payment of compensation for the publication of the name of a police officer subject to disciplinary investigation after a death during a forcible deportation was justified as no need to include the name of the officer in the article) and see the 'photograph' cases discussed above at para 12.285.

[1004] (2001) 31 EHRR 8; see the discussion of this case in H Fenwick and G Phillipson, *Media Freedom under the Human Rights Act* (Oxford University Press, 2006), 188–190.

[1005] Judgment of 14 December 2006; see also *Österreichischer Rundfunk v Austria*, Judgment of 7 December 2006 (injunction preventing publication of a photograph of a politician who had been convicted at an earlier trial was a breach of Art 10) and *Radio Twist as v Slovakia* (2006) 22 BHRC 396 (domestic judgement arising broadcast of illegally made tape of private telephone conversation between two politicians unjustified).

[1006] (2005) 41 EHRR 51.

[1007] *Colombani v France*, Judgment of 25 June 2002, para 65; *Bladet Tromsø and Stensaas v Norway* (2000) 29 EHRR 125, para 65.

15.327 In *Cuc Pascu v Romania*[1008] the applicant published an article in which he accused the Dean of the Faculty of Medicine of Oradea University, also a Member of Parliament, of fraud and plagiarism, describing him among other things as a 'crook' and a 'little law-breaking doctor'. The Court found that the applicant had not succeeded in proving the veracity of his statements before the Romanian courts. Given the lack of factual basis and his position as a journalist, the applicant should have demonstrated the greatest rigour and exercised particular caution before publishing the offending article. In *Standard Verlagsgesellschaft mbH (No. 2) v Austria*[1009] the applicant had published an article stating that Mr Haider had deliberately misled the Regional Government and had acted in breach of the constitution. It had been ordered to black out the impugned statements in the issues still to be disseminated and to publish the court's judgment. By a bare majority the court held that there was no violation.

15.328 The important recent Grand Chamber case of *Lindon, Otchakovsky-Laurens and July v France*[1010] concerned a novel entitled 'Jean-Marie le Pen on Trial' which recounted the trial of a fictional National Front militant who had murdered a young man of North African descent. The novel was based on real events and contained a number of statements about M le Pen—that he was 'the chief of a gang of killers', equated him to Al Capone, suggested that he advocated murder and was a 'vampire who thrives on the bitterness of his electorate' and 'sometimes also on their blood'. The French courts convicted the author and publisher of the novel of defamation and imposed a fine of €2,286 and awarded damages of €3,811 to M le Pen and the National Front, along with an order that the publishers pay for the publication of an announcement of the judgment. A majority of the Grand Chamber (13-4) found that there was no violation of Article 10. The Court accepted that the novel, as a form of artistic expression, was entitled to protection under Article 10 and, since it related to a debate on a matter of general concern, that it constituted political expression of a high value. However, novelists—like anyone else exercising their right to freedom of expression—had 'duties and responsibilities'. The novel was not a work of pure fiction, but included real people and information presented as 'fact'. The publishers had not carried out even basic verification of those facts. The Court took into account that M Le Pen, as a politician, was required to show a high tolerance for criticism and that he was a particularly controversial figure, who had been convicted of a number of speech crimes, including inciting racial hatred. Even so, the descriptions in the novel overstepped permissible limits.

15.329 However, the Court has taken a stricter view of the Article 10(2) justification requirements in cases where the defamatory allegations concern conduct in public office. Thus in *Flux v Moldova*[1011] the applicant had published an allegation of corruption against politicians which was a factual statement, not a value judgment. Although the allegation raised issues of genuine public interest, the applicant had been unable to establish a factual basis for it. The Court, surprisingly, found a breach, taking into account difficulty of proof a year later and the fact that reputation damage fades with time.[1012] This case was decided without

---

[1008] Judgment of 16 September 2008.
[1009] Judgment 22 February 2007.
[1010] (2008) 46 EHRR 35 (GC).
[1011] Judgment of 20 November 2007.
[1012] Ibid, para 31.

consideration of the Article 8 rights of the politicians involved; and, we suggest, is an incorrect application of Article 10 principles.

Claims by public bodies.   There is nothing in the Convention case law to prevent public **15.330** bodies bringing defamation claims. Such claims will, however, be strictly scrutinized under Article 10(2). It has been emphasized that

> the limits of permissible criticism are wider still with regard to the government than in relation to a private citizen or even a politician. In a democratic system the actions or omissions of the Government must be subject to the close scrutiny not only of the legislative and judicial authorities but also of public opinion[1013]

However, interferences resulting from claims made by public bodies have been held to be justified.[1014] Furthermore, defamatory statements must refer to particular individuals and it would be excessive and disproportionate to permit state officials to sue for defamation in connection with statements critical of the administrations where they were not identifiable.

Disclosure of confidential documents.   In *Fressoz and Roire v France*[1015] one of the legiti- **15.331** mate aims for the conviction of applicants for publishing a press article was the protection of the reputation of M Calvert, the chairman of the French car manufacturer, Peugeot. Although the article was intended to contribute to a wider debate, it disclosed details of M Calvert's personal income and tax assessments. The applicants were found guilty of 'the handling of photocopies of tax returns obtained through a breach of professional confidence by an unidentified tax official' and sentenced to substantial fines and damages. The convictions were held to be a disproportionate interference with freedom of expression. A similar result was reached in *Dupuis v France*[1016] in which a journalist had been fined 5,000FRF and ordered to pay 50,000FRF in damages for handling documents from a judicial investigation file obtained in breach of professional confidence. The Court found that much of the information was already in the public domain, that the journalists were contributing to an important public debate and that the penalty had a chilling effect. As a result, there was a breach of Article 10.

These cases can be contrasted with the Grand Chamber case of *Stoll v Switzerland*.[1017] The **15.332** applicant journalist had been convicted of disclosing a secret document, being paper concerning negotiations between the Swiss banks and the World Jewish Congress concerning compensation due to Holocaust victims for unclaimed assets in Swiss banks accounts. The Grand Chamber held there was a legitimate public interest in the information contained in the report as it concerned the actions of public figures dealing with an important issue of foreign policy and the published article was capable of contributing to the public debate. However, the confidentiality of diplomatic reports was vital to the smooth

---

[1013] *Lombardo v Malta,* Judgment of 24 April 2007, para 54 (in that case a successful defamation claim by local council was a violation).

[1014] See eg, *Coutant v France,* Decision of 24 January 2008 (conviction for 'defamation of the national police'—the applicant was a lawyer who issued a press release in strong terms in the context of a terrorist trial).

[1014a] *Dyuldin and Kislov v Russia* (2009) 48 EHRR 6, para 43.

[1015] (2001) 31 EHRR 2.

[1016] (2008) 47 EHRR 22.

[1017] (2007) 47 EHRR 59 (GC).

functioning of international relations. The editing and content of the articles and the misleading information they contained undermined their potential contribution to public debate. The fine of 800CHF imposed on the applicant did not prevent him from expressing his views. In the circumstances, there was no breach of Article 10. This decision is difficult to reconcile with the approach of the Court in *Dupuis* and gives too great weight to the 'form' of the articles.[1018] We suggest that the view of the five dissenting judges is to be preferred.

(f) Defamation and private individuals

15.333 **Introduction.** The Court has considered a large number of cases in which the media has sanctioned in defamation proceedings which did not involve politicians. In these cases, the Court requires the media to prove the truth of factual allegations or, if it cannot do so, to act 'in accordance with the ethics of journalism'. Until recently, the Court approached defamation cases on the basis that Article 10 was the only Convention right in issue and that interferences with it must be carefully scrutinized. The established approach has, however, been fundamentally changed by the recent recognition of reputation as a Convention right, protected by Article 8.[1019] This means that defamation cases must involve the 'balancing' of two competing Convention rights, with neither being assumed to have priority. We will begin by considering the former approach of the Court. We will then consider the recent case law in which Article 8 considerations have been brought into play. Finally, we will deal with the important issue of cases in which journalists are simply quoting or paraphrasing defamatory statements made by others, what can be called 'reportage'.

15.334 **The former approach of the Court.** The Court has, over a number of years, given strong protection to those accused of defamation of private individuals, particularly in areas where the subject matter relates to issues of public interest. The approach which was taken is illustrated by a number of cases.

15.335 In *Bladet Tromso v Norway*[1020] the applicant had published extracts from a government inspector's report accusing seal hunters of inhumane practices. The article formed part a series on the seal hunting industry. Successful domestic defamation proceedings were brought against it but the Court found a breach of Article 10. The applicant had published the report in order to further a legitimate debate, during which different viewpoints had been put, on preserving the future of the seal hunting industry, and did not intend to defame the individual hunters involved. The need to protect the reputation of those hunters was therefore not a pressing social need sufficient to outweigh the public's right to the debate.

15.336 A violation was also found in *Nilsen and Johnsen v Norway*[1021] the President of the Norwegian Police Association had been found guilty of defamation when he had had claimed that a critic of police brutality had fabricated certain allegations. Although the allegations made

---

[1018] As is pointed out in the dissenting opinion of Judge Zagrebelsky (joined in by four others) this appears to the real reason for the criticism of the journalist (Ibid, O-II10).

[1019] See para 12.301ff above.

[1020] (2000) 29 EHRR 125.

[1021] (2000) 30 EHRR 878.

were potentially damaging they had to be seen against background of a public debate involving serious allegations. The comments were matters of opinion rather than fact and had been made in response to comments which were capable of being seen as denigrating or offensive. The fact that the complainant in the domestic proceedings had chosen to take part in the debate in such a way had to be put in the balance, with extremes of language having to be tolerated in that context.

In *Bergens Tidende v Norway*[1022] the applicant had been found liable in defamation as a result of articles relating to complaints about a plastic surgeon. This was also an unjustified interference as the articles raised serious issues affecting public interest, were part of an ongoing debate and were written in good faith and in accordance with ethics of journalism. The interest of the complainant in protecting his professional reputation not sufficient to outweigh important public interest in freedom of press to impart information on matters of legitimate public concern. **15.337**

The applicants in *Tønsbergs Blad As and Haukom v Norway*[1023] were a newspaper and its editor which had been found liable in proceedings brought by a businessman in relation to articles which suggested that they had not complied with requirements intended to control the demand for holiday homes. The articles had been about a matter of public interest and the accusations made were not of the most serious nature. The articles had been based on the views of the local authority and sufficient steps had been taken to verify the truth of the allegations. A subsequent article had withdrawn the allegation. In all the circumstances, the domestic proceedings had placed an excessive burden on the applicants and there was a violation of Article 10. **15.338**

In *Selisto v Finland*[1024] the applicant journalist had published an article concerning the unprofessional behaviour of a surgeon which was alleged to have caused the death of a patient. The articles contained the clear allegation that the surgeon was drunk or suffering from a hangover whilst operating. There was no reliable basis for this allegation and the surgeon had not been prosecuted. The Court held that, although the reporting was one-sided, it was based on public pre-trial records, the surgeon was not named and was provided with an opportunity to comment afterwards. As a result, it was found that the conviction and fine of the applicant (in the total sum of about €2,700) was a violation of Article 10. In a powerful dissenting opinion Judge Bratza expressed the view that the professional reputation of the surgeon had not been given proper weight and that there had been no violation. We suggest that this reasoning is to be preferred. **15.339**

However, even on its former approach, the Court accepted that sanctions were appropriate where serious factual allegations were made without a proper factual basis. Thus, in *Constantinescu v Romania*[1025] an allegation in an article by a trade union leader that certain **15.340**

[1022] (2001) 31 EHRR 16.

[1023] (2008) 46 EHRR 40; see also *Nikowitz v Austria* [2007] EMLR 8 (award of damages for defamation in respect of a satirical article in a weekly magazine was unjustified).

[1024] (2006) 42 EHRR 8.

[1025] (2001) 33 EHRR 33, but note the dissenting opinion of Judge Casadevall who pointed out that the remarks were not devoid of foundation and were made in good faith; see also *Verdens Gang and Aase v Norway*, Decision of 16 October 2001 (defamation in relation to an article criticizing a plastic surgeon, no proof of

teachers were 'receivers of stolen goods' justified an award of damages for defamation. Similarly in *Shabanov and Tren v Russia*[1026] an award of damages and an order for rectification were justified because the publication was a gratuitous attack on the reputation of a public servant where no comment had been sought and no attempt made to verify.[1027]

15.341 **Balancing Articles 8 with 10.** More recently, the Court has emphasized that the importance of balancing the freedom of expression of the media against the reputational rights of others. The Article 8 right to reputation of individuals must be taken into account.[1028] This means that

> protection of reputation entails an obligation for the State to enforce a corresponding right guaranteed by the Convention with the same status as freedom of expression. Any defamatory statement amounts to interference with the right guaranteed by the Convention and can only be justified if it satisfies the requirements of permissible restrictions on the exercise of such right, ie, it must be prescribed by law and necessary in a democratic society, corresponding to a pressing social need, proportionate to the aim pursued, etc. Therefore it will be more difficult to defend a defamatory statement for purposes of Convention protection when it is examined as interference with a right recognized under the Convention, rather than as a necessary restriction on freedom of expression.[1029]

This approach to 'balancing' Article 8 and Article 10 rights has been adopted in a number of recent cases.[1030]

15.342 It should also be noted that, even in the case of companies, the Court has recognized that there are other important competing interests to take into account in Article 10 cases:

> in addition to the public interest in open debate about business practices, there is a competing interest in protecting the commercial success and viability of companies, for the benefit of shareholders and employees, but also for the wider economic good.[1031]

15.343 The case of *Chauvy v France*[1032] concerned a historical book which questioned an account of events of 1943 given by a well known resistance leader, raising the possibility he had

---

factual allegations); and *Falter Zeitschriften GmbH v Austria*, Decision of 8 February 2007 (allegation that politicians had shredded documents to thwart police investigation, finding of defamation justified in absence of journalistic diligence).

[1026] Judgment of 14 December 2006.

[1027] The application also concerned a case in which damages had been awarded for publicising medical information which had been put before the domestic court as part of an unsuccessful defamation action. The ECtHR noted 'the differing contexts of 'public' statements made before a domestic court and the publicity which results from publication in a newspaper' (para 47) and found that, when commenting on this information the applicants were making a gratuitous attack. As a result, there was no violation.

[1028] See, eg *Cumpănă and Mazăre v Romania* (2005) 41 EHRR 14 (GC), para 91.

[1029] *Lindon, Otchakovsky-Laurens and July v France* (2008) 46 EHRR 35 (GC), Concurring Opinion, O-I8.

[1030] Although it is not followed consistently, thus in recent 'defamation' cases such as *Lepojić v Serbia* ((2008) 47 EHRR 56) and *Filipović v Serbia* (Judgment of 20 November 2007) the Court has adopted its former approach, making no mention of Article 8 and finding a violation in respect of domestic judgments against applicants who had made unsupportable allegations of fact.

[1031] *Timpul Info-Magazin and Anghel v Moldova*, Judgment 27 November 2007, para 33.

[1032] (2005) 41 EHRR 29, in relation to Art 8 see para 70 and the Concurring Opinion of Judge Thomason, O-14; see also *Radio France v France* (2005) 40 EHRR 29 (broadcast mentioning an article which alleged

betrayed his comrades. The domestic court convicted the author and publisher of criminal libel and ordered payment of compensation and the publication of a statement in the press. In particular, it found that the author had engaged in insufficient critical analysis of his sources and rejected his plea of good faith. The Court accepted these conclusions finding that the right to reputation of the persons attacked in the book should take precedence over the freedom of expression of the applicants.

In *Flux v Moldova (No 6)*[1033] the applicant newspaper had quoted an anonymous letter alleging that a school principal had taken bribes but had not sought to prove the truth of the allegations. The applicant was ordered to publish an apology and pay a sum of €88. In considering whether this interference was justified the Court pointed out that **15.344**

> Article 10 of the Convention does not . . . guarantee wholly unrestricted freedom of expression even in respect of coverage by the press of matters of serious public concern. Where, as in the present case, there is question of attacking the reputation of individuals and thus undermining their rights as guaranteed in Article 8 of the Convention . . . regard must be had to the fair balance which has to be struck between the competing interests at stake.[1034]

It went on to hold that there was no breach of Article 10.[1035]

In *Alithia Publishing Company and Constantinides v Cyprus*[1036] the applicants had written and published twelve articles alleging that the Minister of Defence had been involved in a conspiracy to misappropriate public funds with armaments traders. They were found to have acted in bad faith and were ordered to pay general and exemplary damages for defamation in the total sum of nearly €60,000. The Court held that domestic 'qualified privilege' defence was prescribed by law and that the interference was necessary in a democratic society. The allegations were factual and, because they were not published in good faith, it was not necessary to examine the question as to whether there were grounds for dispensing with the obligation to verify.[1037] **15.345**

These cases can be contrasted with *White v Sweden*[1038] in which the applicant had been accused of serious criminal offences, including the murder of the Prime Minister, by two Swedish newspapers. His defamation action was unsuccessful and he complained that the domestic courts had failed to give proper protection to his Article 8 right to reputation. The Court considered the balance of the Article 10 rights of the press against the applicant's Article 8 rights. The journalists had acted in good faith and had made proper attempts to verify. In addition, the newspapers had published statements rejecting the allegations and had given the applicant an opportunity to comment. The domestic courts had properly **15.346**

---

that a civil servant had supervised the deportation of Jews in 1942 and 1943, conviction for defamation was a justified interference).

[1033] Judgment of 29 July 2008.

[1034] Ibid, para 25.

[1035] See also *Wołek, Kasprów and Łęski v Poland*, Decision of 21 October 2008 (no breach of Art 10 in respect of a publication alleging contact between the President and a Russian spy which had no factual basis).

[1036] Judgment of 22 May 2008.

[1037] Ibid, para 67.

[1038] (2008) 46 EHRR 3; contrast the judgments in *Pfeifer v Austria* (2009) 48 EHRR 8 and *Petrina v Roumania*, Judgment of 14 October 2008 in which violations of Article 8 were found as a result of unsuccessful domestic defamation actions against the media.

balanced the applicant's rights against the public interest in the relevant matters. In the circumstances, there was no violation of the applicant's Article 8 rights.

15.347 'Reportage'.   News reporting based on interviews is one of the most important ways in which the press can play its vital role as 'public watchdog'. As a result, where the media is reporting statements made by others in relation to matters of public interest it will, in general, be disproportionate to impose sanctions.[1039] A general requirement for journalists systematically and formally to distance themselves from the content of a quotation that might insult or provoke others or damage their reputation is not consistent with Article 10.[1040] Thus, sanctions in respect of defamatory allegations contained in letters from third parties which are quoted or published in the press will, in general, be unjustified.[1041]

15.348 Similar principles apply in relation to questions posed by journalists in interviews in the press or on television.

> In news reporting based on interviews, a distinction also needs to be made according to whether the statements emanate from the journalist or are a quotation of others, since punishment of a journalist for assisting in the dissemination of statements made by another person in an interview would seriously hamper the contribution of the press to discussion of matters of public interest and should not be envisaged unless there are particularly strong reasons for doing so.[1042]

15.349 Thus in the case of *Colaço Mestre v Portugal*[1043] in the course of a television interview concerning bribery of referees in Portugal, the applicant had described an individual as 'the referees' boss' and accused him of insulting two referees. The applicant was fined for defamation and order to pay €3,990 damages. This was held to be an unjustified interference with his Article 10 rights. The interview contributed to a debate which was a matter of public interest and sanctions on a journalist for the way in which questions are put in an interview require particularly strong justification which was not present.

15.350 These 'reportage' principles have been applied even where articles have not been presented in a neutral manner and have partially adopted the quoted material.[1044] However, a journalist who makes the factual allegations of others his own will be obliged to take steps to verify their truth.[1045]

[1039] See *Pedersen v Denmark* (2006) 42 EHRR 24 (GC), para 73; *Jersild v Denmark* (1994) 19 EHRR 1, para 35.

[1040] *Thoma v Luxembourg* (2003) 36 EHRR 21, para 64. *Radio France v France* (2005) 40 EHRR 29, para 37.

[1041] See eg, *Flux v Moldova (No 5)*, Judgment of 1 July 2008 (open letter about abuses by prosecuting and judicial authorities); *Albert-Engelmann Gesellschaft mbH v Austria*, Judgment of 19 January 2006 (defamation award in respect of anonymous letter in a newspaper a breach, fact that newspaper did not distance itself from the allegations was irrelevant); *Verlagsgruppe News GmbH v Austria*, Judgment of 14 December 2006 (publication of the words of a letter which was the subject of a defamation action in an article criticizing politicians was not an adoption of the words).

[1042] *Pedersen v Denmark* (n 1039 above) para 77.

[1043] See Judgment of 26 April 2007, para 31 and *Filatenko v Russia*, Judgment of 6 December 2007, para 41—particularly where the questions are posed on live television.

[1044] See *Standard Verlags GmbH v Austria* (2008) 47 EHRR 58, para 53.

[1045] See *Rumyana Ivanova v Bulgaria*, Judgment of 14 February 2008, para 62; *Verdens Gang and Aase v Norway*, Decision of 16 October 2001.

(g) Protection of journalistic sources

The Court has recognized the importance of the protection of journalists' sources. The **15.351**
Court has made it clear on a number of occasions that

> The protection of journalistic sources is one of the cornerstones of freedom of the press.
> Without such protection, sources may be deterred from assisting the press in informing the
> public on matters of public interest. As a result the vital public-watchdog role of the press
> may be undermined and the ability of the press to provide accurate and reliable information
> may be adversely affected. Having regard to the importance of the protection of journalistic
> sources for press freedom in a democratic society, an interference cannot be compatible with
> Article 10 of the Convention unless it is justified by an overriding requirement in the public
> interest. Limitations on the confidentiality of journalistic sources call for the most careful
> scrutiny by the Court.[1046]

Thus, in *Goodwin v United Kingdom*[1047] an order for the disclosure of a journalistic source **15.352**
on the ground that it would enable an employer to identify a disloyal employee was not justified by an 'overriding requirement in the public interest'. In *Fressoz v France*[1048] the objective of protecting fiscal confidentiality was legitimate but the conviction of journalists for
handling documents obtained in breach of professional confidence was disproportionate.
In *Voskuil v Netherlands*[1049] a sentence of 30 days imprisonment imposed on a journalist
who refused to reveal a source in a criminal trial was an unjustified interference with the
Article 10 rights of the journalist. Although the requirements of a fair trial might justify an
order for disclosure of a source the Court did not consider that it was necessary on the facts
of that case.

The protection extends to pre-publication activities. Thus, in *Dammann v Switzerland*[1050] **15.353**
a journalist had been convicted of procuring the disclosure of official secrets for obtaining
material about criminal convictions (which was not published). The journalist was
fined €325. It was held that this was an unjustified interference—the court took into
account the fact that the convictions could be obtained, at greater costs, by other means
and the fact that the information related to a matter of public interest. The protection also
covers the seizure of a journalist's papers or working materials. Thus, in *Tillack v Belgium*[1051]
there was a violation when the police seized 6 crates of papers, two boxes of files, two com-
puters, four mobile phones and a metal cabinet from a journalist. The Court emphasised
that the right of journalists to protect their sources was not a simple privilege, which could

---

[1046] *Roemen and Schmit v Luxembourg*, Judgment of 25 February 2003, para 46; see also *Goodwin v United
Kingdom*, (1996) 22 EHRR 123, para 39; *Ernst v Belgium*, Decision of 15 July 2003; *Cumpǎnǎ and Mazǎre
v Romania* (2005) 41 EHRR 14 (GC), para 106; *Tillack v Belgium*, Judgment of 27 November 2007, para
53; see also Committee of Ministers, *Recommendation No R (2000) 7 on the right of journalists not to disclose
their sources of information*, cited and relied on in *Voskuil v Netherlands* (2008) 24 BHRC 306, Judgment of 22
November 2007.
[1047] See n 1046 above.
[1048] (2001) 31 EHRR 2.
[1049] See n 1046 above.
[1050] Judgment of 25 April 2006.
[1051] Judgment of 27 November 2007.

be given or withdrawn, depending on whether or not the source was illicit, but was a true attribute of the right to information, to be treated with the greatest circumspection.[1052]

15.354 However, an order for the disclosure of undercover film taken by a journalist is not an order for the disclosure of a journalistic source.[1053] Individuals who are the subject of undercover filming are not 'freely assisting the press to inform the public about matters of public interest or matters concerning others' and the disclosure of their identities does not impact on journalistic sources.

(h) Sanctions

15.355 The nature and severity of the penalties imposed are factors to be taken into account when assessing the proportionality of an interference with the freedom of expression guaranteed by Article 10 and the utmost caution must be exercised 'where the measures taken or sanctions imposed by the national authorities are such as to dissuade the press from taking part in the discussion of matters of legitimate public concern'.[1054] Although the criminalization of defamation is not forbidden under the Convention and may be a proportionate response in the case of speech inciting violence, the Court gives careful consideration to the question as to whether a civil or disciplinary penalty could have been used.[1055] In 2007 the Parliamentary Assembly recommended that prison sentences for defamation should be abolished 'without delay'.[1056]

15.356 Excessive sanctions against the media may mean that finding of defamation which would, otherwise, be proportionate breaches Article 10. In the well known case of *Tolstoy Miloslavsky v United Kingdom*[1057] the applicant had been the defendant in libel proceedings concerning a pamphlet in which he had alleged that the complainant was guilty of war crimes. He had been awarded damages of £1.5 million by a jury. It was held that the award violated Article 10 as the system under which jury set the amount of the award for non-financial damage without guidance contained insufficient safeguards to prevent disproportionately high awards. In *Bobo v Spain*[1058] concerned an employee of state television in Spain who had been dismissed for making critical and abusive remarks about the management of the television station. The Court held that there was no reasonable relationship of proportionality between the sanction imposed and the legitimate aim pursued. Although discipline would have been justified, dismissal was too severe a sanction.

15.357 In *Maronek v Slovakia*,[1059] the Court held that a judgment for defamation in respect of a letter which was made public, and which contained allegations of dishonesty, was a disproportionate interference with the Article 10 rights of the writer who had acted in good faith,

---

[1052] Ibid, para 65.
[1053] *Nordisk film & TV a/s v Denmark* Decision of 8 December 2005.
[1054] *Cumpănă and Mazăre v Romania* (see n 1046 above) para 111.
[1055] See *Raichinov v Bulgaria* Judgment of 20 April 2006, para 50.
[1056] Resolution 1577 (2007) 'Towards decriminalization of defamation'.
[1057] (1995) 20 EHRR 442.
[1058] (2001) 31 EHRR 50.
[1059] (2004) 38 EHRR 5; (2004) 38 EHRR 5; and see also *Steel and Morris v United Kingdom* (2005) 41 EHRR 22, para 96 (award of libel damages of £40,000 against applicants of modest resources disproportionate) and *Pakdemirili v Turkey,* Judgment of 22 February 2005.

raised matters of public interest and most of whose allegations had been published earlier in a newspaper. One of the bases for the decision was the fact that the applicant had been required to pay damages and costs of 25 times the average monthly salary, which in English terms would be roughly £40,000. Insofar as the majority decision is more widely based it was subject to powerful criticism in the Concurring Opinion in which three of the seven judges joined.

These cases can be contrasted with *Independent News and Media v Ireland*[1060] in which a jury libel damages award of IR£300,000 did not breach Article 10. The Court held that the actual safeguards to be employed to ensure that sanctions were not disproportionate were a matter for individual Member States. The jury at first instance were given specific information regarding a comparable case and were told that damages should be substantial. The Supreme Court had reviewed the authorities and had formulated a test that was sufficiently robust to provide an adequate safeguard.

15.358

(7) Justifying interferences with expression for specific legitimate aims

(a) Introduction

The issues which arise when the Court considers whether interferences with expression are 'necessary in a democratic society' can conveniently be considered under the headings of each of the 'legitimate aims' set out in Article 10(2).[1061] Different considerations apply to different aims and the margin of appreciation accorded by the Court can vary, depending on the justification being advanced by the domestic authorities.

15.359

(b) National security

In national security cases the court has often accorded a wide margin of appreciation to national authorities.[1062] In a case in which serious damage can be caused to national security by the disclosure of information an interference with Article 10 rights is likely to be justified.[1063] The termination of the compulsory military service because the applicant was a member and officer of an extreme right wing political party was justified on this ground.[1064]

15.360

The national security 'legitimate aim' featuretd prominently in *The Observer and The Guardian v United Kingdom*[1065] and *Sunday Times v United Kingdom (No 2)*[1066] which considered the legitimacy of injunctions granted to restrain newspapers from publishing information about the British security services which was derived from the manuscript of a proposed book, *Spycatcher*.[1067] The main issue facing the Court in was the compatibility of

15.361

[1060] (2006) 42 EHRR 46.

[1061] For a survey of the case law see Human Rights File No 18, *Freedom of Expression in Europe: Case Law concerning Article 10 of the European Convention on Human Rights* (Council of Europe Publishing, 2007)—this contains useful summaries of admissibility decisions otherwise available only in French.

[1062] See eg, *Choherr v Austria* (1993) 17 EHRR 358.

[1063] See *Hadjianastassiou v Greece* (1992) 16 EHRR 219 (conviction of an air force officer for selling information about a guided missile project to a private company was justified).

[1064] *Erdel v Germany* (2007) 44 EHRR SE23; *Lahr v Germany* (2008) 47 EHRR SE22.

[1065] (1991) 14 EHRR 153.

[1066] (1991) 14 EHRR 229.

[1067] For the history of the English litigation, see para 15.31ff above.

injunctions issued, modified and extended and finally discharged by the House of Lords, with Article 10. Although the book had been published in the United States, the interlocutory injunctions were continued[1068] until the main proceedings were complete. The House of Lords[1069] had refused to restrain the newspapers on grounds that the American publication had destroyed any justification for granting the permanent injunctions. The Commission found that the injunctions had violated Article 10. However, the Court decided that the interlocutory injunctions were not a breach, holding that only their continuation by the House of Lords infringed freedom of expression. Initially, the Government had identified several aims to support the ban. National security was indirectly in issue; it was said that Mr Wright's information was protected as it had been received in confidence; and the injunction was necessary to preserve the Attorney-General's claim to confidentiality, thus maintaining the authority of the judiciary.[1070] The Court found that, prior to the American publication, revelation of the material could be damaging to the Security Service; and that the objectives of protection of national security and of preserving the Attorney-General's claim were legitimate ones, justifying interference in a democratic society. Once the book had been published,[1071] however, this substantially eradicated any justification for continuing the interim injunction to preserve the case of the Attorney-General until trial.[1072] Before the Court of Human Rights, the Government argued that protection of national security required the maintenance of the morale and reputation of the Security Service and that others should be discouraged from breaches of confidentiality such as the publishing of memoirs.[1073] The Court did not directly assess these issues, but decided that the continuation of the injunction had a negative impact on the third party newspapers which was disproportionate to any need to protect the confidence interest.[1074] Judge Walsh, dissenting, pointed out[1075] that the authorities had not established any threat to national security and ought not to invoke this exception on the basis of opinion alone.

15.362　The Commission has also held that restrictions on broadcasting news material about organizations which support terrorism does not contravene Article 10.[1076] On the other hand, there was an unjustified interference with the freedom of expression of soldiers[1077] where they were disciplined for distributing a satirical journal within military barracks in

---

[1068] *A-G v Guardian Newspapers Ltd* [1987] 1 WLR 1248.

[1069] Ibid.

[1070] Protecting the rights of litigants is recognized as an aspect of maintenance of the authority of the judiciary under Art 10(2): *Sunday Times v United Kingdom* (1979) 2 EHRR 245; see para 15.380 below.

[1071] Publication took place in the United States just prior to the continuation of the interlocutory injunctions by the House of Lords.

[1072] See the earlier decision of the Court in *Weber v Switzerland* (1990) 12 EHRR 508, where it held that the defence of prior publication might limit the scope of the restrictions on Article 10.

[1073] *The Observer and The Guardian Newspapers v United Kingdom* (n 1065 above) para 69.

[1074] For an analysis of the *Spycatcher* litigation at Strasbourg see I Leigh, 'Spycatcher in Strasbourg' [1992] PL 200.

[1075] *The Observer and the Guardian Newspapers v United Kingdom* (see n 1065 above) 205, para 4.

[1076] *Purcell v Ireland* (1991) 70 DR 262, EComm HR; *Brind and McLaughlin v United Kingdom* (1994) 77-A DR 42, EComm HR.

[1077] The Court emphasized in *Hadjianastassiou v Greece* (1992) 16 EHRR 219 that freedom of expression under Art 10(1) extended to soldiers just as much as to civilians.

breach of military regulations.[1078] A number of cases have examined whether restrictions on national security grounds to prevent insults to the armed forces,[1079] or statements of support for a terrorist separatist organization[1080] could be justified on national security grounds. In *Grigoriades v Greece*[1081] a conviction violated Article 10 because the insults to the armed forces were contained in a letter to a commanding officer without wider publication, did not attack the recipient or any other individual and had little impact on military discipline.

In *Zana v Turkey*[1082] a prosecution for the applicant's outspoken support for the PKK was **15.363** justified on national security and public safety grounds as part of the fight against terrorism. However, in *Incal v Turkey*[1083] a conviction for 'inciting the people to hatred' breached Article 10; a leaflet was distributed which contained virulent remarks about Government policy but no incitement to violence, hostility or hatred. The Court distinguished the *Zana* case on grounds that the applicant could not be regarded as being in any way responsible for problems caused by terrorism in the province of Izmir. The Court also considered a number of Turkish cases where convictions on terrorist or public safety grounds were said to be disproportionate restrictions on freedom of expression. Most of the applications were held to breach Article 10[1084] although two convictions were justified.[1085]

(c) Territorial integrity

The justification for interfering with expression to maintain 'territorial integrity' has been **15.364** considered less frequently. In *Piermont v France*[1086] the applicant had been excluded from French Polynesia after making a speech supporting anti-nuclear and independence demands of local political parties. Although the interference with her freedom of expression was to prevent disorder and maintain territorial integrity, the interference was disproportionate as the demonstration was non-violent and there was a strong interest in protecting

---

[1078] *Vereinigung Demokratischer Soldaten Österreichs and Bethold Gubi v Austria* (1994) 20 EHRR 55; see also *Vereniging Weekblad 'Bluf' v Netherlands* (1995) 20 EHRR 189 (6-year-old internal review of Dutch security service published in weekly journal, court assessed national security interets and held that the withdrawal and seizure of journal was unjustified).

[1079] *Grigoriades v Greece* (1997) 27 EHRR 464.

[1080] *Zana v Turkey* (1997) 27 EHRR 667.

[1081] (1997) 27 EHRR 464.

[1082] n 1080 above.

[1083] (2000) 29 EHRR 449.

[1084] *Karatas v Turkey*, Judgment of, 8 July 1999 (convictions under Prevention of Terrorism Act for poems concerning Kurdish discontent); *Arslan v Turkey* (2001) 31 EHRR 264 (conviction of author for book maintaining that Kurds were victims of oppression); *Polat v Turkey*, Judgment of 8 July 1999 (conviction for historical epic concerning Kurdish rebel movement); *Ceylan v Turkey* (2000) 30 EHRR 73 (conviction of union leader for Marxist explanation for Kurdish movement); *Okçuoglu v Turkey* (2001) 31 EHRR 10. (conviction for interview expressing views about Kurdish situation); *Gerger v Turkey*, Judgment of 8 July 1999 (conviction for polemic given at funeral of political activists) *Erdogdu v Turkey* (2002) 34 EHRR 1143 (conviction for interview of sociologist in monthly review expressing views about Kurds); *Surek v Turkey (No 2)*, Judgment of 8 July 1999 (conviction for news report identifying officials which were alleged to be terrorist targets); *Surek v Turkey* (2000) 7 BHRC 339 (conviction for interview with a PKK leader).

[1085] *Sürek v Turkey (No 1)*, Judgment of 8 July 1999 (conviction for polemic about Kurdistan); *Surek v Turkey (No 4)*, Judgment of 8 July 1999 (conviction for polemic about Kurdistan).

[1086] (1995) 20 EHRR 301.

political speech. In *Üstün v Turkey*[1087] the prosecution of the publisher of a book for publishing separatist propaganda was for the legitimate aim of the protection of territorial integrity and public order. However, although the book had a hostile tone, it did not 'encourage violence, armed resistance or insurrection' and, bearing in mind the limited scope for restriction on political speech, the reasons for the conviction were insufficient.

(d) Prevention of disorder or crime

15.365 **Introduction.** The prevention of disorder or crime includes (but is not limited to) public disorder. The need to protect public order in the face of terrorist threats is a significant justification for restricting freedom of expression[1088] or international telecommunications.[1089]

15.366 **Military discipline.** In *Engel v Netherlands*[1090] it was held that the disciplining of soldiers for publishing a journal critical the army was justified under Article 10(2) on the basis that it was necessary for the prevention of disorder. Convictions for the distribution of leaflets calling for soldiers to desert[1091] or for the abolition of the army[1092] have been held to be justified. In *Vereinigung Demokratischer Soldaten Österreichs and Gubi v Austria*[1093] an order to stop the circulation of a journal containing items critical of military life to soldiers was a violation. In *Grigoriades v Greece*[1094] a conscripted reserve office sent a letter to his commanding officer stating, inter alia, that the army maintained a criminal and terrorist apparatus. He was convicted of insulting the army. It was held that while the applicant's letter included certain strong and intemperate remarks concerning the armed forces it was not published and the objective impact of on military discipline of the letter was insignificant. As a result, his conviction was not 'necessary in a democratic society'. In *Ergin v Turkey (No 6)*[1095] a conviction for incitement to evade military service was a violation as the words did not 'exhort the use of violence or incite armed resistance or rebellion and they do not constitute hate-speech'[1096] and were published in a general newspaper.

15.367 **Political expression.** Restrictions on political expression, however, are likely to be difficult to justify. Although freedom of political debate is not absolute, the Government must react proportionately and without excess to criticisms made of it.[1097] Thus, in *Steel v United Kingdom*[1098] arresting protesters for breach of the peace was a legitimate restriction on the right of expression because the arrests were intended to prevent disorder and to protect the rights

---

[1087] Judgment of 10 May 2007.
[1088] *Chorherr v Austria* (1993) 17 EHRR 358.
[1089] *Groppera Radio AG v Switzerland* (1990) 12 EHRR 321 and *Autronic AG v Switzerland* (1990) 12 EHRR 485.
[1090] (1979–80) 1 EHRR 647.
[1091] *Arrowsmith v United Kingdom* (1981) 3 EHRR 218.
[1092] *Saszmann v Austria* (1997) 23 EHRR CD46.
[1093] (1994) 20 EHRR 55.
[1094] (1999) 27 EHRR 464.
[1095] (2008) 47 EHRR 36.
[1096] Ibid, para 34.
[1097] *Incal v Turkey* (2000) 29 EHRR 449, paras 52–59: prosecution for publication of a leaflet urging Kurdish population to band together was a violation; see also *Janowski v Poland* (1999) 29 EHRR 705 in which the Court held that conviction of the applicant, for using offensive words to criticize civil servants acting in an official capacity, was justified.
[1098] (1998) 28 EHRR 603.

of others. However, the restrictions were disproportionate since the police could not justify the arrests on the basis that they had reasonable grounds to apprehend a breach of the peace.[1099]

Crime. In *Marlow v United Kingdom*,[1100] the Court concluded that the prosecution of the **15.368** writer of a book which incited others to grow cannabis pursued the legitimate aim of the prevention of crime. In *Ekin v France*[1101] it was held that a ban on the publication and sale of a book about the Basque conflict on the grounds of a potential danger to public order was disproportionate to the legitimate aim. In *Nicol and Selvanayagam v United Kingdom*[1102] it was accepted that the arrest, detention and subsequent imprisonment of protestors who were seeking to disrupt an angling competition was a serious interference with the right of freedom of expression but, in the circumstances, it was not disproportionate. There was a real risk of disorder if similar protests took place and the imprisonment for 21 days was a result of the failure to agree to a bind over which was designed to avoid a 'real risk' of further protest. In *Osmani v Former Yugoslav Republic of Macedonia*[1103] an interference with freedom of expression in the context of incitement to political violence was found to be proportionate and the complaint was therefore inadmissible.

(e) Protection of health or morals

The Court regards 'morals' as having no objective content, and there is no European con- **15.369** sensus to assist in a definition,[1104] the Court has given national courts a wide margin of appreciation, both in deciding the content of 'morals' and in what measures are necessary to protect morals.[1105] While 'morals' may attract strong local feelings,[1106] it is not self evident that local considerations should govern the determination of national standards for protecting morals.

On the other hand, in the *Open Door* case[1107] the Court found Government interference **15.370** unjustifiable. While it is primarily for the state to determine the content of 'morals', the very broad and perpetual injunction to restrain anyone (regardless of age, health reasons or necessity) from seeking advice about abortion was not necessary in a democratic society. The refusal to renew the registration of a health magazine on the ground that it had published unverified medical information was a justified interference.[1108]

(f) Protection of the reputation or the rights of others

Introduction. The protection of the reputation or rights of others provides the entitlement **15.371** for an individual to pursue defamation proceedings. The strictness of the scrutiny applied

---

[1099] Ibid, para 110.
[1100] Decision of 5 December 2000.
[1101] (2002) 35 EHRR 35.
[1102] Decision of 11 January 2001.
[1103] Decision of 11 October 2001.
[1104] *Handyside v United Kingdom* (1976) 1 EHRR 737.
[1105] See eg, ibid, (the sale of the Little Red Schoolbook); and *Müller v Switzerland* (1988)13 EHHR 212.
[1106] In *Handyside v United Kingdom* (see n 1104 above) and *Müller v Switzerland* (see n 1105 above) the Court accepted that a 'pressing social need' was necessary to punish expression for the protection of the morals of relatively small areas of the population.
[1107] *Open Door and Dublin Well Woman v Ireland* (1992) 15 EHRR 244.
[1108] *Vérités Santé Pratique Sarl v France*, Decision of 1 December 2005.

under Article 10(2) will depend on the nature of the expression involved and on the identity of the individuals whose rights are infringed. The 'rights of others' is widely construed.[1109]

15.372 **Politicians and political expression.** The Court has frequently stressed that the limits of acceptable criticism are wider for a politician than a private citizen. A politician lays himself open to close scrutiny of his every word and deed by both journalists and the general public and must display a greater degree of tolerance.[1110] In *Jerusalem v Austria*[1111] the applicant was a member of the Vienna municipal council who suggested that a particular organization was a sect with fascistic tendencies. An injunction was granted to restrain the repetition of her statements. The Court held that this was an unjustified interference was the statements were value judgments which were fair comment on a matter of public interest. More recently in *Filipovi v Serbia*[1112] the applicant stated at a public meeting that Mayor was guilty of embezzlement. It was held that the domestic finding of defamation was unjustified.

15.373 The bounds of permissible criticism of the Government are even wider.[1113] Thus, the upholding of a complaint against a television broadcast which severely criticized the role of Switzerland during the Second World War was an unjustified interference.[1114] Even where there is substantial damage to reputation, a successful claim in defamation may violate Article 10. The cases are discussed in relation to interferences with media freedom of expression.[1115] The applicant stated at a public meeting that Mayor was guilty of embezzlement. It was held that the domestic finding of defamation was unjustified.

15.374 **Religious beliefs.** Where the religious beliefs of others are offended, interferences with freedom of expression may be justified. In *Otto-Preminger-Institute v Austria*[1116] it justified the nation-wide seizure and forfeiture of a film which offended the rights of a local population on religious grounds. The Court found that, as with 'morals', the lack of a uniform conception of religion in European society gave a wide margin of appreciation to the state to determine the necessity of the ban for the protection of the rights of the local people. However, the case differs from the 'morals' cases because the Court accepted the application of 'local' standards to a national level, finding that the nation-wide ban did not exceed the state's margin of appreciation. Similarly, in *Wingrove v United Kingdom*[1117] the refusal of the British Board of Film Classification to grant a licence for the distribution of the film 'Visions of Christ' was justified to protect the rights of Christians. In *IA v Turkey*[1118]

[1109] It includes, for example, the right to respect for religious feelings (*Otto-Preminger-Institute v Austria* (1994) 19 EHRR 34, para 47), and. the right of the general public to receive objective and transparent information (*Monnat v Switzerland,* Judgment of 21 September 2006, para 41).

[1110] See eg, *Lingens v Austria* (1986) 8 EHRR 103 para 42.

[1111] (2003) 37 EHRR 25.

[1112] Judgment of 20 November 2007; and see *Kwiecień v Poland* (2009) 48 EHRR 7 (order for publication of apology and payment of compensation in respect of a widely circulated letter criticizing politician unjustified).

[1113] *Castells v Spain* (1992) 14 EHHR 445, para 46.

[1114] *Monnat v Switzerland* (n 1109 above) paras 56 to 69.

[1115] See para 15.321ff above.

[1116] (1994) 19 EHRR 34.

[1117] (1996) 24 EHRR 1.

[1118] (2007) 45 EHRR 30.

a conviction for blasphemy which originally resulted in a two year prison sentence,[1119] for an abusive attack on Prophet of Islam was held, by a majority of 4:3 not to constitute a violation of Article 10. These cases can be contrasted with the judgment in *Giniewski v France*[1120] in which a conviction for suggesting that a papal encyclical contributed to anti-semitism was held to constitute a breach. The article not 'gratuitously offensive or insulting and does not incite to disrespect or hatred. Nor does it cast doubt in any way on clearly established historical facts'.[1121]

Restrictions on public servants. The protection of the rights of others also permits an interference to ensure 'effective political democracy'. Such interferences are not limited to circumstances in which the stability of the constitutional or political order is threatened.[1122] Thus, in *Ahmed v United Kingdom*[1123] regulations restricting the political activity of local authority employees were a proportionate restriction on freedom of expression. In the special circumstances of the former Eastern bloc countries, restriction on the freedom of police officers to engage in political debate was proportionate.[1124]   **15.374A**

Commercial expression. Interference with commercial expression may also be justified because of its impact on the rights of others. In *Hertel v Switzerland*[1125] the applicant was convicted[1126] for submitting to a scientific journal a research paper on the possible detrimental effects of the use of microwave ovens. Although the legislation, which was 'intended to guarantee, in the interests of all parties concerned, fair, undistorted competition', had the legitimate aim of the protection of the rights of others, the conviction could not be justified as being necessary in a democratic society. The Court emphasized that the wide margin of appreciation given to states in relation to commercial and competition areas must be reduced when the statement of an individual is not made as a matter of purely 'commercial' interest, but is part of a more general debate.   **15.375**

Religious and political advertising. When considering the justification of restrictions on religious advertising the Court accords a wide margin of appreciation to the State. In *Murphy v Ireland*[1126a] a total ban on religious television advertising was justified on the basis that it did not affect other media and a complete relaxation would sit uneasily with religious sensitivities and the principle of neutrality in broadcasting. In contrast, where the advertising is political in nature the restrictions are much more difficult to justify. In *VgT Verein Gegen Tierfabriken v Switzerland*[1126b] a ban on political advertising which prevented   **15.375A**

[1119] Later commuted to a $16 fine.

[1120] (2007) 45 EHRR 23.

[1121] Ibid, para 53; see also *Klein v Slovakia* (2006) 21 BHRC 457 (conviction for defamation for article criticising Catholic archbishop was disproportionate).

[1122] *Ahmed v United Kingdom* (2000) 29 EHRR 1, para 52.

[1123] Ibid, paras 52–54; for the unsuccessful challenge to these regulations in the English courts, see *R v Secretary of State for the Environment, ex p NALGO* [1993] Admin LR 785.

[1124] *Rekvényi v Hungary* (2000) 30 EHRR 519, paras 44–49.

[1125] (1999) 28 EHRR 534.

[1126] The Federal Unfair Competition Act included in its definition of 'unfair acts' the denigration 'of others or the goods, work, services, prices or business of others by making inaccurate, misleading or unnecessarily wounding statements'.

[1126a] (2004) 38 EHRR 13.

[1126b] (2002) 44 EHRR 4.

the applicant from broadcasting a commercial attacking the industrial farming of pigs was held to be unjustified. A similar approach was taken in *TV Vest As v Norway*[1126c] in which a fine on a broadcaster for showing political adverts for the Pensioners Party in breach of a ban on political television advertising was a breach of Article 10. The Pensioners Party received little television coverage and, in the absence of a system of a party political broadcasts, the restriction was not necessary to protect the rights of others.

15.376 **Criticism of civil servants.** In *Janowski v Poland*[1127] a conviction for using insulting words to criticize the actions of municipal guards in a public setting was justifiable as protecting the reputation and rights of the civil servants. Similarly, in *Peree v Netherlands*[1128] the Commission held that the convictions of the applicant for 'insult and slander' for comparing an anti-discrimination organization to the Nazi SA were justifiable. However, the protection afforded to law-enforcement officials cannot be extended to all persons who are employed by the State.[1129] Thus, an order to rectify statements in a private letter criticising a Deputy Governor was an unjustified interference.[1130]

15.377 **Other cases.** Protection of the rights of others was also claimed to justify interfering with freedom of expression in *Lehideux and Isorni v France*.[1131] The applicant was convicted of the 'public defence of war crimes or the crimes of collaboration' after publishing an advertisement seeking to present in a positive light information concerning Marshall Petain to secure a retrial of his case. The interference pursued several legitimate aims including the protection of rights of others and the prevention of disorder or crime but was a disproportionate restriction.[1132] However, it is difficult to justify interference with expression in a purely political context. Thus in *Brasilier v France*[1133] an award of damages of one franc in respect of an attack by one political candidate on another, including accusations of fraud and theft, was found to be an unjustified interference.

(g) Preventing the disclosure of information received in confidence

15.378 **Introduction.** Justification on grounds of prevention of disclosure of information received in confidence overlaps with other legitimate aims. For example, the protection of confidential governmental information may be required 'in the interests of national security' whilst disclosure of private information may be restricted for 'protection of the rights of others'. However, this aim may be relevant in cases concerning confidential Government information which does not affect national security.[1134] The protection of confidential journalistic sources has been considered under this head.[1135]

[1126c] Judgment of 11 December 2008; the United Kingdom Government unsuccessfully intervened to oppose the application on the basis which found favour with the House of Lords in *R (Animal Defenders) v Secretary of State for Culture, Media and Sport* [2008] 2 WLR 781, see para 15.177 above.

[1127] (2000) 29 EHRR 705; see also *Lešník v Slovakia,* Judgment of 11 March 2003, para 53.

[1128] (1998) 28 EHRR CD 158.

[1129] See *Busuioc v Moldova*, Judgment of 21 December 2004, para 64.

[1130] *Zakharov v Russia,* Judgment of 5 October 2006.

[1131] (2000) 30 EHRR 665.

[1132] Ibid, paras 51–58; see also *Chauvy v France* (2005) 41 EHRR 29 and *Radio France v France* (2005) 40 EHRR 29.

[1133] Judgment of 11 April 2006.

[1134] See *X v Germany* (1970) 13 YB, 888, EComm HR.

[1135] See para 15.350ff above.

In *Guja v Moldova*[1136] the applicant had been the head of the press department at the pros- **15.379**
ecutor general's officer and disclosed to the press two letters sent concerning a criminal
investigation against police officers which had been discontinued. He was dismissed. The
Court noted that

> a civil servant, in the course of his work, may become aware of in-house information, includ-
> ing secret information, whose divulgation or publication corresponds to a strong public
> interest. The Court thus considers that the signalling by a civil servant or an employee in the
> public sector of illegal conduct or wrongdoing in the workplace should, in certain circum-
> stances, enjoy protection.[1137]

However, the Court also had to consider the damage suffered by the public authority by the
disclosure, taking into account the public interest in the disclosure of the material.[1138] On
the facts, taking into account the high degree of public interest in pressure being placed on
public prosecutors, the applicant's good faith and the severity of the sanction, the Court
held that the interference was not justified.

(h) Maintaining the authority and impartiality of the judiciary

The need to maintain the authority and impartiality of the judiciary is a ground of justifica- **15.380**
tion for interference and overlaps with the right of an individual to a fair trial 'where publicity would prejudice the interests of justice' under Article 6(1).[1139] Article 10(2) is broader
in scope and pre-trial comments are potentially legitimate under this head. However, in
this context the Court has recognized that account must be taken of the central position
occupied by Article 6.[1140] The term 'judiciary' ('*pouvoir judiciare*') is broad in scope, covering 'all the machinery of justice or the judicial branch of government as well as judges in
their official capacity' and the notion that the courts 'are the proper forum for the ascer-
tainment of legal rights'.[1141]

In the *Sunday Times* case[1142] an injunction had been granted restraining the publication of **15.381**
a newspaper article about the merits of pending Thalidomide litigation, on grounds that it
would prejudice the trial. The Court decided that there was no 'pressing social need' for the
injunction, that there was substantial public interest in the case, that the article used mod-
erate language and that the injunction was broadly framed. The Court took the view that
the 'authority and impartiality of the judiciary' were 'objectively determinable' interests;
and that the margin of appreciation afforded to the state to take measures to protect them
was therefore a narrow one.[1143]

The impact of criticizing the judiciary has also been considered. In *Barfod v Denmark*[1144] **15.382**
the applicant was convicted of defaming two lay judges. This conviction was justified

---

[1136] Judgment of 12 February 2008 (GC).
[1137] Ibid, para 72.
[1138] Ibid, para 76.
[1139] Art 6(1); see para 11.474ff above.
[1140] *Sunday Times v United Kingdom* (1979) 2 EHRR 245, para 55.
[1141] Ibid, para 55 (but does not extend to private remarks concerning judges or prosecutors, see *Raichinov v Bulgaria* Judgment of 20 April 2006, para 45).
[1142] n 1140 above.
[1143] But see *Weber v Switzerland* (1990) 12 EHRR 508.
[1144] (1989) 13 EHRR 493.

despite his arguments that the comments were aimed at the tribunal rather than the individual judges, and that they were part of a wider political tax debate. In *Schöpfer v Switzerland*[1145] the disciplinary punishment of the applicant lawyer was also justifiable where a lawyer publicly criticized the administration of justice in his jurisdiction in criminal proceedings which were then pending before the courts. In *De Haes and Gijsels v Belgium*[1146] journalists argued that the articles, which personally insulted certain members of the judiciary for their handling of child abuse and incest proceedings, were to be seen against the background of the public debate on incest in the region. They argued that the research upon which they were based constituted objective evidence; and that it was only to protect their sources that it had not been presented in court. The Court held that, although the comments were severely critical, they were not disproportionate to the indignation caused by the subject matter of the articles. In *Amihalachioaie v Moldova*[1147] a fine imposed on the chairman of the Bar Council for criticizing a decision of the Constitutional Court was unjustified as the remarks were on an issue of public interest and were not insulting.

15.383   If, however, it is necessary for the state to protect the judiciary and prosecutors from unjustified criticism. Thus in *Lesnik v Slovakia*[1148] a suspended prison sentence for the publication of a letter making serious allegations against a public prosecutor was justified under Article 10(2). In *Perna v Italy*[1149] the applicant journalist, published an article about a Public Prosecutor, a judicial officer, criticizing his political militancy and accused him of taking part in a plan to gain control of the public prosecutors' offices in all Italian cities and of using a criminal-turned-informer to try and destroy the political career of, a former Italian prime minister, The applicant was convicted of aggravated defamation and ordered to pay damages and costs and to publish the judgment. It was held that there had been no breach of Article 10.

15.384   **Speech of lawyers in court.**   Restrictions on the freedom of speech of lawyers in court has been considered in a number of cases. In *Nikula v Finland*[1150] it was held that, while counsel's freedom of expression in court was not unlimited, it could only be lawfully restricted

---

[1145] (2001) 33 EHRR 34.

[1146] (1997) 25 EHRR 1.

[1147] (2005) 40 EHRR 35; (2005) 40 EHRR 35; see also *Kobenter and Standard Verlags GmbH v Austria*, Judgment of 2 November 2006 (conviction for article comparing judge's decision to that of a medieval witch trial a violation as it was a value judgment on a matter of public interest); *Skalka v Poland* (2004) 38 EHRR 1 (conviction and sentence of 8 months' imprisonment for insulting appeal judge was too severe); *Sabou and Pircalab v Romania*, Judgment of 28 September 2004 (conviction for accusing judge of unlawful use of influence not justified because domestic courts had failed to review applicant's supporting evidence) and see *Hrico v Slovakia* (2005) 41 EHRR 18.

[1148] Judgment of 11 March 2003; see also *Kubli v Switzerland*, Decision of 21 February 2002 (fine imposed on a lawyer for the making of defamatory remarks about a magistrate during his own disciplinary process was not a violation) and *Lomakin v Russia*, Decision of 17 November 2005 (conviction of a lawyer for accusing a judge of abusing her position in order to obtain a flat justified as no supporting evidence produced).

[1149] (2004) 39 EHRR 28: but see *Skalka v Poland* (2004) 38 EHRR 1 (conviction for insulting judiciary a violation).

[1150] (2004) 38 EHRR 45; see also *Steur v Netherlands* (2004) 39 EHRR 33 (violation when a lawyer was disciplined for alleging in proceedings that his client had been pressured by the police into making an incriminating statement, although applicant's good faith had not been challenged).

in exceptional circumstances. In the case itself a lawyer had been convicted of defamation following criticism in court of the prosecutor in a case in which both were involved. This was found to be a breach of Article 10. In *Kyprianou v Cyprus*[1151] a defence lawyer sentenced to 5 days imprisonment for comments in court about the actions of the judges in a criminal case. This sentence pursued a legitimate aim as, although lawyers were entitled to comment on administration of justice their criticism should not overstep certain bounds. However, a restriction on defence counsel's freedom of expression could only be accepted in exceptional circumstances and the penalty disproportionately severe. However, the conviction of a lawyer for issuing a press release attacking the conduct of the national police was a justified interference to protect the reputation of a public authority.[1152]

Pre-trial comment. The restriction of pre-trial comment in criminal cases was addressed in **15.385** *Worm v Austria*[1153] where the Court upheld the conviction of a journalist who had written an article which was critical of a former Minister in advance of his trial on charges of tax evasion. The Court held that states were not entitled to restrict all forms of public discussion on matters pending before the courts. It said:

> There is general recognition of the fact that courts cannot operate in a vacuum . . . Provided that it does not overstep the bounds imposed in the interests of the proper administration of justice, reporting, including comment on court proceedings contributes to their publicity and is thus perfectly consonant with the requirements under article 6(1) of the convention that hearings be public.[1154]

The Court drew attention to the role of the media in imparting information, particularly where a public figure is involved. However:

> public figures are entitled to the enjoyment of the guarantees of a fair trial set out in art 6 . . . the limits of permissible comment may not extend to statements which are likely to prejudice, whether intentionally or not, the chances of a person receiving a fair trial or to undermine the confidence of the public in the role of the courts in the administration of criminal justice.[1155]

The conviction was upheld despite the absence of a requirement in domestic law of actual influence on court proceedings. The Commission had taken took a similar view of a pre-hearing restriction in *Channel Four v United Kingdom*[1156] where it held that the broadcasting of contemporaneous reconstructions of the criminal appeal would have an impact both on the right to fair trial and on the reputation of the court.

[1151] (2007) 44 EHRR 27 (GC) see also *Hurter v Switzerland*, Decision of 21 February 2002, (punishment of a lawyer for making serious allegations against the Court of Appeal in documents lodged in court on his client's behalf was held to be proportionate and his claim was inadmissible); see also *Wingerter v Germany*, Decision of 21 March 2002.

[1152] *Coutant v France*, Decision of 24 January 2008.

[1153] (1997) 25 EHRR 454; see generally, H Fenwick and G Phillipson, *Media Freedom under the Human Rights Act* (Oxford University Press, 2006), 185–187.

[1154] *Worm* (n 1153 above) para 50.

[1155] Ibid.

[1156] (1989) 61 DR 285, EComm HR; see also *Hodgson v United Kingdom* (1987) 51 DR 136, EComm HR; *Atkinson Crook and The Independent v United Kingdom* (1990) 67 DR 244, EComm HR (jury trial) and *BBC Scotland v United Kingdom* (1997) 25 EHRR CD 179.

Appendix 1: United Kingdom Article 10 Cases in Strasbourg

(1) Introduction

15.386   A large number of United Kingdom applications based on Article 10 have come before the Commission and the Court. Many of these were unsuccessful, but the Court has on nine occasions found the United Kingdom to be in violation of Article 10.[1157] The United Kingdom Article 10 applications will be considered under six headings: obscenity and blasphemy, contempt of court, defamation, protest, national security and other cases.

(2) Obscenity and blasphemy

15.387   None of the United Kingdom applications under Article 10 in relation to obscenity and blasphemy have been successful. Where there has been doubt as to the 'necessity' of the measures used, the Government has consistently been given the benefit of a 'margin of appreciation'. This is because:

> a wider margin of appreciation is generally available to the contracting states when regulating freedom of expression in relation to matters liable to offend intimate personal convictions within the sphere of morals or, especially, religion.[1158]

The fact that the margin of appreciation given to national authorities has been determinative in these cases means that the Strasbourg jurisprudence will provide less than reliable guidance to the domestic courts when such matters arise because 'margin of appreciation' is not relevant.[1159]

15.388   The leading case of *Handyside v United Kingdom*[1160] concerned the Little Red Schoolbook, a publication which was written for schoolchildren and included a chapter on explicitly sexual topics. The applicant was convicted of an offence under the Obscene Publications Act. The issue for the Court was whether the undoubted interference with freedom of expression of the applicant was 'necessary in a democratic society for the protection of morals'. The Court referred to the 'national margin of appreciation' and said that:

> The Contracting States have each fashioned their approach in the light of the situation obtaining in their respective territories; they have had regard, *inter alia*, to the different views prevailing there about the demands of the protection of morals in a democratic society.[1161]

[1157] *Sunday Times v United Kingdom* (1979) 2 EHRR 245; *Sunday Times v United Kingdom (No 2)* (1991) 14 EHRR 229; *The Observer and The Guardian v United Kingdom* (1991) 14 EHRR 153; *Tolstoy Miloslavsky v United Kingdom* (1995) 20 EHRR 442; *Goodwin v United Kingdom* (1996) 22 EHRR 123; *Bowman v United Kingdom* (1998) 26 EHRR 1; *Steel v United Kingdom* (1998) 28 EHRR 603 (the Art 10 violation incidental to an Art 5 violation); *Hashman and Harrup v United Kingdom* (2000) 30 EHRR 241; *Steel and Morris v United Kingdom* (2005) 41 EHRR 22.

[1158] See *Wingrove v United Kingdom* (1996) 24 EHRR 1, para 58.

[1159] See para 6.57ff above.

[1160] (1976) 1 EHRR 737.

[1161] Ibid, para 57.

On this basis, the Court found that the conviction of the applicant on grounds of obscenity was not a violation of Article 10.[1162] In *S and G v United Kingdom*[1163] the applicant had been convicted of outraging public decency after displaying a model of a human head with earrings made out of freeze dried human foetuses. The Commission found that the application was inadmissible on the basis that, having regard to the margin of appreciation, the view taken by the domestic court was not unreasonable. In *Hoare v United Kingdom*[1164] the applicant complained of a breach of Article 10 as a result of his conviction for publishing obscene articles[1165] under section 2 of the Obscene Publications Act 1959 and his sentence of 30-months' imprisonment. The Commission took the view that the restriction on the applicant's freedom of expression was for a legitimate aim, namely the protection of morals and was not disproportionate.

15.389 The case of *Gay News and Lemon v United Kingdom*[1166] concerned the convictions of the applicant for blasphemous libel. The Commission found that this offence restricted freedom of expression for a legitimate purpose, namely 'the protection of the rights of citizens not to be offended in their religious feelings by publications'.[1167] The Commission also took the view that the offence of blasphemous libel satisfied the test of 'proportionality' inherent in Article 10(2). As a result, the Commission found that the complaint was manifestly ill-founded.

15.390 Blasphemy was again at issue in *Wingrove v United Kingdom*.[1168] A video entitled 'Visions of Ecstasy' depicted St Teresa of Avila in erotic scenes. The British Board of Film Classification had refused the video a distribution certificate. The admitted interference with freedom of expression was held by the Court to be 'prescribed by law', despite the fact that the offence of blasphemy lacked precise legal definition: it took the view that the applicant, with appropriate legal advice, could reasonably have foreseen that the film might fall within the scope of the offence of blasphemy.[1169] The interference was also found to have the legitimate aim of protecting the rights of others: more specifically, 'to provide protection against seriously offensive attacks on matters regarded as sacred by Christians'.[1170] In holding that the restrictions were 'necessary', the Court took into account the fact that:

> there is as yet not sufficient common ground in the legal and social orders of the Member States of the Council of Europe to conclude that a system whereby a State can impose restrictions on the propagation of material on the basis that it is blasphemous is, in itself, unnecessary in a democratic society and thus incompatible with the Convention.[1171]

[1162] For a discussion of the case, see R Lawson and H Schermers (eds), *Leading Cases of the European Court of Human Rights* (Ars Aequi Libri, 1997), 37–42; and see A Lester, 'Freedom of Expression' and R St J Macdonald, 'The Margin of Appreciation' in R St J Macdonald, F Matscher, and H Petzold (eds), *The European System for the Protection of Human Rights* (Nijhoff, 1993).

[1163] Decision of 2 September 1991, the domestic case was *R v Gibson* [1990] 2 QB 619, see para 15.161 above; and see H Fenwick and G Phillipson, *Media Freedom under the Human Rights Act* (Oxford University Press, 2006), 476–477, correctly describing the decision as 'disappointing'.

[1164] [1997] EHRLR 678.

[1165] The articles were hardcore pornographic video tapes distributed by post.

[1166] (1982) 5 EHRR 123.

[1167] Ibid, para 11.

[1168] (1996) 24 EHRR 1.

[1169] Ibid, para 43.

[1170] Ibid, para 48.

[1171] Ibid, para 57.

The Court took into account the wide margin of appreciation for states in relation to matters which are liable to offend intimate personal convictions.[1172]

15.391 In *Perrin v United Kingdom*[1173] the applicant complained about his conviction and sentence for publishing an obscene article on an internet site. The Court was of the view that his conviction and sentence were proportionate to the legitimate aim of protecting morals and the rights of others and the application was inadmissible.

(3) Contempt of court

15.392 One of the best known decisions of the Court is that of *Sunday Times v United Kingdom*[1174] which arose out of the Thalidomide litigation. The Attorney-General obtained an injunction restraining publication of an article commenting on the drug 'Thalidomide' as a contempt of court.[1175] The Court accepted that the rules relating to contempt of court were 'prescribed by law' and had the legitimate aim, under Article 10(2), of 'maintaining the authority . . . of the judiciary'.[1176] However, the Court went on to consider whether the interference by injunction was 'necessary in a democratic society' and concluded that:

> the interference complained of did not correspond to a social need sufficiently pressing to outweigh the public interest in freedom of expression within the meaning of the Convention.[1177]

The restraint was therefore a breach of Article 10. This decision resulted in the Contempt of Court Act 1981. In *Channel Four v United Kingdom*,[1178] on the other hand, a restraint was acceptable where the Commission found that the broadcasting of contemporaneous reconstructions of a criminal appeal would have an impact on both the right to fair trial and the reputation of the court.

15.393 The effect of section 10 of the Contempt of Court Act 1981 was considered by the Court in *Goodwin v United Kingdom*.[1179] Section 10 introduced a presumption against the disclosure of journalists' sources, subject only to a 'legitimate aim' and a 'necessity' test, requirements which mirror Article 10(2) of the Convention. The House of Lords had ordered disclosure of the identity of the source of confidential financial documents stolen from the plaintiff company.[1180] In contrast, the Court decided that the order breached Article 10; it was not 'necessary in a democratic society' because there was no reasonable relationship of proportionality between the order and the legitimate aim of the protection of the rights of the company.

[1172] For a general discussion, see S Ghandi and J James, 'The English Law of Blasphemy and the European Convention on Human Rights', [1998] EHRLR 430.

[1173] Decision of 18 October 2005.

[1174] (1979) 2 EHRR 245.

[1175] The injunction had been granted at first instance, discharged by the Court of Appeal and restored by the House of Lords: see *A-G v Times Newspapers Ltd* [1974] AC 273.

[1176] *Sunday Times v United Kingdom* (see n 1174 above) para 57.

[1177] Ibid, para 67.

[1178] (1989) 61 DR 285, EComm HR; see also *Hodgson v United Kingdom* (1987) 51 DR 136, EComm HR; *Atkinson Crook and The Independent v United Kingdom* (1990) 67 DR 244, EComm HR and *BBC Scotland v United Kingdom* (1997) 25 EHRR CD 179.

[1179] (1996) 22 EHRR 123.

[1180] *X Ltd v Morgan-Grampian (Publishers) Ltd* [1991] 1 AC 1; see para 15.148ff above.

In *Brown v United Kingdom*[1181] the applicant complained that he had been convicted of **15.394** contempt of court in relation to the publication of the name of a rape victim and fined when he was only a director of the publisher of a newspaper without any editorial control. The application was rejected as manifestly ill-founded on the basis that it was legitimate to hold newspaper proprietors in part responsible for the contents of their newspapers when those contents impinged on the rights of others. The applicant's conviction and fine was not a disproportionate interference.

It has been held that the prohibition on disclosure of the deliberations of a jury contained **15.395** in section 8 of the Contempt of Court Act 1981 was a justified interference with the freedom of expression of a juror who gave a newspaper interview about jury deliberations in a high profile fraud case.[1182]

(4) Defamation

The English law of defamation has generated a steady stream of applications under the **15.396** Convention. The case of *Tolstoy Miloslavsky v United Kingdom*[1183] was brought following the notorious libel proceedings in which the jury had awarded Lord Aldington a record £1,500,000 damages because he was alleged to have been involved in war crimes. Article 10 had been infringed as the size of the award could not be justified as being 'necessary in a democratic society'. The Court of Appeal now gives guidance to juries when they consider making awards of damages.[1184]

The applicants in *Steel and Morris v United Kingdom*[1185] were the individual defendants **15.397** to a libel action brought by the McDonalds Corporation in relation to a 1986 leaflet which had attacked the company's business practices.[1186] At an early stage of the litigation they complained that restrictions on their expression were unjustified because the state failed to provide legal aid funding for defamation proceedings, simplified legal procedures and restrictions which would limit damage awards. The Commission declared the complaint inadmissible, commenting that the freedom of expression under Article 10 is not absolute; and does not authorize the publication of defamatory material:

> They have published their views, upon which there was no prior restraint, and, if those views are subsequently found to be libellous, any ensuing sanctions would in principle be justified for the protection of the reputation and rights, within the meaning of Article 10.[1187]

[1181] (2002) 35 EHRR CD17.

[1182] *Associated Newspapers, Steven and Wolman v United Kingdom*, Decision of 30 November 1994 (the Commission left open the question as to whether a prohibition on research into jury deliberations would be justified), for the domestic law, see para 15.101ff above.

[1183] (1995) 20 EHRR 442 see also *Times Newspapers v United Kingdom* (1990) 65 DR 307, EComm HR: similar argument could not be raised by *The Times* because it was not a victim.

[1184] See para 15.69ff above.

[1185] (1993) 18 EHRR CD 172.

[1186] For the domestic decisions see *McDonald's v Steel* [1995] EMLR 527, CA (striking out pleadings); *McDonald's v Steel* unrep, 19 June 1997, Bell J (judgment after trial); *McDonald's v Steel (No 4) Independent*, 10 May 1999, CA.

[1187] *Steel and Morris v United Kingdom* (see n 1185 above) para 2; cf the discussion of the Art 10 position by the Court of Appeal in *McDonalds v Steel (No 4)* (see n 1186 above).

The trial began in 1994 and judgment was given in 1997. The Court of Appeal rejected the applicants' appeal in 1997 and they made a further application to Strasbourg which led to a judgment in May 2005.[1188] The Court of Human Rights held that in view of the length, scale and complexity of the proceedings the unavailability of legal aid meant that there was an unacceptable inequality of arms and hence a breach of Article 6(1).[1189] The lack of procedural fairness and equality also led to a breach of Article 10.[1190] There was also a breach as a result of the disproportionate awards of damages.[1191]

15.398 There have been a number of other challenges to English libel laws. In *Times Newspapers v United Kingdom*[1192] the Commission rejected the applicant's contention that an apology published in a newspaper gave rise to the defence of qualified privilege. In *McVicar v United Kingdom*[1193] the court held that the denial of legal aid to defend defamation proceedings was not a violation of Article 6(1) and, that such ineligibility was not a violation of Article 10. It also held that the burden of proof on a defendant in defamation proceedings constituted a justified restriction on freedom expression under Article 10(2). In *Times Newspapers v United Kingdom (No 2)*[1194] the Court rejected a challenge to *Reynolds* qualified privilege on the grounds that the law was too vague and unpredictable and also rejected the contention that the interference was not, on the facts of the case, necessary in a democratic society. It took into account that the allegations were factual and serious, the sources 'unreliable or cryptic' and the fact that the libel claimant had not be been contacted or given the opportunity to defend himself prior to publication. However, the Court decided that the applicant's complaint about the 'single publication rule' was admissible.

(5) Protest cases

15.399 In *Arrowsmith v United Kingdom*[1195] there was a challenge to the applicant's conviction for distributing leaflets inciting soldiers to disaffection. Article 10 was not breached, as the prosecution served the legitimate purpose of protecting disorder in the army.

15.400 In *Steel v United Kingdom*[1196] the five applicants had been arrested and detained to prevent a breach of the peace while participating in various protests.[1197] It was found that the arrest and detention of the first and second applicants conformed to English law, but that that of the third, fourth and fifth applicants had been unlawful.[1198] The Court considered that the protests of the applicants constituted expressions of opinion and that the measures taken against them were accordingly violations of Article 10,[1199] albeit in pursuit of the legitimate

---

[1188] *Steel and Morris v United Kingdom* (2005) 41 EHRR 22; for discussion of this case see A Hudson, 'Free Speech and Equality of Arms—the decision in *Steel and Morris v United Kingdom*' [2005] EHRLR 301.

[1189] See para 11.430 above.

[1190] *Steel and Morris* (n 1188 above) para 95.

[1191] Ibid, para 96—the awards of £36,000 and £40,000 against each of the applicants were disproportionate in the light of their modest incomes and the lack of financial damage to McDonalds.

[1192] [1997] EHRLR 430; arising out of the case of *Watts v Times Newspapers Ltd* [1997] QB 650.

[1193] (2002) 35 EHRR 22.

[1194] Decision of 11 October 2005: this arose out of *Loutchansky v Times Newspapers* [2002] QB 783.

[1195] (1980) 19 DR 5, EComm HR.

[1196] (1998) 28 EHRR 603.

[1197] For the facts, see ibid, paras 6–38.

[1198] These applicants were, therefore, successful in Art 5 claims, ibid, para 64.

[1199] Ibid, paras 92–93.

aims of prevention of disorder and protection of the rights of others. In relation to the first and second applicants, taking into account the seriousness of their conduct, the apprehensions were 'necessary in a democratic society'. Interference with the other applicants was, however, unlawful and disproportionate, in violation of Article 10.[1200] The arrest and detention of the applicant protestors in *Nicol and Selvanayagam v United Kingdom*[1201] was not a disproportionate interference with their Article 10 rights. It was proportionate to bind them over in the light of the risk of their protest provoking violence and to imprison them for 21 days when they refused to accept a bindover.

In *Hashman and Harrup v United Kingdom*[1202] the Court again considered the impact of a bind over on protesters. The Court held that a bind over made to prevent behaviour *contra bonos mores*[1203] was not sufficiently precise to be fore seeable in accordance with the law under Article 10(2). As result, there was a violation of Article 10. **15.401**

In *Appleby v United Kingdom*[1204] the applicants had been refused permission to collection signatures for a petition in a private shopping centre. They unsuccessfully argued that the State had a positive obligation to protect their right to freedom of expression from interference by the owner of the centre. Article 10 did not include a positive obligation to provide a forum in which to exercise the right.[1205] **15.402**

(6) National security

The well-known *Spycatcher* litigation[1206] led two newspapers to bring applications under Article 10.[1207] The *Observer* and *Guardian* newspapers complained about interlocutory injunctions, granted by Millett J and continued by the House of Lords, which banned publication of excerpts from the book, *Spycatcher*,[1208] on grounds of national security. By the time of the House of Lords decision, the book had been published in the United States and was obtainable in the United Kingdom. In the related cases of *Observer and Guardian v United Kingdom* and *Sunday Times v United Kingdom*[1209] the Court held that the continuation of the injunctions after confidentiality had been lost contravened Article 10. It was accepted, on the other hand, that, until publication in the United States, confidentiality was justified; and it was, therefore, proportionate to find that publication in breach of the injunctions was a contempt.[1210] **15.403**

[1200] Ibid, para 110.
[1201] 11 January 2001.
[1202] (2000) 30 EHRR 241.
[1203] Conduct which is wrong rather than right in the judgment of the majority of contemporary citizens: see *Hughes v Holley* (1986) 86 Cr App R 130.
[1204] (2003) 37 EHRR 38, para 40.
[1205] For discussions of this case see M A Sanderson, 'Free speech in public places: the privatization of human rights in *Appleby v UK*,' (2004) KCLJ 159 and J Rowbottom 'Property and participation: a right of access for expressive activities' [2005] EHRLR 186.
[1206] For a general discussion, see para 15.31ff above.
[1207] For the history of the litigation see *Sunday Times v United Kingdom (No 2)* (1992) 14 EHRR 153, 156–173.
[1208] *A-G v Guardian Newspapers Ltd (No 1)* [1987] 1 WLR 1428.
[1209] (1991) 14 EHRR 153, 229.
[1210] See *Times Newspapers and Neill v United Kingdom* (1992) 15 EHRR CD 49.

15.404   The applicants in *Brind and McLaughlin v United Kingdom*[1211] challenged the Government 'broadcasting ban' on terrorists.[1212] The Commission found that the interference was for the legitimate aim of protecting the interests of national security, and, bearing in mind the margin of appreciation in relation to measures against terrorism, took the view that the ban was not disproportionate.[1213]

15.405   In *Blake v United Kingdom*[1214] the applicant was a convicted spy who had written an autobiography which, although it did not contain confidential information, was the subject of a successful claim by the Crown for restitutionary damages.[1215] He contended that this order was a breach of his Article 10 rights. The Court held that the interference was proportionate, in the light of the fact that he had not been prevented from publishing the book and that the order was closely related to his serious criminal past.

(7) Commercial speech and advertising

15.406   The case of *Colman v United Kingdom*[1216] arose out of the advertising restrictions of the General Medical Council. The Commission found that there was an interference with the freedom of expression of the applicant, but that it had been carried out in pursuit of legitimate aims, namely the protection of the health of patients and the rights of other doctors. The restrictions were held to be necessary.[1217]

15.407   A complaint under Article 10 was held inadmissible in *United Christian Broadcasters Ltd v United Kingdom*[1218] on the basis that the restriction was not disproportionate as religious groups could apply for local licences and that it was necessary to ensure that there was no discrimination in the allocation of the very limited national radio spectrum. In *Marlow v United Kingdom*[1219] the conviction of a writer of a book which incited others to grow cannabis was held to be justified on the ground that the prosecution pursued the legitimate aim of the prevention of crime and was a proportionate response to a 'pressing social need'.

(8) Other applications

15.408   The limits of the concept of 'expression' have been tested in a number of United Kingdom applications. Expression has been held to include television programmes[1220] but not the physical expression of feelings[1221] or the right to vote or stand for election[1222]—in relation to which Article 3 of the First Protocol is the *lex specialis*.[1223]

[1211]   (1994) 18 EHRR CD 76.
[1212]   For the domestic case see *R v Secretary of State for the Home Department, ex p Brand* [1991] 1 AC 696.
[1213]   See also *Brind and McLaughlin v United Kingdom* (n 1211 above).
[1214]   Decision of 25 October 2005; a very limited aspect of the application, in relation to the Art 6(1) 'reasonable time requirement' was held to be admissible and ultimately resulted in a finding of violation, see *Blake v United Kingdom* (2007) 44 EHRR 29.
[1215]   See *A-G v Blake* [2001] 1 AC 268.
[1216]   (1993) 18 EHRR 119.
[1217]   The restrictions were later relaxed and a friendly settlement reached.
[1218]   Decision of 7 November 2000.
[1219]   Decision of 5 December 2000.
[1220]   See eg, *Hodgson v United Kingdom* (1987) 51 DR 136, EComm HR.
[1221]   *X v United Kingdom* (1978) 3 EHRR 63, EComm HR (public displays of affection by homosexuals).
[1222]   *Liberal Party, Mrs R and Mr P v United Kingdom* (1982) 4 EHRR 106, EComm HR.
[1223]   *Hirst v United Kingdom (No.2)* (2006) 42 EHRR 41 (GC), para 89.

In *Bowman v United Kingdom*[1224] the Court had to consider restrictions on freedom of   **15.409**
expression in the context of elections. The applicant anti-abortion campaigner in that case
had been prosecuted under section 75 of the Representation of the People Act 1983 for her
third party expenditure in excess of £5, 'with a view to promoting or procuring the election
of a candidate' during an election period. The applicant had distributed a leaflet setting out
the candidates' respective views on abortion. She was acquitted on technical grounds. The
Court held that the provisions of section 75 were a restriction on freedom of expression. They
were not 'necessary in a democratic society' as they were disproportionate to the legitimate aim
of securing equality between candidates. As a result, there had been a violation of Article 10.

In *B v United Kingdom*[1225] a civil servant was reprimanded by his employers for his partici-   **15.410**
pation in a television programme about safety at a nuclear weapons establishment. The
reprimand was found to be a justified interference with his freedom of expression. This
approach was confirmed in *Ahmed v United Kingdom*,[1226] in which local government
employees unsuccessfully challenged restrictions placed on their political activities by the
Local Government (Political Restrictions) Regulations 1990. Although it was accepted
that there had been an interference with the expression of the applicant, one of the 'rights
of others' which can justify interference with expression is the right to 'effective political
democracy'. Interferences on this ground are not limited to circumstances in which there
is a threat to the stability of the constitutional or political order.[1227] The Court took the view
that the Government had identified a 'pressing social need' to maintain the political neutrality of local government officers and that the interference was not disproportionate.[1228]

The case of *A and Byrne and Twenty-Twenty Television v United Kingdom*[1229] concerned a   **15.411**
challenge to an injunction which prevented the transmission of a television programme
concerning the illegitimate child of a politician. The Commission held that this was a justifiable interference with freedom of expression: the interference was proportionate to the
aim of protecting the welfare of the child. It was justifiable to favour the child's welfare over
any public interest in the programme.

Appendix 2: Human Rights Cases in Scotland

(1) Prior restraint on publication or broadcast

The law on confidentiality was unsuccessfully prayed in aid against publication in *Scotsman*   **15.412**
Publications v Lord Advocate[1230] where it was held by the House of Lords that the detriment
to the public interest caused by the disclosure by a third party of originally confidential

---

[1224] (1998) 26 EHRR 1.
[1225] (1985) 45 DR 41, EComm HR.
[1226] (2000) 29 EHRR 1.
[1227] Ibid, para 52.
[1228] Ibid, paras 61–65; the Court also took into account the fact that whenever the right to freedom of
expression of public servants was in issue, it had to have regard to the 'duties and responsibilities' referred to
in Article 10(2): see para 15.184 above.
[1229] (1997) 25 EHRR CD 159; for the English case see *Re Z (A Minor) (Identification and Restrictions on
Publication)* [1997] Fam 1.
[1230] [1990] AC 812, at 822A–D, 823C–H, 826B–C and 828G–829F.

material was insufficient to outweigh the public interest in freedom of expression and interdict against publication was accordingly refused. The approach taken by the Court of
Human Rights to freedom of expression was said to mirror the pre-existing common law
and the House of Lords made reference to the need to balance Article 10 free expression
rights against claims to Crown confidentiality, although this was not the basis on which the
case was argued and decided in the courts in Scotland.

15.413   The right to freedom of expression and the maintenance of a free press under Article 10 were
successfully relied upon by the publishers of the newspaper 'Business AM'—the defenders in
Dickson Minto WS v Bonnier Media Ltd[1231]—to defeat an application for an interim interdict
seeking the suppression of a newspaper article which suggested that a solicitor might have had
a conflict of interest in acting for a number of named clients in a particular transaction. In
Response Handling Ltd v BBC[1232] the Lord Ordinary refused a motion for interim interdict
brought by a company operating call centres seeking to prevent the BBC from broadcasting
a programme investigating bank account and credit card fraud. The programme contained
video footage covertly recorded in the pursuer's premises by an undercover reporter engaged
by the BBC who had taken a job at the call centre. In taking up the call centre job the reporter
had signed an employment contract which included a confidentiality clause as well as an
express undertaking not to communicate in any way with a member or employee of any
media organization regarding the pursuers' business. The pursuers complained that the
covert footage she had shot which showed her recording details of customer bank accounts
disclosed a substantial amount of confidential information including a number of their
standard employment protocols, working practices and the type of information held by the
pursuers and how it could be obtained by their employees. The defenders in opposing the
interdict relied on Article 10 and section 12(3) of the HRA. In refusing the motion the Lord
Ordinary held that there was a genuine and strong public interest in exploring the extent to
which lapses in security in call centres might contribute to bank account and credit card
fraud. He did not consider that he kind of material which was disclosed in the final version
of the programme could be said to have been highly confidential and notwithstanding that
it had been obtained in breach of contract he did not consider that the pursuers has failed to
meet the standard for prior restraint set out in section 12(3).

15.414   In *X v BBC*[1233] the court granted interim interdict against the BBC to restrain broadcast of
those parts of a documentary film which related to the court appearances and custody of a
seventeen year old dyslexic individual, whose ability to read or write was extremely limited,
who had signed an agreement with the film-makers without any legal advice and, she
alleged, while intoxicated and under the influence of Valium. It was submitted that there
was a real risk that she might come to serious self harm if it was broadcast and a very real
risk existed that she would be subject to physical violence from others. The temporary
judge held that a pursuer's case engaged her rights under Article 8 in relation to images of
and information about her, and the balancing exercise both in respect of Article 8 and

---

[1231]   2002 SLT 776, OH per Lord Carloway.
[1232]   2008 SLT 51, OH per Lord Bracadale.
[1233]   2005 SLT 796, OH.

Article 10, and the balance of convenience test more generally favoured her interests in the maintenance of her privacy over the broadcaster's freedom of expression.

(2) Contempt of court and restrictions on reporting

In *Nicol v Caledonian Newspapers*[1234] it was held by the Lord Ordinary, Lady Paton, that a **15.415** defender's entitlement to plead the defence of qualified privilege and any other common law defence was not removed in the event of breach by the defender of the provisions of section 1(1)(b) of the Judicial Proceedings (Regulation of Reports) Act 1926 restricting publication of certain matters relating to proceedings for the dissolution of marriage since this entitlement was compatible with the Convention in that it was an aspect of the balance between the general interests of the community and the personal rights of the individual.

As the Lord Justice General (Lord Rodger of Earlsferry) observed in *Cox and Griffiths,* **15.416** *Petitioners,*[1235] the Contempt of Court Act 1981 was passed in order to change the domestic law of the United Kingdom so as to bring it into conformity with the interpretation of Article 10 of the Convention by the European Court on Human Rights in *The Sunday Times v UK.*[1236] He accepted that the Act represented a distinct (and novel) shift of the boundary between freedom of expression and the requirements of the due course of justice in favour of freedom of expression and noted:

> That boundary may have been displaced from the familiar place where it once ran; Parliament may have redrawn the boundary at a point which would not have been chosen by those people looking at the matter primarily from the standpoint of the administration of justice. But these factors simply make it all the more important that the courts faithfully observe the boundary which Parliament has settled in order to meet the international obligations of the United Kingdom.

Following *Cox and Griffiths* rights of free expression deriving ultimately from Article 10 **15.417** began increasingly and explicitly to be acknowledged by the Scottish courts in relation to their interpretation and application of their contempt of court jurisdiction.[1237] In *Lord Advocate v Scottish Media Newspapers Ltd.*[1238] the High Court of Justiciary refused an application from the Lord Advocate to find the respondents guilty of contempt of court in publishing an article reporting on the appearance on petition on a charge of deforcement of a Sheriff Officer of a well-known Scottish actor. The newspaper article made reference to the actor as having 'a well documented history of personal set-backs, including drink problems' and stated that 'neighbours have complained in the past about disturbances at his home'. In giving the opinion of the court the Lord Justice General noted, with effect from 20 May 1999 as a result of the coming into force of the Scotland Act, that the Lord Advocate did not the power to 'move the court to grant any remedy which would be incompatible with the European Convention on Human Rights' unless specifically required so to do by a provision of a Westminster statute. The Lord Justice General also reiterated that the

---

[1234] 2002 SC 493, OH.
[1235] 1998 JC 267 at 273.
[1236] (1980) 2 EHRR 245.
[1237] See for example *HM Advocate v Danskin*, 2000 SCCR 101, Sh Ct.
[1238] 1999 SCCR 599.

Contempt of Court Act 1981 fell to be interpreted in a manner which was compatible with the respondents' Article 10 free expression rights. The court found on the facts that there was no substantial risk in the article's publication of it causing serious impediment or prejudice to the course of justice and dismissed the Lord Advocate's application.[1239]

15.418   The courts in Scotland have emphasized, in accordance with this jurisprudence of the Strasbourg Court, that there exists a strong presumption in favour the freedom of the press and broadcaster to make full and accurate contemporaneous reports of court hearings,[1240] such as may outweigh any feared risk of prejudice to the administration of justice.[1241] In *Megrahi v Times Newspapers Limited*[1242] the Lord Justice Clerk observed as follows

> Where a court is asked to prohibit a publication in a case where proceedings are active its task is to determine the effect of the publication on the course of those proceedings. There is nothing in the Act which enjoins the court to apply as the test the perception of others as to whether the course of justice may be affected. The administration of justice has to be robust enough to withstand criticism and misunderstanding.

Lord Coulsfield noted as follows:

> the application of the statutory test [under Section 4(2) of the Contempt of Court Act 1981] must require the court in every instance to look at the publication or intended publication concerned and ask whether it can be seen to involve a real risk of prejudice to the proceedings. Further, I find it difficult to see how it can be suggested that there is such a risk unless the prejudice can be pointed to in some reasonably specific way.

15.419   While there is a right for reporting by the print media of court proceedings, the courts in Scotland have not accepted that there is any well founded (Convention-based) right for any court proceedings (whether criminal or civil) to be video-taped and/or broadcast.[1243] The video-taping and or broadcasting of court proceedings in Scotland remains a matter for the discretion of the Scottish court service and, in particular, the Lord President.[1244]

(3) Pre-trial publicity and prejudice to a fair trial

15.420   It has been said that it is to be presumed that juries will act in accordance with directions from a judge, for example directing them to put out of their minds anything learned from pre-trial publicity. As Lord Prosser observed in *Cox and Griffiths Petitioners*:[1245]

> Our whole system of trial in relation to serious crime proceeds upon the basis that juries are not merely the appropriate people to judge evidence and to come to conclusions upon fact, but that in doing so they will understand and apply the ordinary directions given to them by the trial judge. . . . Juries are healthy bodies. They do not need a germ free atmosphere. Even

---

[1239]   See also *Megrahi and Another v Times Newspapers Limited and Others*, 2000 JC 22, HCJ; *Galbraith v HM Advocate*, 2001 SLT 465.

[1240]   See also *BBC Petitioner*, 2002 JC 27, para 12 in which Lord Rodger strongly emphasized the right of the press and broadcasting media to report on criminal trials over and against the court's inherent contempt of court jurisdiction.

[1241]   See *Galbraith v HM Advocate*, 2001 SLT 465 at para 13.

[1242]   See n 1239 above at 39C–D.

[1243]   See *BBC, Petitioners (No 2)*, 2000 JC 521 on appeal from *BBC, Petitioners (No 1)*, 2000 JC 419.

[1244]   See 'Practice Note: Television in the Courts', 1992 *SLT (News)* 249.

[1245]   1998 JC 267 per Lord Prosser at 274H–275F.

when articles in the press do contain germs of prejudice, it will rarely be appropriate. In my opinion, to bring these to the attention of the court, far less for specific directions to have to be given, far less for the issue to be treated as even potentially one of contempt.

Subsequently, lawyers acting for the two Libyan individuals charged with carrying out **15.421** the Lockerbie bombing sought the protection of the Scottish courts against allegedly prejudicial pre-trial publicity contained in newspaper reports claiming to be based on inside information obtained from foreign intelligence and national security sources. It was argued that action should be taken against such publications with a view to preventing 'trial by newspaper' rather than by a court of law and the possibility of an undermining both of public confidence in the trial process and of the accuseds' confidence in the impartiality of the tribunal trying them. In refusing the Lockerbie accuseds' petition and complaint against the Sunday Times, the High Court of Justiciary chaired by the Lord Justice Clerk held that the newspaper article and editorial complained of did not fall foul of the test of strict liability laid down by section 2(2) of the 1981 Act but rather raised maters of legitimate public discussion. In Lord Cullen's view, standing the existence in this country of 'an independent judiciary, the members of which are well used to concentrating on the evidence and only the evidence which is put before them in the proceedings' there was no undermining of public confidence in the administration of justice. Lord Coulsfield in a concurring judgment said:

> I do not see that much infringement of the principle of freedom of speech would be involved in insisting that, particularly as the time for the commencement of the trial draws near, care should be taken to ensure that it is made clear in any discussion of the trial, or in any discussion in which the question of the guilt of the suspects arises incidentally, that their guilt remains to be determined.[1246]

In *Montgomery v HM Advocate*[1247] the two accused in the second Surjit Singh Chhokar **15.422** murder trial appealed against a decision by the Scottish criminal appeal court, to refuse their claim that the extent of their pre-trial publicity (resulting in part from a public dispute between Lord McCluskey the trial judge in the first Chhokar trial and the then Lord Advocate, Lord Hardie of Blackford, over the propriety of the Crown deciding against putting all three suspects for the murder on trial together) was such as to deprive them of the possibility of a fair trial. The accuseds' appeal in *Montgomery* was unsuccessful, it being held by the Judicial Committee that the criminal appeal court s was correct in its assessment of the effect of the pre-trial publicity in this case as not being such as to prejudice the possibility of the two accuseds' receiving a fair trial. All the judges in *Montgomery* were agreed that the appeal should be dismissed on the basis that the facts did not show any potential breach of the accuseds' fair trial rights. As Lord Hope observed[1248]

> Recent research for the New Zealand Law Commission suggests that the impact of pre-trial publicity and prejudicial media coverage during the trial, even in high profile cases, is minimal.

[1246] *Megrahi and Another v Times Newspapers Limited and Others* (n 1239 above) per Lord Coulsfield at 39C–D.
[1247] [2003] 1 AC 641.
[1248] Ibid, 30C.

(4) Freedom of expression in other areas

15.423 In *Friend v Lord Advocate*[1249] the House of Lords held that Article 10 was not engaged by the statutory ban on fox hunting in Scotland imposed by the Protection of Wild Mammals (Scotland) Act 2002, noting that although the activities the appellant was permitted to carry on were reduced, the Act did not interfere with the holding or expression of beliefs about the practice of hunting, nor was the wearing of the dress that was traditionally associated with it prohibited.

15.424 In *Quinan v Donnelly*[1250] a Member of the Scottish Parliament was charged with committing breach of the peace at a naval base after he had blocked the road leading to the base with a group of others and had refused to move when asked to do so by the police. He argued that protest by action as well as by words was protected under Article 10 and that given the fact that his protest had been peaceful it was submitted that the criminal proceedings against him were not proportionate to the legitimate aims listed in Article 10. In rejecting these arguments the High Court of Justiciary held that where the democratic interest in freedom of expression by elected representatives could be met as readily by such a representative publicly demonstrating lawfully as unlawfully, there was no ground for holding that it was disproportionate to apply the law to him in the same way as to his fellow citizens.

15.425 In *Robertson v HM Advocate*[1251] the High Court of Justiciary held that the conviction of an individual ('the Naked Rambler') for contempt of court in the face of his repeated appearances before the court naked did not constitute a violation of his article 10 rights to free expression. The application of the law of contempt to him was said merely restricted his right to express his views in his chosen manner and if he sought to express the view that an individual had the right to be naked at all times and in all places there was nothing to prevent his doing so orally or in writing while remaining properly dressed in court.

Appendix 3: The Canadian Charter of Rights

(1) Introduction

15.426 The Canadian Charter of Rights and Freedoms, section 2(b) states:

> (2) Everyone has the following fundamental freedoms: . . .
>
> > (b) the freedom of thought, belief, opinion and expression, including freedom of the press and other media of communication.[1252]

The Supreme Court in *Irwin Toy v Quebec*[1253] expressed the view that freedom of expression is to be valued because:

[1249] [2008] HRLR 11, HL.
[1250] 2005 JC 279.
[1251] 2007 SLT 1153.
[1252] See generally, M Russell, 'The Impact of the Charter on Privacy and Freedom of Expression in Canada' in M Colvin ed, *Developing Key Privacy Rights* (Hart, 2002).
[1253] [1989] 1 SCR 927, 976 per Dickson CJ, Larmer and Wilson J; *R v Keegstra* [1990] 3 SCR 697, 762, 763 per Dickson CJ.

(1) seeking and attaining the truth is an inherently good activity; (2) participation in social **15.427** and political decision-making is to be fostered and encouraged; and (3) the diversity in forms of individual self-fulfilment and human flourishing ought to be cultivated.

In *Libman v A-G of Quebec*[1254] the Supreme Court said that:

> It is difficult to imagine a guaranteed right which is more important to a democratic society than freedom of expression. Indeed, a democracy cannot exist without that freedom to express new ideas and to put forward opinions about the functioning of public institutions. The concept of free and uninhibited speech permeates all truly democratic societies. The vital importance of the concept cannot be over-emphasized. No doubt that is the reason why the framers of the constitution set forth s 2(b) in absolute terms which distinguishes it, for example, from s 8 of the Charter which guarantees the qualified right to be secure from unreasonable search. It seems that the rights enshrined in s 2(b) should only be restricted in the *clearest* of circumstances.

Nevertheless, restrictions on the right of expression may be justified under section 1 of the Charter as being such reasonable limits prescribed by law as can be demonstrably justified in a free and democratic society.

The Supreme Court of Canada has defined 'expression' as activity which attempts to con- **15.428** vey meaning.[1255] It therefore includes all forms of art,[1256] commercial expression[1257] and could even extend to parking a car as part of a protest against parking regulations.[1258] Freedom of expression is content neutral so that a statement cannot be deprived of constitutional protection no matter how offensive it is.[1259] Thus, it includes communicating for the purpose of prostitution,[1260] promoting hatred against the Jews (or other racial group),[1261] threats of violence[1262] and a conviction for the offence of publishing false news by denying the Holocaust.[1263] This is consistent with the principle that Charter rights should be given generous interpretation. Expressive activity that takes the forms of violence is not, however, protected by the Charter.

[1254] [1997] 3 SCR 569, 581; see also *UFCW Local 1518 v K Mart Canada Ltd* [1999] 2 SCR 1083, para 21.
[1255] *Irwin Toy v Quebec* [1989] 1 SCR 927, 968; *Re ss 193 and 195.1 of the Criminal Code (Prostitution Reference)* [1990] 1 SCR 1123, 1180; *Rocket v College of Dental Surgeons* [1990] 2 SCR 232, 244; *R v Keegstra* (n 1253 above) 3 SCR 697, 729, 826.
[1256] *Re ss 193 and 195.1 of the Criminal Code (Prostitution Reference)* (see n 1255 above) 1182.
[1257] See para 15.453ff below.
[1258] *Irwin Toy v Quebec* (see n 1255 above) 969.
[1259] *R v Keegstra* [1990] 3 SCR 697. A majority of the Court upheld the offence of promotion hatred under s 1 of the Charter.
[1260] *Re ss 193 and 195.1 of the Criminal Code (Prostitution Reference)* (see n 1255 above). A majoi/ ity of the Court upheld the law under s 1.
[1261] *R v Keegstra* (see n 1253 above) 828.
[1262] Ibid, 733 per Dickson CJ for the majority.
[1263] *R v Zundel* [1992] 2 SCR 731.

(2) Justifiable limitations

(a) The limitation clause

15.429   The limitation provision in section 1 of the Charter applies equally to the freedom of expression as to other Charter rights. 'Prescribed by law'[1264] requires that a law must not be excessively vague,[1265] and the four-stage *Oakes*[1266] test dictates that: first that the legislative objective of the limitation must be justifiable on the grounds of pressing and substantial concerns, secondly, that the law be rationally connected to the objective; thirdly, that the law must impair the right no more than is necessary to accomplish the objective (it is the least drastic means) and finally that the specific means adopted to implement the objective are proportionate (the law must not have a disproportionately severe effect on the persons to whom it applies). The principle of proportionality[1267] ensures that the means be rationally connected with the legislative objective, that the means result in as little impairment of the right or freedom as possible, and that the effects of the measure be proportional to the objective. It is more difficult to justify a complete ban on a form of expression than a partial ban.[1268]

15.430   An application of the proportionality test to expression is exemplified in *Butler*,[1269] where the criminal prohibition of pornographic material breached section 2(b) of the Charter by restricting pornography on the basis of its content.[1270] The prohibition was, nevertheless, justified under section 1 because it was no wider than was necessary to accomplish the goal of preventing harm to society: it did not prohibit sexually explicit material that was neither violent nor degrading; neither did it attack private possession or viewing of the obscene materials or prohibit material that was required by the internal necessities of serious artistic work.

(b) The value of expression

15.431   The Canadian courts do not treat all types of expression as being of equal worth.[1271] Political speech is considered indispensable,[1272] while artistic and commercial speech are less so. Under the Charter the value of the expression becomes relevant only at the stage of the section 1 assessment of the necessity of limitations on it and has nothing to do, in the first instance, with its protection under section 2(b). The approach taken does not, for example, apply special tests to restrictions on commercial expression; instead, the court considers a

---

[1264]   See generally, para 6.215ff above.

[1265]   In *Ontario Film and Video Appreciation Society v Ontario Board of Censors* (1984) 45 OR (2d) 80n a film censorship law was held invalid for failure to supply standards of censorship; *R v Butler* [1992] 1 SCR 452, 491: the Criminal Code prohibition of obscenity was construed not merely as moral disapprobation but as 'the avoidance of harm to society', which gave it sufficient precision to be considered an intelligible standard.

[1266]   *R v Oakes* [1986] 1 SCR 103.

[1267]   See generally, para 6.42ff above.

[1268]   See *Ramsden v Peterborough* [1993] 2 SCR 1085, 1105, 1106; *Ford v Quebec* [1988] 2 SCR 712, 772, 773.

[1269]   Ibid.

[1270]   *R v Butler* [1992] 1 SCR 452.

[1271]   *R v Keegstra* [1990] 3 SCR 697, 760.

[1272]   *Re Alberta Statutes* (1938) SCR 100, 133 per Duff J; *Samur v City of Quebec* [1953] 2 SCR 299.

conflict between expression and the other values said to justify a restriction on expression by examining its social and factual context while taking account of the special features of the expression in question.[1273]

(c) Types of restrictions on expression

Introduction. The expansive definition of expression and the very general terms in which interferences can be justified under section 1[1274] mean that the freedom of expression cases have been argued in a wide variety of contexts. **15.432**

Prior restraint. The Courts have struck down a variety of prior restraints under section 2. **15.433** A prior restraint is a law that prohibits the publication of particular material either absolutely or under a requirement of prior approval by a censor. These include: legislation authorizing film censorship where there were no statutory standards laid down;[1275] an injunction to prohibit peaceful picketing,[1276] a prohibition on the publication of public opinion polls in the final three days of an election campaign,[1277] a prohibition of election advertising on polling day,[1278] and restrictions on the importation of books of an immoral or indecent character.[1279] Expression that is never published cannot contribute in any way to the democratic process, to marketplace of ideas or to personal fulfilment. Courts have generally found that the prior restraint was a limit on freedom of expression, and the issue was whether the restraint could be justified under section 1 of the Charter.[1280]

Defamation. The most controversial issue that has arisen is whether the Charter provides **15.434** constitutional protection to public officials by entitling them to a defence of qualified privilege along the lines of *New York Times v Sullivan*.[1281] In that case the American Supreme Court held that a defendant had a complete defence where statements made concerned the plaintiff's official conduct unless the defendant was guilty of express malice. At common law the mere existence of a public interest in the subject matter of a publication was insufficient to provide a defence of qualified privilege.[1282] There was therefore considerable debate about whether the Charter might affect this principle.[1283]

[1273] *Rocket v Royal College of Dental Surgeons* [1990] 2 SCR 232, 246, 247 per McLachlin J. See also P Hogg, *Constitutional Law of Canada*, (5th edn, Thomson Carswell, 2007), para 43.5(d).

[1274] See para 15.291 above.

[1275] *Ontario Film and Video Appreciation Society v Ontario Board of Censors* (1983) 147 DLR (4th) 766.

[1276] *Halifax Antiques v Hildebrand* (1985) 22 DLR (4th) 289.

[1277] *Thomson Newspapers Co. v Can.* [1998] 1 SCR 877.

[1278] *Harper v Can.* [2004] 1 SCR 827.

[1279] *Luscher v Canada* (1985) 17 DLR (4th) 503.

[1280] See P Hogg (n 1273 above) at para 43.6(a).

[1281] *New York Times v Sullivan* (1964) 376 US 254.

[1282] *Banks v Globe and Mail* (1961) 28 DLR (2d) 343, SCC.

[1283] See M Doody, 'Freedom of the Press, the Canadian Charter of Rights and Freedoms, and a New Category of Qualified Privilege' (1983) 61 Canadian Bar Rev 126; also D Madott, 'Libel Law, Fiction, and the Charter' (1983) 21:4 Osgoode Hall LJ, 741 786–789 (suggesting that the time is ripe for an expanded defence of qualified privilege).

15.435 The question was addressed by the Supreme Court in *Hill v Church of Scientology of Toronto*.[1284] The action was brought by a Crown Attorney in relation to allegations of criminal contempt made by the defendant. The defendant argued that the common law of defamation was contrary to section 2(b) of the Charter. However, the Supreme Court held that the Charter did not have any direct application to non-governmental action.[1285] Nevertheless, it went on to consider how the common law should be interpreted in accordance with Charter values[1286] and concluded that the common law of defamation did so. The Court acknowledged the criticism which the 'actual malice' rule in *New York Times v Sullivan* had attracted[1287] and said per Cory J that:

> The *New York Times v Sullivan* decision has been criticized by judges and academic writers in the United States and elsewhere. It has not been followed in the United Kingdom or Australia. I can see no reason for adopting it in Canada in an action between private litigants. The law of defamation is essentially aimed at the prohibition of the publication of injurious false statements. It is the means by which the individual may protect his or her reputation which may well be the most distinguishing feature of his or her character, personality and, perhaps, identity. I simply cannot see that the law of defamation is unduly restrictive or inhibiting. Surely it is not requiring too much of individuals that they ascertain the truth of the allegations they publish. The law of defamation provides for the defences of fair comment and of qualified privilege in appropriate cases. Those who publish statements should assume a reasonable level of responsibility.[1288]

Recently, the Ontario Court of Appeal in *Cusson* revisited the decision in *Hill* in light of the more recent English decisions in *Reynolds* and *Jameel*.[1289] In *Cusson* the Court held that the defence of responsible journalism should be adopted in Ontario as it gives appropriate weight and recognition to the Charter values of freedom of expression without unduly minimizing the value of protecting individual reputation. The Court of Appeal was clear that to distinguish the Supreme Court's decision in *Hill*: 'the conclusions in *Hill* must be read in the context of the case . . . and, when read in that light, fall well short of a categorical ruling that would preclude reconsideration of the law of defamation in light of *Charter* values'.[1290] Accordingly, the Court of Appeal adopted the defence of responsible journalism on the basis that it better accords the law of defamation with the constitutional right to freedom of expression. The Supreme Court has held that the law of fair comment had to be modified to provide broader accommodation to freedom of expression so that it includes an objective test of honest belief: could any person honestly express that opinion on the proved facts?

[1284] [1995] 2 SCR 1130.

[1285] For a discussion about the application of the Canadian Charter to private litigation, see para 5.81ff above.

[1286] For a discussion of indirect horizontality under the Canadian Charter, see para 5.77ff above.

[1287] Citing academic criticism such as: RA Epstein, 'Was New York Times v Sullivan Wrong?' (1986) 53 U Chi L Rev 782, RP Bezanson, 'Libel Law and the Realities of Litigation: Setting the Record Straight' (1985) 71 Iowa L Rev 226; PN Leval, 'The No-Money, No-Fault Libel Suit: Keeping Sullivan in its Proper Place' (1988) 101 Harv L Rev 1287.

[1288] At para 139, per Cory J; see generally, L Leigh, 'Of Free Speech and Individual Reputation' in I Loveland (ed), *Importing the First Amendment* (Hart Publishing, 1998), 51–68.

[1289] *Cusson v Quan* (2007) 286 DLR (4th) 196, at paras 123–144, leave to appeal to Can SC granted on 3 April 2008.

[1290] Ibid, at para 138.

[1209a] *WIC Radio Ltd v Simpson* 2008 SCC 40 (comparison of claimant to Hitler and Klu Klux Klan protected by defence of fair comment).

The impact of the right to freedom of expression on criminal libel was examined in **15.436**
R v Lucas.[1291] The Supreme Court took the view that the protection of reputation was a
pressing and substantial objective; and that the negligible value of defamatory expression
significantly reduced the burden on the prosecution to demonstrate that the offence minimally impaired expression. In the circumstances the offence was rationally connected to
the legislative objective of protecting the reputation of individuals and was consistent with
the Charter right to freedom of expression.

Contempt of court. The law of contempt of court in Canada is broadly similar to that of **15.437**
Britain. Contempt can be either civil[1292] or criminal in nature. Criminal contempt is a
common law offence[1293] and may be 'direct'[1294] or 'indirect';[1295] it commonly takes the
form of a statement prejudicial to the merits of a case. 'Scandalizing' of the Court, in which
slanderous or insulting remarks are directed at a judge in his official capacity, or impugning
his impartiality, is a form of contempt which has been long recognized but rarely invoked.

In Canada the law of contempt of court has generally favoured the administration of justice **15.438**
over freedom of expression through the press.[1296] Obviously, reasonable criticism of the
court is not a contempt at common law.[1297] However, in *R v Kopyto*[1298] the Ontario Court
of Appeal found that the contempt of scandalizing the court did not survive the adoption
of the Charter (although it may be significant that the statement in question was made by
the defendant after the trial ended). On the other hand, the Supreme Court has held that
an injunction prohibiting a union from picketing the courthouses on the ground that it
was a contempt amounted to a restriction on the right of freedom of expression; but it was
justified under section 1 in order to ensure unimpeded access to the courts.[1299]

Reporting restrictions. Freedom of expression includes freedom of the press to publish **15.439**
proceedings in court. In *Edmonton Journal v Alberta (A-G)*[1300] the Supreme Court held that
provincial legislation prohibiting press reports of matrimonial cases (with some exceptions) violated freedom of expression because the courts must be open to public scrutiny

---

[1291] [1998] 1 SCR 439.

[1292] The Charter will have no application to civil contempt proceedings where the order in question
resolves a dispute between private parties based on the common law. See *Retail, Wholesale and Department
Store Union v Dolphin Delivery* [1986] 2 SCR 573.

[1293] The offence was preserved by s 8 of the Canadian Criminal Code. The absence of a statutory definition of contempt was not a breach of fundamental justice under s 7 (see generally, para 11.645ff above) of the
Charter: see *UNA v Alberta* (1992) 89 DLR (4th) 609.

[1294] A direct contempt is committed in the face of the court by words or acts in the courtroom which are
intended to disrupt proceedings.

[1295] An indirect contempt is committed by words or acts outside the courtroom that are intended to
obstruct the administration of justice.

[1296] For a review of the area of contempt and freedom of expression, see J Watson, 'Badmouthing the
Bench: Is There a Clear and Present Danger? To What?' (1992) 56 Saskatchewan L Rev 113.

[1297] *Hebert v A-G Quebec* [1967] 2 CCC 111.

[1298] (1987) 62 OR (2d) 449. The Court held that criticism of the courts, however unrestrained, made
after a decision had been rendered, was consitutionally protected expression, and a law attempting to restrict
should expression could not be justified under s 1.

[1299] *BCGEU v BC* [1988] 2 SCR 214.

[1300] (1983) 146 DLR (3d) 673.

and to public criticism.[1301] It went on to decide that the restriction was wider than necessary to safeguard the privacy of litigants.

15.440   A provision in the Criminal Code which prohibited disclosure of the identity of the complainant in a sexual assault was challenged in *Canadian Newspapers Company Ltd v Canada (A-G)*.[1302] The Supreme Court took the view that the limitation on expression was justified to foster the victims who needed such an assurance.

15.441   In *Dagenais v Canadian Broadcasting Corporation*[1303] a fictional television programme concerning sexual abuse of children at a Catholic home was restrained from being broadcast. An injunction had been granted in favour of several priests who were charged with offences in circumstances which were very similar to those depicted in the programme. The injunctions were to continue until the last of four trials took place: on the basis of a common law power to prevent a real and substantial risk of interference with the fairness of a trial. However, the Supreme Court took the view that the common law gave too much weight to a fair trial and too little to freedom of expression; the limit on expression was disproportionate since alternative measures could be taken falling short of an injunction: such as adjourning the trial, changing venues, sequestering jurors, allowing challenges for cause and providing strong judicial directions to the jury.[1304] The Supreme Court therefore concluded that the restriction on expression could not be justified under section 1.

15.442   In *R v Mentuck*[1305] the evidence against an accused, who was charged with murder, had been collected by an undercover police officer. Because there were similar operations under way, the Crown applied for an order prohibiting publication of evidence that would disclose the identity of the police officers or the tactics and techniques they used in gathering the evidence. The Court adopted the following principles in determining whether the publication ban was justifiable: first, such an order is necessary in order to prevent a serious risk to the proper administration of justice because reasonable alternative measures will not prevent the risk; and secondly, the salutary effects of the publication ban outweigh the deleterious effects on the rights and interests of the parties and the public, including the effects on the right to free expression, the right of the accused to a fair and public trial, and the efficacy of the administration of justice. Applying that test, the court held that the one year reporting restrictions on the names of the undercover officers were justified, but that the restrictions on the methods used by police were not justified. The publication ban was accordingly upheld as a justifiable limit on freedom of the press only with respect to the identities of the police officers.

15.443   In *Toronto Star Newspapers v Ontario*,[1306] the Supreme Court again affirmed the rule that court proceedings were to be 'open' unless 'disclosure would subvert the ends of justice or unduly impair its proper administration'. The police had obtained warrants to search a

---

[1301] Ibid, 1337.
[1302] [1988] SCR 122.
[1303] [1994] 3 SCR 835.
[1304] Ibid, 881.
[1305] [2001] 3 SCR 442.
[1306] [2005] 2 SCR 188.

meat packing plant and brought a motion for the Court to seal those warrants, and the information on which they were based, on the basis of not wanting to identify the 'whistle blower' who was the police's confidential informant. The Supreme Court quashed the sealing order, subject only to the editing of the material to conceal the identity of the confidential source, because 'once a search warrant is executed, the warrant and the information on which it was issued must be made available to the public unless an applicant seeking a sealing order can demonstrate that public acess would subvert the ends of justice'.[1307]

Freedom of the press also includes the right of the press and the public to be present in court. For example, prohibiting the press from having access to juvenile trials has been tested under the Charter. In *Re Southam and the Queen (No 1)*[1308] the Ontario Court of Appeal held that an absolute bar on access could not be justified as using the least restrictive means of protecting the interests of a child. The legislation was then changed to require juvenile trials to be held in public with the trial judge having a discretion to order a hearing in private. That provision was regarded as a justifiable restriction on expression in *Re Southam and the Queen (No 2)*.[1309]

15.444

In *Canadian Broadcasting Corporation v New Brunswick (A-G)*[1310] the press was excluded from part of a sentencing hearing where the offences committed by a sex offender against young girls were being detailed. Although the power to exclude the press was unconstitutional as a breach of freedom of expression, the Supreme Court took the view that the legislation pursued an important purpose by permitting an exclusion order to be made where openness was inimical to the proper administration of justice; furthermore, La Forest J went on to identify the principles to be applied when the court is requested to exercise its discretion to make reporting restrictions.

15.445

In *Re Vancouver Sun*,[1310a] the Supreme Court of Canada reviewed a 'judicial investigative hearing' that had been held in camera (closed to the public) by a superior court judge. This kind of hearing was an innovation authorized by the Anti-Terrorism Act, a federal statute that was enacted in response to the September 11, 2001 terrorist attacks in the United States. The Supreme Court emphasized that the 'open court principle' was guaranteed by section 2(b) of the Charter. The Supreme Court also adopted the standards of justification of *Dagenais* and *Mentuck* (those cases concerned publication bans) for orders limiting access to court proceedings. That is, a publication ban or an ordering limiting access to court should only be ordered when (a) such an order is necessary in order to prevent a serious risk to the administration of justice, because reasonable alternative measures will not prevent the risks and (b) the salutary effects of the ban outweigh the deleterious effects on the rights and interests of the parties and the public. The burden of displacing the presumption of openness rests on the party seeking the ban. The majority of the Court held in this case that such hearings should have been in open court, but that the hearing judge maintained

15.446

[1307] Ibid, at para 18.
[1308] (1983) 41 OR (2nd) 113.
[1309] (1986) 53 OR (2nd) 663.
[1310] [1996] 3 SCR 480.
[1310a] [2004] 2 SCR 332.

a discretion to exclude the public from parts of the hearing and/or ban publication of parts of the evidence, in accordance with the *Dagenais/Mentuck* principles.[1311]

15.447 **Obscenity and pornography.** The expression cases in the Supreme Court of Canada make clear that pornography, including obscenity, is protected expression in Canada. Pornography can only be identified by reference to its content, and as there are no content restrictions on section 2(b), it follows that pornography is protected by the guarantee. In *R v Butler*[1312] the Supreme Court held that the prohibitions on obscenity breached freedom of expression because they restricted communication on the basis of its content.[1313] However, the restriction was justified to prevent the 'harm associated with the dissemination of pornography'[1314] and therefore upheld under section 1, that is the justification was 'sufficiently pressing and substantial to warrant some restriction on full exercise of the right to freedom of expression'.[1315] Sopinka J held that 'undue' exploitation of sex contemplated material that (1) portrayed explicit sex with violence, or (2) portrayed explicit sex without violence, but in a degrading or dehumanizing manner. Such 'undue' pornography was not unacceptable because it offended morals but because they were perceived by public opinion as being harmful to society, particularly women.[1316]

15.448 The *Butler* case has attracted feminist criticism,[1317] on the basis that the harm done to women by pornography was misunderstood by the Court: its offensiveness lay in the search for a causal link between pornography and violence towards women, and in the fact that the decision requires censorship of sexually explicit material. A similar debate has occurred in relation to prostitution following the *Prostitution Reference*,[1318] in which the Court found that it is legitimate to criminalize public communication for the purpose of prostitution, despite the fact that prostitution itself is clearly legal. While all judges agreed that the criminal provisions did not violate the Charter, there was divergence over whether they could be justified as a limitation under section 1.[1319]

15.449 The case of *R v Sharpe*[1320] concerned an accused person's challenge to the criminalization of 'child pornography'. This was defined to include visual representations that show a person who is under the age of 18 years and is engaged in explicit sexual activity, visual representations the dominant characteristic of which is the depiction, for a sexual purpose, of a

---

[1311] See also P Hogg, *Constitutional Law of Canada* (5th edn, Thomson Carswell, 2007) at para 41.13(c).

[1312] [1992] 1 SCR 452.

[1313] Ibid, 489.

[1314] See J Cameron, 'Abstract Principle v Contextual Conceptions of Harm: A Comment on *R v Butler*' (1992) 37 McGill LJ 1135.

[1315] *R v Butler* (see n 1312 above) 449; see V Ramraj, 'Keegstra, Butler and Positive Liberty: A Glimmer of Hope for the Faithful' 51:2 University of Toronto Faculty of Law Rev, 304, 305.

[1316] Ibid, 479.

[1317] See eg, 'Pornography, Harm and Censorship: A Feminist (Re)Vision of the Right to Freedom of Expression' 52:1 University of Toronto Faculty of Law Rev, 132; R Moon, 'R v Butler: The Limits of the Supreme Court's Feminist Re-Interpretation of Section 163' (1993) 25:2 Ottawa L Rev 361.

[1318] *Re ss 193 and 195.1 of the Criminal Code* [1990] 1 SCR 1123.

[1319] For a discussion of the reasoning of the judges, their construction of the legislative objectives, and imposition of legal moralism generally see D Dyzenhaus, 'Regulating Free Speech' (1991) 23:2 Ottawa L Rev, 289; also *Ontario Film and Video Appreciation Society v Ontario Board of Censors* (1984) 45 OR (2d) 80n.

[1320] [2001] 1 SCR 45.

sexual organ or the anal region of a person under the age of 18 years and written material that advocated sexual activity with a person under the age of 18 years. The Supreme Court upheld that legislation, except for two instances that raised little or no risk of harm to children, namely: (1) written materials or visual representations created and held by the accused alone, exclusively for personal use; and (2) visual recordings created by or depicting the accused that do not depict unlawful sexual activity and are held by the accused exclusively for private use. Otherwise, the prohibitions on child pornography were upheld under section 1.

In *Little Sisters Book and Art Emporium v Canada (Minister of Justice)*[1321] the Supreme Court considered a challenge based on freedom of expression brought by gay rights groups following Customs' seizures of pornographic materials. In particular, the group challenged legislation that prohibited the importation into Canada of books, magazines and pictures that were obscene under the Criminal Code definition. The freedom of expression argument was unsuccessful. The court held that the 'national community standard of tolerance test', for determining whether materials were obscene, did not discriminate against the gay and lesbian community. A concern for minority expression was one of the principal factors which had led to the adoption of the national community test in the first place. The Canadian community specifically recognized in the Charter that equality (and with it, the protection of sexual minorities) is one of the fundamental values of Canadian society. The standard of tolerance of this same Canadian community for obscenity could not be reasonably interpreted as seeking to suppress sexual expression in the homosexual community in a discriminatory way. However, the challenge was successful on the basis that the placing of the burden of proof on the defendant to disprove obscenity did not constitute a reasonable limit on the appellant's freedom of expression. The legislation was, however, otherwise upheld. **15.450**

Racial hatred. Hate propaganda is material that promotes hatred against minority groups. **15.451** The Criminal Code makes it an offence to wilfully promote hatred against 'any section of the public distinguished by colour, race, religion, or ethnic origin'. In *R v Keegstra*[1322] the Supreme Court stated that the objective of the hate propaganda provisions of the Criminal Code was to 'prevent the pain suffered by target group members and to reduce racial, ethnic and religious tension in Canada'.[1323] While such expression was protected by section 2(b) (which protects all expression 'however unpopular, distasteful or contrary to the mainstream', the law was upheld under section 1 of the Charter as a justified restriction on expression. Similarly, in *Ross v New Brunswick School District No 15*[1324] a decision by a human rights tribunal which required a teacher to be removed from his post for disseminating anti-semitic literature was held to be a justified restriction on freedom of expression.

[1321] [2000] 2 SCR 1120.
[1322] [1990] 3 SCR 697; see also *R v Keegstra (No 2)* [1995] 2 SCR 381 and *R v Keegstra (No 3)* [1996] 1 SCR 458.
[1323] *R v Keegstra* (see n 1322 above).
[1324] [1992] 2 SCR 731.

However, in *R v Zundel*[1325] the Supreme Court struck down the conviction for 'spreading false news' of a defendant who had claimed that the Holocaust was a fraud invented by an international Jewish conspiracy. The offence was an unjustified restriction on freedom of expression as the restriction as the doctrine of content-neutrality protects falsehoods as well as truths, particularly since the question of whether a statement is true or false can be determined only be reference to its content. The Court divided four to three on the issue of whether the legislation could be upheld by section 1, with the majority holding that the false-news offence could not be justified under section 1 and the legislation was therefore struck down. The majority struck down the legislation in part because the law was drafted so broadly that it was difficult to identity an objective that was sufficiently important to justify the limit on freedom of expression.

15.452 **Police powers.**   The Supreme Court has considered the use of search warrants to obtain film taken by television crews of a crime in progress in *Canadian Broadcasting Corporation v Lessard*[1326] and *Canadian Broadcasting Corporation v New Brunswick (A-G)*.[1327] It was argued that the search warrants breached freedom of expression because of their 'chilling' effect on newsgathering. The Court said that the constitutional protection of freedom of expression provides a backdrop against which the reasonableness of a search had to be evaluated: the justice should give careful consideration not only to whether a warrant should issue but also to the conditions which might properly be imposed upon any search of media premises. A warrant would impede the media from fulfilling its news gathering functions and should only be issued where there is a compelling state interest. This could only be demonstrated by showing that there was no reasonable alternative source for the information or if the offence was a grave one and there was an urgent need to obtain the information. On the facts, the warrants were upheld, although the majority stressed that the film had already been shown.

15.453 **Commercial expression.**   Because of the need to protect the public against false or misleading claims, and to ensure appropriate warnings of danger and disclosure of other matters (ie food ingredients), the regulation of commercial expression, such as the advertisement, is well recognized under the Charter. The American jurisprudence on commercial expression was analysed by the Supreme Court in *Ford v Quebec (A-G)*[1328] where it held that provincial legislation requiring commercial signs to be in French only was unconstitutional.

15.454 There have been a number of cases which have considered restrictions on advertising. In *Irwin Toy v Quebec*[1329] the issue concerned provincial legislation aimed at advertising for children. The legislation did not ban advertising absolutely; but required, for example, that advertisement of toys and breakfast cereals did not use cartoons. The Supreme Court accepted that a ban directed at children was a sufficiently important purpose to limit expression; and upheld the legislation.

[1325] [1992] 2 SCR 731; For a discussion of the distinction between *Keegstra* and *Zundel* see P Hogg, *Constitutional Law of Canada* (5th edn, Thomson Carswell, 2007), para 43.9.
[1326] [1991] 3 SCR 421.
[1327] [1991] 3 SCR 459.
[1328] [1988] 2 SCR 712.
[1329] [1989] 1 SCR 927.

The acceptability of restricting advertisements by professionals arose in *Rocket v Royal* **15.455**
College of Dental Surgeons.[1330] The Supreme Court concluded that the regulations on dentists were unjustified because they had an impact far broader than was needed to ensure high standards of professional conduct; and prevented advertising information which would be genuinely useful if it was made available to the public.

The important case of *RJR-McDonald v A-G of Canada*[1331] considered the constitutionality **15.456**
of federal legislation banning the advertisement of tobacco and other tobacco products. The Supreme Court struck down the legislation because the restrictions imposed were not carefully tailored to ensure expression was impaired no more than was reasonably necessary.

Commerical signs are also protected by section 2(b). In *R v Guignard*[1332] a municipal by- **15.457**
law in Quebec prevented advertising signs and billboards except in industrial zones of the municipality. The defendant had erected a sign on his property complaining about his insurance company's services. The Supreme Court held struck down the law and held that it infringed his freedom of expression. In *Vann Niagara v Oakville*[1333] the Supreme Court of Canada upheld a law that banned 'billboard signs' thourghout a municipality. Billboard signs were ground signs measuring more than 80 square feet. Because of the definition, smaller signs were not prohibited which left room for commercial expression on those smaller signs. The Supreme Court did strike down as unreasonable a second by-law that banned 'third party signs' (signs that advertised products or services that were not produced on the premises were the sign was located).

Access to public property. Because the Charter does not apply to private individuals,[1334] it **15.458**
cannot create a right to use private property for the purposes of expression.[1335] However, in *Committee for the Commonwealth of Canada v Canada*[1336] the Supreme Court decided that there is a constitutional right to use public property for freedom of expression although the reasoning of different members of the Court varied significantly. Nevertheless, it held that a manager of a Montreal airport had acted unconstitutionally by prohibiting political leaflets from being distributed at the airport

The issue was again considered in *Ramsden v Peterborough.*[1337] In that case a musician **15.459**
advertised performances of his band by placing posters on public property in contravention of a bye-law which forbade posters on public property. The Supreme Court did not attempt to reconcile the different approaches taken in *Committee for the Commonwealth of Canada v Canada;*[1338] instead, it said that, applying any of the views expressed in the earlier decision, postering on public property was protected by the Charter. The Court also

---

[1330] [1990] 1 SCR 232.
[1331] [1995] 3 SCR 199.
[1332] [2002] 1 SCR 472.
[1333] [2003] 3 SCR 158.
[1334] See generally, para 5.77ff above.
[1335] *Committee for the Commonwealth of Canada v Canada* [1991] 1 SCR 139, 228 per McLachlin J.
[1336] [1991] 1 SCR 139.
[1337] [1993] 2 SCR 1084.
[1338] Ibid.

concluded that the limit on expression was not justified under section 1 because it was broader than necessary to accomplish its objective of reducing litter and blight.

15.460 **Picketing.** The Supreme Court has accepted that picketing is entitled to constitutional protection as 'expression' under the Charter. In the *Dolphin Delivery* case[1339] a union challenged the constitutionality of an injunction on secondary picketing where the union had induced a breach of contract. The Court decided that the Charter did not apply to the common law in private litigation.[1340] However, McIntyre J said *obiter* that picketing came within the scope of 'expression' under the Charter;[1341] but went on to decide that the prohibition on secondary picketing could be justified under section 1 in order to prevent industrial conflict spreading beyond the parties in dispute.

15.461 In the *BCGEU v BC*[1342] case, after seeing a picket line outside the Vancouver court house, the Chief Justice of British Columbia of his own motion and without notifying the union issued an injunction restraining the picket. The Supreme Court held that the injunction on the picket restricted freedom of expression; but that limitation on expression was justified so as to ensure unimpeded access to the court.

15.462 Peaceful leafleting of customers by pickets at secondary sites was restrained by an order of the Industrial Relations Council which the union then claimed was a restriction on freedom of expression. The Supreme Court in *Union of Food and Commercial Workers v K Mart Canada*[1343] held that:

> workers, particularly those who are vulnerable, must be able to speak freely on matters that relate to their working conditions. For employees, freedom of expression becomes not only an important but an essential component of labour relations. It is through free expression that vulnerable workers are able to enlist the support of the public in their quest for better conditions of work. Thus their expression can often function as a means of achieving their goals.[1344]

The Court decided that leafleting did not have the same coercive effect as a picket and that, in the circumstances, leafleting was lawful.

15.463 **Political restrictions on public employees.** The restrictions preventing federal civil servants from engaging in work for a Parliamentary candidate or for a federal political party were challenged in *Osborne v Canada*.[1345] The Supreme Court ruled that the restrictions limited freedom of expression and could not be justified under section 1. The objective of maintaining a neutral public service could justify imposing limits; but the legislation did not adopt the least restrictive means of achieving that objective since the range of activities prohibited and employees covered was wider than needed to accomplish the objective.

[1339] *Retail, Wholesale and Department Store Union v Dolphin Delivery* [1986] 2 SCR 573.
[1340] See generally, para 5.79ff above.
[1341] *Dolphin Delivery* (see n 1339 above) 105.
[1342] [1988] 2 SCR 214.
[1343] [1999] 2 SCR 1083.
[1344] Ibid, para 25.
[1345] [1991] 2 SCR 69.

A narrower prohibition would have been sufficient to protect the value of neutrality with less impact on freedom of expression.

Restrictions on the political process. In *Libman v A-G of Quebec*[1346] the Supreme Court considered a challenge to the constitutional validity of spending limits which had been placed on political groups in the campaign periods for referenda. The restrictions on expression were justified to prevent political debate being dominated by the most affluent. However, the limits did not meet the minimum impairment test required under the proportionality principle; the ceiling was so restrictive that it amounted to a total ban on spending by groups who did not meet the criteria in the legislation which authorized campaign spending. In *Harper v Canada*, the Supreme Court, by a majority of six to three, upheld legislation that imposed third-party expenditure restrictions during elections.[1347]

15.464

The prohibition on disseminating information about opinion polls during the last three days of a federal election was examined in *Thomson Newspapers v Canada*.[1348] The Supreme Court held that a total ban was wider than necessary to guard against the influence of inaccurate polls late in an election campaign; and that the benefits of the ban were outweighed by its detrimental effects.

15.465

In *R v Bryan*[1349] the Supreme Court also upheld a section of the Canada Elections Act that banned the publication of voting results until all federal polls closed on election night. Since Canada includes six timezones, the polls necessarily close in the eastern provinces a few hours before they close in the western provinces. The defendant had posted the results from Atlantic Canada on his website before the polls had closed in British Columbia. While the ban did violate section 2(b), it was upheld on the basis that it maintains 'informational equality' among voters and contributes to 'the fairness and reputation of the electoral system as a whole'.

15.466

Appendix 4: The New Zealand Bill of Rights Act

(1) Introduction

Section 14 of the New Zealand Bill of Rights Act 1990 provides:

15.467

> 14. **Freedom of expression**—Everyone has the right to freedom of expression, including the freedom to seek, receive, and impart information and opinions of any kind in any form.

The White Paper which explained the proposed bill described this provision as being of 'central importance' but did not give any detailed analysis and suggested that most laws which were found to infringe freedom of expression would 'no doubt' be held to establish reasonable limitations on the freedom.[1350]

[1346] [1997] 3 SCR 569.
[1347] [2004] 1 SCR 827.
[1348] [1998] 1 SCR 877.
[1349] [2007] SCC 12.
[1350] *A Bill of Rights for New Zealand: A White Paper* (Government Printer, 1985), 79–80; see generally G Huscroft, 'Defamation, Racial Disharmony and Freedom of Expression' in G Huscroft and P Rishworth (eds)

15.468 Section 14 has had an impact in several areas: defamation, contempt of court, reporting restrictions, obscenity, racial hatred and police powers. However, section 14 does not impose any positive duties on the state to ensure freedom of expression.[1351]

15.469 The New Zealand courts have drawn heavily on the case law of the Canadian Charter of Rights and Freedoms.[1352] In *Solicitor-General v Radio NZ Ltd*[1353] the Canadian approach to the scope of the right was adopted, the court stressing that the Bill of Rights protects all expression that conveys or attempts to convey meaning except threats of violence.[1354]

15.470 Freedom of expression under section 14 includes the right to impart information, a feature that it shares with Article 10(1) of the European Convention.[1355] This right provides jurisdiction in an exceptional case for the court to grant a mandatory injunction before trial compelling a defendant to broadcast a correction where he has clearly established that he has been defamed.[1356]

15.471 There is a public interest in freedom of expression which exists over and above the rights of the individual. In *Police v O'Connor*[1357] it was said:

> While the right in section 25(a) (right to fair and public hearing) is couched in terms of an individual right as is Article 14 of the ICCPR, the right to freedom of expression as expressed in section 14 of the NZ Bill of Rights is not. The latter is to be perceived as a public right. While, therefore, the position adopted by the particular defendant will no doubt be significant, it is not a right which he or she can automatically waive. The public interest in freedom of expression is to be recognized apart from the interests of the individual.

(2) Justifiable limitations

(a) Introduction

15.472 The freedoms set out in the New Zealand Bill of Rights Act are subject to such reasonable limits prescribed by law as may be justified in a free and democratic society.[1358]

15.473 The basic principles to be applied when deciding whether a limitation on a right is justified under section 5 were described in *Ministry of Transport v Noort*.[1359] First, the New Zealand

---

Rights and Freedoms (Brooker's, 1995). See, generally, R Tobin 'Privacy and Freedom of Expression in New Zealand' in M Colvin (ed) *Developing Key Privacy Rights* (Hart, 2002).

[1351] *Mendelsson v A-G* [1999] 1 NZLR 268.

[1352] For a comparison of the general features of the New Zealand Bill and the Canadian Charter, see *Solicitor-General v Radio NZ Ltd* [1994] 1 NZLR 48, 60, 61.

[1353] [1994] 1 NZLR 48, 59.

[1354] *Solicitor-General v Radio NZ Ltd* (see n 1352 above) 59 relying on *Irwin Toy Ltd v Quebec* [1989] 1 SCR 927, 970: 'a murderer or rapist cannot invoke freedom of expression in justification of the form of expression he has chosen'; also McIntyre J in *Retail, Wholesale and Department Store Union v Dolphin Delivery* [1986] 2 SCR 573, 588 who said 'that freedom of course, would not extend to protect threats of violence or acts of violence'. However, in *R v Keegstra* [1990] 3 SCR 697, 733 the Supreme Court reversed its views and now accepts that threats of violence are within the scope of expression under the Charter.

[1355] Also with the Universal Declaration of Human Rights, Art 19, and the ICCPR 1966, Art 19(2). Cf the Canadian Charter, s 2(b), and the US First Amendment, which do not specify the right to impart information.

[1356] *TV3 Network Ltd v Eveready New Zealand Ltd* [1993] 3 NZLR 435.

[1357] [1992] 1 NZLR 87.

[1358] See ss 4, 5, and 6 of the New Zealand Bill of Rights Act.

[1359] [1992] 3 NZLR 260, 282–283.

courts have applied the Canadian authorities both on the meaning of 'prescribed by law'[1360] and the general approach to justifying limitations on rights.[1361] Secondly, the burden of proof rests with those seeking to rely on section 5 to demonstrate the reasonableness of the limit and that it can be justified in a free and democratic society. Thirdly, the Court of Appeal defined the process of the inquiry under section 5: it should use the Canadian approach in *R v Oakes* [1362] as a starting point;[1363] and consider all economic, administrative and social implications, taking into account the following factors:

- the significance of values underlying the Bill of Rights;
- the importance of the public interest in the intrusion;
- the limits sought to be placed on the protected freedom; and
- the effectiveness of the restriction in protecting the interests put forward to justify those limits.

15.474 The means used must have a rational relationship with the objective and there must be as little interference as possible with the right or freedom affected:

> Ultimately, whether the limitation in issue can or cannot be demonstrably justified in a free and democratic society is a matter of judgment which the Court is obliged to make on behalf of the society which it serves.[1364]

(b) Restrictions on expression

15.475 **Prior restraint.**   The New Zealand courts have recognized that the principle of freedom of expression means that any applicant seeking an injunction to prevent a legitimate publication faces an uphill task.[1365] In *A-G for England and Wales v R*,[1366] the Court of Appeal declined to grant the British Government an injunction prohibiting publication of a book by an SAS soldier but held that there was no defence to a claim for an account of profits. In refusing an injunction, the court relied in part on the soldier's right to freedom of expression.

15.476 In *Beadle v Allen*[1367] a restraining order was made under the Harassment Act in relation to a former patient who sent large numbers of faxes to her former doctor and others containing allegations of improper treatment and sex abuse. It was held that this order was a justifiable limitation on the appellant's freedom of expression.

15.477 **Defamation.**   In the field of defamation the Bill of Rights Act has been invoked largely in support of decisions favouring expression. However, its impact has been explained in terms

---

[1360] See generally, para 6.215ff above.

[1361] The general approach of the Canadian courts, 'modified to New Zealand conditions', was adopted by the Court of Appeal in *Solicitor-General v Radio New Zealand* [1994] 1 NZLR 48 (reviewing *R v Oakes* [1986] 1 SCR 103 and *Irwin Toy Ltd v Quebec* [1989] 1 SCR 927); see also *Ministry of Transport v Noort* (see n 1246 above).

[1362] n 1361 above.

[1363] See generally, para 15.429 above.

[1364] *Moonen v Film and Literature Board of Review* [2000] 2 NZLR 9, para 18.

[1365] *Board of Trustees of Tuakau College v TVNZ* (1996) 3 HRNZ 87, 96; see also *Beckett & Ors v TV3 Network Services* [2000] NZAR 399 (any prior restraint of free expression must pass a high threshold).

[1366] [2002] 2 NZLR 91; the refusal to grant an injunction was not the subject of an appeal to the Privy Council, which upheld the remainder of the decision [2004] 2 NZLR 577.

[1367] [2000] NZFLR 639.

of providing assistance in areas of uncertainty where the law is developing[1368] and to reinforce long established principles.[1369]

15.478　Thus, in *Quinn v Television New Zealand Ltd* [1370] it was observed that section 14 did not extend the boundaries of the right of expression, affirming the historic common law right of a person to protect his reputation. In particular, it drew attention to section 28 of the Bill of Rights Act which requires that an existing right or freedom should not be abrogated or restricted by reason only that it was not included in the Bill of Rights. On the other hand, in *TV3 Network v Eveready New Zealand Ltd*[1371] a manufacturer which alleged that a television broadcast libelled its produce applied for a mandatory interlocutory injunction to require the television company to broadcast a correction. It held that section 14 did not preclude the court in an exceptional case from providing mandatory injunctive relief; in fact, the statutory definition of expression created a right to impart information and supported the claim for an injunction.

15.479　The question of parliamentary privilege was the subject of the Privy Council decision in *Prebble v Television New Zealand*.[1372] The case arose out of an investigative television programme of a former Government by one of its MPs. When the defendant pleaded particulars of speeches and other statements made by the plaintiff in 'proceedings of Parliament' by way of defence, the plaintiff was successful in having them struck out on grounds of parliamentary privilege. The Court of Appeal ordered a stay of proceedings unless and until parliamentary privilege was waived by both the House and the MP, a solution which precludes both action in defamation by persons maligned by statements in the House and suit by an MP to protect his reputation. The Privy Council held that where the exclusion of privileged material makes it impossible fairly to determine the issue between the parties, a stay of proceedings may be required; but allowed the appeal on the facts because the allegations related to statements which were made outside of the House. However, there has been criticism of the broad approach taken in view of the right to freedom of expression under the Bill of Rights Act.[1373]

15.480　In *Lange v Atkinson and Australian Consolidated Press NZ Ltd* [1374] the Court of Appeal considered section 14 in the context of a claim to qualified privilege in respect of 'political expression' based on *New York Times v Sullivan*.[1375] It took the view that a newspaper report

---

[1368]　*TV3 Network Ltd v Eveready New Zealand Ltd* [1993] 3 NZLR 435.
[1369]　*Auckland Area Health Board v A-G* [1992] 3 NZLR 406 (the jurisdiction to grant interlocutory injunctions to restrain publication of defamatory statements); see also *Quinn v Television New Zealand Ltd* [1995] 3 NZLR 216 which affirmed of historic right to reputation.
[1370]　[1995] 3 NZLR 216.
[1371]　See n 1368 above; see also *TV3 Network Services v Fahey* [1999] 2 NZLR 129 (no injunction to restrain publication of defamatory material where the defendant announced an intention to justify).
[1372]　[1995] 1 AC 321, 332.
[1373]　See eg, R Best, 'Freedom of Speech in Parliament: Constitutional Safeguard or Sword of Oppression?' (1994) 24 VUWLR 91, 97; and see also the comment of Cooke P in his judgment [1993] 3 NZLR 513, 522; and his subsequent analysis of the case in 'A Sketch From the Blue Train. Non-discrimination and Freedom of Expression: The New Zealand Contribution' (1994) NZLJ 10, 13.
[1374]　[1998] 3 NZLR 424 approving [1997] 2 NZLR 22; see also the discussion of this case in *Reynolds v Times Newspapers Ltd* [2001] 2 AC 137.
[1375]　(1964) 376 US 254.

on a matter of public interest could, of itself, give rise to a 'common interest' between the newspaper and the general public in the publication of the report. In particular, it was stressed that:

> a proper interest does exist in respect of statements made about the actions and qualities of those currently or formerly elected to Parliament and those with immediate aspirations to such office, so far as those actions and qualities directly affect or affected their capacity. . .to meet their public responsibilities.[1376]

The Court of Appeal refused to follow the Australian approach[1377] and held that whether or not the defendant had acted reasonably was irrelevant.[1378] However, the plaintiff's appeal was allowed by the Privy Council[1379] which remitted the case back to the New Zealand Court of Appeal to reconsider in the light of the decision of the House of Lords in *Reynolds v Times Newspapers*.[1380]

The matter was reheard by the Court of Appeal[1381] which maintained the position in its **15.481** earlier judgment for the following reasons[1382]

> First, the *Reynolds* decision appears to alter the structure of the law of qualified privilege in a way which adds to the uncertainty and chilling effect almost inevitably present in this area of law. We are not persuaded that in the New Zealand situation matters such as the steps taken to verify the information, the seeking of comment from the person defamed, and the status or source of the information, should fall within the ambit of the enquiry into whether the occasion is privileged. Traditionally such matters are not of concern to that question in the kind of setting presently under discussion. In particular, source and status may be relevant, but only in the area of reports of meetings and suchlike. For the reasons expressed in our earlier judgment, we do not consider it necessary, nor would it be in accord with principle, to import into this enquiry, for the limited purposes of the specific subject matter now under discussion but not otherwise, a specific requirement of reasonableness. . .
>
> Secondly, there are significant differences between the constitutional and political context in New Zealand and in the United Kingdom in which this body of law operates. They reflect societal differences. Thirdly, the position of the press in the two countries does appear to be significantly distinct. And, fourthly, this is an area of law in which Parliament has essentially left it to the courts to develop the governing principles and apply them to the evolving political social and economic conditions.

The qualified privilege defence was held to be available to newspapers which had republished defamatory allegations made by the defendant in relation to the plaintiff's wood preservative products used in the construction of new homes. The Court took into account the fact that the material was of public concern, it was published in an area where most new homes were built and the high incidence of leaky homes and the importance of home ownership.[1383]

[1376] *Lange v Atkinson* (see n 1374 above) 613g–h.
[1377] See para 15.000ff above.
[1378] *Lange v Atkinson and Australian Consolidated Press NZ Ltd* (see n 1374 above) 615a–f; 619e–620c.
[1379] [2000] 2 LRC 802.
[1380] n 1374 above.
[1381] [2000] 3 NZLR 385.
[1382] Ibid, paras 38 and 40.
[1383] *Osmose New Zealand v Wakeling* [2007] 1 NZLR 841.

15.482 **Contempt.** The law of contempt requires the balancing of the right to freedom of expression and the right of an accused to a fair hearing.[1384] As Richardson J said in *Gisborne Herald Co v Solicitor*[1385]

> Freedom of the press as a vehicle for comment on public issues is basic to our democratic system. The assurance of a fair trial by an impartial Court is essential for the preservation of an effective system of justice. Both values have been affirmed by the Bill of Rights. The public interest in the functioning of the Courts invokes both these values. It calls for free expression of information and opinions as to the performance of those public responsibilities. It also calls for determination of disputes by Courts which are free from bias and which make their decisions solely on the evidence judicially brought before them. Full recognition of both these indispensable elements can present difficult problems for the Courts to resolve.

The conflict between expression in the media and the due administration of justice has traditionally been resolved in favour of the right to a fair trial. The protection of the justice system is considered a substantial and pressing concern;[1386] and the sanction of contempt in achieving this objective has been regarded as being reasonable and demonstrably justified.[1387] Where freedom of expression of and fair trial rights cannot both be fully assured then some temporary curtailment of freedom of expression is required to guarantee a fair trial.[1388] If there is a 'significant risk' that an accused will not receive a fair trial then the issue ceases to be one of balancing and an order restricting publication must be granted.[1389]

15.483 **Reporting restrictions.** Prior restraints have been imposed on publication in several cases to ensure a fair trial.[1390] The approach in the past has been to impose restraints very readily. More recently, the courts have shifted markedly towards favouring freedom of the media in both law and practice.[1391] In *R v Chignell and Walker*[1392] the Crown sought to invoke the inherent jurisdiction of the court to restrain a threatened contempt by preventing further public comment concerning an unnamed witness pending a retrial of the accused homicide suspect. The court declined, citing section 14 of the Bill of Rights Act in support of freedom of expression. In *Duff v Communicado*[1393] it was stressed that the relationship between section 14 and contempt is best approached by balancing freedom of expression against the benefits of protecting the administration of justice by examining the facts of each case to see if the particular interference was so serious as to override freedom of expression.

[1384] New Zealand Bill of Rights Act 1990, s 25.

[1385] [1995] 3 NZLR 563, 571.

[1386] *Solicitor-General v Radio NZ Ltd* [1991] 1 NZLR 48: the protection of the due administration of justice, the impartiality and the freedom of deliberation of a jury, the finality of its verdict and preservation of the juror's anonymity are all substantial and pressing concerns of a free and democratic society.

[1387] Ibid, 64.

[1388] See *Gisborne Herald* (see n 1385 above), 575.

[1389] *R v Burns* [2002] 1 NZLR 387, 404, paras 10–11.

[1390] See *Duff v Communicado Ltd* [1996] 2 NZLR 89; *Greenpeace New Zealand v Minister of Fisheries* [1995] 2 NZLR 463; *R v H* [1996] 2 NZLR 487.

[1391] RE Harrison, 'Mass Media and the Criminal Process: Public Service or Public Circus?' (1992) NZLJ 271; for the media response to Harrison see K Hill, 'Freedom of the Media and the Criminal Law' (1992) NZLJ 278; see the pre-Bill of Rights cases cited in support of the changing style of media coverage: *R v Harawira* [1989] 2 NZLR 714; *The Queen v Tamihere* CA 428/90, 21 May 1992; *Solicitor-General v BCNZ* [1987] 2 NZLR 100; *TV New Zealand Ltd v Solicitor-General* [1989] 1 NZLR 1.

[1392] (1990) 6 CRNZ 476.

[1393] (1995) 2 HRNZ 370.

The Court went on to hold that remarks made on radio to put pressure on another litigant in proceedings amounted to a contempt.

Where a person was awaiting trial for murder he had standing to apply for an injunction restraining the publication of an article which might prejudice a fair trial. The rights to freedom of expression and fair trial had to be balanced but when an article strongly suggested that the same person had committed both the murder with which the claimant was charged and another murder there was a real and substantial risk it would prejudice the claimant's trial.[1394] **15.484**

It is a responsibility of the state to ensure that the administration of justice is carried out in public, so as to safeguard against judicial arbitrariness or idiosyncrasy and to maintain public confidence in the system.[1395] This entails not only the admission of the public to judicial proceedings, but also the publication of fair and accurate press reports so that the public can scrutinize the workings of the courts. The right of the public should not be readily restricted,[1396] reflecting the fact that section 14 provides for the news media to publish information and a public right to receive that information; and in the right of an accused, under section 25, to be given a hearing that is public as well as fair. In *R v H*[1397] a prosecution of an adult for gross indecencies against a child was withdrawn. He subsequently sought an order permanently suppressing his identity. The interference on expression was justified; there was no relevant public interest or need to know that the accused had been charged. **15.485**

By contrast, the issue in *Television New Zealand v R*[1398] arose out of a trial where the defendant who had murdered his parents, brother and two sisters wished to adduce certain evidence. An order was made prohibiting publication of the witness and the evidence which was confirmed by the Court of Appeal; however, a television company then applied to rescind the order. The Court of Appeal emphasized that in the absence of compelling evidence to the contrary, criminal justice is public justice; and held that the right to information to the public outweighed the family right to privacy. **15.486**

In *Television New Zealand v R*[1399] the Court of Appeal considered an application by TVNZ for access to a videotaped interview of a convicted murderer which it proposed to use in the course of a documentary on child abuse. The court considered that the principle of open justice and freedom of expression had to be balanced against the legitimate privacy interests of the accused. The court refused to interfere with the judge's refusal to grant the application. A decision to prohibit the publication of the name of a prominent businessman and philanthropist found in possession of substantial quantities of cannabis was quashed in *Lewis v Wilson & Horton Ltd*.[1400] There was no basis upon which it could be concluded that the risk of damage to the appellant outweighed the interests of freedom of expression. **15.487**

[1394] *Burns v Howling at the Moon Magazines* [2002] 1 NZLR 381.
[1395] See *Police v O'Connor* [1992] 1 NZLR 87, 95.
[1396] Ibid.
[1397] [1994] 2 NZLR 143.
[1398] [1996] 3 NZLR 393.
[1399] (2000) 6 HRNZ 192.
[1400] [2001] 2 LRC 205.

15.488 In *R v Burns (Travis)*[1401] the Court of Appeal granted an order suppressing publication of the appellant's name and other details pending the hearing of his appeal against his conviction for murder because of prejudice to a possible re-trial. The order had initially been made because the appellant had been a witness in an earlier murder trial. However, the Court of Appeal refused to continue the order after the appeal had been dismissed.[1402]

15.489 The decision in *National Newspaper Association v Family Court*[1403] considered reporting restrictions in relation to a child suffering from cancer whose parents objected to chemotherapy treatment. The child was taken into hiding and there was widespread public and media interest when the Family Court approved a news release so he could be found. An order was then made suppressing any information relating to the child or the case. The High Court said that great significance should be attached to freedom of the press but that it must bend to the extent necessary to protect the child; and it was necessary to distinguish between mere curiosity and matters of public interest. As a result, any suppression order had to be tailored to intrude only to the extent necessary to ensure that the child's welfare was protected.

15.490 The statutory prohibition on publishing a report of proceeding before the Family Court without the leave of the court was a justified limit on the right to freedom of expression as it protected the best interests of the child and the privacy of disputes and was proportionate to that end.[1404]

15.491 **Search of court records.**   Recent cases have emphasized that the Court rules on the ability of the public and the media to access court records must be applied in light of freedom on expression, including the right to seek information. As a result, applications by media organization to access camera footage of an historic criminal trial (related to the sinking of Greenpeace's ship *The Rainbow Warrior*)[1405] the videotape of an interview conducted by police (the suspect was ultimately acquitted)[1406] and the videotape of the beating of an arrested person at a police station[1407] have been successful (in each case after the conclusion of the relevant criminal proceeding); as was an application by an opposition MP to search the court file in a judicial review proceeding touching on matters on which he was Opposition spokesman (the proceeding not yet having been heard).[1408]

15.492 **Obscenity and pornography.**   The Bill of Rights Act has also had a significant impact on the regulation of obscenity and pornography. The Films, Videos, and Publications Classification Act 1993 regulates the classification of films, videos and publications. The key concept is 'objectionability', which is defined as the description, depiction, expression or dealing with matters such as sex, horror, crime, cruelty or violence in such a manner that

---

[1401] [2002] 1 NZLR 387.

[1402] *R v Burns (Travis) (No 2)* [2002] 1 NZLR 410.

[1403] [1999] 2 NZLR 344.

[1404] *Solicitor-General v Television New Zealand* [2008] NZLFR 209.

[1405] *Mafart v Television New Zealand* [2006] 3 NZLR 534 (CA).

[1406] *Rogers v Television New Zealand* [2008] 2 NZLR 277 (SC).

[1407] *TVWorks Ltd v Parsons* unrep, 29 Sept 2008, Harrison J (the police officers involved had been acquitted by a jury of assaulting the prisoner).

[1408] *McCully v Whangamata Marina Society Inc* [2007] 1 NZLR 185 (CA).

the availability of a publication is likely to be injurious to the public good. In the important case of *Moonen v Film and Literature Board of Review*[1409] the Court of Appeal considered the relationship between section 14 and the 'censorship provisions' of The Films, Video and Publications Classification Act 1993. It was held that these provisions must be given a meaning that impinges as little as possible on freedom of expression.[1410] Following the decision of the Court of Appeal in *Moonen* the Film and Literature Board of Review reconsidered the classification in the light of the judgments and again held that the material was objectionable. Mr Moonen's appeal against that decision was dismissed by the High Court and the Court of Appeal on the basis that there was no error of law.[1411]

In *Living Word Distributors v Human Rights Action Group*[1412] the Court of Appeal con-   **15.493**
sidered an application by a human rights organization which objected to the importation of religious videos which stigmatized homosexuals. The Court of Appeal quashed the decision of the Film and Literature Board of Review banning the videos. In exercising their censorship role the Board had to take a narrow interpretation of the range of matters that fell within the concept of objectionability. Strong views against homosexuality did not fall properly within that concept. Nor, to be consistent with the Bill of Rights Act, should the Act be the basis for the censorship of political and socially contested opinions.

Racial hatred.   In *Zdrahal v Wellington City Council*[1413] the appellant painted swastikas on   **15.494**
the exterior wall and a window of his house, attracting complaints from two neighbours. The Planning Tribunal under the Resource Management Act issued an abatement order, on grounds that the symbols were offensive and objectionable. The Act in question authorized the prohibition of 'anything . . . that in the opinion of the enforcement officer, was likely to be noxious, dangerous, offensive, or objectionable to such an extent that it has or is likely to have an adverse effect on the environment'. The court accepted that the Tribunal was entitled to find that the ordinary person, members of the public, would find the swastikas offensive. The order had been made for a legitimate legislative objective and the means used were proportionate.[1414]

Police powers.   The restrictions on expression resulting from the imposition of a bind over   **15.495**
were considered in *Bracanov v Moss*.[1415] In that case an anti royalist was ordered to enter into a bond to keep the peace because of a royal visit. The court held that any limitations on freedom of expression were justified to ensure a citizen respects the rights and freedoms of others in the community. In *Stemson v Police*[1416] it was held that loud complaints in a benefits offices did not constitute disorderly conduct.[1417] Although the appellant's conduct was troubling to the complainant and to members of the public it was no more than a

---

[1409] (1999) 5 HRNZ 224.
[1410] Overruling *Re News Media Ltd v Film and Literature Review Board* (1997) 4 HRNZ 410.
[1411] *Moonen v Film and Literature Board of Review (No 2)* [2002] NZAR 358 and [2002] 2 NZLR 754.
[1412] [2001] 2 LRC 233 (CA).
[1413] [1995] 1 NZLR 700.
[1414] Applying s 5 as analysed in *MOT v Noort* [1992] 3 NZLR 260.
[1415] [1996] 1 NZLR 445.
[1416] [2002] NZAR 278.
[1417] Under s 4(1)(a) of the Summary Offences Act 1981.

vehement exercise of his right to freedom of expression under section 14. As a result, the appeal against conviction for disorderly conduct was allowed.[1418] A similar point was considered by the Supreme Court in *Brooker v The Police*.[1419] The defendant had been convicted of the offence as a result of knocking on the door of a police constable against whom he had a complaint, singing a song with a guitar in the road while displaying a placard. He refused to desist and was arrested for intimidation. The Supreme Court held that the criminal statute had to be read consistently with section 14 and that, as a result, for behaviour to be 'disorderly', it had to be disruptive of public order. It was also relevant to take into account the fact that the conduct involved a genuine exercise of the right to freedom of expression. Private annoyance was not sufficient. As a result, in the circumstances the defendant's conduct did not constitute 'disorderly conduct'.

15.496   **Expression and privacy.**   In *P v D*[1420] the High Court considered that the public disclosure of private facts which were highly offensive and objectionable to a reasonable person was a breach of privacy. These factors balanced the right to freedom of expression in section 14. There was minimal legitimate public interest in disclosure of the fact that a public figure had been treated in a psychiatric hospital and a permanent injunction was granted. In *L v G*[1421] it was held that the publication of sexually explicit photographs of the claimant was an invasion of her privacy, despite the fact that she could not be identified. Damages of NZ$2,500 were awarded for invasion of privacy.[1422] In *Brown v Attorney-General*[1423] the plaintiff who had a history of sexual offences against young people was released on parole subject to residential conditions. Police officers took his photograph which was put on a flyer distributed in the local community. This resulted in the plaintiff being verbally and physically assaulted and becoming the subject of media interest. It was held that he had a reasonable expectation of privacy and there was no pressing need in the public interest for the full response of the flyer.

15.497   In *R v Mahanga*[1424] the Court of Appeal upheld the trial judge's decision to refuse the media access to a videotaped interview which had been played during the course of a trial. The privacy rights of the convicted person outweighed the interests in open justice and freedom of speech. These interests had been fulfilled during the course of the trial by the opportunity to see the interview being played in court.

15.498   **Broadcasting standards.**   The Broadcasting Standards Authority receives complaints on whether radio and television programmes meet standards set out in statutorily authorized codes. In applying those codes to individual complaints made to it the Authority is required

---

[1418] For a discussion of expression and assembly see R Hart, 'The Mobs are out: the Right to Protest on Public Roads' (2001) 9 University of Auckland Law Review 311.

[1419] [2007] 3 NZLR 91.

[1420] [2001] 2 NZLR 591.

[1421] [2002] DCR 234.

[1422] See generally, R Tobin, 'Privacy and Freedom of Expression in New Zealand', in M Colvin ed, Developing Key Privacy Rights (Hart Publishing, 2002).

[1423] [2006] NZAR 552.

[1424] [2001] 1 NZLR 641.

to do so consistently with section 14.[1425] In *Browne v Canwest TV Works*[1426] the High Court held that the Authority was entitled to find that section 14 considerations outweighed the religious sensibilities of the claimants and that it was for the Authority and not the court to strike the balance.

Appendix 5: Human Rights Cases in South Africa

(1) Introduction

Section 16 of the South African Constitution provides that: **15.499**

16.(1) Everyone has the right to freedom of expression, which includes—
    (a) freedom of the press and other media;
    (b) freedom to receive and impart information and ideas;
    (c) freedom of artistic creativity; and
    (d) academic freedom and freedom of scientific research.
  (2) The right in subsection (1) does not extend to—
    (a) propaganda for war;
    (b) incitement of imminent violence; or
    (c) advocacy of hatred that is based on race, ethnicity, gender or religion, and that constitutes incitement to cause harm.[1427]

In one of the first major decisions dealing with freedom of expression, the Constitutional   **15.500**
Court confirmed the importance of the right, placing it 'at the heart of democracy'.[1428] O'Regan J endorsed the view of freedom of expression as one of a 'web of mutually supporting rights', including freedom of religion, belief and opinion (section 15), the right to dignity (section 10), as well as the right to freedom of association (section 18), the right to vote and to stand for public office (section 19) and the right to assembly (section 17). She went on to comment:

These rights taken together protect the rights of individuals not only individually to form and express opinions, of whatever nature, but to establish associations and groups of like-minded people to foster and propagate such opinions. The rights implicitly recognize the importance, both for a democratic society and for individuals personally, of the ability to form and express opinions, whether individually or collectively, even where those views are controversial. The corollary of the freedom of expression and its related rights is tolerance by society of different views. Tolerance, of course, does not require approbation of a particular view. In essence, it requires the acceptance of the public airing of disagreements and the refusal to silence unpopular views.[1429]

[1425] *Television New Zealand v Viewers for TV Excellence* [2005] 1 NZAR 1 and see generally, *Can West TV Works Ltd v XY* [2008] NZAR 1 and *Television New Zealand v Green* unrep, 11 July 2008, Mallon J.

[1426] [2008] 1 NZLR 654.

[1427] See generally, S Woolman, T Roux, J Klaaren, A Stein, M Chaskalson, and M Bishop (eds) *Constitutional Law of South Africa* (2nd edn, OS 2006), Chap 42.

[1428] *South African National Defence Union v Minister of Defence* 1999 (6) BCLR 615 (CC), para 7. See also *NM v Smith (Freedom of Expression Institute as* Amicus Curiae*)* 2007 (7) BCLR 751 (CC).

[1429] *South African National Defence* (n 1428 above) para 8.

(2) Defamation

15.501   The Constitution has had a profound effect on reform of the common law of defamation.[1430] The guarantee of freedom of speech sits alongside the express protection of both dignity (section 10) and privacy (section 14), which together reflect the strong traditional protection afforded by South African law to reputation.[1431]

15.502   In *Gardener v Whitaker*[1432] it was held that the constitutional guarantee of freedom of expression meant that the plaintiff should now bear the onus of proving the falsity of a defamatory statement and the absence of defences.[1433] In *Holomisa v Argus Newspapers*[1434] the judge held that a defamatory statement regarding 'free and fair' political activity is constitutionally protected even if false, unless a plaintiff can establish that the defendant acted unreasonably. However, in *Buthelezi v South African Broadcasting Corporation*[1435] this approach was criticized on the grounds that it led to the right to freedom of expression being given precedence over the right to reputation. It was suggested that it would be preferable to develop the common law of defamation by expanding the concept of 'public interest' and placing a burden on the defendant to show that he had acted reasonably.

15.503   This conflict of approach was resolved by the Supreme Court of Appeal in *National Media v Bogoshi*,[1436] which radically reformed the law of defamation by jettisoning the previous case law imposing strict liability on the media and replacing it with a test of negligence. The court held that:

> the publication in the press of false defamatory allegations of fact will not be regarded as unlawful if, upon a consideration of all the circumstances of the case, it is found to have been reasonable to publish the particular facts in a particular way and at a particular time.[1437]

In considering reasonableness, account had to be taken of the nature, extent and tone of the allegations.[1438] Greater latitude is allowed in cases of political discussion. The Court held that the burden of establishing that the publication was reasonable was on the defendant, in accordance with the decision in *Buthelezi*. This approach was held to be in conformity with constitutional values.

15.504   In *Khumalo v Holomisa*,[1439] the Constitutional Court confirmed the reasonableness defence created in *Bogoshi*.[1440] The Court commented that, despite the fundamental importance of

---

[1430] See generally D Milo, *Defamation and Freedom of Speech* (Oxford University Press, 2008).

[1431] Ibid, 23–25. See also I Currie and J De Waal *Bill of Rights Handbook* (5th edn, Juta, 2008), 383ff.

[1432] 1994 (5) BCLR 19 (CC); (the Constitutional Court refused leave to appeal on the grounds that no constitutional issue was raised, 15 May 1996).

[1433] Ibid, 37D–H.

[1434] 1996 (6) BCLR 836 (W), Cameron J; see also *Hall v Welz* 1996 (4) SA 1070 (C); *Rivett-Carnac v Wiggins* 1997 (4) BCLR 562 (C).

[1435] (1997) (12) BCLR 1733 (D).

[1436] 1998 (4) SA 1196 (SCA).

[1437] Ibid, 632e–f.

[1438] Ibid, 632f.

[1439] 2002 (8) BCLR 771 (CC).

[1440] For analysis of the way in which the reasonable publication defence has been applied, see Milo (n 1430 above) 196–197.

freedom of expression to a democratic society, it was not a paramount value and had to be construed in the context of other constitutional values, in particular, human dignity, freedom and equality. The law of defamation sought to strike a balance between the value of human dignity and the protection of freedom of expression. The difficulty of proving the truth of defamatory statements and leaving the proof of falsity to the defendant does cause a 'chilling effect' on the publication of information. However, this chilling effect is reduced considerably by the defence of 'reasonable publication' established in *Bogoshi*. The Court concluded:

> to hold . . . that the plaintiffs may never succeed unless they can establish that a defamatory statement was false would clearly put plaintiffs at risk. It would destabilize the careful balance struck between plaintiff's and defendant's interests achieved by the . . . defence of reasonable publication.[1441]

As a result, the applicants had not demonstrated that the common law was inconsistent with the provisions of the constitution.

The leading post-*Bogoshi* case of *Mthembi-Mahanyele v Mail & Guardian Ltd*[1442] shows the **15.505** concern of the courts to protect both freedom of speech and reputation. The Defendant newspaper had published allegations that the cabinet minister was corrupt. The Supreme Court of Appeal unanimously rejected a previous finding of general immunity in so far as criticism and reporting of a cabinet minister's performance, holding that cabinet ministers have the right to claim damages for defamation even in respect of allegations concerning their official conduct.[1443] However, Lewis JA went on to craft a defence of justifiable publication of political information,[1444] such that publication of defamatory matter is not actionable in circumstances where it is justifiable:

> Justifiability is to be determined by having regard to all relevant circumstances, including the interest of the public in being informed; the manner of publication; the tone of the material published; the extent of public concern in the information; the reliability of the source; the steps taken to verify the truth of the information . . . and whether the person defamed has been given the opportunity to comment on the statement before publication. In cases where information is crucial to the public, and is urgent, it may be justifiable to publish without giving an opportunity to comment.[1445]

Applying this test, Lewis JA found that Respondents' publication of the defamatory statement was, in all the circumstances, justifiable.

(3) Pornography

In the first case concerning the regulation of pornographic material, *Case v Ministry of* **15.506** *Safety and Security*,[1446] the majority declined to express an opinion on whether the protection of section 16 encompassed pornography, dealing instead with the law of obscenity in

---

[1441] Ibid, para 44.
[1442] 2004 (11) BCLR 1182 (SCA).
[1443] Ibid, paras 40–42.
[1444] Ibid, paras 64–68. It should be noted that the Court was split with regard to the introduction of the new defence. See further Milo (n 1430 above) 115.
[1445] *Mthembi-Mahanyele* (n 1442 above) para 68.
[1446] 1996 (5) BCLR 609 (CC).

terms of the right to personal privacy. However, two of the judges[1447] held that the protection of section 15 extended to sexually explicit material and the criminal law on obscenity unjustifiably violated that right.

15.507   The question has now been addressed in *De Reuck v Director of Public Prosecutions (Witwatersrand Local Division)*,[1448] which concerned a challenge to the criminalization of production, distribution or possession of child pornography. The Constitutional Court definitively held that section 16 is content-neutral, and rejected the respondent's argument, drawn from US jurisprudence, that child pornography was not 'expression'.[1449] Accordingly, the restrictions on child pornography did limit freedom of expression and could survive only if justified under the limitation clause.

15.508   Unsurprisingly, the Court held unanimously that the limitation of privacy occasioned by the offence was necessary and justified, as the sexual abuse and degradation of children through such pornography was a serious harm.[1450] The legislation also served three legitimate objectives: protecting the dignity of children; stamping out the market for photographs made by abusing children and preventing a reasonable risk that images would be used to harm children. These objectives remained valid in relation to film-makers or researchers, so rejected the appellant's argument for a defence of 'legitimate purpose' if film-makers or researchers were charged with possession or importation of the material concerned.[1451]

(4) Political restrictions on employees

15.509   The case of *South African National Defence Force Union v Minister of Defence*[1452] concerned a law which prohibited members of the armed forces from participating in public protest actions and from joining trade unions. The Court decided that prohibiting participation in acts of public protest violated the right to freedom of expression of Defence Force members. Their rights to receive and express opinions on a wide range of issues, whether in public or private gatherings, was a grave infringement on the fundamental rights of soldiers. Furthermore, such an infringement was unjustifiable, although the Court indicated that a different, narrower legislative provision might be constitutionally justified.

(5) Privilege

15.510   The issue of parliamentary privilege was considered in *De Lille v Speaker of the National Assembly*.[1453] The applicant had named in parliamentary debate eight senior members of the ANC as spies for the apartheid government. The applicant was formally charged with abusing her privilege of freedom of speech, and the House recommended her suspension from the House for 15 days. The applicant succeeded in setting aside that recommendation. The court

---

[1447] Mokgoro and Sachs JJ.
[1448] 2003 (12) BCLR 1333 (CC).
[1449] Ibid, para 48.
[1450] Ibid, paras 60–72.
[1451] Ibid, para 74.
[1452] 1999 (6) BCLR 615 (CC).
[1453] 1998 (7) BCLR 916 (C).

found that the investigation into the applicant's conduct had been flawed and in breach of natural justice. The court held that the nature and exercise of Parliamentary privilege had to be consonant with the Constitution. The court recognized that the principle of separation of powers and the proper exercise of parliamentary privilege was a matter for Parliament alone. Nevertheless, the court could interfere where Parliament improperly exercised that privilege. Furthermore, the suspension of the member was in breach of her freedom of expression.

(6) Contempt of court

In *S v Mamabolo*[1454] the Constitutional Court held that the form of contempt known as **15.511** 'scandalizing the court' was compatible with the constitutional guarantee of freedom of expression although the scope for a conviction was very narrow indeed. It must be shown that the offending conduct, viewed contextually, really was likely to damage the administration of justice. It was, however, held that the summary procedure for dealing with allegations of scandalizing the court was in breach of the constitutional right to a fair trial.

In *Midi Television (Pty) Ltd v Director of Public Prosecutions (Western Cape)*[1455] the Supreme **15.512** Court of Appeal held that although the constitutional right to freedom of expression could be could be abridged in favour of preserving the integrity of the administration of justice it had to be shown that the prejudice that the publication might cause to the administration of justice was demonstrable and substantial and there was a real risk that the prejudice would occur if publication took place. The Court could not require a television company to provide an advance copy of a programme to the DPP in order to enable him to ascertain that there would be no prejudice to the administration of justice.

(7) Censorship of hate speech

The decision of the Constitutional Court in *Islamic Unity Convention v Independent* **15.513** *Broadcasting Authority*[1456] concerned a complaint by the South African Jewish Board of Deputies that a radio interview broadcast by the Islamic Unity Convention was likely to breach a provision in the Code of Conduct of the Independent Broadcasting Authority. That provision prohibited broadcasting likely to prejudice relations between sections of the population. The court held that the code's provision was too intrusive and made serious inroads into the right of freedom of expression, and declared the provision unconstitutional and invalid. The declaration of invalidity was made subject to the proviso that no protection is given to the broadcasting of material that amounts to propaganda for war, the incitement of imminent violence or the advocacy of hatred that is based on race, ethnicity, gender or religion, and that constitutes incitement to cause harm.

[1454] 2001 (5) BCLR 449 (CC).
[1455] [2008] 1 LRC 407.
[1456] 2002 (5) BCLR 433 (CC).

Appendix 6: Human Rights Cases from Other Jurisdictions

(1) Introduction

15.514 The right to freedom of expression is firmly established as a constitutional right in many European countries.[1457] However, the principles of freedom of expression have been most extensively developed in the United States. American authorities have already had a significant impact on the evolution of the common law on defamation[1458] and, although the point is not uncontroversial,[1459] American constitutional principles have provided some guidance on the development of freedom of expression in England and Wales.[1460]

15.515 In particular, the American courts have accorded a high priority to political speech. Freedom of expression is said to create a market place of ideas. As Holmes J said in his famous dissenting judgment in *Abrams v United States*:[1461]

> when men have realized that time has upset many fighting faiths, they may come to believe even more than they believe the very foundations of their own conduct that the ultimate good desired is better reached by a free trade in ideas—that the best of truth is the power of the thought to get itself accepted in the competition of the market, and that truth is the only ground upon which their wishes can be safely carried out.

As a result, free speech promotes the search for truth. It also secures the right of the citizen to participate in the democratic process:

> Those who won our independence believed that the final end of the State was to make men develop their faculties, and that in its government the deliberate forces should prevail over the arbitrary . . . They believed the freedom to think as you will and to speak as you think are means indefensible to the discovery and spread of political truth; that without free speech and assembly, discussion would be futile; that with them, discussion affords ordinarily adequate protection against the dissemination of noxious doctrine; that the greatest menace to freedom is the inert people; that public discussion is a political duty; and that this should be the fundamental principle of American government.[1462]

Thus, Meiklejohn argued that the purpose of freedom of expression is to ensure that self government guaranteed under the American constitution is achieved by self education.[1463]

[1457] See eg, S Micahelowski and L Woods, *German Constitutional Law* (Dartmouth, 1999), Chap 12.

[1458] See eg, *Derbyshire County Council v Times Newspapers Ltd* [1993] AC 534; *Reynolds v Times Newspapers Ltd* [2001] 2 AC 127.

[1459] Sir Stephen Sedley takes a more sceptical view about the value of borrowing ideas from the First Amendment, arguing that freedom of expression is at the head of the queue for judicial protection because the media has the funds to underwrite litigation and that it places no sanctions on the mass media to act responsibly: see Sir Stephen Sedley, 'The First Amendment: A Case for Import Controls?' in I Loveland (ed), *Importing the First Amendment* (Hart Publishing, 1998).

[1460] See eg, E Barendt, 'The Importance of United States Free Speech Jurisprudence' and I Loveland, 'The criminalization of Racial Violence' in I Loveland (ed), *A Special Relationship* (Clarendon Press, 1995); R Singh, *The Future of Human Rights in the United Kingdom* (Hart Publishing, 1997), Chap 4; I Loveland (ed), *Importing the First Amendment* (Hart Publishing, 1998).

[1461] (1919) 250 US 616, 630.

[1462] Brandeis J in *Whitney v California* (1927) 274 US 357, 375.

[1463] See A Meiklejohn, *Free Speech and its Relation to Self Government* (Harper & Sons, 1948); 'The First Amendment is an Absolute' [1961] Sup Ct Rev 245; andsee eg, WJ Brennan, 'The Supreme Court and the Meiklejohn Interpretation of the First Amendment' (1965) 79 Harv L Rev 1; and Sir John Laws, 'Meiklejohn,

Nevertheless, it must be borne in mind that there are important differences in philosophy   **15.516**
and the political culture between England and the United States which limit the value of
directly transposing expression principles.[1464] Furthermore, the drafting of the First
Amendment is very unlike Article 10 since it prohibits interference with freedom of speech
in absolute terms.[1465] A literal interpretation of the First Amendment would permit no
interference with freedom of speech. The absolutist approach to the First Amendment is
most closely associated with Black J. Thus, in his dissenting judgment in the obscenity case
of *Ginzburg v United States*[1466] he said:

> I believe that the Federal Government is without power under the Constitution to put any
> burden on speech or expression of any kind (as distinguished from conduct).

He later explained the position, writing extra-judicially in the following terms:

> Some people regard the prohibitions of the Constitution, even its most unequivocal com-
> mands as mere admonitions . . . and that all constitutional problems are questions of reasona-
> bleness, proximity and review. I cannot accept this approach to the Bill of Rights. It is my
> belief that there *are* 'absolutes' in our Bill of Rights and that they were put there on purpose
> by men who knew what the words meant and meant their prohibitions to be 'absolutes'. . .
> I am discussing here whether liberties *admittedly* covered by the Bill of Rights can neverthe-
> less be abridged on the ground that a superior public interest justifies the abridgement.
> I think the Bill of Rights makes its safeguards superior.[1467]

However, under the First Amendment even political speech is curtailed where there is a   **15.517**
clear and present danger of harm.[1468] Its regulation is subject to strict scrutiny which
must be 'narrowly tailored' to serve a 'compelling governmental interest';[1469] this means,
for example, that First Amendment protection covers lewd epithets[1470] and extends to
symbolic speech such as flag burning[1471] or to demonstrators in Nazi uniforms marching
through a Jewish community.[1472] In practice, the case law of the American Supreme Court
has developed a complex system for justifying limitations on freedom of expression:

---

the First Amendment and Free Speech in English Law' in I Loveland (ed), *Importing the First Amendment*
(Hart Publishing, 1998).

   [1464] C McCrudden, 'The Impact on Freedom of Expression' in B Markesinis, *The Impact of the Human
Rights Bill in English Law* (Oxford University Press, 1998).

   [1465] The case law has developed important implied limitations to free speech; some of the basic principles
are summarized at para 15.346 below.

   [1466] (1966) 383 US 463.

   [1467] HL Black, *A Constitutional Faith* (Knopf, 1968); see also, HL Black, 'Bill of Rights' (1960) 35 New
York University L Rev 865.

   [1468] The test was formulated by Holmes J in *Schenck v United States* (1919) 249 US 47 52; see *Brandenburg
v Ohio* (1969) 395 US 444.

   [1469] The starting point for the strict scrutiny doctrine is the famous passage from the judgment of Stone J
in *United States v Carolene Products* (1938) 304 US 144 footnote 4 which he said that: 'there may be narrower
scope for the operation of the presumption of constitutionality when legislation appears on its face to be
within a *specific prohibition of the Constitution*, such as those of the first ten amendments'.

   [1470] See eg, *Cohen v California* (1973) 403 US 15 where the Supreme Court held that wearing a badge on
a jacket saying 'Fuck the draft' in the corridor of a Los Angeles courtroom could not amount to a criminal
offence because it was protected as free speech.

   [1471] See eg, *Texas v Johnson* (1989) 491 US 397; *United States v Eichman* (1990) 496 US 310.

   [1472] *Smith v Collins* (1978) 436 US 953.

- by imposing content based restrictions where certain types of speech are singled out as not being sufficiently worthy to attract First Amendment protection[1473] (such as speech which is not essential to the exposition of any idea, libel,[1474] obscenity[1475] and insulting or 'fighting' words);[1476]
- by regulating conduct which only incidentally affects speech;[1477] or
- by permitting restrictions on the time, place or manner of expression provided they are 'content neutral'.[1478]

15.518 Nevertheless, there are numerous expression issues which the American case law illuminates including: the distinction between speech and conduct[1479] (and in particular, the protection of symbolic speech such as flag burning);[1480] the degree of protection given to extreme political views[1481] or to commercial speech;[1482] and whether restrictions on expression require greater justification because they apply in a public place.[1483]

[1473] The principles set out in *Chaplinsky v Hampshire* (1942) 315 US 568 268, 269 should now, however, be treated with caution.

[1474] The scope of First Amendment protection depends on whether the plaintiff is a political figure (see *New York Times v Sullivan* (1964) 376 US 254 or a private citizen (see *Gertz v Robert Welch* (1974) 418 US 323).

[1475] Which is confined to hard core pornography: see *Roth v United States* (1957) 354 US 476 and *Miller v California* (1973) 413 US 15.

[1476] The doctrine was radically changed in the controversial decision in *RAV v City of St Paul, Minnesota* (1992) 505 US 377 where a city ordinance against hate crime laws breached the First Amendment because it selectively silenced free speech on the basis of its content; it now seems that only inflammatory words intended to bring about imminent violence are unprotected.

[1477] The distinction between conduct and speech originates in *Thornhill v Alabama* (1940) 310 US 88 where a state law prohibiting all union picketing was constitutionally protected free speech; the principle means that conduct such as a demonstration is characterized as 'speech plus' and is entitled to a lesser degree of First Amendment protection than 'pure speech': see *Cox v Louisiana* (1965) 379 US 559 per Goldberg J at 563. However, the speech/conduct dichotomy is very difficult to maintain: see eg, L Tribe, *American Constitutional Law* (2nd edn, Foundation Press, 1988), 12–7.

[1478] See eg, *Lloyd Corp v Tanner* (1972) 407 US 551 (rejecting First Amendment protection to distributing antiwar leaflets in a shopping centre).

[1479] See eg, *United States v O'Brien* (1968) 391 US 367 (burning a draft card); and see, generally, Tribe (n 1477 above) 12-6, 12-7; E Barendt, *Freedom of Speech* (Clarendon Press, 1985), 41–48.

[1480] See eg, *Texas v Johnson* (1989) 491 US 397; *United States v Eichman* (1990) 496 US 310.

[1481] Unless they are directed at inciting (or producing) imminent lawless action and are likely to incite (or produce) such action; see *Brandenburg v Ohio* (1969) 395 US 444; and see generally, Tribe (n 1477 above) 12–9.

[1482] See the seminal case of *Virginia State Board of Pharmacy v Virginia Citizens Consumer Council* (1976) 425 US 748 which struck down legislation preventing a pharmacist advertising the price of prescription drugs in order to protect the interest of the consumer in the flow of information about prices); and includes the right of professionals to advertise fees on a limited factual basis (see eg, *Bates v Arizona Bar Association* (1977) 435 US 350; *Shapero v Kentucky Bar Association* (1989) 486 US 466); a prohibition against bans on advertising (see eg, *Central Hudson Gas v New York Public Service Commission* (1980) 447 US 557); the right to use the mail to send unsolicited contraceptives (*Bolger v Youngs Drug Products* (1983) 463 US 60); the right to solicit door-to-door within reasonable hours (see eg, *Linmark Associates v Willingboro* (1977) 431 US 85; and see generally, Tribe (n 1477 above) 12–16.

[1483] See eg, *Hague v CIO* (1939) 307 US 496 (leafleting, parades and other speech related uses of street and parks cannot be banned or subjected to a discretionary licence); *Police Department of City of Chicago v Mosley* (1992) 408 US 92 (city cannot enforce ordinance prohibiting picketing within 150 feet of schools); see generally, Tribe (n 1477 above) 12–24.

(2) Antigua and Barbuda

Section 12(1) of the Constitution of Antigua and Barbuda provides that: **15.519**

> Except with his own consent, no person shall be hindered in the enjoyment of his freedom of expression.

Restrictions on this freedom must be reasonably required for various stated objectives and must also be 'reasonably required in a democratic society'.

In *Hector v Attorney-General of Antigua and Barbuda*[1484] the applicant newspaper editor **15.520** had been charged with printing a false statement which was 'likely to cause fear or alarm in or to the public, or to disturb the public peace, or to undermine public confidence in the conduct of public affairs'. The Privy Council accepted his argument that his rights under section 12 of the Constitution had been contravened by this prosecution. Lord Bridge said:

> In a free democratic society it is almost too obvious to need stating that those who hold office in government and who are responsible for public administration must always be open to criticism. Any attempt to stifle or fetter such criticism amounts to political censorship of the most insidious and objectional kind. At the same time it is no less obvious that the very purpose of the criticism levelled at those who have the conduct of public affairs by their political opponents is to undermine public confidence in their stewardship and to persuade the electorate that the opponents would make a better job of it than those presently holding office. In the light of these considerations their Lordships cannot help viewing a statutory provision which criminalizes statements likely to undermine public confidence in the conduct of public affairs with the utmost suspicion.[1485]

The case of *de Freitas v Permanent Secretary of Ministry of Agriculture, Fisheries, Lands and* **15.521** *Housing*[1486] concerned a provision of the Civil Service Act restricting the freedom of expression of civil servants. All civil servants were forbidden to communicate 'any information or expressions of opinion on matters of national or international political controversy'. The Privy Council held that a blanket restraint which imposed the same restrictions on all categories of civil servants was not reasonably required for the proper performance of their functions. In addition, the restriction was not reasonably justifiable in a democratic society.

(3) Australia

The Constitution Act 1900 does not contain a Bill of Rights but, over recent years, the **15.522** High Court has implied a number of rights into it.[1487] In two judgments delivered on 30 September 1992, the High Court found that the system of representative government gave rise to an implied constitutional guarantee of freedom of communication in relation to the

---

[1484] [1990] 2 AC 312.
[1485] Ibid, at 318B–D.
[1486] [1999] AC 69.
[1487] See generally, G Williams, *Human Rights Under the Australian Constitution* (Oxford University Press, 1999), Chap 7.

political and electoral processes.[1488] The right of the electorate to choose members of the legislature carried with it:

> the right to convey and receive information, opinions and arguments concerning such elections and the candidates who are involved in them.[1489]

Breaches of this 'implied freedom' rendered statutes invalid. Thus, in *Nationwide News*[1490] the High Court held that a statute making it an offence to use words calculated to bring a member of the Industrial Relations Commission into disrepute was invalid.[1491] In *Australian Capital Television Pty Ltd v The Commonwealth of Australia*[1492] the High Court held that a statute prohibiting political advertising during federal elections (coupled with 'free time' for established parties) was invalid because it infringed the implied freedom.

15.523 This approach led the High Court in *Theophanus v Herald and Weekly Times Ltd*[1493] to conclude that the law of defamation raised constitutional issues and unduly limited freedom of communication in political matters. They took the view that the defendant who published material relevant to 'political discussion' should have a defence of qualified privilege if he could show that he had acted reasonably. The same principles were applied by the High Court in *Stephens v West Australian Newspapers Ltd*.[1494]

15.524 The decisions in *Theophanus* and *Stephens* were unsuccessfully challenged by the plaintiff in *Lange v Australian Broadcasting Corp*.[1495] In that case, the High Court held that:

> each member of the Australian community has an interest in disseminating and receiving information, opinions and arguments concerning government and political matters that affect the people of Australia. The duty to disseminate such information is simply the correlative of the interest in receiving it.[1496]

As a result, a defence of qualified privilege was available to anyone disseminating such information. However, because the damage from publication to the whole world was potentially very great, the privilege could only be relied on if the defendant was reasonable as well as honest.[1497] In relation to the 'reasonableness requirement', this must depend upon all the circumstances of the case:

[1488] *Nationwide News Pty Ltd v Wills* (1992) 177 CLR 1 and *Australian Capital Television Pty Ltd v The Commonwealth of Australia* (1992) 177 CLR 106 (relying heavily on Canadian authority, see generally Williams (see n 1487 above) 171–173).

[1489] *Australian Capital Television v Commonwealth of Australia* (see n 1488 above) 232.

[1490] See n 1488 above.

[1491] Mason CJ, Dawson, and McHugh JJ held that it was invalid because, applying a proportionality test, it was not within the implied incidental power to legislate on industrial relations matters. Brennan, Deane, Toohey, and Gaudron JJ held that it was invalid because it breached the implied freedom of political communication.

[1492] See n 1488 above.

[1493] (1994) 182 CLR 104.

[1494] (1994) 182 CLR 211; for general discussions of these cases see, I Loveland, '*Sullivan v The New York Times* Goes Down Under' [1996] PL 126; L Leigh, 'Of Free Speech and Individual Reputation' in I Loveland (ed), *Importing the First Amendment* (Hart Publishing, 1998), 62–65.

[1495] (1997) 145 ALR 96; see also *Kruger v Commonwealth* (1997) 146 ALR 126.

[1496] *Lange v Australian Broadcasting Corp* (n 1495 above) at 115.

[1497] Ibid, 116–118.

But, as a general rule, a defendant's conduct in publishing material giving rise to a defamatory imputation will not be reasonable unless the defendant had reasonable grounds for believing that the imputation was true, took proper steps, so far as they were reasonably open, to verify the accuracy of the material and did not believe the imputation to be untrue. Furthermore, the defendant's conduct will not be reasonable unless the defendant has sought a response from the person defamed and published the response made (if any) except in cases where the seeking or publication of a response was not practicable or it was unnecessary to give the plaintiff an opportunity to respond.[1498]

This implied constitutional freedom does not, however, cover all types of discussion which could be described as 'political'. Its purpose is to 'contribute to protecting and reinforcing the system of representative government provided for by the Australian Constitution'.[1499] The freedom has been held to be applicable in relation to criticism of the conduct of members of the Parliament,[1500] the operation of electoral law,[1501] legislation restricting criticism of a public body,[1502] the administration of a Commonwealth ordinance,[1503] and to campaigns for legislative change.[1504] The freedom extends to conduct as well as to speech.[1505] **15.525**

However, the freedom does not extend to advocacy of law breaking. Thus, in *Brown v Classification Review Board*[1506] the Federal Court upheld a decision of the Classification Review Board refusing classification of a publication containing an 'Art of Shoplifting'.[1507] The Classification Code was enacted for the legitimate aim of preventing crime and was compatible with the maintenance of representative and responsible government, was reasonably appropriate and adapted to achieving the legitimate end.[1508] **15.526**

(4) Hong Kong

(a) Introduction

Article 16 of the Hong Kong Bill of Rights Ordinance gives effect to the right to freedom of expression contained in Article 19 of the International Covenant on Civil and Political Rights.[1509] **15.527**

A number of challenges based on the freedom of expression have been unsuccessful in the courts. In *Ming Pao Newspapers v A-G of Hong Kong*[1510] the Privy Council held that the Prevention of Bribery Ordinance, which prohibited the disclosure of details of investigations into bribery offences, was necessary to preserve the integrity of investigations into **15.528**

[1498] Ibid, 118.

[1499] *Levy v Victoria* (1997) 146 ALR 248, 273, 291.

[1500] *Lange v Australian Broadcasting* (n 1495 above) (the New Zealand Parliament).

[1501] *Australian Capital Television Pty Ltd v The Commonwealth of Australia* (1992) 177 CLR 106; *Muldowney v South Australia (State of)* (1996) 186 CLR 352.

[1502] *Nationwide News Pty v Wills* (1992) 177 CLR 1.

[1503] *Kruger v Commonwealth* (1997) 146 ALR 126.

[1504] *Levy v Victoria* (see n 1499 above).

[1505] Ibid, (the entry of protestors into an area in which duck hunting was taking place).

[1506] (1998) 5 BHRC 619, the issues of the limits of the implied constitutional freedom of expression are comprehensively discussed in this case.

[1507] Rendering the publication, sale or distribution of the article an offence.

[1508] Ibid, 631f–g.

[1509] See App J in Vol 2.

[1510] [1996] AC 907.

corruption. Great weight was given to the fact that the Legislative Council and the Hong Kong Court of Appeal had recognized such a need.[1511] In *Chim Sing Chung v Commissioner of Correctional Services*[1512] the Hong Kong Court of Appeal held that the prison authorities' decision to remove racing supplements from newspapers did not violate the applicant's right to receive information under Article 16 because the restriction was 'authorized by law'.

15.529 In *Hong Kong Polytechnic University v Next Magazine Publishing Ltd*[1513] the Hong Kong Court of Appeal rejected an attempt to argue that a university was a 'public authority' which cannot maintain an action in defamation. It was held that the university was entitled to bring an action for defamation to protect its reputation.[1514] In *Re Lee Kwok Hung*[1515] a challenge was brought to a notice issued by the Securities and Futures Commission Ordinance requiring the applicant to attend an interview with an inspector. The challenge based on breach of rights to freedom of expression was rejected. Article 16 was concerned with the right of freedom of opinion and expression, not with providing an immunity from the disclosure of information. In *HKSAR v Ng Kung Siu*[1516] the Court of Appeal held that a law prohibiting the desecration of the national flag was contrary to Article 19 of the ICCPR because it could not be justified as being 'necessary for the protection of public order'.[1517] Legislation prohibiting the possession of child pornography is a justifiable restriction on freedom of expression to protect the victims and society generally.[1518]

15.530 In *Kwong v The Medical Council of Hong Kong*[1519] it was held that various restrictions on advertising by medical practitioners, including restrictions on advertising in newspapers, were contrary to Article 16 as not being 'necessary' for the protection of public health or the reputation of the profession.

(b) Defamation

15.531 In *Cheung Ng Sheong v Eastweek Publisher Ltd*[1520] the unsuccessful defendant in a libel case challenged the award of damages made by the jury. The Court of Appeal held that excessive awards in defamation cases could constitute an impediment to freedom of expression and opinion as guaranteed in Article 16. The Court noted that, although the Bill of Rights did not apply directly to the case as both parties were private individuals, the Court could

---

[1511] The appeal was in fact allowed on the ground that s 30 did not apply when no specific suspect was being investigated.
[1512] (1997) 1 BHRC 394.
[1513] [1996] 2 HKLR 260.
[1514] See generally, Sze Ping-fat, 'Freedom of the Press' (1996) 16 Lit 291; and 'Freedom of the Press Revisited' (1997) 17 Lit 50.
[1515] [1993] HKLR 49.
[1516] (1999) 6 BHRC 591.
[1517] The Court relied on the US 'flag burning' cases, *Texas v Johnson* (1989) 491 US 397 (US SC) and *United States v Eichman* (1990) 496 US 310, US SC; see generally, E Chemerinsky, *Constitutional Law: Principles and Policies* (3rd edn, Aspen, 2006), 1067–1068; E Barendt, *Freedom of Speech* (2nd edn, Oxford University Press, 2005), 84–86.
[1518] *Secretary for Justice v Man Kwong Choi* [2008] HKCU 1089.
[1519] [2008] HKCU 130.
[1520] [1996] 1 LRC 168.

nevertheless take into account the Bill of Rights when interpreting the common law. The Court of Appeal took a similar approach to that of the English Court of Appeal in *Rantzen v Mirror Group Newspapers (1986) Ltd.*[1521]

(c) Contempt of court

In *Secretary for Justice v The Oriental Press Group*[1522] it was held that the offence of **15.532** scandalizing the court was compatible with freedom of expression. That case concerned a newspaper group which, after some unfavourable judicial decisions concerning copyright and obscenity, published a series of articles designed to vilify the judiciary. The articles contained abuse and racist slurs. The staff members of the newspaper group also conducted a 'paparazzi' type pursuit of a senior judge, with 24 hour surveillance of the judge, and reports and photographs being published in the paper. The articles and pursuit led to proceedings for scandalizing the court. The court found the newspaper guilty of scandalizing the court. The court observed that the offence of scandalizing the court existed not only for the benefit of the judiciary, but also to maintain public confidence in the legal system. Permissible criticism had to be distinguished from scurrilous abuse, which might have an effect on the administration of justice. The court stated there was a strong argument that the offence of scandalizing the court had been developed to preserve the rule of law. The offence was not a restriction of freedom of expression since conduct which jeopardised the rule of law could not be said to be an exercise of the right of freedom of expression at all. Even if there was a breach of freedom of expression, the breach was justified with reference to the need for public order.

(5) Human Rights Committee

Article 19 of the International Covenant on Civil and Political Rights provides: **15.533**

> 1. Everyone shall have the right to hold opinions without interference.
>
> 2. Everyone shall have the right to freedom of expression; this right shall include freedom to seek, receive and impart information and ideas of all kinds, regardless of frontiers, either orally, in writing or in print, in the form of art, or through any other media of his choice.
>
> 3. The exercise of the rights provided for in paragraph 2 of this article carries with it special duties and responsibilities. It may therefore be subject to certain restrictions, but these shall only be such as are provided by law and are necessary:
>
>   (a) For respect of the rights or reputations of others;
>
>   (b) For the protection of national security or of public order (ordre public), or of public health or morals.[1523]

Article 20 provides that advocacy of national, racial or religious hatred that constitutes incitement to 'discrimination, hostility or violence' shall be prohibited by law.

[1521] [1994] QB 670.

[1522] [1998] 2 HKLRD 123.

[1523] See App J in Vol 2 for the text.

15.534 Article 19(2) encompasses every form of ideas and expression, including commercial expression and advertising[1524] and non-verbal expression such as protest.[1525] Article 19 has been found to be engaged by the banning of a political party.[1526]

15.535 In *Faurisson v France*[1527] the HRC considered a communication which contested the provisions of a French statute making it an offence to deny the existence of Nazi war crimes. The HRC took the view that restrictions on freedom of expression under Article 19(3) of the Covenant[1528] could relate to the interests of the 'community as a whole'. As the statements made were such as to raise or strengthen anti-semitic feelings, the restriction on the author's freedom of expression were permissible under Art 19(3)(a) and were necessary to serve the struggle against racism.[1529]

15.536 In *Ballantyne v Canada* the Human Rights Committee found that a Quebec law prohibiting the use of English in advertisements had the legitimate objective of preservation of the French language but was, nevertheless, a violation of Article 19. It was not necessary for the legitimate objective in question.

15.537 In its Concluding Observations on the United Kingdom's Report under Article 40 of the Covenant, the HRC commented[1530]

> The State party should re-examine its technical doctrines of libel law, and consider the utility of a so-called, 'public figure', exception, requiring proof by the plaintiff of actual malice in order to go forward on actions concerning reporting on public officials and prominent public figures, as well as limiting the requirement that defendants reimburse a plaintiff's lawyers fees and costs regardless of scale, including Conditional Fee Agreements and so-called 'success fees', especially insofar as these may have forced defendant publications to settle without airing valid defences. The ability to resolve cases through enhanced pleading requirements (eg, requiring a plaintiff to make some preliminary showing of falsity and absence of ordinary journalistic standards) might also be considered.

15.538 These suggestions appear to be influenced by US law and do not directly derive from Article 19 or the Comments on it. It is doubtful whether either a 'public figure' defence or an actual malice requirement can be derived from Article 19 of the Covenant, particularly bearing in mind the express protection against attacks on 'honour and reputation' provided for by Article 17.

(6) India

15.539 By Article 19 the Constitution of India provides:

(1) All citizens shall have the right—

[1524] *Ballantyne v Canada* (Case 358/89), para 11.3.
[1525] *Kivenmaa v Finland* (Case 412/90); but not graffiti on road signs; *SG v France* (Case 347/88).
[1526] *MA v Italy* (Case 117/81).
[1527] (1997) 2 BHRC 1.
[1528] See App J in Vol 2.
[1529] See also *X v Germany* (1982) 29 DR 194, E Comm HR (in which the Commission declared inadmissible a complaint under Art 10 of the Convention against a prohibition on the display and sale of brochures arguing that the Holocaust was a Zionist fabrication).
[1529a] 5 May 1993. Communications Nos 359/1989 and 385/1989; see also *Singer v Canada* Communication No 455/91.
[1530] CCPR/C/GBR/CO/6, 30 July 2008, para 25.

(a) to freedom of speech and expression . . .

Nothing in sub-clause (a) of clause (1) shall affect the operation of any existing law, or prevent the State from making any law, in so far as such law imposes reasonable restrictions on the exercise of the right conferred by the said sub-clause in the interests of the sovereignty and integrity of India, the security of the State, friendly relations with foreign States, public order, decency or morality, or in relation to contempt of court, defamation or incitement to an offence.[1531]

Freedom of expression is a 'preferred right which is always very zealously guarded by the court'.[1532] In the context of Article 19(2), 'reasonableness' is applied to each individual statute impugned and no abstract standard can be laid down: **15.540**

The nature of the right alleged to have been infringed, the underlying purpose of the restrictions imposed, the extent and urgency of the evil sought to be remedied thereby, the disproportion of the imposition, the prevailing conditions at the time, should all enter into the judicial verdict.[1533]

A law which prohibits the circulation of a newspaper in a particular area[1534] or seeks to control the size of a newspaper[1535] will be contrary to Article 19. In *Rajagopal v State of Tamil Nadu JT*[1536] the Supreme Court held that under Article 19 the state had no authority in law to impose prior restraint on publishing which defamed its officials. They went on to hold that: **15.541**

government, local authority and other organs and institutions exercising governmental powers . . . cannot maintain a suit for damages for defaming them.[1537]

The Indian courts have relied on Article 19(2) to uphold a provision which prohibited an election candidate from advocating voting (or not voting) for any person on the ground of his religion or community.[1538] The Court held that the words 'decency' and 'morality' in Article 19(2), which permits the freedom of expression to be limited, should not be confined to sexual morality alone. The Indian Constitution was explicitly secular. Further, promoting hatred between different classes of citizens tended to create public unrest and disturb public order. Given their influence, politicians had a particular duty to be circumspect in their language. **15.542**

(7) Ireland

Article 40.6.1 of the Irish Constitution provides that: **15.543**

The State guarantees liberty for the exercise, subject to public order and morality, of . . .

i. The right of the citizen to express freely their convictions and opinions.

[1531] See generally H M Seervai, *Constitutional Law of India* (4th edn, N M Tripathi Ltd, 1991), Chap 10; and S Kulshreshtha, *Fundamental Rights and the Supreme Court* (Rawat Publications, 1995), 119–131.
[1532] *Odyssey Communication Pvt Lted v Lokvidyavan Sansthan* (1988) 3 SCC 410, 414, para 5; see also *Ramesh Thappar v State of Madras* AIR 1950 SC 124.
[1533] *Madras v V G Row* [1952] SCR 597, 607.
[1534] *Ramesh Thappar v State of Madras* AIR 1950 SC 124.
[1535] *Benett Coleman & Co v Union of India* Air 1973 SC 106.
[1536] (1995) 82 AIR (SC) 264.
[1537] Ibid, 582c.
[1538] *Dr Ramesh Yeshwant Prabhoo v Prabhakar Kashinath* (1996) 1 SCC 130.

> The education of public opinion being, however, a matter of such grave import to the common good, the State shall endeavour to ensure that organs of public opinion, such as the radio, the press, the cinema while preserving their rightful liberty of expression, including criticism of Government policy, shall not be used to undermine public order or morality or the authority of the State.
>
> The publication or utterance of blasphemous, seditious, or indecent matter is an offence, which shall be punishable in accordance with law.

The precise scope of the protections to be found in this article is controversial.[1539]

15.544   A number of 'limitations' on freedom of expression for reasons of 'public order and morality' have been recognized. It is clear that there is a restriction in the interests of 'state security'[1540] and the protection of official secrets.[1541] This extends to protection of the authority of the courts from the publication of 'scandalous' material and from material tending to obstruct the course of justice.

15.545   Freedom of expression is also restricted in the interest of an individual's right to reputation.[1542] In *Hynes-O'Sullivan v O'Driscoll*[1543] the Supreme Court rejected the argument that the constitutional guarantee of freedom of speech meant that qualified privilege should be recognized in a situation in which the defendant honestly but wrongly believed that the person to whom the communication was made had a right to receive it. However, in *Hunter v Gerald Duckworth & Co*[1544] the High Court held that the approach of the House of Lords in *Reynolds v Times Newspapers*[1545] should be adopted in Ireland as the best way to protect the constitutional rights. In *Evans v Carlyle*[1546] the High Court granted an interim injunction to restrain the continuing publication of a defamatory banner, despite the fact that the defendant stated that he proposed to justify at trial. The judge said that

> Against the defendant's freedom to express himself, protected by Article 40.6.1 of the Constitution, . . . plaintiff claims his right to have his good name protected and vindicated as the state is required to do under Article 40.3.2. It is the difficulty of balancing or harmonising these sometimes conflicting rights that has given rise to the description of this particular jurisdiction as one 'of a delicate nature'. Nowadays this rather quaint description might better be expressed as 'of a particularly difficult nature'.

Taking all the circumstances into account, this was an appropriate case for an injunction.

15.546   A broadcasting ban on advertisements with a religious or political aim, or in relation to any industrial dispute, was upheld in *Murphy v IRTC*.[1547] In relation to the challenge based on freedom of religion, the court observed that the ban did not constitute discrimination on

---

[1539] See G W Hogan and G F Whyte, *J M Kelly's: The Irish Constitution* (4rd edn, Butterworths Ireland, 2003) paras 7.5.08 to 7.5.17, 1726–1730.

[1540] Although not to the interest of other states, see *A-G for England and Wales v Brandon Book Publishers* [1986] IR 597.

[1541] See generally, Kelly (n 1539 above) paras 7.5.20ff.

[1542] Protected by Art 40.3.2.

[1543] [1988] IR 436.

[1544] [2003] IEHC 8.

[1545] [2001] 2 AC 127, see para 15.65ff above.

[1546] [2008] IEHC 143.

[1547] [1997] 2 ILRM 467.

the ground of religious belief: as it operated regardless of the particular religion involved. Moreover, to the extent that the ban was a breach of freedom of expression, it was justified. Irish people with religious beliefs tended to belong to different churches, and religious advertising from a different church could be regarded as proselytizing or offensive.[1548]

Freedom of expression issues have arisen in the context of Article 40.3.1 of the Irish Constitution, which provides that: **15.547**

> The State guarantees in its laws to respect, and, as far as is practicable, by its laws to defend and vindicate the personal rights of the citizen.

That Article has been held to include the right to communicate.[1549] The courts have held that it is a justifiable restriction on that right for prisoners' letters to be read by prison staff, but the non-delivery of mail to prisoners as a result of a strike by the prison staff was a breach of that right.[1550]

(8) Namibia

By Article 21(1)(a) of the Constitution of Namibia, all persons have the right to 'freedom of speech and expression, which shall include freedom of the press and other media'. In *Kauesa v Minister of Home Affairs*[1551] the Supreme Court struck down a police regulation that prevented police officers from publicly criticizing the Government. That regulation had been used to penalize a police officer for publicly commenting unfavourably about the affirmative action policies of the police force. The court noted that the police have the same rights of freedom of speech as ordinary citizens; but accepted that that right had to be balanced against the interest of the police in maintaining discipline. However, there was no rational connection between the impugned regulation and that aim. The Court also noted that the fact that some of the appellant's comments were insulting or defamatory or rendered him criminally liable did not automatically deprive him of his right to free speech. **15.548**

(9) Sri Lanka

(a) Introduction

Article 14(1)(a) of the Constitution of Sri Lanka provides that: **15.549**

> Every citizen is entitled to the freedom of speech and expression including publication.[1552]

Article 15(7) permits such restrictions to the right as may be prescribed by law, in the interests of national security, public order and the protection of public health or morality, or for the purpose of securing due recognition and respect for the rights and freedoms of others, or of meeting the just requirements of general welfare in a democratic society. There must be proximate and reasonable nexus between the restriction and the object sought to be

---

[1548] See also *Colgan v IRTC* [1999] 1 ILRM (broadcasting ban applied to group lobbying for change in abortion laws).

[1549] *Attorney-General v Paperlink Ltd* [1984] ILRM 343.

[1550] *Kearney v Minister for Justice* [1986] IR 116.

[1551] [1995] 3 LRC 528.

[1552] See generally, J Wickramaratne, *Fundamental Rights in Sri Lanka* (Navrang, 1996), Chap 7; S Sharvananda, *Fundamental Rights in Sri Lanka* (Arnold's International Printing House, 1993), Chap XII.

achieved by the restriction. Article 15(2) also permits such restrictions as may be prescribed by law in the interests of racial and religious harmony or in relation to parliamentary privilege, contempt of court, defamation or incitement to offence. Freedom of the recipient is included within the freedom of speech and expression. Thus, regular readers of a newspaper which had been banned by emergency regulations had standing to seek relief.[1553]

(b) Public order

15.550 A number of cases have been brought raising issues about freedom of expression. In *Joseph Perera's* case,[1554] a regulation which provided that nobody could distribute leaflets or handbills without police permission was struck down, as giving unguided and unfettered discretion to police. The police regulation of a public meeting was held to be a breach of freedom of expression in *Mohottige v Gunatilleke*.[1555] The organizers of the meeting applied for a police permit to use loudspeakers at the public meeting. The police asked for the names of the speakers, and then issued a permit subject to two conditions, that only the named speakers would be permitted to speak, and that the speakers should refrain from criticizing the Government, any organization, or any individual. The Supreme Court held that both conditions violated the freedom of speech and expression. The Court noted that demanding the names of people beforehand can have the effect of silencing people who may otherwise wish to contribute to proceedings by participating.

(c) Defamation

15.551 The case of *A-G v Siriwardana*[1556] arose out of a defamation case where a newspaper criticized the speech of an MP in Parliament, likening MPs in general to bulls and donkeys. The Supreme Court found the remarks to be defamatory, and rejected the newspaper's defence of fair comment. The Supreme Court did not decide the question of whether the defence of fair comment was available, as the newspaper had not engaged in fair criticism. Likewise, a newspaper which contained a false statement concerning a Supreme Court trial, was penalized.[1557] The Court held that the publication was deliberate and wilful, holding the Court to odium and an undue interference with the administration of justice.[1558]

(d) Media regulation

15.552 In *Siriwardena v Liyanage*[1559] the closure of a newspaper was upheld on the basis that its contents were likely to inflame sections of the community to violence and breaches of the peace, and thereby endanger the maintenance of law and order.[1560] The constitutionality of the establishment of a Sri Lankan Broadcasting Authority was considered in *Athukorale v*

[1553] *Visvalingam v Liyanage* [1985] LRC Const 909.
[1554] *Perera v A-G* [1992] 1 Sri LR 199.
[1555] (1992) 2 Sri LR 246.
[1556] (1978–79–80) 1 Sri LR 377.
[1557] *In the matter of a rule on De Souza* [1916] 18 NLR 41.
[1558] See also *Hulugalle's Case* [1937–39] 39–40 NLR 294 (article which imputed to Supreme Court judge serious breach of duty by taking an unauthorized holiday for the purposes of going to race meetings was disrespectful; press criticism of administration of justice should be honest and in good faith, and not step beyond its bounds).
[1559] [1985] LRC Const 909.
[1560] See also *Visvalingam v Liayanage* FRD (2) 310.

A-G of Sri Lanka.[1561] It decided that the existence of such an authority was not, of itself, a breach of Article 14.[1562] However, it was held that such an authority had to be independent of the Government. Since the proposed authority lacked independence and was susceptible to ministerial interference, the right of freedom of speech was placed in jeopardy.

(e) Other cases

The Sri Lankan Supreme Court held in *Karunaratne v Bandarnaike*[1563] that a member of a **15.553** political party has freedom of expression, and cannot be expelled from the party for voicing unpopular views. An MP had urged the party leadership to hold internal party elections for various party committees. When that course of action failed, he made a statement to a newspaper expressing concerns at the non-holding of elections by a party committed to democracy. The petitioner was expelled by the party after a disciplinary enquiry to which he refused to submit. The Supreme Court held that the petitioner's expulsion was unlawful. While the Court accepted that freedom of speech may be limited by voluntarily joining a political association, the petitioner in this case had made every effort to obtain internal party change, before making a public statement. In the circumstances, his public statement was justified as having been made under the exercise of his freedom of speech and therefore guaranteed under the Constitution. His expulsion was therefore invalid.

(10) Trinidad and Tobago

Section 4 of the Constitution of Trinidad and Tobago recognizes a number of 'fundamental **15.554** human rights and freedoms' including "the right to join political parties and express political views' (section 4(e)) and of 'thought and expression' (section 4(i)). Although there is no constitutional right to establish a broadcasting state, where there had been a failure to ensure the efficient, objective and non-discriminatory handling of licence applications, securing the speedy grant of licences where appropriate and thereby also securing the constitutional right to freedom of expression, an applicant's freedom of expression could be said to have been infringed.[1564]

The purpose of the law of defamation is to hold a balance between freedom of speech and **15.555** the right to reputation. Section 4(e) cannot be read as permitting the expression of any political views provided that the speaker was honest. As a result, the Prime Minister was liable in defamation for making a speech accusing a businessman of racism in circumstances where he did not exercise reasonable care to establish the truth of the allegation.[1565]

[1561] (1997) 2 BHRC 610.
[1562] Relying, inter alia, on *Groppera Radio AG v Switzerland* (1990) 12 EHRR 321 and *Informationseverein Lentia v Austria* (1993) 17 EHRR 93.
[1563] [1993] 2 Sri LR 90.
[1564] *Central Broadcasting Services Ltd v Attorney General* [2007] 2 LRC 19; relying on *Observer Publications Ltd v Matthew* [2001] 4 LRC 288 and *Benjamin v Minister of Information and Broadcasting* [2001] 4 LRC 272.
[1565] *Panday v Gordon* [2006] 3 LRC 252 (PC).

INDEX

Convention rights and freedoms are indexed under
subject e.g. **family life, right to** and **expression,
freedom of.**

Abbreviations used in the subheadings are as follows:-

ECHR – European Convention on Human Rights

HRA – Human Rights Act 1998

RIPA – Regulation of Investigatory Powers Act 2000

abortion 12.272

abuse of power
secret surveillance 12.338

access to documents *see* **documents**

access to information *see* **personal information**

access to medical records 12.282, 12.355, 12.386

access to personal information 12.73–12.77

access to public property 15.458–15.459

admissibility 12.490

adoption records 12.77

advertisements
Australia 15.522
broadcasting 15.177, 15.546
children 15.454
commercial expression 15.223–15.224,
15.294–15.295, 15.453–15.456
freedom of expression 15.223–15.224,
15.294–15.295, 15.406–15.407
Hong Kong 15.530
Ireland 15.546
political 15.177, 15.522, 15.546
professions 15.455, 15.530
property 15.459
religious 15.375A
tobacco 15.456

aerial photography 12.149, 12.508

age of consent
homosexuals 12.380

anti-social behaviour
possession order 12.368, 12.416
Scotland 12.419–12.422
surveillance 12.377

Antigua and Barbuda 15.519–15.521

Anton Piller **orders** 12.366

appeals
contempt of court 15.89
reporting restrictions 15.116
video classification 15.185

armed forces
freedom of expression 15.509
sexual orientation 12.206, 12.382
South Africa 15.509

arrest
freedom of expression 15.367
proportionality 15.367

artificial reproduction *see* **medically assisted
reproduction**

artistic expression 15.287–15.289

assisted reproduction *see* **medically assisted
reproduction**

assisted suicide 12.363, 12.397

association, freedom of
breach of the peace 15.258, 15.260

asylum seekers
privacy 12.428
welfare of detainees 12.220

Australia
advertising 15.522
defamation 15.523–15.524
elections 15.522
expression, freedom of 15.522–15.526
law breaking, advocacy of 15.526
political expression 15.522
privacy 12.509–12.510

bankrupts
privacy of correspondence 12.77C

BBC 15.172, 15.176

blasphemy
blasphemous libel 15.389
ECHR 15.387–15.391
expression, freedom of 15.374, 15.387–15.391
margin of appreciation 15.387, 15.390

bodily/DNA samples 12.385A

breach of confidence
Bonnard v *Perryman* rule 15.30–15.31
employment 12.401
expression, freedom of 15.30–15.35,
15.217–15.218, 15.331–15.333,
15.378–15.379
HRA 12.24, 15.35
injunctions 15.30–15.34
journalists' sources 15.379
marital secrets 12.23
media 15.331–15.333
medical information 12.23
official secrets 15.217–15.218
prevention of crime 12.362
prior restraint 15.32–15.35
privacy 12.22–12.25
public bodies *see* **disclosure**
public domain information 12.39–12.40

371

breach of confidence (*cont.*)
   public interest 12.45–12.48, 15.379
   sexual conduct 12.47
   Spycatcher litigation 15.31–15.34
   surveillance 12.146
   'three part test' 12.22
   untrue information 12.34
   wrong doing, revealing 12.46–12.47
breach of contract 15.29
breach of the peace
   association 15.258, 15.260
   expression, freedom of 15.196, 15.258,
      15.260, 15.400, 15.424
   protestors 15.196, 15.400, 15.424
broadcasting
   access to broadcast time 15.251
   advertising 15.177, 15.546
   BBC 15.172, 15.176
   Broadcasting Standards Commission 12.97,
      15.173
   censorship 15.176
   Code 15.174–15.175
   courts 15.176
   DA Notice system 15.178–15.181
   expression, freedom of 15.171–15.177, 15.251,
      15.262–15.265, 15.498
   Fairness Committee 12.98
   independent 15.173
   Independent Broadcasting Authority 15.172
   Independent Radio Authority 15.173
   Independent Television Commission 15.173
   Ireland 15.546
   judicial oversight 12.102
   monopolies 15.266
   New Zealand Bill of Rights 15.498
   Ofcom 12.98–12.102, 15.173–15.175
   political advertising 15.177
   prior restraint 15.414
   privacy 12.439
   public 15.173
   radio 12.97
   regulation 12.97–12.102, 15.171–15.177
   satellite television 15.252
   television 12.97, 15.252
burden of proof
   defamation 15.52, 15.58

Canadian Charter of Rights
   access to public property 15.458–15.459
   advertising 15.453–15.456, 15.459
   children 15.454
   commercial expression 15.453–15.458
   contempt 15.437–15.438
   criminal libel 15.436
   defamation 15.434–15.436
   documents 12.458–12.460
   elections 15.465–15.466

   employment 15.463
   expression, freedom of 12.439, 15.426–15.466
      justification for restrictions 15.427
      limitation clause 15.429–15.430
      types of restrictions 15.432–15.466
      value of expression 15.431
   goods 12.445–12.446
   images 12.438
   New Zealand Bill of Rights and 12.476,
      12.478
   obscenity 15.430, 15.447–15.450
   picketing 15.460–15.462
   police 15.452
   political process, restrictions on 15.464–15.466
   pornography 15.430, 15.447–15.450
   privacy 12.435–12.471
      reasonable expectation 12.445–12.452
   professions 15.455
   proportionality 15.429–15.430
   public authorities 15.463
   public interest 12.439
   racial hatred 15.451
   reasonableness 12.445–12.452
   referenda 15.464
   reporting restrictions 15.439–15.446
   scandalizing the court 15.437–15.438
   search 12.440–12.443, 12.447–12.448
   seizure 12.440–12.443, 12.447–12.448,
      12.453–12.456
   surveillance 12.449–12.452
   telephone tapping 12.451
   third parties 12.447
   tobacco advertising 15.456
CCTV 12.139, 12.145, 12.279, 12.396
censorship
   BBC 15.176
   DA Notices 15.178–15.181
   expression, freedom of 15.170–15.187
   films 15.182–15.187, 15.390
   media 15.170–15.187
   theatres 15.182
   videos 15.185–15.187, 15.390, 15.492–15.493
census records 12.282
children and young persons
   advertising 15.454
   detention 12.333
   Gillick competency 12.215
   imprisonment 12.333
   medical treatment 12.215, 12.398
   medically assisted reproduction *see* **medically
      assisted reproduction**
   obscenity 15.164–15.165
   paternity
      transsexuals 12.291
   reporting restrictions 15.131–15.140, 15.441,
      15.444–15.445, 15.489–15.490
   sexual offences 15.441, 15.444–15.445

civil proceedings
    contempt of court 15.90
    reporting restrictions 15.105–15.112
      see also **reporting restrictions**
civil rights 12.27
    see also **International Covenant on Civil and Political Rights**
civil servants
    expression, freedom of 15.286, 15.374A, 15.376, 15.410
    political expression 15.286, 15.374A, 15.376, 15.410
closed circuit television 12.139, 12.145, 12.279, 12.396
codes of practice
    broadcasting 15.174–15.175
    media 12.91, 12.94–12.95
    Ofcom Code 12.99–12.102
    Standards Board for England 15.225–15.226
commercial expression 15.375, 15.406–15.407
    advertisements 15.223–15.224, 15.453–15.456
    Canadian Charter of Rights 15.453–15.458
    ECHR 15.290–15.296, 15.302
    see also **advertisements**
common law
    contempt of court 15.81
    defamation 15.435
    expression, freedom of 15.06–15.10, 15.301
    powers of entry 12.130
    privacy 12.13
    seizure 12.135–12.136
    surveillance 12.146–12.150
companies
    defamation 15.54, 15.343
    privacy 12.235
compensation, criminal injuries 12.426
compulsory purchase 12.199
conditional fees
    defamation cases 15.229, 15.537
confidentiality *see* **breach of confidence**
confiscation
    housing 12.195, 12.415
    proceeds of crime 12.415
conscience *see* **religion, thought and conscience, freedom of conscientious objectors**
consent
    Gillick competence 12.215
    medical treatment 12.210–12.213, 12.215
conspiracy to corrupt public morals 15.156–15.157, 15.161
conspiracy to injure
    expression, freedom of 15.41
    injunctions 15.30
contaminated land 12.433
contempt of court
    advance clearance 15.48
    appeals 15.89

    Canadian Charter of Rights 15.437–15.438
    civil 15.81, 15.90
    classification of 15.81
    common law 15.81
    criminal 15.81, 15.83, 15.89, 15.392, 15.437, 15.482
    ECHR 15.87, 15.392–15.395
    expression, freedom of 15.80–15.103, 15.392–15.395, 15.437–15.438, 15.482
    Hong Kong 15.532
    impartiality, imputation 15.99
    injunctions 15.45–15.48, 15.392
    innocent publication defence 15.91
    intentional 15.93–15.96
    journalistic sources, protection of 15.145, 15.393
    judiciary 15.97–15.100, 15.437–15.438, 15.532
    jury deliberations 15.101–15.102, 15.395
    legislation 15.87–15.93
    meaning 15.80
    media 15.83–15.100
    New Zealand Bill of Rights 15.482
    Phillimore Committee 15.86
    prejudicing or impeding proceedings 15.84–15.96, 15.420–15.422
    prior restraint 15.45–15.48, 15.483
    proportionality 15.393–15.394
    scandalizing the court 15.97–15.100, 15.437–15.438, 15.532
    Scotland 15.415–15.418
    South Africa 15.511–15.512
    strict liability 15.84, 15.86–15.92
    sub judice 15.84–15.96
    tribunals 15.82
contracts of employment 12.81
conversion of goods 12.121
copyright 15.29, 15.230–15.233, 15.235
corporations *see* **companies**
correspondence
    bankrupt's 12.77C
    interception of 12.150–12.151
    interference with 12.314–12.319, 12.360–12.361, 12.365, 12.371
    postal 12.314–12.319, 12.332, 12.360–12.361, 12.365, 12.371
    prisoners' rights 12.314–12.319, 12.333, 12.360–12.361, 12.365, 12.371
    screening 12.315, 12.319
    supervision 12.327, 12.333, 12.361
    privileged material 12.347–12.348
    searches and seizures 12.320
    solicitors 12.315, 12.347, 12.360–12.361, 12.371
corruption of public morals 15.156–15.157, 15.161
costs
    conditional fees 15.229, 15.537
    expression cases 15.229

Council of Europe 15.307
courts
   defamation 15.61
   expression, freedom of 15.07
   privacy 12.09–12.10
covert surveillance 12.165–12.169, 12.406,
   12.409–12.410
   RIPA 12.169
   workplace monitoring 12.82
criminal injuries compensation 12.426
criminal law
   contempt of court 15.81, 15.89, 15.437–15.438
   criminalization of private acts 12.331, 12.381,
     12.507
   expression, freedom of 15.19, 15.188–15.211
   obscenity 15.158
   privacy 12.229, 12.262
   see also **criminal proceedings**
criminal libel 15.192–15.195, 15.436
   politicians 15.313, 15.321–15.322
criminal proceedings
   severity of penalty 15.314
   criminal injuries compensation 12.426
   penalties, severity of 15.314
   pre-trial publicity 15.420–15.422
criminalization of private acts 12.331, 12.381,
   12.499, 12.507

DA Notices 15.178–15.181
damages
   criminal injuries compensation 12,426
   defamation 15.69–15.72, 15.104,
     15.396–15.397, 15.531
   expression, freedom of 15.20
   juries 15.69–15.72, 15.531
data protection 12.60–12.72
   adoption records 12.77
   data controller 12.66–12.67, 12.69
   data protection principles 12.65
   data subject's rights 12.66–12.67
   exemptions 12.68, 12.74–12.75
   fee for information 12.67
   filing system 12.64
   individual rights 12.66–12.67
   Information Commissioner 12.69, 12.145
   Information Tribunal 12.69–12.71
   personal information 12.60–12.62,
     12.73–12.77
   photographs 12.144
   Police National Computer 12.72
   privacy 12.60–12.72
   public authorities 12.60
   types of data 12.64
   Younger Committee 12.62
defamation 15.192–15.195
   Australia 15.523–15.524
   Bonnard v *Perryman* rule 15.26–15.29

burden of proof of truth 15.52, 15.58
Canadian Charter of Rights 15.434–15.436
claimants 15.54–15.55
common law 15.435
companies 15.54, 15.343
conditional fees 15.229, 15.537
courts 15.61
criminal libel 15.192–15.195, 15.313,
   15.321–15.322, 15.436
damages 15.69–15.72, 15.104, 15.396–15.397,
   15.531
declaration of falsity 15.73–15.74
ECHR 15.75–15.77, 15.371–15.377,
   15.396–15.398
English law 15.49–15.74
fair comment 15.56, 15.59
funding actions 15.229, 15.397–15.398
governments 15.373
Hong Kong 15.529, 15.531
injunctions 15.26, 15.72, 15.478
Ireland 15.545
juries 15.51, 15.69–15.72, 15.531
justification 15.26, 15.56–15.58
legal aid 15.397–15.398
libel *see* **libel**
local authorities 15.55
malice 15.60, 15.64, 15.434
meaning 15.51–15.53
media *see* **media**
New Zealand Bill of Rights 15.477–15.481
offer to make amends 15.71
other causes of action 15.29
parliament
   immunities 15.61
   privilege 15.479
politicians 15.313, 15.321–15.322,
   15.326–15.329, 15.372
prior restraint 15.26–15.29
privacy 12.34, 12.391–12.394, 12.505
private individuals 15.333–15.336
privilege
   absolute 15.56, 15.61
   parliamentary 15.479
   qualified 15.56, 15.62–15.68, 15.398,
     15.434, 15.523–15.524
public authorities/bodies 15.55, 15.330,
   15.434
public interest 15.56, 15.59, 15.434, 15.480
remedies 15.69–15.74
reputation 15.49–15.50, 15.52, 15.74,
   15.313, 15.341, 15.346, 15.371,
   15.436, 15.478
single publication rule 15.398
slander 15.53
South Africa 15.501–15.505
Sri Lanka 15.551
standing 15.54–15.55

defences
innocent publication 15.91
public good 15.160
public interest 15.216
democratic society, necessary in 15.12, 15.278,
  15.306–15.309
privacy 12.341–12.343
deportation
family life and 12.224, 12.225–12.226
detainees, welfare of 12.220
disabled persons, facilities for 12.255
disclosure 12.284, 12.461–12.463
crime prevention 12.362
criminal conduct
HIV status 12.505
medical information 12.56–12.59
personal information 12.55
presumptions in favour 12.51
public authorities/bodies 12.49–12.59
discretion 12.339, 12.513
discrimination
dismissal, unfair 12.86–12.87
DNA samples 12.385A
documents
access to 12.254, 12.386
collection 12.458–12.460
recovery, from civil proceedings 12.434
seizure 12.137
see also **privacy**
dress codes
employment 12.85
religious belief 12.85
drugs
prisoners' rights 12.372

elections
Australia 15.522
Canadian Charter of Rights 15.465–15.466
expenses 15.205
expression, freedom of 15.205, 15.282, 15.409
India 15.542
employment
Canadian Charter of Rights 15.463
confidential information 12.401
contracts 12.81
dismissal 12.86–12.87
dress codes 12.85
employment tribunals 15.120
expression, freedom of 15.246, 15.260, 15.509
monitoring *see* workplace monitoring
privacy 12.78–12.90, 12.257, 12.300, 12.321,
  12.401, 12.437
private conduct 12.85–12.88
public authorities 15.463
religious belief
  dress code 12.85
residence 12.437

sexual orientation discrimination 12.90
South Africa 15.509
suspected criminal conduct 12.54
telephone calls 12.257, 12.321
unfair dismissal
  privacy 12.86–12.87
waiver of Convention rights 12.81, 12.85
workplace monitoring 12.79–12.84,
  12.138–12.141, 12.257, 12.279, 12.406
employment tribunals
reporting restrictions 15.120
environment
contaminated land 12.433
economic well-being of country 12.351, 12.353,
  12.391–12.393
pollution and the home 12.310
privacy 12.259, 12.310–12.312, 12.351, 12.357,
  12.368, 12.433
European Convention on Human Rights (ECHR)
artistic expression 15.287–15.289
blasphemy 15.387–15.391
commercial expression 15.290–15.296,
  15.302
contempt of court 15.87, 15.392–15.395
defamation 15.75–15.77, 15.371–15.377,
  15.396–15.398
expression, freedom of 15.06, 15.236–15.411
licensing 15.262–15.265, 15.272
media 15.253–15.254
national security 15.403–15.405
obscenity 15.387–15.391
opinions, right to hold 15.248–15.252
political expression 15.282–15.286, 15.297
prisoners' rights 15.220–15.227
privacy 12.01, 12.234–12.369
evidence
admissibility 12.490
collection of 12.453–12.458
irregularly obtained 12.407–12.412
seizure 12.136
see also **witnesses**
expression, freedom of 15.01–15.555
advance clearance 15.48
advertising 15.177, 15.223–15.224, 15.235,
  15.294–15.295, 15.375A, 15.406–15.407,
  15.453–15.456, 15.522, 15.530, 15.546
  see also **advertisements**
Antigua and Barbuda 15.519–15.521
armed forces 15.509
arrest 15.367
artistic expression 15.287–15.289
association and 15.258, 15.260
Australia 15.522–15.526
blasphemous libel 15.389
blasphemy *see* **blasphemy**
breach of confidence *see* **breach of confidence**
breach of contract 15.29

evidence (*cont.*)
  breach of the peace 15.196, 15.258, 15.260,
    15.400, 15.424
  broadcasting
    licensing 15.262–15.265, 15.272
    New Zealand Bill of Rights 15.498
    regulation 15.171–15.177
    right to time for 15.251
  Canadian Charter of Rights 12.439,
    15.426–15.466
  censorship 15.170–15.187
  civil servants 15.286, 15.374A, 15.376, 15.410
  claimants 15.238
  commercial expression *see* **commercial expression**
  common law 15.06–15.10, 15.301
  conditional fee agreements 15.229, 15.537
  conspiracy to injure 15.41
  contempt *see* **contempt of court**
  Convention rights 15.247–15.261
  copyright law 15.29, 15.230–15.233, 15.235
  costs 15.229
  Council of Europe 15.250, 15.307
  court proceedings 15.384
  courts 15.07, 15.19, 15.439–15.446
  crime prevention 15.365–15.368
  criminal law 15.19, 15.188–15.211
  criminal libel 15.192–15.195, 15.313,
    15.321–15.322, 15.436
    politicians 15.313, 15.321–15.322
  damages 15.20
  defamation *see* **defamation**
  definition 15.16, 15.241, 15.428, 15.432
  disorder, prevention of 15.365–15.368
  duties and responsibilities 15.279–15.280
  ECHR 15.06, 15.236–15.411
  elections 15.205, 15.282, 15.409
  employment 15.246, 15.260, 15.509
  English law 15.07–15.24
  European Union law 15.234–15.235
  'everyone' 15.238
  exceptions 15.09
  exclusion from UK 15.14
  expression
    content 15.242–15.243
    definition 15.241
    types 15.281–15.292
    value 15.431
  facts 15.247, 15.314, 15.316–15.320
    verification 15.312
  'glorifying terrorism' 15.207
  government, criticism of 15.373
  harassment 15.43–15.44, 15.204
  hate speech 15.244–15.245, 15.513
  health 15.235, 15.369–15.370
  Holocaust denial 15.451, 15.535
  Hong Kong 15.527–15.532
  HRA 15.11–15.24

Human Rights Committee 15.533–15.538
hunting 15.423
indecency 15.161–15.168
India 15.539–15.542
information
  freedom of 15.227–15.228
  public domain, in 15.49, 15.330
  right to impart 15.248–15.252, 15.470
  see also **information**
injunctions 15.19–15.20, 15.32–15.34, 15.361
innocent publication defence 15.207
interference with right 15.237–15.238, 15.258,
    15.260, 15.267–15.272
  examples 15.272
  justification 15.12, 15.203, 15.273–15.285,
    15.427
  legitimate aims 15.305, 15.359–15.385
  national law 15.300
  necessary in a democratic society 15.12,
    15.278, 15.306–15.309
  prescribed by law 15.299–15.304
International Covenant on Civil and Political
    Rights 15.02
Ireland 15.543–15.547
journalists' sources *see* **journalists' sources,
    protection of**
judiciary 15.261, 15.380–15.383
jury deliberations 15.101–15.102, 15.395
lawyers in court 15.384
margin of appreciation 15.14, 15.239, 15.277,
    15.308–15.309, 15.369
media 15.310–15.358, 15.541
  press freedom 15.10, 15.15, 15.18,
    15.253–15.254, 15.413
  regulation 15.170–15.187
  see also **media**
morality 15.369–15.370
Namibia 15.548
national security 15.360–15.363, 15.403–15.405
New Zealand Bill of Rights 15.467–15.498
obscenity *see* **obscenity; pornography**
offences restricting 15.203–15.207
official secrets 15.212–15.216, 15.544
opinions, right to hold 15.248–15.252
parliamentary privilege 15.61
parliamentary proceedings 15.07
penalties, severity of 15.314
picketing 15.41, 15.433, 15.438, 15.460–15.462
police powers 15.208–15.211, 15.452, 15.495
political advertising 15.177, 15.522, 15.546
political expression *see* **political expression**
political parties 15.553
politicians
  criminal libel 15.313, 15.321–15.322
  defamation 15.326–15.329, 15.372
  private life 15.323–15.325
pornography *see* **obscenity; pornography**

positive obligations 15.255–15.256, 15.402
pre-trial publicity 15.420–15.422
press freedom 15.10, 15.15, 15.18,
    15.253–15.254, 15.413
prior restraint 15.25–15.35, 15.268–15.269,
    15.412–15.414, 15.433, 15.475, 15.483
prisoners' rights 15.220–15.227, 15.547
privacy 12.12, 12.439, 15.496–15.497
private information 15.36–15.39
    misuse 15.78–15.79
proportionality 15.219, 15.367, 15.429–15.430
protests 15.196–15.199, 15.399–15.402
    breach of the peace 15.196, 15.400, 15.424
    designated areas 15.206
    public order 15.197–15.199
public authorities 15.08, 15.463
public domain 15.49, 15.330
public enquiries 15.228
public interest 15.13, 15.22, 15.237, 15.471
public life, conduct in 15.225–15.226
public order 15.197–15.202, 15.550
public property, access to 15.458–15.459
public servants 15.286
racial hatred 15.200–15.202, 15.244,
    15.451, 15.494
religious belief 15.374, 15.375A
remedies 15.19–15.24
'reportage' 15.347–15.350
reporting restrictions *see* **reporting restrictions**
reputation *see* **reputation**
restrictions, types of 15.432–15.466
role of 15.01
sanctions 15.270–15.271
satellites 15.252
Scotland 15.412–15.425
seditious libel 15.190–15.191
seizure 15.208–15.211
South Africa 15.499–15.513
Sri Lanka 15.559–15.553
success fees 15.229, 15.537
territorial integrity 15.364
terrorism 15.362–15.363, 15.365, 15.404
threshold test 15.21
trademark infringement 15.29, 15.42
Trinidad and Tobago 15.554–15.555
UK cases in Strasbourg 15.386–15.411
uniforms 15.517
United States 15.02–15.03, 15.25,
    15.514–15.518
values 15.247, 15.314, 15.316–15.320
extradition 12.227, 12.429–12.440

fair trial
anonymity
    of parties 15.121–15.127, 15.133
    of witnesses 15.128–15.130, 15.142
civil rights 12.27

contempt 15.482
    see also **contempt of court**
    New Zealand Bill of Rights 15.482
    pre-trial publicity 15.420–15.422
    prejudicing 15.420–15.422
    see also **prejudice**
family life, right to
deportation 12.224, 12.225–12.226
fertility treatment *see* **medically assisted**
    reproduction
Fiji 12.511–12.512
film censorship 15.182–15.187, 15.390
forfeiture of obscene material 15.159, 15.168
fox hunting *see* **hunting rights**
France 12.506
freedoms *see under subject e.g.* expression,
    freedom of

gender reassignment *see* **transsexuals**
    see also **margin of appreciation; proportionality**
Germany
    privacy 12.506
Gillick competence 12.215
gypsies
    homes 12.304, 12.390
    possession proceedings 12.189

harassment 15.43–15.44, 15.204
    media 12.94, 12.104, 12.178
    surveillance 12.146, 12.149, 12.178
hate speech 15.244–15.245, 15.513
HIV, disclosure of status 12.505
Holocaust denial 15.451, 15.535
home, respect for 12.117–12.137
    acquisition 12.182–12.183
    caravan 12.306
    civil procedure 12.403
    compulsory purchase 12.199
    confiscation orders 12.195, 12.415
    conversion 12.121
    criminal procedure 12.404
    English law 12.117–12.137
    existing home 12.182
    goods, interference with 12.121
    gypsies 12.304, 12.390
    holiday home 12.306
    'home' concept/meaning 12.180–12.181,
        12.305
    interference with 12.308–12.309
    intrusion into 12.06, 12.117–12.137
    land, interference with 12.120, 12.200
    leases 12.307
    licence to occupy 12.387
    limitations 12.117
    listed buildings 12.417
    noise 12.310–12.311
    planning 12.196–12.198, 12.201

home, respect for (*cont.*)
pollution 12.310
possession orders 12.369, 12.388, 12.416
powers of entry 12.117–12.118,
    12.122–12.129, 12.389
privacy 12.06
proportionality 12.387
retention of goods 12.132–12.137
right to home 12.303–12.312
Scotland 12.399–12.434
seizure 12.118, 12.132–12.137
trespass 12.120, 12.200
United States 12.508
work premises 12.306
see also **housing**
homosexuals *see* **sexual orientation discrimination**
Hong Kong Bill of Rights
advertisements 15.530
contempt of court 15.532
defamation 15.529, 15.531
expression, freedom of 15.527–15.532
privacy 12.513
public authorities 15.529
scandalizing the court 15.532
housing
acquisition 12.182–12.183
anti-social behaviour 12.368, 12.416
compulsory purchase 12.199
concept of home 12.180
confiscation orders 12.195, 12.415
English law 12.180–12.202
gypsies 12.189, 12.304, 12.390
listed buildings 12.417
local authorities 12.184–12.185
planning 12.196–12.198, 12.201
positive obligations 12.185
possession orders 12.369, 12.388,
    12.416
possession proceedings 12.186–12.194
privacy 12.184–12.185, 12.256
private landlords 12.194
provision of 12.256
social landlords 12.184–12.185
see also **home, respect for**
Human Rights Act 1998
breach of confidence 12.24, 15.35
margin of appreciation 15.14
    see also **margin of appreciation**
expression, freedom of 15.533–15.538
Holocaust denial 15.451, 15.535
privacy 12.514–12.516
press freedom 15.15, 15.18
privacy 12.11–12.13, 12.24
hunting rights
expression, freedom of 15.423
private life 12.17, 12.207, 12.427
Scotland 12.427, 15.423

images 12.438
immigration 12.224–12.228, 12.428
impartiality
contempt of court 15.99
judiciary 15.99, 15.261, 15.380–15.383
scandalizing the court 15.99
incitement to racial hatred *see* **racial hatred**
indecency 15.161–15.168
imports 15.168
licensing sex establishments 15.169
malicious communications 15.166
postal services 15.163
public electronic communications 15.167
see also **obscenity**
Independent Broadcasting Authority 15.172
Independent Radio Authority 15.173
Independent Television Commission 15.173
India
access to information 12.517
elections 15.542
expression, freedom of 15.539–15.542
media 15.541
privacy 12.517–12.518
telephone tapping 12.518
information
access to 12.74–12.75, 12.254
claimant 12.37–12.38
collection 12.281–12.283
data protection *see* **data protection**
disclosure *see* **disclosure**
freedom of 15.227–15.228
    access to personal information 12.74–12.75
    education 15.08, 15.544
    educational institutions 15.08, 15.544
    local authorities 15.227–15.228
    public authorities 15.227
    public enquiries 15.228
    see also **access to medical records**
freedom to impart 15.248–15.252, 15.470
how obtained 12.35–12.36
India 12.517
justification for privacy 12.41–12.48
marital 12.23
medical 12.23, 12.29, 12.56–12.59
nature of 12.29–12.34
New Zealand Bill of Rights 15.470
personal *see* **personal information**
privacy *see* **privacy**
private information
    access to 12.74–12.75
    misuse 12.06, 12.18, 12.26–12.77,
        12.105–12.107, 12.367,
        12.385–12.386, 12.400,
        12.507, 15.78–15.79
    publication 15.36–15.39
    public domain 12.39–12.40, 15.49, 15.330
    public interest 12.45–12.48

publication 12.12, 12.109–12.110, 12.285–12.287, 15.36–15.39
reasonable expectation of privacy 12.26, 12.27–12.28, 12.31, 12.33
recovery of documents 12.434
right to impart 15.248–15.252, 15.470
South Africa 12.504
trivial 12.31–12.33
United States 12.507
untrue 12.34
Information Commissioner 12.69, 12.145
injunctions
breach of confidence 15.32–15.34
conspiracy to injure 15.30
contempt 15.45–15.48, 15.392
contra mundum 12.116, 15.38
defamation 15.26, 15.72, 15.478
freedom of expression 15.19–15.20, 15.32–15.34, 15.361
media 12.111–12.113
national security 15.403
official secrets 15.217
picketing 15.460–15.461
privacy 12.12, 12.111–12.113, 15.37–15.39
insolvency
privacy of correspondence 12.77C
interception of communications
complaints 12.163–12.165
correspondence 12.150–12.151, 12.332
grounds 12.160–12.161
privacy 12.150–12.179
RIPA 12.160–12.165
warrant 12.162
see also **surveillance; telephone tapping**
Interception of Communications Tribunal 12.163–12.165
interference with Convention rights
expression, freedom of 15.237–15.238, 15.258, 15.260, 15.267–15.272
examples 15.272
justification 15.12, 15.203, 15.273–15.285, 15.427
legitimate aims 15.305, 15.359–15.385
national law 15.300
necessary in a democratic society 15.12, 15.278, 15.306–15.309
prescribed by law 15.299–15.304
privacy 12.07, 12.26, 12.41–12.48, 12.237, 12.324–12.369
by non-state bodies 12.258–12.263
by private individuals or organizations 12.03
by public authority 12.326–12.333
crime or disorder prevention 12.356–12.362
economic well-being of country 12.351–12.355
factors taken into account 12.44–12.48
in accordance with the law 12.334–12.340

justification 12.07, 12.26, 12.41–12.48, 12.237, 12.324–12.369
legitimate aims 12.350
necessary in a democratic society for a legitimate aim 12.341–12.343
procedural requirements 12.344–12.349
safeguards 12.344–12.349
threshold for 12.328
interference with Convention rights, justification
democratic society *see* **necessary in democratic society**
expression, freedom of 15.12, 15.203, 15.273–15.285, 15.299–15.305, 15.359–15.385, 15.427
legitimate aims *see* **legitimate aims, interference justification**
necessary *see* **necessary in democratic society**
prescribed by law *see* **prescribed by law**
privacy 12.07, 12.26, 12.41–12.48, 12.237, 12.324–12.369
International Covenant on Civil and Political Rights
expression, freedom of 15.02
privacy 12.02
Ireland
advertisements 15.546
broadcasting 15.546
defamation 15.545
expression, freedom of 15.543–15.547
prisoners' rights 15.547
privacy 12.519
religion, thought and conscience, freedom of 15.546
telephone tapping 12.519

journalistic material, seizure of 15.208–15.211
journalists' sources, protection of 15.145–15.152
breach of confidence 15.379
contempt of court 15.145, 15.393
crime or disorder, prevention of 15.147
disclosure 15.145–15.148, 15.351–15.354
exceptions 15.146–15.151
expression, freedom of 15.145–15.148, 15.351–15.354
interests of justice 15.148–15.151
national security 15.147
'newspaper rule' 15.145
pre-publication activities 15.353
proportionality 15.152
judiciary
contempt of court 15.97–15.100, 15.437–15.438, 15.532
criticizing the 15.382–15.383
European Court of Human Rights 15.380–15.383
expression, freedom of 15.261, 15.380–15.383
impartiality 15.99, 15.261, 15.380–15.383
scandalizing the court 15.97–15.100, 15.437–15.438, 15.532

jury trials/juries
contempt 15.89
damages 15.69–15.71, 15.531
defamation 15.51, 15.69–15.71, 15.531
disclosure of deliberations 15.101–15.102,
15.395
reporting restrictions 15.118

land
interference with 12.120
trespass to 12.120, 12.200
see also **home, respect for**
leave requirements
criminal libel 15.194
legal aid 15.397–15.398
legal professional privilege 12.77A-B,
12.128–12.129, 12.471
legitimate aims, interference justification
expression, freedom of 15.305, 15.359–15.385
privacy 12.350
legitimate expectation 12.100, 12.264
lesbians and gays *see* **sexual orientation
discrimination**
libel 15.52
blasphemous 15.389
criminal 15.192–15.195, 15.313, 15.321–15.322,
15.436
licences/licensing
broadcasting 15.262–15.265, 15.272
ECHR 15.262–15.265, 15.272
films 15.183, 15.187, 15.390
local authorities 15.187
listening devices 12.140, 12.151, 12.153, 12.279,
12.376, 12.378
litigation *see* **civil proceedings**
local authorities
compulsory purchase 12.199
defamation 15.55
housing 12.184–12.185
information, freedom of 15.227–15.228
licensing 15.187
see also **public authorities**
locus standi 15.54–15.55
Luxembourg 12.340

malice 15.60, 15.64, 15.434
Malta 12.520
margin of appreciation
blasphemy 15.387, 15.390
expression, freedom of 15.14, 15.239, 15.277,
15.308–15.309, 15.369
HRA 15.14
privacy 12.200, 12.205, 12.237, 12.239,
12.242, 12.245–12.246, 12.251–12.253,
12.257, 12.290, 12.292, 12.298,
12.311–12.312, 12.342, 12.344,
12.365, 12.383

media
breach of confidence 15.331–15.333
censorship *see* **censorship**
children, information concerning 12.114–12.116
codes of practice 12.91, 12.94–12.95
conditional fee agreements 15.229, 15.537
confidential documents 15.331–15.333
contempt of court 15.83–15.100
defamation 15.313, 15.321–15.322
companies 15.343
private individuals 15.333–15.336
public bodies 15.330
qualified privilege 15.65–15.68
democratic society, role in 15.311–15.313
ECHR 15.253–15.254
English law 12.91–12.116
expression, freedom of 15.170–15.187,
15.253–15.254, 15.310–15.358, 15.541
justification for interference 15.310–15.358
facts 15.314, 15.316–15.320
verification of 15.312
films 15.182–15.187, 15.390
grief and shock, intrusion into 12.94
harassment 12.94, 12.104, 12.178
India 15.541
injunctions
contra mundum 12.116, 15.38
interim 12.111–12.113
intrusion 12.05, 12.94
judicial proceedings 12.108
photography 12.103–12.107
politicians
criminal libel 15.313, 15.321–15.322
defamation 15.326
private life 15.323–15.325
Press Complaints Commission 12.10, 12.91,
12.95–12.96
press freedom 15.10, 15.15, 15.18,
15.253–15.254, 15.413
press regulation 12.93–12.96
prior restraint 15.269, 15.414
privacy 12.05, 12.08, 12.91–12.116, 12.402,
12.439, 12.505
English law 12.91–12.116
positive obligation 12.260–12.261
private information 12.105–12.107,
12.109–12.110
public interest 12.94
radio 12.97
regulation 15.170–15.187, 15.552
'reportage' 15.347–15.350
reporting restrictions *see* **reporting restrictions**
sanctions 15.355–15.358
scandalizing the court 15.97–15.100
Scotland 12.402
sources 15.351–15.354
South Africa 12.505

Sri Lanka 15.552
television 12.97
theatres 15.182
values 15.314, 15.316–15.320
videos 15.185–15.187, 15.390
see also **broadcasting; privacy**
medical information 12.23, 12.29
medical records, access to 12.282, 12.355,
  12.386
medical treatment
  children 12.215, 12.398
  consent 12.210–12.213, 12.215
  Gillick competency 12.215
  involuntary 12.425
  privacy 12.210–12.218, 12.425
  withdrawal 12.216
medically assisted reproduction
  identity of parents information 12.77
  prisoners' rights 12.373
  withdrawal of consent 12.208
mental disabilities
  compulsory treatment 12.432
  nearest relatives 12.57, 12.217
  privacy 12.210–12.218, 12.432
military service *see* **armed forces**
minors *see* **children and young persons**
morals and human rights
  corruption of public morals 15.161
  moral integrity 12.209–12.223,
    12.273

names
  privacy 12.252, 12.288, 12.424
  reporting restrictions
    parties 15.121–15.127, 15.133
    witnesses 15.128–15.130
Namibia
  expression, freedom of 15.548
  police 15.548
national security
  DA Notices 15.178–15.181
  ECHR 15.403–15.405
  expression, freedom of 15.360–15.363,
    15.403–15.405
  injunctions 15.403
  journalists' sources 15.147
  privacy 12.350
  surveillance 12.350
  terrorism 15.404
  see also **security services**
necessary in democratic society
  expression, freedom of 15.12, 15.278,
    15.306–15.309
  privacy 12.341–12.343
New Zealand Bill of Rights
  admissibility of evidence 12.490
  broadcasting standards 15.498

Canadian Charter of Rights 12.476, 12.478,
    15.469
  contempt of court 15.482
  defamation 15.477–15.481
  expression, freedom of 15.467–15.498
    justifiable limitations 15.472–15.498
  fair trial 15.482
  Grayson principles 12.482–12.487
  information, right to impart 15.470
  obscenity 15.492–15.493
  police 15.495
  pornography 15.492–15.493
  privacy 12.472–12.493
  racial hatred 15.494
  reasonableness 12.475–12.490
  reporting restrictions 15.483–15.490
  searches 12.475–12.490
  section 21 cases 12.480–12.489
  seizure 12.475–12.490
  surveillance 12.491–12.493
  warrants 12.487
noise
  economic well-being of the
    country 12.391–12.392
  home, right to respect for 12.310–12.311
  privacy 12.391–12.392
nuisance 12.148

obscenity
  Canadian Charter of Rights 15.430,
    15.447–15.450
  children 15.164–15.165
  corruption of public morals 15.161
  criminal offences 15.158
  definition 15.156–15.157
  deprave and corrupt 15.156–15.157
  displays 15.162
  ECHR 15.387–15.391
  European Union law 15.168
  forfeiture 15.159, 15.168
  imports 15.168
  indecency 15.161–15.168
  internet publishing 15.167, 15.391
  legislation 15.154–15.160
  malicious communications 15.166
  New Zealand Bill of Rights 15.492–15.493
  obscene libel 15.161
  outraging public decency 15.161
  penalties 15.158
  postal services, use of 15.163
  public electronic communication 15.167, 15.391
  public good defence 15.160
  'publication' 15.158
  seizure 15.159
  sex establishments, licensing of 15.169
  South Africa 15.506–15.508
  see also **pornography**

Ofcom
broadcasting regulation 12.98–12.102,
   15.173–15.175
Ofcom Code 12.99–12.102
official secrets
breach of confidence 15.217–15.218
criminal law 15.213–15.216
disclosure 15.215
expression, freedom of 15.212–15.216,
   15.544
injunctions 15.217
legislation 15.212–15.216
public interest 15.216, 15.217
opinions, right to hold 15.248–15.252
outraging public decency 15.161

parliament
defamation 15.479
freedom of expression 15.07
immunities 15.61
privilege 15.07, 15.61, 15.479, 15.510
South Africa 15.510
paternity
determination 12.253
transsexuals 12.291
penalties
expression, freedom of 15.314
severity of 15.314
personal autonomy 12.204
personal information
access to 12.73–12.77
data protection 12.60–12.62, 12.73–12.77
disclosure 12.55
information, freedom of 12.74–12.75
privacy 12.73–12.77
receiving information, right to 15.249
see also **private information**
photographs 12.06, 12.30, 12.33, 12.36, 12.438
aerial photography 12.149, 12.508
data protection 12.144
media 12.103–12.107
surveillance 12.139, 12.142–12.144
taking and retaining 12.144
physical integrity 12.209–12.223, 12.269–12.272
picketing
association, freedom of 15.41, 15.433, 15.438,
   15.460–15.462
Canadian Charter of Rights 15.460–15.462
expression, freedom of 15.41, 15.433, 15.438,
   15.460–15.462
injunctions 15.460–15.461
planning
home, respect for 12.196–12.198, 12.201
injunction to enforce decision 12.201
police
Canadian Charter of Rights 15.452
expression, freedom of 15.452, 15.495

journalistic material, seizure of 15.208–15.211
Namibia 15.548
New Zealand Bill of Rights 15.495
powers of entry 12.389
   under warrant 12.122–12.129
seizure 12.132–12.137
surveillance 12.157–12.158, 12.374–12.378
see also **arrest**
Police National Computer 12.72
political expression 15.367, 15.372–15.373,
   15.409–15.411, 15.463–15.465,
   15.515–15.517
Australia 15.522
civil servants 15.286, 15.374A, 15.376,
   15.410
ECHR 15.282–15.286, 15.297
government, criticism of 15.373
New Zealand Bill of Rights 15.480
political parties 15.553
politicians
criminal libel 15.313, 15.321–15.322
defamation 15.326–15.327, 15.372
private life 15.323–15.325
pollution 12.310
pornography
Canadian Charter of Rights 15.430,
   15.447–15.450
expression, freedom of 15.296, 15.430,
   15.447–15.450, 15.492–15.493
privacy and 12.499–12.500
sexual offences 15.448
South Africa 15.506–15.508
see also **obscenity**
possession orders
anti-social behaviour 12.368, 12.416
homes 12.369, 12.388, 12.416
proportionality 12.369, 12.388
possession proceedings 12.186–12.194
balancing interests 12.187–12.192
gypsies 12.189
private landlords 12.194
proportionality 12.192
suspended orders 12.193
powers of entry
common law 12.130
excluded material 12.124
home, respect for 12.117–12.118,
   12.122–12.129, 12.389
police 12.122–12.129, 12.389
privilege 12.124, 12.128
public interest 12.125
searches 12.118, 12.123–12.124, 12.125
special procedure material 12.124
warrants 12.122–12.129
without warrant 12.130–12.131
pre-trial publicity 15.420–15.422
pregnancy 12.272

prejudice
  contempt of court 15.84–15.96
  prejudicing or impeding proceedings 15.84–15.96
  reporting restrictions 15.117–15.118
  sub judice 15.84–15.96
press *see* **media**
Press Complaints Commission 12.10, 12.91,
    12.95–12.96
  judicial oversight 12.96
press freedom 15.10, 15.15, 15.18, 15.253–15.254,
    15.413
  HRA 15.15, 15.18
  prior restraint 15.269, 15.414
prisoners' rights
  children 12.233
  correspondence 12.314–12.319, 12.333,
      12.360–12.361, 12.365, 12.371
  drug testing 12.372
  expression, freedom of 15.220–15.227, 15.547
  medically assisted reproduction 12.373
  privacy 12.221, 12.230–12.233, 12.271, 12.431,
      12.467
  searches 12.467
  solicitors 12.315, 12.360–12.361, 12.371
  telephone calls 12.321
  voting *see* elections
privacy 12.01–12.520
  abortion 12.272
  access to documents 12.254, 12.386
  access to personal information 12.73–12.77
  aerial photography 12.149, 12.508
  assisted suicide 12.363, 12.397
  asylum 12.428
  Australia 12.509–12.510
  bankrupts 12.77C
  bodily samples 12.385A
  broadcasting 12.439
  Canadian Charter of Rights 12.435–12.471
  claimant
    conduct 12.38
    identity 12.37
  common law 12.08–12.13
  compulsory purchase 12.199
  corporations 12.235
  correspondence 12.77C, 12.313–12.323
  courts 12.09–12.10
  crime prevention 12.356–12.362
  criminal law 12.262, 12.299
  criminalization of private acts 12.331, 12.381,
      12.499, 12.507
  data protection *see* **data protection**
  defamation *see* **defamation**
  definition 12.03, 12.05
  disabled facilities 12.255
  disclosure 12.284, 12.461–12.463
    by public bodies 12.49–12.59
    crime prevention 12.362

  HIV status 12.505
    medical information 12.56–12.59
    personal information 12.55
    presumptions in favour 12.51
  discretion 12.339, 12.513
  disorder 12.356–12.362
  DNA sample retention 12.385A
  documents
    access to 12.254, 12.386
    collection 12.458–12.460
    recovery, from civil proceedings 12.434
    seizure 12.137
  dress codes *see* **dress codes**
  ECHR 12.234–12.369
  economic well-being of the
      country 12.391–12.393
  employment 12.78–12.90, 12.257, 12.300,
      12.321, 12.401, 12.437
    dismissal 12.86–12.87
    personal data 12.89
    private conduct 12.85–12.88
    sexual orientation discrimination 12.90
    suspected criminal conduct 12.54
    workplace monitoring 12.79–12.84,
        12.138–12.141, 12.279, 12.406
  English law 12.08–12.233
    Article 8 in courts 12.14–12.19
    common law 12.08–12.13
    employment 12.78–12.90
    housing 12.180–12.202
    intrusion into home 12.117–12.137
    media 12.91–12.116
    surveillance 12.138–12.179
  environment 12.259, 12.310–12.312, 12.351,
      12.357, 12.368, 12.433
  evidence
    admissibility 12.490
    collection 12.453–12.458
    irregularly obtained 12.407–12.412
  expectation of 12.445–12.452, 12.495–12.496
  expression, freedom of 12.12, 12.439,
      15.36–15.39, 15.78–15.79, 15.496–15.497
  extradition 12.227, 12.429–12.440
  failure to act 12.329
  Fiji 12.511–12.512
  France 12.506
  Germany 12.506
  goods 12.445–12.446
  harassment 12.104
  health and morals, protection of 12.363–12.364
  home, intrusion into 12.06, 12.117–12.137
  Hong Kong 12.513
  housing 12.184–12.185, 12.256
    see also **housing**
  HRA and 12.11–12.13, 12.24
  Human Rights Committee 12.514–12.516
  hunting 12.17, 12.207, 12.427

prisoners' rights (*cont.*)
  identity information 12.37, 12.288–12.292
  images 12.438
  immigration 12.224–12.228, 12.428
  India 12.517–12.518
  information
    access to 12.254
    claimant 12.37–12.38
    collection 12.281–12.283
    data protection *see* **data protection**
    disclosure *see* disclosure
    how obtained 12.35–12.36
    justification 12.41–12.48
    marital 12.23
    medical 12.23, 12.29, 12.56–12.59
    nature of 12.29–12.34
    personal 12.55
    private *see* private information
    public interest 12.45–12.48
    publication 12.12, 12.109–12.110,
      12.285–12.287
    reasonable expectation of privacy 12.26,
      12.27–12.28, 12.31, 12.33
    recovery of documents 12.434
    South Africa 12.504
    trivial 12.31–12.33
    untrue 12.34
  injunctions 12.12
    contra mundum 12.116, 15.38
    interim 12.111–12.113
  interception of letters 12.150–12.151
  interference with
    by non-state bodies 12.258–12.263
    by private individuals or organizations 12.03
    by public authority 12.326–12.333
    threshold for 12.328
  International Covenant on Civil and Political
    Rights 12.02
  investigative obligation 12.349
  Ireland 12.519
  justification for interference with 12.07, 12.26,
    12.41–12.48, 12.237, 12.324–12.369
    in accordance with the law 12.334–12.340
    crime or disorder prevention 12.356–12.362
    economic well-being of country 12.351–12.355
    factors taken into account 12.44–12.48
    legitimate aims 12.350
    necessary in a democratic society 12.341–12.343
    procedural requirements 12.344–12.349
    safeguards 12.344–12.349
  legitimate expectation of 12.100, 12.264
  Malta 12.520
  margin of appreciation 12.200, 12.205, 12.237,
    12.239, 12.242, 12.245–12.246,
    12.251–12.253, 12.257, 12.290,
    12.292, 12.298, 12.311–12.312,
    12.342, 12.344, 12.365, 12.383

marital information 12.23
media 12.05, 12.08, 12.402, 12.439
  English law 12.91–12.116
  positive obligation 12.260–12.261
  South Africa 12.505
medical information 12.23, 12.29, 12.56–12.59
medical records 12.282, 12.355, 12.386
medical treatment 12.210–12.218, 12.425
medically assisted reproduction 12.208
mental disabilities 12.210–12.218, 12.432
moral integrity 12.209–12.223, 12.273
name of choice 12.252, 12.288, 12.424
national security 12.350
natural persons 12.235
negative obligations 12.240–12.242
New Zealand Bill of Rights 12.475–12.490
noise 12.391–12.392
obscene material 12.499–12.500
paternity determination 12.253
personal autonomy/identity 12.204–12.208,
  12.266, 12.288–12.298
personal information 12.55, 12.73–12.77
personal or private space 12.274–12.280,
  12.498
personal right 12.444–12.447
photographs 12.06, 12.30, 12.33, 12.36, 12.139,
  12.142–12.144, 12.405–12.406, 12.438
  aerial photography 12.149, 12.508
  media 12.103–12.107
  surveillance 12.139, 12.142–12.144
  taking and retaining 12.144
physical integrity 12.209–12.223, 12.269–12.272
politicians 15.323–15.325
pornography 12.499–12.500
positive obligations 12.240–12.251
  private persons 12.263
  recognition 12.246–12.248
  state inaction 12.249
pregnancy 12.272
Press Complaints Commission 12.10
prisoners' rights 12.221, 12.230–12.233, 12.271,
  12.431, 12.467
private information
  access to 12.74–12.75
  misuse 12.06, 12.18, 12.26–12.77,
    12.105–12.107, 12.367,
    12.385–12.386, 12.400, 12.507
  publication 15.36–15.39
private law 12.05
private life 12.16–12.17
  employees 12.85–12.88
  HRA and 12.11–12.13, 12.17
  scope 12.264–12.302
privilege
  legal professional 12.77A-B, 12.128–12.129,
    12.471
  see also **privilege**

psychological integrity 12.260–12.272
public authorities 12.11, 12.238, 12.323,
    12.324, 12.326–12.333
public domain information 12.39–12.40, 15.49,
    15.330
public interest 12.439
public safety 12.350
Québec Charter of Human Rights and
    Freedoms 12.436
reasonable expectation of 12.26, 12.27–12.28,
    12.31, 12.33
reasonableness 12.449–12.452
recovery of documents 12.434
reform 12.10
reputation 12.19, 12.301–12.302, 12.394
    defamation 15.49–15.50, 15.52, 15.74,
        15.313, 15.341, 15.346, 15.371,
        15.436, 15.478
'respect' 12.15
sado-masochism 12.295, 12.384
Scotland 12.399–12.434
self-fulfilment 12.19, 12.207–12.208, 12.299
sex offenders 12.421–12.422
sexual identity 12.205, 12.423
sexual orientation 12.90, 12.206, 12.294–12.297,
    12.331, 12.364, 12.380–12.382
sexuality 12.47, 12.293–12.297, 12.380–12.384
social activities 12.18, 12.299
South Africa 12.494–12.505
spatial isolation 12.278, 12.498
state 12.03
tape recordings 12.30, 12.153
telephone tapping *see* **telephone tapping**
third parties 12.447
transsexuals 12.250–12.251, 12.291–12.292,
    12.383
trivial information 12.31–12.33
UK cases under Article 8 12.370–12.398
unfair dismissal 12.86–12.87
United States 12.04–12.05
Universal Declaration of Human Rights 12.02
untrue information 12.34
victim test 12.330
video recordings 12.30
workplace monitoring 12.79–12.84,
    12.138–12.141, 12.279, 12.406
    telephone calls 12.257, 12.321
wrong doing, revealing 12.46–12.47
Younger Committee 12.10, 12.62
see also **correspondence; surveillance; telephone
    tapping**
private information
access to 12.74–12.75
misuse 12.06, 12.18, 12.26–12.77,
    12.105–12.107, 12.367, 12.385–12.386,
    12.400, 12.507, 15.78–15.79
publication 15.36–15.39

private life *see* **privacy**
privilege
absolute 15.56, 15.61
Australia 15.523–15.524
defamation 15.56, 15.61, 15.398, 15.434,
    15.479
freedom of expression 15.07
legal professional 12.77A-B, 12.128–12.129,
    12.471
parliamentary 15.07, 15.479, 15.510
powers of entry 12.124, 12.128
qualified 15.56, 15.62–15.65, 15.398, 15.434,
    15.523–15.524
South Africa 15.510
privileged material
correspondence 12.347–12.348
searches 12.124, 12.128–12.129, 12.471
proceeds of crime, confiscation of 12.415
proof, burden of 15.52, 15.58
property
access to 15.458–15.459
advertisements 15.459
Canadian Charter of Rights 15.458–15.459
expression, freedom of 15.458–15.459
home, respect for 12.307
land *see* **land**
proportionality
arrest 15.367
Canadian Charter of Rights 15.429–15.430
contempt 15.393–15.394
expression, freedom of 15.219, 15.367,
    15.429–15.430
home, respect for 12.387
journalists' sources 15.152
possession orders 12.369, 12.388
possession proceedings 12.192
protests
breach of the peace 15.196, 15.400, 15.424
designated areas 15.206
expression, freedom of 15.196–15.199,
    15.399–15.402
public order 15.197–15.199
public authorities
Antigua and Barbuda 15.521
Canadian Charter of Rights 15.463
civil servants 15.286, 15.374A, 15.376, 15.410
data protection 15.60
defamation 15.55, 15.330, 15.529
employment 15.463
expression, freedom of 15.08, 15.463, 15.521
Hong Kong 15.529
information, freedom of 15.227
internal communications system 12.375
privacy 12.11, 12.238, 12.323, 12.324,
    12.326–12.333
sexual orientation discrimination 12.206
surveillance 12.179

public authorities (*cont.*)
  telephone tapping 12.374–12.375
  see also **local authorities**
public interest
  breach of confidence 15.379
  Canadian Charter of Rights 12.439
  defamation 15.56, 15.59, 15.434, 15.480
  expression, freedom of 15.13, 15.22, 15.237,
    15.471
  journalistic material, seizure of 15.210–15.211
  media 12.94
  New Zealand Bill of Rights 15.471
  official secrets 15.217
  powers of entry 12.125
  privacy 12.439
public interest defence 15.216
public life, regulation of conduct in 15.225–15.226
public order 15.197–15.202, 15.550
  protests 15.197–15.199
  racial hatred 15.201
public property, access to 15.458–15.459
publicity, pre-trial 15.420–15.422

Québec Charter of Human Rights and
    Freedoms 12.436

racial hatred
  Canadian Charter of Rights 15.451
  definition 15.200
  expression, freedom of 15.200–15.202, 15.244,
    15.451, 15.494
  Holocaust denial 15.451, 15.535
  marches 15.202
  New Zealand Bill of Rights 15.494
  public order 15.201
radio 12.97
  see also **broadcasting**
rape
  anonymity of complainant 15.141
reasonableness
  Canadian Charter of Rights 12.449–12.452
  New Zealand Bill of Rights 12.475–12.490
  privacy 12.449–12.452
  searches 12.453, 12.464–12.471
  seizure 12.136, 12.453–12.457, 12.464–12.471
referenda 15.464
regulation
  broadcasting 12.97–12.102, 15.171–15.177
  conduct in public life 15.225–15.226
  press 12.93–12.96
  RIPA *see* **Regulation of Investigatory Powers**
    Act 2000
Regulation of Investigatory Powers Act 2000
    12.83–12.84, 12.141, 12.156, 12.159–12.174
  covert surveillance 12.169
  interception of communications 12.160–12.165
  scrutiny of powers 12.171–12.174

  use of material 12.170
Regulation of Investigatory Powers
    Tribunal 12.172–12.174
religion, thought and conscience, freedom of 15.374,
    15.375A
  advertisements 15.375A
  blasphemy *see* **blasphemy**
  buildings *see* **ecclesiastical buildings**
  dress codes 12.85
remedies
  defamation 15.69–15.74
  surveillance 12.146
'reportage' 15.347–15.350
reporting restrictions
  appeals 15.116
  Canadian Charter of Rights 15.439–15.446
  children 15.131–15.140, 15.441, 15.444–15.445,
    15.489–15.490
  civil proceedings 15.105–15.112
  criminal proceedings 12.108, 15.19,
    15.113–15.144
  disclosure material 15.143–15.144
  employment tribunals 15.120
  expression, freedom of 15.19, 15.103–15.144,
    15.385, 15.415–15.416, 15.439–15.446,
    15.483–15.490
  fair trial 15.484
  Heilbron report 15.141
  judicial review 15.116
  jury trials 15.118
  names of parties 15.121–15.127, 15.133
  names of witnesses 15.128–15.130
  New Zealand Bill of Rights 15.483–15.490
  orders 15.103–15.144
  postponement orders 15.117–15.120
  pre-trial comment 15.385
  prejudice 15.117–15.118
  rape case complainant 15.141
  Scotland 15.415–15.417
  sexual offences 15.440–15.442, 15.444–15.445
  tribunals 15.104, 15.120
  undercover police officers 15.442
reproduction *see* **medically assisted reproduction**
reputation
  defamation 15.49–15.50, 15.52, 15.74, 15.313,
    15.341, 15.346, 15.371, 15.436, 15.478
  privacy 12.19, 12.301–12.302, 12.394

sado-masochism 12.295, 12.384
satellite television 15.252
scandalizing the court 15.97–15.100,
    15.437–15.438, 15.532
Scotland
  anti-social behaviour 12.419–12.422
  expression, freedom of 15.412–15.425
  home, respect for 12.399–12.434
  hunting with dogs 12.427, 15.423

pre-trial publicity 15.420–15.422
privacy 12.399–12.434
reporting restrictions 15.415–15.417
surveillance 12.405–12.406
searches
administrative inspections 12.467
Anton Piller orders 12.366
'bedpan vigil' 12.468
Canadian Charter of Rights 12.440–12.443,
12.447–12.448
correspondence 12.320
excluded material 12.124
intrusiveness 12.479
New Zealand Bill of Rights 12.475–12.490
powers of entry 12.118, 12.122–12.129
prisoners' rights 12.467
privileged material 12.124, 12.128–12.129,
12.471
reasonableness 12.453, 12.464–12.471
seizure 12.132–12.137
South Africa 12.501–12.503
special procedure material 12.124
strip 12.468
warrants 12.122–12.129, 12.357, 12.487
security services
surveillance 12.151–12.156, 12.175–12.176,
12.379
see also **national security**
seditious libel 15.190–15.191
seizure
Canadian Charter of Rights 12.440–12.443,
12.447–12.448, 12.453–12.456
common law 12.135–12.136
correspondence 12.320
documents 12.137
evidence 12.136
home, respect for 12.132–12.137
journalistic material 15.210–15.211
New Zealand Bill of Rights 12.475–12.490
obscenity 15.159
police 12.132–12.137, 15.212–15.216
reasonableness 12.134, 12.453–12.457,
12.464–12.471
South Africa 12.501–12.503
sexual identity 12.205, 12.423
sexual offences
children 15.441, 15.444–15.445
pornography 15.448
reporting restrictions 15.440–15.442,
15.444–15.445
sexual orientation discrimination
age of consent 12.380
armed forces 12.206, 12.382
criminalizing private acts 12.331, 12.364,
12.381
ECHR 12.206
employment 12.90

private life, right to 12.206, 12.331, 12.364,
12.380–12.382
public authorities 12.206
South Africa 12.497
sexuality
private life, right to 12.47, 12.293–12.297,
12.380–12.384
slander 15.53
social activities 12.18, 12.299
solicitors
correspondence 12.315, 12.347, 12.360–12.361,
12.371
prisoners' rights 12.315, 12.360–12.361, 12.371
see also **legal professional privilege**
South Africa
armed forces 15.509
contempt 15.511–15.512
defamation 15.501–15.505
discrimination
sexual orientation 12.497
employees, political restrictions on 15.509
expression, freedom of 15.499–15.513
hate speech 15.513
information
privacy 12.504
media 12.505
obscenity 15.506–15.508
parliamentary privilege 15.510
pornography 15.506–15.508
privacy 12.494–12.505
privilege 15.510
search and seizure 12.501–12.503
sexual orientation 12.497
special procedure material 12.124
Sri Lanka
defamation 15.551
expression, freedom of 15.559–15.553
media 15.552
political parties 15.553
public order 15.550
Standards Board for England
Code of Conduct 15.225–15.226
standing 15.54–15.55
strict liability
contempt of court 15.84, 15.86–15.92
strip searches 12.468
sub judice 15.84–15.96
see also **pre-trial publicity; reporting restrictions**
surveillance 12.06, 12.138–12.141, 12.279, 12.332
abuse of power 12.338
aerial photography 12.149, 12.508
authorization 12.157–12.158
breach of confidence 12.146
Canadian Charter of Rights 12.449–12.452
closed circuit television (CCTV) 12.139, 12.145,
12.279, 12.396
common law 12.146–12.150

strict liability (*cont.*)
  covert 12.165–12.169, 12.406, 12.409–12.410
  evidence
    exclusion 12.153
    irregularly obtained 12.407–12.412
  harassment 12.146, 12.149, 12.178
  HRA and 12.179
  Investigatory Powers Tribunal 12.83–12.84,
    12.141
  justification 12.337
  legislation 12.155–12.156
  listening devices 12.140, 12.151, 12.153,
    12.279, 12.376, 12.378
  national security 12.350
  New Zealand Bill of Rights 12.491–12.493
  non-participant 12.491–12.492
  nuisance 12.148
  participant 12.493
  photographs 12.139, 12.142–12.144
  police 12.157–12.158, 12.374–12.378
  Police Act 1997 12.157–12.158
  remedies 12.146
  RIPA 12.83–12.84, 12.141, 12.156,
    12.159–12.174
    covert surveillance 12.169
    interception of communications 12.160–12.165
    scrutiny of powers 12.171–12.174
    use of material 12.170
  Scotland 12.405–12.406
  security services 12.151–12.156, 12.175–12.176,
    12.379
  terrorism 12.177
  tracking devices 12.407
  trespass to land 12.147, 12.149
  United States 12.508
  video 12.377, 12.491
  warrants 12.151, 12.176
  workplace monitoring 12.79–12.84,
    12.138–12.141, 12.279, 12.406
    covert recording 12.82
    warnings 12.80–12.81
  see also **telephone tapping**

telephone calls
  prisoners' rights 12.321
  workplace monitoring 12.257
telephone tapping 12.06, 12.152–12.153, 12.279,
    12.331–12.333, 12.332
  authorization 12.152
  Canadian Charter of Rights 12.451
  civil proceedings 12.413
  criminal proceedings 12.414
  India 12.518
  internal communications system 12.375
  Ireland 12.519
  justification 12.340
  Luxembourg 12.340

  public authorities 12.374–12.375
  Scotland 12.413–12.414
  United States 12.508
television 12.97
  satellite 15.252
  see also **broadcasting**
terrorism
  expression, freedom of 15.207, 15.362–15.363,
    15.365, 15.404
  'glorifying' 15.207
  surveillance 12.177
theatres
  censorship 15.182
third parties
  Canadian Charter of Rights 12.447
  privacy 12.447
thought *see* **religion, thought and conscience,**
    freedom of
tobacco advertising 15.456
trademarks 15.29, 15.42
transsexuals
  birth certificates 12.250, 12.291, 12.383
  children 12.291
  gender reassignment surgery 12.292
  paternity 12.291
  privacy 12.250–12.251, 12.383
trespass to goods 12.121
trespass to land
  enforcement powers 12.200
  home, respect for 12.120, 12.200
  surveillance 12.147, 12.149
tribunals
  contempt of court 15.82
  reporting restrictions 15.120
Trinidad and Tobago
  expression, freedom of 15.554–15.555

unfair dismissal 12.86–12.87
uniforms, political 15.517
United States
  expression, freedom of 15.02–15.03,
    15.514–15.518
  home, respect for 12.508
  information, misuse of 12.507
  privacy 12.04–12.05
  surveillance 12.508
  telephone tapping 12.508
Universal Declaration of Human Rights 12.02

victims 12.330
videos, classification 15.185–15.187, 15.390

waiver of Convention rights
  contracts of employment 12.81, 12.85
war crimes 15.377
warrants
  New Zealand Bill of Rights 12.487

Police and Criminal Evidence Act 1984 12.126
powers of entry 12.122–12.129
search 12.123–12.124, 12.125, 12.357
surveillance 12.151, 12.176
whistleblowing 15.443
witnesses
absent through fear 15.142
anonymity 15.128–15.130, 15.142

in fear 15.142
restrictions on reporting names 15.128–15.130
workplace monitoring 12.79–12.84, 12.138–12.141,
12.279, 12.406

young persons *see* children and young persons
Younger Committee 12.10, 12.62

CONTENTS OF THE LAW OF HUMAN RIGHTS

For reference, we reproduce here the Summary Table of Contents from *The Law of Human Rights*, second edition (OUP 2009, 978-0-19-9579730) from which this chapter is extracted.

VOLUME 1

Table of Cases   xxxvii
Tables of Legislation and Treaties   cclxi

Introduction   1

I THE BACKGROUND TO THE HUMAN RIGHTS ACT

1. The Constitutional Protection of Human Rights   19
2. Unincorporated Human Rights Treaties in Domestic Law   73

II GENERAL PRINCIPLES UNDER THE HUMAN RIGHTS ACT

3. The Human Rights Act: Interpretation and Synopsis   121
4. The Human Rights Act and Statute Law   175
5. Human Rights and Public Authorities   229

III THE CONVENTION RIGHTS

6. General Principles under the Convention   299
7. The Right to Life and the Abolition of the Death Penalty   407
8. Right Not to be Subject to Torture or Inhuman or Degrading Treatment   469
9. Freedom from Slavery, Servitude, and Forced Labour   553
10. The Right to Liberty   573
11. Fair Trial Rights   705
12. The Right to Respect for Privacy and the Home   1005
13. The Right to Marry and to Family Life   1187
14. Freedom of Thought, Conscience, and Religion   1279
15. Freedom of Expression   1359
16. Freedom of Assembly and Association   1547
17. Freedom from Discrimination in Relation to Convention Rights   1617
18. Right to Enjoyment of Possessions   1755

19. The Right to Education   1833

20. Electoral Rights   1885

IV REMEDIES AND PROCEDURES

21. Remedies under the Human Rights Act   1929

22. Human Rights Act Procedure   2001

23. Court of Human Rights Procedure   2055

Index   2091

VOLUME 2

Appendices

United Kingdom Materials
     A. Human Rights Act 1998   1
     B. Rights Brought Home: The Human Rights Bill ((1997) Cm 3782)   19
     C. Practice Direction Under the Human Rights Act 1998
        (PD39 Miscellaneous Provision Relating to Hearings: Extract)   33
     D. Practice Direction (Devolution Issues and Crown Office
        Applications in Wales)   35

European Materials
     E. Convention for the Protection of Human Rights and Fundamental
        Freedoms, with Protocols   47
     F. European Court of Human Rights Rules of Court (July 2006)   71
     G. European Social Charter 1961   105

United Nations Materials
     H. Universal Declaration of Human Rights 1948   119
     I. Convention Relating to the Status of Refugees 1951   123
     J. International Covenant on Civil and Political Rights 1966,
        with Optional Protocol   135
     K. International Covenant on Economic, Social and Cultural Rights 1966   151
     L. International Convention on the Elimination of All Forms
        of Racial Discrimination 1966   159
     M. Convention on the Elimination of All Forms of Discrimination
        against Women 1979   169
     N. Convention on the Rights of Persons with Disabilities 2006   179
     O. Convention on the Rights of the Child 1989   201

Domestic Bills of Rights
- P. Canadian Charter of Rights and Freedoms
  (Part 1, Constitution Act 1982) 215
- Q. Constitution of India 221
- R. Irish Constitution (Chapter XII, Fundamental Rights, Arts 40–44) ... 229
- S. New Zealand Bill of Rights Act 1990 233
- T. Constitution of the Republic of South Africa 1996 239
- U. Constitution of the United States of America: Bill of Rights
  and Thirteenth to Fifteenth Amendments 249